The *American Heritage*®
Children's Thesaurus

by
Paul Hellweg

With the Editors of
the American Heritage® Dictionaries

HOUGHTON MIFFLIN

Boston • New York

ACKNOWLEDGMENTS

Many people were actively involved in the compilation of the thesaurus, and their contributions deserve recognition. The authorial staff included:

Susannah LeBaron, *Contributing Editor*, who helped more than anyone else to set the book's tone. She edited an earlier version of the manuscript and contributed new material to the current version.

Joyce LeBaron, *Contributing Editor*, who also edited an earlier version of the manuscript and contributed new material to the current version. She helped to make the final manuscript age-appropriate for its target audience.

Susan Grossman, *Copyeditor*, who was involved in the preparation of an earlier version of the manuscript. She helped to develop the book's original format and presentation.

Tony Perone, *Copyeditor*, who edited and proofread portions of the original manuscript.

Robyn Battle and **Marvin Vernon**, *Contributors*, who helped in the preparation of the original database.

The editorial and production staff at Houghton Mifflin included:

Margery S. Berube, *Vice President and Director of Lexical Publishing*, who got the project started and oversaw its development.

David R. Pritchard, *Senior Editor*, and **Beth Anderson**, *Associate Editor*, who developed the manuscript into its final form.

Margaret Anne Miles, *Senior Art and Production Coordinator*, who coordinated the artwork.

Katherine Prior, *Administrative Assistant*, who provided administrative and secretarial support.

The author is deeply indebted to all of the above. The thesaurus could not have been completed without their contributions.

ISBN 0-618-28024-3

**Library of Congress
Cataloging-in-Publication Data**

Hellweg, Paul.
   The American Heritage children's thesaurus/by Paul Hellweg with the editors of the American Heritage dictionaries.
      p. cm.
   Summary: Presents over 4000 alphabetically arranged words with several synonyms and an illustrative sentence for each.
    ISBN 0-395-84977-2 (cloth)
    1. English language—Synonyms and antonyms—
Juvenile literature.
[1. English language—Synonyms and antonyms.]
I. Title.
PE1591.H44 1997
423'. 1—dc21   97-12396
                     CIP
Visit our website: www.houghtonmifflinbooks.com

Manufactured in the United States of America

Book design by the Houghton Mifflin Company School Design Department
Cover design by Clifford Stoltze Design; jack and flower cover photographs: © 2003 PhotoDisc, Inc./Getty Images; starfish cover photograph: © School Division, Houghton Mifflin Company/Tony Scarpetta

Table of Contents

How to Use This Thesaurus

What Is a Thesaurus?

A thesaurus is a book of *synonyms*—words that share the same or nearly the same meaning. For example, **clamor, din, racket, sound, tumult,** and **uproar** are all synonyms of the noun **noise,** just as **blow up, expand,** and **swell** are all synonyms of the verb **inflate** and **excellent, fine, magnificent, splendid, superior,** and **terrific** are synonyms of the adjective **superb.** You will find these synonyms and thousands more listed in this thesaurus.

Of course, not every word you can think of has the same meaning as another word. Words that don't have synonyms, such as *uncle* or *spaghetti* or *computer,* are not included in thesauruses. Many words do have synonyms, however, and we have listed more than 4,000 of them as main entries in this book, with over 36,000 synonyms included in all.

Why Use a Thesaurus?

Another way to think of a thesaurus is as a book of *word choices.* Sometimes, especially when you are writing, you might feel that the word you were about to use isn't quite right. Understanding how to use synonyms is one of the secrets of good writing.

For example, maybe you were about to describe a book as *funny,* but that word seemed too ordinary. You could look up the entry for **funny** in this thesaurus and choose a more interesting word such as **amusing, comical, hilarious,** or **humorous.**

Or perhaps your teacher has told you that you use the word *weird* too often in your writing. Looking up **weird** would provide you with **bizarre, eerie, odd, peculiar, strange,** and **unnatural** as words you could use instead.

To see how using synonyms works, imagine that you are writing a letter to your friends in Australia or Brazil who have never even seen snow. You want to describe what a really harsh winter can feel like, so you begin:

> *Of course, winter is normally a **cold** time of the year, but last January was unbelievably **cold**. I would go outside wearing boots and two pairs of socks, and my feet would still feel **cold**! I couldn't wait for spring to arrive so the **cold** weather would end.*

You read your paragraph and realize something seems wrong. Your words just don't communicate the idea you want to get across, and your friends aren't going to think they have been missing much. How can you make the story sound more exciting? At the entry for **cold,** you find

inflate, blow up, expand, swell

chilly, cool, icy, frigid, and **frozen** as choices for other words to use here. It appears you will be able to improve your letter simply by changing a few words:

> *Of course, winter is normally a **cold** time of the year, but last January was unbelievably **frigid**. I would go outside wearing boots and two pairs of socks, and my feet would still feel **frozen**! I couldn't wait for spring to arrive so the **icy** weather would end.*

There is nothing wrong with using the word *cold*, but if you repeat any word too many times in the same paragraph, your writing will probably sound boring no matter how exciting your story is.

How Do You Choose the Best Word?

The choice is yours—but how do you make it? Which is the best word to get your meaning across and to express exactly what you want to say?

Just because a word and its synonym share the same meaning doesn't mean that they can always be substituted for each other. In any particular sentence, some synonyms will probably work better than others. That's why we have designed this thesaurus in a special way to help you think about word choices.

■ First, we include a typical example sentence for every entry word in the book. This gives you a clear idea of how the word is commonly used in writing and speaking.

■ Second, we show you which synonyms fit the example sentence best and which synonyms don't fit quite as well. We do this by dividing the synonym list into

two parts: *best choices*, which are listed first and follow the solid symbol ✦, and *other choices*, which are listed second and follow the open symbol ✧.

Remember, we have divided each list of synonyms for only the particular example sentence that is given in that entry, and you will have to choose which of the other words shown will fit in your own writing.

For example, at the entry for **pale** the example given is *The sky turned **pale** blue as the sun came up.* In this sentence, the best choices for a synonym are **faint** and **light**, while other choices, which would not work so well in this example, are **colorless, dim,** and **whitish**. But maybe you want to describe the sky itself rather than its blue color, and you write the sentence *The sky turned **pale** as the haze settled over the city.* Now, in your sentence, **colorless, dim,** and **whitish** make the best choices while **faint** and **light** are other choices that will work sometimes as a synonym for *pale*, but not in this sentence.

Any time you look for a synonym, keep in mind that all of the available choices for a specific word or meaning may not make the best match for a specific sentence. It's up to *you* to decide which synonyms work best in *your* sentence.

noise, clamor, din, racket

The Main Entry

Let's see how a typical entry in this thesaurus works:

1 The entry word is printed in dark purple type, making it easy to find.

2 The part of speech is printed in italic (slanting) letters.

3 A solid symbol (♦) indicates the best choices. These words fit best in the example sentence that follows the synonym list. Try them!

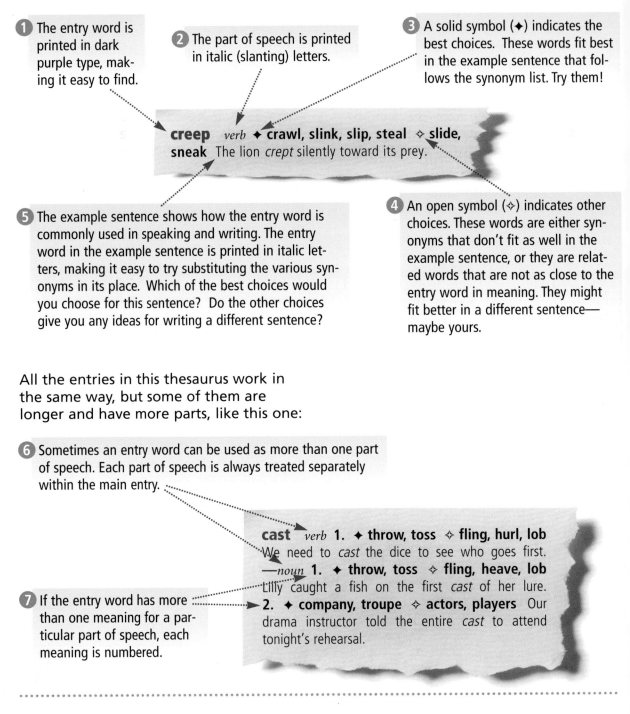

creep *verb* ♦ **crawl, slink, slip, steal** ♦ **slide, sneak** The lion *crept* silently toward its prey.

5 The example sentence shows how the entry word is commonly used in speaking and writing. The entry word in the example sentence is printed in italic letters, making it easy to try substituting the various synonyms in its place. Which of the best choices would you choose for this sentence? Do the other choices give you any ideas for writing a different sentence?

4 An open symbol (♦) indicates other choices. These words are either synonyms that don't fit as well in the example sentence, or they are related words that are not as close to the entry word in meaning. They might fit better in a different sentence—maybe yours.

All the entries in this thesaurus work in the same way, but some of them are longer and have more parts, like this one:

6 Sometimes an entry word can be used as more than one part of speech. Each part of speech is always treated separately within the main entry.

cast *verb* **1.** ♦ **throw, toss** ♦ **fling, hurl, lob** We need to *cast* the dice to see who goes first. —*noun* **1.** ♦ **throw, toss** ♦ **fling, heave, lob** Lilly caught a fish on the first *cast* of her lure. **2.** ♦ **company, troupe** ♦ **actors, players** Our drama instructor told the entire *cast* to attend tonight's rehearsal.

7 If the entry word has more than one meaning for a particular part of speech, each meaning is numbered.

Substituting Synonyms

Many synonyms can be substituted for one another just as they are, but others need to add or change a preposition. In this thesaurus, we have worded the best-choice synonyms in a way that will help you fit them correctly into the example sentence. For instance, in the following entry, you could write "Michelle *condemns* littering" or "Michelle *frowns on* littering" instead of the sample sentence "Michelle *disapproves of* littering":

> **disapprove** *verb* ✦ **condemn, denounce, dislike, frown on, object to** ✧ **criticize** Michelle *disapproves of* littering.

In other cases we have placed a preposition or an article in parentheses as a reminder that it will need to be changed to make that synonym work properly. An example of this kind of entry is **dislike** on page 65.

Antonyms

In addition to synonyms, many English words also have *antonyms*—words that are opposite in meaning. We have included a varied selection of antonyms in this thesaurus, putting them in feature boxes alongside the entry word to which they refer. For example, here is the antonym box for **fresh** on page 97:

Antonyms
fresh *adjective*
1. musty, old, stale
3. dirty, impure, polluted, tainted

Note that numbered lists of antonyms correspond to the numbered definitions in the main entry and may not always be in numerical sequence. Thus **musty, old,** and **stale** are antonyms for the first meaning in the main entry **fresh**, while **dirty, impure, polluted,** and **tainted** are for the third meaning.

Word Groups

We have included some entry words in this thesaurus that do not have actual synonyms but instead have a group of closely related words. For example, there are no words that mean the same thing as *knife*. There are, however, many words that refer to different types of knives, and we have put these related words in Word Group boxes:

> **Word Groups**
>
> A knife is a sharp instrument used for cutting and piercing. Knife is a general term with no true synonyms. Here are some different kinds of knives to investigate in a dictionary:
>
> cleaver, dagger, dirk, jackknife, machete, pocketknife, scalpel, stiletto, switchblade

Word Groups are entered in the same alphabetical order as the main entry words. For example, you will find the Word Group for *knife* on page 133, between the main entries for **kneel** and **knit**.

Homographs

Words with the same spelling but different meanings are called *homographs.* These words are entered separately in the thesaurus, and each is followed by a small raised number, such as **present**[1] and **present**[2] on page 183.

You are a writer

You have to write papers and reports for school. You might want to write a letter to a relative or a friend. Perhaps you keep a diary, or maybe you want to write your thoughts and experiences in a journal when you are on vacation. Surely you've had ideas that mean so much you just have to write them down. You might like creative writing, too. People your age have written poems, stories, even novels. You can too.

In all these cases, this thesaurus will help you find the right words to express your thoughts and keep your writing lively and interesting.

A

abandon *verb* **1.** ✦ **desert, forsake** ✧ **leave, reject** Brittany took home a puppy that someone had *abandoned*. **2.** ✦ **cease, discontinue, give up, quit, stop** Rescuers had to *abandon* their search for the missing plane when night fell.

abandoned *adjective* ✦ **deserted, empty, unoccupied, vacant** ✧ **forgotten** The *abandoned* house had broken windows and an overgrown lawn.

abbreviate *verb* ✦ **condense, contract, shorten** ✧ **compress, reduce** "Doctor" is commonly *abbreviated* as "Dr."

abdicate *verb* ✦ **quit, resign** ✧ **renounce, retire, yield** When the king *abdicated*, his son became the new ruler.

ability *noun* ✦ **capability, skill, talent** ✧ **aptitude, power** Cindy has great *ability* as a soccer player. ▼

able *adjective* ✦ **capable, proficient** ✧ **competent, fit, qualified** Colleen is an *able* storyteller.

abnormal *adjective* ✦ **eccentric, odd, strange, weird** ✧ **uncommon, unusual** My brother thinks that I'm *abnormal* because I like lima beans.

abolish *verb* ✦ **do away with, eliminate** ✧ **cancel, disallow, end** Enrique thinks that homework should be *abolished*.

about *preposition* **1.** ✦ **concerning, regarding** ✧ **involving** I am reading a book *about* dragons and unicorns. **2.** ✦ **approximately, around** ✧ **almost, nearly** Chris has to be home at *about* four o'clock.

above *adverb* ✦ **overhead** ✧ **over** I'm friends with the people who live in the apartment *above*. —*preposition* ✦ **beyond, over, past** Children *above* the age of twelve are full price at our movie theater.

abroad *adverb* ✦ **overseas** ✧ **away, elsewhere** Chelsey spent her summer vacation *abroad*.

abrupt *adjective* **1.** ✦ **hasty, quick, rapid, sudden** ✧ **unexpected** Thomas brought his bicycle to an *abrupt* stop when a dog ran in front of it. **2.** ✦ **curt, impolite, rude, uncivil** ✧ **blunt, gruff** Ms. Hickley warned Marcus not to be *abrupt* with her.

absence *noun* **1.** ✦ **nonattendance (at)** ✧ **truancy** Eugene's *absence* from the choir was due to a cold. **2.** ✦ **lack** ✧ **deficiency, need, shortage, want** The *absence* of fresh snow made our ski trip less enjoyable.

absent *adjective* ✦ **away, gone, missing** ✧ **truant** Karen was *absent* from school today.

absolute *adjective* **1.** ✦ **complete, downright, total, utter** ✧ **perfect, pure** Brian thinks that his little sister is an *absolute* nuisance.

✦ **best choices**
✧ **other choices**

2. ✦ unconditional, unlimited, unrestricted ✧ unqualified Russian czars once ruled with *absolute* power.

absorb *verb* **1. ✦ soak up, take up ✧ hold, retain** Jennifer used a kitchen towel to *absorb* the spilled milk. **2. ✦ take in, understand ✧ assimilate, learn** I listened hard but I couldn't *absorb* what Mr. Santos was telling us.

absorbing *adjective* **✦ captivating, engrossing, fascinating, interesting** Aubrey found the novel so *absorbing* that she recommended it to all her friends.

abstain *verb* **✦ avoid, forgo, keep from, refrain from ✧ pass, resist** Linda has to *abstain from* eating sticky foods now that she has braces.

abstract *adjective* **✦ philosophical, theoretical ✧ obscure, vague** "What do Martians eat for breakfast?" is an *abstract* question.

absurd *adjective* **✦ foolish, ridiculous, senseless, silly, stupid** Eric thinks that the idea of going to school all year long is *absurd*.

abundance *noun* **✦ lot, plenty, profusion, wealth ✧ excess, surplus** The farmer was happy because his orchard produced an *abundance* of apples. ▼

abundant *adjective* **✦ ample, full, generous, plentiful, rich ✧ sufficient** Velma's dog has an *abundant* supply of rawhide bones.

abuse *verb* **✦ mistreat, misuse ✧ harm, hurt, take advantage of** Erika *abused* her brother's trust when she revealed the location of his secret fort. —*noun* **✦ mistreatment, misuse ✧ damage, harm, hurt** Dora's battered tennis racket looks like it has taken a lot of *abuse*.

abyss *noun* **✦ chasm, void ✧ gulf, hole, pit** Cassie became dizzy when she looked over the edge of the *abyss*.

accelerate *verb* **✦ go faster, quicken, speed up ✧ hasten, hurry, rush, speed** The sled suddenly *accelerated* when it hit a patch of ice.

accent *noun* **✦ inflection, pronunciation ✧ emphasis, stress, tone** My friend Heidi speaks English with a German *accent*.

accept *verb* **1. ✦ receive, take, welcome ✧ acquire, gain, get, obtain** Kaye happily *accepted* the kitten I offered her. **2. ✦ acknowledge, agree, believe ✧ admit, affirm, claim** Is there anyone who does not *accept* that the world is round?

acceptable *adjective* **✦ adequate, agreeable, fair, satisfactory, suitable** Ry thought that the two lizards were an *acceptable* trade for his comic book.

access *noun* **✦ admission, entrance, entry ✧ passage** Sara denied her little brother *access* to her room.

accessory *noun* **1. ✦ attachment, extra ✧ addition, supplement** Among the *accessories* Mr. Pounds bought for his new truck were seat covers and cup holders. **2. ✦ accomplice, partner**

◇ **assistant, associate, confederate** The cashier was convicted of being an *accessory* to the robbery.

accident *noun* **1.** ✦ **chance, fluke, fortune, luck** Sir Alexander Fleming discovered penicillin by *accident* when he found mold growing on an unwashed petri dish. **2.** ✦ **crash, mishap** ◇ **disaster, misfortune** Bob broke his arm in a skateboarding *accident*.

accidental *adjective* ✦ **chance, unexpected, unintentional, unplanned** The farmer's *accidental* discovery of oil made him very rich.

acclaim *verb* ✦ **applaud, commend, praise** ◇ **approve, compliment** The movie was *acclaimed* by all the critics. —*noun* ✦ **praise, recognition** ◇ **approval, honor** The author was pleased by the great *acclaim* that her novel received.

accommodate *verb* ✦ **contain, hold** ◇ **house, lodge, shelter** Our classroom *accommodates* twenty-five students.

accompany *verb* ✦ **go with** ◇ **attend, escort, follow, guide** Petra's dad *accompanied* her to the swimming pool.

accomplice *noun* ✦ **accessory, confederate, conspirator** ◇ **helper, partner** Megan and her cousin were *accomplices* in sneaking out to go to the park.

accomplish *verb* ✦ **achieve, attain, complete, realize** ◇ **finish** My mom *accomplished* one of her major goals when she graduated from college last year.

accomplishment *noun* ✦ **achievement, feat** ◇ **success, triumph** Learning to play the saxophone is quite an *accomplishment*.

accord *verb* ✦ **agree with, coincide with, concur with, correspond to, match** Frank's explanation does not *accord with* his sister's. —*noun* ✦ **agreement, concurrence** ◇ **harmony, rapport** Many students and teachers are in *accord* that summer vacation is too short.

account *noun* **1.** ✦ **description, report** ◇ **explanation, story, tale, version** Ahmed gave his parents a detailed *account* of the class field trip. **2.** ✦ **importance, significance, value, worth** Laurie thinks that her brother's opinion is of little *account*. —*verb* ✦ **explain** ◇ **clarify, justify** Antonio's mother asked him if he could *account for* the missing cupcake.

accumulate *verb* ✦ **assemble, collect, gather** ◇ **acquire, gain** Paul has *accumulated* an impressive collection of arrowheads.

accuracy *noun* ✦ **correctness, exactness, precision** Mitsuko strives for *accuracy* when she types.

accurate *adjective* ✦ **correct, exact, precise, right** ◇ **perfect, truthful** Steve always double-checks his math homework to make sure that his answers are *accurate*.

accuse *verb* ✦ **charge (with)** ◇ **allege, blame** Amy *accused* her brother of spying on her.

accustomed *adjective* ✦ **customary, habitual, normal, usual** ◇ **ordinary, routine** In France, the *accustomed* greeting is a kiss on the cheek.

ache *verb* **1.** ✦ **hurt, throb** ◇ **pain, smart, suffer** My arm *aches* from playing tennis all afternoon. **2.** ✦ **desire, long, want** ◇ **covet, crave** Yaakov *aches* to be reunited with his family. —*noun* ✦ **hurt, pain, soreness** ◇ **discomfort** If that *ache* persists, you should see a doctor.

achieve *verb* ✦ **accomplish, attain, fulfill, reach, realize** Arlene recently *achieved* her dream of getting a black belt in tae kwon do.

achievement *noun* ✦ **accomplishment, feat, triumph** ◇ **deed, exploit** Zachary's proudest *achievement* is having won the regional chess tournament.

acknowledge *verb* **1.** ✦ **admit, concede, grant** ◇ **accept, allow** Matt *acknowledges* that Tyrone has a better baseball card collection.

✦ **best choices**
◇ **other choices**

2. ✦ **consider, deem, hold, recognize** Jen is *acknowledged* to be the best writer in our class.

acknowledgment *noun* ✦ **admission, concession, confession** ✧ **acceptance, recognition** Rick's *acknowledgment* that he had been wrong helped us forget our anger at him.

acquaintance *noun* ✦ **associate, colleague, companion** I have many *acquaintances*, but only a few close friends.

acquire *verb* ✦ **attain, gain, get, obtain, procure** ✧ **receive** Robin recently *acquired* a beautiful kachina doll for her collection.

acquit *verb* ✦ **absolve, clear** ✧ **discharge, excuse, forgive** The jury *acquitted* the suspect when the evidence proved his innocence.

act *verb* ✦ **function, operate, work** ✧ **serve** The lawyer *acted* on her client's behalf. —*noun* **1.** ✦ **action, deed, feat** ✧ **accomplishment, achievement** The legendary Hercules performed many heroic *acts*. **2.** ✦ **law, statute** ✧ **bill, decree** Abraham Lincoln's birthday was made a national holiday by an *act* of Congress.

action *noun* ✦ **act, deed** ✧ **accomplishment, effort, performance** Jamal's swift *action* saved the drowning boy's life.

active *adjective* **1.** ✦ **energetic, lively** ✧ **dynamic, industrious** Alice is very *active*, especially on the playground. **2.** ✦ **functioning, operating, working** ✧ **alive** Mount St. Helens is an *active* volcano.

activity *noun* **1.** ✦ **hobby, pastime, project, pursuit** ✧ **endeavor** Sam keeps himself busy with lots of after-school *activities*. **2.** ✦ **bustle, commotion, tumult** ✧ **action, movement** There was a great deal of *activity* on the day of Jonathan's bar mitzvah.

> **Antonyms**
>
> **activity** *noun*
> **2.** calm, lull, peace, quiet, serenity, tranquillity

actor *noun* ✦ **entertainer, performer, player** ✧ **star** Pedro wants to be a movie *actor*.

actual *adjective* ✦ **definite, real, true** ✧ **authentic, certain, genuine** The *actual* size of the universe is still unknown.

actually *adverb* ✦ **genuinely, really, truly** ✧ **indeed** Much to Farrah's amazement, she *actually* enjoyed the field trip to a worm farm.

acute *adjective* **1.** ✦ **keen, powerful, sharp** ✧ **intense, strong** Eagles have *acute* vision. **2.** ✦ **critical, dire, serious, severe, urgent** ✧ **crucial** Our school district has an *acute* shortage of funding.

adapt *verb* ✦ **adjust, conform** ✧ **change, fit** Ling *adapted* quickly to her new school. ▼

add *verb* **1.** ✦ **calculate, compute, total** ✧ **figure, reckon** Lloyd can *add* numbers so fast that we call him a human calculator. **2.** ✦ **include, insert** ✧ **attach, combine, join** Our peanut butter cookie dough looked so rich already that we decided not to *add* chocolate chips.

addiction *noun* ✦ **dependence (on)** ✧ **fixation, obsession, preoccupation** Do you think someone can have an *addiction* to sugar?

addition *noun* ✦ **annex, extension** ✧ **attachment, expansion, increase** When Grandma moved in, we built an *addition* onto our house to make room for her.

additional *adjective* ✦ **added, extra** ✧ **more, supplementary** Cesar makes the *additional* effort necessary to earn straight A's.

address *noun* **1.** ✦ **home, residence** ✧ **abode, location, place** My family moved to a new *address*. **2.** ✦ **speech, talk** ✧ **lecture, sermon** Wendell gave an *address* at the school assembly. —*verb* ✦ **speak to, talk to** ✧ **lecture** The president will *address* the nation tomorrow.

adequate *adjective* ✦ **enough, sufficient** ✧ **satisfactory, suitable** It is important to have *adequate* vitamins and minerals in your diet.

adhere *verb* **1.** ✦ **attach, cling, hold on, stick** ✧ **fasten** There were many burrs *adhering* to my socks after I took a shortcut through the empty lot. **2.** ✦ **follow, keep to, maintain, stick to** ✧ **heed, obey, observe** Success comes to those who *adhere to* their goals.

adjacent *adjective* ✦ **alongside, next to, touching** ✧ **close to, near** Mom thinks it is funny that the diet center is *adjacent to* a donut shop.

adjust *verb* **1.** ✦ **change, correct, regulate, set** ✧ **fix, repair** Anna helped her brother *adjust* the seat height on his bicycle. **2.** ✦ **adapt, conform** ✧ **reconcile, settle** Max had a hard time *adjusting* to boarding school.

adjustment *noun* ✦ **adaptation, alteration, change, modification** A few *adjustments* to the satellite dish improved our television reception.

administer *verb* **1.** ✦ **direct, manage, run, supervise** ✧ **control** My uncle *administered* the summer arts program for the whole city. **2.** ✦ **apply, dispense, give, provide** ✧ **supply** Paramedics *administered* first aid to the injured woman.

admirable *adjective* ✦ **commendable, praiseworthy** ✧ **beneficial, excellent, good, superb** Victoria makes *admirable* use of her spare time by volunteering at the local hospital.

admiration *noun* ✦ **esteem, praise, regard, respect** ✧ **approval, reverence** Cindy earned her competitors' *admiration* when she won the race despite her asthma.

admire *verb* ✦ **esteem, respect** ✧ **honor, revere, venerate** I *admire* Mike for being able to speak three foreign languages.

admit *verb* **1.** ✦ **acknowledge, concede, confess** ✧ **disclose, reveal** Linda *admitted* that she had difficulty remembering the names of all fifty states. **2.** ✦ **accept at** ✧ **include, receive, take** My older sister was just *admitted to* Harvard University.

adorable *adjective* ✦ **charming, delightful, lovable** ✧ **attractive, captivating** Nicole is the only one who thinks that her pet snake is *adorable*.

adore *verb* ✦ **cherish, love, treasure** ✧ **revere, worship** I *adore* my great-aunt because she is loving and wise.

adorn *verb* ✦ **deck, decorate, ornament, trim** Leah *adorned* her old hat with ribbons and flowers.

adult *noun* ✦ **grown-up** ✧ **man, woman** My scout troop requires an *adult* to be present at all meetings and outings. —*adjective* ✦ **full-grown, grown, mature** ✧ **aged, developed** *Adult* blue whales are the world's largest living animals.

advance *verb* **1.** ✦ **move, proceed, progress** ✧ **hasten, speed** The army *advanced* across the field. **2.** ✦ **boost, further, improve** ✧ **assist, benefit** Marie Curie's discoveries *advanced* our knowledge of radioactivity. **3.** ✦ **introduce, offer, propose, suggest** The crackpot scientist *advanced* a

Antonyms
advance *verb*
1. recede, retreat, withdraw
2. hinder, impede, obstruct
3. repress, suppress, withhold
advance *noun*
reversal, setback

✦ **best choices**
✧ **other choices**

theory that the Earth is square. —*noun*
✦ **advancement, development, improvement, progress** ◇ **headway** *Advances* in technology have made computers faster and more powerful.

advantage *noun* ✦ **benefit, blessing** ◇ **asset, edge, help** Theodore helps those who have fewer *advantages* than he does by volunteering at a soup kitchen.

advantageous *adjective* ✦ **beneficial, helpful, useful** ◇ **favorable, valuable** Alice finds it *advantageous* to sit near the front of the classroom.

adventure *noun* ✦ **exploit, feat, venture** ◇ **escapade, experience, undertaking** Going over the rapids in an inner tube was the greatest *adventure* of our trip.

adventurous *adjective* ✦ **bold, brave, courageous, daring, intrepid** The *adventurous* children explored a cemetery after dark.

adversary *noun* ✦ **competitor, opponent, rival** ◇ **enemy, foe** Tom and Natalie are the best of friends, but on the tennis court they are fierce *adversaries*.

adverse *adjective* ✦ **bad, unfavorable** ◇ **unfortunate, unlucky** *Adverse* weather forced us to postpone our baseball game.

advertise *verb* ✦ **announce, promote, publicize** ◇ **feature** Kat *advertised* her lawn-mowing business in the local paper.

advice *noun* ✦ **counsel, guidance, recommendation** ◇ **directions, help, suggestion** Sometimes it's difficult to follow your parents' *advice*.

advise *verb* ✦ **counsel, recommend, suggest** ◇ **caution, warn** My coach *advised* that I try out for swimming instead of diving.

affect *verb* **1.** ✦ **alter, change, modify** ◇ **disturb, transform** The airline strike *affected* my vacation plans. **2.** ✦ **move, stir, touch** ◇ **impress, upset** The sad movie *affected* Sonia deeply.

affection *noun* ✦ **fondness, love, tenderness, warmth** ◇ **devotion** Frank feels great *affection* for his little brother.

affectionate *adjective* ✦ **fond, loving, warm, tender** Olivia is an *affectionate* child who likes to give people hugs.

affirm *verb* ✦ **confirm** ◇ **assert, claim, declare, insist, swear** The witness *affirmed* that the defendant was telling the truth.

afford *verb* **1.** ✦ **pay for** ◇ **manage, support** If I save my allowance, I'll be able to *afford* a new skateboard. **2.** ✦ **furnish, give, provide, supply** ◇ **produce** This window *affords* a fine view of the ocean.

afraid *adjective* **1.** ✦ **fearful, frightened, scared, terrified** Karyn is *afraid* of her neighbor's dog. **2.** ✦ **sorry** ◇ **reluctant, unhappy** I'm *afraid* that I won't be able to attend your party.

after *preposition* ✦ **behind, following** Dessert comes *after* the main course. —*conjunction* ✦ **as soon as, once, when** I can play *after* I've finished my chores. —*adverb* ✦ **afterward, later, next, thereafter** You go on ahead, and I'll come *after*.

again *adverb* ✦ **once more, over** ◇ **often** Hiroshi liked the movie so much that he decided to see it *again*.

against *preposition* **1.** ✦ **facing, into, opposite to, toward** ◇ **across** The trip was bumpy because the plane had to fly *against* a strong headwind. **2.** ✦ **on, upon** Jay leaned his bike *against* the wall. ▶

age *noun* ✦ **epoch, era, period, time** Curt loves to read about the *age* of the dinosaurs. —*verb* ✦ **develop, grow, mature, ripen** ✧ **season** Letting tomatoes *age* on the vine ensures that they will have a better flavor.

aged *adjective* ✦ **elderly, old** ✧ **advanced, ancient, mature** My uncle is now *aged* and living in a nursing home.

agency *noun* ✦ **business, office** ✧ **bureau, department, organization** Doreen's mother works for a real estate *agency*.

agent *noun* **1.** ✦ **representative** ✧ **broker, delegate, negotiator** Nelson's acting *agent* got him a job in a television commercial. **2.** ✦ **cause, force, instrument, medium** ✧ **means, mechanism, power** I think of my two-year-old sister as an *agent* of destruction.

aggravate *verb* **1.** ✦ **intensify, worsen** ✧ **complicate, increase** When I scratched my mosquito bites, I only *aggravated* the itching. **2.** ✦ **annoy, bother, exasperate, irk, irritate** My brother's constant use of the phone *aggravates* my parents.

agile *adjective* ✦ **dexterous, limber, nimble, spry** ✧ **deft, quick** One needs to be very *agile* to excel in gymnastics.

agitate *verb* **1.** ✦ **churn, shake, stir, toss** A washing machine *agitates* clothes in soapy water to get the dirt out of them. **2.** ✦ **disturb, shake up, unsettle, upset** ✧ **arouse, excite, provoke** The speaker's angry remarks *agitated* the audience.

agony *noun* ✦ **anguish, distress, pain, torment** ✧ **suffering** Rosemary was in *agony* when she stubbed her toe a second time.

agree *verb* **1.** ✦ **consent** ✧ **concur** Mom and Dad finally *agreed* to let me go horseback riding. **2.** ✦ **coincide with, concur with, correspond to, fit, match** Susannah's opinion of the movie did not *agree with* mine.

agreement *noun* **1.** ✦ **accord, harmony** ✧ **conformity** My sister and I are usually in *agreement* about what to watch on TV. **2.** ✦ **compact, deal, pact** ✧ **bargain, treaty, understanding** Sarkis and his friend made an *agreement* to settle their argument by flipping a coin.

ahead *adverb* ✦ **in front** ✧ **before, first, leading** Eli pulled *ahead* of the other cyclists just in time to win the race.

aid *verb* ✦ **assist, help** ✧ **support** Dad stopped to *aid* the stranded motorist. —*noun* ✦ **assistance, guidance, help** ✧ **service, support** My first apple pie would have been a disaster without my mother's *aid*.

ailment *noun* ✦ **disease, disorder, illness, sickness** ✧ **affliction** Roger thought that he had a serious *ailment*, but he only had a bad cold.

aim *verb* ✦ **point, sight** ✧ **direct, level** Pete *aimed* at the bull's-eye, but he missed the target entirely. —*noun* ✦ **goal, objective** ✧ **plan, purpose, target** Jeneane's *aim* in life is to become a senator.

air *noun* ✦ **atmosphere, sky** The dragon spread its wings and soared through the *air*. —*verb* **1.** ✦ **ventilate** ✧ **freshen, refresh** This stuffy room needs to be *aired*. **2.** ✦ **communicate, express, voice** ✧ **declare, display** The principal plans to call a meeting for the students to *air* their complaints.

aisle *noun* ✧ **corridor, lane, passage, path, walkway** My little brother got lost in the *aisles* of the grocery store.

alarm *noun* **1.** ✦ **apprehension, dismay, distress, fear, fright, worry** The doctor assured me that tonsillitis is no cause for *alarm*. **2.** ✦ **alert, signal, warning** ✧ **bell, buzzer, horn, siren** When the fire *alarm* went off, we all had to go outside. —*verb* ✦ **frighten, scare, startle** ✧ **dismay, shock** Caroline likes to *alarm* her friends with her daredevil antics.

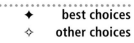

✦   best choices
✧   other choices

alert *adjective* ✦ **attentive, vigilant, watchful** ✧ **observant, ready** The lifeguard at the pool is always *alert* for signs of distress. —*verb* ✦ **advise, notify, warn** ✧ **inform, signal** We were *alerted* to prepare for more flooding. —*noun* ✦ **alarm, signal, warning** ✧ **siren** Everyone ran to their storm cellars when they heard the tornado *alert*.

> ### Word Groups
>
> An **alibi** is a claim that a person was elsewhere when a crime took place. **Alibi** is a very specific term with no true synonyms. Here are some related words to investigate in a dictionary:
>
> account, excuse, explanation, reason, report, statement, story, version

alike *adjective* ✦ **identical, similar, uniform** ✧ **matched** No two snowflakes are *alike* in every detail. —*adverb* ✦ **identically, similarly** ✧ **equally, uniformly** Olga and her twin sister Olivia usually dress *alike*.

alive *adjective* ✦ **live, living** ✧ **active, breathing, existing** Chen found a baby bird, and he kept it *alive* by feeding it worms.

allegiance *noun* ✦ **fidelity, loyalty** ✧ **devotion, obedience** My dog gives his *allegiance* to whoever feeds him.

alliance *noun* ✦ **pact, union** ✧ **agreement, treaty** Dale and Oscar formed an *alliance* against the neighborhood bully.

allied *adjective* ✦ **combined, joint, united** ✧ **associated, connected** The dwarves and elves decided to form an *allied* army to defeat the goblin horde.

allot *verb* ✦ **allocate, allow, assign, give** ✧ **distribute, share** Mrs. Blake *allotted* each pupil five minutes for his or her speech.

allow *verb* ✦ **let, permit** ✧ **approve, authorize** When my mom makes cookies, she always *allows* me to lick the spoon.

ally *verb* ✦ **join, unite** ✧ **associate, combine, unify** The citizen groups *allied* with each other to lobby for a new playground. —*noun* ✦ **partner** ✧ **assistant, associate, colleague** Angela and Eugene were *allies* in the snowball fight.

almost *adverb* ✦ **nearly, practically** ✧ **about, mostly, virtually** Davin *almost* flew off his bicycle when he hit the big pothole.

alone *adjective* ✦ **unaccompanied, unattended** ✧ **isolated, secluded, solitary** Hillary was *alone* all afternoon while her mom ran errands.

aloud *adverb* ✦ **out loud** ✧ **audibly, loudly, openly** Gretchen enjoys reading *aloud* to her little brother. ▼

also *adverb* ✦ **as well, besides, too** ✧ **additionally, furthermore** Everett felt sick because he ate all of the cookies and half the cupcakes *also*.

alter *verb* ✦ **change, modify, transform, vary** ✧ **revise** Chanay's new haircut completely *alters* her appearance.

alternate *verb* ✦ **rotate, shift, switch, take turns** ✧ **vary** My cat *alternates* between sleeping and eating. —*adjective* **1.** ✦ **alternating, every other** ✧ **recurring, successive** Ray mows the yard on *alternate* Sundays. **2.** ✦ **another, different, substitute** The bridge was closed, so we had to take an *alternate* route.

alternative *noun* ✦ **choice, option** ✧ **selection** There are so many *alternatives*, I can't decide which movie to see.

altogether *adverb* ✦ **absolutely, completely, entirely, totally, wholly** Ms. Samuels warned us that we were being *altogether* too rowdy.

always *adverb* ✦ **eternally, forever** ✧ **constantly, perpetually** I will love you *always*.

amateur *noun* ✦ **dabbler, nonprofessional** ✧ **beginner, novice** When it comes to singing, my dad is a total *amateur*.

amaze *verb* ✦ **astonish, astound, impress, surprise** ✧ **shock** Joanne *amazes* me with her ability to remember people's names.

amazement *noun* ✦ **astonishment, awe, bewilderment, surprise, wonder** Imagine my *amazement* when my little brother beat me at chess.

ambition *noun* ✦ **aim, goal, objective** ✧ **desire, wish** Diane's *ambition* is to become a great veterinarian.

ambitious *adjective* **1.** ✦ **aspiring, determined** ✧ **eager, hopeful, purposeful** The *ambitious* actor hopes to land a starring role someday. **2.** ✦ **bold, daring** ✧ **challenging, difficult** The mayor unveiled her *ambitious* plans to build a new civic center.

amble *verb* ✦ **ramble, saunter, stroll, walk** We *ambled* along the river, enjoying the sunny day.

amend *verb* ✦ **alter, change, reform** ✧ **correct, improve, revise** The U.S. Constitution has been periodically *amended*.

amiable *adjective* ✦ **friendly, good-natured, pleasant** ✧ **congenial, sociable** Brennan likes his new school because his classmates are very *amiable*.

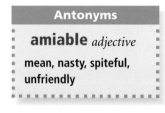

Antonyms

amiable *adjective*

mean, nasty, spiteful, unfriendly

among *preposition* ✦ **amongst, between** ✧ **amid, amidst, with** The bank robbers divided the loot *among* themselves.

amount *noun* ✦ **quantity, sum, total** ✧ **number** The *amount* you owe for dinner is five dollars. —*verb* ✦ **equal, total** ✧ **match, reach** My expenditures for the weekend camping trip *amounted to* thirty-five dollars.

ample *adjective* ✦ **abundant, adequate, enough, plenty of, sufficient** ✧ **plentiful, unlimited** Even though Dave ate two hamburgers, he had *ample* room for dessert.

amplify *verb* ✦ **boost, intensify, strengthen** ✧ **expand, increase** A loudspeaker system *amplified* the band's music.

amuse *verb* ✦ **charm, entertain, please** ✧ **interest** Justine *amused* us with a song she made up.

amusement *noun* ✦ **enjoyment, entertainment, fun** ✧ **mirth, pleasure** The circus provides *amusement* for people of all ages.

amusing *adjective* ✦ **comical, entertaining, funny** ✧ **charming, delightful** Pierre thinks that his sister is *amusing* when she hangs a spoon off her nose.

analyze *verb* ✦ **evaluate, examine, investigate, study** ✧ **judge** In our English class, we *analyzed* the elements of a good novel.

ancestor *noun* ✦ **forebear** ✧ **forefather, foremother** Kevin can trace his *ancestors* clear back to the Middle Ages.

✦   **best choices**
✧   **other choices**

anchor *verb* ✦ attach, fasten, fix, secure ✧ **hold** The climber looked for a safe place to *anchor* her rope.

anger *noun* ✦ **fury, ire, rage, wrath** ✧ **annoyance, irritation** Wanda's *anger* caused her to say things that she later regretted. *—verb* ✦ **incense, infuriate, outrage, upset** ✧ **annoy, offend** It *angers* me when my parents don't listen to my side of the story.

angry *adjective* ✦ **mad, furious, irate, upset** ✧ **annoyed** Gwen was *angry* when she couldn't find her diary.

anguish *noun* ✦ **agony, distress, misery, torment** ✧ **pain, suffering** Dawn, a straight-A student, was in *anguish* over the "D" on her latest report card.

animal *noun* ✦ **beast** ✧ **being, creature** Tara wants to train circus *animals*.

animosity *noun* ✦ **hate, hatred, hostility** ✧ **bitterness, resentment** There was *animosity* between the warring clans.

annex *verb* ✦ **add, attach** ✧ **connect, join, unite** After the war, the victorious country *annexed* some of the loser's territory. *—noun* ✦ **addition, extension, wing** ✧ **branch** The museum built an *annex* to house its new exhibit.

announce *verb* ✦ **declare, proclaim** ✧ **disclose, report, tell** My older brother recently *announced* his engagement.

annoy *verb* ✦ **bother, disturb, irk, irritate** Please don't *annoy* your sister while she's doing her homework.

answer *noun* **1.** ✦ **reply, response** ✧ **acknowledgment** I mailed an *answer* to the birthday party invitation. **2.** ✦ **solution** ✧ **explanation, resolution, result** Jacob thinks that learning to eat insects is the *answer* to world hunger. *—verb* ✦ **reply, respond** ✧ **acknowledge, react** Tricia *answered* with a nod.

anticipate *verb* ✦ **await, expect** ✧ **foresee, predict** Arthur's dog eagerly *anticipates* their evening walks.

antique *noun* ✦ **heirloom** ✧ **artifact, relic, souvenir** This doll is an *antique* that has been handed down from Tracy's great-grandmother.

anxiety *noun* ✦ **apprehension, concern, distress, uneasiness, worry** Claire felt some *anxiety* about giving her first oral report.

anxious *adjective* **1.** ✦ **apprehensive, fearful, nervous, uneasy, worried** Ross was *anxious* about his visit to the dentist. **2.** ✦ **eager, impatient** ✧ **desirous, expectant** Miranda is *anxious* to attend Girl Scout camp.

apathy *noun* ✦ **indifference** ✧ **disinterest, unconcern** Because of Dale's *apathy*, he missed the deadline to sign up for Little League.

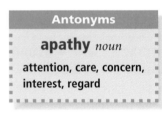

Antonyms

apathy *noun*

attention, care, concern, interest, regard

appall *verb* ✦ **dismay, horrify, shock, stun** The students were *appalled* that their teacher assigned homework over spring break.

apparatus *noun* ✦ **equipment, gear, implements** ✧ **device, machinery** Cayce enjoys using gym *apparatus*, especially the balance beam. ▼

apparel *noun* ✦ **attire, clothes, clothing, garments** Dad is looking for a store that sells *apparel* for tall men.

apparent *adjective* ✦ **clear, evident, obvious, plain** ✧ **visible** It's *apparent* that you don't like these chocolate-covered raisins.

appeal *noun* 1. ✦ **bid, call, entreaty, plea, request** The public television station is making an *appeal* for contributions. 2. ✦ **allure, attraction** ✧ **charm, fascination** Sometimes TV commercials have more *appeal* than the show I'm watching. —*verb* 1. ✦ **ask, beg, plead to** ✧ **pray, request** The earthquake victims *appealed to* the government for assistance. 2. ✦ **attract, fascinate, interest, tempt** Wind surfing *appeals to* Kim.

appear *verb* 1. ✦ **come out, emerge, issue** ✧ **materialize, show up** The moon *appeared* from behind the clouds. 2. ✦ **look, seem** ✧ **act** Jerome *appears* to be enjoying his book.

appearance *noun* 1. ✦ **arrival, emergence** ✧ **coming, entrance** We were thrilled by the sudden *appearance* of dolphins behind the boat. 2. ✦ **look** ✧ **aspect, demeanor, image** Ted always has a neat *appearance*.

appease *verb* ✦ **calm, pacify, quiet, soothe** ✧ **satisfy** The mail carrier *appeased* the barking German shepherd with a dog biscuit.

appendix *noun* ✦ **addition, attachment, supplement** ✧ **index** My math book has an *appendix* that lists answers to the self-test problems.

appetite *noun* ✦ **craving, desire, hunger, taste** ✧ **demand, need** Holly had no *appetite* for the peanut butter and pickle sandwich.

appetizing *adjective* ✦ **appealing, delicious, inviting, pleasing, tempting** During the holidays, our kitchen is filled with *appetizing* aromas.

applaud *verb* ✦ **acclaim, approve, commend, praise** ✧ **cheer** Ms. Taylor *applauded* her class's efforts to win the canned food drive.

applause *noun* ✦ **clapping, ovation** ✧ **acclaim, cheers, praise** The *applause* that followed Mandy's cello recital was very enthusiastic.

appliance *noun* ✦ **apparatus, equipment** ✧ **device, implement** Kitchen *appliances* range from electric can openers to refrigerators.

application *noun* 1. ✦ **function, purpose, use** ✧ **operation, value** A pocketknife has many practical *applications*. 2. ✧ **appeal, petition, request, requisition** Gina's older sister sent *applications* to many different colleges.

apply *verb* 1. ✦ **administer to, put on, spread on** ✧ **deposit, lay** The aloe vera gel Mom *applied to* my burn is sticky. 2. ✦ **employ, exercise, use, utilize** Skyler *applied* all of his strength to open the tightly sealed jar. 3. ✦ **pertain, relate** ✧ **concern, fit, involve, refer** Honesty is an old-fashioned value that still *applies* today.

appoint *verb* ✦ **designate for, name to, select for** ✧ **assign, elect** Esther has been *appointed to* the dance committee.

appointment *noun* 1. ✦ **selection (for)** ✧ **assignment, election, placement** My mother was pleased by her *appointment* to the research board. 2. ✦ **date, engagement** ✧ **booking, meeting** Dad made an *appointment* for me to see the doctor.

appreciate *verb* 1. ✦ **cherish, prize, treasure, value** ✧ **esteem, like** Beatriz *appreciates* the time she is able to spend with her brother when he is home from college. 2. ✦ **comprehend, perceive, understand** ✧ **acknowledge, recognize** I *appreciate* your viewpoint, but you still haven't changed my mind.

appreciation *noun* 1. ✦ **awareness, perception, understanding** ✧ **enjoyment** Bart developed a new *appreciation* of music after starting guitar lessons. 2. ✦ **gratefulness, gratitude, thankfulness, thanks** Sarah expressed her *appreciation* for the gift by writing a thank-you note.

✦ **best choices**
✧ **other choices**

approach *verb* **1.** ✦ **near, reach** ✧ **come, gain** The train slowed down as it *approached* the station. **2.** ✦ **begin, commence, initiate, start, undertake** Colleen *approaches* each chore with a positive attitude. —*noun* **1.** ✦ **method, procedure, system, technique** ✧ **attitude, style** When I have a big project, my *approach* is to do a little work every day. **2.** ✦ **avenue, passage, route** ✧ **entrance, entry** The dwarves guarded all *approaches* to their cave.

appropriate *adjective* ✦ **apt, correct, fitting, proper, suitable** Jocelyn wears *appropriate* shoes when she plays golf. —*verb* ✦ **allocate, allot, assign, authorize** ✧ **devote** Construction will begin as soon as funds are *appropriated*.

approval *noun* **1.** ✦ **admiration, praise, respect** ✧ **acceptance, favor** The crowd cheered with *approval* when the runner got back to her feet and finished the race. **2.** ✦ **agreement, authorization, consent, permission** My parents gave their *approval* when I asked to have a sleepover.

approve *verb* **1.** ✦ **commend, praise, respect** ✧ **accept, appreciate** Jane's parents have always *approved of* her interest in sports. **2.** ✦ **allow, authorize, endorse, permit** My teacher *approved* my report topic.

approximate *adjective* ✦ **close, estimated, rough** ✧ **relative** What is the *approximate* number of people at this party?

approximately *adverb* ✦ **about, nearly, roughly** ✧ **almost** My sister is *approximately* two years younger than I.

area *noun* **1.** ✦ **place, region, terrain, territory** ✧ **district, zone** Pine trees grow best in *areas* that receive a lot of rain. **2.** ✦ **room, space** ✧ **expanse, extent, scope** My chair and desk take up most of the *area* in the study.

argue *verb* **1.** ✦ **contend, plead** ✧ **assert, reason** Jerry *argued* his case for a later bedtime. **2.** ✦ **bicker, fight, quarrel** ✧ **disagree, dispute, feud** Muriel and her brother rarely *argue* because they are so much alike.

argument *noun* **1.** ✦ **disagreement, dispute** ✧ **fight, quarrel, spat** Tom and Leroy resolved their *argument* by flipping a coin. **2.** ✦ **case, reason** ✧ **grounds, justification** Sharyn's *argument* for being allowed to attend the party was that all of her friends were going.

arid *adjective* ✦ **dry** ✧ **barren, parched, waterless** My uncle moved to Arizona because its *arid* climate is very good for his rheumatism. ▼

arise *verb* ✦ **appear, begin, emerge, originate, result, rise** A disagreement *arose* when my friends and I tried to decide which movie to rent.

arm *noun* ✦ **firearm, gun, weapon** ✧ **armament** Paul Revere warned the Massachusetts minutemen to ready their *arms*. —*verb* ✦ **equip, outfit** ✧ **prepare, protect, provide** Sally and Annette *armed* themselves with a supply of snowballs before attacking their friends' fort.

army *noun* ✦ **horde, host, mass, swarm** ✧ **force, troop** We watched in fascination as an *army* of ants descended on the cookie crumbs.

aroma *noun* ✦ **fragrance, odor, scent, smell** I love the *aroma* of freshly baked bread.

around *preposition* ✦ **about, near** I'll be home *around* dinnertime. —*adverb* ✦ **about** ✧ **everywhere** Dena looked *around* until she found her missing barrette.

arouse *verb* ✦ **awaken, excite, kindle, provoke, stimulate, stir** Mr. Winquist's lesson about Native Americans *aroused* my interest.

arrange *verb* **1.** ✦ **order, organize, sort** ✧ **place, position** Our library *arranges* books by the Dewey Decimal System. **2.** ✦ **plan, prepare, schedule** My school *arranged* a field trip to the museum.

arrangement *noun* **1.** ✦ **layout, order** ✧ **distribution, formation, organization** Tori helped her mom plan the seating *arrangement* for their dinner party. **2.** ✦ **plan** ✧ **measure, preparation, provision** My parents made *arrangements* for me to visit my cousins in Hawaii.

arrest *verb* ✦ **apprehend, capture, catch, seize** Police officers *arrested* the robbery suspect. —*noun* ✦ **apprehension, capture** The *arrest* was made by an undercover detective.

arrival *noun* ✦ **appearance, coming** ✧ **approach, entrance** My aunt's unexpected *arrival* was a wonderful surprise.

arrive *verb* ✦ **come, get in, show up** ✧ **appear, approach, reach** When does the next train *arrive*?

arrogant *adjective* ✦ **conceited, disdainful, egotistical, haughty** ✧ **insolent, proud, vain** Andrew became *arrogant* after he was elected class president.

art *noun* ✦ **craft, skill, technique** Anna learned the *art* of calligraphy at school.

article *noun* **1.** ✦ **feature, piece, story** ✧ **essay, review** Zina wrote an *article* about the book fair for her school paper. **2.** ✦ **item, object, piece, thing** ✧ **commodity** Please count the number of *articles* that are in that box.

artificial *adjective* ✦ **fake, imitation, phony, simulated, synthetic** Only an expert can tell *artificial* gems from real ones.

> ### Word Groups
>
> An **artist** is a person who creates works of art. **Artist** is a general term with no true synonyms. Here are some different kinds of artists to investigate in a dictionary:
>
> **artisan, composer, illustrator, musician, painter, sculptor, writer**

ascend *verb* ✦ **climb, mount** ✧ **rise, scale** Renee *ascended* the stairs so that she could slide down the banister.

ascent *noun* ✦ **climb** ✧ **ascension** My uncle has made more than a dozen *ascents* of California's Mount Whitney.

ashamed *adjective* ✦ **embarrassed, guilty** ✧ **humiliated** Conrad felt *ashamed* after he looked at his sister's diary.

ask *verb* **1.** ✦ **request** ✧ **appeal, beg, plead, seek** Bobby *asked for* a camera for his birthday. **2.** ✦ **inquire, query** ✧ **examine, interrogate, question** Let's *ask* if we can talk to the pilot.

asleep *adjective* ✦ **dozing, napping, sleeping, slumbering** ✧ **dormant** My cat is *asleep* on the windowsill.

aspect *noun* ✦ **appearance, look** ✧ **face, surface** Our yard took on a whole new *aspect* when we planted flowers around the edge.

aspire *verb* ✦ **desire, seek, want, wish, yearn** ✧ **crave** James *aspires* to become a champion tennis player.

assassin *noun* ✦ **killer, murderer** ✧ **executioner** One function of the Secret Service is to protect our leaders from would-be *assassins*.

✦ best choices
✧ other choices

assassinate *verb* ✦ **kill, murder, slay** ✧ **execute** President Lincoln was *assassinated* five days after the Civil War ended.

assault *noun* ✦ **attack, strike** ✧ **offensive, onslaught** The soldiers made an *assault* on the enemy fort. —*verb* ✦ **attack** ✧ **bombard, charge, rush, storm** Barry *assaulted* the overgrown grass with his lawn mower.

assemble *verb* 1. ✦ **collect, congregate, gather, rally** ✧ **accumulate** The football team *assembled* around the coach. 2. ✦ **construct, make, put together** ✧ **connect, join** Brad's mother helped him *assemble* his new kite.

assembly *noun* 1. ✦ **gathering, meeting** ✧ **convention, rally** We had a school *assembly* to honor our retiring principal. 2. ✦ **construction** ✧ **connecting, fitting, joining** The directions said that some *assembly* would be required.

assert *verb* ✦ **affirm, announce, claim, declare** ✧ **insist, swear** Karen *asserted* that she planned to stay up until midnight.

asset *noun* 1. ✦ **advantage, aid, benefit, boon, help, strength** Helen's huge vocabulary is a great *asset* when she plays word games. 2. ✦ **possessions, property** ✧ **capital, wealth** My dad's *assets* include two houses and a boat.

assign *verb* 1. ✦ **appoint, designate, name** ✧ **charge, nominate** Rick was *assigned* to be on hall duty for the week. 2. ✦ **give** ✧ **allocate, allot, dispense, distribute** I hope Ms. Fernandez doesn't *assign* us any more book reports.

assignment *noun* ✦ **duty, job, task** ✧ **chore, mission** My *assignment* was to stand guard.

assist *verb* ✦ **aid, help** ✧ **serve, support** Leslie likes to *assist* her dad when he's working in the yard.

Antonyms
assist *verb*
hamper, hinder, impede, obstruct, restrict

assistance *noun* ✦ **aid, help** ✧ **backing, service, support** Tristan gave his mother *assistance* with unloading the groceries. ▼

assistant *noun* ✦ **aide, helper** ✧ **attendant, auxiliary, subordinate** Mrs. Nagel always asks for an *assistant* to help hand out papers.

associate *verb* 1. ✦ **connect to, identify with, link to, relate to** Jack-o'-lanterns and haunted houses are *associated with* Halloween. 2. ✦ **fraternize, mingle, mix, socialize** My parents like to *associate* with a wide variety of people. —*noun* ✦ **colleague, partner, peer** ✧ **confederate** My mother's business *associates* came to our house for dinner.

association *noun* ✦ **club, group, organization, society** ✧ **alliance, league** Margaret Anne is now a member of a national *association* of stamp collectors.

assortment *noun* ✦ **selection, variety** ✧ **array, collection** Breanna gave her teacher an *assortment* of Swiss chocolates.

assume *verb* 1. ✦ **presume, suppose** ✧ **believe, surmise, suspect, think** Lee *assumes* that she will have a party on her birthday. 2. ✦ **take on, undertake** ✧ **acquire, adopt, embrace, take** Keegan had to *assume* more responsibility around the house when his brother left for college.

assure *verb* ✦ **promise** ✧ **confirm, guarantee, pledge** The veterinarian *assured* us that our iguana would be fine.

astonish *verb* ✦ **amaze, astound, stun, surprise** ✧ **startle** Mason *astonished* his parents by cleaning his room without being asked.

astonishment *noun* ✦ **amazement, surprise** ✧ **confusion, disbelief, wonder** I gaped in *astonishment* as the pigeon flew into our car.

athletic *adjective* ✦ **active, energetic, vigorous** Sam is an *athletic* boy who loves to play hockey and other sports.

atmosphere *noun* 1. ✧ **air, sky** The space shuttle takes only a few minutes to exit the Earth's *atmosphere*. ▶ 2. ✦ **feel, feeling, mood, spirit** ✧ **climate, environment** I love the cozy *atmosphere* at this cafe.

atrocious *adjective* ✦ **abominable, bad, dreadful, poor, terrible** ✧ **cruel, wicked** Dad says my table manners are *atrocious*.

attach *verb* ✦ **affix, connect, fasten, join, secure** Kevin helped his sister *attach* a basket to her bicycle.

attachment *noun* 1. ✦ **accessory** ✧ **addition, supplement** Our new vacuum cleaner has an *attachment* for cleaning upholstery. 2. ✦ **bond, tie** ✧ **affection, devotion, love** Rebecca has a strong *attachment* to her best friend.

attack *verb* 1. ✦ **assault, charge, storm** ✧ **assail** Attila the Hun invaded Italy, but he did not *attack* Rome. 2. ✦ **criticize, denounce, fault** ✧ **censure** During the debate, Carlos *attacked* his opponent's argument. —*noun* ✦ **assault, charge, offensive, raid, strike** The enemy forces launched their *attack* at dawn.

attain *verb* ✦ **accomplish, achieve, reach, realize** ✧ **acquire, gain** Kwan *attained* her dream of becoming captain of the swim team.

attempt *verb* ✦ **endeavor, try** ✧ **seek, strive, struggle** I *attempted* to move the table by myself, but I had to ask for help. —*noun* ✦ **effort, try** ✧ **endeavor, venture** Marcy cleared six feet on her first *attempt* at the high jump.

attend *verb* 1. ✦ **go to** ✧ **frequent, visit** Marc *attends* hockey practice after school. 2. ✦ **serve, take care of, tend** ✧ **accompany, escort** When Mrs. Garcia came home from the hospital, she hired two nurses to *attend* her.

attendant *noun* ✦ **assistant, helper** ✧ **aide, servant** The zoo *attendant* gave us directions to the koala bear enclosure.

attention *noun* ✦ **care, heed, regard** ✧ **concentration, notice** When Joel builds model airplanes, gives close *attention* to the details.

attentive *adjective* ✦ **alert, heedful, observant** ✧ **considerate, thoughtful** Everyone was very *attentive* when the fire chief visited our class.

attire *noun* ✦ **apparel, clothing, garments, outfit** ✧ **costume** Charlene wore comfortable *attire* for the plane ride.

attitude *noun* ✦ **outlook, perspective** ✧ **approach, disposition, mood** Nick is fun to work with because he brings a good *attitude* to everything he does.

attract *verb* ✦ **draw, lure, pull** ✧ **charm, entice** Don't leave the food uncovered or it will *attract* flies.

attraction *noun* ✦ **appeal, draw, pull** ✧ **allure, charm** The baby elephants are the main *attraction* at our zoo.

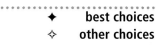

✦   **best choices**
✧   **other choices**

attractive *adjective* ✦ **appealing, beautiful, becoming, lovely, pleasing** Kierra's shirt is an *attractive* shade of green.

audience *noun* ✦ **crowd, onlookers, spectators** ✧ **following** The juggler was so good that he soon attracted an *audience*.

authentic *adjective* ✦ **actual, genuine, real, true** ✧ **valid** Skip claims to have an *authentic* photograph of a UFO.

Word Groups

The author of a written work is its original creator. Author is a general term with no true synonyms. Here are some different kinds of authors to investigate in a dictionary:

essayist, journalist, novelist, playwright, poet, scribe, scriptwriter

---

authority *noun* **1.** ✦ **authorization, control, power, right** ✧ **command, influence** My parents gave me the *authority* to set my own bedtime. **2.** ✦ **expert, specialist** ✧ **master** Shannon is an *authority* on baseball cards.

authorize *verb* ✦ **allow, approve, permit, sanction** ✧ **warrant** The principal *authorized* the field trip.

autograph *noun* ✦ **signature** ✧ **inscription** Michelle asked the basketball star for his *autograph*. —*verb* ✦ **sign** ✧ **endorse, inscribe** The symphony conductor *autographed* my program.

automatic *adjective* ✦ **automated, mechanical, self-acting, self-operating** ✧ **independent** Our electric heater has an *automatic* shutoff as a safety feature.

available *adjective* ✦ **free, obtainable, open** ✧ **accessible, usable** We asked the restaurant hostess if any booths were *available*.

avenue *noun* ✦ **boulevard, road, street, thoroughfare** ✧ **route** We drove down a tree-lined *avenue* on our way to the county courthouse.

average *noun* ✦ **mean, norm, par, standard** Clark's ability in English is above the *average*. —*adjective* **1.** ✧ **mean, middle** The *average* age in our class is eleven years, three months. **2.** ✦ **normal, ordinary, standard, typical, usual** I read that the *average* candy bar has more than two hundred calories.

avoid *verb* ✦ **elude, escape, evade** ✧ **dodge, shun, sidestep** We went to the beach on Wednesday in order to *avoid* the weekend crowds.

award *verb* ✦ **give, grant, present** ✧ **assign, confer** A blue ribbon was *awarded* to Kelly's peach jam at the state fair. ▶ —*noun* ✦ **prize, trophy** ✧ **decoration, honor, medal, tribute** My brother will probably get the *award* for best athlete.

aware *adjective* ✦ **conscious, mindful** ✧ **informed, knowledgeable** April wasn't *aware* that it was her turn to set the table.

awful *adjective* ✦ **abominable, bad, dreadful, hideous, horrible, terrible** Adrienne thinks that ice cream and ketchup would taste *awful* together.

awfully *adverb* ✦ **extremely, immensely, terribly, very** ✧ **greatly** Susan had an *awfully* hard time walking all three dogs at once.

awkward *adjective* **1.** ✦ **clumsy, graceless, inept, uncoordinated, unskilled** Before I took tennis lessons, my serve was *awkward*. **2.** ✦ **cumbersome, difficult, unwieldy** ✧ **unmanageable** The large suitcase was *awkward* to carry.

B

babble *verb* ✦ **chatter, jabber, talk** ✧ **gurgle, murmur** My sister *babbled* on and on about how exciting the plane ride had been. *—noun* ✦ **babbling, burble, gurgle, murmur** ✧ **chatter, jabbering** Listening to the brook's gentle *babble* is very relaxing.

baby *noun* ✦ **babe, infant, newborn** ✧ **toddler** My brother tried to convince me that *babies* are delivered by a stork.

back *noun* ✦ **rear** ✧ **end, reverse, tail** Derek and his friends like to sit at the *back* of the bus. *—adjective* ✦ **hind, rear** ✧ **behind, end, tail** The horse injured its *back* leg landing a jump. *—verb* ✦ **endorse, sponsor, support** ✧ **encourage, help** The local hardware store is *backing* our hockey team by paying for our uniforms.

background *noun* **1.** ✦ **distance** ✧ **landscape, setting, surroundings** Tricia's drawing of a bighorn sheep has mountains in the *background*. **2.** ✦ **experience, training** ✧ **preparation, qualifications** Our new music teacher has some *background* in jazz.

bad *adjective* **1.** ✦ **awful, lousy, poor, terrible** ✧ **imperfect, inferior** During the storm, our television reception was *bad*. **2.** ✦ **disagreeable, nasty, unpleasant** ✧ **disturbing** Rotten eggs have a *bad* odor. **3.** ✦ **disobedient, naughty** ✧ **mean, unruly, wrong** Our dog was *bad* when he dug a big hole in the backyard. **4.** ✦ **damaging, harmful, hurtful** Reading without enough light can be *bad* for your eyes. **5.** ✦ **guilty, regretful, sorry** ✧ **upset** Samantha felt *bad* for yelling at her sister.

baffle *verb* ✦ **bewilder, confuse, mystify, perplex, puzzle, stump** I was *baffled* when my sister refused the cookie I offered her.

bag *noun* ✦ **sack** ✧ **bundle, container, pouch** Jasmine brought her lunch to school in a paper *bag*.

bait *noun* ✦ **lure** ✧ **attraction, magnet, temptation** Many people use worms for *bait* when they fish. *—verb* ✦ **goad, harass, provoke, taunt, tease** ✧ **torment** As Ronald came up to bat, the other team *baited* him with jeers and insults.

balance *noun* **1.** ✦ **equilibrium, stability, steadiness** ✧ **poise** Gunter lost his *balance* while skiing and fell into a snowbank. **2.** ✦ **leftover, remainder, rest** ✧ **difference, residue** Karyn put half her allowance in savings then spent the *balance* on art supplies. *—verb* ✦ **stabilize, steady** ✧ **poise** Molly swayed for a moment but *balanced* herself so she wouldn't fall off the fence. ▶

bald *adjective* ✦ **bare, hairless, smooth** ✧ **barren** My baby sister's head was *bald* for the first few months of her life.

balk *verb* ✦ **refuse, resist, stop** My little brother *balked* when I told him to go down the slide.

ban *verb* ✦ **bar, disallow, forbid, outlaw, prohibit** The city council has *banned* smoking in public places. *—noun* ✦ **prohibition, restriction** ✧ **boycott** I wish there were a *ban* on weekend homework assignments.

band *noun* **1.** ✦ **crew, gang, group, pack, party** ✧ **team** Robin Hood had a *band* of merry men. **2.** ✦ **ensemble, group** ✧ **combo, orchestra** My brother's *band* rehearses in our garage. *—verb* ✦ **join, unite** ✧ **assemble, merge** The citizens *banded* with the police to stop crime.

bandit *noun* ✦ **outlaw, robber, thief** ✧ **criminal** In the Old West, *bandits* frequently robbed trains.

bang *verb* ✦ **beat, hammer, pound** ✧ **strike** My one-year-old cousin likes to *bang* on the table with his spoon.

banish *verb* ✦ **deport, eject, evict, exile, expel** Napoleon was *banished* to the island of Elba.

banquet *noun* ✦ **dinner, feast, meal** My scout troop has an awards *banquet* twice a year.

bar *noun* **1.** ✧ **pole, rail, rod, shaft** The lion gnawed on the iron *bars* of its cage. **2.** ✦ **barrier, impediment, obstacle, obstruction** ✧ **block** Joan's lack of experience was a *bar* to getting the job she wanted. **3.** ✦ **pub, saloon, tavern** ✧ **canteen, lounge, nightclub** In most states, you have to be at least twenty-one years old to enter a *bar*. — *verb* ✦ **forbid, prevent, prohibit, restrict** ✧ **block, obstruct** Randy was *barred* from playing with his friends until he finished his chores.

bare *adjective* ✦ **bald, barren, uncovered** ✧ **empty, naked, vacant** There's a *bare* patch on the lawn where we can't get grass to grow. — *verb* ✦ **expose, reveal, show, uncover** Our new kitten *bared* its little claws when it saw our dog.

barely *adverb* ✦ **hardly, just, scarcely** ✧ **only** The snow *barely* covered the ground.

bargain *noun* **1.** ✦ **agreement, arrangement, pact, promise** ✧ **treaty** My brother and I made a *bargain* to help each other clean our rooms. **2.** ✦ **buy, deal, good buy** ✧ **discount, steal** Mom goes to sales to look for *bargains*. — *verb* ✦ **deal, haggle, negotiate** ✧ **trade** My parents and I *bargained* over the amount of my allowance.

barren *adjective* ✦ **bare, empty** ✧ **infertile, unproductive** Lindsay admired the open views as she hiked up the *barren* hillside.

barrier *noun* ✦ **obstacle, obstruction** ✧ **barricade, blockade** The river was a *barrier* that the fire couldn't cross.

barter *verb* ✦ **exchange, swap, trade** ✧ **bargain** I *bartered* my comic books for Tom's baseball cards.

base *noun* **1.** ✦ **bottom, foundation** ✧ **foot** The *base* of a pyramid is square, but the sides are triangular. **2.** ✧ **camp, headquarters, post, station** My dad works on a military *base*. — *verb* ✦ **found, ground** ✧ **build, construct, establish** Even though the movie was *based* on a true story, I found it hard to believe.

bashful *adjective* ✦ **reserved, shy, timid** ✧ **modest, uncertain** Ara felt *bashful* on his first day at his new school.

basic *adjective* ✦ **elementary, fundamental, primary** ✧ **core, essential, vital** Flour is one of the *basic* ingredients in a cake.

battle *noun* ✦ **combat, conflict, fight, struggle, war** The soldiers were armed and ready for *battle*. — *verb* ✦ **fight, struggle with** ✧ **duel, skirmish** Mary had to *battle* strong winds when she walked to school this morning.

bawl *verb* ✦ **cry, howl, wail** ✧ **shout, shriek, weep** The toddler *bawled* when she couldn't find her teddy bear.

bay *noun* ✦ **cove, harbor** ✧ **inlet, lagoon** The crew anchored their ship in a secluded *bay*.

beach *noun* ✦ **seashore, shore** ✧ **coast, seacoast** Brad looked for shells as he walked along the *beach*.

beacon *noun* ✦ **beam, guide, light, signal** ✧ **landmark, pointer** The street lights were welcome *beacons* as Cayce rode her bicycle home in the dark.

beam *noun* **1.** ✧ **girder, rafter, stud, timber, trestle** Are those *beams* made of pine or cedar? **2.** ✦ **ray** ✧ **gleam, glow, shaft, streak** The flashlight's *beam* became dim as the batteries faded. — *verb* ✦ **gleam, glimmer, radiate, shine** The sun *beamed* from behind the clouds.

bear *verb* **1.** ✦ **carry, hold, shoulder, support** ✧ **sustain, take** Mules can *bear* surprisingly heavy loads. **2.** ✦ **abide, endure, stand, tolerate** ✧ **suffer** Kelly cannot *bear* a messy room. **3.** ✦ **develop, generate, produce** ✧ **deliver, make** Apple trees *bear* fruit in late summer and early fall. ▲

bearing *noun* ✦ **connection (to), relation (to)** ✧ **application, relevance, significance** Our sense of smell has a strong *bearing* on our sense of taste.

beast *noun* ✦ **animal** ✧ **creature, mammal** The lion has been said to be the king of *beasts*.

beat *verb* **1.** ✦ **hit, pound, strike** ✧ **punch, whack** Hail was *beating* the roof. **2.** ✦ **best, conquer, defeat, vanquish, whip** Jessica usually *beats* me at tennis. —*noun* ✦ **pulse, rhythm, throb** ✧ **blow, sound, stroke** Everybody danced to the *beat* of the music.

beautiful *adjective* ✦ **gorgeous, lovely, pretty** ✧ **attractive, pleasing** Your flower arrangement is very *beautiful*.

beckon *verb* ✦ **gesture, motion, signal** ✧ **call, summon** Miguel *beckoned* for us to follow him.

become *verb* ✦ **change into, convert to, grow into, turn into** Caterpillars *become* either moths or butterflies.

becoming *adjective* ✦ **attractive, flattering, pleasing, pretty** ✧ **appropriate** Your dress is very *becoming*.

before *adverb* ✦ **already, previously** ✧ **earlier, formerly** I've seen this episode of the show *before*. —*preposition* ✦ **prior to** ✧ **ahead of, in front of** Mother told me to wash my hands *before* dinner.

beg *verb* ✦ **appeal to, ask, implore, plead with** Mandy *begged* her parents to let her stay up late.

begin *verb* ✦ **commence, start** ✧ **initiate, originate, undertake** Andrea *begins* swimming lessons in July.

beginning *noun* ✦ **commencement, opening, start** ✧ **outset** We found our seats before the *beginning* of the concert.

behavior *noun* ✦ **conduct, manners** ✧ **actions, attitude** My *behavior* always improves when Grandma comes to visit.

behind *preposition* ✦ **in back of** ✧ **after** Marie's cat likes to hide *behind* the couch. —*adverb* ✧ **after, following, in back of** Jill ran so fast that she left all her friends *behind*. ▼

Antonyms
begin *verb*
cease, check, discontinue, finish, halt, quit, stop

behold *verb* ✦ **look at, observe, see, watch, witness** The sunset was beautiful to *behold*.

belief *noun* ✦ **conviction, feeling, opinion, theory, view** It is my *belief* that honesty is the best policy.

believe *verb* ✦ **accept, think** ✧ **hold, presume** Some people *believe* that ghosts are real.

✦   **best choices**
✧   **other choices**

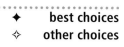

belly *noun* ✦ **abdomen, stomach, tummy** ✧ **underside** Jesse crawled through the grass on his *belly*.

belongings *noun* ✦ **goods, possessions, property, things** ✧ **gear** When my family moved, we packed all our *belongings* into boxes.

below *adverb* ✧ **beneath, lower, under, underneath** From the hilltop, we could see the town *below* us. —*preposition* ✦ **beneath, under, underneath** Sasha's dog is sitting *below* the table, begging for scraps.

bend *verb* ✦ **curve, flex, turn, twist** Marlene likes to *bend* pipe cleaners into little animal shapes. —*noun* ✦ **crook, curve, turn, twist** Kim's house is just past the *bend* in the road.

beneath *preposition* ✦ **below, under, underneath** Rod found his other shoe *beneath* the bed.

beneficial *adjective* ✦ **advantageous, helpful, productive, useful, valuable** Proper nutrition is *beneficial* to your health.

best *adjective* ✦ **finest, greatest, principal** ✧ **foremost, top** Cassandra is my *best* friend. —*adverb* ✦ **most, most of all** ✧ **extremely, fully, greatly** What flavor of ice cream do you like *best*?

bet *noun* ✦ **wager** ✧ **gamble, stake, venture** Mark made a *bet* that he could win the race —*verb* ✦ **wager** ✧ **challenge, chance, dare, gamble** I *bet* Dad that I could beat him at checkers.

betray *verb* ✦ **deceive, double-cross** ✧ **abandon, desert, mislead** I know that Laura won't *betray* me by telling my secret to anyone else.

better *verb* ✦ **enhance, help, improve, strengthen** ✧ **advance** Sometimes you can *better* your grade by doing extra work. —*adjective* ✦ **finer than, preferable to, superior to** ✧ **greater** Homegrown tomatoes taste *better than* store-bought ones. —*adverb* ✦ **more** Robby likes spaghetti *better* than meat loaf.

beware *verb* ✦ **heed, mind, watch out for** ✧ **notice, regard** The swimming hole had a sign that warned people to *beware of* the deep water.

bewilder *verb* ✦ **baffle, confuse, mystify, perplex, puzzle** When Dad and I tried to assemble my new bicycle, the directions completely *bewildered* us.

beyond *preposition* ✦ **after, behind, past** ✧ **across** Our house is just *beyond* that grove of trees.

bias *noun* ✦ **leaning, preference, prejudice** ✧ **inclination, tendency** A good referee has no *bias* toward either team. —*verb* ✦ **distort, influence, prejudice, sway** Don't let my opinion *bias* your decision.

bid *verb* **1.** ✦ **command, direct, instruct, order, tell** ✧ **ask, require** The queen *bid* her servants to kneel in her presence. **2.** ✦ **offer** ✧ **propose** Kay *bid* twelve dollars for the old hat. —*noun* ✦ **offer, offering, proposal** ✧ **estimate** The contractor said that all reasonable *bids* would be considered.

big *adjective* **1.** ✦ **colossal, enormous, gigantic, huge, immense, large** My St. Bernard puppy has *big* paws. **2.** ✦ **important** ✧ **great, major, significant, vital** Our soccer team practiced hard for the *big* game.

bill *noun* **1.** ✦ **check, invoice, statement** ✧ **account** After the meal was over, the waiter brought us our *bill*. **2.** ✧ **draft, measure, program, proposal** The *bill* was approved by both Congress and the Senate.

bind *verb* ✦ **connect, fasten, join, secure** ✧ **tie, wrap** I *bound* the pages of my report together with a stapler. ▼

birth *noun* **1.** ✦ **delivery** ✧ **bearing, child-birth** Baby elephants weigh about 250 pounds at *birth*. **2.** ✦ **beginning, dawn, start** ✧ **creation, emergence** The 200th anniversary of the *birth* of the United States was celebrated in 1976.

bit *noun* ✦ **fragment, particle, piece, scrap, speck** *Bits* of confetti floated through the air. ▼

bite *verb* ✦ **champ, chomp, gnaw, nip** ✧ **nibble** Sean accidentally *bit* his tongue while chewing gum. —*noun* **1.** ✧ **prick, puncture, sting, wound** Try not to scratch those mosquito *bites*. **2.** ✦ **crumb, morsel, mouthful, piece, scrap** ✧ **nibble, taste** I'm so full that I can't eat another *bite*.

bitter *adjective* **1.** ✦ **acrid, biting, pungent, sharp** ✧ **harsh, stinging, unpleasant** Coffee has a *bitter* taste. **2.** ✦ **resentful, sullen** ✧ **angry, hostile, spiteful, upset** Tracy seemed *bitter* when she lost the student council election.

blade *noun* ✦ **cutting edge, edge** Cody's pocketknife has a *blade* that is two inches long.

blame *verb* ✦ **accuse, criticize, fault, reproach** Don't *blame* me if your homework isn't finished on time. —*noun* ✦ **responsibility** ✧ **accountability, fault, guilt** I took the *blame* for the dog getting out of the yard.

blank *adjective* ✦ **empty, unmarked** ✧ **bare, clear, unused, vacant** My math book has *blank* pages for problem solving.

blast *noun* ✦ **bang, burst, roar** ✧ **eruption, explosion** The hunters heard the distant *blast* of a shotgun. —*verb* ✦ **dynamite, explode** ✧ **burst, demolish, detonate** Miners *blasted* their way through the rock.

blaze *noun* ✦ **fire, flames** ✧ **burning, glare, glow** It took firefighters two hours to extinguish the *blaze*. —*verb* ✦ **burn, flame** ✧ **flare, glow, shine** The campfire *blazed* cheerfully.

bleak *adjective* ✦ **depressing, dismal, dreary, forbidding, gloomy, grim** The constant rain made everything look *bleak*.

blemish *noun* ✦ **defect, flaw, imperfection** ✧ **blotch, impurity, stain** Mom got the ceramic pot at a discount because it has a slight *blemish*. —*verb* ✦ **flaw, mar, spoil, tarnish** The gymnast's fall *blemished* his otherwise perfect performance.

blend *verb* ✦ **combine, mix** ✧ **merge, scramble, unite** Patrick *blended* the cake ingredients in a large bowl. —*noun* ✦ **combination, mix, mixture** ✧ **compound, fusion** This shirt is a *blend* of cotton and polyester.

blight *noun* ✦ **affliction, decay, disease, sickness** ✧ **pest, plague** Dad was upset when a *blight* struck his roses.

blind *adjective* **1.** ✦ **sightless** ✧ **unseeing, visionless** My friend is *blind* in one eye. **2.** ✦ **ignorant of, unaware of** ✧ **naive, unknowing, unmindful** We're usually *blind to* our own faults. **3.** ✦ **concealed, hidden, unseen** ✧ **obscure** The hill road had many *blind* curves.

✦   **best choices**
✧   **other choices**

bliss *noun* ✦ delight, ecstasy, happiness, joy Moira's idea of *bliss* is a day all to herself.

blizzard *noun* ✦ snowstorm, winter storm ✧ storm, tempest Yesterday's *blizzard* left huge snowdrifts behind.

block *noun* ✦ chunk, piece ✧ brick, cube, slab, wedge The ancient Egyptians used huge *blocks* of sandstone to build their pyramids. —*verb* ✦ halt, hinder, obstruct, stop ✧ interfere A herd of sheep *blocked* traffic.

> ## Word Groups
>
> A blockade is the closing off of an area to stop people or supplies from getting through. Blockade is a very specific term with no true synonyms. Here are some related words to investigate in a dictionary:
>
> attack, barricade, barrier, encirclement, obstacle, obstruction, siege

bloom *noun* ✦ blossom, flower ✧ bud Cherry trees can have either pink or white *blooms*. —*verb* ✦ blossom, flower ✧ flourish, open, sprout Mom's petunias *bloomed* all summer long.

blow¹ *verb* **1.** ✧ float, flutter, fly, move, sail A fierce wind *blew* tumbleweeds across the road. **2.** ✦ breathe, exhale, puff Christina *blew* on the campfire to get it going. **3.** ✦ blast, dynamite, explode ✧ detonate, erupt Work crews used dynamite to *blow* a tunnel through the mountain.

blow² *noun* ✦ hit, jab, punch, rap, stroke The boxer raised his arms to block the *blows* of his opponent.

bluff *verb* ✦ deceive, delude, fool, mislead, trick My dog's growling often *bluffs* people into thinking that he's fierce. —*noun* ✦ deception, pretense ✧ fake, fraud, lie Jack's claim that he knew karate was just a *bluff* to scare away the bully.

blunder *noun* ✦ error, mistake ✧ oversight, slip I made a *blunder* when I used salt instead of sugar in the cookie dough. —*verb* ✦ stagger, stumble ✧ bungle, flounder Because I was lost in thought, I *blundered* into another pedestrian.

blunt *adjective* **1.** ✦ dull, unsharpened It's hard to cut tomatoes with a *blunt* knife. **2.** ✦ candid, direct, frank, tactless, straightforward Lisa was a little too *blunt* when she voiced her opinion of my new hairdo.

blur *verb* ✦ cloud, dim, obscure ✧ darken, shadow, shroud, veil Mist *blurred* our view of the mountain top.

board *noun* **1.** ✦ plank, slat, timber ✧ beam, panel Dad and I cut the old *boards* into firewood. **2.** ✧ cabinet, committee, council, panel My mother was just elected to the *board* of directors.

boast *verb* ✦ brag, gloat ✧ exaggerate, flaunt Stephanie found it hard not to *boast* about winning the dance competition.

body *noun* **1.** ✦ person, physique ✧ build, figure, form, frame Our gym teacher says that exercise is good for both the *body* and the mind. **2.** ✦ group, mass ✧ assembly, party, society A few soldiers went on ahead, and the main *body* of troops followed behind.

bold *adjective* ✦ audacious, brave, courageous, daring, fearless, heroic A *bold* knight rode forth to slay the dragon.

bolt *noun* **1.** ✦ fastener, pin, rod ✧ rivet, spike I can adjust the height of my bicycle seat by loosening this *bolt*. **2.** ✦ dart, dash, rush, sprint ✧ bound, spring The field mouse made a *bolt* for safety when it saw a hawk. —*verb* **1.** ✦ fasten, latch, lock, secure ✧ bar Please *bolt* the door and turn off the porch light. **2.** ✦ dash, fly, race, run, rush, sprint When I opened the gate, all the horses *bolted* out.

bond *noun* ✦ attachment, connection, link, tie ✧ binding There is a strong *bond* between Pasha and his dog.

bonus *noun* ✦ addition, reward ✧ benefit, gift, prize Mom gave a *bonus* to my allowance because I did extra work around the house last week.

boom *noun* 1. ✦ blast, bang ✧ clap, report, roar, rumble A sonic *boom* shook our windows. 2. ✦ advance, expansion, growth, upswing ✧ boost, prosperity The electronics industry experienced a *boom* when personal computers became popular. —*verb* 1. ✦ crash, roar, rumble ✧ blast, sound Thunder *boomed* in the distance. 2. ✦ flourish, increase, mushroom ✧ prosper, thrive Alaska's population *boomed* when oil was discovered there.

boost *verb* 1. ✦ heft, hoist, lift, raise ✧ push, shove Grandpa *boosted* my sister into his pickup truck. 2. ✦ built up, expand, increase ✧ amplify, hike, improve, raise Winning the first game of the season *boosted* our team's confidence. —*noun* ✦ lift ✧ heft, hoist, push, raise, shove Mr. Dawes gave his niece a *boost* onto her horse. ▶

booty *noun* ✦ loot, pillage, plunder, spoils The pirates buried their *booty* on a deserted island.

border *noun* 1. ✦ edge, margin, perimeter, rim ✧ fringe Kenji planted bamboo around the *border* of his garden. 2. ✦ boundary, frontier ✧ line The Rio Grande River runs along the *border* between the United States and Mexico.

bore *verb* ✦ fatigue, tire, weary ✧ annoy, irritate The assembly *bored* Mario so much that he yawned through the whole thing.

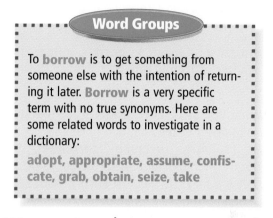

Word Groups

To borrow is to get something from someone else with the intention of returning it later. Borrow is a very specific term with no true synonyms. Here are some related words to investigate in a dictionary:

adopt, appropriate, assume, confiscate, grab, obtain, seize, take

boss *noun* ✦ employer, manager, supervisor ✧ administrator, chief, leader My mother's *boss* just gave her a raise.

bother *verb* ✦ aggravate, annoy, disturb, irritate, pester The hum of the overhead lights really *bothered* me. —*noun* ✦ annoyance, irritation, nuisance, problem ✧ strain The mosquitoes in the backyard were such a *bother* that we had to move into the house.

bottom *noun* ✦ base, foot, lowest point ✧ foundation, ground, seat The visitors paused at the *bottom* of the monument before starting up the many stairs.

bounce *verb* ✦ bound, jump, leap ✧ rebound, recoil, spring We *bounced* up and down on the trampoline. —*noun* ✦ elasticity, rebound, spring A good tennis ball has lots of *bounce*.

bound¹ *verb* ✦ jump, leap, spring ✧ bounce, hop, vault The lamb *bounded* away. —*noun* ✦ jump, leap ✧ hop, spring, vault The deer cleared the stream in a single *bound*.

bound² *noun* ✦ boundary, limit ✧ edge, perimeter We set the *bounds* for the hide-and-seek game.

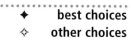

✦ best choices
✧ other choices

bound³ *adjective* **1.** ✦ **obligated, obliged, required** I am *bound* by my promise to help my daughter with her homework. **2.** ✦ **certain, sure** ◇ **destined, fated** I'm *bound* to get a good grade if I study hard.

boundary *noun* ✦ **border, edge, limit, perimeter** ◇ **fringe, rim** My parents planted trees at the *boundary* of our property.

bow *verb* **1.** ◇ **curtsy, kneel, salute, stoop** We all *bowed* to the king and queen. **2.** ✦ **concede, submit, succumb, surrender, yield** ◇ **bend** Owen did not *bow* to the bully's demands for lunch money. —*noun* ◇ **curtsy, nod, salute, greeting** The entire cast of the play came on stage for a final *bow*.

box *noun* ✦ **carton** ◇ **case, container, crate, trunk** Andrea's cat likes to play in cardboard *boxes*. —*verb* ✦ **pack, package** ◇ **crate, wrap** Harriet helped her brother *box* up his books for college.

brace *noun* ✦ **prop, reinforcement, support** ◇ **buttress** The *braces* of the bridge were made of steel. —*verb* ✦ **reinforce, steady, support** ◇ **fortify, strengthen** We used a board to *brace* the old fence.

brag *verb* ✦ **boast** ◇ **bluster, crow, exaggerate, gloat** Wesley *bragged* about how fast he could run around the track.

brake *verb* ✦ **halt, stop** ◇ **decelerate, slow** Juan *braked* suddenly and made skid marks with his bicycle tires.

branch *noun* **1.** ✦ **bough, limb** ◇ **stem** Katherine climbed to the top *branch* of the tree. **2.** ✦ **department, division, extension** ◇ **bureau, chapter** Mom works at the local *branch* of our county library. —*verb* ✦ **divide, fork** ◇ **diverge, part, separate** When the trail *branched*, Casey didn't know which way to go.

brand *noun* **1.** ✦ **kind, make, sort, type, variety** What's your favorite *brand* of cold cereal? **2.** ✦ **label, mark, sign, symbol** ◇ **emblem** The sheriff inspected the steer's *brand* to determine its rightful owner.

brave *adjective* ✦ **courageous, fearless, heroic, plucky, valorous** A *brave* girl rescued the small boy from the river. —*verb* ✦ **endure, face, meet** ◇ **challenge, defy, undergo** The pioneers *braved* many dangers in their westward journey.

break *verb* **1.** ✦ **shatter, smash, splinter** ◇ **crack, fracture** The plate *broke* when I dropped it. **2.** ✦ **breach, violate** ◇ **disregard, ignore, neglect** Gabrielle *broke* her promise to meet me after school. **3.** ✦ **end, halt, stop** ◇ **cease, interrupt** Last week's rain *broke* the long drought. **4.** ✦ **beat, exceed, surpass, top** Jennifer *broke* the school record in the fifty-yard dash. —*noun* **1.** ✦ **rest** ◇ **breather, intermission, pause, recess** I took a *break* from my chores after mowing the lawn. **2.** ✦ **gap, hole, opening** ◇ **crack, split** The sun shone through a *break* in the clouds.

breed *verb* **1.** ✦ **grow, nurture, raise, rear** My aunt *breeds* Siamese cats. **2.** ✦ **cause, create, foster, generate, produce, promote** Fear can often *breed* panic. —*noun* ✦ **kind, sort, strain, type, variety** The poodle is my favorite *breed* of dog. ◄

brief *adjective* **1.** ✦ **fleeting, momentary, quick, short** ✧ **temporary** My neighbor stopped by for a *brief* visit. **2.** ✦ **concise, short, succinct** I sent Uncle Howard a *brief* thank-you note. —*verb* ✦ **advise, inform (about), instruct (about)** ✧ **explain** Our coach *briefed* us on the other team's strengths and weaknesses.

bright *adjective* **1.** ✦ **brilliant, glowing, vivid** ✧ **shining, shiny** Tanya painted her bicycle *bright* yellow. **2.** ✦ **clever, intelligent, quick, smart** Steven is a *bright* boy who reads books above his grade level.

brilliant *adjective* **1.** ✦ **bright, gleaming, shining, sparkling** ✧ **intense, vivid** I polished the silverware to a *brilliant* shine. **2.** ✦ **magnificent, outstanding, remarkable, splendid, superb** Beethoven was a *brilliant* composer.

bring *verb* **1.** ✦ **carry, take** ✧ **bear, deliver, haul, transport** I *bring* my lunch to school every day. **2.** ✦ **bring about, cause, create, generate, make, produce** April showers *bring* May flowers.

brisk *adjective* **1.** ✦ **active, energetic, lively, vigorous** ✧ **quick, swift** My grandma takes *brisk* walks to stay fit and healthy. **2.** ✦ **bracing, crisp, fresh, invigorating, stimulating** The *brisk* wind made my ears numb.

brittle *adjective* ✦ **crisp, delicate, fragile, frail, weak** ✧ **breakable** I was gentle with the old book because its pages were *brittle*.

Antonyms

brittle *adjective*

flexible, firm, mobile, pliable, solid, strong

broad *adjective* ✦ **comprehensive, extensive, wide** ✧ **immense, large, spacious** Sam has gained a *broad* knowledge of birds since he took up bird watching as a hobby.

broken *adjective* **1.** ✦ **cracked, fractured, shattered** ✧ **injured** The doctor put my *broken* arm in a plaster cast. **2.** ✦ **defective, faulty** ✧ **imperfect, out of order** Dad fixed the *broken* lawn mower.

browse *verb* **1.** ✦ **look, scan, skim** ✧ **read, survey** I *browsed* through my comic books. **2.** ✦ **eat, feed, graze** ✧ **crop, nibble** The deer *browsed* in the meadow.

bruise *noun* ✧ **harm, hurt, injure, wound** Anne *bruised* her elbow when she fell off the swing.

brush¹ *verb* **1.** ✦ **clean, curry, groom, smooth** ✧ **polish, sweep** Liana *brushes* her horse every day. **2.** ✦ **graze, skim, touch** ✧ **caress, tickle** A butterfly *brushed* my arm as it flew past.

brush² *noun* ✦ **thicket, underbrush, undergrowth** ✧ **bushes, shrubs** Quails build nests in dense *brush*.

brutal *adjective* ✦ **barbaric, cruel, harsh, merciless, vicious** The *brutal* pirate forced his prisoner to walk the plank.

buckle *noun* ✧ **catch, clasp, fastener, hook** My belt has a brass *buckle*. —*verb* **1.** ✦ **clasp, fasten, hook, secure** Linda *buckled* her rain boots. **2.** ✦ **bend, sag, warp** ✧ **collapse, crumble** The boards on the porch have *buckled* with age.

buddy *noun* ✦ **chum, friend, mate, pal** ✧ **comrade** Last weekend Aaron played baseball with his *buddies*.

budge *verb* ✦ **move, push, shift** ✧ **dislodge, stir** Christopher *budged* the gigantic pumpkin inch by inch. ▼

✦   best choices
✧   other choices

budget *noun* ✦ **allotment** ◇ **allowance, funds, resources** Loretta's *budget* for candy is one dollar a week. —*verb* ✦ **plan, ration, schedule** ◇ **allot, distribute** My parents showed me how to *budget* my allowance so that it lasts all month.

build *verb* ✦ **assemble, construct, make** ◇ **fabricate, manufacture** Joanna and her grandfather *built* a Victorian dollhouse. —*noun* ✦ **body, physique** ◇ **figure, form, shape** He has a good *build* for rock climbing.

bulletin *noun* ✦ **announcement, message, report, statement** ◇ **notification** A news *bulletin* interrupted my television show.

bully *verb* ✦ **domineer over, frighten, harass, intimidate, threaten** Frank doesn't let the bigger kids *bully* him.

bump *verb* ✦ **bang, hit, knock, smack** ◇ **collide, strike** John *bumped* against the corner of the table. —*noun* **1.** ✦ **jar, jolt, thump** ◇ **crash, knock** We felt a slight *bump* as the airplane touched ground. **2.** ✦ **lump, swelling** ◇ **bulge, knob, nodule** A *bump* formed on my leg where the bee stung me.

bunch *noun* ✦ **clump, cluster** ◇ **bundle, crowd, group, quantity** The gorilla ate a *bunch* of bananas. —*verb* ✦ **cluster, flock, gather, herd, huddle** ◇ **collect** Antelope *bunch* together for safety when they see a lion.

bundle *noun* ✦ **bunch, collection** ◇ **batch, pack, package, stack** We took a *bundle* of old newspapers to the recycling center. ▶

burden *noun* **1.** ✦ **cargo, freight, load, weight** ◇ **baggage** Elephants can carry a heavier *burden* than many other animals. **2.** ✦ **difficulty, hardship, strain, trial, worry** I believe that friends help lighten the *burdens* of life. —*verb* ✦ **afflict, load, oppress, tax, weight** Our vacation *burdened* us with many expenses, but we were glad we went anyway.

burglar *noun* ✦ **robber, thief** ◇ **criminal, crook, prowler** The police caught the *burglar* as he came out of the house.

burn *verb* **1.** ✦ **fire, ignite, kindle, torch** ◇ **blaze, combust** The spy *burned* his instructions after reading them. **2.** ✦ **char, scorch, sear, singe** I *burned* the toast.

burst *verb* ✦ **blow up, explode, pop** ◇ **rupture, split** If you don't punch holes in a potato, it will *burst* when you bake it. —*noun* ✦ **eruption, outbreak, outpouring** ◇ **release** There was a *burst* of applause when the magician made the camel disappear.

bury *verb* **1.** ✦ **inter, lay to rest** Brenda *buried* the dead butterfly in the garden. **2.** ✦ **conceal, cover, hide** ◇ **secrete, veil** A pile of laundry *buried* my shoes.

business *noun* **1.** ✦ **industry, profession** ◇ **career, job, occupation, work** Reegan's father used to be in the plumbing *business*. **2.** ✦ **selling, trade, transaction** ◇ **commerce, marketing** This department store does most of its *business* during the holidays. **3.** ✦ **company, firm,**

store ◇ **enterprise, industry, office** My Aunt Di owns her own interior decorating *business*.
4. ✦ **affair, concern, interest** ◇ **duty, responsibility** My mom makes it her *business* to know how I am doing in school.

busy *adjective* ✦ **active, engaged, occupied** ◇ **absorbed** Between homework and after-school activities, Janet is usually *busy*.

but *conjunction* ✦ **however, nevertheless, yet** ◇ **though** I thought that the roller coaster would scare me, *but* I enjoyed it. —*adverb* ✦ **only, just** ◇ **merely, simply** I have *but* three dollars of my birthday money left. —*preposition* ✦ **except, save** Everybody has had the flu *but* me.

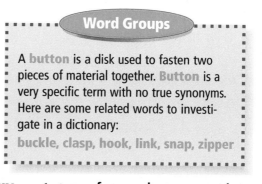

Word Groups

A **button** is a disk used to fasten two pieces of material together. **Button** is a very specific term with no true synonyms. Here are some related words to investigate in a dictionary:
buckle, clasp, hook, link, snap, zipper

buy *verb* ✦ **pay for, purchase** ◇ **acquire, get, obtain** Hiroko used her allowance to *buy* a compact disk.

by *preposition* ✦ **at, before, no later than** Dad has to be at work *by* eight o'clock in the morning.

✦   **best choices**
◇   **other choices**

C

cab *noun* ✦ **taxi, taxicab** ◇ **hired car, limousine** When Mrs. Hixton's car broke down, she took a *cab* to work.

cabin *noun* **1.** ◇ **bungalow, chalet, cottage, hut, lodge** Nathan and his family rented a *cabin* in the woods for their vacation. ▼ **2.** ✦ **berth, compartment, room, stateroom** Francesca and her mom booked a private *cabin* for their cruise to the Greek Islands.

cable *noun* **1.** ✦ **wire** ◇ **chain, line, rope, strand** The telephone pole blew over when its anchoring *cables* broke. **2.** ✦ **cablegram, telegram, wire** ◇ **message** The overseas reporter sent an urgent *cable* to her editor back in the United States.

cafeteria *noun* ✦ **lunchroom** ◇ **cafe, dining room, restaurant, snack bar** Everyone complains about the bland food that our school *cafeteria* serves.

cage *noun* ◇ **cell, coop, enclosure, pen, prison** Rebecca keeps her parrot in a large wire *cage.* —*verb* ✦ **confine, enclose, pen** ◇ **restrain** The zookeeper tried to *cage* an escaped monkey.

calculate *verb* ✦ **compute, determine, figure** ◇ **count, reckon** Melissa *calculated* the total cost of her new skateboard and helmet to be sixty-two dollars.

call *verb* **1.** ✦ **cry, scream, shout, yell** ◇ **hail** Bjorn heard a lost hiker *calling* for help. **2.** ✦ **summon** ◇ **ask, bid, command, order** I have to go now because I hear Dad *calling* me. **3.** ✦ **address** ◇ **designate, label, name, title** We *call* Peter by the nickname "Skyscraper" because he's so tall. **4.** ✦ **dial, phone, ring, telephone** Mom *called* ahead to tell Grandmother we would be a little late. —*noun* ✦ **hail** ◇ **cry, scream, shout, yell** Jamie gets frustrated when her dog ignores her *call.*

calm *adjective* ✦ **collected, cool, self-possessed** ◇ **peaceful, quiet, serene, still, tranquil** Danielle was the only one who remained *calm* when the fire alarm went off. —*verb* ✦ **pacify, quiet, relax, soothe** ◇ **tranquilize** Whenever my cat gets agitated, I *calm* her with hugs.

camouflage *noun* ◇ **cloak, disguise, mask, screen** The soldiers changed the color of their *camouflage* when they moved from jungle to desert. —*verb* ✦ **cloak, conceal, disguise, hide** ◇ **cover** Jeffery used several dead branches to *camouflage* the entrance to his secret fort.

campaign *noun* ✦ **crusade, drive, movement** ◇ **effort, operation** Brooke started a *campaign* to clean up her neighborhood. —*verb* ✦ **run, stump** ◇ **crusade, push** Our mayor is *campaigning* for reelection.

can *noun* ✦ **tin** ◇ **container, jar, receptacle** I had a *can* of soup for lunch today. —*verb* ✦ **jar, preserve** ◇ **bottle, tin** Grandmother decided to *can* most of this year's tomato crop.

cancel *verb* ✦ **drop, stop** ◇ **repeal, revoke, void** Kelsey decided to *cancel* her subscription to *Modern Baby-Sitters.*

candidate *noun* ✦ **contender, nominee, runner** ✧ **applicant** Zachary is a *candidate* for class president.

capable *adjective* ✦ **able, competent** ✧ **apt, qualified, talented** *Capable* teachers are always in demand.

capacity *noun* ✦ **volume** ✧ **content, room, size, space** The *capacity* of a typical oil barrel is fifty-five gallons.

capital *noun* ✦ **assets, cash, funds, money, savings** Mom finally has enough *capital* to start her own business.

captain *noun* ✦ **head, leader** ✧ **chief, commander** Jorge is the *captain* of the league's best football team. ▶ —*verb* ✦ **command, head, lead** ✧ **direct, pilot** Beth's dream is to *captain* a cruise ship someday.

capture *verb* ✦ **seize, take** ✧ **apprehend, catch, hold** Kendra and Gregory tried to *capture* their friends' snow fort. —*noun* ✦ **apprehension, arrest, seizure** The bank robber evaded *capture* for several days, but he was eventually arrested.

car *noun* ✦ **auto, automobile, motor vehicle** ✧ **vehicle** Armand can't wait till he's old enough to drive the family *car*.

care *noun* **1.** ✦ **anxiety, concern, worry** ✧ **burden, fear** Karla's only *care* is her report card. **2.** ✦ **attention, caution** ✧ **effort, heed, wariness** Even though she was performing a routine operation, the surgeon worked with great *care*. **3.** ✦ **charge, custody, keeping, protection** Nicole left her purse in my *care* while she went swimming. —*verb* **1.** ✦ **like** ✧ **desire, love, want, wish** Would you *care for* more ice cream? **2.** ✦ **attend, mind, protect, watch** The neighbors are going to *care for* our pets while we're on vacation.

career *noun* ✦ **job, occupation, vocation, work** ✧ **trade** Keegan hopes to have a *career* in law enforcement.

careful *adjective* ✦ **alert, cautious, vigilant, wary, watchful** I'm always *careful* when I cross a street.

careless *adjective* ✦ **mindless, negligent, thoughtless, unthinking** It was *careless* of the circus performer to leave the tiger's cage unlocked.

carriage *noun* ✦ **buggy, coach** ✧ **cart, wagon** Joseph's family rented a horse-drawn *carriage* to go on a sightseeing tour.

carry *verb* **1.** ✦ **bear, convey, transport** ✧ **bring, move** The campers *carried* everything they needed in their backpacks. **2.** ✦ **maintain, support, sustain** ✧ **continue, extend** My allowance is supposed to *carry* me through the week, but somehow I always run short. **3.** ✦ **furnish, have, stock, supply** ✧ **offer, provide** Renee is looking for a store that *carries* gerbil food.

carve *verb* ✦ **sculpt, whittle** ✧ **cut, form, shape** Grandpa likes to *carve* wooden animals to give as gifts.

case¹ *noun* ✦ **episode, incident, instance** ✧ **example** The police are investigating two separate *cases* of vandalism.

case² *noun* ✦ **box, carton** ✧ **container, crate, package** Mom bought a *case* of root beer for our picnic.

cash *noun* ✦ **currency, money** ✧ **bills, change, coins** Our local market accepts only *cash* or personal checks.

cast *verb* ✦ **throw, toss** ✧ **fling, hurl, lob** We need to *cast* the dice to see who goes first. —*noun* **1.** ✦ **throw, toss** ✧ **fling, heave, lob** Lilly caught a big fish on the first *cast* of her lure. **2.** ✦ **company, troupe** ✧ **actors, players** Our drama instructor told the entire *cast* to attend tonight's rehearsal.

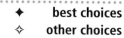

✦ **best choices**
✧ **other choices**

Word Groups

A *castle* is a large building with strong walls and other defenses against attack. *Castle* is a very specific term with no true synonyms. Here are some related words to investigate in a dictionary:

chateau, citadel, fort, fortress, palace, stronghold

casual *adjective* ✦ **informal, relaxed** ◇ **spontaneous, unplanned** My parents invited some friends over for a *casual* dinner.

casualty *noun* ✦ **victim** ◇ **dead, fatality, injured, wounded** The papers reported that there were no *casualties* from the earthquake that hit Oregon yesterday.

catalog *noun* ✦ **directory, index, list, register** ◇ **inventory** Most universities publish *catalogs* that describe the courses they offer. —*verb* ✦ **categorize, classify, list, record** Jenny *cataloged* all of the stamps in her collection.

catastrophe *noun* ✦ **disaster, tragedy** ◇ **accident, misfortune** The sinking of the *Titanic* was a great *catastrophe*.

catch *verb* **1.** ✦ **capture, grab, grasp, seize** My cat *caught* a mouse yesterday. **2.** ✦ **detect, discover, spot** ◇ **surprise** My mother *caught* me sneaking a cookie before dinner. **3.** ✦ **contract, get** ◇ **receive, take** I *caught* the whooping cough from my brother. —*noun* **1.** ✦ **grab, snatch** ◇ **capture, grasp, seizure** Holly made a spectacular *catch* while playing softball with her friends Saturday. **2.** ✦ **clasp, latch** ◇ **bolt, fastener, hook** Dad put a *catch* on the cupboard door to keep it from swinging open.

category *noun* ✦ **class, classification, group, type** ◇ **division, section** Our local video store shelves movies by *category* such as "Westerns" and "Science Fiction."

cause *noun* **1.** ✦ **origin, reason (for)** ◇ **basis, source** Investigators are still trying to determine the *cause* of the accident. **2.** ✦ **goal, principle** ◇ **crusade, purpose** Dad contributes his time and money to support environmental *causes*. —*verb* ✦ **create, generate, produce** ◇ **begin, make** Yesterday's heavy rain *caused* some flooding.

caution *noun* ✦ **attention, care, carefulness, vigilance** The guard used *caution* helping students cross the road. ▼ —*verb* ✦ **advise, warn** ◇ **alert, counsel** Mom *cautions* me to be careful whenever I go swimming.

cautious *adjective* ✦ **attentive, careful, vigilant, wary, watchful** Marcia was very *cautious* the first time she tried the balance beam.

cavity *noun* ✦ **hole, hollow, opening** ◇ **crater, pit** Erosion from running water has left many small *cavities* in the soft rock.

cease *verb* ✦ **quit, stop** ◇ **end, halt, terminate** The officer ordered his men to *cease* firing.

celebrate *verb* ✦ **commemorate, honor, observe** ◇ **keep** Sharon's mother prepared a special feast to *celebrate* Passover.

celebrity *noun* ✦ **star, superstar** ◇ **dignitary, notable** Allison hopes to see some *celebrities* when she visits Hollywood.

cell *noun* ✦ **room** ✧ **cage, chamber, compartment, pen** The sheriff's office has several small *cells* for holding prisoners.

cement *noun* ✦ **concrete, mortar** ✧ **adhesive, glue** Dad used quick-setting *cement* when he built our backyard barbecue. —*verb* ✦ **bond, glue, stick** ✧ **bind, fasten, fix** Kayla *cemented* the lamp's broken pieces back together.

cemetery *noun* ✦ **burial ground, graveyard** ✧ **catacomb, churchyard** We went to the *cemetery* to visit my great-grandfather's grave.

center *noun* ✦ **inside, interior, middle** ✧ **core, nucleus** Jessica prefers chocolate candies that have soft *centers*.

central *adjective* **1.** ✦ **middle** ✧ **inside, interior, midway** Mom grew up on a farm in the *central* part of our state. **2.** ✦ **chief, main, principal** ✧ **key, leading, prime** The librarian at our local branch said that the *central* library has the book I want.

ceremony *noun* ✦ **celebration, rite, ritual, service** ✧ **custom** Darrel attended his uncle's wedding *ceremony*.

certain *adjective* **1.** ✦ **confident, positive, sure** ✧ **satisfied** I am absolutely *certain* that I do not want anchovies on my pizza. **2.** ✦ **definite, particular, precise, specific** On the first day of class, Ms. Yamada said that there were *certain* rules we needed to know.

certainly *adverb* ✦ **definitely, positively, surely, undoubtedly** Juan said that he would *certainly* attend my birthday party.

chain *noun* ✦ **cycle, sequence, series** ✧ **line, progression, set, string, train** The unfortunate *chain* of events started when someone brought a dog to the cat show. —*verb* ✧ **bind, connect, fasten, hold, lock, secure, tie** Esmerelda *chained* her bicycle to a lamppost before she went into the store.

Word Groups

A chair is a piece of furniture built for sitting on. Chair is a general term with no true synonyms. Here are some different kinds of chairs to investigate in a dictionary:

armchair, highchair, love seat, recliner, rocker, stool, throne

---

chairperson *noun* ✦ **chair, chairman, chairwoman** ✧ **director, leader** Kelly's mother is the *chairperson* of a special environmental committee.

challenge *noun* **1.** ✦ **dare** ✧ **bid, call, invitation, summons** After Lauren beat Austin at the video game, she accepted his *challenge* to a rematch. **2.** ✦ **difficulty, test** ✧ **problem, trial** Tyrone finds that math is a real *challenge* for him. —*verb* ✦ **dare** ✧ **bid, call, summon, invite** Sam *challenged* Michael to a game of basketball after school.

champion *noun* ✦ **winner, victor** ✧ **conqueror, hero** The world *champion* earned three gold medals at the Olympics.

chance *noun* **1.** ✦ **accident, luck** ✧ **coincidence, fate, fortune** Wilhelm Roentgen discovered x-rays by *chance*. **2.** ✦ **likelihood, possibility, probability, prospect** There's a good *chance* that the school picnic will be postponed if it rains. **3.** ✦ **occasion, opportunity** ✧ **opening** Please give me a call when you have a *chance*. **4.** ✦ **gamble, risk** ✧ **danger, peril** The police chief warned his officers against taking unnecessary *chances*. —*verb* **1.** ✦ **happen** My birthday *chances* to fall on the same day as my dad's. **2.** ✦ **attempt, hazard, risk, try, venture** Matt wasn't sure if he could ski down the steep slope without falling, but he decided to *chance* it.

change *verb* **1.** ✦ **adjust, alter, modify** ✧ **adapt, shift, vary** When it started to rain, Tiffany *changed* her plans and decided to stay home.

✦ **best choices**
✧ **other choices**

2. ✦ **exchange, replace, substitute, swap, trade** Heather asked us to wait a few minutes while she *changed* her clothes. —*noun* ✦ **alteration, modification, switch, variation** A sudden *change* in the weather forced us to postpone our ball game.

channel *noun* ✦ **course** ✧ **artery, passage, route, streambed** The main *channel* of the Mississippi River is more than 2,300 miles long.

chaos *noun* ✦ **confusion, disorder, turmoil** ✧ **mess, tumult** Our classroom was in total *chaos* the day a substitute teacher told us to do whatever we wanted.

chapter *noun* **1.** ✧ **division, part, portion, section, topic** After reading the first *chapter*, I looked forward to the rest of the book. **2.** ✦ **branch** ✧ **group, unit** The 4-H Club has local *chapters* all over the country.

character *noun* **1.** ✦ **nature, personality** ✧ **attribute, feature, quality, trait** I thought that my dog was timid, but he showed his true *character* when he chased away a burglar. **2.** ✦ **honesty, integrity, morality** ✧ **fiber, honor** I believe that a political leader should be a person who has much *character*.

characteristic *adjective* ✦ **normal, typical** ✧ **distinctive, particular, specific** Cold days are *characteristic* of winter weather in the Midwest. —*noun* ✦ **attribute, feature, quality, trait** I think that Stephanie's kindness is one of her nicest *characteristics*.

charge *verb* **1.** ✦ **ask, bill, demand** ✧ **assess, require** David *charges* a minimum of six dollars for every lawn he mows. **2.** ✦ **push, rush, storm, thrust** ✧ **attack, invade** Our quarterback *charged* through a hole in the other team's defensive line. **3.** ✦ **accuse of, cite for, indict for** ✧ **blame** The suspect was *charged with* one count of armed robbery. —*noun* **1.** ✦ **cost, expense, fee, price** The salesman said that there was no additional *charge* to have our new refrigerator delivered. **2.** ✦ **care, custody** ✧ **guardianship** "While you are in my *charge*," said the baby sitter, "you will not put beans in your ears!" **3.** ✦ **accusation, allegation** ✧ **complaint** The suspect was arrested on a *charge* of shoplifting. **4.** ✦ **assault, attack, rush** ✧ **invasion, offensive** A cavalry *charge* routed the enemy soldiers.

charm *noun* ✦ **appeal** ✧ **allure, attraction, attractiveness, beauty, magnetism** My uncle's log cabin is small, but it has a lot of *charm*. —*verb* ✦ **captivate, delight, enthrall, fascinate, thrill** The clown's silly antics *charmed* everyone in the audience.

charming *adjective* ✦ **attractive, captivating, delightful, enchanting** Ellen has a *charming* smile.

chase *verb* **1.** ✦ **pursue, run after** ✧ **follow, hunt, trail** My dog loves to *chase* rabbits. **2.** ✦ **drive, evict, oust** Mrs. Higgins *chased* us from her yard when she caught us trying to pick some apples. —*noun* ✦ **pursuit** ✧ **hunt, search** Police officers caught the speeding car after a long, dangerous *chase*.

chat *verb* ✦ **converse, talk** ✧ **chatter, discuss, gossip** My mom enjoys *chatting* with her friends over coffee. —*noun* ✦ **conversation, talk** ✧ **discussion, gossip** Aunt Hilda said that she was stopping by for a little *chat*, but she stayed all day.

cheap *adjective* **1.** ✦ **inexpensive, low** ✧ **budget, economical, reasonable, sale** This new Mexican restaurant has great meals at very *cheap* prices. **2.** ✦ **inferior, mediocre, poor, shabby, shoddy** ✧ **useless, worthless** This *cheap* pen keeps running out of ink.

Antonyms
cheap *adjective*
1. costly, expensive, high-priced, precious, pricey
2. excellent, high-quality, select, superior, well-made

cheat *verb* ✦ **defraud, swindle** ✧ **deceive, fool, mislead, trick** The dishonest art dealer *cheated* his customers by selling them forgeries.

check *verb* **1.** ✦ **curb, halt, restrain, stop** ✧ **prevent** Workers built a sandbag dike to *check* the rising floodwater. **2.** ✦ **examine, inspect, survey** ✧ **compare, review, test** We *checked* the motel room to make sure that we weren't forgetting anything. —*noun* **1.** ✦ **under control** ✧ **barrier, block, obstacle, restraint** Elsie counts to ten when she's angry in order to keep her temper *in check*. **2.** ✦ **examination, inspection, investigation** ✧ **study, test** The security guard made routine *checks* of the building. **3.** ✦ **bill, tab** ✧ **receipt, ticket** After we had finished eating, the waiter brought our *check*.

cheer *verb* **1.** ✦ **shout, yell** ✧ **applaud, praise** The crowd *cheered* when our team scored a goal. **2.** ✦ **gladden, hearten** ✧ **comfort, console, encourage** My friend Nancy tried to *cheer* me *up* when I was sick. —*noun* **1.** ✦ **cry, shout, yell** ✧ **applause** When the band began to play its hit song, the *cheers* of the fans grew deafening. **2.** ✦ **cheerfulness, delight, gladness, happiness, joy** My aunt's visits always fill me with *cheer*.

cheerful *adjective* ✦ **gay, glad, happy, joyful, merry** ✧ **pleasant** All of the students were in a *cheerful* mood on the last day of school.

cherish *verb* ✦ **appreciate, prize, revere, treasure, value** Marissa *cherishes* her family more than anything else.

chest *noun* ✦ **trunk** ✧ **box, carton, container, crate** My little brother keeps his toys in a large wooden *chest*.

chew *verb* ✦ **bite, chomp, gnaw, munch, nibble** My puppies like to *chew* on my shoes. ▶

chief *noun* ✦ **director, head, leader, supervisor** ✧ **ruler** The *chief* of our local fire department conducted a safety inspection of our auditorium. —*adjective* ✦ **leading, main, major, primary,**

principal Dad says that his *chief* concern is the welfare of our family.

chiefly *adverb* ✦ **essentially, mainly, mostly, primarily** ✧ **especially** Our house is made *chiefly* of wood.

child *noun* **1.** ✦ **boy, girl, kid, youth** ✧ **baby, juvenile, toddler** We moved from our old house when I was just a young *child*. **2.** ✦ **descendant, offspring** ✧ **daughter, son** Francine is her parents' only *child*.

chill *noun* ✦ **cold, coldness, coolness** ✧ **nip** There was a *chill* in the cabin until we got a fire going. —*adjective* ✦ **chilly, cold, cool** ✧ **frigid, icy** When autumn days turn *chill*, winter is close at hand. —*verb* ✦ **cool, refrigerate** ✧ **freeze, ice** Pudding should be *chilled* before serving.

chilly *adjective* ✦ **chill, cold, cool** ✧ **icy, frigid, nippy** Because the day was *chilly*, Christine wore a wool sweater.

chip *noun* ✦ **fragment, piece, scrap** ✧ **bit** Dad used some wood *chips* to start our campfire. —*verb* ✦ **nick** ✧ **break, crack, splinter** I accidentally *chipped* one of Mom's teacups.

chisel *verb* ✦ **carve, sculpt** ✧ **form, shape** The names on these old tombstones were *chiseled* by hand.

choice *noun* ✦ **alternative, option, selection** ✧ **decision, preference** For dessert there is a *choice* of apple or pumpkin pie. —*adjective* ✦ **excellent, fine, select, special, superior** We had *choice* seats for the concert.

✦   **best choices**
✧   **other choices**

choke *verb* **1.** ✦ **strangle** ✧ **smother, stifle, suffocate** I had to loosen my tie because it was *choking* me. **2.** ✦ **block, clog, close, obstruct, plug** The freeway was *choked* by traffic.

choose *verb* ✦ **pick, select** ✧ **decide, determine** We need to *choose* sides before we can start the game.

chop *verb* ✦ **cut, hack** ✧ **sever, slice, split** Mom *chopped* down the dead tree. —*noun* ✦ **blow, punch, stroke** ✧ **cut, hit** The karate master broke a board with a single *chop* of his hand.

chore *noun* ✦ **duty, job, task** ✧ **assignment, responsibility, work** Brian's daily *chores* include making his bed and setting the dinner table.

chronic *adjective* ✦ **constant, continual, persistent** ✧ **habitual** The asthmatic man had a *chronic* cough.

chubby *adjective* ✦ **plump** ✧ **fat, heavy, stocky, stout** My baby sister has *chubby* legs.

chuckle *verb* ✦ **giggle, laugh** ✧ **snicker, smile** Lynne *chuckled* to herself as she read the Sunday comics. —*noun* ✦ **giggle, laugh** ✧ **snicker, smile** I usually get a *chuckle* out of Grandpa's corny jokes.

chum *noun* ✦ **buddy, friend, pal** ✧ **companion** My uncle said that he was looking forward to seeing his childhood *chums* again.

church *noun* ✦ **house of worship** ✧ **cathedral, chapel, temple** Melinda attends a Bible study class at her *church*.

circle *noun* ✦ **ring** ✧ **disk, hoop, loop** We sat in a *circle* around the campfire. —*verb* ✧ **enclose, loop, ring, surround** I *circled* the correct answers on my math test.

circulate *verb* **1.** ✦ **move** ✧ **flow, swirl, turn** If it gets too hot, turn on a fan to *circulate* the air. **2.** ✦ **disperse, distribute, pass, spread** Victoria *circulated* a petition to change the dress code.

Word Groups

A citizen is an official member of a country, state, or city. Citizen is a very specific term with no true synonyms. Here are some related words to investigate in a dictionary:

civilian, colonist, emigrant, immigrant, inhabitant, native, resident, settler, subject

---

city *noun* ✦ **metropolis, municipality** ✧ **town** Kristin would rather live in a small country village than in a big *city*.

civil *adjective* **1.** ✦ **civic, communal, public** ✧ **civilian** In the United States, *civil* liberties are protected by law. **2.** ✦ **cordial, courteous, polite** ✧ **kind, pleasant** Stuart gave a *civil* answer to the rude question.

civilization *noun* ✦ **culture, society** Most Native American *civilizations* had highly developed religious and social customs.

claim *noun* ✦ **right, title** ✧ **demand, suit** The two princes disagreed over who had legitimate *claim* to the throne. —*verb* **1.** ✦ **demand, occupy, require, take** ✧ **deserve** My after-school activities *claim* so much of my time that I'm almost never home. **2.** ✦ **assert, declare, maintain, profess** ✧ **believe** Whitney *claims* that one of her ancestors was an African king.

clamor *noun* ✦ **commotion, din, noise, uproar** ✧ **disturbance** The *clamor* from our neighbor's party kept me awake until after midnight. —*verb* ✦ **bawl, holler, howl, roar, shout, yell** The audience *clamored* for the rap group to perform another song.

clap *verb* **1.** ✦ **applaud** ✧ **cheer** Everyone *clapped* enthusiastically when the high diver completed his daring ninety-foot jump. **2.** ✦ **pat, slap, smack** ✧ **strike** The whole team *clapped* Kyle on the back after he scored the winning touchdown. —noun ✦ **peal, report** ✧ **boom, crack** We saw the bolt of lightning just seconds before we heard the thunder's loud *clap*.

clarify *verb* ✦ **clear up, explain, simplify** ✧ **define** When Mr. Suarez saw my look of confusion, he *clarified* his directions.

class *noun* **1.** ✦ **category, classification, division, group, kind, sort** The equations were divided into two *classes* based on level of difficulty. **2.** ✦ **course, subject** ✧ **grade, lecture, section** Cassandra's favorite *class* is geography. —*verb* ✦ **arrange, categorize, classify, group, rank** Whales and gorillas can be *classed* together because they are both mammals.

classify *verb* ✦ **arrange, class, organize, rank, sort** Diamonds are *classified* according to their quality.

clean *adjective* ✦ **cleansed, spotless, unsoiled, washed** ✧ **fresh, neat, tidy** We changed into *clean* clothes after running on the muddy field. —*verb* ✦ **cleanse, scrub, wash** ✧ **launder, neaten, tidy** My brother said that it was my turn to *clean* the bathroom.

clear *adjective* **1.** ✦ **bright, cloudless, sunny** ✧ **empty, open, vacant** On a *clear* day, you can see the mountains from here. **2.** ✦ **see-through, translucent, transparent** Milk jugs are usually made of *clear* plastic. **3.** ✦ **apparent, evident, obvious, plain, understandable** Ms. Bergman said that we should make our answers to the test questions as *clear* as possible. —*verb* **1.** ✦ **clean, tidy** ✧ **empty, open** Dad asked me to *clear* the table so he could set it for dinner. **2.** ✦ **absolve, acquit** ✧ **free, release** New evidence *cleared* the couple who had originally been charged with the crime.

clever *adjective* ✦ **alert, bright, intelligent, quick, sharp, smart** The *clever* monkey quickly learned how to unlock the door of its cage.

client *noun* ✦ **customer, patron** ✧ **buyer, shopper** A good accountant is likely to have many *clients*.

cliff *noun* ✦ **bluff, precipice, rock face** ✧ **crag** We saw a brave mountaineer climbing the steep *cliff*. ▶

climate *noun* ✦ **weather** ✧ **atmosphere, environment, nature, temperature** Arizona has a warm and dry *climate*.

climax *noun* ✦ **high point, peak, zenith** ✧ **head, summit** During the movie's *climax*, the heroine slew the dragon and rescued the prince.

climb *verb* **1.** ✦ **ascend, go up, mount, scale** Most expeditions to *climb* Mount Everest take several months. **2.** ✦ **ascend, lift, rise** ✧ **soar** The airplane *climbed* steeply as it cleared the runway. —*noun* ✦ **ascent** It looks like an easy *climb* to the top of that hill.

clip *verb* ✦ **cut, snip** ✧ **crop, trim** Mom usually *clips* coupons out of the Sunday newspaper.

cloak *noun* **1.** ✦ **cape, mantle** ✧ **robe, wrap** In early movies, you could frequently identify the villain by the black *cloak* he wore. **2.** ✦ **cover, screen, veil** ✧ **mask** A *cloak* of fog kept us from seeing the boat. —*verb* ✦ **conceal, cover, hide, screen** ✧ **disguise** The Stealth Bomber has features that *cloak* it from enemy radar.

close *adjective* **1.** ✦ **at hand, imminent, near, nearby** ✧ **next** When the sun began to set, I realized nightfall was *close*. **2.** ✦ **careful, firm, strict, thorough, tight** The lioness kept a *close* watch over her cubs. **3.** ✦ **equal, even** ✧ **alike, narrow, similar** Everyone thought it would be a *close* game, but our team won easily. —*adverb* ✦ **near,**

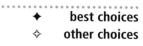
✦ **best choices**
✧ **other choices**

nearby ♦ **almost, closely** Theresa asked me not to sit so *close* to her. —*verb* **1.** ♦ **shut** ♢ **fasten, lock, seal, secure** Dan *closed* his eyes during the scary parts of the movie. **2.** ♦ **complete, conclude, end, finish, stop, wrap up** Our principal *closed* his speech with a funny story. —*noun* ♦ **conclusion, end, finish, stop, termination** Our conversation came to a *close* when Travis said that he had to be going.

cloudy *adjective* ♦ **overcast, sunless** ♢ **dark, dim, hazy, muddy** It was *cloudy* in the morning, but the sun came out in the afternoon.

clown *noun* ♢ **comedian, comic, jester, joker, prankster** My favorite part of the circus is watching the *clowns* perform their hilarious stunts. —*verb* ♦ **fool, play** ♢ **jest, joke, kid** My brother likes to *clown* around by imitating a monkey.

club *noun* **1.** ♢ **bat, mallet, staff, stick** In England, most police officers carry *clubs* instead of guns. **2.** ♦ **association, group, organization, society** Mother's bridge *club* is meeting at our house this afternoon. **3.** ♦ **center, facility** ♢ **hall** Kimberly is taking swimming lessons at the local athletic *club*. —*verb* ♦ **beat, hit, pound, strike** ♢ **batter, hammer** Joey wanted to *club* the snake, but I persuaded him to leave it alone.

clue *noun* ♦ **evidence, lead, sign, trace** ♢ **hint, suggestion** Police said that the burglar left no *clues*.

clumsy *adjective* ♦ **awkward, graceless, uncoordinated** Bill is so *clumsy* that he broke three plates while washing the dishes.

cluster *noun* ♦ **batch, bunch, clump, group** ♢ **bundle** I bought some grapes and ate the entire *cluster*. —*verb* ♦ **assemble, bunch, collect, flock, gather, mass** Whenever the farmer feeds his chickens, they *cluster* around him.

coach *noun* **1.** ♦ **carriage** ♢ **stage, stagecoach** The queen's *coach* was drawn by a team of six gray horses. **2.** ♦ **trainer** ♢ **instructor, manager, teacher** Kyle's father is my baseball *coach*. —*verb* ♦ **drill, instruct, teach, train, tutor** Mother *coached* my little brother on what he should say during our Passover ceremony.

coarse *adjective* ♦ **gritty, rough** ♢ **grainy, sandy, scratchy** Sandpaper has a *coarse* texture.

coast *noun* ♦ **seacoast, seashore, seaside, shore, shoreline** A lighthouse warns ships that the *coast* is near. —*verb* ♦ **glide, slide** ♢ **drift, flow, roll, slip** Kari *coasted* down the steep hill on her bicycle.

coat *noun* **1.** ♦ **jacket** ♢ **overcoat, raincoat, windbreaker, wrap** I always wear a warm *coat* when I walk in the snow. **2.** ♦ **coating, covering, layer** ♢ **surface** When we fixed up our house, we put on a fresh *coat* of paint. —*verb* ♦ **cover** ♢ **smear, spread** A thin layer of frost *coated* the trees.

coax *verb* ♦ **influence, persuade, urge** ♢ **lure** My friends *coaxed* me to join the soccer team.

code *noun* ♦ **regulations, rules, standards** ♢ **law, system** According to the local fire *code*, we can't burn trash in the backyard.

coil *noun* ♦ **reel, roll** ♢ **loop, ring, spiral** The rancher bought a *coil* of barbed wire. —*verb* ♦ **curl, roll, twist, wind, wrap** The python *coiled* itself around a tree branch.

coin *noun* ♦ **change, coinage** Robyn needs some more *coins* for the parking meter. —*verb* ♦ **create, devise, invent, originate** William Shakespeare is said to have *coined* over 1,700 new words.

coincide *verb* ♦ **accord, agree, concur, correspond, match** Steve's opinion of the movie doesn't *coincide* with mine.

coincidence *noun* ♦ **accident, chance** ♢ **fate, luck** It is just a *coincidence* that my best friend and I have the same last name.

cold *adjective* **1.** ✦ **chilly, cool, icy** ✧ **frigid, frozen** A glass of *cold* lemonade tastes wonderful on a hot summer day. **2.** ✦ **aloof, unfriendly** ✧ **haughty** The losing boxer gave the judges a *cold* stare. —*noun* **1.** ✦ **chill, coldness, coolness, iciness** ✧ **freeze** When I went outside without my jacket, I shivered in the *cold*. **2.** ✧ **illness, fever, sickness, virus** Sean had to stay home from school because he had a bad *cold*.

collapse *verb* ✦ **buckle, cave in, crumple, topple** ✧ **fall** The cheap lawn chair *collapsed* when I sat on it. —*noun* ✦ **cave-in** ✧ **breakdown, disintegration, failure** No one knew what caused the tunnel's sudden *collapse*.

colleague *noun* ✦ **associate, coworker, partner** ✧ **aide, comrade** Mom says that what she enjoys most about her job is the friendliness of her *colleagues*.

collect *verb* **1.** ✦ **accumulate, amass, gather** ✧ **assemble** Ever since Dad quit smoking, his old pipes have been *collecting* a lot of dust. **2.** ✦ **acquire, obtain, raise, secure** The government *collects* money through taxes.

collection *noun* ✦ **accumulation, hoard, mass, stockpile** We have a huge *collection* of old magazines down in our basement.

collide *verb* ✦ **bump, crash, hit, slam, smash, strike** The basketball players *collided* when they both ran toward the ball.

collision *noun* ✦ **accident, crash, impact, smashup, wreck** When Mom saw the car coming straight at us, she swerved away in order to avoid a *collision*.

color *noun* ✦ **hue, shade, tinge, tint, tone** My favorite *color* is purple. —*verb* ✦ **dye, paint, stain, tinge, tint** Daniel *colored* two dozen eggs last Easter.

colorful *adjective* ✦ **bright, vivid** ✧ **gaudy, loud** Jason likes to wear *colorful* plaid shirts.

combat *verb* ✦ **battle, fight, struggle against** ✧ **oppose, resist** Our mayor says that her top priority is to *combat* poverty. —*noun* ✦ **battle, war** ✧ **conflict, fight, struggle** The Air Force's newest jet fighter has not been tested in *combat*.

combine *verb* ✦ **blend, mix** ✧ **join, merge, unite** If you *combine* blue and yellow paint, you'll get green.

Antonyms
combine *verb*
detach, divide, segregate, separate, split, sunder

come *verb* **1.** ✦ **approach, go to, move to** ✧ **advance, near** Please *come to* the front of the class when I call your name. **2.** ✦ **appear, arrive, show up** ✧ **reach** My school bus *comes* at seven o'clock in the morning. **3.** ✦ **fall, happen, occur** ✧ **develop** Christmas *comes* only once a year. **4.** ✧ **arise, issue, originate, spring** My friend Olaf *comes* from Norway.

comfort *verb* ✦ **console, soothe** ✧ **ease, pacify, relieve** Whenever I'm feeling bad, my friends try to *comfort* me. —*noun* **1.** ✦ **aid, help, relief, solace, support** It's a real *comfort* to have my sister around the house when Mom and Dad are away. **2.** ✦ **luxury** ✧ **contentment, pleasure, satisfaction** It's possible to camp in *comfort* if you have the proper equipment.

comfortable *adjective* **1.** ✦ **cozy, snug** ✧ **pleasant, pleasurable, satisfying** Cool autumn nights really make me appreciate my warm and *comfortable* bed. **2.** ✦ **calm, easy, relaxed** ✧ **contented, serene** Elizabeth didn't feel *comfortable* the first time she flew on a plane.

comical *adjective* ✦ **amusing, funny, humorous, laughable** ✧ **ridiculous** My puppy is *comical* when he chases his tail.

command *verb* **1.** ✦ **bid, direct, order** ✧ **demand, require** The king *commanded* his knights to defend the realm. **2.** ✦ **head, lead**

✦ best choices
✧ other choices

✧ **control, govern, rule, supervise** A lieutenant *commands* a platoon of approximately forty soldiers. —*noun* **1.** ✦ **demand, direction, order** ✧ **instruction** Sometimes my bossy older sister's requests sound like *commands*. **2.** ✦ **authority, charge, control, power** ✧ **leadership** A naval captain has *command* over both a ship and its crew.

commemorate *verb* ✦ **celebrate, honor** ✧ **keep, observe, remember** The town held a parade to *commemorate* the Chinese New Year. ▼

commence *verb* ✦ **begin, open, start** ✧ **initiate** The graduation ceremony will *commence* at three o'clock.

commend *verb* ✦ **applaud, compliment, praise** ✧ **acclaim, honor** Our teacher *commended* Brad for his excellent attendance.

comment *noun* ✦ **observation, remark, statement** ✧ **note, opinion** Noelle's *comment* that I was an interesting person made me feel good. —*verb* ✦ **express, mention, remark, say, state** All of my friends *commented* that they liked my new sandals.

commerce *noun* ✦ **business, trade** ✧ **exchange, traffic** Many jobs depend upon *commerce* with other states and countries.

commit *verb* **1.** ✦ **carry out, do, perform** ✧ **complete, execute, make** We do not know who *committed* the crime. **2.** ✦ **assign to, confine to, institutionalize in** ✧ **imprison** The emotionally disturbed man was *committed to* a mental hospital for treatment. **3.** ✦ **devote, pledge** ✧ **promise, resolve, vow** My class is *committed* to raising money for the school softball team.

common *adjective* **1.** ✦ **general, universal** ✧ **joint, mutual, shared** It is *common* knowledge that the dinosaurs are extinct. **2.** ✦ **ordinary, routine, simple** ✧ **average, normal, typical, usual** The doctor said that my type of knee injury is very *common*.

commotion *noun* ✦ **clamor, confusion, disturbance, turmoil, uproar** There was a *commotion* in our house when a raccoon came in the pet door.

communicate *verb* ✦ **convey, impart** ✧ **declare, relate, report, state** When my dog dropped his leash in my lap, I knew what he was trying to *communicate* to me.

community *noun* **1.** ✦ **city, neighborhood, town** ✧ **population, public** Our mayor hopes to get the entire *community* involved in his anticrime campaign. **2.** ✦ **body, circle, group, set** ✧ **association, society** The scientific *community* feels that more money should be devoted to research.

compact[1] *adjective* **1.** ✦ **dense, firm, hard, solid, thick** An igloo is made from blocks of snow that are almost as *compact* as ice. **2.** ✦ **little, small** ✧ **cramped, limited, miniature, shrunken, undersized** My uncle's recreational vehicle has a *compact* kitchen. —*verb* ✦ **compress, cram, crush, pack, squeeze** Our kitchen has an appliance that *compacts* trash into small bundles.

compact[2] *noun* ✦ **accord, pact, treaty** ✧ **agreement, deal** The two nations signed a secret *compact* to help defend each other.

companion *noun* ✦ **comrade, friend, partner** ✧ **attendant, escort** It's safer to go hiking if you have a *companion* along.

company *noun* **1.** ✦ **callers, guests, visitors** Mother told me to clean my room because she was expecting *company*. **2.** ✦ **companionship, comradeship, fellowship** ✧ **friendship** Grandpa says that he enjoys my *company* very much. **3.** ✦ **business, establishment, firm** ✧ **corporation** Moira works for a small *company* that makes gardening supplies. **4.** ✦ **troupe** ✧ **band, corps, group, party, troop** A traveling ballet *company* will perform in our town next week.

compare *verb* **1.** ✦ **consider, contrast, relate** ✧ **analyze, examine** Before we bought a new computer, we went to several stores to *compare* prices. **2.** ✦ **compete with, equal, match** ✧ **resemble** Swimming in a pool is fun, but it can't *compare with* actually going to the beach.

comparison *noun* **1.** ✦ **assessment, evaluation, ranking, rating** ✧ **judgment** A *comparison* of the two stereos quickly revealed which one had the better sound. **2.** ✦ **resemblance, similarity** ✧ **connection, relationship** To me, there's no *comparison* between a frozen pizza and a fresh one from my favorite pizzeria.

compassion *noun* ✦ **concern, mercy, sympathy** ✧ **love, tenderness** Good doctors have *compassion* for their patients.

compel *verb* ✦ **drive, force, oblige, require** ✧ **cause, make** Bad weather *compelled* us to change our vacation plans.

compete *verb* ✦ **contend, take part** ✧ **challenge, rival, strive, vie** Natasha will *compete* in next Saturday's golf tournament.

competent *adjective* ✦ **able, capable, good, qualified, proficient, skilled** A *competent* typist rarely makes mistakes.

competition *noun* **1.** ✦ **rivalry** ✧ **conflict, contention, struggle** The *competition* at the Olympics is intense. **2.** ✦ **contest, meet** ✧ **game, match, tournament** Mr. Walker's class will have a spelling *competition* next week.

compile *verb* ✦ **accumulate, assemble, collect, gather, put together** Astrid *compiled* a list of people she wanted to invite to her birthday party.

complain *verb* ✦ **grumble** ✧ **criticize, denounce, object, protest** During last week's heat wave, many people *complained* about the temperature.

complaint *noun* ✦ **criticism, objection, protest** ✧ **dissatisfaction** Claudia really loved the book; her only *complaint* was that it was too short.

complete *adjective* **1.** ✦ **whole** ✧ **entire, full, total** When I dealt the game, I discovered that the card deck wasn't *complete*. **2.** ✦ **absolute, perfect, thorough, utter** ✧ **sheer** The camping trip was a *complete* disaster because of the rainstorm. —*verb* ✦ **conclude, end, finish, wrap up** ✧ **accomplish, fulfill** Grace *completed* her book report two weeks before it was due.

complex *adjective* ✦ **complicated, difficult, hard, intricate** ✧ **elaborate, involved** A jigsaw puzzle with 5,000 pieces is too *complex* for my tastes.

complicate *verb* ✦ **confuse, mix up, muddle** ✧ **handicap, involve** Please don't *complicate* our game by adding all those new rules.

complicated *adjective* ✦ **complex, difficult, hard, intricate** ✧ **involved** My new computer program is so *complicated* that I haven't been able to figure it out yet.

compliment *noun* ✦ **acclaim, praise** ✧ **admiration, approval, flattery** The *compliments* Mary received for her performance in the school play pleased her very much. —*verb* ✦ **admire, commend, praise** ✧ **approve, flatter** Randolph was pleased when I *complimented* his cooking.

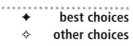

✦ **best choices**
✧ **other choices**

comply *verb* ✦ **abide by, follow, obey** ◇ **observe, respect** The emperor expected everyone to *comply with* his wishes.

compose *verb* **1.** ✦ **constitute, fashion, form, make, make up** Hydrogen and oxygen are the elements that *compose* water. **2.** ✦ **author, create, make, produce, write** ◇ **devise, invent** Jaclyn *composed* a poem to read for her mom's birthday. **3.** ✦ **calm, quiet, relax, settle, soothe** The actor took a few minutes to *compose* himself before the performance.

compound *noun* ✦ **mixture** ◇ **blend, combination, union** Richard's first attempt to make soup resulted in the creation of an unknown *compound* that had an incredibly foul smell. —*verb* ✦ **blend, combine, mix** ◇ **join, link** The witch made her potion by *compounding* rat tails, frog toes, and snake tongues.

comprehend *verb* ✦ **grasp, know, perceive, understand** ◇ **fathom** I know how to use my computer, but I don't really *comprehend* how it works.

comprehensive *adjective* ✦ **complete, full, thorough** ◇ **broad, large** This history book has a *comprehensive* index that lists every subject covered.

comprise *verb* ✦ **contain, include, incorporate** ◇ **embrace, involve** Japan *comprises* more than 3,500 islands.

compromise *noun* ✦ **arrangement, bargain, concession, settlement** My allowance of five dollars a week is a *compromise*: I wanted more, but Mom thought I needed less. —*verb* ✦ **meet halfway** ◇ **concede, give in, negotiate, settle** When Margaret and I couldn't agree which restaurant to go to, we *compromised* by getting a pizza to eat in. ▶

compulsory *adjective* ✦ **mandatory, necessary, required** ◇ **imperative** Wearing your seat belt is *compulsory* in most states.

compute *verb* ✦ **calculate, determine, figure, reckon** ◇ **estimate** Marla *computed* the average of 106, 111, 125, and 130.

comrade *noun* ✦ **buddy, companion, friend, pal, partner** Dad has stayed in touch with many of his army *comrades*.

conceal *verb* ✦ **hide, cover, mask, screen** ◇ **camouflage** The top of the mountain was *concealed* by clouds.

concede *verb* **1.** ✦ **acknowledge, admit, agree, confess, grant** We *conceded* that we were lost and asked for directions. **2.** ✦ **give up, surrender, yield** ◇ **give in, resign** The candidate *conceded* the election before the final votes were counted.

conceited *adjective* ✦ **arrogant, haughty, self-centered, vain** The *conceited* artist claimed that he was the best painter around.

conceive *verb* ✦ **envision, imagine, picture, think of** ◇ **form** Sir Isaac Newton is said to have *conceived of* gravity when he saw an apple fall.

concentrate *verb* **1.** ✦ **focus** ◇ **apply, contemplate, dedicate, devote, think** I was *concentrating* on piano practice and didn't hear the doorbell. **2.** ✦ **center, cluster, focus** ◇ **collect, gather** The motion picture industry is *concentrated* in Southern California.

concept *noun* ✦ **conception, idea, notion, theory** ◇ **thought** Jules Verne wrote about the *concept* of space flight nearly a century before it became a reality.

concern *verb* **1.** ✦ **affect, interest, involve, pertain to** The principal said that she would be speaking on a subject that *concerns* all of us. **2.** ✦ **distress by, disturb by, trouble by, worry about**

◆ **bother** We were *concerned about* Grandfather's health until the doctors said that he would be fine. —*noun* **1.** ◆ **affair, business, matter** ◇ **consideration, interest** Religious beliefs are a private *concern*. **2.** ◆ **apprehension, anxiety, worry** ◇ **care, trouble** Amy took the stray cat home because she felt *concern* for its well-being.

concert *noun* ◆ **performance** ◇ **program, recital, show** I want to go to next week's *concert* because my friend is in the orchestra.

concise *adjective* ◆ **brief, condensed, short, succinct** Our assignment is to write a *concise* report of no more than 150 words.

conclude *verb* **1.** ◆ **close, complete, end, finish, terminate** The celebration *concluded* with a display of fireworks. **2.** ◆ **decide, deduce, determine, resolve, settle** ◇ **assume** The doctor *concluded* that I was in excellent health.

conclusion *noun* **1.** ◆ **close, end, finish, termination** ◇ **finale** The start of the movie was boring, but the *conclusion* was very exciting. **2.** ◆ **decision, deduction, determination, judgment** ◇ **opinion** The detective's *conclusion* was that the butler had committed the crime.

concrete *adjective* ◆ **actual, definite, real, tangible** ◇ **firm, solid** Judge Goodwin ruled that the case could not be tried unless the police found some *concrete* evidence.

concur *verb* ◆ **agree with, assent to** ◇ **accord, approve, consent** I *concur with* your opinion of the television program.

condemn *verb* **1.** ◆ **attack, criticize, denounce** ◇ **blame** In last week's sermon, our minister *condemned* the use of illegal drugs. **2.** ◆ **doom, sentence** ◇ con-

Antonyms

condemn *verb*
1. admire, applaud, commend, esteem, extol, honor, praise
2. acquit, clear, excuse, forgive, pardon

vict, punish During the Roman Empire, prisoners were frequently *condemned* to serve as galley slaves.

condense *verb* ◆ **abbreviate, abridge, crop, reduce, shorten** ◇ **curtail, thicken** The editor *condensed* the author's book by cutting out five chapters.

condition *noun* **1.** ◆ **form, order, repair, shape, state** Mom and Dad are looking for a used car that's in good *condition*. **2.** ◆ **ailment, disease, illness, malady, sickness** ◇ **affliction** Anyone with a heart *condition* should be under a doctor's care. ▶ **3.** ◆ **qualification, provision, requirement, restriction** Dad said that I could go to Joe's house for dinner with the *condition* that I would be home by eight o'clock. —*verb* ◆ **prepare, ready, shape, train** ◇ **adapt** The coach began *conditioning* the team on the first day of practice.

conduct *verb* **1.** ◆ **direct, guide, lead, steer** ◇ **escort, usher** A flight attendant *conducted* us to our seats. **2.** ◆ **acquit, behave** ◇ **act, bear, carry** Joan said that I *conducted* myself perfectly when she took me to visit her friends. —*noun* ◆ **attitude, behavior, manner** ◇ **actions, ways** Our school gives an award to the student who has the best *conduct*.

confer *verb* **1.** ◆ **consult, deliberate** ◇ **discuss, speak, talk** Dad *conferred* with his lawyer before signing the business contract. **2.** ◆ **award to, give to, grant to, present to** A special prize was *conferred on* the hometown hero by the mayor of the city.

conference *noun* ◆ **consultation, discussion, interview, meeting, talk** Mom is scheduled to have a *conference* with my teacher next week.

confess *verb* ◆ **acknowledge, admit, concede, disclose, reveal** My little sister *confessed* that she ate the last cupcake.

◆ best choices
◇ other choices

confide *verb* ✦ **disclose, reveal, tell, whisper** ✧ **commit, entrust, turn over** My best friend *confided* a secret to me because she knows that I'll never tell anyone.

confidence *noun* **1.** ✦ **aplomb, assurance, self-confidence, self-reliance** ✧ **poise** After practicing at home, I was able to stand up in front of my class and speak with *confidence*. **2.** ✦ **faith, reliance, trust** ✧ **belief** We have complete *confidence* in our family dentist.

confident *adjective* ✦ **certain, positive, sure** ✧ **assured** George is *confident* that he will pass tomorrow's math test.

confidential *adjective* ✦ **classified, restricted, secret** ✧ **personal, private** Dad keeps his *confidential* files locked up whenever he is away from his office.

confine *verb* ✦ **hold, limit, restrain, restrict** ✧ **detain, imprison** We built a fence to *confine* our dogs to the backyard.

confirm *verb* ✦ **support, uphold, verify** ✧ **approve, certify** When we consulted a second doctor, she *confirmed* the original diagnosis.

confiscate *verb* ✦ **appropriate, seize, take, take away** Mom *confiscated* our firecrackers before we had a chance to use them.

conflict *noun* **1.** ✦ **fight, war** ✧ **battle, combat, warfare** The Vietnam War was the longest *conflict* in American history. **2.** ✦ **argument, clash, disagreement** ✧ **feud, struggle** The President tried to stay out of the *conflict* that arose among his advisors. —*verb* ✦ **contradict, differ from, disagree with, vary from** ✧ **clash** The second witness gave testimony that *conflicted with* what the first witness had said.

conform *verb* ✦ **agree with, comply with, correspond to, follow** ✧ **obey, observe** We have to wear clothing that *conforms to* our school's new dress code.

confront *verb* ✦ **challenge, defy, face** ✧ **encounter, meet** When I *confronted* the growling dog, it turned tail and ran away.

confuse *verb* **1.** ✦ **bewilder, mystify, perplex, puzzle** My friend's map *confused* me, and I ended up going in the wrong direction. **2.** ✦ **mistake, mix up** ✧ **jumble, misjudge** Ground squirrels look so much like chipmunks that people often *confuse* the two.

confusion *noun* ✦ **chaos, disorder, turmoil** ✧ **bewilderment, perplexity** There was much *confusion* when our plane landed in the wrong city.

congratulate *verb* ✦ **applaud, cheer, compliment, praise** ✧ **honor** We all *congratulated* Mallory when she won the short-story contest.

connect *verb* **1.** ✦ **join, link** ✧ **attach, couple, fasten, unite** The Channel Tunnel *connects* Great Britain with France. **2.** ✦ **associate, equate, identify, relate** It was hard for me to *connect* names and faces when I first joined my scout troop.

connection *noun* **1.** ✦ **coupling** ✧ **bond, junction, union** Our car wouldn't start because the battery *connection* was loose. **2.** ✦ **association, link, relation, relationship** The police said that there was no apparent *connection* between the two bank robberies.

conquer *verb* ✦ **defeat, overcome, subdue** ✧ **beat, triumph** Rome *conquered* England during the first century A.D.

conscious *adjective* **1.** ✦ **aware, knowledgeable, mindful** ✧ **alert, awake** The man gradually became *conscious* of the fact that he was not alone in the haunted house. **2.** ✦ **deliberate, intentional, planned, purposeful** Benjamin has been making a *conscious* effort to improve his grade in social studies.

consecutive *adjective* ✦ **continual, continuous, successive, uninterrupted** During our vacation last year, it rained for four *consecutive* days and nights.

consent *verb* ✦ **agree, assent** ✧ **allow, approve, authorize, permit** I finally *consented* to let my brother ride my bike. —*noun* ✦ **agreement, approval, assent, authorization, permission** Mom said that I had to get Mr. Thompson's *consent* before I could cut through his backyard.

consequence *noun* ✦ **result** ✧ **aftermath, effect, end, outcome, product** Patrick missed his bus and as a *consequence* had to walk to school.

conservative *adjective* ✦ **conventional, reasonable, standard, traditional** Mom wore a *conservative* gray suit to her business meeting.

conserve *verb* ✦ **preserve, save** ✧ **keep, maintain, protect** We were asked to *conserve* water during the long drought.

> **Antonyms**
>
> **conserve** *verb*
>
> consume, misuse, spend, squander, use up, waste

consider *verb* **1.** ✦ **contemplate, deliberate, ponder, reflect on, think about** Before I make a decision, I need to *consider* the options. **2.** ✦ **believe, judge, reckon, regard (as), view (as)** Everyone in the class *considers* Amber to be the top student. **3.** ✦ **allow for, heed, note, remember** The veterinarian said that my cat was in excellent condition, if you *consider* his age.

considerable *adjective* ✦ **extensive, great, significant, substantial** ✧ **large** The famous earthquake that hit San Francisco in 1906 caused *considerable* damage.

considerate *adjective* ✦ **kind, polite, thoughtful** ✧ **attentive, friendly** It was very *considerate* of Patricia to send me such a nice get-well card.

consideration *noun* **1.** ✦ **deliberation, reflection, study, thought** After much *considera-*

tion, my parents have decided to buy a new house. **2.** ✦ **concern, factor, issue, point** ✧ **circumstance** When planning a camping trip, the weather is an important *consideration*. **3.** ✦ **concern, regard, respect** ✧ **courtesy, thoughtfulness** Amanda always shows *consideration* for other people's feelings.

consist *verb* ✦ **comprise, contain, include, incorporate** The spelling test *consisted of* twenty words.

consolidate *verb* ✦ **combine, join, link, merge, unite** ✧ **connect** Mr. Smith *consolidated* his debts by getting one bank loan that covered everything.

conspicuous *adjective* ✦ **noticeable, obvious, prominent, recognizable** ✧ **clear, evident, plain, visible** A giraffe's long neck is its most *conspicuous* feature.

conspiracy *noun* ✦ **plan, plot, scheme** ✧ **intrigue** Several generals were heavily involved in a *conspiracy* to overthrow their country's corrupt government.

constant *adjective* ✦ **ceaseless, continuous, endless, perpetual** A newborn infant requires almost *constant* attention.

construct *verb* ✦ **build, fabricate, make** ✧ **assemble, manufacture** Linda helped her dad *construct* their new garage.

consult *verb* ✦ **confer, deliberate, discuss** ✧ **speak, talk** Dad *consulted* with my mom and me before accepting an out-of-state transfer.

consume *verb* **1.** ✦ **devour, down, eat, swallow** ✧ **digest, feed** The giant anteater of South America can *consume* over 30,000 ants in a day. **2.** ✦ **destroy, devour, use up, waste** ✧ **exhaust, finish** The forest fire *consumed* more than five hundred acres of parkland.

contact *noun* ✧ **connection, encounter, meeting, touch, union** Our counselor has warned

✦ **best choices**
✧ **other choices**

us to avoid *contact* with the poison ivy that grows around camp. **—verb ✦ communicate with ✧ connect, reach, touch** When Krista was sick, her mom *contacted* a doctor for advice.

contain *verb* **1. ✦ have, include ✧ bear, carry, hold** Mom doesn't like to eat mayonnaise because it *contains* so much fat. **2. ✦ check, control, limit, restrain, stop, suppress** Firefighters were able to *contain* the blaze before it destroyed the building.

contaminate *verb* **✦ dirty, foul, pollute, spoil, taint ✧ poison** The oil spill *contaminated* several miles of shoreline.

contemplate *verb* **✦ consider, deliberate, ponder, reflect on, think about** My older sister is *contemplating* getting an apartment on her own.

contempt *noun* **✦ disdain, disrespect, scorn ✧ disgust, hatred** The haughty queen felt *contempt* for all of her subjects.

contend *verb* **1. ✦ battle, combat, fight, struggle with, wrestle** We had to *contend with* a lot of mosquitoes on our last kayaking trip. **2. ✦ compete, vie ✧ challenge, contest, strive** The runners are *contending* for a chance to go to the state championship. **3. ✦ affirm, argue, assert, claim, declare, say, state** Gary *contends* that he is a better swimmer than Peter.

content *adjective* **✦ contented, happy, pleased, satisfied ✧ gratified** Mrs. Hopson said that anyone who wasn't *content* with his or her grade could take the test again. **—noun ✦ contentment, happiness, pleasure, satisfaction** Uncle Fred sighed with *content* after he finished dessert. **—verb ✦ appease, gratify, satisfy ✧ delight, please** Because Jordan couldn't go to the ball game, he had to *content* himself with watching it on television.

contented *adjective* **✦ content, gratified, happy, pleased, satisfied** The *contented* baby fell asleep in her mother's arms.

contest *noun* **✦ competition, meet, tournament ✧ fight, struggle** Chloe took first place in our school's spelling *contest*. **—verb ✦ challenge, dispute ✧ oppose, resist, struggle** The losing candidate *contested* the election results by calling for a recount.

continual *adjective* **✦ constant, continuous, perpetual, persistent, steady** It's hard to concentrate with these *continual* interruptions.

continue *verb* **1. ✦ endure, go on, last, persist, stay** The drought is expected to *continue* for the remainder of this year. **2. ✦ carry on with, pick up, resume ✧ renew, restart** The speaker paused for a moment and then *continued* his lecture.

continuous *adjective* **✦ constant, continual, endless, nonstop, perpetual** The human brain needs a *continuous* supply of oxygen-rich blood.

contract *noun* **✦ agreement, arrangement, compact ✧ bargain, deal** When my parents bought a new car, they signed a *contract* that committed them to making monthly payments. **—verb 1. ✦ compress, shorten ✧ decrease, reduce, shrink** Your muscles *contract* when you lift a heavy object. **2. ✦ agree, pledge, promise, undertake ✧ vow** The disposal company *contracted* to pick up our trash once a week. **3. ✦ catch, develop, get ✧ acquire** My uncle *contracted* malaria while traveling in Central America.

contradict *verb* **✦ challenge, deny, dispute, refute ✧ disagree** Peter *contradicted* his little brother's claim that the moon is made of cheese.

contrary *adjective* **1. ✦ contradictory, counter, opposite ✧ different, opposed** *Contrary* to popular belief, wolves do not howl at the moon. **2. ✦ headstrong, obstinate, perverse, stubborn** My *contrary* dog never comes when I call him.

contrast *verb* **✦ compare, oppose ✧ differ, distinguish, vary** Latoya has written a report that *contrasts* the lives of African-Americans today to

✦ **best choices**
✧ **other choices**

those of her ancestors. —*noun* ✦ **counterpoint, difference (from)** ◇ **comparison** The coolness of the air-conditioned room was a refreshing *contrast* to the heat outside.

Antonyms
contrast *noun*
agreement, harmony, likeness, resemblance, similarity, uniformity

contribute *verb* **1.** ✦ **donate, give, grant, present** ◇ **furnish, supply** Ramona's class raised one hundred dollars to *contribute* to a local charity. **2.** ✦ **add to, influence** ◇ **aid, cause, help, make** The gold-medal gymnast said that her parents' support *contributed to* her success.

contribution *noun* ✦ **donation, gift, offering, present** ◇ **payment** Jason made a five-dollar *contribution* to the American Red Cross.

contrive *verb* ✦ **concoct, create, design, devise, invent** ◇ **plan, scheme** Richard *contrived* a mousetrap out of a board and a tin can.

control *verb* **1.** ✦ **direct, govern, manage, rule, supervise** My dad owns a small business, and he *controls* all of its operations. **2.** ✦ **check, curb, restrain, subdue, suppress** Cindy's dentist advised her to brush regularly and *control* her sweet tooth. ▼ —*noun* **1.** ✦ **authority, command, direction, power, rule** The amount we are allowed to spend is under the treasurer's *control*. **2.** ✦ **check, curb, regulation, restraint, restriction** The mayor is trying to impose strict *controls* on public spending.

controversy *noun* ✦ **argument, debate, disagreement, dispute** The President's plan to raise taxes was a source of much *controversy*.

convene *verb* ✦ **assemble, congregate, gather, meet** ◇ **rally** The school board will *convene* next week to discuss the hiring of a new assistant principal.

convenience *noun* ✦ **advantage, benefit, comfort, ease** ◇ **aid, help, use** The local bank installed an automated teller machine for the *convenience* of its customers.

convenient *adjective* ✦ **advantageous, beneficial, helpful, useful** ◇ **suitable** Mom thinks that it is very *convenient* to live around the corner from a supermarket.

conventional *adjective* ✦ **customary, normal, regular, standard, usual** My parents thought about getting married in a hot air balloon, but they settled on a *conventional* wedding in a church.

conversation *noun* ✦ **discussion, talk** ◇ **chat, conference, speech** I had a long *conversation* with my brother when he got home from summer camp.

converse *verb* ✦ **chat, speak, talk** ◇ **confer, discuss** The two men spent the morning *conversing* about the weather and their grandchildren.

convert *verb* ✦ **change, modify, transform, turn** ◇ **alter, switch** The big mansion on the edge of town has been *converted* into a museum. —*noun* ✦ **believer (in), follower (of), recruit** ◇ **disciple** Marshall is a new *convert* to environmental causes such as recycling.

convey *verb* **1.** ✦ **bring, carry, transport** ◇ **bear, move** The ancient Romans built an elaborate system of aqueducts to *convey* water to their cities. **2.** ✦ **communicate, express, relate, state** ◇ **disclose** I searched for the right words to *convey* my thoughts.

45

convict *verb* ✦ **condemn, sentence** ◇ **find guilty, judge** The jury *convicted* the defendant on two counts of armed robbery. —*noun* ✦ **inmate, prisoner** ◇ **captive, criminal, felon** Three *convicts* escaped from the state prison.

convince *verb* ✦ **assure, persuade, satisfy** ◇ **impress, sway** Your story has *convinced* me that you are telling the truth.

cook *verb* ✦ **make, prepare** ◇ **bake, broil, fry, grill, microwave, roast** Dad said that he would *cook* dinner tonight.

cool *adjective* **1.** ✦ **chill, chilly** ◇ **cold, icy, frigid** It was warm on the beach, but the wind off the ocean was *cool*. **2.** ✦ **calm, collected, composed, unflappable** When the plane went into a spin, the pilot remained *cool* and quickly regained control. **3.** ✦ **aloof, distant, reserved, unfriendly** ◇ **haughty** Anthony's *cool* stare turned into a warm smile when I apologized for having offended him. —*verb* ✦ **chill** ◇ **freeze, frost, ice, refrigerate** We *cooled* the soda by putting the bottle in the mountain stream.

cooperate *verb* ✦ **collaborate** ◇ **coordinate, join, participate, unite** If we *cooperate*, we can clean out the garage in no time.

cooperation *noun* ✦ **participation, teamwork** ◇ **aid, help, support** Keeping the schoolyard free of litter requires the *cooperation* of all students.

coordinate *verb* ✦ **adapt, conform, integrate, harmonize, unite** Good swimmers *coordinate* their breathing with the rhythm of their strokes.

cope *verb* ✦ **contend with, deal with, handle, manage** ◇ **control** The babysitter had a tough time *coping with* five children at once.

copy *noun* ✦ **double, duplicate, reproduction** ◇ **imitation** Medieval monks created beautiful hand-drawn *copies* of important manuscripts. —*verb* **1.** ✦ **duplicate, reproduce, write down** Our teacher asked us to *copy* the vocabulary words that she had written on the chalkboard. **2.** ✦ **follow, imitate, mimic** ◇ **fake, repeat, steal** Many writers have *copied* the style of Ernest Hemingway.

cord *noun* ✦ **string, twine** ◇ **line, rope, thread** Ethan used a length of *cord* to tie up the bundle of newspapers.

cordial *adjective* ✦ **courteous, friendly, nice, pleasant, warm** I'm always *cordial* to Aunt Emma, though it isn't easy when she pinches my cheeks.

core *noun* **1.** ◇ **kernel, nut, seed** We put our apple *cores* in the compost pile. **2.** ✦ **center, middle** ◇ **essence, heart, nucleus** The Earth's *core* is a ball of solid iron and nickel.

corner *noun* **1.** ✦ **edge** ◇ **angle, bend, end** Jessica folded the *corner* of a page to mark her place in the book. **2.** ✦ **intersection, junction** Eric lives near the *corner* of First and Maple streets.

corporation *noun* ✦ **business, company, firm** ◇ **enterprise** Serena works for a *corporation* that develops computer software.

correct *verb* ✦ **fix, remedy, repair** ◇ **adjust, amend, improve** These eyeglasses will *correct* your vision. ▶ —*adjective* **1.** ✦ **accurate, exact, precise, right, true** The *correct* spelling of most words can be found in a good dictionary. **2.** ✦ **decent, proper, respectable, right** ◇ **appropriate, fitting** The *correct* thing to do is to return the lost wallet to its rightful owner.

correction *noun* ◇ **adjustment, amendment, improvement, remedy, revision** I made a lot of spelling *corrections* before I handed in the final copy of my report.

correspond *verb* **1.** ✦ **agree, concur, fit, match** ◇ **accord** The newspaper article does not *correspond* with what I saw on the television news.

2. ✦ **communicate with, exchange letters with, write to** Holly regularly *corresponds with* her pen pal in Sweden.

corridor *noun* ✦ **hall, hallway** ✧ **aisle, passage, passageway** The principal's office is at the end of the main *corridor*.

corrode *verb* ✦ **eat away, erode, wear away** ✧ **rust** Acid rain *corrodes* railroad tracks, stone buildings, statues, and much more.

corrupt *adjective* ✦ **crooked, dishonest, immoral** ✧ **evil, wicked** The *corrupt* boxer accepted a bribe to lose the big fight. —*verb* ✦ **degrade, warp** ✧ **contaminate, pollute, taint** Some people fear that too much violence on television can *corrupt* a person's values.

cost *noun* **1.** ✦ **charge, expense, price** ✧ **amount, payment** If you buy these sunglasses, the case will be included at no extra *cost*. **2.** ✦ **loss, penalty, sacrifice** ✧ **damage, injury** The general believed that the enemy had to be defeated at any *cost*.

costume *noun* ✦ **attire, dress, outfit** ✧ **disguise** Harold's little brother plans to wear a dinosaur *costume* to the Halloween party. ▶

counsel *noun* ✦ **advice, guidance, recommendation** ✧ **suggestion** When deciding which piece to play, Sean asked his flute teacher for *counsel*. —*verb* ✦ **advise, guide** ✧ **direct, recommend** My school has a person available to *counsel* any students who are having problems.

count *verb* **1.** ✦ **add up, tally, total** ✧ **calculate, compute** The chaperone *counted* heads to make sure that everyone was present. **2.** ✦ **have worth, matter, signify** ✧ **consider, regard** The last basket didn't *count* because the shot was made after the buzzer went off. **3.** ✦ **depend on, rely on, trust** Erin said that we could *count on* her to help with the party decorations. —*noun* ✦ **tally** ✧ **calculation** The final ballot *count* revealed that Michelle had won the class election.

counter *adjective* ✦ **contrary , opposite, the reverse (of)** ✧ **contradictory, opposing** Desiree's opinion of Kevin's haircut is *counter* to mine. —*verb* ✦ **oppose** ✧ **answer, respond, return** Lindsey *countered* my suggestion that we get a pizza by proposing hamburgers instead.

counterfeit *verb* ✦ **fake, forge** ✧ **copy, reproduce** Federal agents arrested the criminal who had been *counterfeiting* twenty-dollar bills. —*adjective* ✦ **fake, false, forged, imitation, phony** These *counterfeit* bills don't look very much like the real thing. —*noun* ✦ **fake, forgery, imitation** ✧ **reproduction** This stock certificate looks real, but it is a *counterfeit*.

✦   **best choices**
✧   **other choices**

country *noun* **1. ✦ nation, state ✧ domain, kingdom, realm** Mexico and Canada are the two *countries* that share borders with the United States. **2. ✦ land, terrain, territory ✧ district, region** California's vast Central Valley is good farming *country.* **3. ✦ countryside, rural area ✧ farmland, provinces** Uncle Gene sold his condominium in the city and bought a house in the *country.*

couple *noun* **✦ duo, pair, twosome ✧ team** Fourteen *couples* entered the dance contest. —*verb* **✦ attach, connect, fasten ✧ join, link, unite** I helped Dad *couple* the horse trailer to our pickup truck.

courage *noun* **✦ bravery, fearlessness, heroism, mettle, valor** The firefighter showed great *courage* when she entered the burning building to rescue an elderly man.

courageous *adjective* **✦ brave, fearless, gallant, heroic, valiant** The *courageous* boy climbed a tree to rescue his neighbor's cat.

course *noun* **1. ✦ chain, order, progression, series** We are studying the *course* of events that led up to the Revolutionary War. **2. ✦ bearing, direction, heading, path, route, track, way** The ocean liner changed *course* to avoid running into an iceberg. **3. ✦ class, seminar, subject ✧ lecture, lesson** Bryan's mom is taking a creative writing *course* at the university that meets once a week. —*verb* **✦ flow, run, stream ✧ gush, race** Tears were *coursing* down the woman's cheeks while she chopped the onion.

Antonyms
courteous *adjective*
discourteous, disrespectful, ill-mannered, impolite, impudent, rude

courteous *adjective* **✦ civil, considerate, mannerly, polite, respectful, well-mannered** A *courteous* driver let Dad pull into the lane.

cover *verb* **1. ✦ blanket, coat ✧ cloak, hide, layer, screen** After the volcano erupted, a thick layer of ash *covered* the ground for miles around. **2. ✦ comprise, contain, include, occupy** My aunt and uncle's ranch *covers* more than 5,000 acres. **3. ✦ cross, journey, pass over, travel** The backpackers *covered* ten miles on their first day of hiking. —*noun* **1. ✦ protection, refuge, shelter ✧ asylum, concealment, screen** The rabbit took *cover* under a bush. **2. ✦ lid, top ✧ cap, covering, crown** Please put the *cover* on the kettle so the water will boil faster.

covet *verb* **✦ crave, desire, want, wish for ✧ envy** I think my dog *covets* my peanut butter sandwich.

cozy *adjective* **✦ comfortable, pleasant, snug, warm ✧ easy, safe, secure** We felt *cozy* in front of the fireplace as we listened to the sound of the wind and rain outside.

crack *verb* **1. ✦ snap ✧ bang, beat, slap, pop** The horses reared when the cowboy *cracked* his whip. **2. ✦ break, fracture, splinter, split ✧ rupture** A passing car kicked up a piece of gravel that *cracked* our windshield. —*noun* **1. ✦ bang, report ✧ burst, clap, pop, snap** The deer ran for cover when it heard the loud *crack* of a rifle. **2. ✦ break, chink, crevice, gap, split ✧ cleft, fissure, opening** The boy peeked through a *crack* in the fence.

craft *noun* **1. ✦ ability, art, expertise, skill, talent** The embroidery on this scarf was done with great *craft.* **2. ✦ job, occupation, profession, trade, work** Violin-making is a difficult *craft* to learn. **3. ✦ boat, ship, vessel ✧ aircraft, airplane, plane** The Coast Guard warned all small *craft* to stay in port during the storm.

cram *verb* **✦ jam, load, pack, squeeze, stuff ✧ force** Alyssa *crammed* all her stuffed animals onto one shelf.

cramp *noun* **✦ contraction, convulsion, spasm ✧ kink, twitch** Cody awoke in the middle of the night with a *cramp* in his leg. —*verb* **✦ con-**

tract, **convulse** Jennifer stretches before dance practice to keep her muscles from *cramping*.

cranky *adjective* ✦ **cross, grouchy, grumpy, irritable** My little brother gets *cranky* if he doesn't take an afternoon nap.

crash *verb* ✦ **bump against, collide with, hit, smash into** My radio-controlled car *crashed into* a tree. —*noun* **1.** ✦ **bang, slam, smash** ✧ **clatter, racket** I accidentally dropped a bowling ball, and it hit the floor with a loud *crash*. **2.** ✦ **accident, smash, smashup, wreck** ✧ **collision** The pilot parachuted to safety, but his plane was destroyed in the *crash*.

crave *verb* ✦ **covet, desire, hunger for, long for, want, yearn for** After eating freeze-dried foods for two weeks, the backpackers *craved* fresh fruits and vegetables.

crawl *verb* ✦ **creep, inch** ✧ **drag, slither, wriggle** I watched a snail *crawl* across the patio. —*noun* ✧ **creep, plod, walk, trudge** Traffic slowed to a *crawl* during rush hour.

crazy *adjective* **1.** ✦ **absurd, dumb, foolish, silly, stupid** ✧ **insane, mad** Putting ice cream on your pizza was a *crazy* thing to do. **2.** ✦ **enthusiastic, excited, mad, passionate, wild** ✧ **ardent** Ronisha is *crazy* about rap music.

crease *noun* ✦ **fold, wrinkle** ✧ **line, pleat** Dad ironed the *creases* out of his new shirt. ◄ —*verb* ✦ **fold** ✧ **crinkle, pleat, wrinkle** It's easier to tear a piece of paper in half if you *crease* it first.

create *verb* ✦ **generate, make, produce** ✧ **design, devise, invent** The new factory is expected to *create* a lot of jobs.

creation *noun* **1.** ✦ **formation, making, production** ✧ **development, establishment, generation** The *creation* of a seven-layer cake can take

many hours from start to finish. **2.** ✦ **achievement, product, work** ✧ **invention, masterpiece** Mark's latest *creation* is a clay sculpture of a flying dragon.

creative *adjective* ✦ **ingenious, imaginative, inventive** ✧ **resourceful** The *creative* teacher was always thinking up new and interesting things to do in her classroom.

creature *noun* ✦ **animal, beast, being** ✧ **person** Unicorns are mythical *creatures* revered for their beauty and grace.

credit *noun* ✦ **acclaim, acknowledgement, praise, recognition** ✧ **honor** Betty gave her sister *credit* for all the great party preparations.

creed *noun* ✦ **doctrine, principle, teaching** ✧ **belief, faith** The *creed* of my family demands that we always tell the truth.

creek *noun* ✦ **brook** ✧ **rill, spring, stream** Emilio and his brother are down at the *creek* trying to catch tadpoles.

creep *verb* ✦ **crawl, slink, slip, steal** ✧ **slide, sneak** The lion *crept* silently toward its prey.

crest *noun* ✦ **peak, summit, tip, top** Lynn climbed to the *crest* of a hill to get a better view of the skyline.

crew *noun* ✦ **gang, group, team** ✧ **band, company, staff** I joined the *crew* that was cleaning up the schoolyard. ▼

✦ **best choices**
✧ **other choices**

crime *noun* **1.** ✦ **offense, violation** ✧ **felony, misdemeanor** Shoplifting is a *crime*. **2.** ✦ **outrage, shame** ✧ **sin, vice, wrong, wrongdoing** It would be a *crime* to throw away these old clothes when there are so many people who could use them.

criminal *noun* ✦ **crook, felon, lawbreaker** ✧ **gangster, outlaw** Police are searching for the *criminal* who robbed the local convenience store. —*adjective* ✦ **illegal, lawless, unlawful** ✧ **dishonest, wrong** Stealing a car is a *criminal* act.

cripple *verb* ✦ **damage, disable** ✧ **hurt, injure, weaken** A heavy snowstorm *crippled* the city's transportation system.

crisis *noun* ✦ **emergency** ✧ **predicament, problem, trouble** There was a financial *crisis* when the county government ran out of money.

critical *adjective* **1.** ✦ **disapproving, condemning** ✧ **judgmental** The librarian was *critical* of the plan to save money by ordering fewer books. **2.** ✦ **acute, dangerous, desperate, grave, serious** We experienced a *critical* shortage of water during last year's drought.

criticize *verb* ✦ **evaluate, judge** ✧ **attack, condemn, denounce** How can you *criticize* that movie when you haven't seen it?

crook *noun* ✦ **cheat, criminal, swindler, thief** ✧ **scoundrel, villain** That *crook* is trying to sell fake lottery tickets.

crop *noun* ✦ **harvest, yield** ✧ **growth, produce, production** Farmers are expecting a good *crop* of rice this year. —*verb* ✦ **clip, cut, shear, trim** ✧ **mow, prune** The barber *cropped* your hair pretty short.

cross *noun* ✦ **hybrid** ✧ **blend, combination, mixture** Alexandra's dog is a *cross* between a golden retriever and a Siberian husky. —*verb* **1.** ✦ **move across, transit, travel over** ✧ **pass** An airplane can *cross* the United States in about five

hours. **2.** ✦ **converge, intersect, join, meet** ✧ **crisscross** The intersection where the two busy streets *cross* would be a good place to build a gas station. —*adjective* ✦ **angry, annoyed, mad** ✧ **grouchy, grumpy, irritable** When the man was late to work several days in a row, his supervisor was *cross* with him.

crouch *verb* ✦ **squat, stoop** ✧ **bend, huddle, hunch, kneel** Theresa had to *crouch* to get under the railing.

crowd *noun* ✦ **flock, horde, mob, multitude, swarm, throng** A *crowd* of people gathered to watch the parade. —*verb* ✦ **cluster around, flock around, gather around, mob** Fans *crowded around* the television star, trying to get his autograph.

crude *adjective* **1.** ✦ **coarse, makeshift, rough, simple** ✧ **unfinished** My brother used old boards and packing crates to make a *crude* desk. **2.** ✦ **impolite, rude, tasteless, uncivilized** Aunt Margie says that she will not tolerate *crude* behavior at her dinner table.

cruel *adjective* ✦ **brutal, heartless, mean, ruthless, unkind** Dianne firmly believes that people should never be *cruel* to animals.

Antonyms
cruel *adjective*
compassionate, forgiving, gentle, kind, soft, softhearted, tender

cruise *verb* ✦ **navigate, sail, travel, voyage** ✧ **roam, wander** We *cruised* out to Catalina Island in our neighbor's sailboat. —*noun* ✦ **boat trip, sail, voyage** ✧ **jaunt** Mom and Dad went on a *cruise* for their anniversary.

crumble *verb* ✦ **break, crunch, crush, mash** ✧ **grind** I like to *crumble* my crackers before putting them in my soup.

crumple *verb* **1.** ✦ **crease, crinkle, rumple, wrinkle** Lucas *crumpled* his clothes when he packed his suitcase carelessly. **2.** ✦ **buckle, col-**

lapse, fall, topple, tumble Aunt Hortense *crumpled* to the floor when she heard that she had inherited Uncle Delwin's pet hippopotamus.

crush *verb* **1.** ✦ **compress, mash, press, squash, squeeze** ✧ **trample** I always *crush* my aluminum cans before recycling them. **2.** ✦ **extinguish, quench, subdue, suppress** ✧ **defeat, destroy, overwhelm, vanquish** The dictator tried to *crush* all opposition.

cry *verb* **1.** ✦ **shed tears, sob, weep** ✧ **wail** If weddings are happy occasions, why do so many people *cry* at them? **2.** ✦ **bellow, call, shout, yell** ✧ **bawl, scream** Sara *cried* out a warning when she saw the car come around the corner too fast. —*noun* ✦ **call, scream, shout, yell** The woman gave a *cry* of delight when she saw her long lost brother.

cuddle *verb* ✦ **nestle, snuggle** ✧ **embrace, hug, pet** My baby sister likes to *cuddle* with her teddy bear.

culprit *noun* ✦ **guilty party, offender** ✧ **convict, criminal, lawbreaker, outlaw** Someone ate my ice cream, and I won't rest until I find the *culprit*!

cultivate *verb* **1.** ✦ **grow, raise** ✧ **farm, plant, till** The French are famous for *cultivating* fine grapes. ▶ **2.** ✦ **foster, nourish** ✧ **develop, improve, promote** Reading can help you to *cultivate* your mind.

culture *noun* ✦ **civilization, customs, society** ✧ **cultivation, refinement** We are studying the *culture* of ancient Greece.

cunning *adjective* ✦ **clever, crafty, shrewd, sly, tricky** The *cunning* spy was able to avoid being captured.

cure *noun* ✦ **remedy** ✧ **medicine, therapy, treatment** Medical researchers have yet to find a *cure* for the common cold. —*verb* ✦ **heal, remedy** ✧ **help, improve, relieve** These aspirin should *cure* your headache.

curious *adjective* **1.** ✦ **inquisitive, interested (in)** ✧ **inquiring** The entire class was *curious* about our new teacher. **2.** ✦ **peculiar, odd, remarkable, strange, unusual, weird** The pack rat has the *curious* habit of stealing a shiny object and leaving a stone or twig in its place.

currency *noun* ✦ **cash, legal tender, money** When we traveled to Mexico, we had to exchange our U.S. dollars for Mexican *currency*.

current *adjective* ✦ **contemporary, latest, new, up-to-date** ✧ **modern, present** Kimberly went to a bookstore to get the *current* issue of her favorite magazine. —*noun* ✦ **flow** ✧ **course, stream, tide** Many birds use air *currents* to glide across the sky.

curse *noun* **1.** ✦ **hex, oath, spell** ✧ **jinx** The witch's *curse* changed the handsome prince into a frog. **2.** ✦ **affliction, evil, ill, woe** Tad claims that pollution and overcrowding are two *curses* of modern civilization. —*verb* **1.** ✦ **afflict, plague, torment, torture, trouble** Poor Uncle Bertrand seems to be *cursed* with an incredible run of bad luck. **2.** ✦ **condemn, denounce** ✧ **swear** The farmer *cursed* the tornado that had destroyed his barn and ruined his crops.

curve *noun* ✦ **arc, bend, crook, turn, twist** There are a lot of dangerous *curves* in the road ahead. —*verb* ✦ **bend, swerve, turn, twist, wind** The trail *curves* around the base of that hill.

cushion *noun* ✧ **mat, pad, pillow** Our couch needs new *cushions*. —*verb* ✦ **dampen, deaden, lessen, soften, suppress** Our thick carpet *cushioned* my fall from the chair.

custody *noun* ✦ **care, charge, keeping, guardianship, supervision** My grandparents had

✦ **best choices**
✧ **other choices**

temporary *custody* of me while my parents were away on business.

custom   *noun*   ✦ **practice, rule, tradition** ✧ **habit, routine** Many Jewish Americans observe the *custom* of not eating or drinking on the day of Yom Kippur.

customary   *adjective*   ✦ **common, normal, routine, standard, traditional, usual** It is *customary* to leave a tip when dining in a restaurant.

customer   *noun*   ✦ **buyer, consumer, shopper** ✧ **client, patron** The department store was swamped with *customers* on the day of its big back-to-school sale.

cut   *verb*   **1.** ✦ **carve, slice** ✧ **chop, pierce, sever, slit** Please use this knife to *cut* the melon. **2.** ✦ **clip, crop, snip, trim** ✧ **mow, prune, shorten** Mom *cuts* my hair twice a month. ▶ **3.** ✦ **halt, interrupt, stop** ✧ **end, quit** Dad *cut* the engine and allowed the minivan to coast to a stop. **4.** ✦ **curtail, decrease, lower, reduce** ✧ **remove** The candidate promised to *cut* taxes. —*noun* **1.** ✧ **gash, slash, wound** The doctor said that my *cut* would not require stitches. **2.** ✦ **cut-**

back, decrease, reduction ✧ **decline, fall** Because of recent *cuts* in the state budget, no new highways will be built this year.

cute   *adjective*   ✦ **adorable, attractive, charming, pretty** ✧ **beautiful** My baby cousin looks *cute* in her Easter dress.

cycle   *noun*   ✦ **chain, course, period, phase, sequence, series** A caterpillar is just one stage in the life *cycle* of a butterfly or moth.

D

dab *verb* ✦ **daub, pat, slap, smear, swab, wipe** Colin *dabbed* some grease on his bicycle chain. —*noun* ✦ **bit, drop, pat, touch** ✧ **speck** Nikki put on a *dab* of perfume.

dabble *verb* ✦ **putter, tinker** ✧ **play, toy** Darryl likes to *dabble* with his chemistry set.

dainty *adjective* **1.** ✦ **delicate, exquisite, fine** ✧ **elegant, pretty** Those ballet slippers look *dainty*, but in fact they are very sturdy and strong. ▶ **2.** ✦ **choosy, finicky, fussy, particular** ✧ **discriminating** My cousin is such a *dainty* eater that we never know what to fix for her.

damage *noun* ✦ **destruction, harm, hurt, injury** ✧ **loss** A hailstorm did serious *damage* to the lilies in our garden. —*verb* ✦ **harm, hurt, impair, injure** ✧ **ravage, wreck** The boat was *damaged* slightly in the storm.

damp *adjective* ✦ **moist, wet** ✧ **clammy, dripping, soaked, soggy** After soccer practice, Byron's shirt was *damp* with perspiration.

dance *verb* ✦ **cavort, frolic, gambol, prance, skip** ✧ **jiggle, shake, sway** My dog *dances* with joy whenever I ask him if he wants to go for a walk. —*noun* ✧ **ball, formal, hop, party, prom** Are you going to the *dance* next Saturday?

danger *noun* ✦ **in jeopardy, in peril, at risk** ✧ **hazard, threat** The officer put her own life *in danger* when she rescued the driver from the burning car.

dangerous *adjective* ✦ **hazardous, perilous, risky, unsafe** ✧ **chancy** Riding a bicycle at night can be very *dangerous*.

dangle *verb* ✦ **hang, suspend, swing** ✧ **droop, sag** Melanie *dangled* a toy mouse in front of her cat.

dare *verb* **1.** ✦ **challenge, defy** ✧ **goad, provoke, taunt** Andrea *dared* her friend to ring the doorbell on the haunted house. **2.** ✦ **venture** ✧ **attempt, brave, face, risk** Only when I was done with my chores did I *dare* to ask Mom for a raise in my allowance. —*noun* ✦ **challenge** ✧ **bet, provocation, taunt** Edward accepted his sister's *dare* to jump into the swimming pool with his clothes on.

daring *adjective* ✦ **bold, brave, courageous, fearless, gallant** The band of warriors made a *daring* attack against their enemy. —*noun* ✦ **boldness, bravery, courage, nerve, valor** The spy was told that her mission would require great skill and *daring*.

Antonyms
daring *adjective*
afraid, anxious, cowardly, fearful, nervous, scared, shy, timid
daring *noun*
anxiety, cowardice, fear, nervousness, shyness, timidity

dark *adjective* **1.** ✦ **dim, murky, unlit** ✧ **black, gloomy, inky, sunless** I could barely see my way along the *dark* hallway. **2.** ✧ **black, brown, dusky, tan** Some Arctic animals have *dark* coats in summer that turn white in the winter. —*noun* **1.** ✦ **darkness, dimness, murk** ✧ **blackness, gloom, gloominess** When the lights went out, Terrence groped around in the *dark* to find a flashlight. **2.** ✦ **dusk, evening, night, nightfall, nighttime** Dad said that I could play at Julie's as long as I was home by *dark*.

✦   **best choices**
✧   **other choices**

darling   *noun*   ✦ **beloved, dear, precious, sweetheart** ◇ **favorite, pet** Grandma always calls me her *darling*. —*adjective* **1.** ✦ **beloved, cherished, dear, dearest, loved, treasured** ◇ **favorite** This is Tinkerbell, my *darling* cat. **2.** ✦ **adorable, charming, cute, enchanting, sweet** Spencer bought his baby sister a *darling* little stuffed penguin.

dart   *verb*   ✦ **bolt, dash, hurry, race, run, scurry, zip** I caught a glimpse of a mouse as it *darted* under the sofa.

dash   *verb*   **1.** ✦ **bolt, race, run, rush, speed, sprint** Timothy *dashed* across the finish line to win the race. **2.** ✦ **fling, hurl, knock, slam, smash, throw** A large wave *dashed* our rowboat against the pier. —*noun* **1.** ✦ **bolt, run, rush, sprint** ◇ **beeline** The rabbit made a *dash* for safety when it saw a fox. **2.** ✦ **bit, pinch, touch, trace** ◇ **drop** The soup tasted bland, so I added a *dash* of pepper.

data   *noun*   ✦ **facts, figures, information, statistics** ◇ **evidence** The scientist collected a mass of *data* to prove her theory.

date   *noun*   **1.** ◇ **day, month, time, year** The *date* of the first manned spaceflight was April 12, 1961. **2.** ✦ **appointment, engagement** ◇ **meeting, rendezvous** Dad made a *date* to go golfing next Saturday. **3.** ✦ **companion, escort** ◇ **boyfriend, girlfriend** My older sister and her *date* went to a movie.

dawn   *noun*   **1.** ✦ **daybreak, first light, sunrise, sunup** ◇ **daylight, morning, twilight** Brittany has to get up before *dawn* to get to swimming practice on time. **2.** ✦ **arrival, beginning, birth, commencement, origin, start** The invention of the steam engine marked the *dawn* of the Industrial Age.

day   *noun*   **1.** ✦ **daytime** ◇ **daylight** Most owls sleep during the *day* and hunt for food at night. **2.** ✦ **age, epoch, era, period, time** ◇ **generation** In my great-grandfather's *day*, people did not have televisions.

daze   *verb*   ✦ **bewilder, confuse, stun, stupefy** ◇ **numb, shock** A blow on the head momentarily *dazed* the soccer player. —*noun* ✦ **haze, muddle, stupor, trance** ◇ **astonishment, bewilderment, confusion** I was in a *daze* after staying up all night at the sleepover.

dead   *adjective*   **1.** ✦ **deceased, expired, lifeless, perished** ◇ **departed** I found a *dead* bug in the swimming pool. **2.** ✦ **exhausted, inactive, inoperative, worn out** ◇ **useless** My flashlight won't work because the batteries are *dead*. **3.** ✦ **absolute, complete, entire, total, utter** There was *dead* silence in the classroom when Mr. Pennington announced a pop quiz. —*adverb* **1.** ✦ **absolutely, completely, entirely, thoroughly, totally** My neighbor is *dead* certain that she saw a ghost in her basement. **2.** ✦ **directly, right, straight** ◇ **exactly, precisely** The lookout gave a cry of warning when he saw another ship *dead* ahead.

deadly   *adjective*   ✦ **fatal, lethal, mortal** ◇ **destructive, harmful** In the fourteenth century, a *deadly* plague killed almost half of the people in Europe.

deal   *verb*   **1.** ✦ **concern, have to do with, treat** ◇ **consider, involve** Geology *deals with* the history of the earth. **2.** ✦ **buy and sell, sell, trade in** ◇ **market, traffic** My dad's store *deals in* both new and used books. **3.** ✦ **allot, distribute, give out, hand out** ◇ **administer, deliver** Mom *dealt out* the weekly chore assignments. **4.** ✦ **cope with, handle** I might need some help *dealing with* this problem. —*noun* ✦ **agreement, arrangement, bargain, contract** I made a *deal* with Seth to trade my comic books for his baseball cards.

death   *noun*   ✦ **dying, loss, passing** ◇ **departure, end, extinction** Tiffany was saddened by the *death* of her grandfather.

debate *noun* ✦ **discussion** ✧ **argument, disagreement, dispute** The candidates held a *debate* on television. —*verb* ✦ **discuss** ✧ **argue, dispute, quarrel** The city council *debated* for several weeks before finally voting the new tax into law.

debt *noun* ✦ **liability, obligation** ✧ **bill, claim, dues** My sister loaned me five dollars, and I plan to pay off my *debt* by next week.

decay *noun* 1. ✦ **decomposition, rot** ✧ **corrosion, spoilage** The main cause of tooth *decay* is bacteria. 2. ✦ **collapse, dilapidation, ruin** ✧ **decline** The old barn was in a state of *decay*. —*verb* ✦ **break down, decompose, rot** ✧ **corrode, disintegrate, spoil** The fallen leaves and twigs *decayed* into soil.

deceive *verb* ✦ **fool, mislead, trick** ✧ **betray, cheat** An opossum sometimes *deceives* its enemies by pretending to be dead.

decent *adjective* 1. ✦ **appropriate, fit, proper, seemly, suitable** ✧ **respectable, virtuous**

The *decent* thing to do is to apologize to your friend for missing her party. 2. ✦ **considerate, generous, kind, nice, thoughtful** It was *decent* of Janine to offer to give you help with your homework. 3. ✦ **adequate, fair, passable, reasonable, satisfactory** ✧ **mediocre, ordinary** Grandpa can make *decent* cookies, but Grandma bakes a better pie. ▲

decide *verb* 1. ✦ **conclude, determine** ✧ **choose, resolve, select** I *decided* that one ride on the giant roller coaster was enough for me. 2. ✦ **judge, rule, settle** ✧ **decree** The jury *decided* in favor of the defendant.

decision *noun* ✦ **choice, conclusion, judgment, selection** ✧ **resolution, ruling, verdict** The judges of the poetry contest were ready to announce their *decision*.

decisive *adjective* 1. ✦ **conclusive, deciding, definite** ✧ **significant** The winning candidate defeated his opponent by a *decisive* margin. 2. ✦ **determined, firm, resolute** ✧ **positive** The *decisive* woman quickly picked out the movie she wanted to rent.

declare *verb* 1. ✦ **affirm, assert, claim, say, state** ✧ **swear** Sandra *declared* that she was telling the truth. 2. ✦ **announce, decree, proclaim, pronounce** The governor *declared* a state of emergency after the earthquake.

decline *verb* 1. ✦ **refuse, reject, turn down** ✧ **deny, spurn** Mary *declined* my invitation to go to a movie. 2. ✦ **decrease, diminish, lessen, subside, wane** ✧ **sink, weaken** My interest in skateboarding *declined* after I crashed into a wall. —*noun* ✦ **decrease, downturn, drop, reduction, slump** ✧ **wane** There has been a *decline* in the demand for typewriters since the introduction of the computer.

decorate *verb* ✦ **adorn, ornament, trim** ✧ **beautify, fix up** We *decorated* our Christmas tree with red and white lights.

decrease *verb* ✦ **diminish, lessen, lower, reduce** ✧ **drop, dwindle** Dad's doctor advised him to *decrease* the amount of fat in his diet. —*noun* ✦ **cutback, decline, drop, reduction, slump** ✧ **loss** During the long drought, there was a definite *decrease* in umbrella sales.

decree *noun* ✦ **command, declaration, law, mandate, order, proclamation** ✧ **decision** The dictator issued a *decree* that made his birthday a national holiday. —*verb* ✦ **command, mandate, order, proclaim, rule** ✧ **announce, decide** The queen *decreed* that all the books in the kingdom should be burned.

✦ **best choices**
✧ **other choices**

dedicate   *verb*   ✦ **commit, devote, give** ✧ **apply, pledge, surrender**   Mother Teresa *dedicated* her life to helping poor and needy people.

deduct   *verb*   ✦ **remove, subtract, take, take off** ✧ **withdraw**   My brother said that he would *deduct* two dollars from what I owed him if I'd clean his bike.

deed   *noun*   ✦ **act, action, exploit, feat** ✧ **accomplishment**   This movie is based on Sir Lancelot's heroic *deeds*.

deep   *adjective*   **1.** ✧ **bottomless, cavernous, low, yawning**   The pirates buried their treasure in a *deep* hole.   **2.** ✦ **great, intense, powerful, profound, strong**   Chelsea has a *deep* respect for people who volunteer their time to help others. **3.** ✦ **absorbed, engrossed, lost** ✧ **occupied, preoccupied**   Whenever I'm *deep* in thought, I don't hear what's going on around me.   **4.** ✦ **difficult, obscure, profound** ✧ **mysterious, subtle** Alec likes to discuss *deep* subjects, such as philosophy and religion.

defeat   *verb*   ✦ **beat, conquer, overcome, vanquish** ✧ **crush, rout**   The United States achieved independence by *defeating* England in the Revolutionary War.   —*noun* ✦ **beating, failure, loss** ✧ **downfall, rout, upset**   My favorite football team has suffered three *defeats* in the first five games.

Antonyms
defeat *noun*
conquest, success, supremacy, triumph, victory

defect   *noun*   ✦ **blemish, fault, flaw, imperfection** ✧ **weakness**   This diamond didn't cost very much because it has a *defect*.

defective   *adjective*   ✦ **faulty, flawed, imperfect** ✧ **broken, incomplete**   Our new TV was *defective*, so we returned it.

defend   *verb*   **1.** ✦ **guard, protect, safeguard** ✧ **preserve, secure**   The commander called for reinforcements to help *defend* the fort.   **2.** ✦ **maintain, support, sustain, uphold** ✧ **champion, endorse**   The scientist used facts and figures to *defend* his new theory.

defense   *noun*   ✦ **guard, protection, safeguard** ✧ **preservation, security**   The best *defense* against cavities is to brush your teeth after every meal.

defer   *verb*   ✦ **delay, postpone, put off, suspend** ✧ **wait**   I *deferred* making my decision about summer camp until I knew where my friends were going.

defiance   *noun*   ✦ **disobedience, rebellion, resistance** ✧ **opposition**   When my little sister refused to clean her room, she was sent to bed early as punishment for her *defiance*.

deficiency   *noun*   ✦ **lack, scarcity, shortage** ✧ **inadequacy, need**   If you drink a lot of milk, you are unlikely to have a calcium *deficiency*. ▶

define   *verb*   ✦ **characterize, describe, explain, interpret**   My dad *defines* happiness as a weekend fishing trip.

definite   *adjective*   ✦ **certain, clear, positive, sure, unqualified** ✧ **absolute, exact**   Instead of saying "maybe," I wish you would give me a *definite* "yes" or "no."

definition *noun* ✦ **meaning** ✧ **description, explanation, interpretation, sense** If you don't know what a word means, you can look up its *definition* in a dictionary.

deform *verb* ✦ **disfigure, distort** ✧ **contort, damage, twist** Is it true that you can *deform* your spine by slouching too much?

defy *verb* **1.** ✦ **challenge, dare** ✧ **brave, confront, face** Derek *defied* me to beat him at his new computer game. **2.** ✦ **disobey, oppose, resist** ✧ **disregard, ignore, withstand** My little brother *defied* our parents by refusing to turn off the television.

degrade *verb* ✦ **disgrace, dishonor, lower, shame** ✧ **cheapen** Nicole refused to *degrade* herself by cheating, even though she had a perfect opportunity.

degree *noun* **1.** ✦ **grade, level, measure, order** ✧ **class, phase, stage, step** Kelly's gymnastic routine has a high *degree* of difficulty. **2.** ✦ **amount, extent** ✧ **range, scope** There is a certain *degree* of truth in what he said, but it's not the whole story.

dejected *adjective* ✦ **depressed, gloomy, sad, unhappy** ✧ **discouraged** We all felt a little *dejected* when we learned that our favorite teacher was leaving.

delay *verb* **1.** ✦ **postpone, put off** ✧ **defer, interrupt, suspend** We had to *delay* the opening of our play by one week because several of the actors caught colds. **2.** ✦ **detain, hinder, hold up, impede, slow** ✧ **obstruct, retard** The bus was *delayed* by heavy traffic. —*noun* ✦ **holdup, pause, wait** ✧ **lag, postponement, stop** The pilot announced that there would be a half-hour *delay* before takeoff.

delegate *noun* ✦ **appointee, deputy, representative** ✧ **agent, ambassador** Our class elected Anthony to be our *delegate* to the student council. —*verb* ✦ **appoint, assign, designate,**

name ✧ **commission** Our coach *delegated* Jennifer to bring the refreshments for the next game.

deliberate *adjective* ✦ **intentional, willful** ✧ **careful, planned, thoughtful** The man pretended to be joking, but he was actually making a *deliberate* insult. —*verb* ✦ **confer, consider, debate, discuss** ✧ **reflect, study** The jury *deliberated* for several days before reaching a verdict.

delicate *adjective* **1.** ✦ **dainty, exquisite, fine** ✧ **elegant, nice** The child in the painting has *delicate* features. **2.** ✦ **demanding, difficult, sensitive, touchy, tricky** Repairing a watch is a *delicate* task. **3.** ✦ **breakable, fragile** ✧ **brittle, flimsy, frail, weak** Eggs break easily because their shells are *delicate.*

delicious *adjective* ✦ **appetizing, savory, tasty** ✧ **good** Those strawberries look *delicious.*

delight *noun* ✦ **gladness, happiness, joy, pleasure, rapture** ✧ **enjoyment** Francisco was filled with *delight* when he saw his new in-line skates. —*verb* ✦ **cheer, gladden, please, thrill** ✧ **enchant, gratify** Nothing *delights* me more than going shopping with my friends.

delightful *adjective* ✦ **charming, enjoyable, happy, pleasant, pleasing** Rachel and her friends had a *delightful* day at the beach.

deliver *verb* **1.** ✦ **bring, carry, convey, ship, transport** ✧ **provide, supply** Your order will be *delivered* to your door. ◄ **2.** ✦ **administer, deal, give** ✧ **hurl, launch, throw** The prize-winning boxer *delivered* a knockout punch to his opponent. **3.** ✦ **give, present** ✧ **communicate, say,**

✦   **best choices**
✧   **other choices**

speak The new President will *deliver* his inaugural address tomorrow. **4. ✦ free, liberate, release, rescue, save** The hostages never lost hope of being *delivered* from their captors.

demand *verb* **1. ✦ appeal for, insist on** ✧ **claim, order, request** The workers *demanded* a raise in pay. **2. ✦ call for, compel, need, require** ✧ **necessitate** This problem is so serious that it *demands* our immediate attention. —*noun* **1. ✦ appeal, call** ✧ **command, order, request** The players tried their best to meet the coach's *demand* for better teamwork. **2. ✦ interest (in), market, need** ✧ **requirement** There isn't much *demand* for records now that most people have either CD or cassette players.

demolish *verb* **✦ destroy, devastate, level ruin, wreck** ✧ **tear down** A tornado *demolished* the farmer's barn.

demon *noun* **✦ devil, evil spirit, fiend** ✧ **beast, monster** Justin dressed up as a *demon* for Halloween.

demonstrate *verb* **1. ✦ display, show** ✧ **describe, explain, illustrate, teach** Ms. Ramsey *demonstrated* the proper way to hold a camera. ▼ **2. ✦ march, protest, rally** ✧ **parade, picket** A group of students and teachers *demonstrated* against the building of a highway next to their school.

demonstration *noun* **1. ✦ display, presentation, show** ✧ **explanation, illustration, lesson** A salesperson gave us a *demonstration* of how the new camcorder worked. **2. ✦ march, protest, rally** ✧ **meeting, sit-in** We're holding a *demonstration* to protest against the shortening of our summer vacation.

den *noun* **✦ lair** ✧ **cave, nest, retreat, shelter** A wolf's *den* is usually an underground burrow.

denote *verb* **✦ designate, indicate, mean, symbolize** ✧ **point out, show** A skull and crossbones on a sign usually *denotes* danger.

denounce *verb* **✦ condemn, criticize, disapprove of** ✧ **assail, attack, curse** My parents strongly *denounce* the use of illegal drugs.

dense *adjective* **✦ compact, solid, thick, tight** ✧ **crowded, heavy, packed** The rabbit ran into a *dense* thicket just in time to escape from the hungry coyote.

Antonyms
dense *adjective*
meager, scanty, scattered, sparse, thin

deny *verb* **1. ✦ dispute** ✧ **contradict, disagree, protest** The suspect *denied* that he had committed the crime. **2. ✦ disallow, forbid, refuse, reject, veto** ✧ **withhold** My parents *denied* my request to stay out late.

depart *verb* **✦ go, leave, move out** ✧ **embark, exit** My bus *departs* at three o'clock.

department *noun* **✦ area, division, section** ✧ **branch, bureau, unit** Whenever we go shopping, my brother and I always head straight for the toy *department*.

departure *noun* **✦ going, leaving** ✧ **exit, start, withdrawal** Our *departure* will be delayed because the airport has been closed by fog.

depend *verb* **1. ✦ hang on, hinge on, rest on** Whether or not I go to the movie *depends on* how much homework I get done. **2.** ✦ **count on, rely on, trust** ✧ **believe in** Mom *depends on* me to feed the pets.

dependable *adjective* ✦ **faithful, reliable, responsible, trustworthy, trusty** A *dependable* friend is someone who will always be there in time of need.

depict *verb* ✦ **describe, picture, portray, show** ✧ **represent** This film *depicts* the life of George Washington.

deposit *verb* ✦ **leave, place, put, put down, set** ✧ **accumulate** The wind *deposited* a pile of leaves on our doorstep. —*noun* **1.** ✦ **assets, cash, money** ✧ **savings** The *deposits* in my bank account total 325 dollars. **2.** ✦ **down payment, installment** ✧ **pledge, security** Christine made a ten-dollar *deposit* toward the jacket she wanted. **3.** ✦ **lode, vein** ✧ **accumulation, layer, sediment** The miner was excited when he found a large *deposit* of silver.

depress *verb* **1.** ✦ **deject, discourage, dishearten, sadden, weary** Long spells of rainy weather always seem to *depress* me. **2.** ✦ **press, push** ✧ **flatten, lower, thrust** You *depress* the Escape key to take you back to the main menu.

depression *noun* **1.** ✦ **dejection, despair, gloom, melancholy, sadness** The *depression* I felt when we moved from our old neighborhood ended once I made new friends. **2.** ✦ **cavity, hole, hollow, indentation** ✧ **dent** When Travis turned the rock over, he found that the *depression* underneath was full of ants. **3.** ✦ **economic decline** ✧ **crash, recession, slump** Many people lose their jobs during a *depression*.

deprive *verb* ✦ **rob, strip** ✧ **deny, refuse, withhold** Don't let your worries *deprive* you of sleep.

derive *verb* ✦ **draw, gain, get, obtain, receive, take** Haley *derives* a lot of satisfaction from helping other people.

descend *verb* **1.** ✦ **come down, drop, fall, sink** ✧ **dip** The parachute *descended* slowly to the ground. **2.** ✦ **come** ✧ **derive, issue, originate, spring** My friend Sawa *is descended* from Miwok Indian ancestors.

Word Groups

A **descendant** is a person who is related to a particular ancestor. **Descendant** is a very specific term with no true synonyms. Here are some related words to investigate in a dictionary:

child, grandchild, heir, kin, offspring, progeny

---

descent *noun* **1.** ✦ **decline** ✧ **dip, dive, drop, fall** We stood on our balcony and watched the sun's *descent* toward the horizon. **2.** ✦ **ancestry, heritage, lineage, origin, parentage** Afshin is of Iranian *descent*.

describe *verb* ✦ **recount, relate, tell about** ✧ **depict, recite, report** Lori *described* her trip to Hawaii in vivid detail.

description *noun* ✦ **depiction, portrayal** ✧ **account, report, statement** I recognized the wombat at the zoo from its *description* in my new encyclopedia.

desert *verb* ✦ **abandon, forsake, give up, leave, quit** The birds *deserted* their nest when they flew south for the winter.

deserve *verb* ✦ **earn, merit, rate, warrant** ✧ **gain, win** Patrick *deserved* a rest after cleaning out the garage.

design *noun* ✦ **diagram, pattern, plan** ✧ **blueprint, drawing, sketch** This *design* shows how to build your own kite at home. —*verb* ✦ **conceive, devise, plan** ✧ **create, fashion, invent** Joshua *designed* and built a model space station for his science project.

✦   **best choices**
✧   **other choices**

designate *verb* **1.** ✦ **indicate, mark, point out, show, specify** Brenda tied balloons to a telephone pole to *designate* where her party was being held. **2.** ✦ **appoint, choose, name, select** ✧ **elect, nominate** Mr. Lopez *designated* Kay to represent our class at the school assembly.

desirable *adjective* ✦ **agreeable, attractive, good, nice, pleasing** ✧ **beneficial, worthwhile** Many people believe that small towns are *desirable* places to live.

desire *noun* ✦ **longing, wish, yearning** ✧ **ambition, craving, goal** My *desire* is for the world to live in peace. —*verb* ✦ **covet, crave, long for, want, wish for** Sandy *desires* a parakeet as a pet. ◄

despair *noun* ✦ **desperation, discouragement, dismay, hopelessness** We looked at each other in *despair* as we realized that we were stranded on the island. —*verb* ✦ **give up hope, lose hope** ✧ **resign, surrender** Ashley *despaired* of ever finding the lost library book.

desperate *adjective* **1.** ✦ **frantic, frenzied, mad, urgent** ✧ **drastic** I got up late and made a *desperate* attempt to get to school on time. **2.** ✦ **bold, daring, rash, reckless, risky** ✧ **hopeless** The convict hatched a *desperate* scheme to escape from prison.

despise *verb* ✦ **detest, dislike, hate, loathe** ✧ **scorn** I *despise* people who mistreat their pets.

destination *noun* ✦ **stop, stopping place** ✧ **end, goal** This plane will make two stops before it reaches its final *destination*.

destroy *verb* ✦ **annihilate, demolish, devastate, level, ruin, wreck** In this movie, a giant octopus *destroys* most of downtown Tokyo.

destruction *noun* ✦ **devastation, havoc, ruin, wreckage** ✧ **loss** The hurricane caused widespread *destruction*.

detach *verb* ✦ **remove, take off, unfasten** ✧ **disassemble, disconnect, separate** If you want to get your bike into this trunk, you'll have to *detach* its wheels.

detail *noun* ✦ **element, feature, item, part, particular** David's model of a steam locomotive is authentic in every *detail*. —*verb* ✦ **describe, itemize, recite, recount, specify** Molly's long letter *detailed* everything that she had been doing at summer camp.

detain *verb* **1.** ✦ **delay, hinder, hold up, impede, slow** ✧ **obstruct, retard** We were *detained* by heavy traffic. **2.** ✦ **confine, hold, keep, restrain** ✧ **arrest** Police officers *detained* the suspect for questioning.

detect *verb* ✦ **discover, find, notice, spot** ✧ **expose, reveal** An odor is added to natural gas to help people *detect* leaks.

deter *verb* ✦ **discourage, hinder, prevent, stop** ✧ **restrain** Car alarms are supposed to *deter* thieves.

determine *verb* **1.** ✦ **decide, resolve, settle** ✧ **affect, choose, influence** This field goal attempt will *determine* which team wins the game. **2.** ✦ **detect, discover, find out, learn** ✧ **conclude** Investigators are trying to *determine* what caused the fire.

determined *adjective* ✦ **intent, persevering, purposeful, steadfast** ✧ **firm, tough** Only the most *determined* players will be able to make it to the final competition.

detest *verb* ✦ **despise, dislike, hate, loathe** Amanda says that she *detests* washing dishes.

detour *noun* ✦ **alternate route** ✧ **bypass, byway** We had to take a *detour* because the bridge was closed.

devastate *verb* ✦ **demolish, destroy, ravage, ruin, wreck** The city of Pompeii was *devastated* by the eruption of Mount Vesuvius in 79 A.D.

develop *verb* **1.** ✦ **build up, expand, improve** ◇ **grow, increase, mature** Reading is one of the best ways to *develop* your mind. **2.** ✦ **acquire, form** ◇ **establish, gain, generate** I *developed* an interest in swimming while at camp last summer.

development *noun* ✦ **creation, production** ◇ **advancement, evolution, growth, progress** Scientists are always working on the *development* of newer and more effective medicines.

device *noun* **1.** ✦ **gadget, tool** ◇ **apparatus, appliance, instrument** Sometimes I think that the safety pin is the most practical *device* ever invented. **2.** ✦ **gimmick, maneuver, trick** ◇ **plan, plot, scheme** A tantrum is often just a *device* for getting attention.

devise *verb* ✦ **concoct, contrive, create, fashion, invent, make** ◇ **plan** Anthony is trying to *devise* a robot that will clean his room and do his homework.

devote *verb* ✦ **apply, commit, dedicate, give** ◇ **direct, focus** Dian Fossey *devoted* her life to studying and protecting the endangered mountain gorilla.

devoted *adjective* ✦ **committed, dedicated, faithful, loyal, true** The two girls are *devoted* friends.

devotion *noun* ✦ **affection, fondness, love, loyalty** ◇ **attachment, liking** The bride and groom exchanged rings as a token of their *devotion*.

devour *verb* ✦ **consume, eat, eat up, gobble** ◇ **swallow** John was so hungry that he *devoured* an entire pizza.

devout *adjective* ✦ **pious, religious, reverent** ◇ **earnest, sincere** *Devout* Muslims pray five times every day.

diagram *noun* ✦ **chart, design, drawing** ◇ **model, outline, pattern, plan, scheme** This *diagram* shows the parts of the human digestive system. —*verb* ✦ **draw, illustrate, picture, portray, sketch** ◇ **map, show** The basketball coach used a chalkboard to *diagram* how the zone defense is supposed to work.

dialogue *noun* ◇ **conversation, discussion, script, speech, talk** I loved the movie's *dialogue* because the actors sounded exactly like my friends and me.

Word Groups

A *diary* is a daily written account of one's thoughts and experiences. *Diary* is a very specific word with no true synonyms. Here are some related words to investigate in a dictionary:

chronicle, daybook, journal, log, notebook, record, yearbook

dictate *verb* **1.** ✦ **read aloud** ◇ **pronounce, say, speak, utter** The lawyer *dictated* a letter to her secretary. **2.** ✦ **command, decree, direct, order, prescribe** The tyrant had so much power that he was able to *dictate* how the government should be run.

die *verb* **1.** ✦ **expire, perish** ◇ **depart, pass away, succumb** My African violet *died* because I forgot to water it. **2.** ✦ **diminish, ebb, fade, subside, wane** The sound of the train's whistle gradually *died away* in the distance.

differ *verb* **1.** ✦ **vary** ◇ **alter, change, contrast** These two cars *differ* in price because one has air conditioning and the other doesn't. **2.** ✦ **clash, conflict, disagree, vary** ◇ **contradict, oppose** We all wanted to dine out, but our opinions *differed* when we tried to choose a restaurant.

difference *noun* **1.** ✦ **contrast, dissimilarity, distinction, variation** A big *difference* between

✦ **best choices**
◇ **other choices**

whales and sharks is that whales are mammals and sharks are fish. **2.** ✧ **balance, remainder** The *difference* between 11 and 7 is 4. **3.** ✦ **disagreement, dissension** ✧ **dispute, quarrel** Dylan and Curtis settled their *differences* and became friends again.

different *adjective* **1.** ✦ **contrasting, dissimilar, unlike, varied** My mother and I have *different* opinions about when I should go to bed. **2.** ✦ **distinct, separate** ✧ **diverse, individual, unique** Mom and Dad are both teachers, but they work at *different* schools.

difficult *adjective* **1.** ✦ **demanding, hard, rough, tough** ✧ **strenuous, tedious** The scientist said that sending astronauts to Mars would be *difficult*, but not impossible. **2.** ✦ **obstinate, perverse, stubborn** ✧ **unmanageable, unruly** When Jason refused to play by our rules, we told him to quit being so *difficult*.

difficulty *noun* ✦ **hardship, obstacle, problem, trouble** ✧ **adversity** The Pilgrims who founded Plymouth Colony overcame many *difficulties*, including food shortages and harsh weather.

dig *verb* **1.** ✦ **excavate** ✧ **burrow, scoop, shovel** Workers *dug* a deep trench for the new pipeline. ▼ **2.** ✦ **delve, probe, search** ✧ **investigate, research** Robert *dug* through an encyclopedia to find the facts that he needed for his science report.

digest *verb* ✦ **absorb, assimilate, take up** ✧ **consume, eat** The Venus flytrap is an unusual plant that can trap and *digest* insects.

dignified *adjective* ✦ **formal, proper, solemn, stately** ✧ **elegant, noble** The queen spoke with an authoritative and *dignified* tone.

dignity *noun* ✦ **formality, seriousness, solemnity** ✧ **honor, prestige** Judges typically preside over their courts with *dignity*.

diligent *adjective* ✦ **industrious, persevering** ✧ **careful, earnest, steadfast** The best way to improve your grades is to become more *diligent* in your studying.

dilute *verb* ✦ **cut, thin, water down** ✧ **mix, weaken** A can of condensed soup should be *diluted* with water before cooking.

dim *adjective* **1.** ✦ **low, faint, weak** ✧ **dark, murky, soft** Brendan strained his eyes when he tried to read in the *dim* light. **2.** ✦ **blurry, faint, hazy, indistinct, unclear, vague** On misty days, Seattle residents can see only the *dim* outline of nearby Mt. Rainier. —*verb* ✦ **darken, lower, reduce** ✧ **blur, dull** In a movie theater, the lights are *dimmed* just before the film starts.

dimension *noun* ✦ **measurements, proportions, size** ✧ **expanse, extent** We need to know the window's *dimensions* so that we can buy curtains of the proper size.

diminish *verb* ✦ **abate, decrease, ebb, lessen, wane** ✧ **lower, reduce** Dustin's enthusiasm for playing football *diminished* after he had been tackled a few times.

din *noun* ✦ **clamor, noise, racket, tumult, uproar** The barking dogs made so much *din* that I couldn't sleep.

dine *verb* ✦ **eat, have supper** ✧ **consume, feast, feed, sup** Mom said that she was tired of cooking, and she suggested that we *dine* at a restaurant tonight.

dingy *adjective* ✦ **dirty, grimy, soiled** ✧ **dark, drab, gloomy** I couldn't see out of the *dingy* window on the subway.

dip *verb* **1.** ✦ **dunk, immerse, submerge** ✧ **douse, duck** Lindsey *dipped* her hand in the bath water to see if it was the right temperature.

2. ✦ **descend, drop, sink** ✧ **fall, lower, settle, slump** The hawk *dipped* out of sight behind the ridge of the mountain. —*noun* **1.** ✦ **plunge, swim** ✧ **immersion, soak** José suggested that we all come over and take a *dip* in his pool to cool off. ▲ **2.** ✦ **depression** ✧ **drop, fall, hollow, slope** The driver slowed down when he saw a big *dip* in the road.

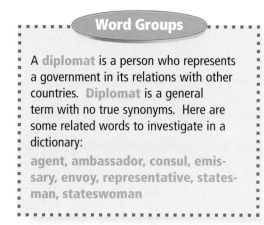

> ### Word Groups
>
> A **diplomat** is a person who represents a government in its relations with other countries. **Diplomat** is a general term with no true synonyms. Here are some related words to investigate in a dictionary:
>
> **agent, ambassador, consul, emissary, envoy, representative, statesman, stateswoman**

direct *verb* **1.** ✦ **guide, lead, point, show, steer** ✧ **aim** Could you *direct* me to the bathroom? **2.** ✦ **administer, control, govern, manage, run, supervise** A store's manager *directs* the activities of the other employees. **3.** ✦ **command, instruct, order, tell** ✧ **bid** The police officer *directed* everyone to stand back. —*adjective* ✦ **short, straight** ✧ **through, unswerving** The *direct* route to the coast is about an hour shorter than the scenic road.

direction *noun* **1.** ✦ **control, guidance, leadership, management, supervision** Our school paper is under the *direction* of the new English teacher. **2.** ✦ **guideline, instruction** ✧ **command, order, rule** Mr. Weiss told his class to follow the *directions* printed at the top of the page. **3.** ✦ **course** ✧ **path, route, track, way** The wind blew in a northerly *direction*.

directly *adverb* **1.** ✦ **right, straight** ✧ **exactly, precisely** Brittany's house is *directly* across the street from mine. **2.** ✦ **immediately, promptly, right** ✧ **shortly, soon** I have a doctor's appointment *directly* after school.

dirt *noun* **1.** ✦ **earth, loam, soil** ✧ **ground** Reggie raises earthworms in a bucket of *dirt*. **2.** ✦ **filth, grime** ✧ **dust, mire, mud, soil** I got a lot of *dirt* on my pants when I played in the garage.

dirty *adjective* **1.** ✦ **filthy, grimy, soiled, unclean** ✧ **messy** My hands were *dirty* after I worked in the garden. **2.** ✦ **angry, bitter, hostile, resentful** ✧ **low, mean** Scott gave me a *dirty* look when he lost the game.

disadvantage *noun* ✦ **drawback, handicap, liability, problem, weakness** Flying is the fastest way to travel, but it has the *disadvantage* of being expensive.

disagree *verb* ✦ **differ, dissent** ✧ **argue, oppose, quarrel** Juan and I always seem to *disagree* over which movie we want to see.

disagreeable *adjective* **1.** ✦ **bad, distasteful, offensive, repulsive, unpleasant** Rotten eggs have a *disagreeable* odor. **2.** ✦ **cross, grouchy, grumpy, irritable, quarrelsome, unfriendly** Kirsten is in a *disagreeable* mood because she didn't get much sleep last night.

disagreement *noun* **1.** ✦ **conflict, opposition** ✧ **difference, dissension** These two books

✦ **best choices**
✧ **other choices**

are in *disagreement* over who really discovered America. **2.** ✦ **argument, dispute, fight, quarrel** ✧ **feud** My parents had a big *disagreement*, but they finally worked it out.

disappear *verb* **1.** ✦ **vanish** ✧ **dissolve, evaporate, fade away** The wizard *disappeared* in a puff of smoke. **2.** ✦ **become extinct, die out, perish** ✧ **end, expire, stop** The wooly mammoth *disappeared* about 10,000 years ago.

disappoint *verb* ✦ **let down** ✧ **displease, fail, frustrate, sadden** You will *disappoint* your brother if you don't take him to the park.

disappointment *noun* **1.** ✧ **displeasure, dissatisfaction, frustration, regret** Jesse tried to hide his *disappointment* when his dad postponed their fishing trip. **2.** ✦ **letdown** ✧ **disaster, failure** The sequel to my favorite movie turned out to be a real *disappointment*.

disapprove *verb* ✦ **condemn, denounce, dislike, frown on, object to** ✧ **criticize** Michelle *disapproves of* littering.

disaster *noun* ✦ **calamity, catastrophe, tragedy** ✧ **accident, misfortune, trouble** One of the biggest natural *disasters* ever was the eruption of the Krakatoa volcano in 1883.

disbelief *noun* ✦ **doubt, skepticism, unbelief** ✧ **distrust, rejection** The sailors' tales of giant sea serpents were met with *disbelief*.

discard *verb* ✦ **dispose of, dump, eliminate, throw out** ✧ **abandon** We *discarded* a lot of old junk from the basement.

discharge *verb* **1.** ✦ **let out, unload** ✧ **disembark, dump, empty** The flight from Houston will *discharge* its passengers at gate 17. **2.** ✦ **dismiss, release** ✧ **excuse, excel, remove** The doctor *discharged* her patient from the hospital. **3.** ✦ **eject, emit, expel, gush, pour** ✧ **drain, leak** The broken fire hydrant *discharged* water all over the street. —*noun* ✦ **dismissal, release** ✧ **expulsion, liberation, termination** The soldier received an honorable *discharge*.

disciple *noun* ✦ **believer, devotee, follower** ✧ **pupil, student, supporter** The religious leader had many *disciples*.

discipline *noun* **1.** ✦ **self-control** ✧ **exercise, practice, preparation, training** It takes a lot of *discipline* to write a book. **2.** ✦ **correction, punishment** ✧ **control, penalty** Mother's typical form of *discipline* is to send me to my room. —*verb* **1.** ✦ **drill, instruct, teach, train** ✧ **coach, educate** The captain *disciplined* his crew to be expert sailors. **2.** ✦ **correct, punish** ✧ **penalize** Mary is not allowed to *discipline* her little brother.

disclose *verb* ✦ **expose, reveal, tell** ✧ **relate, report, show** The reporter refused to *disclose* the source of her information.

discomfort *noun* ✦ **pain** ✧ **annoyance, distress, irritation, misery, suffering** Headaches can cause a lot of *discomfort*.

discontinue *verb* ✦ **cease, end, halt, stop, suspend, terminate** I *discontinued* my subscription to the magazine.

discord *noun* ✦ **conflict, disagreement, disharmony, dispute, dissent** The meeting ended in *discord* with everybody shouting at each other.

discount *noun* ✦ **deduction, reduction** ✧ **cut, decrease, markdown** Senior citizens receive a *discount* at most movie theaters.

discourage *verb* **1.** ✦ **daunt, dishearten, intimidate** ✧ **bother, depress** The minor fall did not *discourage* the climber, and she continued on to the top of the cliff. **2.** ✦ **deter, dissuade** ✧ **prevent, restrain, warn** The city started an ad campaign to *discourage* young people from smoking.

discover *verb* ✦ **find, locate** ✧ **detect, identify, notice, recognize** The Spanish explorer Ponce de León hoped to *discover* the legendary Fountain of Youth.

discovery *noun* ✦ **detection, identification** ◇ **finding, location** Madame Curie won a Nobel Prize in 1911 for her *discovery* of radium.

discuss *verb* ✦ **confer about, talk about** ◇ **debate, deliberate** Mom met with my teacher to *discuss* my progress at school.

discussion *noun* ✦ **dialogue, talk** ◇ **conference, conversation, debate** Our class had a *discussion* about the movie we had seen in social studies. ▼

disease *noun* ✦ **affliction, ailment, disorder, illness, malady, sickness** Modern medicine can prevent many *diseases*.

disgrace *noun* **1.** ✦ **dishonor, humiliation, shame** The politician had to resign in *disgrace* when the public learned that she had accepted a bribe. **2.** ✦ **embarrassment, scandal** ◇ **blemish, stain** Laura thinks it's a *disgrace* that there are so many homeless people in America. —*verb* ✦ **dishonor, humiliate, shame** ◇ **embarrass, tarnish** The warrior's cowardice *disgraced* his entire tribe.

disguise *noun* ✦ **costume, getup, outfit** ◇ **camouflage, cover, mask** I put the finishing touches on my alien *disguise*. —*verb* ✦ **costume, dress** ◇ **camouflage, conceal, cover, mask** Jeremy went to the Halloween party *disguised* as a pirate.

disgust *noun* ✦ **nausea, queasiness, revulsion** ◇ **annoyance, aversion, distaste** I was filled with *disgust* when my little brother put a worm in my cereal. —*verb* ✦ **appall, nauseate, repel, revolt, sicken** My sister says that my messy room *disgusts* her.

dishonest *adjective* ✦ **deceitful, untruthful** ◇ **corrupt, crooked, fraudulent** A person who tells lies is *dishonest*.

disintegrate *verb* ✦ **break up, crumble, fragment, shatter, splinter** The spaceship *disintegrated* when it collided with the asteroid.

dislike *verb* ✦ **despise, detest, hate, loathe** ◇ **scorn** I really *dislike* people who are rude. —*noun* ✦ **aversion (to), distaste (for), revulsion (toward)** ◇ **hatred** I have a great *dislike* of soggy corn flakes.

dismal *adjective* ✦ **bleak, cheerless, dark, depressing, dreary, gloomy** Rain clouds made the sky look *dismal*.

dismay *verb* ✦ **alarm, daunt, distress** ◇ **appall, frighten, scare** The picnickers were *dismayed* to see the approaching storm. —*noun* ✦ **alarm, anxiety, apprehension, distress** ◇ **dread, fright** I was filled with *dismay* when I realized I'd locked myself out of the apartment.

dismiss *verb* **1.** ✦ **excuse, free, release** Paul was *dismissed* from gym class for two weeks because he had a broken toe. **2.** ✦ **discharge, drop, lay off, terminate** ◇ **expel, fire, oust** Because sales were slow, the company had to *dismiss* several employees.

disobedient *adjective* ✦ **defiant, rebellious** ◇ **naughty, stubborn, unruly** My brother was being *disobedient* when he refused to clean his room.

disobey *verb* ✦ **break, disregard, ignore, violate** ◇ **defy, rebel, resist** The driver was fined for *disobeying* the speed limit.

✦ **best choices**
◇ **other choices**

disorder *noun* **1.** ✦ **chaos, commotion, confusion, turmoil** ◇ **jumble** The soldiers retreated in *disorder* when the enemy attacked. **2.** ✦ **affliction, ailment, disease, illness, malady, sickness** Asthma is a breathing *disorder*.

disorderly *adjective* **1.** ✦ **cluttered, disorganized, messy, untidy** Our hall closet is a *disorderly* jumble of hats, coats, boots, and umbrellas. **2.** ✦ **disruptive, improper, unruly** ◇ **obstinate, unlawful** Kevin had to stay after school because of his *disorderly* behavior in class.

dispel *verb* ✦ **banish, drive away, put an end to** ◇ **disperse, erase, scatter** The flight attendant helped to *dispel* my fear of flying.

dispense *verb* ✦ **allot, distribute, give out, hand out** ◇ **administer, award** Every Monday, Dad *dispenses* our weekly allowances.

disperse *verb* ✦ **break up, dissipate, scatter** ◇ **disband, dispel** High winds caused the clouds to *disperse*.

display *verb* ✦ **demonstrate, exhibit, reveal, show** The firefighter *displayed* great courage by saving the man from the burning building. —*noun* ✦ **show, spectacle** ◇ **demonstration, exhibit, exhibition, scene** Everyone enjoyed the New Year's fireworks *display*.

dispose *verb* ✦ **discard, dispense with, throw away** ◇ **dump, junk, scrap** Mom *disposed of* our old magazines and newspapers at the recycling center.

dispute *verb* **1.** ✦ **argue, clash, quarrel, squabble** ◇ **contend, debate** Keith and his brother *disputed* over whose turn it was to take out the garbage. **2.** ✦ **challenge, contest, doubt, oppose, question** ◇ **contradict** Mary *disputes* my claim that I am stronger than she is. —*noun* **1.** ✦ **argument, contention, disagreement, quarrel** ◇ **conflict, controversy, fight, hostility** The two countries found a peaceful solution to their *dispute*.

disregard *verb* ✦ **ignore, overlook** ◇ **forget, neglect, slight** We *disregarded* the instructions for the board game and made up our own rules.

disrupt *verb* ✦ **disturb, interfere with, interrupt, upset** ◇ **confuse, mess up** The fans *disrupted* the rock concert when they rushed onto the stage.

dissent *verb* ✦ **be opposed, differ, disagree, vote no** ◇ **contradict, dispute, protest** Congress was unable to approve the controversial bill because so many senators *dissented*. —*noun* ✦ **difference, disagreement, dissension, opposition** ◇ **protest** The *dissent* among the jurors could not be settled, and they told the judge that they had failed to reach a verdict.

dissolve *verb* ✦ **liquefy** ◇ **disintegrate, melt, mix, soften** The directions on the medicine bottle said to *dissolve* two tablets in a glass of water.

distance *noun* ✦ **interval, length, space** ◇ **gap, span, stretch** The shortest *distance* between two points is a straight line.

distant *adjective* ✦ **far, faraway, far-off, remote** ◇ **removed, separate** We could hear the *distant* thunder of the waterfall. ▶

distinct *adjective* **1.** ✦ **clear, definite, obvious, unmistakable** ◇ **apparent** A *distinct* aroma of baking bread filled the house. **2.** ✦ **different, dissimilar, individual, separate, singular, unlike** It's easy to tell Corey apart from his twin brother because they have such *distinct* personalities.

distinguish *verb* **1. ✦ determine, discriminate, know, tell ✧ divide, separate** You have to learn to *distinguish* right from wrong. **2. ✦ identify, make out, perceive, recognize, tell** I could see someone approaching though the fog, but I couldn't *distinguish* who it was. **3. ✦ honor ✧ dignify, glorify** Christina *distinguished* herself by winning a short story contest.

distort *verb* **1. ✦ bend, contort, deform, twist, warp ✧ ruin, wreck** Don't leave videocassettes in the sun because heat can *distort* them. **2. ✦ change, falsify, misrepresent, twist ✧ deceive, mislead** Supermarket tabloids are famous for *distorting* the truth.

distract *verb* **✦ bother, disturb, interrupt ✧ divert, interfere** My sister closed her door so the noise from the TV wouldn't *distract* her.

distress *noun* **1. ✦ anguish, anxiety, concern, worry ✧ pain, sorrow, suffering** Donald's mischievousness is a constant source of *distress* to his parents. **2. ✦ danger, peril, trouble ✧ difficulty, need** This old-time movie is about a hero who rescues a damsel in *distress*. **—verb ✦ concern, disturb, trouble, upset, worry** I don't want to *distress* you, but I think you should know that they're towing your car.

distribute *verb* **1. ✦ allot, dispense, give out, hand out, issue ✧ divide** Our local charity *distributes* food to needy families. **2. ✦ disperse, spread ✧ scatter** Please *distribute* the icing evenly over the entire cake.

district *noun* **✦ area, quarter, section, zone ✧ neighborhood, region** New York's financial *district* is located on Wall Street.

disturb *verb* **1. ✦ disarrange, disorder, disorganize ✧ handle, move, touch** I was careful not to *disturb* any of the papers on Mom's desk. **2. ✦ distress, perturb, trouble, upset, worry** My parents were *disturbed* when I got home after dark. **3. ✦ annoy, bother, distract, interrupt**

✧ disrupt, interfere Please don't *disturb* me while I'm doing my homework.

disturbance *noun* **1. ✦ disruption, distraction, interference, interruption ✧ bother** Dad loves his den because it's a quiet place where he can work without *disturbance*. **2. ✦ commotion, tumult, turmoil, uproar ✧ riot** Andre's hamster created quite a *disturbance* when it got loose in Mr. Silverman's classroom.

dive *verb* **✦ leap, plunge ✧ descend, drop, sink, submerge** We *dove* into the pool at the start of the race. ▼ **—noun ✦ descent, plunge ✧ dip, drop, fall** The test pilot wanted to see how the new jet would perform in a steep *dive*.

diverse *adjective* **✦ assorted, different, dissimilar, various ✧ miscellaneous** One of the strengths of the United States is the *diverse* backgrounds of its citizens.

divert *verb* **1. ✦ redirect, shift ✧ sidetrack, swing, turn aside, veer** Bad weather caused our Chicago flight to be *diverted* to Indianapolis. **2. ✦ amuse, distract, entertain, occupy ✧ delight** The street musicians *diverted* us while we stood in line at the theater.

divide *noun* **1. ✦ cut, separate, split ✧ part, segment** We *divided* the pizza into six equal pieces. **2. ✦ deal out, distribute, portion, share, split up** The bank robbers *divided* their loot among themselves.

---

divine *adjective* ✦ **holy, religious, sacred** ✧ **heavenly** The *divine* scripture of the Islamic religion is known as the Koran.

division *noun* **1.** ✦ **segmentation, separation** ✧ **split** The *division* of the year into twelve months is an ancient custom. **2.** ✦ **branch, department, section** ✧ **component, part, segment** Mom works for the sales and marketing *division* of her company. **3.** ✦ **divider, partition** ✧ **border, boundary, frontier** Dad built a counter to serve as a *division* between our kitchen and dining room.

divorce *noun* ✧ **breakup, separation, split** I was glad that my friend's parents decided not to get a *divorce.* —*verb* ✧ **break up, part, separate, split** The young couple *divorced* after only three months of marriage.

do *verb* **1.** ✦ **accomplish, execute, perform** ✧ **act, behave, conduct** Soldiers are expected to *do* whatever they're told. **2.** ✦ **compose, create, fashion, make, produce** ✧ **design, form** My artist friend is *doing* a portrait of me. **3.** ✦ **bring about, lead to, result in** ✧ **cause, give, perform** Complaining won't *do* any good. **4.** ✦ **figure out, solve, work out** ✧ **complete, resolve** Grandpa likes to *do* crossword puzzles. **5.** ✦ **be fine, serve, suffice** ✧ **answer, satisfy, suit** Those tennis shoes will *do* for the hike, though boots would be better. **6.** ✦ **fare, make out, manage** ✧ **continue** How are you *doing* with your dance lessons?

docile *adjective* ✦ **gentle, manageable, meek, obedient, tame** ✧ **mild** I'm not going to get on that horse unless he's very *docile.*

doctor *noun* ✦ **physician** ✧ **healer, intern, surgeon** Mom took me to see the *doctor* because I had a fever.

doctrine *noun* ✦ **principle, teaching, tenet** ✧ **belief, creed** I am studying the *doctrines* of my religion.

Word Groups

A **document** is an official paper containing information or proof. **Document** is a general term with no true synonyms. Here are some related words to investigate in a dictionary:

certificate, contract, deed, license, memo, petition, record, testament, will

---

dodge *verb* ✦ **duck, move aside, shift, sidestep, swerve** ✧ **avoid, escape, evade** I stayed dry because I *dodged* when my friend threw a water balloon at me.

domain *noun* ✦ **realm, territory** ✧ **property, region** The king extended his *domain* by conquering two neighboring countries.

domestic *adjective* **1.** ✦ **family, home, household** ✧ **residential** The Coopers rarely go out because they're happiest in a *domestic* setting. **2.** ✦ **tame** ✧ **docile, obedient, trained** Horses and cows are *domestic* animals. ▼

dominant *adjective* ✦ **controlling, leading, main, principal** ✧ **commanding** The young wolf did not dare challenge the *dominant* member of the pack.

dominate *verb* ✦ **control, lead, rule** ✧ **command, direct, govern** Among many animals, it is the strongest male that *dominates* the group.

donate *verb* ✦ **contribute, give, present** ✧ **award, confer** Trevor *donated* half his allowance to his troop's fund-raising drive.

donation *noun* ✦ **contribution, gift, offering** ✧ **present** The charity received *donations* from all over the world.

donor *noun* ✦ **contributor, donator** ✧ **giver** The Red Cross has issued a national appeal for blood *donors*.

doom *noun* ✦ **destiny, end, fate, ruin** ✧ **death** When the knight saw the fierce dragon, he thought that he was facing his *doom*. —*verb* ✦ **condemn, destine, fate** ✧ **finish, ruin** When the vampire was caught outdoors after sunrise, he was *doomed* to die.

door *noun* ✦ **doorway, entrance, entry, gateway, threshold** A good education can be the *door* to success.

dosage *noun* ✦ **amount, measure, portion, quantity** When using any medicine, you should read the label to determine the proper *dosage*.

doubt *verb* ✦ **disbelieve, distrust, question** ✧ **challenge, dispute** I *doubt* that ghosts really exist. —*noun* ✦ **misgiving, question, suspicion, uncertainty** I have some *doubts* about whether he's telling the truth.

doubtful *adjective* ✦ **improbable, questionable, unlikely** ✧ **uncertain, unclear** It's *doubtful* that I'll be ready in time.

down *adverb* ✦ **downward** ✧ **below, beneath, under** I glanced *down* and saw a four-leaf clover. —*preposition* ✦ **along** ✧ **into, through** We walked *down* the block to the video store. —*verb* **1.** ✦ **bring down, shoot down** ✧ **fell, hit, strike** The fighter pilot *downed* two enemy aircraft. **2.** ✦ **drink, gulp, guzzle, swal-** low ✧ **bolt, gobble** Brandon *downed* three glasses of water after the basketball game.

doze *verb* ✦ **drowse, nap, sleep, slumber, snooze** My cat likes to *doze* on the couch.

drab *adjective* ✦ **colorless, dreary, dull, somber** ✧ **uninteresting** Cindy thought that her desk was too *drab*, so she painted it bright yellow.

draft *noun* **1.** ✦ **breeze** ✧ **air, current, wind** If the *draft* is bothering you, feel free to close the window. **2.** ✦ **version** ✧ **outline, plan, sketch** The author spent an entire year writing the first *draft* of her novel. —*verb* ✦ **outline, plan** ✧ **diagram, draw, sketch** I *drafted* my report on note cards and then typed it on regular paper.

drag *verb* **1.** ✦ **draw, haul, pull, tow, tug** ✧ **lug** My little sister came into the room *dragging* her teddy bear behind her. ▶ **2.** ✦ **plod, trudge** ✧ **crawl, creep, dawdle, straggle** The weary hikers *dragged* into camp and collapsed in front of the fire.

drain *verb* **1.** ✦ **draw off, let out** ✧ **discharge, flow, leak** Dad *drained* the oil from the car. **2.** ✦ **consume, deplete, exhaust, sap, use up** ✧ **empty** The long swim *drained* all my strength.

dramatic *adjective* ✦ **exciting, impressive, sensational, spectacular, thrilling** I like that movie that ends with a *dramatic* high-speed chase scene.

drastic *adjective* ✦ **extreme, radical, rash, severe** ✧ **powerful, strong** Starving yourself is a *drastic* way to lose weight.

draw *verb* **1.** ✦ **drag, haul, pull, tow, tug** Pioneers used horses, oxen, or mules to *draw* their covered wagons. **2.** ✦ **extract, remove, take** ✧ **produce, summon** Let's pick teams by *drawing*

✦ **best choices**
✧ **other choices**

names from a hat. **3.** ✦ **sketch** ✧ **create, diagram, outline, trace** Ry *drew* a picture of a superhero. **4.** ✦ **attract, lure, pull in** ✧ **get, obtain, receive** The department store's big sale *drew* hundreds of shoppers. —*noun* ✦ **deadlock, stalemate, standoff, tie** If the score is still tied after overtime in professional hockey, the game is declared a *draw*.

drawback *noun* ✦ **disadvantage, problem (with), trouble (with)** ✧ **defect, difficulty** There are *drawbacks* to living in both the country and the city.

> **Antonyms**
>
> **drawback** *noun*
>
> advantage, benefit, blessing, convenience, favor, profit

dread *noun* ✦ **apprehension, fear, fright, horror, terror** Just thinking about rattlesnakes fills me with *dread*. —*verb* ✦ **be afraid of, fear** ✧ **concern, worry** I used to *dread* going to summer camp, but then I discovered how much fun it can be.

dreadful *adjective* ✦ **awful, frightful, horrible, terrible** ✧ **bad, wicked** No one dared go outside as long as the *dreadful* giant ruled the land.

dream *noun* ✦ **ambition, aspiration, goal, hope** ✧ **vision** Deborah's *dream* is to become an astronaut. —*verb* ✦ **imagine, suppose, think** ✧ **conceive, fantasize** I never *dreamed* that I'd win the spelling bee.

dreary *adjective* ✦ **bleak, cheerless, dismal, dull, gloomy, somber** Leah thinks that *dreary* winter days are best spent at home by the fireplace.

drench *verb* ✦ **douse, saturate, soak, wet** A sudden downpour *drenched* me as I walked home from school.

dress *noun* **1.** ✦ **frock** ✧ **gown** Sarah bought a new *dress* to wear to her friend's party. **2.** ✦ **apparel, attire, clothes, clothing, garments** The dinner invitation stated that formal

dress was required. —*verb* ✦ **attire, clothe, outfit** ✧ **adorn, trim** Stella *dressed* her younger sister warmly to go sledding.

drift *verb* **1.** ✦ **cruise, float, sail** ✧ **idle, meander, wander** The hot-air balloon *drifted* over a hill. **2.** ✦ **accumulate, collect, mass, pile up** ✧ **stack** The wind caused the snow to *drift* against our front door. —*noun* ✧ **bank, heap, mound, pile** ✧ **hill, mass** These *drifts* were formed by big waves that carried sand onto the beach.

drill *noun* ✦ **exercise, practice, rehearsal, training** ✧ **study** Los Angeles schools hold regular earthquake *drills*. —*verb* **1.** ✦ **bore** ✧ **penetrate, pierce, puncture** The rancher *drilled* a well in order to get water for her cattle. **2.** ✦ **coach, instruct** ✧ **practice, rehearse, teach, train** I helped Adam prepare for his history test by *drilling* him on the names of the Presidents.

drink *verb* ✦ **down, gulp, guzzle, sip, swallow** Kara *drinks* a glass of orange juice every morning. —*noun* **1.** ✦ **beverage** ✧ **fluid, liquid** Luke's favorite *drink* is homemade lemonade. **2.** ✦ **sip, swallow** ✧ **cup, glass** May I have a *drink* of water?

drive *verb* **1.** ✦ **control, operate, run, steer** ✧ **pilot** Uncle Walter showed me how to *drive* his tractor. **2.** ✧ **bus, chauffeur, convey, transport** Mom *drove* me to school today. **3.** ✦ **compel, force, press, push, shove** The climber tried to make it to the top of the mountain, but he was *driven* back by high winds. **4.** ✦ **hit, knock, propel** ✧ **pound, strike** My dad can *drive* a golf ball almost 300 yards. —*noun* **1.** ✦ **excursion, ride** ✧ **journey, tour, trip** My family enjoys taking weekend *drives* in the country. **2.** ✦ **campaign, movement** ✧ **cause, crusade, effort** Our school is sponsoring a *drive* to collect money for new playground equipment.

droop *verb* ✦ **bend, drop, hang down, sag, slump** ✧ **wilt** Heavy snow caused the tree branches to *droop*.

drop *noun* **1.** ✦ **bead, droplet, globule** ✧ **dribble, drip, trickle** *Drops* of sweat formed on my forehead in the hot sun. **2.** ✦ **decline, decrease, dip, reduction** There's been a *drop* in the price of corn due to an abundant harvest. **3.** ✦ **descent, fall, plunge** ✧ **slope** It's a long *drop* from the top of the cliff to the river below. —*verb* **1.** ✦ **descend, fall, plunge, sink** ✧ **lower, reduce** The temperature *dropped* more than thirty degrees last night. **2.** ✦ **eliminate, leave out, omit, remove** ✧ **skip** We'll have to *drop* one of these poems from the literary magazine because there isn't enough room for both. **3.** ✦ **cease, discontinue, end, stop, terminate** When Lisa joined a softball league, she had to *drop* her piano lessons.

drown *verb* **1.** ✦ **douse, drench, saturate, soak** ✧ **wet** I like to *drown* my pancakes in maple syrup. ▼ **2.** ✦ **overpower, overwhelm** ✧ **smother, stifle, submerge** The audience's applause *drowned out* the speaker's final words.

drowsy *adjective* ✦ **sleepy, tired** ✧ **groggy, listless** If you feel so *drowsy*, why don't you take a nap?

drug *noun* **1.** ✦ **medication, medicine, pharmaceutical** ✧ **remedy** Aspirin is one of the most commonly used *drugs* in America. **2.** ✦ **substance** ✧ **depressant, narcotic, stimulant** People who deal in illegal *drugs* run the risk of imprisonment.

drunk *adjective* ✦ **drunken, intoxicated** ✧ **groggy, impaired** *Drunk* drivers cause a lot of serious accidents.

dry *adjective* ✦ **arid, parched, rainless, waterless** ✧ **thirsty** Deserts can be hot or cold, but they're always *dry*.

duck *verb* **1.** ✦ **bend, crouch, stoop** ✧ **drop, lower** Gina *ducked* behind a bush during the hide-and-seek game. **2.** ✦ **avoid, dodge, elude, escape, evade** The politician *ducked* reporters by sneaking out the back door.

due *adjective* **1.** ✦ **adequate, appropriate, fitting, proper, suitable** Use *due* care when handling a knife. **2.** ✦ **anticipated, expected, scheduled** Dad's plane is *due* at three o'clock. —*adverb* ✦ **directly, straight** ✧ **dead, exactly, right** We drove *due* east across the desert.

dull *adjective* **1.** ✦ **blunt, unsharpened** ✧ **edgeless** It's hard to cut cleanly with a *dull* blade. **2.** ✦ **boring, monotonous, tedious, tiresome, uninteresting** Robyn fell asleep during the *dull* film. —*verb* ✦ **blunt, dim, diminish, lessen, reduce** ✧ **fade** Age has *dulled* our cat's eyesight.

dumb *adjective* ✦ **crazy, foolish, silly, stupid, unintelligent** I made a *dumb* mistake when I said to you that George Washington was the mother of his country.

dummy *noun* **1.** ✧ **doll, figure, marionette, model, puppet** The ventriloquist's *dummy* has a funny-looking head. **2.** ✦ **fake, imitation** ✧ **copy** You can't open this drawer because it's a *dummy*.

dump *verb* ✦ **deposit, drop, empty, pour out, unload** I was taking a nap on the beach when my sister *dumped* a bucket of water on me. —*noun* ✦ **junkyard, rubbish heap, trash pile** ✧ **landfill** Dad and I took a load of trash to the *dump*.

duplicate *noun* ✦ **copy, reproduction** ✧ **double, image, replica** I made a *duplicate* of

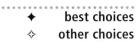

✦   best choices
✧   other choices

my book report in case something happened to the original. —*verb* ✦ **copy, imitate, repeat, reproduce** ◇ **simulate** The scientist is *duplicating* her original experiment to see if she can get the same results. ◀

durable *adjective* ✦ **enduring, firm, lasting, long-lasting** ◇ **permanent, strong, sturdy** Kate and I have a *durable* friendship that has lasted ever since we first knew each other.

duration *noun* ✦ **length** ◇ **course, period, span, term, time** I spent the *duration* of my summer vacation on a farm in Vermont.

dusk *noun* ✦ **evening, nightfall, sundown, sunset, twilight** Mom said that I could play in the park but that I had to be home by *dusk*.

duty *noun* **1.** ✦ **assignment, job, obligation, responsibility, task** A police officer's *duties* include enforcing the law and keeping the peace. **2.** ✦ **tariff, tax** ◇ **fee, levy** Mom had to pay a *duty* on the pearls that she brought back from Japan.

dwell *verb* ✦ **abide, live, reside** ◇ **inhabit** People have *dwelled* in cities for thousands of years.

dwindle *verb* ✦ **decrease, diminish, shrink, thin out** ◇ **decline, ebb, lessen, reduce** The crowd began to *dwindle* before the game was over.

Antonyms
dwindle *verb*
build, expand, flourish, grow, increase, sprout, swell

dye *noun* ✦ **coloring** ◇ **color, pigment, stain, tint** This red *dye* is guaranteed not to fade. —*verb* ✦ **color, tint** ◇ **shade, stain** My class is going to *dye* T-shirts as an art project.

dynamic *adjective* ✦ **active, energetic, forceful, lively, vigorous** The *dynamic* performer had the whole audience singing along with her.

E

eager *adjective* ✦ **avid, impatient, keen** ✧ **anxious, enthusiastic** Caitlin is *eager* for summer vacation to begin.

early *adjective* ✦ **beginning** ✧ **first, initial, opening** My oldest brother is in his *early* twenties. —*adverb* ✦ **ahead, before, beforehand, in advance** ✧ **prematurely** Alexandra arrived *early* and helped us with the party decorations.

earn *verb* **1.** ✦ **get, make, receive** ✧ **collect, gain** Michael *earns* twenty dollars a week delivering newspapers. **2.** ✦ **gain, win** ✧ **deserve, merit** Susannah *earned* our admiration when her essay was printed in a national magazine.

earth *noun* **1.** ✦ **world** ✧ **planet** Soviet astronaut Yuri Gagarin was the first person to orbit the *Earth*. **2.** ✦ **dirt, loam, soil** ✧ **ground, land** Most gardeners enjoy the smell and feel of rich, moist *earth*.

ease *noun* **1.** ✦ **comfort, leisure, relaxation, rest** ✧ **contentment** My cat Lulu lives a life of total *ease*. **2.** ✦ **easiness, facility** ✧ **adroitness, dexterity** Anna won the race with *ease*. —*verb* ✦ **lessen, lighten, relieve, soothe** ✧ **comfort** The nurse's cheerful words helped to *ease* my fear when I got my flu shot.

easy *adjective* **1.** ✦ **simple, uncomplicated** ✧ **effortless, light** Marie picked an *easy* pattern for her first sewing project. **2.** ✦ **carefree, comfortable, cozy, pleasant** ✧ **prosperous** My grandparents have been enjoying an *easy* life since they retired. **3.** ✦ **lenient, undemanding** ✧ **casual, informal, tolerant** Our coach was *easy* on us for the first two or three practices of the season.

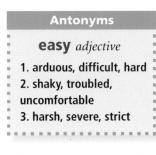

Antonyms

easy *adjective*

1. arduous, difficult, hard
2. shaky, troubled, uncomfortable
3. harsh, severe, strict

eat *verb* **1.** ✦ **consume, devour, swallow** ✧ **dine, feast, feed** An adult elephant *eats* as much as one thousand pounds of food every day. **2.** ✦ **corrode, erode, wear away** ✧ **destroy, waste** Sea water has been slowly *eating away* the boat's iron anchor.

ebb *verb* **1.** ✦ **flow back, recede, retreat, withdraw** ✧ **subside** When the tide *ebbed*, I went looking for seashells. **2.** ✦ **decline, decrease, diminish, lessen** ✧ **reduce** The runner was only halfway through the race when his strength began to *ebb*.

echo *noun* ✦ **reflection, reverberation** ✧ **answer, repetition, response** The quiet *echo* of voices could be heard throughout the museum. —*verb* ✦ **reflect, resound, ring** ✧ **rebound, repeat** The crowd's cheers *echoed* loudly in the gymnasium.

eclipse *verb* **1.** ✦ **block, conceal, hide, obscure, shadow** ✧ **darken, dim** When the moon passes between the sun and the Earth, the sun is *eclipsed*. **2.** ✦ **exceed, outdo, overshadow, surpass** ✧ **excel** At the art contest, Matt's drawing was so good that it totally *eclipsed* all the other entries.

economical *adjective* ✦ **frugal, thrifty** ✧ **careful, cheap, prudent, saving** Waiting until a store puts its merchandise on sale is an *economical* way of shopping.

edge *noun* **1.** ✦ **border, fringe, margin, side** ✧ **rim** The lake has a beautiful sandy beach along its southern *edge*. **2.** ✦ **advantage** ✧ **asset, benefit, head start** Victoria's height gives her a definite *edge* when she plays basketball. —*verb* **1.** ✦ **creep, ease, inch, slide** ✧ **budge, glide, move** Alex *edged* away from the growling dog. **2.** ✦ **border, outline, trim** ✧ **decorate** Mrs. Schwartz decided to *edge* her gravel driveway with red bricks.

✦ **best choices**
✧ **other choices**

edit *verb* ✦ **revise, rewrite** ✧ **check, correct, proofread** I had to *edit* my book report so that it would fit on two pages.

educate *verb* ✦ **instruct, teach** ✧ **coach, train, tutor** A teacher's main job is to *educate* his or her students.

education *noun* ✦ **knowledge, learning, schooling** ✧ **information, instruction** *Education* can help you get an interesting job.

eerie *adjective* ✦ **spooky, strange, uncanny, weird** ✧ **frightening, scary** We heard *eerie* noises coming from the old abandoned house.

effect *noun* **1.** ✦ **consequence, end, outcome, result** ✧ **conclusion** Tooth decay is one of the bad *effects* of eating too much candy. **2.** ✦ **impact, influence** ✧ **impression, significance** Improving my study habits had a positive *effect* on my grades. —*verb* ✦ **accomplish, achieve, bring about, cause, make** The development of electricity *effected* many changes in the way people live.

effective *adjective* **1.** ✦ **efficient, practical, productive** ✧ **successful** Gary makes *effective* use of his study time. **2.** ✦ **in effect, operational, operative** ✧ **active, functioning, real** Our teacher said that her new grading policy will be *effective* for the rest of the year.

efficient *adjective* ✦ **effective, practical, productive** ✧ **competent, proficient** When microchips were developed, computers became much more *efficient*.

effort *noun* **1.** ✦ **exertion, labor, toil, work** ✧ **strain, struggle** Painting the garage took more *effort* than we anticipated. **2.** ✦ **attempt, endeavor** ✧ **try** Jeffrey is making an *effort* to do better in school.

eject *verb* ✦ **discharge, expel, force out, spew** ✧ **remove** The geyser *ejected* a spray of hot water and steam.

elaborate *adjective* ✦ **complex, complicated, detailed, intricate** ✧ **fancy, thorough** Isaac's parents made *elaborate* preparations for his bar mitzvah. —*verb* ✦ **amplify, develop, enlarge upon, expand, explain** ✧ **add to, improve** When Joanna gave a brief answer, her tutor asked her to *elaborate on* it.

elastic *adjective* ✦ **stretchable** ✧ **adaptable, flexible, pliable** My gym shorts have an *elastic* waistband.

elder *adjective* ✦ **older** ✧ **senior** My *elder* sister is in high school. —*noun* ✦ **senior** ✧ **senior citizen** Mr. Carter says that young people can learn a lot by listening to their *elders*. ▶

elderly *adjective* ✦ **aged, aging, old** ✧ **mature** Our *elderly* neighbor has been retired for twenty years.

elect *verb* **1.** ✦ **vote** ✧ **appoint, designate, name, nominate** We *elected* Nathan to be our class president. **2.** ✦ **choose, decide, opt** ✧ **prefer, select** Kayla *elected* to go to the park rather than stay home.

elegant *adjective* ✦ **exquisite, fancy, stylish** ✧ **fine, graceful, grand** Mom wore an *elegant* dress to go to the opera.

element *noun* ✦ **component, factor, feature, ingredient, part** ✧ **item, piece** The basic *elements* of a successful movie include an interesting story and good acting.

elementary *adjective* ✦ **basic, beginning, fundamental, introductory** ✧ **simple** We studied nouns and verbs as part of our class in *elementary* grammar.

elevate *verb* ✦ **lift, raise** ✧ **boost, hoist, pick up** The nurse *elevated* the patient's legs to make him more comfortable.

eligible *adjective* ✦ **qualified** ✧ **acceptable, fit, suitable, worthy** In the United States, citizens have to be eighteen years old before they are *eligible* to vote.

eliminate *verb* ✦ **drop, exclude, leave out, omit, remove** ✧ **discard** It's a good idea to *eliminate* excess sugar from your diet.

elude *verb* ✦ **avoid, dodge, duck, escape, evade** ✧ **lose, shun** James won our tag game when he successfully *eluded* all of the other players.

embarrass *verb* ✦ **discomfort, disconcert, fluster** ✧ **humiliate, shame** Mom has promised to never *embarrass* me by showing my baby pictures to my friends.

embarrassment *noun* ✦ **awkwardness, discomfort** ✧ **shame, shyness, uneasiness** Kristi blushed in *embarrassment* as she read her poem in front of our class.

emblem *noun* ✦ **insignia, sign, symbol** ✧ **badge, token** Canada's official *emblem* is the maple leaf.

embrace *verb* **1.** ✦ **clasp, hug** ✧ **cuddle, grip, hold, squeeze** The couple *embraced* each other at the end of their wedding ceremony. **2.** ✦ **accept, adopt, endorse** ✧ **choose, welcome** By the fifth century A.D., most of the Roman world had *embraced* Christianity. **3.** ✦ **comprise, contain, embody, encompass, include** ✧ **cover, hold** The United Kingdom *embraces* four countries: England, Wales, Scotland, and Northern Ireland. —*noun* ✦ **clasp, hug** ✧ **caress, pat, squeeze** Grandpa gave us each a warm *embrace* and a kiss on the cheek.

emerge *verb* ✦ **appear, come out, materialize** ✧ **arise, surface** After the storm, the sun *emerged* from behind a rain cloud.

emergency *noun* ✦ **crisis** ✧ **accident, difficulty, predicament, trouble** Mom wrote down the phone number where she could be reached in case of an *emergency*.

emigrate *verb* ✦ **migrate, move, relocate** ✧ **immigrate** Yoshiko has relatives in Japan who are planning to *emigrate* to the United States.

eminent *adjective* ✦ **distinguished, famous, outstanding, prominent, top** Thomas Edison was an *eminent* scientist and inventor.

emit *verb* ✦ **discharge, expel, give off, release** ✧ **vent** That factory *emits* too much air pollution.

emotion *noun* ✦ **feeling, sentiment** ✧ **affection, passion** I get filled with *emotion* every time I watch the end of that movie.

Word Groups

An **emperor** is a man who is the ruler of an empire. **Emperor** is a very specific term with no true synonyms. Here are some related words to investigate in a dictionary:

empress, king, majesty, monarch, queen, ruler, sovereign

emphasis *noun* ✦ **attention, importance, significance, stress, weight** Our gym teacher puts a lot of *emphasis* on just having fun.

emphasize *verb* ✦ **accentuate, feature, highlight, stress** Mr. Calloway *emphasizes* creativity in his classroom.

employ *verb* **1.** ✦ **engage, hire, take on** ✧ **enlist, retain** The new factory will *employ* three hundred workers. **2.** ✦ **use, utilize** ✧ **apply, exercise, operate** Early computers were bulky because they *employed* vacuum tubes instead of transistors and microchips.

✦   best choices
✧   other choices

employee *noun* ✦ **worker** ✧ **assistant, helper, laborer, staff** My aunt's travel agency has five *employees*.

employer *noun* ✦ **boss, manager, supervisor** ✧ **business, company** Ms. Kaplan's *employer* gave her a promotion and a raise.

empty *adjective* **1.** ✦ **bare, unoccupied, vacant** ✧ **blank, clear** You can use this *empty* shelf for your shell collection. **2.** ✦ **hollow, idle, meaningless** ✧ **insincere, useless** My dog is quite harmless, and his growling is just an *empty* threat. —*verb* ✦ **clean out, clear, clear out** ✧ **evacuate, vacate** We had to *empty* the closet before we could paint it.

enchant *verb* **1.** ✦ **bewitch, charm** The witch *enchanted* the prince by turning him into a frog. **2.** ✦ **captivate, delight, entrance, fascinate, intrigue** The storyteller *enchanted* his audience with tales of danger and romance.

enclose *verb* **1.** ✦ **close in, envelop, surround** ✧ **circle, cover, wall in** Our back porch is *enclosed* by screens. **2.** ✦ **include, insert, put in** ✧ **add** Grandma and Grandpa *enclosed* a check with my birthday card.

encounter *noun* ✦ **contact, meeting** ✧ **brush, confrontation** Most of Lewis and Clark's *encounters* with Indians were peaceful. —*verb* ✦ **come across, meet, run into** ✧ **experience, face** Darla is one of the nicest people I've ever *encountered*.

encourage *verb* **1.** ✦ **inspire, motivate, persuade, stimulate** ✧ **urge** The praise I got from my music teacher finally *encouraged* me to enter the state competition. **2.** ✦ **advance, foster, further, promote** ✧ **help** Regular exercise *encourages* good health.

> **Antonyms**
>
> **encourage** *verb*
>
> 1. deter, discourage
> 2. hinder, impede, inhibit, obstruct, retard

end *noun* **1.** ✦ **edge, extremity** ✧ **border, limit, margin** This highway runs from one *end* of the continent to the other. **2.** ✦ **conclusion, ending, finish** ✧ **close, finale** I read the entire book from beginning to *end* in one afternoon. **3.** ✦ **aim, goal, objective, purpose** ✧ **intent** The movie's villain would stop at nothing to achieve his *end*. —*verb* ✦ **conclude, finish, halt, stop** ✧ **close, complete** The game will *end* at sunset, regardless of the score.

endeavor *verb* **1.** ✦ **attempt, seek, strive, try, undertake** ✧ **struggle** I believe that everyone should *endeavor* to be as good a person as possible. —*noun* ✦ **attempt, effort, try** ✧ **exertion, pains, struggle, undertaking** Hamilton's *endeavor* to improve his poor handwriting finally met with success.

endorse *verb* ✦ **approve, back, champion, support** ✧ **allow** The principal *endorsed* the teachers' request for a pay raise.

endure *verb* **1.** ✦ **bear, suffer, take, tolerate, withstand** When Amy broke her arm, she *endured* the pain without complaining. **2.** ✦ **continue, last, persist, remain, survive** The Roman empire *endured* for hundreds of years before it was finally conquered.

enemy *noun* ✦ **adversary, antagonist, assailant, attacker, competitor, foe, opponent** ✧ **rival** In the American Civil War, the North and the South were *enemies*.

energetic *adjective* ✦ **active, dynamic, lively, spirited, vigorous** Rita is one of our most *energetic* soccer players.

energy *noun* ✦ **pep, spirit, vigor, vitality** ✧ **force, power, strength** Benjamin is so full of *energy* that he has a hard time sitting still.

enforce *verb* ✦ **administer, apply, impose** ✧ **accomplish, perform** A team of lifeguards *enforces* the safety rules at our school's swimming pool.

engage *verb* **1.** ✦ **employ, enlist, hire, retain** ✧ **take on** Mr. Willis *engaged* a consultant to help him start his new business. **2.** ✦ **absorb, fascinate, interest, involve** ✧ **occupy** Grandpa and I were so *engaged* in my new computer game that we lost all track of time. ▼

engagement *noun* ✦ **appointment, date** ✧ **commitment, meeting** My parents made a dinner *engagement* for Saturday night.

engrave *verb* ✦ **carve, cut, inscribe** ✧ **etch, stamp** The jeweler *engraved* my name on my new silver bracelet.

enhance *verb* ✦ **heighten, increase, intensify** ✧ **improve, strengthen** Grandma uses herbs to *enhance* the flavor of her spaghetti sauce.

enjoy *verb* **1.** ✦ **delight in, like, love, relish** ✧ **appreciate** Gregory really *enjoys* playing his guitar. **2.** ✦ **have, possess** ✧ **hold, own** Despite our cat's age, he still *enjoys* good health.

enjoyment *noun* ✦ **amusement, delight, joy, pleasure** ✧ **satisfaction** Tara gets more *enjoyment* from going to a live concert than from watching a band on TV.

enlarge *verb* ✦ **expand, extend** ✧ **amplify, augment, increase** The city is planning to *enlarge* the airport by building two new runways.

enlighten *verb* ✦ **educate, inform, instruct, teach** ✧ **notify, tell** The movie *enlightened* us about the traditional way of life of Indian peoples of the rain forest.

enlist *verb* **1.** ✦ **enter, join, sign up for** ✧ **enroll, volunteer** My older sister *enlisted in* the U.S. Air Force. **2.** ✦ **engage, obtain, procure, recruit, secure** Dad *enlisted* our help in picking out a present for Mom.

enormous *adjective* ✦ **giant, gigantic, huge, immense, tremendous** ✧ **big, large, vast** Tyrannosaurus was an *enormous* dinosaur.

enough *adjective* ✦ **adequate, sufficient** ✧ **ample, satisfactory** Brandi is saving her allowance until she has *enough* money to buy a new softball glove.

enrage *verb* ✦ **anger, incense, infuriate, madden** ✧ **provoke** The man was *enraged* when he found that his car had been stolen.

enrich *verb* ✦ **better, develop, enhance, improve, refine** A good education will *enrich* your mind.

enroll *verb* ✦ **enter, join, register for, sign up for** ✧ **enlist** Hannah wants to *enroll in* a ballet class.

ensure *verb* ✦ **check, confirm, insure, make sure** ✧ **assure, guarantee** Please *ensure* that your seat belt is properly fastened.

enter *verb* **1.** ✦ **come in, go in** ✧ **penetrate** In Japan, it's polite to take off your shoes before *entering* someone's house. **2.** ✦ **begin, start** ✧ **enroll, join, register** Luis will be *entering* the sixth grade next fall. **3.** ✦ **list, post, record, write** ✧ **file, insert** Mr. Knowles *entered* our test scores in his grade book.

enterprise *noun* ✦ **endeavor, project, undertaking, venture** ✧ **task** Amundsen's journey to the South Pole by dogsled in 1911 was a daring *enterprise*.

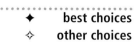

✦ **best choices**
✧ **other choices**

entertain *verb* ✦ **amuse, delight, divert** ✧ **interest, occupy** When our TV was broken, we had to find some other way to *entertain* ourselves.

entertainment *noun* ✦ **amusement, diversion, enjoyment, fun, pleasure** My friend and I play video games for *entertainment*.

enthusiasm *noun* ✦ **eagerness, excitement** ✧ **fire, passion, zest** The class showed great *enthusiasm* when the teacher announced a field trip to a movie studio.

enthusiastic *adjective* ✦ **ardent, avid, eager, passionate** ✧ **earnest** My dog always gives me an *enthusiastic* welcome when I get home.

entire *adjective* ✦ **complete, whole** ✧ **full, total** I'm so hungry that I could eat an *entire* pizza.

entitle *verb* **1.** ✦ **call, name, title** ✧ **designate, dub, label** Jamie read an article *entitled* "101 Ways to Give Your Dog a Bath Without Getting Yourself Wet." **2.** ✦ **allow, authorize, permit, qualify** In the United States, all adult citizens are *entitled* to vote.

entrance *noun* **1.** ✦ **appearance, entry** ✧ **admission, approach, arrival** Everyone kneeled down and bowed when the queen made her *entrance*. **2.** ✦ **entry, entryway, gate** ✧ **door, doorway, passageway** There was a long line at the *entrance* to the stadium.

entry *noun* **1.** ✦ **appearance, entrance** ✧ **admission, approach, arrival** Loud applause greeted the orchestra's *entry* onto the stage. **2.** ✦ **door, doorway, entrance, entryway, passageway** ✧ **gate** The treasure room had a secret *entry* that was hidden behind a bookcase. **3.** ✦ **posting, record** ✧ **note, statement** At the end of each day, the ship's captain made an *entry* in his logbook.

envelop *verb* ✦ **cloak, cover, shroud, surround, wrap** ✧ **hood** The silky cocoon completely *enveloped* the caterpillar.

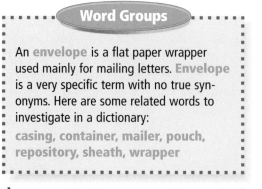

Word Groups

An **envelope** is a flat paper wrapper used mainly for mailing letters. **Envelope** is a very specific term with no true synonyms. Here are some related words to investigate in a dictionary:

casing, container, mailer, pouch, repository, sheath, wrapper

envious *adjective* ✦ **covetous, jealous** ✧ **desirous, resentful** Marla gave the birds an *envious* look because she wished that she had wings to fly too.

environment *noun* ✦ **atmosphere, conditions, setting, surroundings** ✧ **locality** Our school library provides a quiet *environment* for studying.

envy *noun* ✦ **jealousy** ✧ **desire, greed, resentment** I was filled with *envy* when my neighbors got a new puppy. *—verb* ✦ **be jealous of** ✧ **begrudge, covet, resent** Everyone on the basketball team *envies* Walt because he's so tall.

episode *noun* **1.** ✦ **development, event, incident, occurrence** ✧ **occasion** The building of the transcontinental railroad was an important *episode* in the history of the West. **2.** ✦ **installment** ✧ **chapter, show** We'll have to watch next week's *episode* to find out who committed the crime.

equal *adjective* ✦ **equivalent, even, identical, (the) same** ✧ **like, similar** I dealt an *equal* number of cards to each player. *—noun* ✦ **equivalent, match, peer** ✧ **parallel** The undefeated boxer has yet to meet his *equal* in the ring. *—verb* ✦ **amount to, constitute, make, make up** ✧ **correspond, match** Four quarters *equal* one dollar.

equip *verb* ✦ **furnish, outfit, provide, supply** ✧ **stock** The mountaineers *equipped* themselves with ropes and safety harnesses.

equipment *noun* ✦ **apparatus, gear, supplies** ✧ **furnishings, materials, things** The local department store is having a sale on sports *equipment*. ◄

equivalent *adjective* ✦ **equal, even, identical, the same** ✧ **like, similar** My brother and I are assigned *equivalent* amounts of housework. —*noun* ✦ **counterpart of, equal of, same as** ✧ **match** I know that one cup is the *equivalent of* eight ounces.

era *noun* ✦ **age, epoch, period, time** ✧ **day** The Victorian *era* is named after Queen Victoria, who ruled Great Britain from 1837 to 1901.

erase *verb* ✦ **rub out, wipe off** ✧ **blot, cancel, clear, delete, remove** The teacher asked Allison to *erase* everything on the blackboard.

erect *adjective* ✦ **straight, upright, vertical** *Erect* posture is good for your back. —*verb* ✦ **build, construct, put up, raise** ✧ **make** The farmer and his neighbors *erected* a new barn.

erode *verb* ✦ **wear, wear away** ✧ **carve, corrode, eat** The wind *eroded* the rocks into interesting shapes.

errand *noun* ✦ **assignment, chore, commission, job, mission, task** Kurt went out to do an *errand* for his mother.

erratic *adjective* ✦ **changeable, irregular, unpredictable, variable** ✧ **bizarre, odd** The weather has been so *erratic* lately that I never know if it's going to rain or shine.

error *noun* ✦ **mistake, slip** ✧ **blunder, fault, flaw, lapse, oversight** Brad made only one *error* on his spelling test.

erupt *verb* ✦ **break, burst, explode** ✧ **blow up** The audience *erupted* into laughter.

escape *verb* 1. ✦ **break out, get away, run away** ✧ **flee** The tiger *escaped* from its cage. 2. ✦ **elude, evade, get by** ✧ **avoid, dodge, get out of** Nothing *escapes* our teacher's attention. —*noun* ✦ **breakout, getaway** ✧ **departure, flight** The convicts made their *escape* on a dark and stormy night.

escort *noun* ✦ **attendant, companion** ✧ **guard, guide** My parents won't let me go to the dance without an *escort*. —*verb* ✦ **conduct, guide, lead** ✧ **accompany, attend** The usher *escorted* us to our seats.

especially *adverb* ✦ **chiefly, mainly, particularly, primarily** ✧ **very** I like all desserts, but I am *especially* fond of chocolate cake.

essay *noun* ✦ **composition, paper** ✧ **article, report, theme** Our teacher asked everyone to write an *essay* about his or her favorite book.

essence *noun* ✦ **basis, core, heart** ✧ **nature, substance** The *essence* of democracy is the right to choose your own government.

essential *adjective* ✦ **basic, critical, important, necessary, vital** Proper nutrition is *essential* to maintaining good health.

establish *verb* 1. ✦ **build, create, found, institute, start** My uncle would like to *establish* his own business. 2. ✦ **confirm, demonstrate, prove, show, verify** Medical research has *established* the fact that smoking is hazardous to your health.

establishment *noun* 1. ✦ **creation, development, formation** ✧ **start** Our city is raising funds for the *establishment* of a new community college. 2. ✦ **business, company, enterprise**

✦ **best choices**
✧ **other choices**

◇ **institution, organization** Mr. Lee works for an *establishment* that makes and sells vacuum cleaners.

esteem *verb* ✦ **admire, appreciate, honor, respect, value** Albert Einstein is *esteemed* for his contributions to science. —*noun* ✦ **admiration, honor, regard, respect** ◇ **reverence** Everyone holds Jaclyn in high *esteem* because she's honest and dependable.

estimate *verb* ✦ **calculate, figure, guess, judge** ◇ **evaluate** Garrett *estimated* that about a thousand people attended the concert. —*noun* ✦ **appraisal, assessment, calculation, evaluation** ◇ **guess** The mechanic gave Mom an *estimate* on the cost of repairing our car.

eternal *adjective* ✦ **endless, everlasting, perpetual, timeless** ◇ **constant, continual** I liked that poem about the *eternal* rhythm of the seasons.

Antonyms
eternal *adjective*
brief, concise, fleeting, momentary, short, temporary, transitory

etiquette *noun* ✦ **manners** ◇ **convention, courtesy, custom** Chewing with your mouth open is not good *etiquette*.

evacuate *verb* ✦ **abandon, exit, get out of, leave, vacate** ◇ **clear, empty** We had a drill to see how quickly we could *evacuate* the school building in case of emergency.

evade *verb* ✦ **avoid, dodge, elude, escape, lose** The criminal tried to *evade* the police officers who were pursuing him.

evaluate *verb* ✦ **appraise, assess, judge, rate** ◇ **calculate, value** A panel of judges *evaluated* our gymnastic performances to determine who would go on to the state competition.

evaporate *verb* ✦ **disappear, dissipate, fade, vanish** My boredom *evaporated* when my friend came over to play.

even *adjective* **1.** ✦ **equal, identical, the same** ◇ **like, similar** I cut the strips of paper into *even* lengths. **2.** ✦ **flat, level, smooth** ◇ **horizontal, straight** It's easier to walk along an *even* path than over rocky fields. **3.** ✦ **constant, regular, steady, unchanging, uniform** When you relax, your heart beats at an *even* rate. —*adverb* ✦ **still, yet** ◇ **actually, indeed** I was encouraged to try *even* harder when my teacher told me how much I had improved. —*verb* ✦ **balance, equalize, tie** ◇ **equal, level, match** Matthew's home run *evened* the score.

evening *noun* ✦ **dusk, nightfall, twilight** ◇ **sundown, sunset, night** The wind died down toward *evening*.

event *noun* **1.** ✦ **happening, incident, occasion, occurrence** ◇ **circumstance** Visiting the Holocaust Memorial Museum was an important *event* in my life. **2.** ✦ **competition, contest, match** ◇ **game** Tasha won three *events* at last week's swim meet.

ever *adverb* ✦ **always, forever** ◇ **continuously, eternally** Snow White married the prince, and they lived happily *ever* after.

everlasting *adjective* ✦ **ceaseless, endless, enduring, eternal, perpetual, unending** ◇ **immortal** The knight made a vow of *everlasting* loyalty to his king and queen.

every *adjective* ✦ **each** ◇ **all, any** Please answer *every* question to the best of your ability.

everyday *adjective* ✦ **common, familiar, frequent, ordinary, regular, usual** I'm too tired to make even little *everyday* decisions like what to wear and what to eat for lunch.

Antonyms
everyday *adjective*
exceptional, infrequent, occasional, rare, remarkable, uncommon, unusual

evidence *noun* ✦ **facts, grounds, information, proof** ◇ **indication, sign** There wasn't enough *evidence* to convict the defendant of the crime so he was released.

evident *adjective* ✦ **apparent, certain, clear, obvious, plain, visible** It's *evident* from the dullness of my pencil that I need to sharpen it.

evil *adjective* ✦ **bad, base, immoral, wicked** ✧ **harmful, wrong** I read a story about an *evil* wizard who turns everybody into toads. —*noun* ✦ **immorality, sin, wickedness** ✧ **crime, harm, wrong** It is often said that the love of money is the root of all *evil*.

evolve *verb* ✦ **derive, develop, emerge, result** ✧ **change, grow** Darwin's theory states that present-day plants and animals *evolved* from earlier forms.

exact *adjective* ✦ **accurate, correct, faithful, precise, true** ✧ **right** I made an *exact* copy of the drawing.

exactly *adverb* ✦ **just, precisely** ✧ **absolutely, completely, quite** Thanks for the present! It's *exactly* what I wanted.

exaggerate *verb* ✦ **overstate** ✧ **expand, inflate, magnify** Richard was *exaggerating* when he said that he had a million and one comic books in his collection.

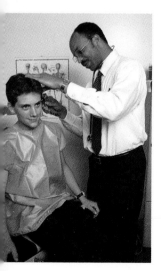

examination *noun* 1. ✦ **check, checkup, inspection** ✧ **review, study, survey** Jared's doctor gave him a complete *examination* before he went away to camp for summer vacation. ◀ 2. ✦ **exam, quiz, test** Ms. Rosenberg said that our *examination* would consist entirely of true-or-false questions.

examine *verb* 1. ✦ **check, inspect, study** ✧ **analyze, investigate** The jeweler *examined* the sapphire very closely. 2. ✦ **interrogate, query, question** ✧ **ask, inquire, quiz** The police *examined* the suspect to see if she had an alibi.

example *noun* ✦ **sample, specimen** ✧ **case, instance, model** This bracelet is a fine *example* of the silver and turquoise jewelry made by Navajos.

exasperate *verb* ✦ **aggravate, annoy, bother, irritate** ✧ **disturb** Sometimes my little brother *exasperates* me.

excavate *verb* ✦ **dig up, uncover, unearth** ✧ **hollow, mine** Archaeologists *excavated* King Tutankhamen's tomb in 1922.

exceed *verb* ✦ **beat, better, outdo, pass, surpass, top** Mary's performance at the track meet *exceeded* her expectations.

excel *verb* ✦ **dominate, stand out** ✧ **exceed, outdo, surpass** William *excels* in football, but he is only an average basketball player.

excellence *noun* ✦ **distinction, merit, superiority** ✧ **quality** Vanessa received an award for scholastic *excellence*.

excellent *adjective* ✦ **fine, great, outstanding, splendid, superb, superior** This is an *excellent* day for a picnic.

except *preposition* ✦ **besides, but, excluding, other than** Dominique likes all vegetables *except* spinach and broccoli.

exceptional *adjective* ✦ **extraordinary, remarkable, uncommon, unusual** ✧ **rare** When it snowed in July, everyone commented on the *exceptional* weather.

excess *noun* ✦ **oversupply, surplus** We gave our neighbors the *excess* from our vegetable garden. —*adjective* ✦ **excessive, extra, surplus** ✧ **spare** Dad trimmed the *excess* fat off the steaks before he cooked them.

✦   best choices
✧   other choices

excessive *adjective* ✦ **extravagant, extreme, undue, unreasonable** ◇ **lavish, profuse** Mom thinks twelve hours a week is an *excessive* amount of television.

exchange *verb* ✦ **swap, switch, trade** ◇ **barter, change, substitute** Meg and I like to *exchange* comic books once we've read them. —*noun* ✦ **barter, swap, switch, trade** ◇ **substitution** My baseball bat for Troy's hockey stick seemed like a fair *exchange*.

excite *verb* ✦ **arouse, rouse, stimulate, stir, thrill** ◇ **agitate, provoke** The home run *excited* the team's fans.

exciting *adjective* ✦ **dramatic, rousing, stirring, thrilling** ◇ **sensational** It was an *exciting* moment when Neil Armstrong set foot on the moon.

> **Antonyms**
>
> **exciting** *adjective*
>
> boring, dreary, dull, monotonous, routine, tedious

exclaim *verb* ✦ **call, cry, shout, yell** ◇ **bellow, roar, scream** "Watch out!" I *exclaimed* as the bookshelf started to tip over.

exclude *verb* ✦ **ban, bar, keep out** ◇ **forbid, omit, prohibit** The rule *excludes* bigger children from the kiddie pool.

excursion *noun* ✦ **jaunt, outing, trip** ◇ **journey, tour** Next weekend we're taking an *excursion* to the beach.

excuse *verb* 1. ✦ **disregard, forgive, overlook, pardon** Please *excuse* my messy room. 2. ✦ **exempt, let off, release** ◇ **dismiss, relieve, spare** I was *excused* from school because I had a doctor's appointment. —*noun* ✦ **explanation, reason** ◇ **alibi, story** The teacher accepted my *excuse* for being tardy.

execute *verb* 1. ✦ **accomplish, carry out, perform** ◇ **achieve, do** The goalie *executed* a difficult save. 2. ✦ **put to death** ◇ **kill, murder, slay** The traitor was *executed* by a firing squad.

executive *noun* ✦ **administrator, director, manager, officer, official** The company's top *executives* meet once a week. —*adjective* ✦ **directorial, managerial, supervisory** My dad has an *executive* position at the local bank.

exempt *verb* ✦ **excuse, free, release, relieve** ◇ **dismiss** The government *exempts* most charities from the requirement to pay taxes.

exercise *noun* 1. ✦ **application, employment, use** ◇ **operation** The best way to stay on a diet is through the *exercise* of self-control. 2. ✦ **activity, workout** ◇ **drill, practice, training** Bicycling and swimming are excellent forms of physical *exercise*. —*verb* 1. ✦ **apply, employ, use, utilize** Always *exercise* caution when you cross a street. 2. ✦ **work out** ◇ **drill, practice, train** Mom *exercises* by jogging three miles every other day.

exert *verb* ✦ **apply, employ, exercise, use, utilize** Dad had to *exert* a lot of willpower in order to quit smoking.

exhaust *verb* 1. ✦ **consume, finish, use up** ◇ **drain, spend** The campers quickly *exhausted* their supply of firewood. 2. ✦ **fatigue, tire, wear out, weary** ◇ **weaken** The long, hard workout *exhausted* me.

exhaustion *noun* ✦ **fatigue, tiredness, weariness** ◇ **weakness** We were in a state of total *exhaustion* by the end of the game.

exhibit *verb* ✦ **display, present, show** ◇ **demonstrate, reveal** Arnold *exhibited* his rabbits at the county fair. —*noun* ✦ **display, exhibition, show** ◇ **presentation** Megan's watercolors were put on *exhibit* in the school lobby.

exhilarate *verb* ✦ **energize, invigorate, stimulate, vitalize** ◇ **elate, excite** The cold winter air *exhilarated* the skiers.

exile *noun* ✦ **banishment, expulsion** ◇ **deportation, removal** The rebel leader was punished by permanent *exile* from his homeland. —*verb* ✦ **banish, expel** ◇ **deport, oust, remove** The fallen dictator was *exiled* to a distant country.

exist *verb* ✦ **live, survive** ◇ **continue, dwell, last** A fish cannot *exist* out of water.

existence *noun* **1.** ✦ **life, survival** ◇ **being, living** Pollution can threaten the *existence* of certain animals. **2.** ✦ **actuality, fact, occurrence, reality** ◇ **presence** Some people believe in the *existence* of ghosts.

exit *noun* **1.** ✦ **outlet, way out** ◇ **door, opening, passage** Try to sit near the window on the train that serves as an emergency *exit*. **2.** ✦ **departure, escape, retreat** ◇ **withdrawal** When a skunk came in the front door, everyone made a hasty *exit* out the back door. —*verb* ✦ **depart, go out, leave** ◇ **retreat, withdraw** A flight attendant told the passengers to *exit* at the rear of the plane.

expand *noun* ✦ **enlarge, grow, increase, swell** ◇ **extend** A balloon *expands* when you blow air into it.

expect *verb* ✦ **anticipate, count on, depend on** ◇ **assume, await, presume** The weather forecaster said that we could *expect* rain. ▼

expedition *noun* **1.** ✦ **journey, trip** ◇ **safari, voyage** Angela dreams of going on a scientific *expedition* to the jungles of the Amazon basin. **2.** ✦ **group, party, team** ◇ **band, company, troop** The members of Coronado's *expedition* were the first Europeans to see the Grand Canyon.

expel *noun* ✦ **eject, throw out** ◇ **banish, discharge, dismiss** The principal *expelled* the student who was caught selling illegal drugs on the high school campus.

expense *noun* ✦ **cost, price** ◇ **amount, charge, payment** Dad said that we can't afford the *expense* of a new car.

expensive *adjective* ✦ **costly, high-priced** ◇ **rich, valuable** My friend likes *expensive* clothes, but I prefer blue jeans and T-shirts.

experience *noun* **1.** ✦ **adventure, event, incident, occasion** ◇ **affair, ordeal** Rafting down the river was an *experience* I'll never forget. **2.** ✦ **background, practice, training** ◇ **knowledge, skill** My father has a lot of *experience* as a carpenter. —*verb* ✦ **encounter, have, meet, undergo** ◇ **know, see** Did you *experience* any difficulty in finding your way here?

experiment *noun* ✦ **test, trial** ◇ **demonstration, research** Our class did an *experiment* to find out which is heavier, oil or water. —*verb* ✦ **test, try, try out** ◇ **analyze, examine, investigate** I'm *experimenting with* different recipes to see which makes the best fruit pancakes.

experimental *adjective* ✦ **test, trial** ◇ **beginning, early, initial** It's a dangerous job to fly *experimental* aircraft.

expert *noun* ✦ **authority** ◇ **master, professional, specialist** That archaeologist is an *expert* on prehistoric stone tools. —*adjective* ✦ **adept, proficient, skilled, skillful** ◇ **experienced, knowledgeable** This fine gold watch was made by an *expert* craftsperson.

✦ **best choices**
◇ **other choices**

expire *verb* **1.** ✦ **cease, end, finish, lapse, stop** My magazine subscription will *expire* in two months. **2.** ✦ **die, perish, succumb** ✧ **depart, pass away** The wounded soldier *expired* before help could arrive.

explain *verb* **1.** ✦ **clarify, define, describe** ✧ **demonstrate, interpret** Our teacher *explained* the difference between a frog and a toad. **2.** ✦ **account for, justify** ✧ **excuse** Can you *explain* why you are so late?

explode *verb* ✦ **blow up, burst, go off** ✧ **blast, discharge, erupt** The firecracker *exploded* with a loud bang.

exploit *noun* ✦ **act, adventure, deed, feat** ✧ **achievement, stunt** Davy Crockett's *exploits* have been written about in many books. —*verb* ✦ **control, manipulate, take advantage of, use** ✧ **abuse, misuse** The politician *exploited* the media in order to get as much favorable press coverage as possible.

explore *verb* **1.** ✧ **discover, scout, search, survey, travel, wander** Sir Henry Stanley *explored* much of central Africa in the late 1800's. **2.** ✦ **examine, investigate, look into, research** My Boy Scout troop is *exploring* ways to raise some money.

explosion *noun* **1.** ✦ **blast, detonation, discharge** ✧ **bang, burst** When workers dynamited the old building, the *explosion* could be heard for miles. **2.** ✦ **eruption, outbreak, outburst** ✧ **boom, spurt** There's been an *explosion* of interest in the Internet in recent years.

expose *verb* **1.** ✦ **subject** ✧ **bare, open, uncover** The campers were *exposed* to the rain when their tent blew down. **2.** ✦ **disclose, reveal, show**

Antonyms
expose *verb*
2. cloak, conceal, cover, disguise, hide, mask, obscure

✧ **display, exhibit** A reporter *exposed* the politician's lies.

express *verb* ✦ **declare, indicate, state, voice** ✧ **reveal, show, speak** Everybody *expressed* a preference for pizza. —*adjective* **1.** ✦ **definite, distinct, particular, special, specific** This room was built for the *express* purpose of storing historical documents. **2.** ✦ **fast, quick, rapid, speedy** ✧ **direct** If you want to get there quickly, take the *express* train.

expression *noun* **1.** ✦ **gesture, indication, sign, token** ✧ **declaration, statement** On Valentine's Day, it is customary to give either flowers or candy as an *expression* of love. **2.** ✦ **look** ✧ **air, appearance, aspect** I knew by the *expression* on Kelly's face that she was in a good mood. **3.** ✦ **phrase, saying** ✧ **motto, proverb, term** "Break a leg" is a common *expression* for wishing an actor good luck.

exquisite *adjective* ✦ **beautiful, delicate, elegant, fine, lovely** That silver necklace in the store window is *exquisite*.

extend *verb* **1.** ✦ **expand, lengthen, open, stretch out** ✧ **grow, increase** This ladder can be *extended* to a length of twelve feet. **2.** ✦ **reach, stretch** ✧ **carry, go, run, spread** The ocean *extends* much farther than the eye can see. **3.** ✦ **give, offer, present (with)** ✧ **grant, submit** I *extended* them an invitation to my party.

extensive *adjective* ✦ **considerable, great, wide, widespread** ✧ **broad, huge, vast** The earthquake caused *extensive* damage.

exterior *adjective* ✦ **external, outer, outside** ✧ **outdoor** Many castles have *exterior* walls that are separate from the central stronghold. —*noun* ✦ **outside** ✧ **cover, face, surface** The *exterior* of our building is brick.

exterminate *verb* ✦ **annihilate, destroy, eliminate, kill** ✧ **extinguish** We had to *exterminate* the termites that were damaging our house.

external *adjective* ✦ **exterior, outer, outside, surface** All insects have six legs and an *external* skeleton.

extinct *adjective* ✦ **vanished** ◇ **dead, deceased, gone, nonexistent** The museum has lots of fossils of *extinct* animals and plants.

extinguish *verb* **1.** ✦ **douse, put out, quench, smother** We used both water and dirt to *extinguish* our campfire. **2.** ✦ **destroy, eliminate, end, erase, wipe out** ◇ **abolish, suppress** Last night's defeat *extinguished* our hopes of winning the championship.

extra *adjective* ✦ **additional, spare, surplus** ◇ **more, new, other** Dad keeps a flashlight and *extra* batteries in his car. —*adverb* ✦ **especially, very** ◇ **greatly, highly, most** We made the chili with *extra* lean ground beef. —*noun* ✦ **accessory, attachment** ◇ **addition, bonus, supplement** Our new car came with many *extras*, including a sunroof and a CD player.

extract *verb* ✦ **draw out, pull, remove, take out, withdraw** ◇ **pluck** I used a pair of tweezers to *extract* the splinter from my hand. —*noun*

✦ **concentrate, essence** ◇ **juice, oil** A few drops of vanilla *extract* can flavor a whole batch of cookie dough.

extraordinary *adjective* ✦ **exceptional, great, outstanding, remarkable, unusual** ◇ **amazing, rare** Hercules was a mythological hero known for his *extraordinary* strength.

extravagant *adjective* ✦ **excessive, indulgent, lavish, wasteful** ◇ **costly, extreme** Buying ten pairs of shoes at a time would definitely be *extravagant*.

extreme *adjective* **1.** ✦ **great, intense, tremendous, unusual** ◇ **excessive, extravagant** California's Death Valley is known for its *extreme* heat. **2.** ✦ **far, farthest, outermost, remotest** ◇ **final, last** Pluto is located at the *extreme* edge of our solar system.

eye *verb* ✦ **observe, regard, watch** ◇ **stare, survey, view** The mouse didn't know that it was being *eyed* by a cat.

eyesight *noun* ✦ **sight, vision** ◇ **seeing** I wear contact lenses to correct my *eyesight*.

✦ **best choices**
◇ **other choices**

F

fable *noun* ✦ **legend, story, tale** ✧ **myth, yarn** The *fable* about the boy who cried wolf teaches the importance of telling the truth.

fabric *noun* ✦ **cloth, material** ✧ **textile** I sewed together squares of *fabric* to make a quilt.

fabulous *adjective* ✦ **amazing, astonishing, fantastic, incredible, unbelievable** The old prospector told *fabulous* tales about the riches that he had discovered.

face *noun* **1.** ✦ **countenance, expression, look** ✧ **appearance** I could tell by Kathleen's *face* that she was not happy. **2.** ✦ **front, surface** ✧ **exterior** The climbers went straight up the cliff's *face*. —*verb* **1.** ✦ **look, point** ✧ **front, overlook** Traditional Navajo homes *face* east to receive blessings from the rising sun. **2.** ✦ **brave, challenge, confront, encounter, meet** Police officers sometimes have to *face* danger in the line of duty.

facility *noun* **1.** ✦ **ease, effortlessness, fluency** Sean ice-skates with great *facility*. **2.** ✦ **equipment** ✧ **convenience, resource** Our apartment building has laundry *facilities* in the basement. ◄

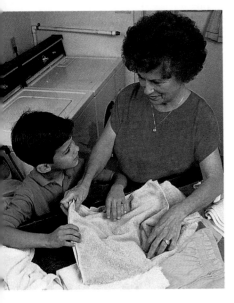

fact *noun* **1.** ✦ **data, information** ✧ **detail, particular** Nathan used an encyclopedia to look up *facts* for his science report. **2.** ✦ **actuality, certainty, reality, truth** It is a *fact* that insects have six legs.

factor *noun* ✦ **consideration** ✧ **circumstance, component, detail, ingredient, element, part** Bad weather was the main *factor* in canceling the picnic.

factory *noun* ✦ **plant** ✧ **mill, workshop** In our town there is a *factory* where cars and trucks are made.

factual *adjective* ✦ **accurate, correct, real, true, valid** The book gave a *factual* account of President Kennedy's life.

fad *noun* ✦ **craze, fashion, trend** ✧ **rage, style** Breakdancing was a popular *fad* in the 1980's.

fade *verb* **1.** ✦ **dim, dull, pale** ✧ **age, wither** Sunlight caused our curtains to *fade*. **2.** ✦ **decline, die away, diminish, lessen, wane** When the thunder began to *fade away*, we knew that the storm was almost over.

fail *verb* **1.** ✦ **fall short, miss** ✧ **lose** The pole vaulter *failed* on his first attempt to clear the bar. **2.** ✦ **neglect, omit** ✧ **avoid, ignore** My grandmother never *fails* to notice how much I've grown. **3.** ✦ **decline, diminish, dwindle, wane, weaken** My dog is getting old, and his hearing is beginning to *fail*.

failure *noun* **1.** ✧ **breakdown, defeat, lack of success, miss** Denise's *failure* to win the race did not discourage her. **2.** ✦ **dud, flop, loss** ✧ **disappointment, mess, ruin** My first cake was a *failure*, but my second was a success.

faint *adjective* **1.** ✦ **dim, feeble, indistinct, low, soft, weak** The flashlight's *faint* beam told Cara that the batteries were almost dead. **2.** ✦ **dizzy, giddy, lightheaded** Brett felt *faint* after climbing ten flights of stairs. —*verb* ✦ **black out, pass out, swoon** ✧ **collapse, keel over** The man *fainted* when he heard that he had won three million dollars.

fair *adjective* **1.** ✦ **attractive, beautiful, lovely, pretty** ✧ **charming** Welcome to our *fair* city. **2.** ✦ **light, pale** ✧ **blonde, white** Erin sunburns easily because she has a very *fair* complexion. **3.** ✦ **bright, clear, cloudless, fine, sunny**

◇ **favorable, mild** The forecast is for *fair* weather this weekend. **4.** ✦ **impartial, just, objective, unbiased** ◇ **equitable, indifferent, square** Ms. Gomez is always *fair* when she grades her students. **5.** ✦ **adequate, average, decent, moderate, satisfactory** There's a *fair* chance that Dad will be home early tonight.

faith *noun* **1.** ✦ **confidence, trust** ◇ **dependence, reliance** Our coach told the team that she has *faith* in us. **2.** ✦ **belief, creed, religion** ◇ **doctrine** In the United States, people of all *faiths* are allowed to worship freely.

faithful *adjective* ✦ **devoted, loyal, staunch, steadfast, true** ◇ **constant, resolute** My dog is my *faithful* companion.

fake *verb* ✦ **imitate, feign, simulate** ◇ **counterfeit, pretend** Katie sometimes *fakes* a foreign accent to amuse her friends. —*noun* ✦ **counterfeit, imitation, forgery** ◇ **fraud, phony** Only an expert can tell that this diamond is a *fake*. —*adjective* ✦ **counterfeit, false, imitation, phony** My coat is lined with *fake* fur.

fall *verb* **1.** ✦ **drop, pitch, plunge, topple, tumble** I bumped into the lamp, and it *fell* to the floor. **2.** ✦ **surrender** ◇ **submit, succumb, yield** Rome *fell* to barbarians in the year 476 A.D. **3.** ✦ **decrease, diminish, lower** ◇ **ebb, lessen, reduce** John's voice *fell* to a whisper when he told me his secret. **4.** ✦ **arrive, come, happen, occur, take place** My birthday *falls* on a Tuesday this year. —*noun* **1.** ✦ **descent, dive, drop, plunge, spill, tumble** The climber's safety rope stopped her *fall*. **2.** ✦ **descent, tumble** ◇ **plunge** Democracy was restored after the dictator's *fall* from power.

false *adjective* ✦ **inaccurate, incorrect, untrue, wrong** ◇ **mistaken** The dishonest witness gave *false* testimony.

Antonyms
false *adjective*
authentic, correct, genuine, real, right, true

fame *noun* ✦ **celebrity, recognition, renown** ◇ **glory, popularity** Charles Lindbergh won *fame* by being the first person to fly solo across the Atlantic Ocean.

familiar *adjective* **1.** ✦ **common, everyday, frequent, regular, routine, well-known** Swings and jungle gyms are *familiar* sights at playgrounds. **2.** ✦ **acquainted, aware (of), knowledgeable (about)** ◇ **informed** Are you *familiar* with the song "Happy Birthday to You"? **3.** ✦ **close, friendly, sociable** ◇ **intimate** I am on *familiar* terms with most of the other students in my grade.

family *noun* **1.** ✦ **household, kin, relations, relatives** On Rosh Hashanah, Benjamin's *family* goes to temple together. **2.** ✦ **class, division, group, order** The violin and cello are part of the *family* of stringed instruments.

famine *noun* ✦ **food shortage** ◇ **hunger, starvation** The United Nations sent food to the country that was experiencing a *famine*.

famous *adjective* ✦ **celebrated, prominent, renowned, well-known** ◇ **popular** Abraham Lincoln was one of the most *famous* U.S. Presidents.

fan *noun* ✦ **admirer, devotee, enthusiast** ◇ **follower, lover** *Fans* mobbed the rock star in an attempt to get his autograph.

fancy *noun* **1.** ✦ **idea, impulse, notion, thought, whim** I had a sudden *fancy* to go for a walk in the rain. **2.** ✦ **fondness, liking** ◇ **desire, longing, want** Melissa had a *fancy* for the baby rabbit from the moment she saw it. —*adjective* ✦ **decorative, elaborate, elegant, extravagant, intricate** Mom bought some *fancy* stationery for writing thank-you notes.

fantastic *adjective* **1.** ✦ **bizarre, odd, strange, unbelievable, weird** Terry told me a *fantastic* story about her next-door neighbor being a Martian. **2.** ✦ **marvelous, remarkable, superb, terrific, wonderful** Ethan has more than 10,000 baseball cards in his *fantastic* collection.

✦   best choices
◇   other choices

fantasy *noun* ✦ **daydream, dream, vision** ✧ **fancy, imagination** I have a *fantasy* in which I am the first astronaut to travel to Jupiter.

far *adverb* ✦ **considerably, much, significantly** ✧ **greatly** The book was *far* more interesting than I expected. —*adjective* ✦ **distant, faraway, remote** ✧ **long, removed** Dinosaurs lived in the *far* past.

fare *noun* ✦ **charge, cost, fee, price, toll** ✧ **cost, price** I paid the *fare* as soon as I boarded the bus. —*verb* ✦ **do, get along, manage** ✧ **progress, prosper, thrive** Marnie says that she is *faring* well at her new job.

farm *noun* ✧ **field, garden, homestead, plantation, ranch, spread** My uncle grows corn and soybeans on his *farm*. —*verb* ✦ **cultivate, grow, harvest, plant, till** People first began to *farm* crops more than ten thousand years ago.

fascinate *verb* ✦ **captivate, enthrall, entrance, intrigue** ✧ **charm, enchant** The astronaut *fascinated* us with tales of his adventures in outer space.

fashion *noun* 1. ✦ **manner, method, style, way** ✧ **system** Hold the chopsticks in this *fashion*. 2. ✦ **craze, custom, fad, style, trend** At my school, the current *fashion* is to wear your baseball cap backwards. —*verb* ✦ **build, construct, fabricate, form, make, shape** Joyce used paper-mâché to *fashion* a two-foot-tall giraffe.

fast *adjective* 1. ✦ **fleet, quick, rapid, speedy, swift** The cheetah is the *fastest* animal on land. 2. ✦ **firm, fixed, secure, strong, tight** Whenever I go on a carnival ride, I keep a *fast* grip on the safety bar. ▶ 3. ✦ **faithful, loyal, steadfast, true** ✧ **steady** Alicia and Erica have been *fast* friends ever since they met in kindergarten. —*adverb* 1. ✦ **quickly, rapidly, speedily, swiftly** I like to walk *fast*. 2. ✦ **firmly, hard, securely, soundly, tightly** The gum was stuck *fast* to the bottom of my shoe.

fasten *noun* ✦ **attach, connect, fix, secure** ✧ **bind, tie** Make sure the shelf is tightly *fastened* to the wall.

fat *noun* ✦ **grease, oil** ✧ **lard, tallow** French fries contain a lot of *fat*. —*adjective* ✦ **heavy, obese, overweight, plump, stout** Dad started exercising because he thought that he was getting *fat*.

fatal *adjective* ✦ **deadly, lethal, mortal, terminal** Black widow spider bites are almost never *fatal* to humans.

fate *noun* ✦ **destiny, fortune, luck** Mom says that *fate* smiled on her the day she met Dad.

fatigue *noun* ✦ **exhaustion, tiredness, weakness, weariness** Byron's *fatigue* was caused by lack of sleep. —*verb* ✦ **drain, exhaust, tire, wear (out), weary** The long walk across town *fatigued* me.

fault *noun* 1. ✦ **responsibility** ✧ **blame, guilt, offense** It's my *fault* that the dishes aren't done yet. 2. ✦ **defect, flaw, imperfection, shortcoming** ✧ **error, mistake** My computer is not working right because there's a *fault* in its programming.

favor *noun* **1.** ✦ **courtesy, good deed, kindness, service** My brother did me a *favor* by helping me study for my history test. **2.** ✦ **acceptance, admiration, approval, liking, support** The politician worked hard to win the voters' *favor*. —*verb* **1.** ✦ **accommodate, gratify, indulge, oblige, reward** The pianist *favored* her audience with two encores. **2.** ✦ **like, prefer, support** ✧ **approve, encourage** Which of the two proposals do you *favor*?

favorable *adjective* ✦ **advantageous, appropriate, good** ✧ **beneficial, helpful** The weather conditions today are *favorable* for skiing.

favorite *noun* ✦ **first choice, ideal, love, pick, preference** Licorice-flavored jelly beans are my *favorites*. —*adjective* ✦ **dearest, favored, preferred, special** Deborah's *favorite* book is *The Wind in the Willows*.

fear *noun* ✦ **anxiety, dread, fright, panic, terror** I experienced a brief moment of *fear* when the lights went out. —*verb* ✦ **be afraid of, be scared of, dread** My daredevil friend seemingly *feared* nothing.

fearless *adjective* ✦ **bold, brave, courageous, gallant, heroic, valiant** The *fearless* mouse plucked a thorn from the lion's paw.

feast *noun* ✦ **banquet** ✧ **dinner, meal** Shantay's family enjoys a special *feast* to celebrate Kwanzaa. —*verb* ✦ **banquet, dine, feed** ✧ **devour, eat** We *feast* on roast turkey every Thanksgiving.

feat *noun* ✦ **act, deed, exploit, stunt** ✧ **achievement** The magician performed a truly remarkable *feat* when he pulled an elephant out of his hat.

feature *noun* ✦ **attribute, characteristic, quality, trait** Many *features* of the house reminded me of the last place we lived. —*verb* ✦ **emphasize, highlight, promote** ✧ **star, stress** The concert will *feature* folk songs from around the world.

fee *noun* ✦ **charge, toll** ✧ **cost, payment, price** Dad had to pay a *fee* to park our car at the fairground.

feeble *adjective* ✦ **dim, faint, weak** ✧ **fragile, frail** The room was completely dark except for the *feeble* light of a single candle.

feed *verb* **1.** ✦ **nourish** ✧ **maintain, satisfy, sustain** This lasagna is big enough to *feed* ten people. **2.** ✦ **consume, devour, eat** ✧ **live, subsist** Polar bears *feed on* seals and fish. —*noun* ✦ **fodder, food, forage, provisions** The farmer used some of his corn crop as *feed* for his cattle.

feel *verb* **1.** ✦ **handle, touch** ✧ **rub, stroke** The doctor *felt* my arm to see if it was broken. **2.** ✦ **detect, notice, perceive, sense** I *feel* a headache coming on. **3.** ✦ **believe, hold, think** ✧ **consider, know** I *feel* that my parents are usually fair. —*noun* ✦ **feeling, touch** ✧ **sensation** Kayla loves the *feel* of her hamster's fur.

feeling *noun* **1.** ✦ **awareness, perception, sensation** ✧ **feel, touch** I had no *feeling* in my foot when it went to sleep. **2.** ✦ **sense** ✧ **emotion, mood, sentiment** Eric had a *feeling* of pride when his article was printed in the school paper. **3.** ✦ **belief, idea, notion** ✧ **opinion, thought** I have a *feeling* that it's going to rain today.

fell *verb* ✦ **chop down, cut down, drop, hew, level** Maria helped her father *fell* the dead tree in the backyard.

fence *noun* ✦ **barrier** ✧ **wall** Our landlord installed a *fence* between our house and the neighbor's driveway.

ferocious *adjective* ✦ **brutal, cruel, fierce, savage, vicious** ✧ **wild** Judging by their teeth and claws, velociraptors must have been *ferocious* dinosaurs.

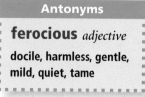

Antonyms

ferocious *adjective*
docile, harmless, gentle, mild, quiet, tame

✦ **best choices**
✧ **other choices**

fertile *adjective* ✦ fruitful, productive, rich ✧ bountiful The farmland in Illinois is very *fertile*.

festival *noun* ✦ celebration, jubilee ✧ holiday, ritual Our youth center sponsored a *festival* where we tasted foods from all over the world. ▶

fetch *verb* ✦ go for, go get, retrieve ✧ bring, carry When Jamie plays with her dog, she throws a stick for him to *fetch*.

feud *noun* ✦ disagreement, dispute, fight, quarrel ✧ conflict The cousins didn't speak to each other because of a family *feud*.

few *adjective* ✧ limited, occasional, rare, scant, scarce I felt a few drops, but it didn't really rain.

fib *noun* ✦ falsehood, lie, untruth ✧ fiction, story, tale I told a *fib* when I said that I knew a famous rock star. —*verb* ✦ falsify, lie about ✧ exaggerate, misrepresent I don't think people should *fib* about their age in order to get into the movie theater.

fiction *noun* ✦ concoction, fantasy, invention ✧ fable, story, tale I couldn't tell if Brent's story was fact or *fiction*.

field *noun* 1. ✦ clearing ✧ ground, meadow, pasture, plot, tract I like to play in the vacant *field* beside my house. 2. ✦ athletic field ✧ arena, court, stadium, track Our football coach made us sprint up and down the *field*. 3. ✦ area, domain, realm, subject ✧ occupation, profession Dr. Seuss was a leading author in the *field* of children's literature.

fierce *adjective* 1. ✦ dangerous, ferocious, savage, vicious ✧ wild Mother bears can be very *fierce* when their cubs are threatened. 2. ✦ extreme, high, powerful, strong, violent Antarctica's *fierce* winds have been clocked at more than two hundred miles per hour.

fight *noun* 1. ✦ scrap, scuffle, struggle ✧ battle, combat My cat and the neighborhood

Foods of the World Festival

stray got into a *fight* last night. 2. ✦ disagreement, dispute, quarrel, squabble ✧ feud My sister and I had a *fight* over whose turn it was to use the computer. —*verb* 1. ✦ battle, combat, contend, oppose, struggle Americans *fought* against each other in the Civil War. 2. ✦ argue, bicker, dispute, quarrel, squabble Let's not *fight* over what television show we watch.

figure *noun* 1. ✦ digit, number, numeral Antonio can add up a long list of *figures* in his head. 2. ✦ design, pattern ✧ drawing, illustration The cover of my math book is decorated with geometric *figures*. 3. ✦ form, shape, silhouette ✧ contour, outline I could see two *figures* walking in the distance. 4. ✦ dignitary, leader, notable, personality ✧ character, person The Secretary-General of the United Nations is an important world *figure*. —*verb* ✦ calculate, compute, reckon ✧ estimate, solve I helped Mom *figure out* how much we should tip the waiter.

file *noun* 1. ✦ document, record ✧ data, information Doctors keep medical *files* on all of their patients. 2. ✦ column, line, row, string I saw a long *file* of ants heading toward our picnic basket. —*verb* 1. ✦ arrange, classify, organize, sort ✧ deposit, rank, store Catalog cards are *filed* in alphabetical order. 2. ✦ enter, register,

submit (to) ✧ **apply, seek** After Dad was in a car accident, he *filed* a claim with his insurance company. **3.** ✦ **march, parade, troop, walk** During fire drills, we have to *file* out of the building in an orderly manner.

fill *verb* **1.** ✦ **jam, load, pack, stock, stuff** Jacob *filled* his suitcase with clothes and books. ▼ **2.** ✦ **occupy** ✧ **act, function, perform, serve** Faisal volunteered to *fill* the office of student-council chair until someone could be elected. **3.** ✦ **plug, seal, stop up** ✧ **block, close** The dentist *filled* my cavity. **4.** ✦ **fulfill, supply** ✧ **furnish, meet, provide** The clerk said that it would take fifteen minutes to *fill* our order.

filter *noun* ✧ **screen, sieve, strainer** Dad installed a *filter* to purify our drinking water. —*verb* **1.** ✦ **clear, cleanse, purify, screen, strain** When firefighters enter smoke-filled buildings, they wear masks to *filter* their air. **2.** ✦ **flow, seep** ✧ **drain, leak, ooze, trickle** Sunlight *filtered* down through the leaves and branches.

filthy *adjective* ✦ **dirty, grimy, grubby, muddy, soiled** ✧ **messy, unkempt** My friends and I were *filthy* after we played field hockey on the muddy field.

final *adjective* **1.** ✦ **closing, concluding, last** ✧ **ending, finishing** I missed the *final* part of the movie because I fell asleep. **2.** ✦ **conclusive, deci-** sive, definite ✧ **authoritative** Decisions made by referees or umpires are *final*.

finale *noun* ✦ **climax, close, conclusion, finish** ✧ **end** The concert's grand *finale* included stirring music and lots of fireworks.

find *verb* **1.** ✦ **come upon, detect, locate, spot** ✧ **recover, retrieve** Travis *found* a beautiful conch shell at the beach. **2.** ✦ **determine, discover, learn, perceive, see** Have you *found* the answer to my riddle yet?

fine *adjective* **1.** ✦ **little, minute, small, tiny** ✧ **light, thin** You can use a magnifying glass to read the *fine* print in this unabridged dictionary. **2.** ✦ **excellent, good, splendid, superb, superior, terrific** It's a *fine* day for a picnic. —*adverb* ✦ **excellently, nicely, splendidly, well** Christina was getting along *fine* at summer camp until she fell in the poison ivy.

finish *verb* **1.** ✦ **accomplish, complete, conclude, end** ✧ **close** Mitchell *finished* his chores in almost no time at all. **2.** ✦ **consume, exhaust, use up** ✧ **drain, empty** The drive to Springfield *finished* the gas in our tank. —*noun* ✦ **close, completion, conclusion, end, ending** I missed the start of the race, but I saw the *finish*.

Antonyms
finish *verb*
1. arise, begin, commence, launch, start
finish *noun*
beginning, inception, opening, start

fire *noun* **1.** ✧ **blaze, burning, combustion, flame** Smokey the Bear warns us about the dangers of forest *fires*. **2.** ✦ **gunfire, firing, shooting, shots** The soldiers were exposed to enemy *fire*. —*verb* **1.** ✦ **ignite, kindle, light** ✧ **spark** Dad used special matches to *fire* our wood-burning stove. **2.** ✦ **shoot** ✧ **discharge** The gunfighter kept in practice by *firing* at empty bottles. **3.** ✦ **discharge, dismiss, drop, let go, release** Timothy was *fired* because he was always late to work.

✦ **best choices**
✧ **other choices**

firm¹ *adjective* **1.** ✦ **hard, rigid, solid, stiff** ◇ **compact, dense** I like to sleep on a *firm* mattress. **2.** ✦ **certain, definite, steadfast, steady, unwavering** Bethany is *firm* in her beliefs. **3.** ✦ **fast, secure, steady, strong, sure, tight** Keep a *firm* grip on the rope.

firm² *noun* ✦ **business, company, corporation, enterprise, establishment** More than a dozen lawyers work for that *firm*.

first *noun* ✦ **beginning, outset, start** ◇ **origin** The night was dark at *first*, but then the moon came out. —*adjective* ✦ **earliest, initial, original** Amelia Earhart was the *first* woman to fly across the Atlantic Ocean. —*adverb* ✦ **initially, originally** ◇ **firstly** When did you *first* learn to walk?

fit *verb* **1.** ✦ **conform to, correspond to, match, suit** ◇ **agree** Your clothes *fit* the occasion perfectly. **2.** ✦ **equip, furnish, outfit** ◇ **provide, supply** We're having our living room *fitted* with new drapes. —*adjective* **1.** ✦ **appropriate, correct, proper, right, suitable** At the end of a party, it is *fit* to thank the host or hostess. **2.** ✦ **healthy, robust, strong, well** ◇ **hale, sound** I exercise regularly to stay *fit*.

fix *verb* **1.** ✦ **anchor, install, secure** ◇ **attach, fasten** The fence posts are *fixed* in concrete. **2.** ✦ **arrange, conclude, determine, establish, settle** Before we left the dentist's office, Mom *fixed* a time for my next appointment. **3.** ✦ **mend, repair** ◇ **correct, patch, remedy** Dad *fixed* our toaster. —*noun* ✦ **jam, plight, predicament** ◇ **difficulty, trouble** I was in a *fix* when I couldn't find my homework.

flag *noun* ✦ **banner, ensign, pennant, standard** A pirate's *flag* usually has a white skull and crossbones on a black background. —*verb* ✦ **hail, signal** ◇ **gesture, motion, wave** When we ran out of gas, Dad *flagged* a passing car for assistance.

flame *noun* ✦ **blaze, fire** ◇ **glow, light** Moths are attracted to a candle's *flame*.

flap *verb* ✦ **flutter, wave** ◇ **beat, fly, swing** The *flag* was flapping in the wind.

flash *verb* **1.** ✦ **blaze, flame, flare, gleam** ◇ **glimmer, shimmer** We hurried home as lightning *flashed* on the horizon. **2.** ✦ **dash, fly, hurry, race, rush, speed** ◇ **hasten** Race cars *flashed* by the grandstand. —*noun* **1.** ✦ **blaze, burst, flare, gleam** ◇ **glimmer, shimmer** The fireworks exploded with colorful *flashes* and a lot of noise. **2.** ✦ **jiffy, instant, moment, second** Don't worry, I'll be back in a *flash*.

flat *adjective* **1.** ✦ **even, smooth** ◇ **horizontal, level** Dad sanded the tabletop until it was perfectly *flat*. **2.** ✦ **fixed, set, uniform** ◇ **constant, firm** The restaurant charges a *flat* rate for delivery, regardless of how much food is ordered. **3.** ✦ **bland, flavorless, tasteless** ◇ **dull, stale** If you think that the soup seems *flat*, add a little salt.

> | **Antonyms** |
> |---|
> | **flat** *adjective* |
> | 1. coarse, craggy, jagged, rugged, uneven 3. delicious, flavorful, luscious, savory, tasty, toothsome |

flatter *verb* ✦ **compliment, praise** ◇ **charm, gratify, please** Do you really think that I look like a movie star, or are you just *flattering* me?

flavor *noun* ✦ **tang, taste** ◇ **relish, savor, zest** What did you put in the salad dressing to give it such a great *flavor*? —*verb* ✦ **season, spice** When Dad makes chili, he *flavors* it with pepper and barbecue sauce.

flaw *noun* ✦ **blemish, defect, fault, imperfection** ◇ **shortcoming** This sweater is inexpensive because it has a *flaw*.

flee *noun* ✦ **leave, run away, take off** ◇ **depart** The mice *fled* when they saw a cat enter the room.

fleet *adjective* ✦ **fast, quick, rapid, speedy, swift** Pony-express riders were so *fleet* that they could carry mail from Missouri to California in under ten days.

flexible   *adjective*   **1.** ✦ **bendable, pliable** ✧ **elastic, springy**   My fishing pole is made of *flexible* plastic.   **2.** ✦ **adaptable, adjustable, changeable, variable**   Mom's job has *flexible* hours, so she's able to be with us when we need her.

flicker   *verb* ✦ **blink, flash, glimmer, twinkle, wink** ✧ **flutter**   Hundreds of lightning bugs *flickered* in the dark.   —*noun* ✦ **flare, flash, glimmer** ✧ **ray, spark**   There was a *flicker* of lightning in the stormy sky.

flight   *noun*   **1.** ✦ **flying** ✧ **gliding, soaring**   Ostriches, emus, and a few other birds are incapable of *flight*.   **2.** ✦ **formation, squadron, wing** ✧ **flock, swarm**   We watched in awe as a *flight* of jets passed overhead.

flimsy   *adjective* ✦ **fragile, frail, thin, weak** ✧ **feeble**   Tissue paper is too *flimsy* for making paper airplanes.

flinch   *verb* ✦ **cringe, draw back, recoil, shrink back** ✧ **cower, wince**   Patrick *flinched* as a snowball went whizzing past his head.

fling   *verb* ✦ **heave, hurl, pitch, throw, toss**   The angry toddler *flung* his toy across the room.   —*noun* ✦ **cast, heave, pitch, throw, toss**   When I played horseshoes with Grandpa, he got a ringer on his first *fling*.

float   *verb* ✦ **drift, glide, sail, skim**   Devin's model boat *floated* all the way across the pond.

flock   *noun* ✦ **herd** ✧ **crowd, group, pack, swarm, throng**   A shepherd watches over a *flock* of sheep. ▶ —*verb* ✦ **collect, crowd, gather, press, swarm, throng**   The young campers *flocked* around their counselor.

flood   *noun* ✦ **deluge, overflow, torrent** ✧ **stream, tide**   This room has so many windows that on sunny days it is filled with a *flood* of light.   —*verb* ✦ **cover, deluge, drown, fill, overflow,**

submerge   After the great storm, water *flooded* all of the valley's low-lying farmland.

floor   *noun*   **1.** ✦ **bottom** ✧ **base, bed, ground**   Stalagmites form on cave *floors*.   **2.** ✦ **level, story** ✧ **deck, tier**   My classroom is on the second *floor* of our school building.   —*verb* ✦ **drop, fell, flatten, knock down, level**   The boxer *floored* his opponent with a single punch.

flow   *verb* ✦ **gush, pour, run, spill, stream**   The river *flows* rapidly after a heavy rain.   —*noun* ✦ **current, river, stream, tide**   There was a steady *flow* of traffic on the busy highway.

flower   *noun* ✦ **bloom, blossom** ✧ **bud**   Dad gave Mom a bouquet of *flowers* last Valentine's Day.   —*verb* ✦ **bloom, blossom** ✧ **bud**   Cherry trees *flower* in the springtime.

fluid   *noun* ✦ **liquid**   When I was sick, the doctor told me to drink a lot of *fluids*.   —*adjective* ✦ **liquid, runny, watery** ✧ **flowing**   Freshly-mixed concrete is *fluid*, but it becomes hard when it sets.

flush   *verb*   **1.** ✦ **blush, color, redden** ✧ **glow**   Charles *flushed* when I told him how nice he looked.   **2.** ✦ **cleanse, drown, flood, rinse out, wash out**   Dad used a garden hose to *flush out* our rain gutters.   —*noun* ✦ **color, glow, rosiness** ✧ **blush, redness**   Ginger's face had a healthy *flush* after basketball practice.

✦   best choices
✧   other choices

fly *verb* **1. ✦ take flight ✧ glide, sail, soar, wing** Pterodactyls were reptiles that could *fly*. **2. ✦ bolt, dash, hasten, hurry, run, rush** My cat *flew* to the kitchen when he heard me opening his can of food.

focus *noun* **✦ center, core, heart, hub, seat** Bridgette enjoyed being the *focus* of attention at her birthday party. **—***verb* **✦ address (to), center, concentrate, devote (to), direct, fix, give (to)** Samantha *focused* her attention on the computer screen.

foe *noun* **✦ adversary, antagonist, enemy, opponent, rival** The two senators were political *foes*.

fog *noun* **✦ haze, mist ✧ cloud, vapor, whiteout** The captain would not set sail until the *fog* lifted. **—***verb* **✦ blur, cloud, mist ✧ blanket, obscure** Steam from the kettle *fogged* our kitchen windows.

foggy *adjective* **1. ✦ hazy, misty, murky ✧ cloudy** The airport had to be closed because the day was so *foggy*. **2. ✦ confused, dim, fuzzy, indistinct, unclear, vague** I have only a *foggy* recollection of my dream.

foil *verb* **✦ check, defeat, frustrate, hinder, thwart** An alert police officer *foiled* the gang's attempt to paint graffiti on the storefront.

fold *verb* **1. ✦ bend, crease, double over ✧ pleat** Danielle *folded* the note and put it into her pocket. **2. ✧ clasp, close, gather, tuck, wrap** The photographer told me to *fold* my arms for the picture. **—***noun* **✦ crease, pleat, wrinkle** I ironed the *folds* out of my new blouse.

follow *verb* **1. ✦ come after, succeed ✧ go after, replace, trail** February *follows* January. **2. ✦ abide by, heed, obey, observe, regard** Our softball game was a success because everybody *followed* the rules. **3. ✦ catch, comprehend, get, grasp, understand** I wasn't able to *follow* what you were saying.

fond *adjective* **✦ affectionate, devoted, loving, warm ✧ close** Keith gave a *fond* greeting to his pet rat.

fool *noun* **✦ dummy, idiot, moron, simpleton** A *fool* and his money are soon parted. **—***verb* **1. ✦ deceive, trick ✧ bluff, mislead** My friend *fooled* me into thinking that today was his birthday. **2. ✦ jest, joke, kid, tease ✧ pretend** I was only *fooling* when I said that I hate ice cream.

foolish *adjective* **✦ dumb, silly, stupid ✧ crazy, senseless, unwise** I felt *foolish* when I put my shirt on backwards.

foot *noun* **✦ base, bottom ✧ foundation** There's a lake near the *foot* of the mountain.

forbid *verb* **✦ ban, bar, disallow, outlaw, prevent, prohibit** The rules *forbid* swimming without a lifeguard.

force *noun* **1. ✦ energy, might, power, strength, vigor** The wind blew with so much *force* that it knocked down our power lines. **2. ✧ body, crew, gang, group, team, unit** The company has a work *force* of about fifty people. **—***verb* **1. ✦ compel, obligate, oblige, require ✧ make** Darkness *forced* us to stop our baseball game. **2. ✦ break, pry ✧ drive, press, push, thrust** The door was stuck, and I had to *force* it open.

forceful *adjective* **✦ dynamic, effective, powerful, strong, vigorous** The governor drew large crowds because he was such a *forceful* speaker.

forecast *verb* ✦ **call for, foretell, predict, project** ✧ **anticipate** The weather bureau is *forecasting* snow for tomorrow. —*noun* ✦ **outlook, projection** ✧ **prediction, prophecy** The economic *forecast* is for lower prices and higher wages.

foreign *adjective* ✦ **alien** ✧ **distant, exotic, faraway, remote** Liam speaks English with a *foreign* accent.

forest *noun* ✦ **woods, woodland** ✧ **grove, thicket, timberland** *Forests* provide food and shelter for many animals.

foretell *verb* ✦ **forecast, foresee, predict, project, tell** Do you believe that some people can *foretell* the future?

forever *adverb* ✦ **always, eternally, perpetually** ✧ **constantly, continuously** I wish summer vacation would last *forever*.

forfeit *verb* ✦ **give up, lose, sacrifice, surrender** ✧ **drop, yield** The customer had to *forfeit* his deposit when he canceled his order.

forge *verb* **1.** ✦ **fashion, form, make, mold, shape** ✧ **create** By practicing regularly, Gary has *forged* himself into a strong badminton player. **2.** ✦ **copy, counterfeit, fake, falsify** The expert discovered that the painting had been *forged*.

forget *verb* ✦ **fail to remember** ✧ **disregard, neglect, overlook** Don't *forget* your card when you go to the library.

forgive *verb* ✦ **excuse, pardon** ✧ **acquit, clear, condone** Please *forgive* me for interrupting you.

form *noun* **1.** ✦ **design, figure, shape** ✧ **outline, pattern** Mother and I made a cake in the *form* of a snowman. **2.** ✦ **kind, sort, type, variety** Television is a popular *form* of entertainment. **3.** ✦ **document, paper, sheet** ✧ **application, questionnaire** The catalog came with a *form* for placing orders. —*verb* **1.** ✦ **create, fashion, make, shape** ✧ **produce** The city council voted to

form a new school district. **2.** ✦ **appear, develop, grow, materialize** Mold has *formed* on this old loaf of bread.

formal *adjective* ✦ **official, proper** ✧ **conventional, regular** Bill is one of the smartest people I ever met, but he never had a *formal* education.

formation *noun* ✦ **arrangement, design, pattern** ✧ **layout, order** Derek saw a cloud *formation* that looked like a horse.

former *adjective* ✦ **past, previous** ✧ **earlier, preceding, prior** Mr. Barrett took over our class when our *former* teacher was promoted to principal.

forsake *verb* ✦ **abandon, desert, disown, leave, quit** I love my country, and I will never *forsake* it.

fort *noun* ✦ **fortification, fortress, stockade, stronghold** In the Old West, *forts* were usually made of logs.

forth *adverb* ✦ **forward, on, onward, out, outward** The cavalry soldiers rode *forth* to meet the enemy.

fortunate *adjective* ✦ **blessed, favored, lucky** ✧ **happy, well-off** I feel *fortunate* that my best friend lives next door.

fortune *noun* **1.** ✦ **chance, destiny, fate, luck** *Fortune* was with us when we won the big football game. **2.** ✧ **riches, treasure, wealth** The museum contains a *fortune* in paintings. ▼

✦ **best choices**
✧ **other choices**

forward *adjective* ✦ **front** ◇ **advance, fore, head, leading** My seat is in the plane's *forward* cabin. —*adverb* ✦ **forth, out** ◇ **ahead, before, onward** Please step *forward* when your name is called. —*verb* ✦ **deliver, dispatch, send, ship, transmit** Mom asked the principal to *forward* my records to my new school.

foul *adjective* **1.** ✦ **disgusting, nasty, offensive, repulsive, revolting, sickening** Rotten eggs have a *foul* odor. **2.** ✦ **bad, blustery, rainy, stormy, wet** ◇ **threatening** We had to cancel our soccer game because of *foul* weather.

found *verb* ✦ **create, establish, institute, start** ◇ **originate** My friends and I decided to *found* a computer club. ▶

foundation *noun* **1.** ✦ **basis, framework, root** ◇ **cause, reason** Reading, writing, and arithmetic are the traditional *foundations* of a good education. **2.** ✦ **base, bottom** ◇ **bed, foot, support** The *foundation* of our house is made of concrete blocks.

fraction *noun* ✦ **part, portion, section** ◇ **piece, share** Only a small *fraction* of the class forgot to bring something for show-and-tell.

fracture *noun* ✦ **break, crack** ◇ **rupture, separation, split** The school nurse showed us how to splint a *fracture*. —*verb* ✦ **break, crack, shatter, splinter, split** The bone *fractured* in two places.

fragile *adjective* ✦ **breakable, brittle, delicate** ◇ **feeble, frail, weak** If you mail something that's *fragile*, be sure to pack it very carefully.

> **Antonyms**
>
> **fragile** *adjective*
>
> hardy, robust, rugged, strong, sturdy, tough

fragment *noun* ✦ **bit, chip, piece, scrap** ◇ **part, portion** The archaeologist found a *fragment* of pottery.

frail *adjective* **1.** ✦ **feeble, infirm, sickly, weak** Teddy Roosevelt is remembered as a robust man, but he was *frail* as a child. **2.** ✦ **brittle, delicate, flimsy, fragile** Flowers that have been dried and pressed are very *frail*.

frame *noun* **1.** ✦ **framework, framing, shell** ◇ **mount, mounting** My new bicycle has a steel *frame* that is much sturdier than my old one. **2.** ✦ **body, build, form, physique** Darrell is a good wrestler in part because he has a small, wiry *frame*. —*verb* ✦ **border, enclose, mount** ◇ **assemble, build** Mom *framed* her college diploma and hung it on the wall of her office.

frantic *adjective* ✦ **agitated, distressed, excited, frenzied** ◇ **wild** The mother robin became *frantic* when she saw a hawk circling over her nest.

fraud *noun* **1.** ✦ **deceit, deception, trickery** ◇ **swindle, swindling** If an advertiser makes false claims about a product, he or she is guilty of *fraud*. **2.** ✦ **fake, faker, impostor, phony, pretender** ◇ **swindler** One of the characters in the book *The Adventures of Huckleberry Finn* claims to be a king, but he's actually a *fraud*.

fray *verb* ✦ **come apart, unravel, wear** ◇ **shred, tear** The cuffs on my shirt are beginning to *fray*.

free *adjective* **1.** ✦ **independent, liberated, self-governing** ◇ **unconfined** The former slave rejoiced when he became a *free* man. **2.** ✦ **clear, empty** ◇ **open, vacant, void** The doctor said that my cut was *free* of infection. **3.** ✦ **complimentary, free of charge, gratis, on the house** If you rent two movies, the third one is *free*. —*verb* ✦ **let go, liberate, release, set free** ◇ **emancipate** We *freed* the rabbit that was caught in our garden netting.

freedom *noun* ✦ **independence, liberty** ✧ **emancipation** My grandparents came to the United States in part so they would have the *freedom* to practice their religious beliefs.

freeze *verb* **1.** ✦ **ice over, ice up** ✧ **chill, frost, nip** The river *freezes* in winter. **2.** ✦ **halt, stand still, stop** ✧ **stay** The deer *froze* when it saw the car's headlights.

frenzy *noun* ✦ **furor, turmoil** ✧ **agitation, commotion, excitement** I was in a *frenzy* trying to finish my report on time.

frequent *adjective* ✦ **constant, numerous, repeated** ✧ **regular, routine, usual** While working on my research paper, I made *frequent* trips to the library.

fresh *adjective* **1.** ✦ **new, unspoiled** ✧ **current, recent** The local supermarket always has *fresh* fruits and vegetables. **2.** ✦ **additional, another, new** ✧ **different, more** Mom thinks that our house needs a *fresh* coat of paint. **3.** ✦ **clean, invigorating, pure, refreshing** ✧ **healthy** Charlotte opened a window as wide as possible to let some *fresh* air into her room.

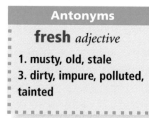

Antonyms

fresh *adjective*

1. musty, old, stale
3. dirty, impure, polluted, tainted

friction *noun* **1.** ✦ **abrasion, grinding, rubbing, scraping** If your foot rubs against your shoe, the *friction* can produce a blister. **2.** ✦ **antagonism, conflict, disagreement, discord, tension** There was constant *friction* between the bossy director and his conceited star.

friend *noun* ✦ **buddy, comrade, pal** ✧ **acquaintance, companion** Erica and Kristi have been good *friends* for years.

friendship *noun* ✦ **companionship, comradeship, fellowship** ✧ **intimacy** Your *friendship* is important to me.

fright *noun* ✦ **alarm, apprehension, dread, fear, panic, terror** The scary movie filled me with *fright*.

frighten *verb* ✦ **alarm, intimidate, scare, terrify** ✧ **startle** Shawna confessed that flying on a plane *frightened* her.

frigid *adjective* ✦ **cold, freezing, icy** ✧ **chill, chilly, cool** A *frigid* wind blew swiftly over the Arctic tundra.

fringe *noun* ✦ **border, edge, margin, rim** The people on the *fringes* of the crowd weren't paying attention to the speaker.

frolic *verb* ✦ **play, romp** ✧ **prance** The kittens often *frolic* with each other.

front *noun* ✦ **beginning, head, start** ✧ **fore, forepart, lead** Locomotives are often at the *front* of a train. ▶ —*adjective* ✦ **first, foremost, initial** ✧ **beginning, fore** Al likes to sit in the *front* row of the classroom.

frontier *noun* ✦ **border, borderland, boundary** ✧ **edge, outpost, outskirts, territory** The *frontier* between the United States and Canada is not fortified.

frosting *noun* ✦ **glaze, icing** ✧ **topping** Julia thinks that the best part of a cupcake is the *frosting*.

frown *verb* ✦ **grimace, scowl** ✧ **pout** I *frowned* at my brother when he bragged about his grades. —*noun* ✦ **grimace, pout, scowl** The clown painted a *frown* on his face.

frustrate *verb* **1.** ✦ **defeat, foil, thwart, ruin** ✧ **cancel, prevent** The falling snow *frustrated* my efforts to keep the driveway clear. **2.** ✦ **disappoint, discourage, upset** My inability to advance

✦ **best choices**
✧ **other choices**

to a higher level in this computer game is beginning to *frustrate* me!

fugitive *noun* ✦ **escapee, runaway** ✧ **outlaw, refugee** Police finally caught the *fugitive* who had escaped from prison.

fulfill *verb* **1.** ✦ **accomplish, achieve, realize** Aunt Yvonne has *fulfilled* her lifelong dream of owning her own bookstore. **2.** ✦ **answer, fill, finish, meet, satisfy** Corey has *fulfilled* all of the requirements to get his next scouting badge.

full *adjective* **1.** ✦ **filled, loaded, packed, stuffed** I couldn't find a seat because the bus was *full*. **2.** ✦ **complete, entire, whole** ✧ **comprehensive, thorough** You need a *full* deck of cards to play "Go Fish." —*adverb* ✦ **completely, entirely, thoroughly, wholly** The ship turned *full* about and sailed off in the opposite direction.

fumble *verb* ✦ **blunder, feel, flounder, grope, stumble** Alex *fumbled* around in the dark for a flashlight.

function *noun* **1.** ✦ **job, purpose, role, task** ✧ **operation, use** One *function* of a judge is to preside over trials. **2.** ✦ **affair, ceremony, meeting, ritual** ✧ **celebration** The President has to attend many political *functions*. —*verb* ✦ **act, operate, perform, serve, work** ✧ **run** This soap *functions* as a stain remover and a cleanser.

fund *noun* ✦ **account, holding, reserve** ✧ **stock, supply** Mom makes monthly contributions to her retirement *fund*.

fundamental *adjective* ✦ **basic, essential, key, major, primary** Addition is a *fundamental* part of mathematics. —*noun* ✦ **basic, essential, foundation, principle** I learned the *fundamentals* of making jam from a cookbook.

funny *adjective* **1.** ✦ **amusing, comical, hilarious, humorous** Allison told us a *funny* story. **2.** ✦ **curious, odd, peculiar, strange, unusual,**

weird There is a *funny* smell coming from the refrigerator.

furious *adjective* **1.** ✦ **angry, enraged, irate, mad, wrathful** The *furious* bear stood on its hind legs and roared. **2.** ✦ **fierce, strong, turbulent, violent, wild** The *furious* gale knocked down a lot of trees.

furnish *verb* **1.** ✦ **equip, fit, outfit** ✧ **decorate** Dad *furnished* his office with bookshelves and a desk. **2.** ✦ **give, provide, supply** ✧ **deliver, present** Uncle Bill offered to *furnish* the tools that I need to start my own lawn-mowing business.

further *adverb* ✦ **additionally, longer, more** ✧ **also, yet** I'll have to study the problem *further* before I can give you any advice. —*adjective* ✦ **added, additional, extra, more, new, other** The television announcer said to stay tuned for *further* details. —*verb* ✦ **advance, forward, promote** ✧ **aid, assist, support** My parents have helped to *further* my interest in music.

fury *noun* **1.** ✦ **anger, ire, furor, rage, wrath** I was filled with *fury* when my computer crashed. **2.** ✦ **ferocity, intensity, severity, violence** The storm raged with awesome *fury*.

Antonyms
fury *noun*
1. bliss, happiness, joy, rapture, satisfaction

fuse *verb* ✦ **blend, combine, melt, merge, mix** Bronze is made by *fusing* copper and tin.

fuss *noun* ✦ **bother, bustle, commotion, disturbance, stir** Dad made quite a *fuss* over me when I won the science fair, but I didn't mind. —*verb* ✦ **fret, worry** ✧ **bustle** The whole family *fussed* over the new baby when she had a cold.

future *adjective* ✦ **approaching, coming, forthcoming, prospective** ✧ **later** My friends and I like to plan our *future* activities well in advance.

gadget *noun* ✦ **apparatus, appliance, device, implement, tool** Dad just bought a *gadget* that automatically peels apples.

gain *verb* ✦ **acquire, attain, get, pick up** ✧ **reach, win** I *gained* a lot of experience working in the library last summer. —*noun* ✦ **advance** ✧ **addition, improvement, increase** The quarterback carried the ball for a *gain* of fifteen yards.

gale *noun* ✦ **wind, windstorm** ✧ **squall, storm, tempest** The *gale* blew with so much fury that several small boats almost capsized.

gallant *adjective* ✦ **brave, courageous, daring, heroic, valiant** Firefighters made a *gallant* attempt to save the burning building.

gallop *noun* ✧ **canter, jog, run, trot** Victoria exercises her horse by taking it for a *gallop*. —*verb* ✦ **fly, race, rush, speed, zoom** The summer is *galloping* by, and soon I'll be back in school.

gamble *verb* ✦ **bet, wager** ✧ **chance, risk** I *gambled* twenty-five cents on my favorite football team. —*noun* ✦ **chance, risk** ✧ **bet, wager** We took a *gamble* with the weather when we went picnicking on a cloudy day.

game *noun* **1.** ✧ **amusement, entertainment, fun, play, recreation, sport** Amanda's favorite *game* is hide-and-seek. **2.** ✦ **competition, contest** ✧ **match, meet, race, tournament** The Super Bowl is the most important *game* of the football season.

gang *noun* ✦ **band, pack, ring** ✧ **crew, crowd, group, mob** Jesse James led a famous *gang* of outlaws.

gap *noun* ✦ **opening, space** ✧ **break, crack, hole** My rabbit has a big *gap* between its two front teeth.

garbage *noun* ✦ **refuse, rubbish, trash, waste** Whose turn is it to take the *garbage* out?

garment *noun* ✦ **apparel, attire, clothes, clothing** Mom buys all of her dresses at a shop that specializes in women's *garments*.

gasp *verb* ✦ **gulp, pant** ✧ **huff, puff, wheeze** Jordan *gasped* for air after he swam a pool length under water. —*noun* ✦ **gulp, pant, puff** ✧ **wheeze** I was breathing in short *gasps* by the time I ran up the fourth flight of stairs.

gate *noun* ✧ **door, doorway, entrance, entry, gateway** I made sure that the *gate* was closed so that the dog wouldn't get out.

gather *verb* **1.** ✦ **accumulate, assemble, cluster, collect, group** Pigeons *gathered* around the woman who was tossing out bread crumbs. **2.** ✦ **harvest, pick, pluck** ✧ **garner, glean, reap** Let's go out to the woods and *gather* some blueberries.

gathering *noun* ✦ **assembly, meeting** ✧ **company, crowd, group** We are having a family *gathering* next Thanksgiving.

gauge *noun* ✦ **mark, measure** ✧ **meter** How we survive a month of travel together will be a *gauge* of our friendship. —*verb* ✦ **calculate, measure** ✧ **estimate, figure, judge** It is difficult to *gauge* the speed of the wind unless you have the right equipment.

gaunt *adjective* ✦ **bony, lean, skinny, thin** Many wild animals become *gaunt* during winter because their food is scarce.

gay *adjective* ✦ **cheerful, happy, jolly, merry, mirthful** Everyone was in a *gay* mood at the Halloween party.

gaze *verb* ✦ **look, stare** ✧ **eye, gape, gawk** It was such a beautiful night that I couldn't stop *gazing* at the stars. —*noun* ✦ **eye, look, stare** ✧ **gape** When the teacher's *gaze* fell on me, I knew that she was going to ask me a question.

✦	**best choices**
✧	**other choices**

gear *noun* ✦ **apparatus, equipment, outfit, stuff, things** ◇ **tackle** The campers all carried their own *gear* to the campsite. ◀

gem *noun* 1. ✦ **gemstone, jewel, precious stone** The king's crown was covered with diamonds and other *gems*. 2. ✦ **marvel, masterpiece, prize, treasure, wonder** Evan has some real *gems* in his comic-book collection.

general *adjective* 1. ✦ **common, whole** ◇ **total, universal** The museum's library is open to the *general* public three days a week. 2. ✦ **broad, overall, widespread** ◇ **popular** There was *general* satisfaction with the plan, though a few people were still unhappy. 3. ✦ **normal, routine, usual** ◇ **typical** With computers, it's a *general* rule that you should save your work often in case the program crashes.

generally *adverb* 1. ✦ **normally, routinely, typically, usually** ◇ **often** I *generally* have cereal and toast for breakfast. 2. ✦ **broadly, commonly, popularly, widely** It is not *generally* known that Russia is only thirty-six miles away from Alaska.

generate *verb* ✦ **create, make, produce** ◇ **develop, form** A fire *generates* both heat and light.

generous *adjective* ✦ **considerate, kind, thoughtful, unselfish** Ms. Taylor said that she appreciated my *generous* offer to help clean our classroom.

genius *noun* 1. ✦ **ace, expert, master, wizard** ◇ **prodigy** My older sister is a real *genius* with computers. 2. ✦ **ability, brilliance, creativity, talent** ◇ **gift, intelligence** Mozart's operas are widely thought to be works of great *genius*.

gentle *adjective* 1. ✦ **light, low, mild, moderate, slight, soft** A *gentle* breeze made the evening cool and pleasant. 2. ✦ **docile, tame** ◇ **easy, kind, tender** Our dog is very *gentle* when she plays with us.

genuine *adjective* ✦ **actual, authentic, real, true** ◇ **legitimate** Kevin's dad has a *genuine* Model-T Ford.

gesture *noun* ✦ **motion, movement, sign, signal** ◇ **indication** Police officers use hand and arm *gestures* to direct traffic. —*verb* ✦ **motion, sign, signal** ◇ **indicate, wave** Mom *gestured* for us to be quiet as we tiptoed into the baby's room.

get *verb* 1. ✦ **become, grow, turn** ◇ **develop** It's *getting* cold out. 2. ✦ **arrive, reach, show up** ◇ **approach, come** When will the bus *get* here? 3. ✦ **go, move, travel** ◇ **proceed** I use my bicycle to *get* around. 4. ✦ **acquire, obtain, receive** ◇ **earn, gain, win** Jennifer *got* a tape player for her birthday. 5. ✦ **fetch, pick up** ◇ **capture, catch, go after** Please *get* some peanut butter when you go to the store. 6. ✦ **convince, influence, persuade** ◇ **urge** I'll see if I can *get* my parents to let you stay over tonight. 7. ✦ **catch, comprehend, grasp, understand** I didn't *get* the joke at first.

ghastly *adjective* ✦ **dreadful, gruesome, hideous, horrible, terrible** The *ghastly* monster was half human and half bug.

ghost *noun* ✦ **phantom, specter, spirit, spook** ◇ **bogeyman, hobgoblin** The house was supposed to be haunted by two *ghosts*.

giant *adjective* ✦ **colossal, enormous, gigantic, huge, immense, mighty** Across the way is a *giant* oak that is taller than our house.

gift *noun* 1. ✦ **contribution, donation, present** ◇ **offering** The man gave a *gift* of one thousand dollars to his favorite charity. 2. ✦ **aptitude, faculty, knack, talent** ◇ **ability** My sister has a *gift* for making people laugh.

gifted *adjective* ✦ **talented** ◇ **accomplished, capable, expert, skilled, skillful** Aunt Janet is a *gifted* photographer.

gigantic *adjective* ✦ **colossal, enormous, giant, huge, immense, tremendous** Redwoods are *gigantic* trees that can grow to be over 350 feet high.

giggle *verb* ✦ **laugh, titter** ◇ **cackle, chuckle, guffaw, snicker** The girls *giggled* nervously when they saw the handsome young movie star. —*noun* ✦ **chuckle, laugh, laughter, snicker** ◇ **cackle** *Giggles* filled the room when someone cracked a joke while we were taking a test.

give *verb* **1.** ✦ **present (with)** ◇ **contribute, donate, hand out** My brother *gave* me his old baseball glove. **2.** ✦ **hand, pass** ◇ **deliver, hand over, let have, provide** Please *give* me a glass of water. **3.** ✦ **accord, allow, grant** ◇ **offer, permit** My teacher *gave* me an extra day to complete my homework. **4.** ✦ **furnish, provide, supply** ◇ **make, produce, yield** This bulb doesn't *give* enough light to read by. **5.** ✦ **have, hold, stage** ◇ **do, perform** Let's *give* a party to surprise Mom on her birthday.

glad *adjective* ✦ **delighted, happy, pleased** ◇ **cheerful, joyful** I'm always *glad* when it's time for art class.

glamorous *adjective* ✦ **exciting, fascinating** ◇ **attractive, charming, lovely** Directing movies sounds like a *glamorous* career to me.

glance *verb* ✦ **look, peek, peep** ◇ **glimpse** I *glanced* into the oven to see if the brownies were done. —*noun* ✦ **look, peek, peep** ◇ **glimpse** One *glance* at the test told Raymond that it would be easy.

glare *verb* **1.** ✦ **glower, scowl, stare** ◇ **frown, gaze** The librarian *glared* at the students who were talking loudly. **2.** ✦ **blaze, flash, shine** ◇ **dazzle, glisten, sparkle** Sunlight *glared* off the snow and ice. —*noun* **1.** ✦ **scowl, stare** ◇ **frown, gaze** My cat gave me a *glare* when I served him the wrong food. **2.** ✦ **blaze, glow, light, shine** ◇ **brilliance, dazzle** The *glare* from the rocket's engines could be seen for miles.

glaring *adjective* **1.** ✦ **blinding, bright, brilliant, dazzling** The *glaring* sunlight made my eyes water. **2.** ✦ **conspicuous, evident, noticeable, obvious** I made a *glaring* error on my spelling test.

gleam *noun* ✦ **flash, flicker, glimmer, twinkle** ◇ **glow** The campers saw the distant *gleam* of someone's lantern. —*verb* ✦ **glisten, glow, shine, sparkle** ◇ **radiate** Grandma and I polished the silver tea set until it *gleamed*.

glee *noun* ✦ **delight, gladness, happiness, joy** ◇ **merriment, mirth** My sister cried out with *glee* when she saw the kitten that Dad brought home.

Antonyms
glee *noun*
anguish, grief, misery, sadness, sorrow, woe

glide *verb* ✦ **coast, sail, soar** ◇ **flow, slide, slip** The eagle *glided* through the sky above us. ◄

glimmer *noun* ✦ **flash, flicker, gleam** ◇ **glow, twinkle** The campfire's dying embers gave off faint *glimmers* of reddish light. —*verb* ✦ **gleam, flash, flicker, sparkle, twinkle** ◇ **shine** Stars *glimmered* in the night sky.

glimpse *noun* ✦ **peek (at), peep (at)** ◇ **glance** Blake had a *glimpse* of the cardinal before it flew away. —*verb* ✦ **detect, make out, spot, spy** ◇ **see** I barely *glimpsed* the mayor in the crowd.

glitter *noun* ✦ **brilliance, radiance, sparkle** ◇ **light, shine** The *glitter* of the sun on the water looked like diamonds. —*verb* ✦ **glisten, shine, sparkle, twinkle** ◇ **flash, flicker** The city *glitters* at night with the lights of buildings and traffic.

✦ **best choices**
◇ **other choices**

gloat *verb* ✦ **exult** ✧ **boast, brag, crow** Marcus was very glad to have won the race, but he didn't *gloat* over his victory.

globe *noun* **1.** ✦ **ball, sphere** Our kitchen light is covered by a glass *globe*. **2.** ✦ **earth, planet, world** My grandparents' travels have taken them all over the *globe*. ◀

gloom *noun* **1.** ✦ **dark, darkness, dimness, murk** ✧ **blackness, bleakness** We couldn't see very far in the *gloom* of the long tunnel. **2.** ✦ **dejection, glumness, sadness, unhappiness** ✧ **depression** I was filled with *gloom* when I thought of my best friend moving far away.

gloomy *adjective* **1.** ✦ **bleak, dark, dismal, dreary, somber** The castle was cold and *gloomy*. **2.** ✦ **dejected, glum, sad, unhappy** ✧ **depressed, sullen** Juan has been in a *gloomy* mood ever since his team lost in the playoffs.

glorious *adjective* ✦ **amazing, gorgeous, incredible, magnificent, marvelous, splendid, stunning, superb** The Grand Canyon is one of the most *glorious* sights I've ever seen.

glory *noun* **1.** ✦ **fame, honor, praise, prestige** ✧ **distinction** The knight's heroic deeds brought him much *glory*. **2.** ✦ **grandeur, magnificence, splendor** ✧ **majesty** The sun rose in a blaze of *glory*.

glow *verb* ✦ **shine** ✧ **beam, gleam, glimmer** My alarm clock has a dial that *glows* in the dark. —*noun* ✦ **gleam, glimmer, light, radiance** ✧ **glare, shine** The room was lit by the *glow* of a single candle.

glue *noun* ✦ **adhesive** ✧ **cement, mucilage, paste, rubber cement** I needed to use just a drop of *glue* to repair my model airplane. —*verb* ✦ **paste, stick** ✧ **cement, fasten, gum** Rhianna *glued* the new pictures of her family's cross-country trip into her scrapbook.

gnaw *verb* ✦ **bite, chew, nibble** ✧ **eat, munch** Our dog is in trouble for *gnawing* on Dad's shoes.

go *verb* **1.** ✧ **journey, move, proceed, progress, travel** Maureen likes to *go* to her friend's house after school. **2.** ✦ **depart, leave, run along** ✧ **exit, pull out, quit, retire, withdraw** I have to *go* now. **3.** ✦ **lead** ✧ **extend, head, reach, run** Where does this road *go*? **4.** ✦ **fare** ✧ **happen, occur, result** How did things *go* at school today? **5.** ✦ **pass, slip away** ✧ **elapse, lapse** The summer *went by* too fast. **6.** ✦ **fit, match, suit** ✧ **agree, belong** Does this tie *go with* my jacket and shirt?

goal *noun* ✦ **aim, ambition, objective** ✧ **end, purpose** My *goal* is to read five books this summer.

gobble *verb* ✦ **bolt, gulp, wolf** ✧ **devour, eat** It's not polite to *gobble* your food.

good *adjective* **1.** ✦ **enjoyable, fine, nice** ✧ **excellent, great** That was a *good* movie we just saw. **2.** ✦ **advantageous, beneficial** ✧ **favorable, helpful, useful** A *good* diet includes lots of fruits and vegetables. **3.** ✦ **able, capable, competent, skilled, skillful** Ms. Blanchard is a *good* teacher. **4.** ✦ **dependable, reliable, sound, trustworthy** My bicycle is old, but it's still *good*. **5.** ✦ **nice, obedient, well-behaved** ✧ **honorable, virtuous** When my dog is *good*, I give her a treat. —*noun* ✦ **advantage, benefit, interest, welfare** Our coach urges us to play for the *good* of the team.

gorge *noun* ✧ **canyon, chasm, gulch, ravine, valley** A river runs through the *gorge*. —*verb* ✦ **cram, fill, stuff** ✧ **devour, eat, indulge** We *gorged* ourselves with cake and ice cream at my birthday party.

gorgeous *adjective* ✦ **beautiful, glorious, magnificent, splendid** ✧ **handsome, lovely, pretty** It was such a *gorgeous* and sunny day that we spent the whole afternoon at the park.

gossip *noun* ✦ **hearsay, rumor** ✧ **scandal, slander** I read some *gossip* about my favorite movie star in the fan magazine. —*verb* ✦ **chatter, chitchat, jabber, talk** ✧ **tattle, whisper** We sat around all morning long *gossiping* about last night's party.

govern *verb* ✦ **direct, lead, manage, run** ✧ **control, rule** In a democracy, public elections determine who will *govern* the country.

government *noun* ✦ **regulation, rule** ✧ **administration, regime, state** Monarchies, democracies, and republics are three different forms of national *government*.

gown *noun* ✦ **dress** ✧ **frock** Mom still has her wedding *gown*.

grab *verb* ✦ **clutch, grasp, seize, snatch** ✧ **pluck, take** I had to *grab* my little brother's hand to keep him from stepping off the curb. —*noun* ✦ **lunge, snatch** ✧ **clutch, grasp, pass** Stephanie made a *grab* for the frog, but it was too fast for her and got away.

grace *noun* 1. ✦ **ease, elegance, gracefulness, polish** ✧ **charm** The figure skater performed with remarkable *grace*. 2. ✦ **decency, manners, politeness** ✧ **kindness** He at least had the *grace* to apologize for his careless behavior. —*verb* ✦ **adorn, decorate** ✧ **dignify, favor, honor** The bank lobby had several beautiful paintings *gracing* its walls.

graceful *adjective* ✦ **refined, smooth** ✧ **agile, charming, elegant, lovely** Amber's dive was so *graceful* that she hardly made a splash.

> **Antonyms**
>
> **graceful** *adjective*
> awkward, clumsy, gawky, uncoordinated

gracious *adjective* ✦ **cordial, courteous, hospitable, kind, polite** The Browns are always *gracious* hosts at their annual holiday party.

grade *noun* 1. ✦ **category, degree, level, rank** ✧ **kind, type** Sandpaper comes in different *grades* of coarseness. 2. ✦ **incline, pitch, slant, slope** I had to walk my bicycle up the hill because the *grade* was so steep. 3. ✦ **mark, score** ✧ **evaluation, rating** Cheyenne got the best *grade* on yesterday's test. —*verb* 1. ✦ **categorize, classify, order, rank, sort** Lumber is *graded* according to its quality. 2. ✦ **mark, score** ✧ **evaluate, rate** Ms. Gontero *grades* our papers in red ink. 3. ✦ **even out, flatten, level, smooth** Before construction can begin, the lot will have to be *graded*.

gradual *adjective* ✦ **moderate, slow, steady** ✧ **even, regular** The mountaineers made *gradual* progress up the steep slope.

graduate *verb* 1. ✧ **complete, finish, pass** Both of my parents went to college, but only Mom *graduated*. 2. ✦ **mark off** ✧ **arrange, divide, measure** This measuring cup is *graduated* in ounces.

grand *adjective* 1. ✦ **excellent, great, splendid, superb, wonderful** We had a *grand* time on our trip to Washington, D.C. 2. ✦ **luxurious, magnificent, majestic, stately** The dance will be held in the palace's *grand* ballroom.

grant *verb* 1. ✦ **accord, allow, award, give, permit** ✧ **authorize** The genie of the lamp *granted* Aladdin three wishes. 2. ✦ **acknowledge, admit, agree, concede** I'll *grant* that you're a faster runner than I am. —*noun* ✦ **contribution, donation, gift** ✧ **allotment, award** Our school just received a *grant* to buy computers for all the classrooms.

grasp *verb* 1. ✦ **comprehend, perceive, see, understand** ✧ **know** Do you *grasp* the meaning of this poem? 2. ✦ **clasp, clutch, grab, grip,**

✦ best choices
✧ other choices

seize We all *grasped* the rope tightly and pulled to win the tug-of-war. ▼ —*noun* **1.** ✦ **clasp, clutch, grip, hold** ✧ **possession** Nicholas caught a garter snake, but it wriggled out of his *grasp*. **2.** ✦ **comprehension, perception, understanding** ✧ **knowledge** I think I have a good *grasp* of the situation.

grateful *adjective* ✦ **appreciative, thankful** ✧ **gratified, pleased** Mom was *grateful* when I said I'd help her cook dinner.

gratify *verb* ✦ **cheer, delight, gladden, please** The librarian said that it *gratifies* him to see me so interested in reading.

gratitude *noun* ✦ **appreciation, gratefulness, thankfulness, thanks** When the actress won the award, she expressed her *gratitude* to everyone who had been of help.

grave *noun* **1.** ✦ **serious, severe, significant, weighty** ✧ **critical** In our school, cheating is a *grave* offense. **2.** ✦ **serious, sober, solemn, somber** ✧ **thoughtful** The reporter described the accident in a *grave* tone of voice.

graze¹ *verb* ✦ **browse** ✧ **crop, eat, feed, forage** A flock of sheep was *grazing* in the pasture.

graze² *verb* ✦ **brush, scrape, swipe, touch** ✧ **glance off, skim** The thorn just *grazed* my leg as I passed.

grease *noun* **1.** ✦ **drippings, fat, lard** ✧ **tallow** Some people fry their eggs in bacon *grease*. **2.** ✦ **lubricant, oil** ✧ **petroleum** Mom was covered with *grease* after working on our car. —*verb* ✦ **lubricate, oil** I *greased* the hinges of the squeaky door.

great *adjective* **1.** ✦ **big, enormous, huge, large** ✧ **vast** Elephants are known for their *great* size. **2.** ✦ **excellent, important, notable, outstanding, remarkable** Many people think Franklin D. Roosevelt was a *great* President.

greed *noun* ✦ **craving, desire, hunger, longing** Trick-or-treating brings out my *greed* for candy.

greet *verb* ✦ **hail, salute** ✧ **meet, welcome** I *greeted* Tina with a wave of my hand.

grief *noun* ✦ **heartache, sadness, sorrow** ✧ **despair, distress** *Grief* is a natural response to the death of a loved one.

grieve *verb* ✦ **mourn, sorrow** ✧ **cry, weep** Everyone at the funeral *grieved* for the friend they had lost.

grim *adjective* ✦ **hard, harsh, severe, stern** ✧ **firm, stubborn** The judge had a *grim* look on his face.

grime *noun* ✦ **dirt, filth** ✧ **dust, mire, mud, soil** The garage windows were covered with *grime*.

grimy *adjective* ✦ **dirty, filthy, grubby, soiled** ✧ **messy, unclean** I was all *grimy* after helping Dad clean out the basement.

grin *verb* ✦ **beam, smile** My little sister *grinned* happily when I offered her a piggyback ride. —*noun* ✦ **smile** I could tell from Leticia's *grin* that she was in a good mood.

grind *verb* **1.** ✦ **mill, pulverize** ✧ **crumble, crush, powder** Millstones were once used to *grind* grain into flour. **2.** ✦ **file, rub, scrape** ✧ **grate, polish, rasp, sand, sharpen, smooth** Early peoples made stone axes by *grinding* the ax head against a sandstone slab.

grip *noun* ✦ **clasp, grasp, hold** ✧ **clutch** My tennis instructor told me to keep a firm *grip* on the racket. —*verb* ✦ **clasp, clutch, grasp, hold** ✧ **grab, seize** The baseball player *gripped* his bat tightly. ◀

grit *noun* ✦ **dirt, dust, sand** ✧ **debris** The wind blew a piece of *grit* into my eye. —*verb* ✦ **clamp, clench** ✧ **gnash, grate, grind** Daniel *grits* his teeth whenever he gets a shot.

groan *verb* ✦ **moan, sigh** ✧ **complain, gripe, grumble** Shana *groaned* when she saw all the homework she had to do. —*noun* ✦ **cry, moan, sigh** ✧ **sob** The traveler gave a *groan* of relief when he set down his heavy luggage.

groom *verb* ✦ **tend** ✧ **brush, clean, comb** Tracey *grooms* her horse after every ride.

groove *noun* ✦ **channel, slot** ✧ **cut, furrow, rut, trench** My school desk has a *groove* for holding pencils.

grope *verb* ✦ **feel, fumble** ✧ **poke, probe** The theater was so dark that I had to *grope* for my seat.

gross *adjective* **1.** ✦ **flagrant, glaring, obvious, plain** ✧ **extreme** The tabloid article contained nothing but *gross* lies. **2.** ✦ **disgusting, offensive, repulsive, revolting** The smell from the garbage can was really *gross*.

grotesque *adjective* ✦ **bizarre, strange, unnatural, weird** ✧ **ugly** The mythical Cerberus was a *grotesque* dog that had three heads.

grouchy *adjective* ✦ **bad-tempered, cranky, cross, grumpy, irritable** My little brother becomes *grouchy* if he doesn't take a nap.

ground *noun* **1.** ✦ **land** ✧ **dirt, earth, soil** I was glad to be back on the *ground* after our bumpy flight. **2.** ✧ **field, lot, property, terrain, yard** Our band uses the football field as a parade *ground*. **3.** ✦ **basis, cause, evidence, reason** ✧ **motive** The lawyer believed that there was not sufficient *ground* for taking the case to court. —*verb* ✦ **base, establish, found** ✧ **build, fix, rest** The French Revolution was *grounded* on the principles of liberty, equality, and fraternity.

group *noun* **1.** ✦ **bunch, cluster, crowd** ✧ **batch, gang, party** A *group* of students gathered on the playground. **2.** ✦ **category, class** ✧ **branch, grade, set** Fruits and vegetables form one of the basic food *groups*. —*verb* ✦ **arrange, classify, organize, sort** ✧ **distribute, divide** The clothes were *grouped* by size.

grove *noun* ✦ **stand, thicket** ✧ **forest, orchard** There's a little *grove* of oak trees by the duck pond in back of the school.

grow *verb* **1.** ✦ **enlarge, expand, increase, swell** ✧ **develop** The population in our town is *growing* rapidly. **2.** ✦ **flourish, live, thrive** ✧ **arise, sprout** Weeds can *grow* almost anywhere. **3.** ✦ **cultivate, plant, produce, raise** ✧ **breed, farm** Aztec farmers *grew* corn, tomatoes, and chilies. **4.** ✦ **become, come to be, get, turn** It *grows* light just before dawn.

growl *noun* ✦ **bark, bellow, grunt, roar, snarl** We heard a low *growl* in the dark. —*verb* ✦ **bark, bellow, grunt, roar, snarl** Did you know that raccoons and opossums can *growl*?

growth *noun* **1.** ✦ **development, expansion, increase** ✧ **advance, progress** The mayor was

✦ **best choices**
✧ **other choices**

pleased by the rapid *growth* of new businesses in the town. **2. ✦ accumulation, buildup ✧ collection, mass** There was a thick *growth* of weeds around the abandoned house. ▼

grudge *noun* ✧ **hard feelings, ill will, malice, spite, resentment** Anthony doesn't stay mad long, and he never holds a *grudge*.

gruesome *adjective* ✦ **ghastly, grim, hideous, horrible, shocking, terrible** There was story on the news last night about a *gruesome* accident.

gruff *adjective* ✦ **abrupt, curt, harsh, stern ✧ impolite, rude** Papa Bear spoke to Goldilocks in a *gruff* manner.

grumble *verb* ✦ **complain, gripe, whine ✧ moan, mutter** My brother *grumbles* when he has to go to bed early.

grumpy *adjective* ✦ **bad-tempered, cranky, cross, grouchy, irritable** The player was *grumpy* because he had to sit out the first half of the game.

guarantee *noun* ✦ **assurance, promise ✧ pledge, warranty** There are no *guarantees* when it comes to predicting the weather. —*verb* ✦ **certify ✧ assure, pledge, promise, warrant** The victory *guarantees* that our team will be in the finals.

guard *verb* ✦ **defend, protect, safeguard, shield ✧ preserve, watch** One of the missions of the Secret Service is to *guard* the President. —*noun* **1. ✧ caretaker, lookout, sentry** This bank is protected by three armed *guards*. **2. ✦ security ✧ control, protection, watch** Police kept the two prisoners under *guard*. **3. ✦ protector ✧ defense, safeguard, shield** Baseball catchers wear shin *guards*.

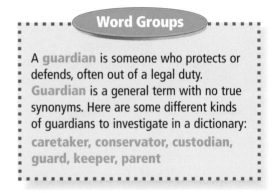

Word Groups

A **guardian** is someone who protects or defends, often out of a legal duty. **Guardian** is a general term with no true synonyms. Here are some different kinds of guardians to investigate in a dictionary: **caretaker, conservator, custodian, guard, keeper, parent**

guess *verb* **1. ✦ estimate, judge, reckon ✧ calculate** Can you *guess* how many marbles are in this jar? **2. ✦ assume, suppose, surmise ✧ believe, think** Since Leslie is not here yet, I *guess* she's not coming to school today. —*noun* ✦ **belief, opinion, speculation ✧ assumption, estimate** It's my *guess* that we'll have a mild winter this year.

guest *noun* **1. ✦ company ✧ visitor** We have *guests* coming for dinner tonight. **2. ✧ customer, lodger, tenant** This hotel can accommodate more than 250 *guests*.

guide *noun* ✦ **leader ✧ escort, scout** A park ranger was our *guide* for the nature hike. —*verb* ✦ **conduct, escort, lead ✧ direct, steer, usher** Our teacher *guided* us through the museum.

guilt *noun* ✦ **blame, fault, offense** The jury ruled that the defendant was free of *guilt*.

guilty *adjective* **1. ✦ at fault, blameworthy, responsible, wrong** The suspect claimed that she was not *guilty*. **2. ✦ contrite, regretful, remorseful, sorry** I felt *guilty* when I forgot my friend's birthday.

gulf *noun* **1.** ✧ **bay, inlet, lagoon, sound** The explorers made a map of the newly discovered *gulf*. **2.** ✦ **difference, disparity, gap, separation, split** There's a big *gulf* between the richest and the poorest members of our society.

gullible *adjective* ✦ **believing, trustful, trusting, unsuspecting** When I was younger, I was so *gullible* that I believed the moon was made out of cheese.

gully *noun* ✦ **channel** ✧ **ditch, ravine, trench** The rain created *gullies* in the hillside.

gulp *verb* ✦ **bolt, gobble, wolf** ✧ **guzzle, swallow** When I offered my dog a taste of my ice cream, he *gulped* down the whole cone. —*noun* ✦ **mouthful, swallow** ✧ **sip** Craig was so thirsty that he downed a glass of water in just three *gulps*.

gush *verb* ✦ **flow, pour, run, rush, stream, surge** Water *gushed* from the broken fire hydrant.

gust *noun* ✦ **blast** ✧ **blow, breeze, draft** A strong *gust* of wind knocked down the power line to our house.

gutter *noun* ✦ **ditch, drain** ✧ **channel, pipe, trough** Rainwater pools up in our yard because our street doesn't have *gutters*.

guy *noun* ✦ **fellow, person** ✧ **boy, lad, man** Your brother is a great *guy*.

✦   **best choices**
✧   **other choices**

H

habit *noun* ✦ **custom, practice, routine** ✧ **mannerism, trait** Gregory has the *habit* of doing his homework before dinner.

habitual *adjective* ✦ **customary, normal, regular, routine, usual** Everyone in my family has a *habitual* place at the dinner table.

hack *verb* ✦ **chop, slash, whack** ✧ **cut, slice** Jessica *hacked* at the weeds with a garden hoe.

hail *verb* ✦ **flag, signal** ✧ **call, greet, summon** Dad *hailed* a passing driver when our car broke down.

hall *noun* **1.** ✦ **corridor, hallway, passageway** I'll meet you in the *hall* as soon as class is over. **2.** ✦ **auditorium, building, chamber, gallery** ✧ **room** University classes are often taught in huge *halls*.

halt *noun* ✦ **pause, rest, stop** ✧ **break, recess** The runner came to a *halt* to retie her shoelace. —*verb* ✦ **stop** ✧ **cease, discontinue, pause, rest** The cavalry soldiers rode for a long time before an officer ordered them to *halt*.

hammer *verb* ✦ **beat, pound, strike, tap, thump** The blacksmith *hammered* the horseshoe into shape.

hamper *verb* ✦ **hinder, impede, obstruct, restrain, restrict** The rain *hampered* our efforts to light a campfire.

hand *noun* **1.** ✦ **aid, assistance, help, support** Let's all give Mom *a hand* with washing the windows. **2.** ✦ **assistant, employee, helper, laborer, worker** The rancher hired extra *hands* to help with the roundup. ◄ **3.** ✦ **part, role, share** ✧ **piece** Everyone on the team had a *hand* in winning the game. —*verb* ✦ **give, pass** ✧ **convey, deliver, transfer, turn over** I *handed* a pencil to my friend.

handicap *noun* ✦ **disadvantage, drawback, hindrance** ✧ **disability** We tried to arrive early, but the snow was a *handicap*. —*verb* ✦ **burden, hamper, hinder, impede, restrain** The competitor was *handicapped* by a sore ankle.

handle *noun* ✦ **grip, handgrip** ✧ **arm, shaft, stem** This shovel has a wooden *handle*. —*verb* **1.** ✦ **grasp, grip, hold** ✧ **feel, touch** I *handled* the crystal bowl with care. **2.** ✦ **command, control, direct, manage, supervise** Dominique *handles* her horse well.

handsome *adjective* ✦ **attractive, beautiful, fine, lovely** ✧ **good-looking** Scott's new suit is made of a *handsome* material.

handy *adjective* **1.** ✦ **expert, proficient, skilled, skillful** Dad is *handy* with carpentry tools. **2.** ✦ **accessible, available, close, convenient, nearby** It is smart to keep a flashlight *handy* during a storm in case the electricity goes off. **3.** ✦ **efficient, helpful, practical, useful** An almanac is a *handy* reference book.

hang *verb* **1.** ✦ **dangle, swing** ✧ **attach, fasten, suspend** My swing *hangs* from a tree limb. **2.** ✦ **lynch, string up** ✧ **execute** In the Old West, outlaws were often *hanged*.

haphazard *adjective* ✦ **careless, chance, disorganized, random, unplanned** The videos were in *haphazard* stacks on the shelf.

happen *verb* ✦ **arise, develop, occur, take place** ✧ **chance** What *happened* in school when I was absent?

happiness *noun* ✦ **bliss, cheer, delight, gladness, joy, pleasure** Drawing in my sketchbook always fills me with *happiness*.

happy *adjective* **1.** ✦ **delighted, glad, pleased** ✧ **satisfied, thrilled** I'm *happy* to make your acquaintance. **2.** ✦ **joyful, joyous, pleasing** ✧ **cheerful, gay** Have you heard the *happy* news that our class is going on a field trip next week?

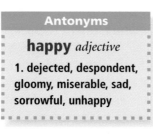

Antonyms

happy *adjective*

1. dejected, despondent, gloomy, miserable, sad, sorrowful, unhappy

harass *verb* ✦ **annoy, bother, disturb, pester, trouble** Ants and flies frequently *harass* picnickers.

harbor *noun* ✦ **port** ✧ **bay, cove, inlet, lagoon** Two tugboats guided the ocean liner into the *harbor*.

hard *adjective* **1.** ✦ **firm, solid** ✧ **rigid, stiff** That bed is much *harder* than it looks. **2.** ✦ **forceful, heavy, powerful, severe, strong** I arrived at home just before a *hard* rain began to fall. **3.** ✦ **difficult, laborious, rough, tough** We had a *hard* time driving up the slick mountain road. —*adverb* **1.** ✦ **diligently, earnestly, intently** I worked *hard* to memorize all the state capitals. **2.** ✦ **energetically, forcefully, heavily, powerfully** You have to pull *hard* on that drawer because it sticks.

hardly *adverb* ✦ **barely, just, scarcely** ✧ **only** I can *hardly* hear you.

hardship *noun* ✦ **adversity, difficulty, trouble** ✧ **danger, misfortune** The Pilgrims experienced many *hardships* during their first winter in America.

hardy *adjective* ✦ **robust, strong, sturdy, tough** ✧ **fit, healthy** The *hardy* tree in our yard survived a hurricane that uprooted many other trees in the neighborhood.

harm *noun* ✦ **hurt, injury** ✧ **damage, misfortune** Automobile seat belts help protect passengers from *harm*. —*verb* ✦ **hurt, injure** ✧ **damage, mar** My dog won't *harm* you.

harmful *adjective* ✦ **damaging, injurious, unhealthy** ✧ **bad, dangerous** Exposure to too much sunlight is *harmful*.

harmless *adjective* ✦ **nontoxic, safe** ✧ **innocent** Some berries are poisonous, but many others are *harmless*.

harmony *noun* ✦ **accord, agreement, concord, peace** ✧ **rapport, tune, unity** Maureen and Ivana worked in *harmony* on their current events report.

harsh *adjective* **1.** ✦ **coarse, grating, hoarse, jarring** A blue jay has a *harsh* cry. **2.** ✦ **bitter, brutal, cruel, hard, rough, severe** We had a *harsh* winter last year.

harvest *noun* ✦ **crop, yield** ✧ **produce, product** There is an abundant *harvest* of oranges in Florida. —*verb* ✦ **gather, reap** ✧ **collect, garner, glean, pick** Winter wheat is planted in the fall and *harvested* in the spring or early summer.

haste *noun* ✦ **rapidity, speed** ✧ **hurry, hustle, quickness** I ran home with great *haste* when I realized that I was late for dinner.

hasten *verb* ✦ **dash, hurry, race, run, rush, speed** Todd *hastened* to answer the phone.

Antonyms

hasten *verb*

delay, hestitate, lag, loiter, slow, tarry

hasty *adjective* ✦ **fast, hurried, quick, rapid, speedy, swift** Caleb and his friends made a *hasty* retreat when they saw the bull running towards them.

hatch *verb* ✦ **concoct, create, devise, invent, make up, plot** My friends and I *hatched* a plan to give a surprise party for Ian.

hate *verb* ✦ **despise, detest, dislike, loathe** Kristen *hates* taking out the garbage.

hatred *noun* ✦ **disgust, dislike, loathing** ✧ **animosity, hate** Steven's *hatred* of lima beans increases every time he has to eat them.

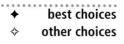
✦ **best choices**
✧ **other choices**

haughty *adjective* ✦ **arrogant, conceited, proud, vain** I feel sorry for the *haughty* queen in the story of Snow White.

haul *verb* **1.** ✦ **drag, draw, pull, tow, tug** It took four men to *haul* the piano up a flight of stairs. **2.** ✦ **carry, convey, move, transport, truck** Dad hired a truck to *haul* our furniture to our new house. —*noun* ✦ **cargo, catch, load, take, yield** ◇ **booty** The fishermen sailed back to port with a large *haul* of fish.

haunt *verb* **1.** ✦ **obsess, torment, trouble, worry** My first piano recital was so embarrassing that the memory of it still *haunts* me. **2.** ◇ **dwell in, infest, inhabit, possess, visit** This show is about a phantom that *haunts* an opera house.

have *verb* **1.** ✦ **own, possess** ◇ **hold, keep** Nicole *has* a hamster and a parakeet. **2.** ✦ **comprise, contain, embrace, include** ◇ **involve** A week *has* seven days. **3.** ✦ **accept, take** ◇ **acquire, get, obtain, receive** Will you *have* another piece of cake? **4.** ✦ **experience** ◇ **encounter, endure, know, meet, see, undergo** Did you *have* a good day at the beach? **5.** ✦ **need** ◇ **must, ought, should** I *have* to go home right after school today.

haven *noun* ✦ **refuge, retreat, sanctuary, shelter** ◇ **asylum** My room is my *haven*.

hazard *noun* ✦ **danger, peril, risk** ◇ **threat** The beekeeper said that an occasional sting is one of the *hazards* of his occupation. ◀

hazardous *adjective* ✦ **dangerous, perilous, risky, unsafe** Playing with matches is *hazardous*.

hazy *adjective* **1.** ✦ **cloudy, foggy, misty, overcast** The sky was *hazy* this morning when I left for school. **2.** ✦ **dim, faint, indistinct, uncertain,** vague I have only a *hazy* recollection of my early childhood.

head *noun* **1.** ✦ **brain, mind** ◇ **aptitude, instinct, talent** Grandma says that you have to use your *head* to solve a crossword puzzle. **2.** ✦ **boss, chief, director, leader, manager** Mom is the *head* of her company's publicity department. **3.** ✦ **beginning, front, start** ◇ **top** A high school band marched at the *head* of the parade. —*adjective* ✦ **chief, leading, main, principal, top** The *head* counselor gave our cabin a tour of Camp Wilderness when we first arrived. —*verb* **1.** ✦ **aim, direct, guide, steer, turn** We *headed* our sailboat into the wind. **2.** ✦ **direct, govern, lead, manage, run, supervise** Tyler will *head* this year's student council.

heal *verb* ✦ **mend, recover, restore** ◇ **cure, remedy** The doctor said that my broken arm will *heal* in six weeks or less.

health *noun* ✦ **welfare, well-being** ◇ **haleness, wellness** Ginnie says that yoga helps her to maintain her *health*.

healthy *adjective* **1.** ✦ **fit, hale, well** ◇ **sound** I was sick last week, but I'm *healthy* now. **2.** ✦ **healthful, nourishing, wholesome** ◇ **beneficial, helpful** Vegetables and fruits are important parts of a *healthy* diet.

heap *noun* ✦ **mass, mound, pile, stack** ◇ **hill** Dad and I raked the leaves into a big *heap*. —*verb* ✦ **load, lump, mound, pile, stack** ◇ **pack** Grandma always *heaps* lots of food onto my plate.

hear *verb* ✦ **attend to, heed, listen to** The Captain called for the crew's attention by saying, "Now *hear* this."

heart *noun* **1.** ✦ **soul** ◇ **emotion, feeling, sentiment, sympathy** Ashley has a kind *heart* and is considerate of others. **2.** ✦ **courage, mettle, nerve, pluck, spirit** Our team has a lot of *heart*. **3.** ✦ **center, core, middle** ◇ **essence, nucleus** We went for a hike through the *heart* of the forest.

heat *noun* ✦ **hotness, warmth** ✧ **temperature** That fire is putting out a lot of *heat*. —*verb* ✦ **warm, warm up** I'll set the table while you *heat* the soup.

heave *verb* **1.** ✦ **hoist, lift, pick up, raise** ✧ **boost** It took two strong men to *heave* the ship's anchor. **2.** ✦ **fling, hurl, pitch, throw, toss** Timothy *heaved* a big rock into the pond just to see the splash.

heaven *noun* ✦ **bliss, ecstasy, paradise** ✧ **joy, rapture** Joyce was in *heaven* when she got to meet her favorite author.

heavenly *adjective* ✦ **blissful, delightful, marvelous, pleasing, wonderful** The roses have a *heavenly* scent.

heavy *adjective* **1.** ✦ **massive, weighty** ✧ **big, bulky, huge, large** Philip helped his mother lift the *heavy* trunk. ▼ **2.** ✦ **abundant, ample, bountiful, plentiful** ✧ **extreme** We will be able to go skiing this weekend if the snow is *heavy* enough. **3.** ✦ **demanding, difficult, hard, laborious, rigorous, tough** Digging a deep ditch is *heavy* work.

hedge *noun* ✦ **hedgerow** ✧ **bushes, shrubbery, thicket** There's a tall *hedge* between our yard and our neighbor's. —*verb* ✦ **edge, enclose, ring, surround** ✧ **fence** Mom *hedged* our garden with rose bushes.

heed *verb* ✦ **follow, mind, obey, observe, regard** ✧ **listen to** Everyone is expected to *heed* traffic laws.

height *noun* **1.** ✦ **elevation** ✧ **altitude** The *height* of the Empire State Building is 1,250 feet. **2.** ✦ **climax, crest, peak, top, zenith** At the *height* of the baseball season, there are games almost every day.

help *verb* **1.** ✦ **aid, assist** ✧ **benefit, serve, support** Shelley helps her parents in the garden. **2.** ✦ **ease, improve, relieve** Kevin's mother gave him a cup of ginger tea to *help* his upset stomach. —*noun* ✦ **aid, assistance** ✧ **hand, support** When it came time to move the piano, Dad asked for my *help*.

helpful *adjective* ✦ **handy, useful, valuable** ✧ **beneficial, practical** Mom says that I am very *helpful* when we go grocery shopping together.

helpless *adjective* ✦ **defenseless, dependent** ✧ **feeble, weak** Baby kittens are *helpless* for about eight weeks after birth.

herd *noun* ✦ **drove** ✧ **group, horde, pack, swarm, throng** My grandmother has a *herd* of dairy cows. —*verb* ✦ **drive, guide, lead, round up** ✧ **collect, gather** Collies were once bred for the purpose of *herding* sheep.

heritage *noun* ✦ **inheritance, legacy, tradition** ✧ **ancestry** Gabriela and her family brought a rich *heritage* of language and customs when they immigrated from Venezuela.

hero *noun* ✦ **champion, heroine, idol, inspiration, role model** Some of my *heroes* are real people, and some are from stories and legends.

heroic *adjective* ✦ **bold, brave, courageous, fearless, gallant, valiant** Sir Lancelot was a *heroic* knight of King Arthur's court.

hesitant *adjective* ✦ **reluctant** ✧ **doubtful, indecisive, uncertain** I was *hesitant* to go in the baby's room while she was sleeping.

hesitate *verb* ✦ **delay, falter, pause, wait, waver** ✧ **balk** Brianna and her friends *hesitated* a moment before entering the carnival's haunted house.

Antonyms
hestitant *adjective*
certain, decisive, definite, positive, secure, sure

hide *verb* ✦ **conceal, cover up, mask, screen, veil** My uncle wears a wig to *hide* his bald spot.

hideous *adjective* ✦ **disgusting, ghastly, gruesome, horrible, repulsive, ugly** I bought a *hideous* mask to wear to the Halloween party.

high *adjective* **1.** ✦ **tall** ◇ **big, lofty, towering** Did you know that Mount Everest is 29,028 feet *high*? **2.** ✦ **excessive, extreme, fierce, furious, heavy, strong** A hurricane's *high* winds can do considerable damage. **3.** ✦ **eminent, important, leading, prominent** ◇ **chief** Harry has a *high* position in our volunteer group because he is one of the original members. **4.** ✦ **piercing, sharp, shrill, treble** I call my dog with a whistle that has a *high* pitch. —*noun* ✦ **maximum, peak, zenith** ◇ **top** Test scores in our school reached an all-time *high* last year.

highway *noun* ✦ **expressway, freeway, interstate, turnpike** ◇ **road** Will this *highway* take us to Indianapolis?

hike *verb* ✦ **travel, trek, walk** ◇ **march, ramble, stroll** The backpackers *hiked* seventeen miles to reach the top of the mountain. —*noun* ✦ **ramble, stroll, trek, walk** ◇ **trip** Tara enjoys taking *hikes* through the hills behind her house.

hill *noun* ✦ **knoll** ◇ **elevation, hilltop, promontory, rise** Lisa rode her bike down the *hill* at a dangerous speed.

hinder *verb* ✦ **bog down, hamper, impede, obstruct, slow down** ◇ **stall** Heavy snow *hindered* the flow of traffic.

hint *noun* ✦ **clue, cue, tip** ◇ **sign, suggestion** I was able to guess the answer to my sister's riddle even though she refused to give me any *hints*. —*verb* ✦ **imply, indicate, insinuate, suggest** ◇ **mention** I *hinted* that I would like a new bike for my birthday.

hire *verb* **1.** ✦ **employ, engage, retain, take on** ◇ **enlist** I wish I could *hire* someone to clean my room. **2.** ✦ **charter, lease, rent** Dad *hired* a limousine to surprise Mom on her birthday.

history *noun* ✦ **background, past** ◇ **account, chronicle, record, story** My grandparents are a great source for learning my family's *history*.

hit *verb* **1.** ✦ **beat, club, hammer, knock, pound, strike** Jason *hit* the nail into the board with just two blows. ▶ **2.** ✦ **affect, impress, occur to** ◇ **influence, move, touch** The significance of the skull and crossbones on the ship's flag *hit* me at once. —*noun* **1.** ✦ **blow, impact, strike** ◇ **bang, crack, knock, shot, swat** Erin's arrow scored a direct *hit* on the bull's-eye. **2.** ✦ **sensation, smash, success, triumph** Ryan's article for the school paper about school spirit was a big *hit* with his classmates.

hitch *verb* ✦ **attach, fasten, harness, join, tie** "*Hitch* your wagon to a star" is an old saying that means you should follow your dreams. —*noun* ✦ **difficulty, mishap, problem, snag** ◇ **delay** Luckily our trip to the mountains went off without a *hitch*.

hoard *noun* ✦ **stock, stockpile, store, supply, treasure** The dragon kept a watchful eye on its *hoard* of gold coins. —*verb* ✦ **lay away, stockpile, store** ◇ **accumulate, gather** Squirrels *hoard* nuts for the winter.

hoarse *adjective* ✦ **coarse, croaking, harsh, husky, raspy, rough, scratchy** ◇ **grating, jarring** A *hoarse* voice is a common symptom of a sore throat.

hoax *noun* ✦ **joke, prank, trick** ✧ **deception, fraud** My dad always thinks of a funny *hoax* to pull on April Fools' Day.

hobby *noun* ✦ **pastime** ✧ **amusement, diversion, pursuit, recreation** Shannon's *hobby* is collecting stamps.

hoist *verb* ✦ **haul up, lift, raise, run up** ✧ **boost, elevate** I was chosen to help *hoist* the flag this morning.

hold *verb* **1.** ✦ **clasp, clutch, grasp, grip, squeeze** Patrick *held* the bat with both hands. **2.** ✦ **accommodate, contain, include** ✧ **comprise** This carton *holds* a dozen eggs. **3.** ✦ **bear, carry, support, take** The porch swing will *hold* the weight of two people. **4.** ✦ **continue, endure, last, persist, remain, stay** I hope that this good weather will *hold* for a few more days. **5.** ✦ **conduct, give, have, stage** ✧ **direct, run** We are planning to *hold* a garage sale next Saturday. —*noun* ✦ **clasp, clutch, grasp, grip** I kept a firm *hold* on the ladder.

hole *noun* **1.** ✦ **breach, gap, opening, slit, slot** We did not know how our dog was getting out of the yard until we discovered a *hole* in the fence. **2.** ✧ **cavity, crater, depression, hollow, pit** Natalie helped her dad dig *holes* for their new rose bushes.

holiday *noun* **1.** ✦ **celebration, festival, jubilee** ✧ **holy day** The Fourth of July is a *holiday* that celebrates the United States' independence. **2.** ✦ **break, leave, recess, vacation** We are going to visit my grandparents during the summer *holiday*.

hollow *adjective* ✦ **empty, unfilled** ✧ **sunken, vacant, void** Some people say you can hear the ocean roar when you hold a *hollow* seashell to your ear. —*noun* ✦ **cavity, hole, pocket** ✧ **crater, depression** Raccoons sometimes make their dens in the *hollows* of trees. —*verb* ✦ **dig, scoop, shovel** ✧ **excavate, remove** A dugout is

a type of canoe that is made by *hollowing* out a large log.

holy *adjective* ✦ **divine, religious, sacred** Ahmed is studying the Koran, which is the Muslim *holy* book.

home *noun* **1.** ✦ **abode, dwelling, house, residence** ✧ **lodging** Several new *homes* are being built in our neighborhood. **2.** ✦ **asylum, hospital, institution** ✧ **shelter** Our elderly neighbor just moved to a nursing *home*.

homely *noun* ✦ **plain, ugly, unattractive, unlovely** I think turtles are *homely*.

honest *adjective* ✦ **good, honorable, trustworthy, upright, upstanding** ✧ **truthful** An *honest* person would return a lost wallet to its rightful owner.

honesty *noun* ✦ **integrity, truthfulness** ✧ **honor, trustworthiness** When I told Mom that I broke her vase, she thanked me for my *honesty*.

honor *noun* **1.** ✦ **acclaim, award, distinction, laurels** ✧ **praise** The straight-A student graduated with *honors*. **2.** ✦ **honesty, integrity, virtue** ✧ **dignity, reputation** A sense of *honor* makes us want to do the right thing. —*verb* ✦ **acclaim, celebrate, commend, hail, praise, recognize** This memorial *honors* the men and women who died in the Vietnam War.

hook *noun* ✦ **catch, clasp, fastener** There is a *hook* undone on the back of your dress. —*verb* ✦ **catch, fasten, latch, secure** ✧ **attach** Please *hook* the screen door so it will stay closed.

hop *verb* ✦ **bounce, bound, jump, leap, skip, spring** Shaun *hopped* his way to first prize in the sack race. —*noun* ✦ **bounce, bound, jump, leap, skip, spring** The robin moved across the lawn in *short* hops.

hope *verb* ✦ **wish** ✧ **anticipate, expect, look forward to, pray** Stacy *hopes* to get a new computer game for her birthday. —*noun* ✦ **desire,**

✦ best choices
✧ other choices

113

dream, longing, wish ◇ expectation Amber's *hope* is that she will win the tennis tournament next week.

hopeful *adjective* **1.** ✦ **confident, expectant, optimistic** Aunt Lori is *hopeful* that she will find a good job now that she has finished college. **2.** ✦ **encouraging, favorable, good, heartening, promising** The doctor said that there were many *hopeful* signs that the patient would soon make a full recovery.

hopeless *adjective* ✦ **desperate, forlorn, futile** ◇ **despairing, pessimistic** We were in a *hopeless* situation when we were behind by fifty points at halftime.

horde *noun* ✦ **crowd, herd, mob, pack, swarm, throng** There was a *horde* of people downtown at the celebration. ▼

horrible *adjective* ✦ **awful, dreadful, frightful, ghastly, grim, horrid, terrible** I have *horrible* nightmares after reading ghost stories.

horrid *adjective* ✦ **ghastly, grim, gruesome, hideous, horrible, revolting** Melissa made a *horrid* face at her brother, but he only laughed.

horror *noun* ✦ **alarm, dread, fear, fright, panic, terror** Angie had a feeling of *horror* when she saw her dog run in front of a moving car.

host *noun* ✦ **hostess, receptionist** ◇ **entertainer** Melinda is going to be one of the *hosts* at our school's open house.

hostile *adjective* ✦ **antagonistic, belligerent** ◇ **malicious, unfriendly** A *hostile* force had the soldiers surrounded.

hot *adjective* **1.** ✦ **scorching, searing, sizzling, sweltering, torrid** On *hot* summer days, Tyler likes to cool off by going swimming in the lake. **2.** ✦ **sharp, spicy, zesty** ◇ **acrid, biting** Dad likes to put *hot* sauce on his hamburgers. **3.** ✦ **angry, fiery, intense, passionate** ◇ **ardent** Some people have *hot* tempers.

Word Groups

A hotel provides a place for people to stay in return for payment. Hotel is a general term with no true synonyms. Here are some different kinds of hotels to investigate in a dictionary:

bed-and-breakfast, hostel, inn, lodge, motel, motor inn, resort

hound *noun* ✦ **dog, hunting dog** The *hounds* began baying when they caught the fox's scent. —*verb* ✦ **badger, bother, harass, nag, pester, prod** Sometimes I *hound* my mom to let me stay up late.

house *noun* **1.** ✦ **abode, dwelling, home, residence** Ronald lives in a small *house* that has just two bedrooms. **2.** ✦ **place** ◇ **building, hall, structure** A Jewish *house* of worship is called a synagogue. —*verb* ✦ **lodge, put up, shelter** ◇ **board, dwell, reside** The horses are *housed* in the barn.

hover *verb* **1.** ✦ **hang, poise** ◇ **flap, flutter, pause** The butterfly *hovered* over a flower. **2.** ✦ **hang around, linger, loiter** We *hovered* near the kitchen, hoping for a snack.

however *conjunction* ✦ **but, nevertheless, still, yet** ◇ **though** My library book is not due until next week; *however*, I plan to return it today.

howl *noun* ✦ **cry, scream, wail, yell, yowl** Bryce let out a *howl* of pain when he stubbed his toe. —*verb* ✦ **bay, wail, yowl** ◇ **bawl, bellow, cry, scream** Wolves *howl* at night to keep in touch with other members of their pack.

hub *noun* ✦ **center, headquarters, seat** ◇ **core, middle** Kansas City, Missouri, is a transportation *hub* because many railroads and highways meet there.

huddle *noun* ✦ **bunch, clump, cluster, mass** ◇ **group** The team formed a *huddle* and gave a cheer. —*verb* ✦ **bunch, cluster, crowd, flock, gather** Sheep *huddle* together for warmth.

hue *noun* ✦ **color, shade, tint, tone** I would like that coat in a darker *hue*.

hug *verb* ✦ **clasp, embrace, hold, squeeze** ◇ **cuddle** Grandmother always *hugs* me because she is so happy to see me. —*noun* ✦ **clasp, embrace, squeeze** My dad gave me a big *hug* when he returned from his trip.

huge *adjective* ✦ **big, enormous, gigantic, immense, large, massive** We usually think of dinosaurs as being *huge*, but some were as small as chickens.

humane *adjective* ✦ **compassionate, kind, merciful, tender** ◇ **good** It is important to be *humane* to your pets.

humble *adjective* 1. ✦ **modest, unassuming** ◇ **bashful, meek, shy** I tried to be *humble* when I won the track and field award so people wouldn't think I was showing off. 2. ✦ **common, simple** ◇ **lowly, mean, obscure, poor** My grandfather is proud of his *humble* background.

humid *adjective* ✦ **damp, moist, muggy, steamy** ◇ **clammy, soggy** The bathroom was *humid* after I took a long shower.

humiliate *verb* ✦ **disgrace, embarrass, shame** ◇ **dishonor** I was *humiliated* when I forgot my lines during the school play.

humor *noun* 1. ✦ **comedy, fun, wit** ◇ **amusement, funniness** A good sense of *humor* makes life more enjoyable. 2. ✦ **mood, temper** ◇ **disposition, nature** Kendra has been in a good *humor* ever since she was chosen to play in the chess tournament. —*verb* ✦ **cater to, indulge, pamper, spoil** I *humor* my parakeets by whistling to them all the time.

humorous *adjective* ✦ **amusing, comic, comical, funny, witty** Clayton told us a *humorous* story that made us laugh.

hump *noun* ✦ **bulge, bump, lump, mound, swelling** Grizzly bears have *humps* on their backs.

Antonyms
humorous *adjective*
grave, grim, serious, sober, solemn, somber

hunch *noun* ✦ **feeling, idea, impression, notion, suspicion** I had a *hunch* that we would be having a quiz today.

hunger *noun* ✦ **hungriness, starvation** ◇ **appetite, famine** Kara found a kitten that was weak from *hunger*. —*verb* ✦ **crave, desire, long for, want, yearn for** Some people *hunger for* praise and recognition.

hungry *adjective* 1. ✦ **famished, ravenous, starved, starving** Ronald was *hungry* after the long canoe trip. 2. ✦ **avid, eager, greedy, needful, yearning** I am always *hungry* for a new book by my favorite author.

hunt *verb* 1. ✦ **chase, pursue, stalk, track, trail** ◇ **kill, shoot** Dominique thinks that people should *hunt* wild animals with cameras instead of guns. 2. ✦ **look, search, seek** ◇ **probe** I helped Mom *hunt* for her missing keys. —*noun* ✦ **quest, search** ◇ **chase, pursuit** Alex would love to go on a *hunt* for buried treasure.

hurdle *noun* ✦ **bar, barrier, difficulty, impediment, obstacle, obstruction, problem** Getting

✦ **best choices**
◇ **other choices**

the President's signature is the last *hurdle* a bill faces before it becomes law. —*verb* ✦ **jump, leap, spring over, vault** In a steeplechase, horses have to *hurdle* hedges, walls, and other obstacles.

hurl *verb* ✦ **fling, heave, launch, pitch, throw, toss** The little dog *hurled* himself into the air to make the catch. ▼

hurry *verb* ✦ **dash, hasten, fly, race, run, rush, speed** I grabbed my jacket as I *hurried* out of the house. —*noun* ✦ **rush** ◇ **dispatch, haste, quickness** Kiara was in a *hurry* to get home before her favorite television show started.

hurt *verb* **1.** ✦ **ache, smart** ◇ **pain, suffer** My arms *hurt* from all the push-ups I did yesterday. **2.** ✦ **damage, harm, impair, injure, ruin, spoil** All of this bad weather is *hurting* the local tourist trade.

hustle *verb* ✦ **hasten, hurry, race, run, rush, speed** The basketball players *hustled* up and down the court.

hut *noun* ✦ **shack, shanty, shed, shelter** ◇ **cabin** Some ski resorts have warming *huts*.

hysterical *adjective* ✦ **excited, frantic, frenzied, panic-stricken, upset** Some people become *hysterical* when they see a snake.

I

idea *noun* ✦ **notion, opinion, thought** ✧ **belief, concept** Everyone had a different *idea* about where we should go for vacation.

ideal *noun* ✦ **dream, wish** ✧ **aim, ambition, goal** My *ideal* is to somehow make the world a better place. —*adjective* ✦ **excellent, fitting, perfect** ✧ **satisfactory, suitable** This field is *ideal* for playing softball.

identical *adjective* ✦ **matching** ✧ **equal, exact, like, same** My parents gave my brother and me *identical* wristwatches.

identify *verb* ✦ **distinguish, know, recognize** ✧ **describe, pinpoint** Javier had no problem *identifying* his dog at the animal shelter.

idiot *noun* ✦ **dummy, dunce, fool** Grandpa said that he felt like an *idiot* the time he went golfing and forgot to bring his clubs.

idle *adjective* **1.** ✦ **inactive, unused** ✧ **inert, vacant** The town's snowplow stood *idle* all summer long. **2.** ✦ **lazy, shiftless, slothful** I'd hate to be an *idle* kid who sat around doing nothing all day. **3.** ✦ **empty, hollow, useless** ✧ **vain, worthless** It's better to try to change things than to just make *idle* complaints. —*verb* ✦ **dawdle, while** ✧ **loaf, lounge, waste** William likes to *idle* away rainy days by playing computer games.

idol *noun* **1.** ✦ **image, statue** ✧ **deity, god, goddess** The archaeologist found a gold *idol* in the ruins of an ancient temple. **2.** ✦ **hero, heroine** ✧ **celebrity, star** Dylan's *idol* is a prizewinning biologist.

ignite *verb* ✦ **burn, combust, kindle, light** ✧ **flame** Dry leaves *ignite* easily.

ignorant *adjective* **1.** ✦ **uneducated, untaught** ✧ **illiterate** When I started taking cooking lessons I felt *ignorant*, but by the end of the year I had learned many skills. **2.** ✦ **unaware,** unconscious, uninformed ✧ **unfamiliar** Many pioneers were *ignorant* of the dangers that they would have to face.

ignore *verb* ✦ **disregard, forget about, overlook** ✧ **neglect** I tried to *ignore* the sound of the loud party.

ill *adjective* **1.** ✦ **sick, unwell** ✧ **ailing, unhealthy** Brittany felt *ill* and went to bed early. **2.** ✦ **adverse, bad** ✧ **evil, harmful, unfavorable** It's an old superstition that spilling salt will bring *ill* fortune. —*noun* ✦ **affliction, evil, misery, misfortune, trouble** Poverty is one of the *ills* that affect society today.

illegal *adjective* ✦ **criminal, illicit, unlawful** ✧ **lawless, prohibited, wrongful** Vandalism is *illegal*.

illness *noun* ✦ **ailment, malady, sickness** ✧ **affliction, disease** Keith's *illness* caused him to miss two days of school.

illuminate *verb* ✦ **light, light up** ✧ **brighten, lighten** Floodlights *illuminated* the entire baseball field.

illusion *noun* ✦ **falsehood, misbelief, misconception, mistake** ✧ **delusion, mirage** The notion that money can buy happiness is an *illusion*.

illustrate *verb* **1.** ✦ **clarify, demonstrate, explain** ✧ **show** The teacher *illustrated* her point by giving several specific examples. **2.** ✧ **adorn, decorate, draw, paint, sketch** *Where the Wild Things Are* was written and *illustrated* by Maurice Sendak.

image *noun* ✦ **likeness, picture, portrait** ✧ **reflection, resemblance** A dollar bill bears the *image* of George Washington.

imaginary *adjective* ✦ **fictional, legendary, nonexistent, unreal** Dragons and unicorns are *imaginary* creatures.

✦ **best choices**
✧ **other choices**

imagination *noun* **1.** ✦ **fancy, fantasy, mind** ✧ **impression, notion, thought** I have an invisible friend who exists only in my *imagination*. **2.** ✦ **creativity, originality** ✧ **inspiration, vision** When my teacher read my short story, she said that I have a lot of *imagination*.

imagine *verb* **1.** ✦ **picture, visualize** ✧ **conceive, fancy, fantasize** As I listened to the story, I could *imagine* the whole scene perfectly. **2.** ✦ **assume, guess, presume, suppose** ✧ **suspect, think** I *imagine* you'll want to know all the details about what happened at the party.

imitate *verb* ✦ **copy, mimic, reproduce** ✧ **duplicate, repeat** Television comedians often *imitate* the voices of famous people.

imitation *noun* ✦ **copy, duplicate, likeness, replica, reproduction** This statue is an *imitation* of an authentic Egyptian artifact.

immature *adjective* ✦ **babyish, childish, juvenile** ✧ **foolish, infantile, young, youthful** It was *immature* of me to think that I could always get my own way.

immediate *adjective* **1.** ✦ **instant, prompt, quick, speedy, swift** ✧ **sudden** This medicine is guaranteed to give *immediate* relief. **2.** ✦ **close, near** ✧ **adjacent, direct, next** My aunt is planning a small wedding, and only the *immediate* family will be invited.

Antonyms
immediate *adjective*
1. deferred, delayed, late, overdue, slow, tardy
2. distant, faraway, remote, removed

immediately *adverb* ✦ **at once, instantly, now, promptly, right away** We need to leave *immediately* or we'll be late.

immense *adjective* ✦ **colossal, enormous, gigantic, huge, massive** ✧ **large, vast** The volcano erupted with enough force to hurl *immense* boulders into the air.

immerse *verb* **1.** ✦ **dip, douse, dunk, plunge, submerge** ✧ **soak** Clean the fruits and vegetables by *immersing* them in water. ▶ **2.** ✦ **absorb by, engage with, interest in, involve with, occupy with** Lauren was so deeply *immersed in* her video game that she lost track of the time.

immigrate *verb* ✦ **migrate, move, relocate** ✧ **colonize, settle** Lian and her family *immigrated* to the United States from Vietnam.

imminent *adjective* ✦ **at hand, close, near, looming** ✧ **immediate, inevitable** Defeat seemed *imminent*, but we won the game by scoring a touchdown at the last moment.

immoral *adjective* ✦ **bad, wrong** ✧ **evil, sinful, wicked** Most people would agree that cheating is *immoral*.

immortal *adjective* ✦ **eternal, everlasting, undying** ✧ **ceaseless, endless** According to ancient Greek religion, Zeus was the king of the *immortal* gods. ▶

immune *adjective* ✦ **resistant** ✧ **exempt, free, protected, safe** Some lucky people are *immune* to poison ivy.

impact *noun* **1.** ✦ **collision, crash** ✧ **blow, contact, jolt** This crater was formed by the *impact* of a meteor. **2.** ✦ **effect, influence** ✧ **force, impression, meaning** That book had a strong *impact* on my life.

impair *verb* ✦ de-crease, hinder, re-duce ✧ damage, harm, hurt, injure Clipping a bird's wing feathers *impairs* its ability to fly.

impartial *adjective* ✦ fair, neutral, objective, unbiased ✧ just A good referee is *impartial*.

impatient *adjective* 1. ✦ anxious, avid, eager, keen ✧ restless I am *impatient* to get back to school. 2. ✦ annoyed, exasperated, irri-tated ✧ intolerant The *impatient* driver kept honking her horn at the pedestrians in the crosswalk.

imperative *adjective* ✦ dire, essential, mandatory, necessary, urgent It was *imperative* for the deep-sea diver to return to the surface because she was low on air.

imperfect *adjective* ✦ defective, deficient, faulty, flawed ✧ incomplete *Imperfect* vision can usually be corrected with eyeglasses.

imperial *adjective* ✧ majestic, regal, royal, sovereign, stately The emperor was protected by his *imperial* guard.

implement *noun* ✦ device, instrument, tool ✧ object, utensil Pencils and pens are writing *implements*.

imply *verb* ✦ hint, indicate, suggest ✧ mean, signify Randy's expression *implied* that he disagreed with what I said.

impolite *adjective* ✦ discourteous, disre-spectful, inconsiderate, rude It is *impolite* to chew with your mouth open.

important *adjective* 1. ✦ big, critical, signif-icant ✧ meaningful, serious, valuable Mom has an *important* meeting at work today. 2. ✦ dis-tinguished, eminent, influential, prominent ✧ powerful The most *important* guests were seat-ed at the head of the table.

impose *verb* 1. ✦ assess, decree, levy, place, put ✧ dictate The city council *imposed* a new tax on luxury items. 2. ✦ bother, inconvenience, intrude on, trouble I'd love to stay for dinner, if you're sure I wouldn't be *imposing on* you.

impossible *adjective* ✦ unattainable ✧ impractical, futile, hopeless It's *impossible* to be in two places at one time.

impostor *noun* ✦ fake, fraud, phony, pre-tender The man claimed to be a movie star, but he was an *impostor* who had never done any acting.

impress *verb* ✦ affect, awe, move, strike ✧ influence, touch Seeing Saturn's rings through the telescope really *impressed* me.

impression *noun* 1. ✦ effect, impact ✧ appearance, image, influence The new teacher made a good *impression* on her first day at school. 2. ✦ feeling, hunch, idea, notion ✧ suspicion I have the *impression* that you're ready to go now. 3. ✦ imprint, indentation, outline ✧ mark, stamp This rock contains the fossilized *impression* of a leaf.

impressive *adjective* ✦ affecting, awesome, moving, stirring ✧ influential, touching The Grand Canyon is an *impressive* sight. ▼

improper *adjective* ✦ **inappropriate, unfit, unsuitable** ◇ **incorrect, wrong** Sweatpants are *improper* attire for a formal wedding.

improve *verb* ✦ **better, develop, help** ◇ **perfect, polish, refine** Rasheeda's visit to America *improved* her English.

improvement *noun* ✦ **advance, upgrade (from)** ◇ **change, enhancement, progress, revision** Our new car is a big *improvement* over the one we used to have.

improvise *verb* ✦ **concoct, contrive, devise** ◇ **invent, originate** My brother *improvised* a toy airplane using a milk carton and some coat hangers.

impulse *noun* ✦ **urge, whim** ◇ **inclination, motive, stimulus** Carleton was acting on a generous *impulse* when he shared his dessert with a friend.

impulsive *adjective* ✦ **hasty, impetuous, rash, reckless** ◇ **foolish, spontaneous** I soon regretted my *impulsive* offer to baby-sit all day for the kids next door.

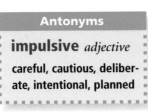

Antonyms

impulsive *adjective*

careful, cautious, deliberate, intentional, planned

in *preposition* ✦ **inside, into, within** ◇ **at, to** Please put your jacket *in* the closet.

inaccurate *adjective* ✦ **false, incorrect, mistaken, wrong** ◇ **faulty** The tabloid article was full of *inaccurate* information.

inappropriate *adjective* ✦ **improper, unfit, unsuitable** ◇ **incorrect, wrong** Yolanda's school has a strict dress code, and blue jeans are considered *inappropriate*.

inaugurate *verb* **1.** ✦ **induct, install** The new President will be *inaugurated* next month. **2.** ✦ **begin, commence, initiate, start** ◇ **introduce, open** Postal service was *inaugurated* in the United States in 1710.

incapable *adjective* ◇ **helpless, incompetent, powerless, unable, unfit** Whales are *incapable* of breathing underwater.

incense *verb* ✦ **anger, enrage, infuriate, madden** ◇ **irritate** It *incenses* me when someone cuts in front of me in a line.

incentive *noun* ✦ **encouragement, inducement, motivation, spur, stimulus** ◇ **reason** The store offered big discounts as an *incentive* to bring in new customers.

incident *noun* ✦ **affair, event, experience, happening, occurrence** Debrah didn't remember the funny *incident* until I reminded her.

incline *verb* ✦ **lean, slant, slope, tilt, tip** ◇ **list** The Leaning Tower of Pisa *inclines* more than fourteen feet to one side. —*noun* ✦ **grade, rise, slope** ◇ **hill** Monique walked her bike down the steep *incline*.

include *verb* ✦ **cover, encompass, take in** ◇ **contain, hold, involve** The price of the meal *includes* one medium drink and a dessert.

income *noun* ✦ **money** ◇ **earnings, pay, resources, wage** My sister's after-school job is her main source of *income*.

incompetent *adjective* ✦ **inadequate, incapable, unqualified, unskilled** ◇ **inefficient** It's hard to learn from an *incompetent* teacher.

incomplete *adjective* ✦ **deficient, lacking, partial, unfinished** ◇ **fragmentary, spotty** Jeremy's coin collection is *incomplete* because he's missing a couple of rare pennies. ▶

inconvenience *noun* ✦ **annoyance, bother, difficulty** ✧ **drawback, trouble** It was a real *inconvenience* when we lost the television's remote control. —*verb* ✦ **bother, disturb, trouble** ✧ **annoy, upset** Would it *inconvenience* you to give me a ride home?

incorrect *adjective* ✦ **false, inaccurate, mistaken, untrue, wrong** The *incorrect* answers are marked with red ink.

increase *verb* ✦ **amplify, augment, boost, enlarge, expand** ✧ **grow, multiply, swell** Regular practice will *increase* our chances of winning. —*noun* ✦ **expansion, gain, growth, rise** ✧ **advance, raise** The world is experiencing a population *increase* of almost ninety million people per year.

incredible *adjective* **1.** ✦ **inconceivable, unbelievable, unconvincing** ✧ **improbable** Your excuse about aliens stealing your homework is *incredible*. **2.** ✦ **amazing, astonishing, extraordinary, fantastic** ✧ **fabulous** The hurricane struck land with *incredible* fury.

indeed *adverb* ✦ **certainly, definitely, positively, really, truly** You are *indeed* my best friend.

indefinite *adjective* ✦ **open, uncertain, unclear, undecided, vague** ✧ **doubtful** My plans for the weekend are still *indefinite*.

independence *noun* ✦ **freedom, liberty, self-reliance** I had a feeling of *independence* the first time I walked to school by myself.

independent *adjective* **1.** ✦ **autonomous, free, self-governing, sovereign** ✧ **liberated** The United States became an *independent* nation on September 3, 1783. **2.** ✦ **self-reliant, self-sufficient** When I decided on my own to join the debate club, I felt very *independent*.

indicate *verb* ✦ **designate, mark, point out, reveal, show** The pirate put a big "X" on his map to *indicate* where the treasure was buried.

indifferent *adjective* ✦ **apathetic (toward), unconcerned (about), uninterested (in)** ✧ **detached, neutral** How could anyone be *indifferent* to the suffering of others?

indirect *adjective* **1.** ✦ **roundabout** ✧ **long, rambling, winding** Ryan was in no hurry so he took an *indirect* route home. **2.** ✦ **ambiguous, evasive, vague** The politician gave an *indirect* answer to the embarrassing question.

individual *adjective* **1.** ✦ **separate, single** ✧ **lone, sole, solitary.** This store allows you to buy candy in bulk or by the *individual* piece. **2.** ✦ **personal, private** ✧ **distinctive, particular, special** Which movies we enjoy is a matter of *individual* taste. —*noun* ✦ **person** ✧ **being, creature, fellow, human, soul** Lara is a much more thoughtful *individual* than most people realize.

indulge *verb* ✦ **appease, gratify, satisfy** ✧ **baby, pamper, spoil** Ricky *indulged* his craving for ice cream by having a chocolate sundae.

industrious *adjective* ✦ **active, busy, diligent, energetic, productive** Beavers are considered to be *industrious* animals.

industry *noun* ✦ **business** ✧ **commerce, trade** The American automobile *industry* is centered in Detroit.

inert *adjective* ✦ **immobile, motionless, still, unmoving** ✧ **lifeless** An opossum will sometimes lie *inert* in order to trick its enemies into thinking that it is dead.

inevitable *adjective* ✦ **certain, inescapable, sure, unavoidable** It was *inevitable* that my little brother would want a jacket just like mine.

inexpensive *adjective* ✦ **cheap, economical, low-cost, low-priced** ✧ **reasonable** An animal shelter is an *inexpensive* place to get a pet.

inexperienced *adjective* ✦ **green, new, raw, untried** ✧ **unskilled, untrained** Our football team is composed mostly of *inexperienced* players.

✦   **best choices**
✧   **other choices**

infant *noun* ✦ baby, newborn ✧ child, toddler, tot The *infant* slept peacefully in its crib.

Word Groups

To **infect** someone is to transmit an illness to them. **Infect** is a very specific term with no true synonyms. Here are some related words to investigate in a dictionary:

afflict, contaminate, poison, pollute, soil, taint

---

infectious *adjective* ✦ contagious ✧ catching, spreading Vaccines are helpful in preventing the spread of many *infectious* diseases.

infer *verb* ✦ conclude, deduce, gather, presume ✧ know, understand I *infer* from your smile that you are in a good mood.

inferior *adjective* 1. ✦ lesser, lower, secondary, subordinate ✧ under Silver is *inferior* in value to gold. 2. ✦ mediocre, poor, substandard ✧ bad This radio is inexpensive because it is of *inferior* quality.

infinite *adjective* ✦ boundless, endless, limitless, unlimited The number of stars in the night sky is seemingly *infinite*.

inflate *verb* ✦ blow up ✧ expand, swell Shay can *inflate* a balloon with just one breath. ◄

influence *noun* ✦ effect, impact ✧ control, force, power, sway, weight The librarian has had a great *influence* on the kinds of books my sister and I like to read. —*verb* ✦ affect, alter, change, shape ✧ determine, sway Television has greatly *influenced* the way Americans get their news.

influential *adjective* ✦ important, powerful ✧ forceful, persuasive Newspapers are very *influential* because so many people read them.

inform *verb* ✦ advise, notify, tell ✧ relate, report I called my parents to *inform* them that I was at a friend's house.

informal *adjective* ✦ casual, easygoing, simple, relaxed ✧ spontaneous I had an *informal* dinner at my friend's house.

information *noun* ✦ data, facts, knowledge ✧ learning, news Benjamin needs to find *information* about Venus and Mars for his science report.

infrequent *adjective* ✦ rare, uncommon, unusual ✧ isolated, occasional Total solar eclipses are *infrequent* events.

infuriate *verb* ✦ anger, enrage, incense, madden ✧ provoke You really *infuriate* me when you call me names.

Antonyms

infuriate *verb*

calm, comfort, compose, ease, pacify, soothe

ingredient *noun* ✦ component, constituent, element ✧ factor, part Milk and ice cream are the main *ingredients* of a milk shake.

inhabit *verb* ✦ abide in, dwell in, live in, occupy, reside in Adrian discovered that a mouse was *inhabiting* a shoebox in his closet.

inheritance *noun* ✦ legacy ✧ estate, heritage I received a gold ring as part of my *inheritance* from my great-grandmother.

initial *adjective* ✦ earliest, first, original ✧ beginning, introductory My *initial* opinion of Andrea changed when I got to know her better.

initiate *verb* 1. ✦ begin, commence, launch, start ✧ establish, introduce Our history teacher *initiated* the discussion by asking us questions. **2.** ✦ **induct** ✧ **admit, install, receive** Douglas recited the Scout Oath when he was *initiated* into the Boy Scouts.

injure *verb* ✦ **harm, hurt, wound** ✧ **damage, impair** If you're not careful, you can *injure* yourself when you use a pair of scissors.

injury *noun* ✦ **hurt, wound** ✧ **damage, harm** Seth received only a minor *injury* when he fell off his bike.

injustice *noun* ✦ **offense, outrage, wrong** ✧ **crime, misdeed, unfairness** Sending an innocent person to prison is a terrible *injustice*.

inner *adjective* ✦ **inside, interior** ✧ **central, internal, inward** Did you know that the *inner* bark of a willow tree is edible?

innocent *adjective* ✦ **blameless, guiltless, not guilty** ✧ **faultless** According to the law, a person is *innocent* until proven guilty.

inquire *verb* ✦ **ask** ✧ **examine, query, question, quiz** My parents *inquired* about the house that was for sale.

inquisitive *adjective* ✦ **curious, inquiring, investigative, questioning** ✧ **nosy, prying, snoopy** It is easy to think of questions in class when you have an *inquisitive* mind.

insane *adjective* **1.** ✦ **mentally ill** ✧ **crazy, mad** Doctors determined that the man was legally *insane*. **2.** ✦ **dumb, foolish, ridiculous, silly, stupid** I think you're *insane* to go out in this horrible weather.

insecure *adjective* ✦ **shaky, unstable, unsteady, wobbly** ✧ **dangerous, weak** Charles felt that the tall stack of dominoes was too *insecure* to risk adding to.

insert *verb* ✦ **put in** ✧ **enter, inject, introduce** To unlock the drawer, *insert* the key and turn it to the left.

inside *noun* ✦ **interior** ✧ **center, core, middle** The *inside* of Cynthia's jewelry box is lined with red velvet. —*adjective* ✦ **inner, interior** ✧ **central, internal** I prefer to use the *inside* lane when I run laps on the school track.

insignia *noun* ✦ **badge, emblem** ✧ **crest, mark, sign, symbol** A three-leaf clover is the official *insignia* of the Girl Scouts of America.

insignificant *adjective* ✦ **meaningless, petty, trifling, trivial, unimportant** The teacher said that my mistake was too *insignificant* to worry about.

insincere *adjective* ✦ **artificial, phony, pretended** ✧ **deceitful, dishonest** I could tell that her smile was *insincere*.

insist *verb* **1.** ✦ **demand, require** ✧ **command, urge** The teacher *insisted* that homework assignments be turned in on time. **2.** ✦ **affirm, assert, claim, contend, declare, state** The lawyer *insisted* that his client was innocent.

inspect *verb* ✦ **check, examine, observe, survey** ✧ **investigate, study** Schools are *inspected* regularly by fire department officials.

inspection *noun* ✦ **check, checkup, examination, review, survey** Commercial airplanes undergo regular safety *inspections*.

inspiration *noun* **1.** ✦ **encouragement, incentive, motivation** ✧ **stimulation, vigor** The coach's dramatic speech at halftime gave *inspiration* to his players. **2.** ✦ **concept, idea, revelation, vision** ✧ **brainstorm, creativity** Some inventors say that they have gotten their best *inspirations* from dreams.

inspire *verb* ✦ **encourage, motivate, prompt, stimulate, stir, urge** The crowd's cheers *inspired* the runner to try harder.

install *verb* ✦ **put in, set up** ✧ **establish, locate, place, position** Dad had a hard time *installing* the new air conditioner.

✦ **best choices**
✧ **other choices**

instance *noun* ◆ **case, occasion, time** ◇ **example, illustration, sample, situation** I can think of only one *instance* all year long when I was late for school.

instant *noun* ◆ **minute, moment, second** ◇ **flash, jiffy** I saw the deer for just an *instant* before it disappeared into the forest. —*adjective* ◆ **immediate, prompt** ◇ **fast, quick, swift** Our school play was an *instant* success.

instantly *adverb* ◆ **at once, immediately, right away** ◇ **directly, now, quickly** When Tyrell picked up the phone, he recognized the principal's voice *instantly*.

instead *adverb* ◆ **in place of, rather than** ◇ **alternatively** We decided to go bowling *instead of* seeing a movie.

instinct *noun* ◆ **feeling, hunch, intuition** ◇ **impulse, tendency, urge** Mom says that if I follow my *instincts*, I'll always do the right thing.

institute *verb* ◆ **establish, organize, set up, start** ◇ **found, originate** The city government *instituted* a new recycling program. ▶ —*noun* ◆ **academy, institution, school** ◇ **establishment, foundation** My sister wants to study at an art *institute* after she graduates from high school.

institution *noun* ◆ **academy, institute, school** ◇ **establishment, foundation** Colleges and universities are *institutions* of higher education.

instruct *verb* **1.** ◆ **coach, educate, guide, teach, train** ◇ **inform** Jenny's skydiving coach *instructed* her in the proper use of a parachute. **2.** ◆ **bid, command, direct, order, tell** The spy received a secret message that *instructed* her to return home.

instruction *noun* **1.** ◆ **guidance, teaching, training** ◇ **education, lesson, schooling** You'll need some *instruction* before you can use this computer. **2.** ◆ **command, direction, order** ◇ **mandate** The captain expected his men to follow his *instructions*.

instrument *noun* ◆ **device, implement, mechanism, tool** ◇ **utensil** A barometer is an *instrument* for measuring atmospheric pressure.

insult *verb* ◆ **affront, offend** ◇ **humiliate, scorn, snub, taunt** I did not mean to *insult* you. —*noun* ◆ **affront, offense** ◇ **scorn, snub, taunt** It was an *insult* to my intelligence to expect me to believe that excuse.

Antonyms
insult *verb*
acclaim, applaud, commend, compliment, flatter, laud, praise

integrity *noun* ◆ **character, honesty, principle** ◇ **honor, virtue** It takes *integrity* to tell the truth when you know you'll be punished for it.

intellectual *adjective* ◆ **learned, scholarly** ◇ **intelligent, mental, thoughtful** The library subscribes to several *intellectual* magazines about science and philosophy. —*noun* ◆ **brain, mind, scholar, thinker** ◇ **genius, sage** Albert Einstein was one of the greatest *intellectuals* of the twentieth century.

intelligence *noun* ◆ **brains, brightness, cleverness, intellect, mind** Tonya doesn't know how to play chess, but she has the *intelligence* to learn.

intelligent *adjective* ◆ **alert, bright, brilliant, clever, smart** ◇ **wise** Only the most *intelligent* students understood Ms. Dubie's explanation the first time around.

intend *verb* ◆ **aim, expect, mean, plan, propose** ◇ **hope, wish** What to you *intend* to do this summer?

intense *adjective* ✦ **extreme, fierce, great, strong, terrible, terrific** ✧ **furious, heightened, violent** The continent of Antarctica is known for its *intense* cold.

intensity *noun* ✦ **energy, ferocity, fury, power, strength, violence** The forest fire burned with great *intensity*.

intent *adjective* ✦ **absorbed, attentive, determined, earnest** ✧ **deep, resolute** Joshua had an *intent* look on his face as he worked on the difficult problem. —*noun* ✦ **aim, ambition, goal, intention, objective** ✧ **end, purpose** It is my *intent* to go to college someday.

intentional *adjective* ✦ **deliberate, intended** ✧ **planned, premeditated, voluntary** Doctors take an oath in which they promise to never do any *intentional* harm to anyone.

intercept *verb* ✦ **cut off, head off** ✧ **block, catch, seize, stop** Two fighter planes were sent to *intercept* the enemy aircraft.

interest *noun* **1.** ✦ **attention, curiosity** ✧ **care, concern, notice, regard** I watched with *interest* to see if my sister could beat the computer at checkers. **2.** ✦ **activity, hobby, pastime, pursuit** ✧ **recreation** Robyn's *interests* include reading books and playing soccer. **3.** ✦ **(to) advantage, (to) benefit, (for) good** ✧ **profit, welfare** It is in the *interest* of the team for all players to practice as hard as they can. —*verb* ✦ **attract, engage, intrigue, fascinate** ✧ **absorb** Everything about airplanes *interests* me.

interesting *adjective* ✦ **absorbing, appealing, entertaining, fascinating, gripping, riveting** The most *interesting* part of the book was when the main character went swimming with a pod of dolphins.

interfere *verb* ✦ **interrupt, intervene, meddle** ✧ **disturb, hinder, tamper** My friends were having a private talk, and I knew that I shouldn't *interfere*.

interior *noun* ✦ **inside** ✧ **center, core, heart, middle** There's a diagram in my geography book showing the *interior* of a volcano. —*adjective* ✦ **inner, inside, internal** Our science teacher took a telephone apart to show us the *interior* structure.

intermediate *adjective* ✦ **halfway, middle, midway** ✧ **central, median, medium** A cocoon is the *intermediate* stage between a caterpillar and a butterfly.

intermission *noun* ✦ **break, pause, recess** ✧ **rest, stop, time-out** There will be a brief *intermission* halfway through the play.

internal *adjective* ✦ **inner, inside, interior** The *internal* workings of a clock are very complicated.

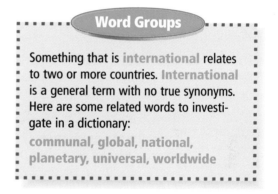

Word Groups

Something that is international relates to two or more countries. International is a general term with no true synonyms. Here are some related words to investigate in a dictionary:

communal, global, national, planetary, universal, worldwide

interpret *verb* ✦ **decipher, explain, understand** ✧ **clarify, define** Rachel is reading a book about how to *interpret* dreams.

interrupt *verb* ✦ **break into, cut off, halt, stop** ✧ **disturb, hinder, interfere** The alarm clock *interrupted* my dream. ▶

interval *noun* ✦ **period, span, spell, stretch** ✧ **break, gap, pause, space** There was an *interval* of warm weather between the two huge snowstorms.

✦ best choices
✧ other choices

interview *noun* ✦ **conference, consultation** ◇ **discussion, meeting, talk** Our teacher is scheduling *interviews* with all of our parents. —*verb* ✦ **talk to** ◇ **examine, interrogate, question** Colin had to do a report on law enforcement, so he *interviewed* a police officer.

intolerant *adjective* ✦ **biased, close-minded, narrow-minded, prejudiced** I try not to be *intolerant* when I meet people whose beliefs are different from my own.

intricate *adjective* ✦ **complex, complicated, detailed, elaborate** ◇ **fancy** A computer program has many *intricate* parts that all have to work together.

Antonyms
intricate *adjective*
clear, elementary, modest, plain, simple, straightforward

intrigue *verb* ✦ **fascinate, interest** ◇ **attract, excite** Many people are *intrigued* by the possibility that there might be life on other planets.

introduce *verb* **1.** ✦ **present** ◇ **acquaint, announce** Janine *introduced* herself to her new neighbor. ◀ **2.** ✦ **begin, launch, start** ◇ **establish, originate, put forth** Mr. Nolan *introduced* the unit on electricity by showing us how a battery works.

invade *verb* ✦ **assault, attack, overrun, penetrate** ◇ **occupy, raid** Germany *invaded* Russia during World War II.

invaluable *adjective* ✦ **precious, priceless, valuable, worthy** ◇ **expensive** Reading and writing are *invaluable* skills.

invasion *noun* ✦ **assault, attack** ◇ **aggression, offensive, raid** The Great Wall of China was built to protect the country from foreign *invasion*.

invent *verb* ✦ **devise, develop, originate** ◇ **concoct, contrive, create, dream up** The telephone was *invented* by Alexander Graham Bell in 1876. ▶

invention *noun* ✦ **development** ◇ **creation, production** Thomas Edison is credited with the *invention* of the first practical light bulb.

inventory *noun* **1.** ✦ **list, record** ◇ **catalog, file, register, summary** The teachers made an *inventory* of all classroom supplies. **2.** ✦ **stock, stockpile, store, supply** ◇ **reserve** The department store had a sale to reduce its *inventory* of winter clothing.

investigate *verb* ✦ **analyze, examine, inspect, study** ◇ **explore, follow, probe** The police are *investigating* clues related to last week's robbery.

invisible *adjective* ✦ **indistinguishable, unnoticeable, unobservable** ◇ **concealed, disguised, hidden** The snowshoe rabbit was almost *invisible* against the white snowdrift.

invite *verb* ✦ **ask** ◇ **bid, request, summon** Cassandra *invited* two of her friends to spend the night at her house.

involuntary *adjective* ✦ **automatic, spontaneous** ◇ **impulsive, instinctive** Breathing and digestion are *involuntary* actions.

involve *verb* **1.** ✦ **call for, include, require** ◇ **contain, have** Dad's job *involves* a lot of traveling. **2.** ✦ **absorb in, engage in, immerse in, occupy with** We were so *involved* in our conversation that we didn't hear the phone ring.

irregular *adjective* ✦ **unequal, uneven, variable** ◇ **abnormal, unusual** The patient had an *irregular* heartbeat.

irritate *verb* **1.** ✦ **annoy, bother, disturb, exasperate, provoke** ◇ **anger** That noisy car alarm is beginning to *irritate* me. **2.** ✦ **aggravate, inflame** ◇ **hurt, worsen** You'll only *irritate* that mosquito bite if you continue to scratch it.

island *noun* ✦ **isle, islet** ◇ **archipelago, atoll** There's a little *island* in the center of the lake.

isolate *verb* ✦ **quarantine, segregate, separate, set apart** The veterinarian *isolated* the sick puppy so that it wouldn't infect any other animals.

issue *noun* ✦ **matter, question, subject, topic** ◇ **problem** Health care is an *issue* that affects everyone. —*verb* ✦ **dispense, distribute, give out, hand out** ◇ **deliver, release** The coach *issued* new uniforms to everyone on the team.

item *noun* **1.** ✦ **article, object, thing** ◇ **element, particular** Before she started to pack, Kimberly made a list of the *items* that she needed for her trip abroad. **2.** ✦ **account, article, entry, feature, report, story** Did you read the *item* in the paper about our school concert?

itemize *verb* ✦ **detail, document, list, record** ◇ **catalog** This receipt *itemizes* everything that we bought.

✦   **best choices**
◇   **other choices**

J

jab *verb* ✦ **poke, push, stab, thrust** ✧ **nudge, prod** Lindsay *jabbed* her fork into the baked potato. —*noun* ✦ **blow, punch** ✧ **nudge, poke, strike** The boxer threw a series of quick *jabs* at his opponent's stomach.

jacket *noun* **1.** ✧ **coat, parka, windbreaker** Ray took a warm *jacket* with him to the football game. ◄ **2.** ✦ **cover, dust jacket, wrapper** ✧ **case, container, sheath** Dustin keeps his special comic books in protective plastic *jackets*.

jagged *adjective* ✦ **pointed, ragged, uneven** ✧ **notched, rough** Alexis accidentally cut her finger on a *jagged* piece of broken glass.

jail *noun* ✦ **jailhouse, prison** ✧ **pen, penitentiary** The sheriff kept the outlaws in *jail*. —*verb* ✦ **imprison, lock up** ✧ **confine, detain** The police have arrested and *jailed* two suspects.

jam *verb* ✦ **cram, crowd, load, pack, press, squeeze, stuff, wedge** My sister tried to *jam* more clothes into her suitcase. —*noun* **1.** ✧ **barrier, blockage, congestion, crush, obstruction** A log *jam* blocked the river. **2.** ✦ **difficulty, plight, predicament, trouble** ✧ **problem** The tourists were in a real *jam* when they lost all of their money.

jar¹ *noun* ✧ **bottle, container, jug, vase, vessel** Dad keeps his loose change in a *jar* on his desk.

jar² *verb* **1.** ✦ **jolt, rattle, rock, shake, vibrate** The earthquake *jarred* our house but didn't cause any damage. **2.** ✦ **grate on, irritate, upset** ✧ **annoy, disturb** The sound of chalk scraping on a blackboard *jars* my nerves. —*noun* ✦ **bounce, bump, jolt, jounce** ✧ **crash, impact** I felt repeated *jars* as we drove down the bumpy dirt road.

jealous *adjective* **1.** ✧ **angry, anxious, insecure, possessive, threatened** Madeline was *jealous* when her parents paid extra attention to her baby brother. **2.** ✦ **covetous, envious** ✧ **resentful** Who wouldn't be *jealous* of your fantastic new computer?

jealousy *noun* ✦ **envy** ✧ **grudge, resentment, spite** The man was filled with *jealousy* when his neighbor won the lottery.

jeer *verb* ✦ **laugh at, mock, ridicule, taunt** ✧ **insult** I thought the comedian was very good, but some people in the audience *jeered at* him.

jeopardy *noun* ✦ **danger, peril** ✧ **risk, threat** Police officers sometimes place their lives in *jeopardy* in order to protect the public.

jerk *verb* ✦ **pull, tear, tug, wrench, yank** Alexandra's dog *jerked* the leash out of her hand and ran off after a cat. —*noun* ✦ **bump, jolt, lurch, snap** ✧ **pull, tug, yank** The roller coaster started with a *jerk* and then quickly picked up speed.

jest *noun* ✦ **gag, joke** ✧ **hoax, prank, trick** I hope your statement that dinner would be three hours late was a *jest*. —*verb* ✦ **fool, joke, kid, tease** Grandpa was *jesting* when he said that mice are the best bait for catfish.

jet *noun* ✦ **spray, spurt, squirt, stream** ✧ **flow** An erupting geyser shoots a *jet* of boiling water high into the air.

jewel *noun* ✦ **gem, gemstone, precious stone** ✧ **ornament** Emeralds and sapphires are my favorite *jewels*. ►

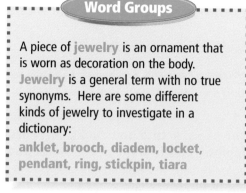

Word Groups

A piece of jewelry is an ornament that is worn as decoration on the body. Jewelry is a general term with no true synonyms. Here are some different kinds of jewelry to investigate in a dictionary:

anklet, brooch, diadem, locket, pendant, ring, stickpin, tiara

jiffy *noun* ✦ **flash, instant, minute, moment, second** Lunch will be ready in a *jiffy*.

jingle *verb* ✦ **chime, clink, ring, tinkle** ✧ **jangle** The bell on the shop door *jingled* as I entered. —*noun* ✦ **chime, clink, ring, tinkle** ✧ **jangle** I enjoy listening to the *jingle* of our wind chimes.

job *noun* 1. ✦ **assignment, chore, duty, task** ✧ **obligation** My sister's *job* is to clear the table, and mine is to wash the dishes. 2. ✦ **position, situation** ✧ **employment, occupation, work** Mom just got a *job* as a computer programmer.

jog *verb* ✦ **lope, run, trot** ✧ **sprint** Whitney *jogged* around the track. —*noun* ✦ **run** ✧ **dash, race, sprint** I like to go for a *jog* first thing in the morning.

join *verb* 1. ✦ **attach, connect, fasten, link, unite** A special coupling mechanism is used to *join* railroad cars. ▼ 2. ✦ **ally, assemble, combine,**

merge, unite ✧ **associate** The two scout troops *joined* together to paint the playground equipment. 3. ✦ **enlist in, enroll in, enter, sign up for** My little sister plans to *join* my singing group as soon as she's old enough.

joint *noun* ✦ **junction, seam** ✧ **connection, link, union** The clacking sound that a train makes is caused by the wheels rolling over *joints* in the track. —*adjective* ✦ **common, mutual, shared** ✧ **combined** Mom deposited Dad's paycheck in their *joint* bank account.

joke *noun* ✦ **jest** ✧ **gag, prank, trick** The honoree started her speech with a *joke*. —*verb* ✦ **fool, jest, kid, tease** I was *joking* when I said that I wanted a peanut-butter pizza.

jolly *adjective* ✦ **cheerful, gay, gleeful, happy, jovial, merry** Our *jolly* neighbor is always smiling and laughing.

jolt *verb* ✦ **bounce, bump, jar, jerk, lurch, shake** We were almost *jolted* out of our seats when our car hit a big pothole. —*noun* 1. ✦ **bounce, bump, jerk, lurch** ✧ **jar, shake** The plane landed with a small *jolt*. 2. ✦ **shock, surprise** ✧ **blow** I got a big *jolt* when I looked at my new haircut.

jostle *verb* ✦ **bump, crowd, joggle, press, push, shove** The pigs *jostled* each other as they tried to get to their feeding trough.

jot *verb* ✦ **note, record, register, write** We keep a notepad next to the telephone on which to *jot* messages.

journal *noun* 1. ✧ **chronicle, diary, log, record** Lewis and Clark described many interesting plants and animals in the *journals* they kept on their expedition. 2. ✦ **magazine, periodical, publication** ✧ **newspaper, paper** I read an article about ancient Greece in a history *journal*.

journalist *noun* ✦ **correspondent, newsperson, reporter** ✧ **writer** A *journalist* interviewed the mayor for a newspaper article.

✦   **best choices**
✧   **other choices**

journey *noun* ◆ **expedition, trip** ◇ **excursion, tour, voyage** Marco Polo's famous *journey* to China lasted twenty-four years. —*verb* ◆ **ramble, roam, tour, travel, trek** ◇ **go** Ashley would love to *journey* through South America.

jovial *adjective* ◆ **cheerful, gay, gleeful, jolly, merry, mirthful** A *jovial* clown with a big smile greeted everyone who entered the circus tent.

joy *noun* ◆ **delight, ecstacy, glee, happiness** ◇ **enjoyment, pleasure** Christopher was filled with *joy* when he was allowed to stay an extra two weeks at camp.

joyful *adjective* ◆ **blissful, cheerful, glad, happy, joyous, merry** This Thanksgiving was especially *joyful* because the whole family was able to be together.

jubilant *adjective* ◆ **delighted, ecstatic, exultant, thrilled** ◇ **triumphant** The prospector was *jubilant* when he discovered a rich vein of gold.

judge *noun* 1. ◆ **justice, magistrate** My new family and I were very happy when the *judge* finalized my adoption. 2. ◆ **critic, evaluator, reviewer** ◇ **referee, umpire** I was a *judge* for our school art contest. —*verb* ◆ **assess, decide, determine** ◇ **decree, rule, try** The defendant's guilt or innocence will be *judged* in a court of law.

judgment *noun* 1. ◆ **conclusion, decision, finding, ruling, verdict** The *judgment* of a court is always based on the existing laws as well as the evidence presented. ▶

2. ◆ **common sense, sense** ◇ **prudence, wisdom** I am glad to have parents who respect my *judgment*.

jug *noun* ◇ **bottle, flask, jar, pitcher, vessel** We bought a *jug* of maple syrup while vacationing in Maine.

juggle *verb* ◆ **toss and catch** ◇ **maneuver, manipulate, shuffle** The circus performer was able to *juggle* five balls while riding a bicycle.

jumble *verb* ◆ **mess up, muddle, scramble** ◇ **confuse, disorder** I *jumbled* everything in my closet while looking for my skateboard. —*noun* ◆ **clutter, mess, muddle, tangle** ◇ **chaos, confusion, disarray, disorder** Cody left a *jumble* of dirty clothes on the floor of his room.

Antonyms
jumble *verb*
assemble, classify, distribute, group, order, organize, sort
jumble *noun*
collection, pattern, plan, sequence, set, system

jumbo *adjective* ◆ **colossal, enormous, gigantic, huge, immense, large** I ordered a *jumbo* plate of French fries.

jump *verb* ◆ **bound, hop, hurdle, leap, spring, vault** The squirrel *jumped* out of the cyclist's way. —*noun* ◆ **bound, hop, leap, spring, vault** Chad cleared the pole on his first *jump*.

junction *noun* ◆ **intersection, joining, linking, meeting, union** St. Louis is located at the *junction* of the Mississippi and Missouri rivers.

jungle *noun* ◆ **rain forest, tropical forest** ◇ **brush, wilderness** *Jungles* are humid because they receive a lot of rain.

junior *adjective* 1. ◆ **adolescent, juvenile** ◇ **youthful** Caroline entered the *junior* division of the surfing tournament. 2. ◆ **minor, secondary,**

subordinate ◇ **lesser, lower, under** Even though Moira is only a *junior* member of our club, she is one of the most active.

junk *noun* ✦ **debris, garbage, litter, refuse, rubbish, trash** To clear the lot for our community garden we had to throw away a lot of *junk*.

just *adjective* ✦ **fair, impartial, objective, unbiased** ◇ **honest, right** This judge is known for making *just* decisions. —*adverb*

1. ✦ **exactly, precisely** ◇ **completely, entirely, perfectly** Mom says that I look *just* like her Great-Uncle Raymond.
2. ✦ **recently** ◇ **lately, now, presently** The free concert had *just* started when we arrived at the park.

Antonyms
just *adjective*
biased, narrow-minded, one-sided, partial, prejudiced, unfair

3. ✦ **barely, hardly, only, scarcely** You'll *just* have time to get to the store before it closes.

justice *noun* ✦ **fairness, justness, rightness** ◇ **honesty** If *justice* is to be achieved, the innocent man must be released.

justify *verb* ✦ **confirm, support, sustain, uphold, validate, verify** Lisa *justified* my trust when she returned the book that I had loaned her.

jut *verb* ✦ **extend, hang, protrude, stick out** ◇ **bulge, project** The rude passenger sat so that his legs *jutted* into the aisle of the bus.

juvenile *adjective* ✦ **immature, young, youthful** ◇ **childish, infant** *Juvenile* elephants stay with their mothers for up to ten years. —*noun* ✦ **child, minor, youngster, youth** ◇ **boy, girl** *Juveniles* under the age of eighteen may not sign a legal contract.

✦   **best choices**
◇   **other choices**

K

keen *adjective* **1.** ✦ **acute, perceptive, sensitive, sharp** ✧ **fine, quick** Bears have a *keen* sense of smell. **2.** ✦ **ardent, avid, eager, enthusiastic** ✧ **excited** Jeremiah is a *keen* moviegoer.

keep *verb* **1.** ✦ **have, hold, maintain, retain** Mom said that I could *keep* the pen I had borrowed from her. **2.** ✦ **continue, persevere in, persist in** ✧ **remain, stay** I *keep* trying to improve my time for running the one-hundred yard dash. **3.** ✦ **place, store** ✧ **carry, stock** Where do you *keep* the mayonnaise and mustard? **4.** ✦ **adhere to, fulfill, honor, observe** ✧ **obey** Matthew *kept* his promise to send me a postcard from his trip. **5.** ✦ **prevent, restrain, stop** ✧ **hinder, impede** A storm *kept* us from going sailing. —*noun* ✦ **livelihood, living, room and board, upkeep** ✧ **income, support** The nanny earned her *keep* by caring for three small children.

keg *noun* ✦ **barrel, cask** ✧ **drum, tank, tub** Carpenters used to buy their nails by the *keg*. ▶

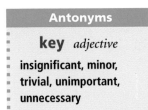

kettle *noun* ✦ **caldron, pot** ✧ **vat, vessel** In colonial times, a *kettle* of hot water was usually kept hanging in the fireplace.

key *noun* **1.** ✦ **answer, clue, explanation, guide, means** ✧ **solution** The *key* to solving this riddle is to listen carefully to its exact wording. **2.** ✦ **formula, means, path, route, secret, ticket, way** Hard work is frequently the *key* to success. —*adjective* ✦ **chief, leading, main, major, top** ✧ **essential, necessary** Your contribution was a *key* factor in making our carnival such a success.

> ### Antonyms
> **key** *adjective*
> insignificant, minor, trivial, unimportant, unnecessary

kick *verb* ✦ **boot** ✧ **hit, knock, strike, tap** Dennis *kicked* the ball and scored a goal. —*noun* ✦ **nudge, poke** ✧ **blow, hit, knock, stroke** Carolyn gave her horse a gentle *kick* in the ribs to get it moving.

kid *noun* ✦ **child, youngster, youth** ✧ **boy, girl, juvenile** Some of the neighborhood *kids* got together to play a game of hide-and-seek. —*verb* ✦ **tease** ✧ **fool, jest, joke, ridicule** I like to *kid* my sister about her boyfriend.

kidnap *verb* ✦ **abduct, carry off, snatch, steal** ✧ **capture, seize** My brother *kidnapped* my favorite doll and demanded a candy bar as ransom.

kill *verb* **1.** ✦ **exterminate, slay** ✧ **assassinate, execute, murder, slaughter** I don't like to *kill* spiders, so I catch them and take them outside. **2.** ✦ **destroy, eliminate, end, extinguish, ruin, wipe out** My injury *killed* any chance that I might have had to win the race. —*noun* ✦ **prey, victim** ✧ **game** The lioness stood guard over her *kill*.

kin *noun* ✦ **family, kinfolk, relations, relatives** Rosa hopes that all of her *kin* can make it to the next family reunion.

kind[1] *adjective* ✦ **considerate, generous, good, goodhearted, helpful** ✧ **gentle** A *kind* woman helped me pick up all the books that I had dropped.

kind[2] *noun* ✦ **category, class, manner, sort, type, variety** There are two *kinds* of pandas—the giant panda and the red panda.

kindle *verb* **1.** ✦ **ignite, light** ✧ **burn, fire** I used a match and some crumpled newspaper to *kindle* our campfire. **2.** ✦ **arouse, awake, inspire, stir, stimulate** My friend *kindled* my interest in computers.

kindly *adjective* ✦ **benevolent, good, goodhearted, humane, kind, kindhearted** The Tin

Woodman is one of many *kindly* characters in *The Wonderful Wizard of Oz* by L. Frank Baum. *—adverb* ✦ **generously, thoughtfully** ✧ **courteously, graciously, politely** My friend *kindly* offered to help me with my homework when she found out I was having trouble.

kindness *noun* ✦ **charity, compassion, decency, goodwill, humanity** ✧ **generosity** Mary believes that all animals should be treated with *kindness*.

king *noun* ✦ **monarch, sovereign, ruler** ✧ **lord** Henry VIII was the *king* of England from 1509 to 1547. ▼

kink *noun* **1.** ✦ **bend, curl, twist** ✧ **coil, knot, tangle** The garden hose had a *kink* in it. **2.** ✦ **cramp, knot, pain, pang, spasm** Jason got a *kink* in his back when he tried to lift a heavy box.

kit *noun* ✦ **outfit, set** ✧ **equipment, materials, tools** Jenna bought a sewing *kit* as a gift for her cousin.

knack *noun* ✦ **aptitude, flair, gift, talent** ✧ **ability, skill** My friend Libby has a *knack* for drawing funny cartoon characters.

kneel *verb* ✧ **bend, bow, crouch, stoop** I *knelt* down to look at the kittens.

Word Groups

A **knife** is a sharp instrument used for cutting and piercing. **Knife** is a general term with no true synonyms. Here are some different kinds of knives to investigate in a dictionary:

cleaver, dagger, dirk, jackknife, machete, pocketknife, scalpel, stiletto, switchblade

knit *verb* **1.** ✧ **crochet, sew, stitch, weave** My baby sitter is teaching me how to *knit* a scarf. ▼ **2.** ✦ **heal, mend** ✧ **attach, join, unite** The doctor said that my broken arm should *knit* in about six weeks.

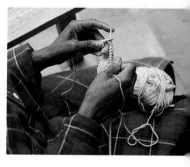

knob *noun* ✦ **handle** ✧ **button, dial, grip, handhold** Our kitchen cabinets have white plastic *knobs* on them.

knock *verb* ✦ **hit, smash, strike** ✧ **beat, pound, rap, tap** Dionne *knocked* her head against the new light fixture. *—noun* ✦ **rap, tap, thump** ✧ **blow, hit, punch, stroke** I just heard a *knock* at the door.

✦   **best choices**
✧   **other choices**

knot *noun* **1.** ◇ **bow, braid, hitch, loop, splice, tie** I'm having a lot of trouble getting this *knot* out of my jump rope. ▶

2. ✦ **gnarl, kink, lump, snag, snarl, tangle** Lisette brushed the *knots* out of her sister's hair. **3.** ✦ **band, batch, bunch, clump, cluster, clutch, group, swarm** A *knot* of people gathered around the musician who was playing on the corner.

know *verb* **1.** ✦ **comprehend, grasp, understand** ◇ **apprehend, fathom** Do you *know* how to read a map? **2.** ✦ **distinguish, identify, perceive** ◇ **notice, recognize** My cousin said that I'd *know* her by her bright green suitcase.

knowledge *noun* **1.** ✦ **data, facts, ideas, information, learning, wisdom** An encyclopedia is a storehouse of *knowledge*. **2.** ✦ **awareness, comprehension, consciousness, understanding** The *knowledge* that skydiving is dangerous keeps many people from trying the sport.

L

label *noun* ✦ **marker, sticker, tag, ticket** ✧ **seal** Emily put a *label* on each item in the yard sale. —*verb* ✦ **mark, tag** ✧ **classify, describe, identify, name** Nadia *labeled* each leaf that she collected for her science project.

labor *noun* **1.** ✦ **exertion, toil, work** ✧ **drudgery, effort** It took years of *labor* to dig the canal. **2.** ✦ **help, laborers, workers, workmen, workwomen** ✧ **crew, employees** The company is a success because it uses highly skilled *labor*. —*verb* ✦ **toil, work** ✧ **strain, strive, struggle** The highway crew *labored* all week to get the road repaired.

lack *verb* ✧ **miss, need, require, want** Our town *lacks* the money to build a new public swimming pool. —*noun* ✦ **deficiency, scarcity, shortage** ✧ **need, want** Not many plants grow in the desert because of the *lack* of rainfall.

lad *noun* ✦ **boy, young man, youngster, youth** My grandfather likes to tell stories about his adventures as a *lad*.

laden *adjective* ✦ **burdened, loaded, weighed down** ✧ **full** The mule train was *laden* with heavy sacks of food and other supplies.

lag *verb* ✦ **dawdle, linger, poke along, trail** ✧ **delay, loiter** I *lagged* behind my friends on our walk home from school because I was tired. —*noun* ✦ **break, pause** ✧ **delay, hesitation, interruption, interval** There was a *lag* in the conversation when we all ran out of things to say.

lair *noun* ✦ **den** ✧ **burrow, refuge, nest** A wolf's *lair* is commonly a hole dug in the ground.

lake *noun* ✧ **pond, pool, reservoir, sea** These *lakes* were formed when the glaciers melted at the end of the Ice Age.

lame *adjective* **1.** ✦ **crippled** ✧ **disabled, handicapped** My dog was *lame* in his front left leg until his paw finally healed. **2.** ✦ **feeble, poor, unconvincing, unsatisfactory, weak** No one laughed at the *lame* joke.

lance *noun* ✦ **spear** ✧ **harpoon, javelin** The horse soldiers were armed with swords and *lances*. —*verb* ✦ **cut, cut open, pierce, prick, puncture** Mom *lanced* my blister with a needle.

land *noun* **1.** ✦ **country, nation, state** ✧ **region, territory** America is sometimes called the *land* of opportunity. **2.** ✦ **earth, ground, soil** ✧ **property, real estate** This is good *land* for growing soybeans. —*verb* **1.** ✦ **alight, set down, touch down** ✧ **arrive, disembark** Astronauts first *landed* on the moon on July 20, 1969. ▼ **2.** ✦ **gain, get, obtain, secure, win** ✧ **catch** The basketball star just *landed* a big five-year contract.

lane *noun* ✦ **road** ✧ **avenue, path, route, street** My grandparents live on a country *lane* that is lined with oak trees.

language   *noun* **1. ✦ tongue ◇ dialect, speech** My best friend can speak two *languages*. **2. ◇ communication, expression, symbolism** American Indians used sign *language* to communicate with other tribes.

lapse   *noun* **1. ✦ failure, slip ◇ blunder, error, mistake** I had a memory *lapse* and couldn't remember my classmate's name. **2. ✦ gap, interruption, interval, pause ◇ lull** Kamilah started taking ballet lessons again after a *lapse* of six months. —*verb* **✦ fall, slide, slip, sink ◇ decline, fade** The baby squirmed for a while, but finally she *lapsed* into sleep.

large   *adjective* **✦ big, considerable, sizable ◇ enormous, huge, immense, vast** A *large* crowd attended the free rock concert.

lark   *noun* **✦ adventure, affair, celebration ◇ caper, prank** Adrian expects that his summer vacation will be a carefree *lark*.

lash¹   *noun* **✦ blow, hit, rap, smack, stroke** It took just one *lash* of the whip to get the mule moving. —*verb* **✦ move, thrash, wave, whip ◇ beat, hit, strike** A violent wind *lashed* the trees back and forth.

lash²   *verb* **✦ bind, fasten, secure, strap, tie** The driver used rope to *lash* the cargo to the truck.

lass   *noun* **✦ girl, young lady, young woman** The young man married a *lass* from a neighboring village.

last¹   *adjective* **1. ✦ closing, concluding, ending, final ◇ terminal** The *last* episode of my favorite television series airs tonight. **2. ✦ latest, most recent ◇ newest, preceding, previous** I can't remember the name of the *last* movie I saw.

last²   *verb* **✦ continue, endure, go on, persist ◇ remain, stay** Does anyone know how long this rain is supposed to *last*?

latch   *noun* **✦ catch ◇ bar, bolt, clamp, hook, lock** The *latch* on the screen door needs to be replaced. —*verb* **✦ fasten, secure ◇ bar, bolt, close, lock, shut** Be sure to *latch* the gate when you leave.

late   *adjective* **1. ✦ belated, delayed, tardy ◇ overdue, slow** Larry got a *late* start but managed to finish all of his chores before dinner. **2. ✦ most recent, newest ◇ fresh, modern** Have you read that author's *latest* book? —*adverb* **◇ behind, belatedly, tardily** Brittany arrived at the party two hours *late*.

lately   *adverb* **✦ of late, recently ◇ currently, presently** The weather has been hot *lately*.

latter   *adjective* **✦ end, final, last, later ◇ rear, terminal** Where I live, it usually gets cold by the *latter* part of October.

Word Groups

To *laugh* is to express amusement or scorn by making sounds in the throat. *Laugh* is a general term with no true synonyms. Here are some words describing different kinds of laughing:

cackle, chortle, chuckle, giggle, guffaw, howl, roar, snicker, snigger

---

laughable   *adjective* **✦ amusing, comical, funny, humorous ◇ ridiculous** My uncle thought his mistake was *laughable* when he discovered that his socks didn't match.

launch   *verb* **1. ✦ put in orbit ◇ fire, propel, send off, shoot** The Soviet Union *launched* the world's first satellite on October 4, 1957. **2. ✦ begin, commence, initiate, open, start ◇ originate** The mayor held a press conference to *launch* her campaign for reelection.

launder   *verb* **✦ clean, cleanse, wash ◇ scrub** I usually help Mom *launder* our clothes.

lavish   *adjective* **✦ abundant, extravagant, fancy, sumptuous ◇ luxurious** The cruise ship was famous for its *lavish* meals. —*verb* ✦ **heap, pour, shower** ✧ **squander, waste** Liz *lavishes* a lot of care and attention on her pet.

law *noun* ✦ **ordinance, regulation, rule, statute** ✧ **bill, decree** If you break a traffic *law*, you usually have to pay a fine.

lawful *adjective* ✦ **authorized, legal, legitimate, rightful** ✧ **just** The stolen car was returned to its *lawful* owner.

lawyer *noun* ✦ **attorney, counsel, counselor, legal advisor** People in America have the legal right to be represented by a *lawyer*.

lay *verb* ✦ **deposit, leave, place, put, set** Please *lay* the package on the table.

layer *noun* ✦ **coat, coating, cover, covering** ✧ **blanket** The chocolate cake had a thick *layer* of vanilla icing.

lazy *adjective* ✦ **idle, inactive, listless, slothful, sluggish** *Lazy* people don't get much done.

lead *verb* **1.** ✦ **conduct, direct, escort, guide** ✧ **show, steer** A search dog *led* rescuers to the lost child. **2.** ✦ **go, run** ✧ **extend, reach, stretch** This path *leads* straight to the beach. **3.** ✦ **command, direct** ✧ **govern, manage, supervise** General Robert E. Lee *led* the Confederate army during the American Civil War. —*noun* ✦ **fore, front** ✧ **advance, head** Raymond was in the *lead* as the runners began the last lap.

leader *noun* ✦ **chief, director, head** ✧ **ruler, supervisor** I'm the *leader* of the refreshment committee for next week's dance.

league *noun* ✦ **alliance, association, union** ✧ **group, organization** The countries formed a *league* for common defense.

leak *noun* ✦ **crack, hole, opening** ✧ **break, chink, puncture** They finally fixed the *leak* in our school's roof. —*verb* **1.** ✦ **drip, flow, ooze, seep** ✧ **escape, spill** Oil slowly *leaked* from the car's

engine. **2.** ✦ **disclose, release, reveal, tell** Someone on the governor's staff has been *leaking* secrets to the press.

lean[1] *verb* ✦ **incline, slant, slope, tilt** ✧ **tip** The telephone pole was *leaning* dangerously after the storm.

lean[2] *adjective* ✦ **skinny, slender, slim, spare, thin** ✧ **gaunt** The athlete was *lean* and muscular.

leap *verb* ✦ **hop, jump, spring** ✧ **bounce, bound, skip, vault** A kangaroo can *leap* over twenty-five feet with a single bound. —*noun* ✦ **bound, hop, jump, spring** ✧ **bounce, skip, vault** The deer made a graceful *leap* over the fallen tree.

learn *verb* **1.** ✦ **study** ✧ **grasp, master, memorize, understand** Amber is *learning* how to use a computer. **2.** ✦ **determine, discover, find out** ✧ **detect, hear, realize** The doctors hoped to *learn* how to cure the mysterious disease.

lease *noun* ✦ **agreement, contract** ✧ **arrangement, deal** We signed a one-year *lease* for our new apartment. —*verb* ✦ **rent** ✧ **charter, hire** Mom didn't want to buy a new car, so she *leased* one for six months instead.

leash *noun* ✧ **chain, cord, rein, rope, strap, tether** Kristin put a *leash* on her pet iguana and took it for a walk around her front yard. —*verb* ✧ **chain, hold, rein, restrain, tether, tie up** You will have to *leash* your dog if you want to take him to the park.

least *adjective* ✦ **slightest, smallest, tiniest** ✧ **fewest, minimum** Of all my pets, my hamster requires the *least* amount of food.

leave[1] *verb* **1.** ✦ **depart, go, set out, start out** ✧ **exit, take off** I have to *leave* by 7 o'clock to catch the school bus. **2.** ✦ **keep** ✧ **maintain, retain, sustain** Please *leave* the door unlocked. **3.** ✦ **will** ✧ **endow, entrust, give, hand down** The millionaire *left* her entire fortune to charity.

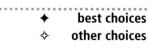

✦ **best choices**
✧ **other choices**

leave² *noun* ◆ **furlough, liberty** ◇ **absence, holiday, vacation** The soldier was home on *leave*.

lecture *noun* ◆ **address, speech, talk** ◇ **lesson** The forest ranger gave a *lecture* on bird identification. —*verb* ◆ **address, speak to, talk to** ◇ **preach, teach** A police officer *lectured* our class about the dangers of using drugs and alcohol.

ledge *noun* ◆ **shelf** ◇ **edge, projection, ridge** Eagles often build their nests on small, rocky *ledges*.

legal *adjective* ◆ **lawful, legitimate** ◇ **allowable, permissible** The *legal* voting age in the United States is eighteen.

legend *noun* ◆ **fable, folklore, mythology, story, tale** ◇ **myth,** According to *legend*, Robin Hood robbed from the rich in order to give to the poor.

legendary *adjective* ◆ **fabled, fabulous** ◇ **celebrated, mythical, mythological** El Dorado was a *legendary* city whose streets were said to be paved with gold.

legible *adjective* ◆ **clear, distinct, readable** ◇ **understandable** Jason is practicing his penmanship in order to make his handwriting more *legible*. ◀

legion *noun* ◆ **crowd, flock, horde, multitude, swarm, throng** The singer has a *legion* of fans who attend all of his concerts.

legitimate *adjective* ◆ **proper, valid** ◇ **justifiable, lawful, legal, official** Cameron had a *legitimate* reason for not attending school.

leisure *noun* ◆ **downtime, free time** ◇ **ease, recreation, relaxation, rest** The busy doctor had very little *leisure*.

lend *verb* ◇ **extend, furnish, give, provide, supply** Davey *lent* me his bicycle for the afternoon.

length *noun* 1. ◆ **extent, size** ◇ **distance, measure, reach, space** Tyrannosaurus rex had teeth that were up to seven inches in *length*. 2. ◆ **duration** ◇ **period, span, term** Summer vacation is usually about three months in *length*.

lengthen *verb* ◆ **extend, stretch** ◇ **expand, increase, prolong, protract** Pulling on a piece of taffy will *lengthen* it.

lenient *adjective* ◆ **easy, merciful, mild, tolerant** ◇ **gentle, kind** The judge was known for giving *lenient* sentences.

less *adjective* ◆ **limited, reduced, shortened** ◇ **fewer, lower, smaller** I have *less* time to play now that school has started.

lessen *verb* ◆ **decrease, diminish, lower, reduce** ◇ **shrink** This medicine should *lessen* the pain of your headache.

lesson *noun* ◆ **education, instruction** ◇ **class, schooling, teaching** My older brother is taking driving *lessons*.

let *verb* ◆ **allow (to), permit (to)** ◇ **approve, authorize, grant, sanction** My parents *let* me stay up late on weekend nights.

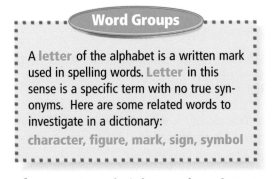

Word Groups

A letter of the alphabet is a written mark used in spelling words. Letter in this sense is a specific term with no true synonyms. Here are some related words to investigate in a dictionary:

character, figure, mark, sign, symbol

level *noun* 1. ◆ **height, mark, point, stage** ◇ **altitude, depth, elevation** The flood waters reached a *level* that was thirty feet above normal. 2. ◆ **degree, grade, standard** ◇ **position,**

rank, step Mandy reads at the same *level* as a high school student. —*adjective* **1.** ✦ **even, flat, horizontal** ✧ **smooth, straight, plane** We don't have any *level* ground in the yard for planting a garden. **2.** ✦ **even, flush** ✧ **aligned, equal, parallel** The top of my little brother's head is *level* with my shoulder. —*verb* **1.** ✦ **even out, grade, smooth** ✧ **flatten** A park employee used a rake to *level* the sand in the children's play area. **2.** ✦ **demolish, destroy, knock down, tear down, wreck** Construction workers *leveled* several old buildings in order to clear the site.

liable *adjective* **1.** ✦ **accountable, answerable, responsible** ✧ **obligated** If you lose a library book, you might be held *liable* for the replacement cost. **2.** ✦ **apt, likely, prone** ✧ **inclined, open, probable** You're *liable* to get wet if you don't take your umbrella.

liar *noun* ✦ **fibber** ✧ **storyteller** You can believe anything that Toni says because she's not a *liar*.

liberal *adjective* **1.** ✦ **abundant, ample, generous, plentiful** ✧ **full, lavish** This sapling needs *liberal* amounts of water to help it grow. **2.** ✦ **broad, open-minded, progressive, tolerant, unbiased** My parents have *liberal* ideas about raising children.

liberty *noun* **1.** ✦ **freedom, independence, sovereignty** ✧ **self-government** Mexico won its *liberty* from Spain in 1821. **2.** ✦ **freedom, privilege, right** ✧ **authorization, permission** Free speech is one of the *liberties* guaranteed by the Bill of Rights.

license *noun* ✦ **certificate** ✧ **authorization, permission, permit** My older sister and her fiancé just got their marriage *license*. —*verb* ✦ **certify** ✧ **allow, authorize, permit, qualify** Teachers must be *licensed* by the state.

lid *noun* ✦ **cover, top** ✧ **cap, stopper** I used a screwdriver to pry the *lid* off the can of paint.

lie[1] *verb* **1.** ✦ **lie down, recline, stretch out** ✧ **sprawl** Brian likes to *lie* on the couch when he watches television. **2.** ✦ **be located, be situated, sit** ✧ **exist, rest** The lake where I swam yesterday *lies* just beyond that grove of trees.

lie[2] *noun* ✦ **falsehood, fib, untruth** No one has ever known Rachelle to deliberately tell a *lie*. —*verb* ✦ **fib** ✧ **deceive, distort, falsify, mislead** Sometimes I am tempted to *lie* about my age.

life *noun* **1.** ✦ **into existence** ✧ **animation, being, vitality** Only in cartoons can a toy come *to life*. **2.** ✦ **lifetime, time** ✧ **days, duration, term** I've only been outside the United States once in my *life*. **3.** ✦ **human, human being, individual, person** ✧ **soul** Luckily, no *lives* were lost when the ship sank. **4.** ✦ **energy, high spirits, liveliness, spirit, vigor, vitality** My puppy is so full of *life* that he can never sit still.

lift *verb* **1.** ✦ **hoist, pick up, raise** ✧ **boost, elevate, heave** This crate is too heavy for me to *lift* by myself. **2.** ✦ **ascend, climb, rise** ✧ **soar, take off** Airplanes have to gain sufficient speed before they can *lift* into the air. **3.** ✦ **disappear, disperse, dissipate** ✧ **scatter, vanish** The fog *lifted* at noon. —*noun* ✦ **boost, hoist** ✧ **heave** My little sister couldn't reach the water fountain, so I gave her a *lift*.

light[1] *noun* **1.** ✦ **glow, illumination, radiance** ✧ **brilliance, shine** The river looked silver in the *light* of the moon. **2.** ✦ **aspect, perspective, regard** ✧ **angle, facet** I saw things in a different *light* after hearing Meg's side of the story. —*adjective* **1.** ✦ **bright** ✧ **brilliant, illuminated, radiant, sunny** My bedroom is very *light* when I open the curtains. **2.** ✦ **pale** ✧ **fair, whitish** I painted the water *light* blue and the fish bright yellow. —*verb* **1.** ✦ **ignite, kindle** ✧ **burn, fire, set fire to** Gabriel *lit* the campfire while I got the marshmallows. **2.** ✦ **brighten, illuminate** ✧ **lighten, shine** Do you think one lamp will be enough to *light* the entire room?

✦   **best choices**
✧   **other choices**

light² *adjective* **1.** ◆ **lightweight** ◇ **scant, slight, underweight** My dog is *light* enough that I can easily pick her up. **2.** ◆ **gentle, moderate, soft** ◇ **faint, mild, weak** Yesterday's *light* rain barely got the ground wet. **3.** ◆ **easy, simple** ◇ **effortless, moderate, undemanding** Our teacher gave us a *light* homework assignment on the first day back at school after break.

lighten¹ *verb* ◆ **brighten, light up** ◇ **illuminate, shine** The sky began to *lighten* just before the sun appeared.

lighten² *verb* ◆ **make lighter** ◇ **empty, lessen, reduce, unload** The box was too heavy for me to lift, so I *lightened* it by removing some of the contents.

like¹ *verb* ◆ **enjoy** ◇ **admire, adore, fancy, love, relish** I *like* playing ball after school.

like² *preposition* ◆ **identical to, the same as, similar to** Your computer is *like* mine except for the mouse. —*adjective* ◆ **comparable, equal, identical, matching, similar** We got five inches of snow yesterday and a *like* amount today.

likely *adjective* **1.** ◆ **apt, expected, liable** ◇ **destined, inclined, probable** The weather report said that the storm is *likely* to hit tomorrow morning. **2.** ◆ **acceptable, appropriate, fit, proper, reasonable, suitable** The mother cat began looking for a *likely* spot in which to have her kittens. —*adverb* ◆ **presumably, probably** ◇ **doubtless, no doubt, seemingly** I'll *likely* be late, so don't wait for me.

limit *noun* **1.** ◆ **limitation, restriction** ◇ **ceiling, end, maximum** There is a *limit* on how many fish you are allowed to catch in this lake. **2.** ◆ **boundary, bounds** ◇ **border, edge, extent, extreme** Before we play hide-and-seek, we agree on the *limits* beyond which no one is allowed to go. —*verb* ◆ **confine, restrict** ◇ **check, restrain, set** The coach decided to *limit* the basketball team to ten players.

limp *verb* ◆ **hobble** ◇ **shuffle, stagger, stumble, waddle** I *limped* around for two days after I sprained my ankle. —*noun* ◆ **hobble** ◇ **shuffle, stagger, waddle** Our old dog walks with a *limp*. —*adjective* ◆ **droopy, floppy** ◇ **loose, slack, soft, weak** Flowers get *limp* if you don't water them.

line *noun* **1.** ◆ **streak, strip, stripe** ◇ **band, bar, mark** White *lines* were painted on the pavement to indicate parking places. **2.** ◆ **border, boundary, limit** ◇ **edge, margin** This fence sits right on our property *line*. **3.** ◆ **column, file, row** ◇ **rank** The class formed two *lines* to march to the auditorium. **4.** ◆ **cable, wire** ◇ **cord, rope, strand, string** Our telephone doesn't work because the *lines* are down. **5.** ◆ **card, letter, message, note, postcard** Please drop me a *line* while you're on vacation. **6.** ◆ **assortment, range** ◇ **kind, make, type, variety** This store carries a full *line* of cameras and video equipment.

linger *verb* ◆ **continue, endure, go on, last, persist, remain, stay** ◇ **delay** According to the weather report, the thunderstorms should be over today, but a few light showers may *linger* through tomorrow morning.

link *noun* ◆ **association, connection, relationship** ◇ **bond, tie** Detectives found no apparent *links* between the two robberies. —*verb* ◆ **connect, join, unite** ◇ **attach, combine, fasten** The Brooklyn Bridge *links* Brooklyn with Manhattan Island.

lip *noun* ◆ **brim, rim** ◇ **border, edge** The *lip* of a cup or mug is usually smooth and rounded.

liquid *noun* ◆ **fluid** ◇ **solution** Water, oil, and milk are all *liquids*. —*adjective* ◆ **fluid** ◇ **flowing, molten, runny, watery, wet** Some rockets use *liquid* oxygen as part of their fuel.

list *noun* ◆ **record** ◇ **catalog, file, inventory, register** Before Mom and I went to the mall, I made a *list* of all my tapes and CDs so that I wouldn't buy something I already had. —*verb* ✦ **itemize, write down** ✧ **catalog, file, record, register** Our English teacher asked us to *list* all of the books that we read over the summer.

listen *verb* ✦ **pay attention** ✧ **hear, heed, mind** When our teacher gave us our assignment, she told us to *listen* carefully to the directions.

litter *noun* ✦ **debris, refuse, rubbish, trash** ✧ **junk, mess** My Girl Scout troop volunteered to pick up the *litter* along the lakeshore. —*verb* ✦ **clutter, mess up** ✧ **cover, scatter** Our living room was *littered* with wrapping paper after my birthday party.

little *adjective* **1.** ✦ **small, tiny, wee** ✧ **miniature, minute** A Chihuahua is a very *little* dog. **2.** ✦ **brief, limited, short** ✧ **scant, slight** I only have a *little* time left before my report is due. —*adverb* ✦ **slightly, somewhat** ✧ **barely, hardly, scarcely** I was getting *a little* tired of leftover lasagna. —*noun* ✦ **bit, portion** ✧ **particle, speck, touch, trace** Conor reads a *little* of his book every night.

live¹ *verb* **1.** ✦ **exist, survive** ✧ **be, continue, last, thrive** Human beings need food, water, and air to *live*. **2.** ✦ **dwell in, inhabit, occupy, reside in** ✧ **stay** Kathleen and her family *live in* a three-bedroom apartment.

live² *adjective* ✦ **alive, living** ✧ **breathing, conscious, existing** Yogurt is made by adding *live* bacteria to milk.

lively *adjective* ✦ **dynamic, energetic, spirited, vigorous** ✧ **active, brisk** The *lively* music made me want to dance.

living *adjective* ✦ **alive, live** ✧ **breathing, conscious, existing** I believe that all *living* creatures should be treated with respect. —*noun* **1.** ✦ **existence, life** ✧ **being, existing** I love city *living*. **2.** ✦ **income, livelihood** ✧ **career, keep, occupation, support** Aunt Joyce makes her *living* as a writer.

load *noun* ✦ **burden, weight** ✧ **cargo, freight, shipment** Camels can carry heavy *loads* on their backs for long distances without needing water. —*verb* ✦ **fill, pack** ✧ **heap, pile, stuff** We'll be ready to leave on vacation as soon as we finish *loading* the car. ▼

loaf *verb* ✦ **idle, lounge, relax** ✧ **loiter, rest** I plan on *loafing* around the house for the first few days of summer vacation.

loan *noun* ✧ **advance, allowance, credit** I asked my sister for a *loan* so that I could go to the movies.

loathe *verb* ✦ **despise, detest, dislike, hate** I don't mind most chores, but I *loathe* cleaning out the basement.

loathsome *adjective* ✦ **disgusting, hateful, hideous, revolting** ✧ **nasty** The movie was about some *loathsome* creatures that came out of the swamp at night.

local *adjective* ✦ **community, neighborhood** ✧ **close, near, nearby** I get most of my reading material from the *local* library.

locate *verb* **1.** ✦ **detect, discover, find** ✧ **spot** Moles rely mainly on smell and touch to *locate* food. **2.** ✦ **place, position, put, set,**

situate This looks like a good place to *locate* our lemonade stand.

location *noun* ✦ **address, place, site, spot** ✧ **locality, point, position** Our school will be moving to a new *location* next year.

lock *noun* ✧ **bolt, catch, clasp, hook, latch, padlock** Dad changed the broken *lock* on our garage door today. —*verb* **1.** ✦ **secure** ✧ **bar, bolt, fasten, latch** Did you *lock* the car doors? **2.** ✦ **couple, fasten, interlock, join, link** ✧ **grasp, hold, entwine** The plastic blocks are designed to *lock* together.

> ### Antonyms
> **lock** *verb*
> **1.** open, open up, unclose, unfasten, unlock
> **2.** free, liberate, loose, release, uncouple

lodge *noun* ✦ **cabin, cottage** ✧ **chalet, inn, hotel, shelter** I spent a lot of my time at camp in the crafts *lodge*. —*verb* **1.** ✦ **reside, stay** ✧ **accommodate, house** My cousin Chris plans to *lodge* in hostels on his bike trip through Europe. **2.** ✦ **catch, snag, stick, wedge** ✧ **fix, snare** My kite is *lodged* in the branches of that tree.

lofty *adjective* ✦ **high, tall, towering** ✧ **sky-high, soaring** The mountain's *lofty* summit was hidden by clouds.

logical *adjective* ✦ **intelligent, rational, reasonable, sensible, sound** If you are hungry, the *logical* thing to do would be to eat something. ◀

loiter *verb* ✦ **dally, dawdle, dilly-dally, idle, lag, linger** ✧ **delay, pause** John told me that he was in a hurry and did not have time to *loiter*.

lone *adjective* ✦ **single, sole, solitary** ✧ **alone, individual, lonely** A *lone* pear tree grew in the middle of the open field.

lonely *adjective* **1.** ✦ **companionless, lonesome, solitary** ✧ **alone, lone, single** The old hermit in this story leads a *lonely* life. **2.** ✦ **deserted, desolate, forlorn** ✧ **isolated, remote, secluded** This desert is a *lonely* place.

long[1] *adjective* ✦ **extended, extensive, lengthy, prolonged** ✧ **big, great, large** We spent a *long* time going over the answers to the math test.

long[2] *verb* ✦ **ache, desire, want, wish, yearn** ✧ **crave** Grandmother *longs* to visit her childhood home in Italy.

look *verb* **1.** ✦ **hunt, search, seek** ✧ **explore** I'll help you *look* for your missing book as soon as I finish clearing the table. **2.** ✦ **gaze at, observe, see, view, watch** ✧ **glance** I like to climb the tower in the park and *look at* the people below. **3.** ✦ **appear, seem** ✧ **resemble** Do you think this shirt *looks* nice enough to wear to the party? —*noun* **1.** ✦ **glance, glimpse, peek** ✧ **gaze, inspection, view** I took a *look* out the window to see if my ride had come. **2.** ✦ **appearance, expression** ✧ **bearing, manner** The parents of the sick boy had a worried *look*.

loom *verb* ✦ **appear, arise, materialize, take shape** ✧ **emerge** Storm clouds *loomed* on the horizon.

loop *noun* ✦ **circle, coil, ring** ✧ **spiral** The cowboy slipped a *loop* of rope over the bull's horns. —*verb* ✦ **circle, coil, turn, twist** ✧ **bend** The climber anchored her rope by *looping* it around a tree.

loose *adjective* **1.** ✦ **free, unattached, unbound, unfastened, untied** The boat came *loose* and floated down the stream. **2.** ✦ **at liberty, free, unconfined, unrestrained** Dad called the police about a big dog that was *loose* in our neighborhood. **3.** ✦ **baggy, roomy, slack** ✧ **big, comfortable, oversize** Daniel likes to wear *loose* clothing when he plays tennis.

loosen *verb* ✦ **slacken, untighten** ◇ **ease, relax, untie** My necktie was too tight, so I *loosened* it.

loot *noun* ✦ **booty, plunder, spoils** ◇ **haul, treasure** The robbers hid their *loot* in the hollow of an old tree. —*verb* ✦ **plunder, sack** ◇ **raid, rob, steal** The pirates *looted* the town and took any valuables back to their ships.

lose *verb* 1. ✦ **mislay, misplace** ◇ **forget, miss** Damon is always *losing* his car keys. 2. ✦ **be defeated** ◇ **forfeit, succumb, surrender, yield** Our team won the first two games but *lost* in the semifinals.

loss *noun* 1. ✦ **reduction** ◇ **removal, shrinkage** Dad is on a diet, and he is pleased with his weight *loss*. 2. ✦ **misfortune, setback** ◇ **damage, injury, suffering, trouble** It was a great *loss* for our school when two of the best teachers moved away.

lost *adjective* 1. ✦ **mislaid, misplaced, missing** ◇ **absent, gone** I found my *lost* sweater under the bed. 2. ✦ **absorbed, deep, occupied** ◇ **distracted** I didn't hear you come in because I was *lost* in thought.

lot *noun* 1. ✦ **an abundance of, lots of, many, numerous, plenty of** ◇ **much** Hannah received *a lot of* presents for her birthday this year. 2. ✦ **batch, set** ◇ **bunch, collection, group** The store will be receiving a new *lot* of furniture tomorrow. 3. ✦ **parcel, plot, tract** ◇ **land, property, real estate** My parents bought our house and the vacant *lot* next door at the same time.

loud *adjective* 1. ✦ **deafening, noisy** ◇ **blaring, roaring, shrill** The band was so *loud* that my friends and I could hardly hear each other speak. 2. ✦ **bright, flashy, gaudy, showy** John bought a *loud* T-shirt that has orange lettering on a purple background.

love *noun* ✦ **affection, fondness, liking** ◇ **tenderness, warmth** Arthur has had a *love* for reading as long as he can remember. —*verb* 1. ✦ **adore, cherish** ◇ **treasure, worship** My cat is grumpy sometimes, but I *love* him anyway. 2. ✦ **enjoy, like, relish** ◇ **fancy** I *love* going to the movies with my friends.

lovely *adjective* ✦ **adorable, attractive, beautiful, enchanting, pretty** That is a *lovely* dress you're wearing.

loving *adjective* ✦ **affectionate, caring, devoted, tender** We have a warm, *loving* family.

low *adjective* 1. ✦ **short** ◇ **little, shallow, small** The horse easily jumped over the *low* fence. 2. ✦ **bad, inadequate, inferior, poor** This job has excellent benefits, but the pay is *low*. 3. ✦ **hushed, quiet, soft, subdued** The two friends spoke to each other in *low* voices in the museum. 4. ✦ **dejected, depressed, downcast, gloomy, sad, unhappy** Ariane has been feeling a little *low* ever since her best friend moved away.

lower *verb* 1. ✦ **drop, let down** ◇ **descend, sink** The stage crew *lowered* the curtain after the final act. 2. ✦ **decrease, diminish, lessen, reduce** The teacher will *lower* our grades if our reports are late.

loyal *adjective* ✦ **dependable, devoted, faithful, steadfast, true, trustworthy** A *loyal* friend will stand by you even when you have troubles.

loyalty *noun* ✦ **allegiance, devotion, faithfulness** ◇ **dependability** The king knew that he could count on the *loyalty* of his knights.

luck *noun* 1. ✦ **chance, fortune** ◇ **destiny, fate** I prefer games of skill over games of *luck*. 2. ✦ **good fortune, good luck** ◇ **favor, success** Finding a four-leaf clover is said to bring *luck*.

lucky *adjective* ✦ **fortunate, successful** ◇ **favorable, happy** I made a *lucky* guess on the quiz and chose the right answer.

lug *verb* ✦ **bear, carry, haul** ◇ **drag, tow, tug** I *lugged* the heavy groceries up two flights of stairs.

✦ **best choices**
◇ **other choices**

luggage *noun* ✦ **baggage, bags, suitcases** ✧ **belongings, gear** A porter helped us carry our *luggage* to the train. ◄

lull *verb* ✦ **calm, quiet, settle, soothe** ✧ **pacify** The soft music *lulled* me so much that I fell asleep. —*noun* ✦ **break, lapse, pause** ✧ **calm, hush, quiet** The rain started up again after a brief *lull*.

lump *noun* **1.** ✦ **chunk, clump, hunk, mass, piece** ✧ **wad** Grandfather uses a hoe to break up the *lumps* of dirt in his garden. **2.** ✦ **bulge, bump, swelling** ✧ **knot** The bee sting raised a big *lump* on my arm.

lunge *noun* ✦ **charge, dive, pounce, rush, spring** When I dangled a toy mouse in front of my kitten, she made a *lunge* for it. —*verb* ✦ **charge, dive, jump, leap, spring** ✧ **pounce, thrust** Stephanie *lunged* forward to catch the lamp as it started to fall to the floor.

lure *noun* ✦ **attraction, draw, invitation, temptation** ✧ **bait** The *lure* of adventure makes some people want to travel and see new places. —*verb* ✦ **attract, draw, pull, tempt** ✧ **hook, invite** We were *lured* into the bakery by the wonderful smells coming from within.

lush *adjective* ✦ **abundant, dense, luxuriant, rich, sumptuous, thick** We saw deer browsing on the *lush* grass of a mountain meadow.

luster *noun* ✦ **brilliance, gloss, glow, radiance, shine** We admired the *luster* of the ancient statues in the museum.

luxurious *adjective* ✦ **elegant, magnificent, splendid, sumptuous** ✧ **expensive, rich** The princess wore a *luxurious* gown to the grand ball.

Antonyms
luxurious *adjective*
cheap, poor, ragged, shabby, threadbare, wo

luxury *noun* **1.** ✦ **pleasure, treat** ✧ **delight, enjoyment** Dining at an expensive restaurant is a rare *luxury* for us. **2.** ✦ **affluence, comfort, extravagance, splendor** ✧ **riches, wealth** The wealthy movie star lived in *luxury*.

M

machine *noun* ✦ **appliance, device, mechanism** ✧ **engine, motor** Our neighbor uses a *machine* to blow leaves off her lawn.

mad *adjective* **1.** ✦ **angry, furious, incensed, indignant** ✧ **upset** I was *mad* when my sister borrowed my skateboard without asking. **2.** ✦ **crazy, insane** ✧ **delirious, foolish, idiotic** This movie is about a *mad* scientist who travels through time. **3.** ✦ **ardent, enthusiastic, excited, fanatic, wild** There was a *mad* scramble to score in the final seconds of the game.

magazine *noun* ✦ **journal, periodical, publication** ✧ **newsletter** Kari subscribes to a *magazine* for horse lovers.

magic *noun* ✦ **witchcraft, wizardry** ✧ **charm, enchantment** The genie used *magic* to grant people their three wishes. —*adjective* ✦ **magical** ✧ **charming, enchanting, fascinating** Kyle likes to perform *magic* tricks.

magician *noun* ✦ **entertainer** ✧ **enchanter, witch, wizard** The *magician* pulled a rabbit out of his hat.

magnetic *adjective* ✦ **appealing, captivating, charismatic, charming, fascinating** The actor was known for his *magnetic* personality as well as his acting ability.

magnificent *adjective* ✦ **beautiful, fantastic, glorious, grand, splendid, wonderful** A peacock looks *magnificent* when it spreads its tail feathers.

magnify *verb* ✦ **enlarge** ✧ **boost, expand, grow, increase, inflate** Whenever Grandpa reads, he wears glasses that *magnify* the print.

mail *noun* ✧ **cards, letters, messages, packages** More *mail* is delivered during the Christmas season than at any other time of the year. —*verb* ✦ **post, send** ✧ **dispatch, forward, ship, transmit** Please *mail* this letter for me.

main *adjective* ✦ **chief, major, primary, principal** ✧ **head, leading** This is the *main* road leading into town.

mainly *adverb* ✦ **chiefly, generally, mostly, primarily, usually** Jill likes all types of books, but she *mainly* reads science fiction novels.

maintain *verb* **1.** ✦ **keep, preserve, retain, sustain** ✧ **continue** Mom exercises to *maintain* her health. **2.** ✦ **care for, look after** ✧ **fix, repair, service** My brother and I help *maintain* the yard. **3.** ✦ **affirm, assert, claim, declare, insist, state** Throughout his trial, the defendant *maintained* that he was innocent.

majestic *adjective* ✦ **grand, impressive, magnificent, splendid** ✧ **dignified, stately** Redwoods are *majestic* trees that can grow to be more than three hundred feet tall.

major *adjective* ✦ **chief, leading, main, primary** ✧ **first, foremost** My *major* focus this year has been improving my math skills.

make *verb* **1.** ✦ **create, fashion, produce** ✧ **build, form, manufacture** Aunt Geraldine *made* me a needlepoint pillow for my birthday. ▶ **2.** ✦ **cause (to), compel (to), force (to)** ✧ **bring, bring about** Peeling onions always *makes* my eyes water. **3.** ✦ **acquire, earn, get, obtain** ✧ **gain, receive** Keith *makes* enough money by mowing lawns to buy his own clothes. **4.** ✦ **add up to, amount to, come to, equal, total** Four quarts *make* one gallon. —*noun* ✦ **brand, kind, model, style, type, variety** Dad liked his old car so much that he got a new one of the same *make*.

✦ **best choices**
✧ **other choices**

mammoth *adjective* ✦ **colossal, enormous, gigantic, huge, immense, large** Sending astronauts to the moon is a *mammoth* undertaking.

man *noun* ✦ **fellow, gentleman, guy** ◇ **male** A kind *man* helped us fix our flat tire.

manage *verb* **1.** ✦ **administer, control, direct, run, supervise** My aunt *manages* a flower shop. **2.** ✦ **fare, get by, succeed** ◇ **accomplish, achieve, do, function** Although it won't be easy to carry all my luggage, I'll *manage* somehow.

management *noun* ✦ **control, direction, leadership, supervision** ◇ **administration** The restaurant reopened under new *management*.

manager *noun* ✦ **administrator, director, head, supervisor** ◇ **boss, leader** When my brother applied for a sales job, he had to speak to the store's *manager*.

maneuver *noun* ✦ **move, movement, turn** ◇ **action, play, stunt** The marching band executed a series of complicated *maneuvers*. —*verb* ✦ **guide, move, navigate, pilot, steer** The pilot carefully *maneuvered* his riverboat past a sandbar.

manner *noun* ✦ **fashion, style, way** ◇ **method, system** My parents have taught me to speak in a polite *manner* to everyone.

Word Groups

A **mansion** is a large stately house. **Mansion** is a general term with no true synonyms. Here are some related words to investigate in a dictionary:

chateau, estate, hacienda, hall, manor, plantation, villa

---

manual *adjective* ✦ **physical** ◇ **hand-operated, human** Gardening is a *manual* activity. —*noun* ✦ **guide, guidebook, handbook** ◇ **text, textbook** Samuel read the instruction *manual* before assembling his new bicycle.

manufacture *verb* ✦ **assemble, build, construct, make, produce** ◇ **create** Our class toured a factory that *manufactures* air conditioners.

many *adjective* ✦ **countless, numerous, several** ◇ **endless** There are *many* interesting books in our school library.

map *noun* ✦ **chart, plan** ◇ **diagram, drawing, graph, sketch** We used a *map* of the city to find our hotel. —*verb* ✦ **chart** ◇ **diagram, draw, plot, sketch** Astronomers use images received from spacecraft to *map* the planet Mars.

mar *verb* ✦ **blemish, damage, flaw, spoil** ◇ **injure, impair** The surface of the antique writing table was *marred* by a long scratch.

march *verb* ✦ **parade** ◇ **hike, stride, stroll, walk** My school band will *march* in this year's Memorial Day festivities. —*noun* ✦ **parade, procession** ◇ **hike, trek, walk** Some local environmentalists are planning a *march* to celebrate the new wildlife sanctuary.

margin *noun* **1.** ✦ **border, edge, fringe** ◇ **boundary, rim** Our teacher writes comments along the *margins* of our papers. **2.** ✦ **range, space, surplus** ◇ **freedom, room** Bryan allowed a *margin* of fifteen minutes to cover any delay in getting to the performance.

mark *noun* **1.** ✦ **blemish, spot, stain** ◇ **impression, imprint** The wet glass left a *mark* on the table. **2.** ✦ **indication, sign, symbol, token** ◇ **emblem** Everyone stood up as a *mark* of respect when the senator entered the room. **3.** ✦ **goal, objective, target** ◇ **aim, end** I tried to hit the tree with a snowball, but I missed my *mark*. **4.** ✦ **grade, rating, score** ◇ **evaluation** I earned a better *mark* on this test than I did on the last one. —*verb* **1.** ✦ **blemish, mar, spot, stain** ◇ **scar** Be careful not to *mark* the freshly waxed floor. **2.** ✦ **designate, identify, indicate, point out, show** Flags were used to *mark* the corners of the playing field. **3.** ✦ **correct, grade, rate, score**

◇ **evaluate** Joshua helped our teacher *mark* the spelling tests.

market *noun* **1.** ✦ **grocery, store, supermarket** ◇ **marketplace, shop** Could you get me a candy bar when you go to the *market*? **2.** ✦ **call, demand, need** ◇ **business, commerce, trade** There is a very large *market* for health foods in this city. —*verb* ✦ **sell** ◇ **offer, peddle, trade** These television sets are *marketed* worldwide.

marriage *noun* ✦ **matrimony, wedlock** ◇ **match, union, wedding** The man and woman were joined in *marriage*.

marry *verb* ✦ **wed** ◇ **join, unite** My aunt is planning to *marry* her fiancé next June.

marshal *noun* ✦ **law officer, officer** ◇ **sheriff** Wyatt Earp was a famous federal *marshal* back in the 1880's. —*verb* ✦ **arrange, array, order, organize** The colonel *marshaled* his troops for inspection.

marvel *noun* ✦ **wonder** ◇ **astonishment, curiosity, miracle, sensation** Egypt's ancient *marvels* include the Sphinx and the Great Pyramid of Cheops. —*verb* ✦ **admire, wonder at** ◇ **gape, gaze, stare** Visitors to the Grand Canyon usually pause to *marvel at* its great length and depth.

marvelous *adjective* ✦ **amazing, fantastic, incredible, outstanding, wonderful** My friend Erica is a *marvelous* singer.

mash *verb* ✦ **crush, smash, squash** ◇ **pound, pulverize** *Mash* the garlic before you add it to the pasta sauce.

mask *noun* ✦ **disguise** ◇ **camouflage, cloak, cover, veil** Donald wore a gorilla *mask* to the costume party. —*verb* ✦ **camouflage, conceal, cover up, disguise, hide** Whenever Paul has to

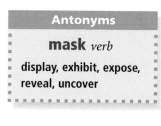

Antonyms

mask *verb*

display, exhibit, expose, reveal, uncover

eat fish, he *masks* its flavor by adding lots of lemon and butter.

mass *noun* **1.** ✦ **batch, bunch, heap, pile** ◇ **clump, lump** The plow left a big *mass* of snow in front of our house. **2.** ✦ **bulk, size, volume** ◇ **extent, magnitude, weight** The *mass* of a blue whale is much greater than that of a goldfish. —*verb* ✦ **accumulate, assemble, cluster, collect, gather** I knew that a storm was coming when I saw dark clouds *massing* on the horizon.

massacre *noun* ✦ **killing, slaughter, slaying** ◇ **mass murder** Many people are outraged by the *massacre* of baby seals. —*verb* ✦ **kill, slaughter, slay** ◇ **murder** African elephants are being *massacred* for their ivory tusks.

massage *noun* ✦ **rubdown** ◇ **back rub, rub** The doctor prescribed *massages* as part of the athlete's physical therapy. —*verb* ✦ **knead, rub** ◇ **stroke** I *massaged* my neck to ease the stiffness.

massive *adjective* ✦ **enormous, gigantic, huge, immense** ◇ **bulky, heavy** Mount Rushmore is famous for its *massive* portraits of four U.S. Presidents.

master *noun* **1.** ✦ **owner** ◇ **leader, lord, ruler, superior** A well-trained dog will always obey its *master*. **2.** ✦ **expert, genius, professional, wizard** ◇ **authority** The chef was a *master* at creating new dishes. —*adjective* **1.** ✦ **accomplished, competent, expert, professional, skilled** My mother has a dresser that was made by a *master* carpenter. **2.** ✦ **chief, main, primary, principal** ◇ **major** The *master* bedroom in my grandparents' house is much larger than the other bedrooms. —*verb* ✦ **grasp, learn, pick up** ◇ **command, conquer, control** My little brother has yet to *master* the art of riding a bicycle.

match *noun* **1.** ✦ **companion, counterpart, mate** Dad's striped tie is a good *match* for his white shirt. **2.** ✦ **double, equal, equivalent** We need a *match* for the bedroom wallpaper so we can fix a

✦ best choices
◇ other choices

tear. **3.** ✦ **competition, contest, game** ✧ **meet, tournament** I played well, but Tobias won our tennis *match*. —*verb* **1.** ✦ **agree with, correspond to, duplicate, resemble** This paint *matches* the color of our curtains. **2.** ✦ **compare with, equal, rival** ✧ **challenge** No one on their team can *match* our quarterback.

material *noun* **1.** ✦ **matter, stuff, substance** ✧ **component, element, ingredient** Wood is often used as building *material*. **2.** ✦ **cloth, fabric, textile** Mona picked out *material* for a new dress. —*adjective* ✦ **concrete, physical, real, solid** ✧ **bodily** Anything that you can see or touch is a part of the *material* world.

matter *noun* **1.** ✦ **material, substance** ✧ **components, elements, stuff** A space that has no *matter* is known as a vacuum. **2.** ✦ **affair, business, concern, issue, point, subject** Mom went to the bank to take care of some financial *matters*. **3.** ✦ **difficulty, problem, trouble** ✧ **predicament** What's the *matter* with my singing voice? —*verb* ✦ **be important** ✧ **affect, concern, count, influence** It *matters* to me that you remembered my birthday. ◀

mature *adjective* **1.** ✦ **adult, full-grown, grown** ✧ **ready, ripe** A *mature* elephant can weigh as much as five tons. **2.** ✦ **adult, developed, experienced, grown-up** ✧ **wise** Robyn's parents feel that she is *mature* enough to stay at home without a baby sitter. —*verb* ✦ **develop, evolve, grow** ✧ **age, ripen** Most trees *mature* very slowly.

maximum *noun* ✦ **ceiling, limit** ✧ **most, peak, top, zenith** This elevator is designed to carry a *maximum* of twenty people. —*adjective* ✦ **best, greatest, supreme, top** ✧ **biggest, largest** A Boeing 747 jetliner can reach a *maximum* speed of more than five-hundred miles per hour.

maybe *adverb* ✦ **conceivably, perhaps, possibly** *Maybe* my mom will let me go to the fair.

maze *noun* ✦ **network, web** ✧ **knot, snarl, tangle** Carlsbad Caverns is a complex *maze* of interconnecting tunnels and chambers.

meager *adjective* ✦ **inadequate, poor, scant, scanty, small, sparse** The coyote is thin because his winter food supply was *meager*.

meal *noun* ✦ **banquet, feast** ✧ **breakfast, dinner, lunch, supper** Jessica prepared a Thanksgiving *meal* large enough to feed her entire extended family.

mean[1] *verb* **1.** ✦ **denote, indicate, signify** ✧ **designate, imply** A red traffic light *means* that drivers are supposed to stop. **2.** ✦ **aim, expect, intend, plan, propose** ✧ **want** What do you *mean* to do about that stray dog you brought home?

mean[2] *adjective* ✦ **cruel, malicious, nasty, rotten, rude, unkind** The *mean* man screamed at us to get out of his way.

mean[3] *noun* ✦ **average, center, medium, middle** ✧ **norm** The best speed for driving is a *mean* between too fast and too slow. —*adjective* ✦ **central, intermediate, middle** ✧ **average** The *mean* score on our last quiz was 75.

meaning *noun* ✦ **idea, intent, message, purpose, significance** ✧ **sense** I read the story twice, but I still don't understand its *meaning*.

measure *verb* ✦ **calculate, compute, figure** ✧ **count, gauge, rule** We *measured* the size of our garage to see if a pickup truck would fit. —*noun* **1.** ✦ **amount, portion, share** ✧ **dimension, extent, size** This brownie recipe calls for equal *measures* of flour and sugar. **2.** ✦ **gauge, rule, test** ✧ **scale, standard, unit, yardstick** An IQ test is not always a true *measure* of a person's intelligence. **3.** ✦ **action, procedure, step** ✧ **course, move** We took *measures* to keep Fido out of our neighbor's yard.

mechanism *noun* ✦ **apparatus, device** ✧ **instrument, machine, tool** Our VCR has a *mechanism* that automatically rewinds and ejects the tapes.

medal *noun* ✧ **award, badge, decoration** During the 1972 Olympics swimmer Mark Spitz won seven gold *medals*.

meddle *verb* ✦ **interfere, intervene** ✧ **fool, mess, tamper** It's not polite to *meddle* in other people's affairs.

medicine *noun* ✦ **drug, medication, prescription** ✧ **cure, remedy** The doctor gave me *medicine* that helped bring my temperature back to normal.

meditate *verb* ✦ **consider, contemplate, deliberate, ponder, reflect on, think about** Ginny *meditated on* whether or not to skip a grade for a long time before deciding.

medium *noun* 1. ✦ **environment, setting, substance** Moist soil in a dark room is the perfect *medium* for growing mushrooms. 2. ✦ **agency, agent, instrument, means** ✧ **tool, vehicle** Gold was commonly used as a *medium* of exchange before paper money was introduced. —*adjective* ✦ **average, intermediate, middle** ✧ **moderate, normal** These shirts come in small, *medium*, and large sizes.

meet *verb* 1. ✦ **come together, cross, intersect** ✧ **connect, join, link** A new truck stop was built at the spot where the two highways *meet*. 2. ✦ **get together with, see** ✧ **contact, encounter, greet** I plan to *meet* my friends at the donut shop after school. 3. ✦ **assemble, congregate, convene** ✧ **collect, gather** Kendra's chess club *meets* once a week. 4. ✦ **fill, fulfill, satisfy** ✧ **equal, reach** My brother received a letter saying that he *meets* all the university's admission requirements. —*noun* ✦ **competition, contest, match, tournament** ✧ **event** My friend Ian will be competing in next week's swim *meet*.

meeting *noun* ✦ **assembly, conference, gathering** ✧ **affair, session** The *meeting* will begin as soon as everyone gets here.

melancholy *noun* ✦ **dejection, depression, gloom, sadness, unhappiness** A feeling of *melancholy* came over me as I listened to the sad song. —*adjective* ✦ **depressing, dreary, gloomy, sad, sorrowful** The *melancholy* movie made me cry.

mellow *adjective* ✦ **gentle, mild, smooth, soft, soothing, sweet** The mother sang a *mellow* tune to lull her baby to sleep.

melody *noun* ✦ **music, tune** ✧ **refrain, song** I was awakened by the *melody* of a robin chirping outside my window.

melt *verb* ✦ **thaw** ✧ **disappear, dissolve, fade, soften** My snowman began to *melt* as soon as the sun came out.

member *noun* ✦ **associate, participant** ✧ **constituent, part, piece** Danielle is our science club's newest *member*.

memorable *adjective* ✦ **important, noteworthy, remarkable, significant, unforgettable** My aunt said that her college graduation was the most *memorable* event of her life.

memorial *noun* ✦ **monument, shrine** ✧ **remembrance, tribute** This *memorial* honors the Americans who died in the Vietnam War. —*adjective* ✦ **commemorative** ✧ **testimonial** The city will hold a *memorial* service for the police officers who died in the line of duty last month.

memory *noun* ✦ **recollection, remembrance** ✧ **recall, thought** The earliest *memory* I have is of my father reading me a story.

menace *noun* ✦ **danger, hazard, threat** ✧ **peril, risk** Our cat is a *menace* to any bird that enters our yard. —*verb* ✦ **endanger, imperil, threaten** ✧ **frighten, scare** The shepherd protected his sheep from the wolf that *menaced* them.

✦ **best choices**
✧ **other choices**

mend *verb* **1.** ✦ **fix, patch, repair** ◇ **correct, restore** The crew *mended* the ship's torn sails. **2.** ✦ **cure, heal, recover** ◇ **improve** The doctor said that my broken hand would *mend* in about six weeks.

mental *adjective* ✦ **intellectual** ◇ **rational, reasoning, thinking** Jacqueline enjoys solving riddles because she likes the *mental* challenge.

mention *verb* ✦ **disclose, remark, say** ◇ **declare, state, tell** Courtney *mentioned* that she would be away next weekend. —*noun* ✦ **comment, note, notice, reference, remark, statement** Last night's thunderstorm received only a brief *mention* on the morning news.

menu *noun* ✦ **index, list** ◇ **inventory, register, table** Andre scanned the list of programs on his computer's *menu*.

merchandise *noun* ✦ **goods, products, stock, wares** ◇ **articles, things** All the sale *merchandise* is marked with a red tag.

merchant *noun* ✦ **retailer, shopkeeper, storekeeper** ◇ **dealer, trader** Several *merchants* have shops on my block.

mercy *noun* ✦ **charity, compassion, kindness** ◇ **pity, sympathy** I showed *mercy* to the cricket by putting it outside.

mere *adjective* ✦ **insignificant, minor, plain, simple** ◇ **only, scant** I had a bike accident, but a *mere* scratch was my only injury.

Antonyms

merge *verb*

break, divide, part, separate, split

merge *verb* ✦ **combine, come together, join, meet** ◇ **link, unite** I know of a good fishing spot where two creeks *merge*.

merit *noun* ✦ **value, virtue, worth** ◇ **benefit, quality** Ms. Jansen said that my story idea has real *merit*. —*verb* ✦ **deserve, justify, rate** ◇ **earn, gain, get** The whole club thinks that your proposal *merits* further consideration.

merry *adjective* ✦ **cheerful, gay, happy, jolly, jovial, mirthful** Everyone at the party was in a *merry* mood.

mess *noun* ✦ **clutter, litter** ◇ **disorganization, eyesore** I am cleaning up the *mess* I left in the kitchen. —*verb* ✦ **disarrange, disorder, muss** ◇ **clutter, dirty, litter** The wind *messed up* Jonah's hair.

message *noun* ✦ **communication, statement** ◇ **note, notice, report** Victoria wasn't home when I called, so I left a *message* on her answering machine.

messenger *noun* ✦ **courier** ◇ **carrier, delivery person, emissary** The duchess gave the letter to her most trusted *messenger*.

messy *adjective* ✦ **cluttered, disorderly, disorganized, untidy** ◇ **sloppy** I cleaned up my *messy* room.

method *noun* ✦ **manner, mode, style** ◇ **fashion, system, technique, way** Traveling by bus is just one of the many *methods* of transportation available to us.

middle *noun* ✦ **center, core, inside** ◇ **heart, midpoint** These candies have soft *middles*. —*adjective* ✦ **center, central** ◇ **inner, inside, intermediate** Daryl held up three straws, and I picked the *middle* one.

mighty *adjective* ✦ **powerful, strong, sturdy** ◇ **colossal, gigantic, huge** Crocodiles have *mighty* jaws for crushing their prey.

migrate *verb* ✦ **immigrate, journey, move, travel** ◇ **emigrate, wander** The American West was settled by pioneers who *migrated* from the East.

mild *adjective* ✦ **delicate, gentle** ◇ **calm, easy, moderate, pleasant, smooth, soft** We use a *mild* detergent that doesn't fade our clothes.

mimic *verb* ✦ **copy, echo, imitate, repeat** ◇ **mock** My parrot *mimics* a lot of what he hears.

mind *noun* ✦ brain, intellect ◇ head, intelligence, thinking A good education helps to develop a person's *mind*. —*verb* **1.** ✦ care, object ◇ disapprove, dislike, resent Do you *mind* if I borrow your sweater? **2.** ✦ attend to, care for, look after, tend, watch Who is going to *mind* the cat while we're away? **3.** ✦ heed, listen to, obey ◇ follow Mom and Dad told us to *mind* our sitter.

mine *noun* ◇ excavation, hole, pit, quarry, shaft, tunnel My grandfather once worked in a silver *mine* in Idaho. —*verb* ✦ dig up, excavate, quarry ◇ extract More gold is *mined* in South Africa than anywhere else in the world.

mingle *verb* ✦ blend, combine, join, mix ◇ merge, unite When I saw the bear I felt fear *mingled* with awe.

miniature *adjective* ✦ little, minute, small, tiny, wee Anthony has a collection of *miniature* cars.

minimum *adjective* ✦ lowest, slowest ◇ least, littlest, slightest, smallest The *minimum* speed at which this airplane can be flown is seventy miles per hour.

minor *adjective* ✦ insignificant, petty, slight, small, trivial, unimportant ◇ lesser The fact that we were fifteen minutes late is a *minor* problem compared to the fact that the museum is closed today. —*noun* ✦ adolescent, child, juvenile, youngster, youth *Minors* cannot vote in state or federal elections.

minute[1] *noun* ✦ instant, jiffy, moment, second, trice, twinkling I'll be with you in just a *minute*.

minute[2] *adjective* ✦ little, small, tiny, wee ◇ microscopic, miniature The bug was so *minute* that I almost couldn't see it.

miracle *noun* ✦ marvel, wonder ◇ sensation, surprise It was a *miracle* that no one was injured in the car wreck.

miraculous *adjective* ✦ amazing, extraordinary, incredible, marvelous, remarkable The gravely ill man made a *miraculous* recovery.

miscellaneous *adjective* ✦ assorted, different, diverse, mixed, varied, various The top drawer contains *miscellaneous* art supplies.

mischief *noun* ✦ misbehavior, misconduct, trouble ◇ damage, harm, injury I wonder what kind of *mischief* my cousin is up to now.

mischievous *adjective* ✦ annoying, bad, misbehaving, naughty, troublesome The *mischievous* puppy chewed up two pairs of shoes.

miserable *adjective* **1.** ✦ dejected, desolate, gloomy, sad, unhappy, wretched Mirabelle felt *miserable* when she couldn't find her trombone. **2.** ✦ awful, bad, lousy, poor, rotten ◇ inferior, unsatisfactory I had *miserable* luck the last time we played checkers.

misery *noun* ✦ distress, hardship, misfortune, sorrow, suffering, torment The avalanche victims endured much *misery* before help arrived.

misfortune *noun* **1.** ✦ bad luck, ill fortune, ill luck We had the *misfortune* to get a flat tire just as we were leaving for our trip. ▶ **2.** ✦ blow, catastrophe, disaster, tragedy ◇ trouble The loss of our best player was a great *misfortune* for our volleyball team.

misgiving *noun* ✦ anxiety, concern, doubt, fear, worry ◇ suspicion Alex has some *misgivings* about doing a back dive off the high board.

mislead *verb* ✦ deceive, fool, trick ◇ misinform The advertisement

✦ **best choices**
◇ **other choices**

misled people into thinking that the exercise machine would be easy to use.

misplace *verb* ✦ **lose, mislay** ✧ **forget, miss** Tyrone occasionally *misplaces* his eyeglasses.

miss *verb* **1.** ✦ **forget, neglect, overlook, skip** ✧ **drop, let go** Nathaniel fell asleep on the subway and *missed* his stop. **2.** ✦ **long for, want, yearn for** ✧ **crave, desire** I *missed* my family while I was away at summer camp. **3.** ✦ **avoid, dodge, escape, evade** ✧ **lose** We'll *miss* the lunch-hour rush if we go to the restaurant early.

mission *noun* **1.** ✦ **assignment, job, objective, task** ✧ **obligation, responsibility** The spy's *mission* was to gather information about the enemy. **2.** ✦ **commission, delegation, task force** ✧ **embassy** The United Nations sent a peacekeeping *mission* to help stop the war.

mist *noun* ✦ **cloud, fog, haze** ✧ **drizzle, vapor** A heavy *mist* hung in the air just before sunrise. —*verb* ✦ **cloud, fog, steam** ✧ **drizzle, sprinkle** The bathroom mirror *mists* up whenever anyone takes a hot shower.

mistake *noun* ✦ **error** ✧ **blunder, fault, lapse, slip** I made only one *mistake* on my spelling test. —*verb* ✦ **confuse (with), mix up (with)** ✧ **misinterpret** I *mistook* Jo for her twin sister.

mistaken *adjective* ✦ **false, faulty, inaccurate, incorrect, wrong** People once had the *mistaken* belief that the Earth was flat.

mistreat *verb* ✦ **abuse, harm, hurt, injure** ✧ **damage** People should never *mistreat* their pets.

misty *adjective* ✦ **cloudy, foggy, hazy** ✧ **dim, murky, vague** We were not able to see the lunar eclipse because the evening was *misty*.

misunderstand *verb* ✦ **confuse, misinterpret** ✧ **misjudge, mistake** I had trouble finding my friend's house because I *misunderstood* her directions.

misunderstanding *noun* ✦ **misconception, mix-up** ✧ **confusion, error, mistake** There was a *misunderstanding* about the time of our meeting.

mix *verb* ✦ **blend, combine, merge, scramble, stir** ✧ **mingle** Did you know that concrete is made by *mixing* cement with gravel and water? —*noun* ✦ **assortment, combination, mixture, variety** ✧ **jumble** There was an interesting *mix* of food at our potluck supper.

mixture *noun* ✦ **blend, combination, compound, mix** ✧ **assortment** My favorite drink is a *mixture* of iced tea and lemonade.

moan *noun* ✦ **groan, howl, wail, yowl** ✧ **sob, whimper** I heard an eerie *moan* that turned out to be the wind. —*verb* ✦ **groan, howl, wail, yowl** ✧ **cry, sigh** Every Halloween my brother walks around the house *moaning* like a ghost.

mob *noun* ✦ **crowd, horde, mass, pack, swarm, throng** ✧ **group** There was a *mob* of people at the shopping mall on the day before Christmas. —*verb* ✦ **crowd around, press toward, surround, swarm around, throng around** Dozens of shouting reporters *mobbed* the politician.

mobile *adjective* ✦ **movable, portable, transportable, traveling** Volunteers set up a *mobile* kitchen to help feed the homeless.

mock *verb* ✦ **insult, jeer, laugh at, ridicule, taunt, tease** Many people *mocked* early aviators by saying that if humans were meant to fly, they would have wings. —*adjective* ✦ **artificial, imitation, simulated** ✧ **fake, false** The film crew built a *mock* spaceship for the science-fiction movie.

mode *noun* ✦ **manner, means, method, style, system, way** ✧ **fashion, procedure** Steamboats and stagecoaches are two old-fashioned *modes* of transportation.

model *noun* 1. ✦ **miniature, replica** ✧ **copy, duplicate, imitation** Michael likes to build plastic *models* of military airplanes. 2. ✦ **design, kind, style, type, variety, version** We traded in our old car for a newer *model*. 3. ✦ **example, ideal, pattern, prototype** ✧ **paragon, subject** Laynie's research is a *model* of good scholarship. —*verb* ✦ **design, fashion, make, shape** ✧ **copy, imitate** The courthouse building was *modeled* after an ancient Greek temple. —*adjective* ✦ **ideal, good, perfect** ✧ **representative, standard, typical** Donald believes that being active in community affairs is part of being a *model* citizen.

moderate *adjective* ✦ **modest, reasonable** ✧ **average, medium, temperate** This store sells quality merchandise at *moderate* prices. —*verb* ✦ **control, restrain, tame, tone down** ✧ **lessen, reduce** My uncle has to *moderate* his eating habits for health reasons.

modern *adjective* ✦ **contemporary, current, new, present, recent** ✧ **fresh** High-rise office buildings are a *modern* form of architecture.

modest *adjective* 1. ✦ **humble, quiet, reserved** ✧ **shy, silent** The research scientist was *modest* about her many discoveries. 2. ✦ **limited, moderate, small** ✧ **average, reasonable** My grandparents live on a *modest* income now that they have retired.

modify *verb* ✦ **adjust, alter, change, revise, vary** ✧ **reorganize, transform** The weather forced us to *modify* our vacation plans.

moist *adjective* ✦ **damp, wet** ✧ **humid, soggy** Matthew used a *moist* rag to clean the dirt off his bicycle.

moisten *verb* ✦ **dampen, soak, wet** ✧ **drench, rinse, wash, water** *Moisten* the sponge before you wipe the counter.

moisture *noun* ✦ **dampness, liquid, water, wetness** ✧ **fluid** Try to keep your books dry because *moisture* will harm them.

mold¹ *noun* ✦ **form** ✧ **shape, pattern** Candles are made by pouring hot wax into a *mold*. —*verb* ✦ **fashion, form, make, shape** ✧ **build, forge** Alexa took a small lump of clay and *molded* it into a bead.

mold² *noun* ✦ **fungus** ✧ **blight, rot** There's *mold* on this loaf of bread.

moment *noun* ✦ **jiffy, minute, second** ✧ **flash, instant** The doctor will be with you in a *moment*.

momentous *adjective* ✦ **historic, important, major, significant** ✧ **serious** The lunar landing on July 20, 1969, was a *momentous* occasion.

momentum *noun* ✦ **speed, velocity** ✧ **energy, force, power** The bicyclist gained *momentum* as he coasted down the hill.

monarch *noun* ✦ **queen, ruler, sovereign** ✧ **king** Queen Elizabeth I was England's *monarch* from 1558 to 1603.

money *noun* ✦ **cash, currency** ✧ **funds, revenue, riches, wealth** DeShaun intends to save all of the *money* that he earns until he has enough for a new guitar.

monitor *noun* ✦ **overseer** ✧ **director, guide, supervisor** Our school selects older students to be hallway *monitors*. —*verb* ✦ **check, observe, supervise, watch** ✧ **control** Doctors closely *monitored* the seriously ill patient.

monotonous *adjective* ✦ **boring, dull, tedious, tiresome** ✧ **dreary, routine** The long plane trip was *monotonous*.

monster *noun* ✦ **beast, creature** ✧ **brute, demon, fiend, giant** My favorite movie *monster* is a giant lizard that destroys Tokyo.

monstrous *adjective* 1. ✦ **colossal, enormous, gigantic, huge, immense, mammoth** The sailboat was almost capsized by a *monstrous* wave. 2. ✦ **frightening, gruesome, hideous, horrible,**

✦ **best choices**
✧ **other choices**

terrifying ◇ ugly According to folklore, ogres are *monstrous* creatures that eat human beings.

monument *noun* ✦ memorial, shrine ◇ testament, tribute This statue is a *monument* to the pioneers who founded our town.

mood *noun* ✦ attitude, disposition, frame of mind ◇ spirit, temper When my *mood* is cheerful in the morning, I am usually happy all day long.

moody *adjective* ✦ gloomy, melancholy, sulky, sullen ◇ unstable Janine prefers to be by herself when she feels *moody*.

moor *verb* ✦ fasten, fix, lash, secure, tie ◇ anchor The crew *moored* their ship to the dock. ◀

mop *verb* ✦ clean, sponge, wipe ◇ scrub, wash Please *mop* up the spilled milk.

moral *adjective* ✦ good, honest, honorable, upright, virtuous A *moral* person does not lie or cheat. —*noun* ✦ lesson, meaning, message, teaching ◇ proverb A fable is a story that has a *moral*.

morale *noun* ✦ attitude, confidence, spirit ◇ mood, self-esteem *Morale* at our school has really improved since we got a new principal.

more *adjective* ✦ additional, extra ◇ added, another, new, other Do you need *more* time to finish? —*noun* ◇ addition, another, extra, increase, supplement When we ran out of bagels, Mom went to the bakery to get some *more*. —*adverb* ✦ additionally, further ◇ better, beyond, still, too, yet Our coach said that we will have to practice *more*.

morsel *noun* ✦ bit, bite, crumb, piece ◇ fragment, scrap When we were finished with the cake, there wasn't a *morsel* left.

mortal *adjective* ✦ deadly, fatal, lethal, terminal A lion delivers a *mortal* wound by biting its prey in the back of the neck. —*noun* ✦ human, human being ◇ man, person, woman In Roman mythology, Hercules was a *mortal* who possessed godlike strength.

most *adjective* ✦ greater, greatest, maximum ◇ better, best, top The person with the *most* strength will probably win the weightlifting contest. —*noun* ✦ almost all, nearly all ◇ majority, maximum, peak Shannon spends *most* of his allowance on comic books. —*adverb* ✦ exceedingly, extremely, quite, very ◇ extra, notably Everyone in the audience thought that the magician's performance was *most* impressive.

mostly *adverb* ✦ chiefly, largely, mainly, primarily My archery class is *mostly* girls, but a few boys also attend.

motion *noun* ✦ flux, movement ◇ action, activity, move, stir Because sharks are very heavy, they have to remain in constant *motion* or they will sink. —*verb* ✦ beckon, gesture, indicate, signal ◇ direct My aunt *motioned* to me to sit down beside her.

motive *noun* ✦ aim (in), cause, incentive, motivation, objective (in), purpose, reason Dad's *motive* for taking an exercise class was to look good for his high school reunion.

motor *noun* ✦ engine, power source ◇ machine, mechanism, power plant My model airplane has a miniature battery-powered *motor*. —*adjective* ✦ mobile, moving, traveling ◇ mechanized, motorized My grandparents are driving through Alaska in their *motor* home.

motto *noun* ✦ maxim, saying, slogan ◇ expression, principle, rule The Boy Scout *motto* is "Be Prepared."

mound *noun* ✦ heap, hill, mass, pile, stack ◇ mountain Some species of ants form huge *mounds* of soil when they dig their nests.

mount *verb* **1. ✦ build, grow, increase, rise ✧ ascend, climb, lift** Excitement *mounted* as the swimmers neared the finish line. **2. ✦ install, place, position ✧ exhibit, frame, show** Dad *mounted* a pair of antique snowshoes above our fireplace. ◄

mountain *noun* **1. ✦ mount, peak, summit ✧ hill, mound** We camped at the base of a majestic snow-capped *mountain*. **2. ✦ heap, mass, mound, pile, stack ✧ abundance, accumulation** We have a *mountain* of trash that we need to take to the dump.

mourn *verb* **✦ grieve, sorrow ✧ cry, despair, suffer** It is natural to *mourn* when someone we care about dies.

move *verb* **1. ✦ carry, convey, shift ✧ change, go, transport** Sydney *moved* her chair closer to the television. **2. ✦ relocate, transfer ✧ depart, leave, travel** My uncle recently *moved* from New York to Iowa. **3. ✦ affect, disturb, stir, touch** I was deeply *moved* by the tragic love story that I just finished reading. **4. ✦ cause, influence, inspire, motivate, persuade, stimulate** What *moved* you to join the karate club? *—noun* **✦ motion, movement ✧ action, maneuver, step** The police officer ordered the suspect to stand still and not make a *move*.

movement *noun* **1. ✦ motion, stirring ✧ action, activity, move, shift** A sudden *movement* in the bushes caught Darla's attention. **2. ✦ campaign, crusade, drive ✧ group, organization** There is a *movement* in my neighborhood to start a community garden.

movie *noun* **✦ film, motion picture ✧ feature, picture, show** My favorite *movie* will soon be available on video.

mow *verb* **✦ clip, cut, trim ✧ crop, shear** The grass is too wet to *mow* right now.

mud *noun* **✦ mire, muck, slime ✧ dirt** We always wear our boots when we walk in the *mud*. ▼

muffle *verb* **✦ dampen, silence, soften, stifle, suppress** I put my hand over my mouth to *muffle* my laughter.

muggy *adjective* **✦ clammy, humid, sticky ✧ damp, moist** I never feel like doing much on hot, *muggy* days.

multiply *verb* **✦ build up, expand, grow, increase, mount, swell** The difficulties of the climb *multiplied* as the mountaineers got close to the summit.

multitude *noun* **✦ crowd, horde, mass, pack, swarm, throng** A *multitude* of tourists boarded the ferryboat.

mumble *verb* **✦ murmur, mutter, whisper** It's hard for me to understand you when you *mumble*.

munch *verb* **✦ eat, snack on ✧ bite, chew, gnaw** Brandon loves to *munch on* potato chips while he watches television.

murder *noun* **✦ homicide, killing, slaying ✧ assassination, massacre** The suspect has been

✦ best choices
✧ other choices

charged with attempted *murder*. —*verb* ✦ **assassinate, kill, slay** ✧ **massacre, slaughter** President Abraham Lincoln was *murdered* by John Wilkes Booth on April 14, 1865.

Word Groups

Music is a pleasing or meaningful combination of sounds. **Music** is a general term with no true synonyms. Here are some different forms of music to investigate in a dictionary:

air, harmony, lyrics, melody, singing, song, strain, tune

must *verb* ✦ **have to, need to** ✧ **ought to, should** Our book reports *must* be turned in no later than next Wednesday.

mutiny *noun* ✦ **rebellion, revolt, uprising** ✧ **revolution, riot** The pirates staged a *mutiny* because their captain refused to share his treasure. —*verb* ✦ **rebel, revolt** ✧ **resist, riot** The sailors *mutinied* and took over the ship.

mutual *adjective* ✦ **common, joint, shared** ✧ **general, related** My best friend and I have a *mutual* love of dancing.

mystery *noun* ✦ **puzzle, question, riddle** ✧ **problem, secret** The reason why so many ships have been lost in the Devil's Triangle is an unsolved *mystery*.

mystify *verb* ✦ **baffle, bewilder, confuse, perplex, puzzle** Easter Island's huge statues *mystify* archaeologists because no one knows why the statues were made.

myth *noun* ✦ **folk tale, legend, story** ✧ **fable** There are *myths* from many cultures describing how the world was made.

mythical *adjective* ✦ **fabled, fanciful, fantastic, fictitious, imaginary, legendary** ✧ **unreal** Shangri-la is a *mythical* paradise where people never grow old.

mythology *noun* ✦ **myth** ✧ **folklore, legend, lore, tradition** In Greek *mythology*, Poseidon was the god of the sea.

N

nag *verb* ✦ **badger, bother, hound, pester** ✧ **annoy, complain, scold** My parents don't *nag* me as long as I get my chores done on time.

> **Word Groups**
>
> A **nail** is a pointed piece of metal that is hammered into pieces of wood to fasten them. **Nail** is a very specific term with no true synonyms. Here are some related words to investigate in a dictionary:
> brad, peg, pin, spike, tack

naked *adjective* 1. ✦ **bare, nude, unclad, unclothed** ✧ **exposed, uncovered** My little brother ran *naked* through the house after his bath. 2. ✦ **unaided, unassisted** ✧ **natural, plain, simple** Bacteria are too small to be seen by the *naked* eye.

name *noun* 1. ✦ **designation** ✧ **label, term, title** The *name* of the tallest mountain in the world is Mount Everest. 2. ✦ **reputation** ✧ **character, distinction, fame** My brother wants to go to a college that has a good *name*. —*verb* 1. ✦ **call, designate** ✧ **label, term, title** Susannah *named* her cat Kittyhawk. 2. ✦ **identify, itemize, list, specify** ✧ **mention** Can you *name* all seven of the Seven Dwarves? 3. ✦ **appoint, choose, designate, select** ✧ **elect** We have to *name* someone to represent us on the student council.

nap *noun* ✦ **catnap, doze, rest, snooze** ✧ **siesta, sleep** I used to take a *nap* every afternoon when I was little. —*verb* ✦ **catnap, doze, drowse, sleep, snooze** Our turtle is *napping* in the sun.

narcotic *noun* ✧ **drug, medicine, painkiller** Doctors sometimes prescribe *narcotics* for patients who are in great pain.

narrate *verb* ✦ **describe, recount, relate, tell** ✧ **recite, report** In the book I just read, an old sailor *narrates* his adventures on the high seas.

narrow *adjective* 1. ✦ **confined, cramped, snug, tight** ✧ **slender, thin** The cavers inched their way along the *narrow* passage. 2. ✦ **meager, slim, small** ✧ **close, limited** The horse won the race by a *narrow* margin. —*verb* ✦ **taper** ✧ **contract, reduce, tighten** The road *narrows* as it goes through the tunnel.

nasty *adjective* 1. ✦ **cruel, evil, hateful, mean, vicious, wicked** The movie audience cheered when the *nasty* villain was defeated. 2. ✦ **awful, bad, disgusting, foul, offensive, unpleasant** There's a *nasty* smell coming from the garbage can. 3. ✦ **dangerous, serious, severe** ✧ **harmful, injurious** The skier took a *nasty* fall.

nation *noun* ✦ **country, state** ✧ **domain, land, realm, republic** Canada and Mexico are the two *nations* that border on the United States.

natural *adjective* 1. ✦ **inborn, instinctive** ✧ **hereditary, inherited** Dogs have a *natural* tendency to chase anything that runs away from them. 2. ✦ **lifelike, native, realistic** ✧ **normal, regular, typical** The San Diego zoo is famous for displaying animals in their *natural* surroundings.

naturally *adverb* 1. ✦ **normally, regularly** ✧ **genuinely, routinely, typically** I felt nervous having a solo part in the play, but I tried to just speak *naturally*. 2. ✦ **clearly, obviously, of course** ✧ **certainly, logically, surely** *Naturally*, we'll be having turkey for Thanksgiving dinner.

nature *noun* 1. ✦ **the environment, the outdoors** ✧ **creation, universe, wilderness, world** Our class is taking a field trip to a state park to learn more about *nature*. 2. ✦ **character, disposition, makeup, personality** ✧ **essence, quality** I like people who have a gentle *nature*.

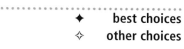

✦   best choices
✧   other choices

naughty *adjective* ✦ **bad, disobedient, unruly** ✧ **impish, mischievous** My little sister was being *naughty* when she threw her food onto the floor.

nausea *noun* ✦ **upset stomach** ✧ **indigestion, sickness** My *nausea* was probably caused by eating too much just before I got on the roller coaster.

nautical *adjective* ✦ **boating, marine, maritime, naval, sailing** "Forecastle" is a *nautical* term that refers to the forward part of a ship's deck.

navigate *verb* ✦ **pilot, steer** ✧ **direct, guide, maneuver** Early sailors *navigated* by using the stars as a guide.

navy *noun* ✦ **armada, fleet, naval forces** England's *navy* gained control of the seas by defeating the Spanish in 1588.

near *adjective* 1. ✦ **approaching, at hand, coming, imminent** Winter is *near* when the days begin to be shorter and colder. 2. ✦ **close** ✧ **adjacent, adjoining, immediate, nearby** We live in the country, and our *nearest* neighbor is two miles away.

nearly *adverb* ✦ **about, almost, approximately, roughly, virtually** My older brother is *nearly* as tall as my dad.

neat *adjective* 1. ✦ **orderly, organized, precise, tidy** ✧ **clean** Richard stacked his baseball cards in *neat* piles. 2. ✦ **clever, deft, skillful** ✧ **fine, great, wonderful** Grandpa showed me a really *neat* magic trick.

necessary *adjective* ✦ **essential, needed, required** ✧ **imperative, important, urgent** My art teacher said that she would furnish all of the *necessary* supplies for making masks.

necessity *noun* ✦ **essential, must, requirement** ✧ **condition, fundamental** Water is a *necessity* for all life on the Earth.

need *noun* 1. ✦ **essential, necessity, requirement, want** ✧ **resource** Pioneer families had to provide most of their *needs* themselves. 2. ✦ **call, necessity** ✧ **demand, obligation** There is no *need* for further discussion of this matter. —*verb* ✦ **desire, require, want** ✧ **demand, lack** We *need* two more players for our team.

needless *adjective* ✦ **pointless, useless** ✧ **unnecessary** It is *needless* to ask me again because I have made up my mind.

needy *adjective* ✦ **destitute, impoverished, penniless, poor, poverty-stricken** Every year at Thanksgiving our school holds a drive to collect food for *needy* families.

negative *adjective* ✦ **adverse, bad, unfavorable** ✧ **pessimistic, unsatisfactory** The movie received many *negative* reviews.

neglect *verb* ✦ **fail, forget** ✧ **disregard, ignore, overlook, skip** The man's phone was disconnected because he *neglected* to pay the bill. —*noun* ✦ **disregard, inattention, indifference, oversight** The dilapidated old barn has suffered from years of *neglect*.

negligent *adjective* ✦ **careless, inattentive** ✧ **forgetful, indifferent, irresponsible** The *negligent* driver got a ticket for running a red light.

negotiate *verb* ✦ **arrange, bargain, determine, settle** ✧ **confer, discuss** The details of the agreement still have to be *negotiated*.

neighborhood *noun* ✦ **area, community, district, locality** ✧ **block, street** We have lived in the same *neighborhood* for ten years.

nerve *noun* ✦ **bravery, courage, daring, pluck** ✧ **mettle, spirit** It took a lot of *nerve* to ski down the expert trail.

nervous *adjective* ✦ **anxious, distressed, fearful, tense, uneasy, upset** Loud noises make my cat very *nervous*.

Antonyms
nervous *adjective*
calm, collected, cool, relaxed, serene

nestle *verb* ✦ **clasp, cuddle, embrace, snuggle** ✧ **hug, squeeze** My cousin always goes to sleep with his teddy bear *nestled* in his arms. ▼

neutral *adjective* **1.** ✦ **impartial, unbiased** ✧ **detached, indifferent, uninvolved** A referee is supposed to be *neutral* so that each team has an equal chance of winning. **2.** ✦ **bland, drab, flat, indistinct, ordinary, plain** My dentist's office is painted a *neutral* color.

nevertheless *adverb* ✦ **anyway, even so, nonetheless, regardless** ✧ **however, still, yet** I didn't feel very well this morning, but I went to school *nevertheless*.

new *adjective* **1.** ✦ **brand-new** ✧ **current, latest, modern, recent** Everyone in the family wants to use our *new* camcorder. **2.** ✦ **fresh, unfamiliar, unknown** ✧ **different, strange** There are several *new* students in my class this year. **3.** ✦ **different, novel, original, unique, unusual** Tyler and I have an idea for a *new* way to recycle old soda bottles.

newly *adverb* ✦ **just, freshly, lately, recently** Samantha loves her *newly* redecorated bedroom.

news *noun* ✦ **information, report, story, word** ✧ **intelligence, knowledge** Have you heard the *news* about the movie that is going to be made in our town?

next *adjective* ✦ **coming, following, subsequent** ✧ **adjacent, close** I mailed Melinda's letter on Tuesday, and she got it the *next* day. —*adverb* ✧ **after, afterward, hereafter, later, subse-**

quently I've seen this movie before, but I don't remember what happens *next*.

nibble *verb* ✦ **chew, gnaw, munch** ✧ **bite** My rabbit *nibbled* on the carrot that I gave him. —*noun* ✦ **bite, taste** ✧ **bit, morsel** The mouse took one *nibble* of the cheese and decided that he liked it.

nice *adjective* **1.** ✦ **agreeable, delightful, enjoyable, good, pleasant, pleasing** Roses have a *nice* smell. **2.** ✦ **decent, kind, thoughtful** ✧ **courteous, polite, proper** It was *nice* of you to share your umbrella with me.

nick *noun* ✦ **chip, cut, dent, notch, scar, scratch** The antique table was in perfect condition except for a few *nicks* on its legs. —*verb* ✦ **cut, scratch** ✧ **chip, dent, mar, notch, scar** Dad *nicked* himself while shaving this morning.

night *noun* ✦ **dark, nighttime** ✧ **evening, nightfall, sundown** I like to see fireflies in the *night*.

nimble *adjective* ✦ **agile, deft, lively, quick, spry, swift** ✧ **clever** You have to have *nimble* fingers to play a guitar.

noble *adjective* **1.** ✦ **aristocratic, highborn, royal** ✧ **upper-class** The prince was required to marry a woman who was of *noble* birth. **2.** ✦ **honorable, moral, selfless** ✧ **courageous, excellent, generous** Helping the homeless is a *noble* cause. **3.** ✦ **grand, imposing, magnificent, majestic, stately** The Sierra Nevada is a chain of *noble* mountains. —*noun* ✦ **aristocrat** ✧ **lady, lord, nobleman, noblewoman** *Nobles* came from all over the land to attend the queen's coronation.

noise *noun* ✦ **clamor, din, racket, sound** ✧ **tumult, uproar** The *noise* from my computer game woke my little sister.

noisy *adjective* ✦ **loud** ✧ **blaring, booming, clamorous, deafening** Dad's old lawnmower is really *noisy*.

✦ best choices
✧ other choices

nominate *verb* ✦ **choose, designate, name, propose, select** ✧ **appoint** We *nominated* three candidates for the office of class president.

nonsense *noun* ✦ **absurdity, craziness, foolishness, silliness** ✧ **stupidity** As we sat around the table, we made up a funny story that was pure *nonsense*.

normal *adjective* ✦ **average, ordinary, regular, standard, typical, usual** The river returned to its *normal* level one week after the flood.

notable *adjective* ✦ **eminent, famous, great, important, memorable, noteworthy** The signing of the Declaration of Independence was a *notable* event in American history.

notch *noun* ✦ **groove, indentation, nick** ✧ **chip, cut, dent** An arrow has a *notch* on its end in order to get a better grip on the bowstring. —*verb* ✦ **cut, nick** ✧ **chip, chop, scratch** When you build a log cabin you have to *notch* the logs so that they fit together snugly.

note *noun* **1.** ✦ **card, letter, message** ✧ **communication** I sent Claudia a *note* thanking her for my birthday present. **2.** ✦ **comment, observation, remark** ✧ **memorandum, record** The teacher made a few *notes* in the margin of my book report. **3.** ✦ **hint, indication, suggestion, trace** ✧ **evidence, sign** There was a *note* of sadness in Gina's voice when she told us that she was moving away. —*verb* ✦ **notice, observe** ✧ **perceive, regard, see** Please *note* that your appointment is for three o'clock.

nothing *noun* ✦ **naught, nought, zero** ✧ **not anything** The final score was ten to *nothing*.

notice *verb* ✦ **note, observe, see, spot** ✧ **perceive, recognize** Did you *notice* the flock of chickadees in the yard? —*noun* **1.** ✦ **attention, consideration, heed, regard** ✧ **observation** I was happy that my work received such favorable *notice*. **2.** ✦ **announcement, declaration, statement** ✧ **bulletin, pronouncement** Mom received a *notice* that said she had to report for jury duty. **3.** ✦ **notification, warning** ✧ **information, instruction** We gave the landlord a month's *notice* before we moved out of our apartment.

notify *verb* ✦ **advise, alert, inform, tell** ✧ **instruct, mention** We *notified* the post office that we were going on vacation.

notion *noun* ✦ **belief, idea, thought** ✧ **concept, opinion** My little brother has somehow gotten the *notion* that there's a monster in his closet.

notorious *adjective* ✦ **infamous, scandalous** ✧ **famous, leading, well-known** Edward Teach, known also as Blackbeard, was a *notorious* pirate.

nourish *verb* ✦ **feed, maintain, supply, sustain** ✧ **provide, support** Your blood *nourishes* your body by carrying oxygen and nutrients to every living cell.

nourishment *noun* ✦ **feed, food** ✧ **nutrition, provision, support** All baby animals need *nourishment* to grow. ▼

novel *adjective* ✦ **different, fresh, new, original, unusual** ✧ **odd, uncommon, unique** Someone came up with a *novel* idea for turning old automobile tires into pavement.

Antonyms
novel *adjective*
common, familiar, ordinary, usual, well-known

novelty *noun* ✦ **freshness, newness** ✧ **originality, strangeness, uniqueness** Some people lose interest in new undertakings once the *novelty* wears off.

now *adverb* ✦ **at once, directly, immediately, instantly, right away** If I don't leave *now*, I'll be late for school.

nucleus *noun* ✦ **center, core** ✧ **focus, heart, kernel, seed** This year's team will be formed around a *nucleus* of returning players.

nudge *verb* ✦ **prod, propel, push** ✧ **jab, poke, shove, touch** The tugboat *nudged* the ocean liner away from the pier. —*noun* ✦ **poke, prod, push** ✧ **jab, shove, touch** Jodi gave me a *nudge* with her elbow.

nuisance *noun* ✦ **aggravation, annoyance, bother, irritation, pest** That barking dog is a real *nuisance*.

numb *adjective* ✦ **unfeeling** ✧ **asleep, dead, deadened, frozen** My ears were *numb* from walking in a cold wind. —*verb* ✦ **blunt, deaden, dull** ✧ **chill, freeze** The dentist gave me a shot to help *numb* the pain.

number *noun* **1.** ✦ **digit, numeral** ✧ **character, figure, sign, symbol** My watch has big *numbers* on it so it is easy to read. **2.** ✦ **amount, quantity** ✧ **sum, total** Five is the maximum *number* of players that a basketball team can have on the court at one time. **3.** ✦ **collection, company, crowd, group** ✧ **multitude** A large *number* of guests attended my sister's wedding.

numeral *noun* ✦ **digit, number** ✧ **character, figure, sign, symbol** Our car's license plate is a combination of letters and *numerals*.

numerous *adjective* ✦ **abundant, many, plentiful, profuse** ✧ **infinite** On a clear night, the stars are too *numerous* to be counted.

nurse *verb* ✦ **care for, take care of, tend, treat** ✧ **aid, nourish** Heidi found an injured owl and *nursed* it till it was able to fly again.

nutrition *noun* ✦ **diet, food, nourishment** ✧ **nutriment** Good *nutrition* is essential to a healthy and active life.

nutritious *adjective* ✦ **healthful, healthy, nourishing, wholesome** Fresh fruits and vegetables are *nutritious* foods. ▶

nuzzle *verb* ✦ **cuddle, nestle, snuggle** ✧ **press, rub, touch** My kitten likes to *nuzzle* against me when she's in an affectionate mood.

O

oath *noun* ✦ **pledge, vow** ✧ **affirmation, assertion, declaration, promise, statement** The Knights of the Round Table took an *oath* of loyalty to King Arthur.

obedient *adjective* ✦ **dutiful, loyal** ✧ **conscientious, submissive** The queen rewarded her most *obedient* servants with extra pay.

obese *adjective* ✦ **fat, heavy, overweight, plump, stout** The vet told us to put our cat on a diet because he's getting *obese*.

obey *verb* ✦ **carry out, follow, heed** ✧ **fulfill, observe, respect** Soldiers are expected to *obey* the orders given by an officer.

object *noun* **1.** ✦ **article, item, thing** ✧ **device** This antique store has many unusual *objects* for sale. **2.** ✦ **focus, subject, target** ✧ **mark** I was the *object* of much attention when I won the contest and got to appear on television. **3.** ✦ **aim, goal, objective** ✧ **end, purpose** The *object* of chess is to checkmate your opponent's king. —*verb* ✦ **complain about, dispute, protest** ✧ **argue, challenge, oppose** The ball player *objected to* the umpire's decision.

objection *noun* ✦ **complaint, protest** ✧ **argument, challenge, opposition** If there are no *objections* from the other club members, I'll open the meeting with a poem I wrote.

objective *adjective* ✦ **fair, impartial, just, unbiased** ✧ **honest, sincere** The referee was careful to be *objective* when making her calls. —*noun* ✦ **aim, goal, object** ✧ **end, purpose** The *objective* of this game is to capture the other team's flag.

obligation *noun* ✦ **commitment, duty, requirement, responsibility** ✧ **promise** Police officers have an *obligation* to uphold the law.

oblige *verb* ✦ **obligate, require** ✧ **compel, force, make** Now that I have joined the band, I am *obliged* to practice every day.

obscure *adjective* **1.** ✦ **unclear, vague** ✧ **hidden, indistinct** The meaning of this sentence is very *obscure*. **2.** ✦ **minor, unheard-of, unknown** ✧ **insignificant, unimportant** The actress isn't a big star because all of her roles have been in *obscure* movies. —*verb* ✦ **block, conceal, cover, hide, screen** ✧ **veil** In a solar eclipse, the moon *obscures* the sun.

observation *noun* **1.** ✦ **examination, inspection, study** ✧ **view, watch** Scientists made a careful *observation* of the whales' feeding habits. **2.** ✦ **comment, remark, statement** ✧ **opinion, view** My friend made an interesting *observation* about the new album we'd been listening to.

observe *verb* **1.** ✦ **notice, see, spot** ✧ **watch, witness** Mom called the fire department when she *observed* smoke coming from our neighbor's garage. **2.** ✦ **abide by, comply with, follow, heed, keep, obey** ✧ **respect** The referee warned both boxers to *observe* the rules at all times.

obstacle *noun* ✦ **barrier, difficulty, hurdle, impediment** ✧ **barricade, block, check** The biggest *obstacle* I had to overcome in making new friends was my shyness.

obstinate *adjective* ✦ **headstrong, stubborn** ✧ **uncontrollable, unruly** The *obstinate* mule refused to budge.

obstruct *verb* ✦ **block, close (up), stop (up)** ✧ **bar, delay, prevent** Our rain gutter overflowed because leaves were *obstructing* it. ◄

obstruction *noun* ✦ **barrier, block, hindrance, impediment, obstacle** ✧ **bar, blockage, check, clog, hurdle** The fallen tree was an *obstruction* to traffic. ▼

obtain *verb* ✦ **acquire, attain, gain, get** ✧ **earn** You have to be sixteen years old before you can *obtain* a driver's license.

obvious *adjective* ✦ **clear, distinct, evident, unmistakable** ✧ **apparent, plain** Our volleyball team has an *obvious* advantage because we have taller players.

Antonyms
obvious *adjective*
ambiguous, hidden, obscure, unclear, vague

occasion *noun* **1.** ✦ **event, happening, incident, time** ✧ **circumstance** Our grandparents' fiftieth anniversary is an important *occasion* for the entire family. **2.** ✦ **chance, opportunity** ✧ **excuse, possibility** I haven't had many *occasions* to play tennis this summer.

occasional *adjective* ✦ **infrequent, odd, periodic, random** ✧ **irregular, rare, uncommon** The weather has been fine except for an *occasional* afternoon shower.

occupant *noun* ✦ **inhabitant, resident** ✧ **renter, tenant** The former *occupants* left the apartment very clean.

occupation *noun* **1.** ✦ **job, profession, work** ✧ **business, career** My father's *occupation* is teaching school. **2.** ✦ **control, possession, rule** ✧ **capture, conquest** China was under Japanese *occupation* during World War II.

occupy *verb* **1.** ✦ **dwell in, inhabit, live in, reside in** Uncle Bob and Aunt Connie have *occupied* the same house for more than twenty years. **2.** ✦ **engage, fill, use up** ✧ **busy, employ** Raymond's schoolwork *occupies* a lot of his time. **3.** ✦ **take control of, take possession of** ✧ **capture, command, conquer, seize** During the War of 1812, British troops briefly *occupied* Washington, D.C.

occur *verb* ✦ **happen, result, take place** ✧ **appear, develop** Thunder *occurs* when the heat from a flash of lightning expands the surrounding air.

occurrence *noun* ✦ **event, experience, incident** ✧ **affair, development, occasion** The local airport is very busy, and flight delays are a common *occurrence*.

odd *adjective* **1.** ✦ **curious, peculiar, strange, unusual** ✧ **outlandish, weird** Mr. Gilbert has the *odd* habit of scratching his ear whenever he's thinking. **2.** ✦ **lone, single, unmatched** ✧ **extra, leftover, surplus** I have several *odd* socks that are missing their mates. **3.** ✦ **miscellaneous, various** ✧ **chance, irregular, occasional** Alex earns extra money by doing *odd* jobs at the hardware store after school.

odor *noun* ✦ **scent, smell** ✧ **aroma, fragrance, stench, stink** Onions and garlic have a strong *odor*.

offend *verb* ✦ **anger, annoy, displease, insult, irritate, upset** ✧ **disgust, outrage** My friend was *offended* when I forgot to meet her at the movies as planned.

offense *noun* **1.** ✦ **crime, misdeed, violation** ✧ **error, sin, wrong** Jaywalking is only a minor *offense*. **2.** ✦ **disrespect, insult** ✧ **indignation,**

✦ best choices
✧ other choices

outrage, resentment I meant no *offense* when I said that you look different today.

offensive *adjective* 1. ✦ atrocious, disgusting, foul, nasty, revolting, unpleasant Sulphur hot springs have an *offensive* odor similar to that of rotten eggs. 2. ✦ discourteous, disrespectful, insulting, rude Krista is so tactful that she can point out a person's faults without being *offensive*. —*noun* ✦ assault, attack ✧ aggression, charge, strike The generals hoped that their big *offensive* would end the war.

offer *verb* 1. ✦ volunteer ✧ propose, submit Amelia *offered* to help clean up after the party. 2. ✦ furnish, present, provide, supply ✧ give Our city *offers* a wide variety of cultural activities. —*noun* ✦ bid, proposal, proposition ✧ suggestion Davin accepted my *offer* to buy his old baseball glove.

office *noun* 1. ✧ department, headquarters, room, shop, workplace The principal will be back in her *office* this afternoon. 2. ✦ position, post ✧ job, role, situation, task Aaron is running for the *office* of class president.

official *adjective* ✦ authorized, formal, legitimate, proper ✧ real, true An ambassador is an *official* representative from one country to another. —*noun* ✦ officer ✧ administrator, director, executive, leader The President is the highest elected *official* in the United States.

often *adverb* ✦ commonly, frequently, regularly ✧ generally, usually The zipper on my backpack *often* gets stuck.

old *adjective* 1. ✦ aged, elderly, senior ✧ ancient, antique, mature Social Security was created primarily to benefit *old* people after they retire. 2. ✦ rundown, used, worn, worn-out These shoes are so *old* that they're starting to fall apart. 3. ✦ former, past, previous ✧ late, onetime It's been six years since we moved from our *old* house to the one we live in now.

omen *noun* ✦ indication, sign, token ✧ prediction, prophecy Some people think that finding a four-leaf clover is an *omen* of good luck.

omit *verb* ✦ exclude, forget, neglect, skip ✧ drop, eliminate I want to hear everything that happened at the party, so please don't *omit* any details.

once *adverb* ✦ at one time, formerly, previously ✧ already, before, earlier Dinosaurs were *once* the largest creatures living on the Earth.

only *adjective* ✦ lone, one, single, sole, solitary ✧ individual, unique Jaron is the *only* student who earned a perfect score on the math quiz. —*adverb* ✦ just, merely, simply, solely Leanne has two brothers, but *only* one sister.

ooze *verb* ✦ drain, dribble, drip, leak, seep, trickle Sap *oozed* from the tree's broken branch.

open *adjective* 1. ✦ ajar, unclosed ✧ unfastened, unlocked Somebody left the window *open*, and our parakeet got out. 2. ✦ uncapped, uncovered, unsealed ✧ exposed, unprotected Don't leave the soda bottle *open* or all the fizz will go out. 3. ✦ empty, vacant ✧ bare, clear, wide Damon and his friends like to play baseball in the *open* field behind his house. 4. ✦ accessible, available ✧ free, public This contest is only *open* to students under the age of twelve. —*verb* 1. ✦ unfasten, untie, unwrap ✧ free, release My little sister eagerly *opened* her birthday presents. ▶ 2. ✦ begin, commence, start ✧ initiate School *opens* on the day after Labor Day.

operate *verb* **1. ✦ function, perform, run, work ✧ go** Our VCR isn't *operating* properly. **2. ✦ drive, handle, use ✧ manage, work** The farmer taught his daughter how to *operate* a tractor.

operation *noun* **✦ action, functioning, performance, working ✧ effect, use** This new factory has computers that control the *operation* of most of its machinery. ▼

opinion *noun* **✦ belief, conviction, judgment, view ✧ idea** In my *opinion*, *Charlotte's Web* is one of the best books ever written.

opponent *noun* **✦ adversary, competitor, rival ✧ enemy, foe** Randy defeated two *opponents* to become our class president.

opportunity *noun* **✦ chance, occasion ✧ moment, situation, time** I haven't had an *opportunity* to fly my new kite yet.

oppose *verb* **✦ disagree with, disapprove of, object to, protest, resist ✧ contest, deny, fight** I wonder if my parents will *oppose* my idea to dye my hair green.

opposite *adjective* **1. ✦ facing, opposing ✧ other** The football teams lined up on *opposite* sides of the field. **2. ✦ contradictory, contrary, reverse ✧ conflicting, different** "Up" and "down" have *opposite* meanings.

opposition *noun* **✦ disagreement (with), disapproval (of), objection ✧ defiance, resis-** tance Local residents have expressed *opposition* to the proposal to build a new freeway exit.

optimistic *adjective* **✦ confident, hopeful, positive, trusting ✧ cheerful** The drama teacher was *optimistic* that the school play would be a great success.

optional *adjective* **✦ elective, voluntary ✧ free, possible** Gym class is *optional* at my school, but I take it anyway.

oral *adjective* **✦ spoken, verbal ✧ vocal, voiced** I have to give an *oral* report about three books by my favorite author.

Antonyms
optional *adjective*
compulsory, mandatory, necessary, obligatory, required

orbit *noun* **✦ revolution ✧ circuit, course, path, rotation, trajectory** Russia's *Sputnik I* was the first artificial satellite to be placed in *orbit* around the Earth. —*verb* **✦ circle, revolve around ✧ rotate, spin, turn** The Earth *orbits* the sun once every year.

ordeal *noun* **✦ difficulty, hardship, trial, trouble ✧ experience** The shipwrecked sailors said that the worst part of their *ordeal* was going without food and water.

order *noun* **1. ✦ condition, form, repair, shape, state** The pilot checked her plane to ensure that all the equipment was in working *order*. **2. ✦ arrangement, classification, sequence ✧ pattern, system** I put my books in alphabetical *order* by author. **3. ✦ calm, control, discipline, peace, quiet** The teacher had trouble restoring *order* after a bird flew in the classroom window. **4. ✦ command, direction, instruction ✧ demand, rule** The soldier received an *order* to report to his commanding officer. —*verb* **1. ✦ command, direct, instruct, tell ✧ force, require** The firefighters *ordered* everyone to leave the building immediately. **2. ✦ ask for, request ✧ buy, purchase, reserve** We *ordered* a large pizza with extra cheese.

✦	best choices
✧	other choices

orderly *adjective* **1.** ✦ **methodical, neat, organized, regular** ✧ **clean, tidy** The band marched in *orderly* lines. **2.** ✦ **calm, disciplined, peaceful, quiet, well-behaved** The fans remained *orderly* even though the concert did not start on time.

ordinarily *adverb* ✦ **generally, normally, typically, usually** ✧ **customarily, regularly, routinely** Dad is on vacation this week, but *ordinarily* he would be at work now.

ordinary *adjective* **1.** ✦ **average, normal, regular, standard, typical, usual** On an *ordinary* day, school begins at 8 o'clock in the morning. **2.** ✦ **common, everyday, modest, plain, simple** We were surprised to see the famous actress dressed in *ordinary* clothes.

organization *noun* **1.** ✦ **arrangement, planning** ✧ **design, form, order, structure** The entire sixth-grade class helped with the *organization* of this year's school picnic. **2.** ✦ **association, group, society** ✧ **club, league, party** Gloria joined an *organization* that works to protect endangered species.

organize *verb* **1.** ✦ **arrange, categorize, classify, group, order, sort** I need to *organize* the stamps in my stamp collection. **2.** ✦ **establish, form, set up, start** ✧ **create, develop, found, institute** Our class *organized* a tree-planting campaign to celebrate Arbor Day.

origin *noun* ✦ **beginning, source, start** ✧ **basis, cause, foundation** The explorers traveled up the river to find its *origin*.

original *adjective* **1.** ✦ **first, initial** ✧ **beginning, early, primary** Our car still has its *original* coat of paint. **2.** ✦ **fresh, imaginative, new, novel, unique, unusual** The idea for your story should be *original*, not copied from something you've read.

originate *verb* ✦ **begin, commence, start** ✧ **create, introduce, invent** The use of paper money *originated* in China almost one thousand years ago.

ornament *noun* ✦ **decoration, trimming** ✧ **accessory** Mom bought a box of new *ornaments* for our Christmas tree. —*verb* ✦ **adorn, decorate** ✧ **beautify, enhance, trim** The castle was *ornamented* with bright flags and banners.

other *adjective* ✦ **additional, alternate, different, more** ✧ **extra, new** Does this shirt come in any *other* colors?

ought *auxiliary verb* ✦ **should** ✧ **have, must, need** As long as I'm at the pet store, I *ought to* buy some rabbit food.

oust *verb* ✦ **eject, expel, remove** ✧ **banish, evict** The city council voted to *oust* the corrupt mayor.

out *adverb* ✦ **outdoors, outside** My little brother and his friends went *out* to play. —*adjective* ✦ **dead, gone** ✧ **absent, done, finished, over** I can't use my computer because the power is *out*.

outbreak *noun* ✦ **epidemic, surge** ✧ **eruption, outburst, uprising** Measles vaccinations can help prevent *outbreaks* of the disease.

outburst *noun* ✦ **burst, eruption, outbreak** ✧ **flood, gush, torrent** I apologized to Tina for my earlier *outburst* of anger.

outcome *noun* ✦ **conclusion, end, result** ✧ **aftermath, consequence** I couldn't wait to hear about the *outcome* of the game.

outdo *verb* ✦ **beat, better, exceed, surpass, top** ✧ **excel** Shantay is determined to *outdo* her previous personal record for the long jump.

outer *adjective* ✦ **exterior, external, outside** ✧ **outward** Crabs, lobsters, and clams all have hard *outer* shells for protection.

outfit *noun* ✦ **clothing, dress, garb** ✧ **equipment, gear** A hunter's *outfit* usually includes a brightly-colored vest and cap. —*verb* ✦ **equip,**

provision, supply ✧ furnish, provide, stock We went shopping to *outfit* ourselves for the week-long canoe trip.

outing *noun* ✦ excursion, jaunt, tour, trip ✧ expedition Yolanda's scout troop is taking an *outing* to Catalina Island.

outlaw *noun* ✦ bandit, criminal, crook, robber ✧ gangster Billy the Kid was a notorious *outlaw* of the Old West. —*verb* ✦ abolish, ban, forbid, prohibit ✧ banish, prevent The Eighteenth Amendment to the U.S. Constitution *outlawed* the sale of alcoholic beverages.

outlet *noun* ✦ channel, release, vent ✧ exit, opening, passage Marie took up painting as an *outlet* for her creative energy.

outline *noun* 1. ✦ contour, profile, silhouette ✧ form, shape I like to see the *outline* of the mountains against the evening sky. 2. ✦ draft, plan, sketch, summary Giving a speech is easier if you have an *outline* to follow. —*verb* ✦ plan out, sketch, summarize ✧ draft, draw up The author *outlined* the plot of his new novel.

outlook *noun* 1. ✦ attitude (toward), perspective, view (of), viewpoint A positive *outlook* on life can help you get through a bad day. 2. ✦ forecast, prediction, prospect ✧ chance, future The weatherman said that the *outlook* for the next few days is not very good.

output *noun* ✦ production, productivity ✧ harvest, yield The companies that make exercise equipment have recently been increasing their *output*.

outrage *noun* ✦ anger, fury, indignation ✧ resentment, wrath The principal expressed her *outrage* when she learned that the school budget was to be cut. —*verb* ✦ anger, incense, offend ✧ affront, insult, shock We were *outraged* when we saw the polluted beach.

outrageous *adjective* ✦ despicable, disgraceful, offensive, shameful, shocking The movie star said that the scandal was based on an *outrageous* lie.

outside *noun* ✦ exterior ✧ face, front, surface We painted the *outside* of the old shed. ▼ —*adjective* ✦ exterior, external, outer, outward These caramels have an *outside* layer of chocolate.

outstanding *adjective* ✦ excellent, exceptional, remarkable, superior Ms. Walsh said I did an *outstanding* job on my science project.

over *preposition* ✦ above, beyond, past ✧ across Joe hit the ball *over* the outfield fence. —*adjective* ✦ finished ✧ complete, done, through The movie was *over* in time for supper.

overcast *adjective* ✦ cloudy, gray ✧ dark, hazy, misty, murky The sky was *overcast* all day long, but it never rained.

overcome *verb* ✦ beat, conquer, defeat, master, surmount ✧ win Jocelyn worked hard to *overcome* her shyness.

overdue *adjective* ✧ behind, late, tardy I have three *overdue* books that I must get back to the library by tonight.

✦ best choices
✧ other choices

overflow *verb* ✦ **cascade, flood, gush, pour, spill** When I accidentally left the bathtub faucet on, water *overflowed* onto the floor.

overhaul *verb* ✦ **fix, rebuild, repair, service** ✧ **examine, inspect** Mechanics *overhauled* the plane's jet engines.

overlook *verb* ✦ **miss, neglect, pass over, skip** ✧ **disregard, forget, omit** I *overlooked* two misspelled words when I proofread my report.

overrule *verb* ✦ **disallow, reject** ✧ **repeal, revoke, veto** The judge *overruled* most of the lawyer's objections.

oversight *noun* ✦ **blunder, error, lapse, mistake, slip** ✧ **fault, neglect** It was an unfortunate *oversight* to forget to take a tape recorder to the interview.

overtake *verb* ✦ **catch, catch up with, pass** ✧ **beat, reach, surpass** The motorboat easily *overtook* our rowboat.

overthrow *verb* ✦ **bring down, oust, remove, topple** ✧ **conquer, defeat, destroy** The people rose up to *overthrow* their oppressive dictator. —*noun* ✦ **downfall, ouster, removal** ✧ **collapse, defeat** The king's aides plotted his *overthrow*.

overturn *verb* ✦ **capsize, roll over, turn over, upset** ✧ **spill, topple** A kayak is a type of canoe that can be easily righted if it *overturns*.

overweight *adjective* ✦ **fat, heavy, obese, plump, stout** The doctor recommended more exercise and fewer snacks between meals so I would not become *overweight*.

overwhelm *verb* ✦ **crush, defeat, overpower, overrun** ✧ **destroy, wipe out** The attacking army quickly *overwhelmed* the small band of defenders.

own *verb* ✦ **have, possess** ✧ **hold, keep, retain** I *own* more than one hundred books.

P

pace *noun* **1.** ✦ **step, stride** ✧ **gait** The treasure is buried fifteen *paces* north of an old oak tree. **2.** ✦ **rate, speed, velocity** ✧ **motion, movement** Olivia can run at a faster *pace* than I can. —*verb* ✦ **step, stride, tread, walk** ✧ **march** The lion *paced* back and forth in its cage.

pack *noun* **1.** ✦ **package** ✧ **bag, bundle, carton, container, parcel** Please get me a *pack* of gum when you go to the store. **2.** ✦ **band, bunch, group** ✧ **gang, herd, mob** We could hear a *pack* of coyotes howling in the distance. —*verb* ✦ **cram, crowd, load, squeeze, stuff** ✧ **fill** Kwame had so many items *packed* in his duffel bag that he could barely get it to close.

package *noun* ✦ **box, carton, parcel** ✧ **bundle, container, pack** The mail carrier left a *package* on our front porch.

pact *noun* ✦ **accord, agreement, alliance, treaty** ✧ **bargain, deal** The two nations signed a *pact* to help defend each other.

pad *noun* **1.** ✦ **cushion, mat** ✧ **mattress, pillow** We used a blanket and a foam *pad* to make a bed for our dog. **2.** ✦ **notepad, tablet** ✧ **notebook** Each student received two pencils and a *pad* of paper.

pageant *noun* ✦ **play, show, spectacle** ✧ **celebration, parade, procession** I'll be playing a Pilgrim in this year's Thanksgiving *pageant*.

pail *noun* ✦ **bucket** ✧ **can, container, vessel** Arielle uses a plastic *pail* to carry water to her flower garden.

pain *noun* **1.** ✦ **ache, hurt, pang, soreness, stitch** ✧ **discomfort** I felt a sudden *pain* in my side from running. **2.** ✦ **agony, anguish, distress, misery, suffering** Losing a good friend can cause a lot of *pain*. —*verb* ✦ **distress, hurt, trouble** ✧ **injure, wound** It *pains* me to see you so unhappy.

paint *noun* ✧ **coloring, dye, pigment, stain, tint** Mom put two coats of green *paint* on our old picnic table. —*verb* ✦ **color, tint** ✧ **cover, decorate, dye, shade** The clown *painted* his face red and white.

painting *noun* ✦ **picture, portrait** ✧ **canvas, drawing, oil, sketch** One of the world's most famous *paintings* is the *Mona Lisa* by Leonardo da Vinci.

pair *noun* ✦ **couple, duo, twosome** ✧ **combination, team, unit** I think you and I would make a good *pair*. —*verb* ✦ **couple, join, match, team** ✧ **combine, mate** The coach *paired* the wrestlers according to their weight.

pal *noun* ✦ **buddy, chum, companion, comrade, friend** George and I have been *pals* for years.

pale *adjective* ✦ **faint, light** ✧ **colorless, dim, whitish** The sky turned *pale* blue as the sun came up.

pamper *verb* ✦ **baby, cater to, coddle, indulge, spoil** Aunt Grace *pampers* her cat by feeding it fresh tuna and chicken.

pamphlet *noun* ✦ **booklet, brochure** ✧ **book, text** My new bicycle came with a *pamphlet* on safety tips.

> ## Word Groups
>
> A **pan** is an open container used for cooking. **Pan** is a general term with no true synonyms. Here are some different kinds of pans to investigate in a dictionary:
>
> broiler, casserole, frying pan, griddle, roaster, saucepan, skillet

panel *noun* ✦ **group** ✧ **assembly, board, commission, committee** The talk show featured a *panel* of teachers who discussed ways to improve educational quality.

pang *noun* ✦ ache, pain, twinge ✧ discomfort, smart, throe I get hunger *pangs* if I go too long without eating.

panic *noun* ✦ alarm, dread, fear, fright, terror ✧ distress I felt a sudden *panic* when I thought the car was going to go off the road. —*verb* ✦ alarm, frighten, scare, terrify ✧ terrorize The horse galloped away after a rattlesnake *panicked* it.

pant *verb* ✦ gasp, huff, puff, wheeze ✧ heave We were all *panting* hard after running three laps around the track.

pants *noun* ✦ slacks, trousers ✧ blue jeans, dungarees, jeans Some of the girls wore *pants* while others wore dresses.

paper *noun* **1.** ✦ stationery, writing paper ✧ page, parchment, sheet I need some nice *paper* on which to write thank-you letters. **2.** ✦ document ✧ certificate, contract, deed Mom and Dad had to sign a bunch of *papers* when they bought our new house. **3.** ✦ newspaper ✧ gazette, journal, periodical, publication Our local *paper* is called *The Daily Enterprise*. **4.** ✦ composition, essay, report, theme ✧ article I have to select a President and write a *paper* about his life.

parade *noun* ✧ march, procession Our school band was in this year's Thanksgiving *parade*. ▶ —*verb* ✦ file, march, stride ✧ step, stroll, walk The graduating students *paraded* across the stage to pick up their diplomas.

paradise *noun* ✦ heaven ✧ bliss, delight, ecstasy, glory Many people think that Hawaii is a tropical *paradise*.

parallel *adjective* **1.** ✧ aligned, alongside, even, side by side The rails of a railroad track are *parallel* to each other. **2.** ✦ corresponding, equivalent, like, similar ✧ alike The two scientists are conducting *parallel* experiments to see if they can get the same results. —*noun* ✦ likeness, resemblance, similarity ✧ comparison There are some obvious *parallels* between the two bank robberies. —*verb* ✦ correspond to, equal, match ✧ resemble The subjects covered in home schooling *parallel* those taught in public schools.

paralyze *verb* ✦ cripple, disable, immobilize ✧ numb, stun A massive power failure *paralyzed* the entire West Coast.

parcel *noun* ✦ package ✧ box, bundle, carton, container, pack The post office delivers millions of *parcels* every year.

parch *verb* ✦ dehydrate, dry out ✧ burn, roast, scorch, wither The long drought has *parched* all the corn fields.

pardon *verb* ✦ excuse, forgive ✧ absolve, overlook, tolerate Please *pardon* my barging in like this. —*noun* ✦ forgiveness ✧ excuse, mercy I beg your *pardon*, but I didn't mean to bump into you.

pare *verb* ✦ peel ✧ cut, skin, strip, trim Wesley helped his mom *pare* apples for the pie she was baking.

part *noun* **1.** ✦ element, portion, section, segment ✧ piece Some *parts* of the book were

better than others. **2.** ◆ **piece, share** ◇ **duty, responsibility, role, task** Everyone did their *part* to help clean up the classroom. —*verb* ◆ **divide, separate, split** ◇ **break up, open** The ax *parted* the wood right down the middle.

partial *adjective* **1.** ◆ **incomplete, limited, part** ◇ **fragmentary, unfinished** I only got *partial* credit for my report because I forgot to illustrate it. **2.** ◆ **biased, one-sided, prejudiced, unfair** ◇ **unjust** A good referee is never *partial*.

participate *verb* ◆ **join, take part** ◇ **contribute, cooperate, share** Everybody *participated* in the sing-along.

particle *noun* ◆ **bit, fragment, grain, piece, scrap, speck, trace** The dog ate every last *particle* of food in his dish.

particular *adjective* **1.** ◆ **close, detailed, special, specific** ◇ **thorough, unusual** Whenever I get ready to go out, I pay *particular* attention to my hair. **2.** ◆ **choosy, fussy, picky** ◇ **careful, demanding** Because Carly is a vegetarian, she's very *particular* about what she eats. —*noun* ◆ **detail, fact, point, specific** ◇ **circumstance, item** Please tell me all the *particulars* about your trip to Mexico.

partition *noun* ◆ **barrier, divider, screen** ◇ **wall** Some libraries have *partitions* between desks so that patrons can study in privacy. —*verb* ◆ **divide, section, separate** ◇ **break up, cut, split** Dad *partitioned* off part of the garage to make a workshop for himself.

partly *adverb* ◆ **partially, partway, slightly, somewhat** Please leave the window *partly* open until the room cools off.

partner *noun* ◆ **associate, colleague** ◇ **ally, companion, mate** My dad and my uncle are business *partners*.

partnership *noun* ◆ **alliance, association** ◇ **business, company** Larry and I both wanted to set up a lemonade stand, so we decided to form a *partnership*.

party *noun* **1.** ◆ **celebration** ◇ **festivity, get-together, social** We're going to give our parents a surprise *party* for their anniversary. **2.** ◆ **group** ◇ **band, bunch, company, crowd, gang** Ask the waiter if he can seat our entire *party* at one table.

pass *verb* **1.** ◆ **go, proceed, travel** ◇ **journey, move, progress** The parade will *pass* along Forest Street and turn onto Monument Avenue. **2.** ◆ **cease, end, go away, lapse** ◇ **depart, die, expire** If you take these aspirin, your pain should soon *pass*. **3.** ◆ **give, hand** ◇ **convey, deliver, transmit** Please *pass* me the butter. **4.** ◆ **complete, fulfill, satisfy** ◇ **accomplish, achieve** My older sister just *passed* all the requirements to get her driver's license. **5.** ◆ **adopt, approve, ratify, sanction** ◇ **confirm** The state legislature *passed* a bill requiring all bicyclists to wear helmets.

passage *noun* **1.** ◆ **course, flow, movement, passing** ◇ **journey, travel** You will grow taller with the *passage* of time. **2.** ◆ **corridor, passageway, walkway** ◇ **channel, path, route** There is an underground *passage* that connects these two buildings. **3.** ◆ **part, portion, section, segment, selection** Our teacher read us a *passage* from her favorite book.

passenger *noun* ◆ **rider, traveler** ◇ **commuter, tourist** A Boeing 747 can carry more than five hundred *passengers*.

passion *noun* ◆ **emotion, enthusiasm, feeling, fire, intensity** Mr. Yoon spoke with *passion* about the play he is directing.

passionate *adjective* ◆ **emotional, forceful, heated, intense, moving** The charity's spokesperson made a *passionate* plea for donations.

past *adjective* ◆ **preceding, previous, prior** ◇ **finished, former, gone** I've been pretty busy for the *past* few days. —*noun* ◆ **former times,**

◆ **best choices**
◇ **other choices**

previous times ◇ **yesterday, yesteryear** Audrey studies harder now than she did in the *past*. —*preposition* ✦ **after, beyond** ◇ **behind, over** To get to the municipal swimming pool, turn left just *past* the library.

paste *noun* ✦ **adhesive, cement, glue, mucilage** This *paste* is not as sticky as the kind we used to get. —*verb* ✦ **cement, glue, stick** ◇ **attach, fasten** Melanie *pasted* a photograph into her scrapbook.

pastime *noun* ✦ **amusement, diversion, entertainment** ◇ **hobby, recreation** Baseball is one of America's most popular *pastimes*. ▼

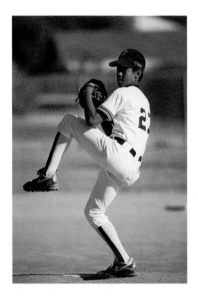

pasture *noun* ✦ **field, meadow** ◇ **clearing, grassland** Floyd's morning chore was to put the cows out to graze in the *pasture*.

pat *verb* ✦ **pet, stroke, tap** ◇ **caress, cuddle, fondle, rub** My dog Ruby seems to like being *patted* on the head.

patch *noun* ✦ **area, space, spot** ◇ **lot, stretch, tract** There were some *patches* of ice on our driveway this morning. —*verb* ✦ **cover, mend** ◇ **fix, repair, restore** I tried to *patch* the hole in my blue jeans.

path *noun* ✦ **pathway, trail, walk, walkway** ◇ **course, route** This *path* goes all the way around the lake.

pathetic *adjective* ✦ **forlorn, heartbreaking, moving, pitiful, sad, touching** ◇ **miserable, unfortunate** The lost puppy looked so *pathetic* that I decided to take it home.

patience *noun* ✦ **calmness, restraint, self-control, tolerance, serenity** When the concert didn't start on time, the audience waited with admirable *patience*.

patient *adjective* ✦ **calm, serene, tolerant, understanding** ◇ **gentle** Emily is a popular baby sitter because she is very *patient* with young children.

Antonyms
patient *adjective*
anxious, hasty, impatient, restless, uneasy

patrol *verb* ✦ **police** ◇ **defend, guard, protect, supervise, watch** The sheriff said that more deputies would be made available to *patrol* the streets after dark.

patron *noun* ✦ **client, customer** ◇ **backer, sponsor, supporter** The barber shop has dozens of regular *patrons* who have been coming there for many years.

pattern *noun* **1.** ✦ **arrangement, design** ◇ **figure, form, shape** The shadows of the trees made a pretty *pattern* on the snow. **2.** ✦ **guide, model, standard** ◇ **example, ideal, sample** Making a dress is easier if you have a *pattern* to follow. —*verb* ✦ **fashion after, form after, model on** ◇ **copy, follow, imitate** This museum building is *patterned after* a medieval castle.

pause *noun* ✦ **break, interruption, lull** ◇ **delay, halt, rest, stop** There was a brief *pause* in our conversation. —*verb* ✦ **cease, halt, hesitate, stop** ◇ **delay, rest, wait** The speaker *paused* for a moment to glance at his notes.

pave *verb* ✦ **coat, cover, surface, top** ✧ **tar** We had our driveway *paved* with asphalt.

pay *verb* ✦ **compensate, give, render, reward (with)** ✧ **earn, gain, get** What will you *pay* me to mow the lawn for you? —*noun* ✦ **compensation, earnings, money, salary, wages** ✧ **fee** An experienced restaurant cook can get very good *pay*.

peace *noun* 1. ✧ **accord, armistice, harmony, neutrality, truce** There has always been *peace* between the United States and Canada. 2. ✦ **calm, peacefulness, quiet, serenity, tranquility** Dad loves the sense of *peace* that he finds on his fishing trips to the North Woods.

peaceful *noun* 1. ✦ **nonviolent, peaceable** ✧ **friendly, neutral** Switzerland is a *peaceful* country that hasn't been at war since 1848. 2. ✦ **calm, placid, quiet, restful, serene, tranquil** I found a *peaceful* spot in the park in which to read my book.

peak *noun* 1. ✦ **crest, crown, summit, tip, top** ✧ **roof** The mountain's *peak* was covered with snow. 2. ✦ **climax, height, top, zenith** ✧ **limit, maximum** The actress is now at the *peak* of her career.

peculiar *adjective* ✦ **curious, odd, strange, unusual** ✧ **distinctive, unique** The duck-billed platypus has a *peculiar* mouth that looks like a bird's beak.

peddle *verb* ✦ **hawk, market, sell** ✧ **barter, trade** Vendors were *peddling* caps, pennants, and other souvenirs at the baseball stadium.

pedestrian *noun* ✦ **walker** ✧ **hiker, stroller** The sidewalk was crowded with *pedestrians* enjoying the warm weather.

peek *verb* ✦ **glance, look, peep** ✧ **glimpse, peer** I *peeked* into the closet to see if that's where Mom hid my presents. ▶ —*noun* ✦ **glance, glimpse, look, peep** I was tempted to take a *peek* at my sister's diary, but I knew that I shouldn't.

peer[1] *verb* ✦ **gaze, look, stare** ✧ **examine, inspect, scan** Bryce *peered* into the stream to see if he could spot any fish.

peer[2] *noun* ✦ **associate, colleague, equal** ✧ **counterpart, teammate** The young doctor gained the respect of her *peers*.

pelt[1] *noun* ✦ **coat, hide, skin** ✧ **fur, hair** Fur coats are made from the *pelts* of animals such as mink and fox.

pelt[2] *verb* ✦ **batter, beat, hammer, hit, pummel, strike** ✧ **knock, tap** We listened to the hail *pelting* the roof.

pen *noun* ✦ **enclosure** ✧ **cage, coop, corral, stockade** Close the gate to the *pen* or the pigs will get out. —*verb* ✦ **cage, confine, coop, enclose, shut away, shut up** ✧ **corral** We *penned* the geese for the night.

penalize *verb* ✦ **discipline, punish** ✧ **correct, fine** Players who are late to practice will be *penalized* by running two laps around the field.

penalty *noun* ✦ **punishment** ✧ **correction, discipline, fine** The *penalty* for disrupting class is staying after school.

penetrate *verb* ✦ **enter, pass through, pierce** ✧ **perforate, puncture** An arrow can *penetrate* several inches of wood.

pennant *noun* ✧ **banner, colors, flag, standard, streamer** David collects the *pennants* of his favorite baseball and football teams.

people *noun* 1. ✦ **human beings, humans, individuals, persons** ✧ **folks** There are nearly six billion *people* living on the planet Earth. 2. ✦ **citizens, populace, public**

✧ **community, nation, society** The *people* voted in favor of the new recycling law.

perceive *verb* **1.** ✦ **discover, note, notice, observe, see, tell** Can you *perceive* any difference between the two twins? **2.** ✦ **comprehend, grasp, realize, understand** ✧ **know** The teacher quickly *perceived* that some students had not understood her directions.

percentage *noun* ✦ **fraction, part, percent, proportion, share** ✧ **ratio** A large *percentage* of the voters are opposed to the new tax.

perfect *adjective* **1.** ✦ **accurate, complete, exact, precise** ✧ **correct, right** I traced a *perfect* copy of the design on the album cover. **2.** ✦ **faultless, flawless** My aunt can speak *perfect* Russian. **3.** ✦ **excellent, ideal, superlative** ✧ **fine, good** This is a *perfect* day for a picnic. —*verb*

✦ **develop, polish, refine** ✧ **accomplish, achieve, complete** The gymnast *perfected* his technique by practicing several hours every day. ▲

perform *verb* **1.** ✦ **accomplish, carry out, complete, do** ✧ **achieve, fulfill** The surgeon *performed* five operations in one day. **2.** ✦ **enact, give, present** ✧ **act, play, portray** Our class will *perform* Shakespeare's *Romeo and Juliet*.

perhaps *adverb* ✦ **conceivably, maybe, possibly** *Perhaps* we'll be able to get together tomorrow night.

peril *noun* ✦ **danger, hazard, risk, threat** ✧ **jeopardy, menace** The explorers faced many *perils* on their journey across Antarctica.

period *noun* ✦ **interval, span, spell, stretch, time** ✧ **era, phase, season** We've been having a *period* of rainy weather.

perish *verb* ✦ **die, expire, pass away, succumb** ✧ **cease, end, vanish** Many animals *perished* in the forest fire.

permanent *adjective* ✦ **durable, enduring, lasting, long-lasting** ✧ **constant, stable** I have a *permanent* scar on my arm where I cut it when I fell off my bike.

permit *verb* **1.** ✦ **allow, authorize** ✧ **approve, consent, let, tolerate** In soccer, only the goalkeeper is *permitted* to touch the ball with his or her hands. **2.** ✦ **allow, be favorable, oblige** If the weather *permits*, we can go swimming. —*noun* ✦ **authorization, license, permission, sanction** ✧ **pass** My brother has a learner's *permit* that allows him to drive a car if an adult is present.

perplex *verb* ✦ **baffle, bewilder, confuse, mystify, puzzle, stump** The horse's strange behavior *perplexed* its owner.

persecute *verb* ✦ **harass, oppress, punish** ✧ **abuse, torment, wrong** Throughout history, many religious groups have been *persecuted* for their beliefs.

persist *verb* ✦ **continue, endure, go on, last** ✧ **persevere, remain** The hailstorm *persisted* long enough to damage most of the crops.

persistent *adjective* **1.** ✦ **determined, firm, insistent, persevering, steadfast** The *persistent* salesman would not take "no" for an answer. **2.** ✦ **chronic, continuing, lasting, lingering, long-lived** ✧ **constant** Mom took me to the doctor because I had a *persistent* cough.

person *noun* ✦ **human, human being, individual** ✧ **man, woman** In July of 1969, astronaut

Neil Armstrong became the first *person* to set foot on the moon.

personal *adjective*
✦ **intimate, private** ✧ **individual, own, particular, peculiar** I keep my *personal* thoughts in my diary, which I don't let anyone read.

personality *noun* ✦ **character, disposition, identity, makeup, nature** ✧ **qualities, traits** The twin brothers may look alike, but they have very different *personalities*.

perspective *noun* ✦ **context, proportion, relation** ✧ **outlook, viewpoint** To put the size of a blue whale into *perspective*, a fully-grown one can weigh as much as two thousand men.

perspire *verb* ✦ **sweat** ✧ **drip, flush, lather, secrete** Christopher was *perspiring* heavily after he finished the mile run.

persuade *verb* ✦ **coax, convince, get, influence, sway, talk (into)** ✧ **urge** I'm trying to *persuade* my parents to let me go on the overnight camping trip.

pertain *verb* ✦ **apply to, bear on, concern, refer to, regard, relate to** The judge would only allow testimony that *pertained to* the case that was currently being tried.

pessimistic *adjective* ✦ **dark, dim, discouraging, dismal, gloomy, glum** ✧ **doubtful, hopeless** The movie we saw takes a *pessimistic* view of human nature.

pest *noun* ✦ **annoyance, bother, irritation, nuisance** ✧ **trouble** My little brother can be a big *pest* when he won't leave me alone.

pester *verb* ✦ **annoy, bother, disturb, harass, irritate, torment, trouble** Please don't *pester* me while I'm trying to do my homework.

pet *noun* ✦ **darling, dear, favorite** I hope no one thinks that I'm the teacher's *pet* just because she has been kind to me. —*adjective* ✦ **cherished, favored, favorite, preferred, special** ✧ **precious** Dad's *pet* project is the canoe that he's been working on for years. —*verb* ✦ **caress, fondle, stroke** ✧ **cuddle, pat** My cat purrs when I *pet* her. ▶

petition *noun* ✦ **appeal, plea, proposal, request** ✧ **application** Hundreds of parents signed a *petition* asking the city to hire more teachers. —*verb* ✦ **appeal to, apply to, ask, call upon, entreat** ✧ **request** The scientists *petitioned* the government for more money to support their research.

petrify *verb* **1.** ✧ **dry, harden, set, solidify** Under the right conditions, wood will *petrify* into stone. **2.** ✦ **frighten, horrify, scare, terrify** ✧ **alarm, shock** The monster movie *petrified* me.

petty *adjective* **1.** ✦ **insignificant, minor, small, trifling, trivial, unimportant** Samantha doesn't let *petty* problems bother her. **2.** ✦ **mean, narrow-minded, small-minded, spiteful** ✧ **stingy** Gossip is spread by *petty* people.

phantom *noun* ✦ **ghost, specter, spirit** ✧ **spook, vision** According to the legend, a *phantom* haunted the old mansion on the hill.

phase *noun* ✦ **period, stage** ✧ **condition, development, level, state** A tadpole is one *phase* in the life cycle of a frog.

phony *adjective* ✦ **artificial, counterfeit, fake, false, pretended** ✧ **unreal** The actor's *phony* accent didn't fool anyone. —*noun* ✦ **fake, fraud, impostor, pretender** ✧ **forgery, hoax, imitation** The woman claimed to be a fortuneteller, but she turned out to be just another *phony*.

✦ **best choices**
✧ **other choices**

photograph *noun* ✦ **photo, picture, snap-shot** ✧ **image, portrait** Grandma has dozens of family *photographs* on display in her home.

phrase *noun* ✦ **expression** ✧ **clause, idiom, motto, saying, slogan** The word "good-bye" is derived from the *phrase* "God be with you." —*verb* ✦ **express, formulate, present, put, state, word** Perhaps your question will be easier to answer if you *phrase* it differently.

physical *adjective* **1.** ✦ **bodily** ✧ **living, personal** Athletes exercise regularly to maintain their *physical* fitness. **2.** ✦ **concrete, material, solid, substantial** ✧ **actual, real** Anything that you can touch is a *physical* object.

physician *noun* ✦ **doctor, medical doctor** ✧ **healer, intern** If your cold doesn't go away soon, you should see a *physician*.

pick *verb* **1.** ✦ **choose, decide on, elect, select** We *picked* Jacqueline to be the captain of our soccer team. **2.** ✦ **collect, gather, harvest, pluck** ✧ **garner, reap** I helped our next-door neighbor *pick* raspberries. ◀ —*noun* ✦ **choice, preference, selection** ✧ **best, prize** You can take your *pick* of any piece of candy in the box.

picture *noun* **1.** ✦ **image, portrait** ✧ **drawing, painting, photograph** Do you want me to draw your *picture*? **2.** ✦ **film, motion picture, movie** ✧ **cinema, feature, show** My favorite movie won an award for Best *Picture*. —*verb* ✦ **conceive, envision, imagine, visualize** ✧ **see, think** I'm trying to *picture* what my room will look like with new curtains and wallpaper.

piece *noun* ✦ **part, portion, section, segment** ✧ **share, unit** I cut the cake into six *pieces*.

pier *noun* ✦ **dock, jetty, wharf** ✧ **breakwater, quay** Several gift shops and a seafood restaurant are located out on the *pier*.

pierce *verb* ✦ **penetrate, prick, puncture, stick** ✧ **cut, gash, stab** The nurse said I would hardly feel it when the needle *pierced* my skin.

pile *noun* ✦ **heap, lump, mass, mound, stack** ✧ **accumulation, collection** I changed in a hurry and left my old clothes in a *pile* on the floor. —*verb* ✦ **heap, lump, mass, mound, stack** ✧ **accumulate, collect** We *piled* all the cushions on the floor and jumped on them.

pill *noun* ✦ **capsule, tablet** ✧ **medication, medicine** I take a vitamin *pill* every morning.

pillar *noun* ✦ **column** ✧ **post, prop, support** Our courthouse has two big *pillars* on either side of the door.

Word Groups

A **pillow** is a case filled with something soft and used to support or cushion. **Pillow** is a general term with no true synonyms. Here are some different kinds of pillows to investigate in a dictionary: **bolster, cushion, headrest, pad, sham**

---

pilot *noun* **1.** ✧ **airman, aviator, captain, flyer** Small aircraft usually require only one *pilot*. **2.** ✧ **guide, helmsman, navigator, steersman** As the ship neared land, a licensed *pilot* came on board to guide it into port. —*verb* ✦ **fly, operate** ✧ **guide, navigate, steer** I'd love to learn how to *pilot* an airplane.

pin *noun* ✦ **brooch** ✧ **clip, ornament, stickpin, tiepin** Chelsey wore a silver and turquoise *pin* that was shaped like a little dolphin. —*verb* **1.** ✦ **attach, fasten, fix, secure, stick** ✧ **staple**

I have lots of buttons *pinned* to my backpack.
2. ✦ hold, press ✧ clasp, restrain The wrestler won the match by *pinning* his opponent to the mat.

pinch *verb* **✦ squeeze ✧ compress, cramp, crush, nip** I accidentally *pinched* my hand in the front door. —*noun* **1. ✦ squeeze ✧ nip** My friend gave me a playful *pinch* on the arm. **2. ✦ bit, dash, speck, trace ✧ little** Dad added a *pinch* of salt to his bowl of chili. **3. ✦ crisis, emergency, predicament ✧ difficulty, trouble** This umbrella isn't very good, but it will do in a *pinch*.

pioneer *noun* **1. ✦ settler ✧ colonist, explorer, frontiersman, pathfinder, scout** During the nineteenth century, many *pioneers* made the difficult journey westward across North America. **2. ✦ developer, forerunner, founder, originator ✧ creator** The Wright brothers were among the *pioneers* of aviation.

pious *noun* **✦ devout, religious, reverent ✧ holy, saintly** The *pious* man went to church every day.

pirate *noun* **✦ buccaneer, privateer ✧ outlaw, plunderer, robber** *Pirates* sometimes attacked coastal cities as well as ships at sea.

pistol *noun* **✦ handgun ✧ firearm, gun, revolver, side arm** Police officers are usually armed with *pistols*.

pit¹ *noun* **✦ cavity, excavation, hole ✧ basin, crater, shaft, well** The prospectors dug a *pit* for their garbage a short distance from camp. —*verb* **✦ match, oppose, set ✧ counter, play off** In wrestling matches, people of about the same weight are *pitted* against each other.

pit² *noun* **✦ kernel, seed ✧ nut, stone** We put the avocado *pit* in a glass of water to see if it would grow.

pitch *verb* **1. ✦ cast, fling, heave, hurl, throw, toss** I *pitched* the stone far out into the lake. **2. ✦ erect, put up, raise, set up ✧ establish, place** This looks like a good spot to *pitch* our tent. **3. ✦ heave, rock, roll, toss ✧ lurch, plunge** Waves *pitched* our rowboat back and forth. —*noun* **1. ✦ throw, toss ✧ cast, delivery, fling, heave** The batter hit a home run on the first *pitch*. **2. ✦ degree, level, point ✧ height, peak** The crowd reached a high *pitch* of excitement as the band began to play. **3. ✦ angle, grade, incline, slant, slope, tilt** The roof of a Swiss chalet has a steep *pitch* so that snow will slide off easily.

pitiful *adjective* **✦ forlorn, heartbreaking, moving, pathetic, sad** The injured bird looked *pitiful*, but we were able to nurse it back to health.

pity *noun* **✦ compassion, mercy, sympathy ✧ charity, kindness** Many people donated clothes and money out of *pity* for the hurricane victims. —*verb* **✦ feel sorry for ✧ sympathize** I love my neighborhood so much that I sometimes *pity* people who don't live here.

pivot *verb* **✦ swing, swivel, turn ✧ revolve, rotate, swerve** I learned how to *pivot* my skateboard left or right on its back wheels.

place *noun* **1. ✦ area, location, point, position, site, spot** This is a good *place* to plant the rosebush. **2. ✦ district, locale, locality, region ✧ vicinity** My uncle thinks that Cape Cod is a great *place* to live. **3. ✦ home, house, residence ✧ abode, dwelling, quarters** Mom invited some friends to our *place* for dinner. ▲ **4. ✦ position, post, rank, station ✧ situation, status** George Washington occupies a *place* of honor in our country's history. —*verb* **1. ✦ locate, position, put, set, situate ✧ arrange, deposit** Please *place* a chair at each end of the table. **2. ✦ identify, recognize, remember ✧ connect, know** I know I've seen that boy before, but I just can't *place* him.

✦ best choices
✧ other choices

placid *adjective* ✦ **calm, peaceful, quiet, serene, tranquil, undisturbed** The lake is *placid* and smooth whenever the wind dies down.

plague *noun* **1.** ✦ **disease, epidemic** ✧ **illness, infection, outbreak, sickness** A deadly *plague* hit Europe in the mid-fourteenth century. **2.** ✦ **affliction, burden, curse, hardship, ill, problem, trouble** Poverty and crime are two *plagues* that society is trying to overcome. —*verb* ✦ **afflict, burden, curse, torment, trouble** ✧ **annoy, bother** The patient was *plagued* by a cough that lasted all winter long.

plain *adjective* **1.** ✦ **apparent, clear, distinct, evident, obvious, unmistakable** You have made your meaning perfectly *plain*. **2.** ✦ **common, everyday, ordinary, standard** ✧ **average, routine** Many police detectives wear *plain* clothes instead of a uniform. **3.** ✦ **frank, honest, simple, sincere, straightforward** ✧ **absolute, total** Please tell me the *plain* truth. —*noun* ✦ **grassland, prairie** ✧ **field, plateau, steppe** Enormous herds of buffalo once roamed the North American *plains*.

plan *noun* ✦ **aim, goal, intent, intention** ✧ **design, scheme, strategy** My brother's *plan* is to go to college after he graduates from high school. —*verb* ✦ **arrange, design, devise, organize** ✧ **aim, intend, propose** Kristin and I helped *plan* the class field trip.

plane *noun* **1.** ✦ **degree, grade, level, stage** ✧ **condition, rank** Ancient Chinese civilization reached a very high *plane* of development. **2.** ✦ **aircraft, airplane** ✧ **airliner, jet** Hundreds of *planes* land at Los Angeles International Airport every day.

plant *noun* **1.** ✧ **bush, grass, herb, shrub, tree, vegetable** We have lots of different *plants* in our garden. **2.** ✦ **factory** ✧ **facility, mill, shop, works** My father works at an automobile *plant*. —*verb* ✦ **seed, sow** ✧ **farm, grow, raise** Winter wheat is *planted* in the fall.

play *verb* **1.** ✦ **amuse (oneself), entertain (oneself)** ✧ **frolic, romp** I have the whole afternoon to *play* with my friends. **2.** ✦ **compete, participate, take part** ✧ **contend** Everyone on our soccer team got a chance to *play* in yesterday's game. **3.** ✦ **act, perform, portray, represent** ✧ **impersonate** Caitlin is going to *play* Snow White in our show. —*noun* **1.** ✦ **drama, performance, show, theatrical** Every student will have a role in the class *play*. **2.** ✦ **amusement, diversion, entertainment, fun, pleasure, recreation** If you get your chores done in the morning, there will be time for *play* in the afternoon.

playful *adjective* ✦ **energetic, frisky, frolicsome, lively** ✧ **amusing, joking** My kitten is always in a *playful* mood.

plea *noun* ✦ **appeal, petition, request** ✧ **cry, prayer** The Red Cross made a *plea* for donations of warm clothing.

plead *verb* ✦ **appeal, beg, entreat, implore** ✧ **ask, request** My little sister *pleaded* for a puppy of her very own.

pleasant *adjective* ✦ **agreeable, delightful, enjoyable, nice, pleasing, pleasurable** I like springtime because the days are warm and *pleasant*.

please *verb* **1.** ✦ **delight, gladden, gratify** ✧ **cheer, satisfy** Steven's parents were *pleased* when his project won first place in the science fair. **2.** ✦ **choose, desire, like, prefer, want, will, wish** My grandparents gave me twenty-five dollars to buy whatever I *please* for my birthday.

pleasure *noun* ✦ **enjoyment, delight, gladness, happiness, joy** ✧ **cheer, satisfaction** My little brother laughs with *pleasure* when I give him a piggyback ride.

pledge *noun* ✦ **agreement, commitment, promise** ✧ **contract, oath, vow** My parents made a *pledge* to contribute money to the homeless shelter. —*verb* ✦ **affirm, promise, swear, vow** ✧ **agree, guarantee** In our Scout meetings, we *pledge* allegiance to the flag of the United States of America.

plenty   *noun*   ✦ **an abundance, a great deal, lots, a quantity**   ✧ **enough, much, sufficient** We have *plenty* of food for tomorrow's picnic.

plod   *verb*   ✦ **drag, toil, tramp, trudge** ✧ **tread, walk**   We *plodded* wearily up the stairs of the Washington Monument.

plot   *noun*   **1.**   ✦ **lot, parcel, tract**   ✧ **area, ground, land, space**   Grandpa has a small *plot* of land that he uses for a vegetable garden. **2.**   ✦ **story, story line**   ✧ **narrative, theme** This novel has an exciting *plot* about traveling in a time machine. **3.**   ✦ **conspiracy, intrigue, plan, scheme** ✧ **design**   There was a *plot*   to overthrow the cruel dictator. —*verb*   ✦ **con-spire, intrigue, plan, scheme** ✧ **contrive**   The bandits were *plotting* to rob a bank.

plug   *noun*   ✦ **stopper**   ✧ **block, cork, filling** Pull the *plug* to let water drain out of the sink.

Antonyms

plug *verb*

clear, free, open,
unblock, unimpede

—*verb*   ✦ **block, close, cover, fill, seal, stop, stuff** Mom tried to *plug* the leak in the pipe until the plumber could come.

plump   *adjective*   ✦ **fat, stout, well-fed** ✧ **beefy, bulky, chubby, fleshy, full, obese**   Dad picked out a nice *plump* turkey for our Thanksgiving dinner.

plunder   *verb*   ✦ **loot, pillage, raid, sack** ✧ **rob, steal**   About 1,000 years ago, Vikings *plun-dered* Europe's coastal villages.   —*noun*   ✦ **booty,** loot, pillage, spoils   ✧ **treasure, winnings**   The pirates divided their *plunder* into equal shares.

plunge   *verb*   **1.**   ✦ **dive, jump, leap**   ✧ **dip, immerse, submerge**   I ran down the path and *plunged* into the pond.   **2.**   ✦ **drop, fall, pitch, tumble**   ✧ **descend, topple**   The climber would have *plunged* fifty feet if her rope hadn't caught her.   ◄ —*noun*   ✦ **dip, dive, swim**   ✧ **drop, fall, jump, leap**   Dad enjoys taking a *plunge* in our pool after work.

pocket   *noun*   ✦ **cavity, cham-ber, hole, hollow**   ✧ **compart-ment, receptacle**   The miner found a *pocket* of gold.   —*adjec-tive*   ✦ **compact, concise, little, portable, small**   ✧ **miniature**   My *pocket* encyclopedia has a lot of useful information in it.

point   *noun*   **1.**   ✦ **end, tip**   ✧ **head, peak, prong, spike, top**   Your pencil will write better if you sharpen its *point*.   **2.**   ✦ **cape, headland, promontory**   ✧ **peninsula**   A lighthouse sits out on the end of this *point*.   **3.**   ✦ **locality, location, place, position, site, spot**   There are many *points* of interest in Yellowstone National Park.   **4.**   ✦ **in-stant, moment, time**   ✧ **period**   At this *point* in the school year the first report cards are given out. **5.**   ✦ **item, matter, particular, subject, topic**   The mayor's speech covered many important *points*. **6.**   ✦ **purpose, reason**   ✧ **aim, end, idea, objec-tive**   There isn't much *point* in watering the lawn on a rainy day.   —*verb*   **1.**   ✦ **aim, direct**   ✧ **turn**   You have to *point* the remote control straight at the tele-vision or it won't work.   **2.**   ✦ **designate, indicate, show**   ✧ **mention, name**   The tour guide *pointed* out many interesting sights.

poise   *verb*   ✦ **balance, perch**   ✧ **hang, hover, suspend**   Amy was *poised* for a moment on the edge of the diving board before she jumped. —*noun*   ✦ **assurance, composure, confidence,**

✦   **best choices**
✧   **other choices**

self-control It's not easy to maintain your *poise* while speaking in front of a large group.

poisonous *adjective* ✦ **toxic** ◇ **dangerous, deadly, fatal, lethal, venomous** Most insecticides are *poisonous* to humans.

poke *verb* **1.** ✦ **dig, jab, prod, stab, stick, thrust** ◇ **hit, nudge** Dylan accidentally *poked* his finger in my eye. **2.** ✦ **stick, thrust** ◇ **push, shove** The gopher *poked* its head cautiously out of its hole.

policy *noun* ✦ **guidelines, procedure, rules** ◇ **code, custom, practice** According to school *policy*, students may not take a medication unless they have the nurse's approval.

polish *verb* **1.** ✦ **buff, shine** ◇ **brighten, clean, rub, wax** Grandmother always *polishes* her silverware before she hosts big family dinners. **2.** ✦ **improve, perfect, refine, touch up** ◇ **enhance, smooth** The President's aides spent several weeks *polishing* his inauguration speech. —*noun* **1.** ✦ **gloss, glow, luster, shine** ◇ **glaze, sparkle** I buffed my shoes until they had a beautiful *polish*. **2.** ✦ **elegance, grace, refinement, style** ◇ **class** The actor worked hard to give *polish* to his performance.

polite *adjective* ✦ **civil, considerate, courteous, respectful, well-mannered** A *polite* person treats everyone with respect.

poll *noun* ✦ **survey** ◇ **census, sampling** The latest *poll* shows that the senator is likely to be reelected. —*verb* ✦ **interview, question, survey** ◇ **examine, sample** One hundred students were *polled* about their summer vacation plans.

pollute *verb* ✦ **contaminate, foul** ◇ **dirty, poison, soil, stain** The exhaust from cars and trucks *pollutes* the air.

ponder *verb* ✦ **consider, contemplate, think about** ◇ **deliberate, reflect** Let's *ponder* the situation a while longer before we decide what to do.

poor *adjective* **1.** ✦ **destitute, impoverished, needy, penniless, poverty-stricken** This shelter provides free meals for people who are too *poor* to buy their own food. **2.** ✦ **bad, deficient, inadequate, inferior, unsatisfactory** ◇ **worthless** You can't get a good crop out of *poor* soil. **3.** ✦ **pathetic, pitiful, unfortunate, unlucky, wretched** That *poor* cat was abandoned by its owners.

popular *adjective* **1.** ✦ **general, public, widespread** ◇ **democratic, universal** Due to *popular* demand, the circus will stay in town for another week. **2.** ✦ **favored, preferred, well-liked** ◇ **favorite, leading** Soccer is a *popular* sport in most parts of the world.

popularity *noun* ✦ **acceptance, acclaim, celebrity, fame, favor, support** That singer is currently enjoying great *popularity*.

population *noun* ✦ **citizenry, populace** ◇ **inhabitants, people, residents** The little village where my father grew up has a *population* of almost two hundred people.

portable *adjective* ✦ **movable, transportable** ◇ **compact, light, lightweight** Laptop computers are small enough to be easily *portable*.

Antonyms
portable *adjective*
firm, fixed, immovable, permanent, stationary, steadfast

portion *noun* ✦ **fraction, part, share** ◇ **piece, section, segment** Andrea saves a *portion* of her weekly allowance. —*verb* ✦ **deal out, dispense, distribute, divide, parcel out** ◇ **disperse** We *portioned out* the snacks so that everyone got an equal share.

portray *verb* **1.** ✦ **characterize, depict, describe, represent, show** ◇ **picture** History books often *portray* Thomas Jefferson as an effective and honest President. **2.** ✦ **act, perform, play**

◇ **impersonate** Rebecca is going to *portray* an evil queen in our school play.

pose *verb* 1. ✦ **sit** ◇ **model, stand** Once a year, we get dressed up and *pose* for a family portrait. 2. ✦ **impersonate, masquerade as, pass for, pretend to be** ◇ **act, feign** The man was able to get into the sold-out concert by *posing as* a reporter. 3. ✦ **advance, present, propose, raise, state, suggest** Matthew *posed* a philosophical question that no one could answer. —*noun* ✦ **position** ◇ **attitude, posture, stance** As the ballet ended, all of the dancers held their *poses* until the curtain came down.

position *noun* 1. ✦ **location, place, site, spot, station** ◇ **area, orientation** The parade will be able to start as soon as all of the floats are in their proper *positions*. 2. ✦ **condition, situation, state** ◇ **circumstances, status** I'm not in a very good *position* to ask my sister for a favor because she's still mad at me. 3. ✦ **belief, conviction, feeling, opinion, stand, view** In this interview the senator states her *position* on the new tax bill. 4. ✦ **appointment, job, post, office** ◇ **employment, duty** In 1933, Frances Perkins became the first woman to hold a cabinet *position* in the United States government.

positive *adjective* 1. ✦ **favorable, good, optimistic** ◇ **constructive, helpful** Our teacher always has something *positive* to say about our work. 2. ✦ **certain, confident, convinced, definite, sure** I'm *positive* that I have seen this movie before.

possess *verb* ✦ **have, hold, own** ◇ **command, control** Our local library *possesses* more books than I can ever hope to read.

possession *noun* 1. ✦ **custody, ownership, title** ◇ **control, hold** We will be able to take *possession* of our new condominium any day now. 2. ✦ **belonging** ◇ **asset, effect, property, resource** My most valuable *possession* is a quilt that my great-grandmother made.

possibility *noun* ✦ **chance, likelihood, probability, prospect** ◇ **odds** There's a good *possibility* that we'll get out of school early because it's the day before winter break.

possible *adjective* ✦ **conceivable, potential, workable** ◇ **likely, probable** There is more than one *possible* solution to this riddle.

post[1] *noun* ◇ **column, picket, pillar, pole, prop, stake** The fence *posts* were spaced ten feet apart. —*verb* ✦ **attach, fasten, place, put** ◇ **install, set** Room assignments will be *posted* on the bulletin board.

post[2] *noun* 1. ✦ **base, camp, garrison, station** ◇ **fort, headquarters** The soldiers returned to their *post* after the maneuvers. 2. ✦ **appointment, assignment, office, position** ◇ **duty, job** Dad knows someone who was just given an important *post* in the state government. —*verb* ✦ **place, position, situate, station** ◇ **assign** Two guards were *posted* near the bank's entrance.

post[3] *verb* ✦ **advise, brief, inform, notify** ◇ **report, tell** I'm interested in hearing about how you're doing, so please keep me *posted*.

postpone *verb* ✦ **defer, delay, put off** ◇ **hold, stay, suspend** The weather forced us to *postpone* our picnic.

potential *adjective* ✦ **likely, possible, probable, promising** ◇ **conceivable** I had a *potential* buyer for my bike, but she changed her mind.

pounce *verb* ✦ **jump, leap, spring** ◇ **ambush, attack, strike** The cat *pounced* on the terrified mouse.

pound *verb* ✦ **batter, beat, hammer, hit, pummel, strike** ◇ **punch, thrash, wallop** The impatient man *pounded* the door of the elevator with his fists.

pour *verb* ✦ **cascade, flow, run, rush, stream** ◇ **gush, surge** After a heavy rain, water *poured* over the top of the dam.

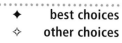

✦ **best choices**
◇ **other choices**

poverty *noun* ✦ destitution, neediness, pennilessness ✧ lack, need, want The actor had to endure years of *poverty* before he finally started to get good roles.

power *noun* 1. ✦ ability, capability, might, strength ✧ energy, force Superman has the *power* to leap tall buildings and stop speeding vehicles. 2. ✦ authority, command, control ✧ dominion, mastery, rule The election will decide which party will be in *power*. —*verb* ✦ activate, operate, run ✧ energize My model car is *powered* by batteries. ◄

powerful *adjective* ✦ effective, forceful, influential, strong, vigorous ✧ heavy, mighty The speaker presented a *powerful* argument in favor of ending the war.

Antonyms

powerful *adjective*

feeble, frail, helpless, ineffectual, weak

---

practical *adjective* ✦ helpful, realistic, sensible, sound, useful, worthwhile ✧ efficient Your suggestion to stick the button on my coat with chewing gum was not very *practical*.

practice *verb* 1. ✦ drill, rehearse, train ✧ discipline, exercise, study The marching band is *practicing* for next Saturday's performance. 2. ✦ apply, employ, perform, use ✧ do, follow, observe *Practicing* good oral hygiene helps to prevent tooth decay. —*noun* 1. ✦ preparation, rehearsal, training ✧ discipline, study It takes a lot of *practice* to become a good drummer. 2. ✦ custom, habit, routine ✧ rule, tradition, way It is our *practice* to have dinner at 6 P.M. every day. 3. ✦ action, execution, operation, use

✧ **performance** The school will soon put its new procedures into *practice*.

praise *noun* ✦ acclaim, commendation, compliments, recognition ✧ approval Katherine received a lot of *praise* for her outstanding science project. —*verb* ✦ acclaim, commend, compliment, congratulate ✧ approve, honor The conductor *praised* our orchestra for having played so well. ►

pray *verb* ✦ desire, hope for, long for, want, wish for, yearn for ✧ appeal, beg, implore, plead The farmer *prayed for* rain.

precaution *noun* ✦ safeguard, safety measure ✧ care, caution, prevention If you take a few simple *precautions*, this sport can be quite safe.

precede *verb* ✦ come before, go before, usher in ✧ lead, introduce High winds and dark clouds *preceded* the thunderstorm.

precious *adjective* ✦ costly, expensive, valuable ✧ invaluable, priceless, rare Diamonds and emeralds are *precious* stones.

precise *adjective* ✦ exact, specific ✧ accurate, correct, definite, true What were her *precise* words?

precision *noun* ✦ accuracy, correctness, exactness, preciseness ✧ attention, care, carefulness A computer can perform calculations with great speed and *precision*.

predicament *noun* ✦ crisis, fix, jam, mess ✧ difficulty, problem, trouble The man was in a *predicament* when he locked his keys in his car.

predict *verb* ✦ **forecast, foresee, foretell, prophesy, see, tell** ✧ **project** The foretuneteller at the carnival claimed to be able to *predict* the future in a crystal ball.

preface *noun* ✦ **foreword, introduction** ✧ **beginning, overture, prelude** The *preface* to this history book includes a discussion of the author's background.

prefer *verb* ✦ **like** ✧ **choose, elect, favor, pick, select** Which would you *prefer*, frozen yogurt or ice cream?

preference *noun* ✦ **choice, desire, pick, selection** ✧ **fancy, favorite, liking** My *preference* is to go to a movie rather than stay home and watch television.

prejudice *noun* ✦ **bias, one-sidedness, partiality** ✧ **intolerance, unfairness** Judges must be without *prejudice* if they are to render fair verdicts. —*verb* ✦ **bias** ✧ **influence, sway, turn against** Don't be *prejudiced* against the movie just because you don't like one of the actors.

preliminary *adjective* ✦ **beginning, introductory, opening, preparatory, starting** The speaker made a few *preliminary* remarks before addressing his main topic.

premature *adjective* ✦ **early, hasty, untimely** ✧ **impulsive, rash** The swimmer was disqualified for making a *premature* start.

prepare *verb* ✦ **fix, get ready, make** ✧ **arrange, form, organize** Amber likes to help her parents *prepare* dinner.

presence *noun* **1.** ✦ **appearance, existence, occurrence** ✧ **attendance, being** The *presence* of smoke usually means that there is a fire. **2.** ✦ **company, vicinity** ✧ **midst, nearness, neighborhood** There are some things that my parents won't discuss in my *presence*.

present¹ *adjective* **1.** ✦ **current, existing, present-day** ✧ **immediate, latest, recent** Mom wants to quit her *present* job and try to find a better one. **2.** ✦ **at hand, attending, here** ✧ **near, nearby, there** The meeting will start as soon as everyone is *present*.

present² *verb* **1.** ✦ **award, confer, give** ✧ **donate, grant, offer** The field hockey coach will now *present* the trophy for Best Athlete. **2.** ✦ **introduce, make known** ✧ **acquaint** The visiting nobleman was *presented* to the queen. **3.** ✦ **display, exhibit, furnish, produce, show** ✧ **perform, provide** The lawyer *presented* evidence that proved the innocence of his client. —*noun* ✦ **gift** ✧ **donation, favor, grant, offering** I got this shirt as a birthday *present*.

preserve *verb* ✦ **conserve, maintain, protect, save** ✧ **guard, safeguard** Everyone should help to *preserve* our natural resources. —*noun* **1.** ✧ **jam, jelly, marmalade** Nicholas likes to put strawberry *preserves* on his toast. **2.** ✦ **refuge, reservation, reserve, sanctuary** ✧ **park** Our class is taking a field trip to a wildlife *preserve*.

press *verb* **1.** ✦ **depress, push** ✧ **compress, crush, squeeze** *Press* this button to start the elevator. ▶ **2.** ✦ **iron** ✧ **flatten, smooth, steam** Mom showed me how to *press* my own shirts and pants. **3.** ✦ **beg, entreat, urge** ✧ **demand, insist, plead** My friend *pressed* me to stay for dinner.

pressure *noun* **1.** ✦ **strain, weight** ✧ **compression, force, power, strength** The shelf sagged under the *pressure* of the heavy books. **2.** ✦ **strain, stress** ✧ **anxiety, distress, tension** Ann-Marie was under a lot of *pressure* to get her book report done on time.

prestige *noun* ✦ **distinction, importance, influence, status** ◇ **reputation** The President occupies a position of *prestige* in the United States government.

presume *verb* ✦ **assume, believe, suppose, surmise, think** ◇ **guess, imagine** I stopped by my friend's house because I *presumed* that he would be home.

pretend *verb* **1.** ✦ **fake, feign, simulate** ◇ **act, claim, pose** I *pretended* to be asleep so that my brother wouldn't bother me. **2.** ✦ **fantasize, imagine, make believe, play** ◇ **act, masquerade** My friends and I sometimes *pretend* that we are superheroes.

pretty *adjective* ✦ **attractive, beautiful, lovely** ◇ **cute, good-looking, handsome, sweet** Which of the tropical fish do you think is the *prettiest*? —*adverb* ✦ **fairly, quite, rather, somewhat, very** ◇ **reasonably** It's *pretty* cold out for a spring day.

prevent *verb* ✦ **forestall, halt, head off, stop** ◇ **avoid, hinder, obstruct** Only you can *prevent* forest fires.

previous *adjective* ✦ **earlier, former, past, prior, preceding** Only people with *previous* experience should apply for this job.

prey *noun* ✦ **catch, game, kill** ◇ **target, victim** The tiger pounced on its *prey*. —*verb* ✦ **eat, feed on, hunt, live on, pursue** ◇ **attack, seize** Spiders *prey on* flies and other small insects.

price *noun* ✦ **charge (for), cost** ◇ **amount, expense, value, worth** The *price* of admission at our town movie theater just went up. —*verb* ✦ **appraise, assess, estimate, evaluate, value** The merchant *priced* the diamond necklace at three thousand dollars.

priceless *adjective* ✦ **invaluable, precious, valuable** ◇ **costly, expensive** The museum has several works of art that are rare and *priceless*.

pride *noun* **1.** ✦ **self-esteem, self-respect** ◇ **dignity, honor** The author's *pride* was hurt when she failed to win the writing contest. **2.** ✦ **fulfillment, satisfaction** ◇ **delight, enjoyment, pleasure** Dad takes great *pride* in his ability to fix things around the house. **3.** ✦ **arrogance, conceit, self-importance, vanity** ◇ **insolence** The man didn't apologize for making a mistake because he had too much *pride*.

primary *adjective* **1.** ✦ **beginning, earliest, first, initial, original** The project is still in its *primary* stage of development. **2.** ✦ **chief, foremost, leading, main, prime, principal, top** My *primary* interests are reading books, listening to music, and playing soccer.

primitive *adjective* ✦ **crude, rough, simple** ◇ **ancient, basic, early, prehistoric, raw** Archaeologists have found *primitive* stone tools that are more than 2.5 million years old.

principal *adjective* ✦ **foremost, key, leading, main, major, primary, top** The *principal* crop in our region is potatoes. —*noun* ◇ **administrator, chief, director, head, leader, ruler** The *principal* of our school was once a teacher herself.

Antonyms
principal *adjective*
inferior, irrelevant, lesser, minor, secondary

principle *noun* **1.** ✦ **assumption, axiom, fundamental, rule, standard** ◇ **law** The United States is founded on the *principle* that all people are created equal. **2.** ✦ **character, honesty, integrity, morality, virtue** ◇ **honor** A person of high *principle* is not likely to lie, steal, or cheat.

print *verb* **1.** ✦ **imprint** ◇ **engrave, letter, mark, stamp** Tib had her name and address *printed* on her new stationery. **2.** ✦ **issue, publish, release** ◇ **reissue, reprint** The publisher *printed* ten thousand copies of the new cookbook. —*noun* **1.** ✦ **impression, imprint** ◇ **mark, stamp** My dog left a paw *print* in the wet cement.

2. ✦ **letters, printing, type** ✧ **text, writing** Grandpa prefers to read books that have large *print*.
3. ✧ **engraving, etching, illustration, photograph, reproduction** These *prints* have been signed and numbered by the artist.

prior *adjective* ✦ **earlier, former, past, preceding, previous** The beginner's class is for people who have no *prior* experience using a computer.

prison *noun* ✦ **jail, penitentiary** ✧ **brig, cell, dungeon, pen, stockade** The thief was caught and sent to *prison*.

private *adjective* **1.** ✦ **individual, personal** ✧ **exclusive, reserved, restricted** I like to have *private* time to write in my journal every day.
2. ✦ **confidential, secret** ✧ **classified, concealed, hidden** My best friend and I have a *private* meeting place that no one else knows about.

privilege *noun* ✦ **advantage, benefit, right** ✧ **freedom, liberty** The company's top executives enjoy certain *privileges* that are not available to other employees.

prize *noun* ✦ **award, premium, reward, winnings** ✧ **recognition, trophy** The *prize* for first place was a scholarship for five hundred dollars.
—*adjective* ✦ **acclaimed, champion, winning** ✧ **cherished, top, valued** The rancher's *prize* bull won a blue ribbon at the county fair. —*verb* ✦ **cherish, esteem, treasure, value** ✧ **admire, appreciate** Lawrence has one coin in his collection that he *prizes* more than all the others.

probable *adjective* ✦ **likely, presumed** ✧ **apparent, possible, reasonable** Investigators are trying to determine the fire's *probable* cause.

probe *noun* ✦ **inquiry, investigation** ✧ **examination, exploration, research** The police *probe* revealed that several people were involved in the crime. —*verb* ✦ **examine, inspect, investigate, search** ✧ **explore, study** The dentist *probed* inside my mouth to see if I had any problems with my teeth.

problem *noun* **1.** ✦ **question** ✧ **mystery, puzzle, riddle** I need some help with this math *problem*. **2.** ✦ **complication, difficulty, trouble** ✧ **issue, predicament** It took us a few days to work all of the *problems* out of our new computer system.

procedure *noun* ✦ **method, process, technique, way** ✧ **course, policy, system** Luckily we have a booklet that explains the *procedure* for programming our VCR.

proceed *verb* ✦ **advance, continue, go on, move on, progress** ✧ **start** When drivers encounter a flashing red light, they must come to a full stop before *proceeding*.

process *noun* ✦ **method, procedure, system, technique, way** ✧ **formula, operation** In 1856, Henry Bessemer developed a new *process* for making steel from cast iron. —*verb* ✦ **deal with, handle, treat** ✧ **alter, prepare, ready** The college admissions office *processes* thousands of applications every year.

proclaim *verb* ✦ **announce, declare, state** ✧ **call, claim, profess** The judge *proclaimed* Robyn and Christopher to be the winners of the spelling bee.

procure *verb* ✦ **acquire, gain, get, obtain, secure** ✧ **buy, win** The coin collector finally managed to *procure* the rare silver dollar that he had long desired.

Antonyms
procure *verb*
drop, forfeit, give up, lose, sell

prod *verb* **1.** ✦ **jab, nudge, poke** ✧ **dig, push, thrust** When the mule refused to budge, its owner *prodded* it with a stick.
2. ✦ **goad, motivate, nag, prompt, urge** ✧ **encourage, inspire** No one has to *prod* me to do my homework.

produce *verb* **1.** ✦ **furnish, give, provide, supply, yield** ✧ **bear** This well *produces* more than one hundred barrels of oil every day.
2. ✦ **assemble, make, manufacture** ✧ **build,**

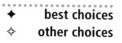
✦ **best choices**
✧ **other choices**

construct, create Dad works at a factory that *produces* microwave ovens. **3.** ✦ **bring forward, bring out** ✧ **display, exhibit, present, show** The magician reached into his hat and *produced* a rabbit.

product *noun* ✦ **commodity, goods, merchandise** ✧ **outcome, produce, result** This store carries televisions, stereos, and other electronic *products*.

profess *verb* ✦ **affirm, announce, declare, proclaim, state** ✧ **confirm** Some people are persecuted for openly *professing* their beliefs.

profession *noun* **1.** ✦ **calling, career, field, occupation, vocation** ✧ **business, job, work** Medicine and law are *professions* that require years of specialized education. ▼ **2.** ✦ **affirmation, announcement, declaration, pledge, statement** The jury did not believe the defendant's *profession* of innocence.

profile *noun* ✦ **side view** ✧ **contour, outline, portrait, silhouette** A *profile* of Abraham Lincoln appears on U.S. pennies.

profit *noun* **1.** ✦ **advantage, benefit, use, value** ✧ **good, improvement** The time you spend in school now will be of *profit* to you in the future. **2.** ✦ **earnings, gains, returns** ✧ **income, money, pay, revenue** *Profits* for computer makers are expected to grow this year. —*verb* ✦ **benefit, gain** ✧ **advance, earn, help, improve** A lot of companies will *profit* from the plan to lower corporate taxes.

profound *adjective* **1.** ✦ **deep, thoughtful, wise** ✧ **intellectual, intelligent, knowledgeable** The historian's book presented some *profound* insights into the effects of war. **2.** ✦ **deep, great, intense, strong, thorough, total** I have *profound* admiration for people who risk their lives to rescue others from danger.

program *noun* **1.** ✦ **show** ✧ **performance, presentation, production, series** My favorite television *program* airs at 7 o'clock tonight. **2.** ✦ **plan, policy, procedure** ✧ **arrangement, list, schedule** Our school just started a *program* to help students learn how to use computers.

progress *noun* ✦ **advancement, headway, improvement** ✧ **development, growth** I'm not making much *progress* with the saxophone so far. —*verb* ✦ **advance, go forward, move, proceed** ✧ **develop, grow, improve** Work on the new gymnasium is *progressing* at a steady pace.

prohibit *verb* ✦ **ban, disallow, forbid** ✧ **outlaw, prevent, restrict, stop** Parking is *prohibited* on this street.

project *noun* ✦ **enterprise, task, undertaking** ✧ **design, plan, scheme** Dad's latest *project* is to build an outdoor barbecue. —*verb* ✦ **extend, jut, protrude, stick out** ✧ **bulge, overhang** The rocky promontory *projected* several hundred feet into the water.

prolong *verb* ✦ **draw out, extend, lengthen, protract, stretch out** We decided to *prolong* our visit for two more days.

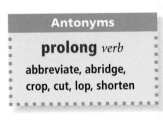

Antonyms

prolong *verb*

abbreviate, abridge, crop, cut, lop, shorten

prominent *adjective* **1.** ✦ **conspicuous, evident, noticeable, obvious, visible** The two skyscrapers are the most *prominent* buildings in the whole city. **2.** ✦ **distinguished, eminent, important, notable, outstanding** ✧ **famous, great** The mayor invited several *prominent* citizens to lunch to discuss the future of the city.

promise *noun* **1.** ✦ **oath, pledge, vow, word** ✧ **assurance, commitment** People trust Stephanie because she always keeps her *promise*. **2.** ✦ **hope, possibility, prospect** ✧ **ability, capacity, talent** The rookie baseball player showed a lot of *promise*. —*verb* ✦ **pledge, swear, vow** ✧ **agree, assure, guarantee** You may borrow my video game if you *promise* to return it tomorrow.

promote *verb* **1.** ✦ **aid, assist, encourage, foster, further, support** Proper eating habits *promote* good health. **2.** ✦ **advance, elevate, move up, raise** ✧ **graduate** The store *promoted* two sales clerks to management positions.

prompt *adjective* ✦ **punctual, quick, rapid, swift, timely** ✧ **immediate, instant** This restaurant is known for its *prompt* service. —*verb* ✦ **cause, inspire, motivate, prod, stimulate** ✧ **arouse** My curiosity *prompted* me to skip to the last page of the book.

prone *adjective* **1.** ✦ **face down, flat, horizontal** ✧ **reclining** Everyone lay in a *prone* position, waiting for the coach's command to start doing pushups. **2.** ✦ **apt, given, inclined, liable, likely** ✧ **subject** People sometimes tell me that I'm *prone* to talk too much.

pronounce *verb* **1.** ✦ **articulate, enunciate, say, utter** ✧ **express, speak** Gabrielle has a hard time *pronouncing* the name Rumpelstiltskin. **2.** ✦ **announce, declare, decree, proclaim, state** The judge *pronounced* a verdict of "not guilty."

pronounced *adjective* ✦ **distinct, evident, noticeable, obvious, strong** ✧ **clear, plain** The tourist spoke English with a *pronounced* accent.

proof *noun* ✦ **authentication, certification, documentation, evidence, verification** Andrea had to show *proof* of her citizenship before she could get a passport.

propel *verb* ✦ **drive, move, run** ✧ **launch, operate, push, start, thrust** My little brother has a toy airplane that is *propelled* by a rubber band.

proper *adjective* ✦ **appropriate, correct, fitting, right, suitable** ✧ **apt, useful** If you wear the *proper* clothing, you can stay warm and dry on stormy days.

property *noun* **1.** ✦ **assets, belongings, effects, goods, possessions, things** My personal *property* includes all of my clothes, books, toys, and stuffed animals. **2.** ✦ **land, real estate** ✧ **acreage, estate, plot, tract** My grandparents bought a piece of *property* out in the country. **3.** ✦ **attribute, characteristic, feature, quality, trait** ✧ **element, part** Heat and light are *properties* of fire.

prophecy *noun* ✦ **foretelling, prediction** ✧ **forecast, vision, warning** The wizard made a *prophecy* that the king's reign would be long and prosperous.

prophesy *verb* ✦ **foresee, foretell, predict** ✧ **forecast, warn** A fortuneteller *prophesied* that I will someday be a famous athlete.

proportion *noun* **1.** ✦ **measure, ratio** ✧ **amount, degree, extent, size** The *proportion* of milk to ice cream in a milk shake is usually about 2 to 1. **2.** ✦ **balance, perspective, relation, symmetry** ✧ **harmony** In the funhouse mirror, my features appeared to be out of *proportion*.

proposal *noun* **1.** ✦ **offer, proposition, request** ✧ **invitation, suggestion** The princess accepted the duke's *proposal* of marriage. **2.** ✦ **idea, plan, recommendation, scheme** ✧ **program, project** The city council is studying the mayor's *proposal* to hire more police officers.

propose *verb* **1.** ✦ **present, offer, recommend, submit, suggest** ✧ **introduce** I *proposed*

✦   best choices
✧   other choices

the idea that we order pizza and chocolate ice cream for dinner tonight. **2. ✦ aim, expect, intend, mean, plan ✧ contemplate** My older brother *proposes* to go to college after he graduates from high school.

prospect *noun* **✦ chance, expectation, hope, possibility ✧ anticipation, outlook** Megan was excited by the *prospect* of getting her own computer. —*verb* **✦ explore, look, probe, search, seek** In 1849, thousands of people journeyed to California to *prospect* for gold.

prosper *verb* **✦ boom, flourish, thrive ✧ gain, increase, succeed** The town *prospered* when an automobile factory was built nearby.

Antonyms
prosper *verb*
decline, dwindle, fade, fail, weaken

prosperity *noun* **✦ affluence, comfort, ease ✧ fortune, riches, success, wealth** The author lived in *prosperity* after her book became an international bestseller.

protect *verb* **✦ defend, guard, safeguard, shield ✧ preserve, save** A bear can be very dangerous when *protecting* its cubs.

protection *noun* **✦ safekeeping, safety, security ✧ cover, defense, refuge, shelter** When my little sister gets scared, she runs to Mom for *protection*.

protest *noun* **✦ challenge, complaint, objection ✧ demonstration, disagreement, opposition** *Protests* have been made by people who are opposed to the new power plant. —*verb* **✦ argue against, challenge, oppose ✧ complain, demonstrate** Our coach loudly *protested* the umpire's decision.

proud *adjective* **1. ✦ pleased with, satisfied with ✧ delighted, glad, happy** Mom said that she was *proud of* me because I stuck up for my friend. **2. ✦ arrogant, conceited, haughty, self-**

important, vain The *proud* nobleman refused to socialize with common people.

prove *verb* **✦ certify, confirm, demonstrate, establish, show, verify** My birth certificate *proves* that I'm eleven years old.

proverb *noun* **✦ adage, saying ✧ moral, motto, rule** "The early bird gets the worm" is a *proverb* that late sleepers may not appreciate.

provide *verb* **✦ contribute, furnish, supply ✧ bring, deliver, give, produce** My parents are *providing* the dessert for our church's potluck dinner tonight.

provoke *verb* **1. ✦ cause, incite, produce, set off, start ✧ arouse, prompt** That bully is always trying to *provoke* a fight. **2. ✦ aggravate, anger, annoy, bother, disturb, irritate** Our dog is usually gentle, but he growls at people who *provoke* him.

prowl *verb* **✦ creep, lurk, slink, sneak, stalk, steal ✧ roam** We saw a raccoon *prowling* around our garbage can.

prudent *adjective* **✦ careful, cautious, sensible, thoughtful, wary, wise** *Prudent* pilots always check their airplanes before takeoff.

Antonyms
prudent *adjective*
foolhardy, hasty, impulsive, madcap, rash

pry¹ *verb* **✦ force, lever, lift, raise ✧ break, move, work** I used a screwdriver to *pry* the lid off the paint can.

pry² *verb* **✦ interfere, meddle, nose, snoop ✧ investigate, poke** My friend said she didn't want to talk about why she was upset, so I decided not to *pry*.

public *adjective* **✦ civic, civil, communal, community ✧ common, general** Patrick feels that we have a *public* duty not to litter. —*noun* **✦ citizens, community, people, populace**

⬧ **everyone** The university museum is open to the *public* on weekends only.

publish *verb* ✦ **bring out, issue, put out, release** ⬧ **print** I can't wait for my favorite author to *publish* another book.

pull *verb* **1.** ✦ **drag, draw, haul, tow** ⬧ **lug, tug** Dad's pickup truck can *pull* a horse trailer. **2.** ✦ **draw out, extract, remove, take out** ⬧ **pluck, yank** The dentist said that she might have to *pull* my loose tooth if it doesn't fall out soon on its own. **3.** ✦ **rip, shred, tear, tug** ⬧ **break, divide, separate** The puppy *pulled* Bartholomew's old sock to pieces. —*noun* ✦ **jerk, tug, wrench, yank** ⬧ **drag** The fisherman hooked a fish by giving the line a quick *pull*.

pulse *noun* ✦ **beat, throb** ⬧ **rhythm, stroke, vibration** When I hold my breath I can feel the *pulse* of my blood in my veins.

punch *verb* ✦ **box, hit, jab, knock, strike** ⬧ **poke, wallop** The boxer tried to *punch* his opponent in the jaw. —*noun* ✦ **blow, hit, jab** ⬧ **poke, smack, thrust** The *punch* missed because the other boxer ducked.

punctual *adjective* ✦ **on time, prompt, timely** ⬧ **dependable, reliable** The nurse urged me to be *punctual* for my appointment with the doctor.

puncture *verb* ✦ **penetrate, perforate, pierce** ⬧ **cut, prick, stick** A piece of glass *punctured* my bicycle tire. —*noun* ✦ **hole, perforation, prick** ⬧ **break, cut, opening** Fortunately I had a repair kit, and I was able to patch the *puncture* in my bike tire.

punish *verb* ✦ **admonish, discipline, penalize** ⬧ **correct, sentence** I try to avoid doing anything that my parents will *punish* me for.

punishment *noun* ✦ **discipline, penalty** ⬧ **correction, payment, sentence** The usual *punishment* for misbehaving in class is to stay after school to serve detention.

pupil *noun* ✦ **student** ⬧ **learner, scholar, schoolboy, schoolgirl** Counting myself, there are fifteen *pupils* in my class.

Word Groups

A **puppet** is a toy that looks like a person or animal and is designed to be moved around. **Puppet** is a general term with no true synonyms. Here are some different kinds of puppets to investigate in a dictionary:

doll, dummy, figurine, mannequin, marionette

purchase *verb* ✦ **buy** ⬧ **acquire, get, obtain, procure** Robert is saving his money until he has enough to *purchase* a new skateboard. —*noun* ✦ **acquisition, buy** ⬧ **asset, possession, property** Though I could have afforded more, I made only one *purchase* at the music store.

pure *adjective* **1.** ✦ **genuine, real, undiluted, unmixed** ⬧ **plain, simple** Cheryl's new necklace is made of *pure* gold. **2.** ✦ **absolute, complete, sheer, thorough, total, utter** Grandpa thinks that the whole idea of UFO abductions is *pure* nonsense.

purify *verb* ✦ **clean, cleanse, decontaminate, filter** ⬧ **sterilize** Dad installed a filter on the furnace in order to *purify* the air in our house.

purpose *noun* ✦ **aim, goal, intent, intention, objective, point** ⬧ **design, end** The *purpose* of my visit is to ask you a favor.

pursue *verb* **1.** ✦ **chase, follow, go after** ⬧ **hunt, track, trail** A police officer *pursued* the thief on foot. **2.** ✦ **strive for, work for** ⬧ **lead, live, undertake** My older sister is *pursuing* her dream of becoming a veterinarian.

pursuit *noun* **1.** ✦ **chase** ⬧ **following, hunt, quest, search** A rabbit dashed across the yard with

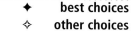
✦ best choices
⬧ other choices

189

two dogs in *pursuit*. **2.** ✦ **activity, hobby, pastime** ✧ **job, occupation, vocation** Fishing is Dad's favorite leisure *pursuit*.

push *verb* **1.** ✦ **depress, press** ✧ **force, move, nudge, shove, thrust** *Push* this button to turn on the VCR. **2.** ✦ **encourage, pressure, prod, prompt, urge** ✧ **coerce** The mayor is *pushing* the city council to adopt new parking regulations. —*noun* **1.** ✦ **shove** ✧ **jolt, nudge, poke, pressure, thrust** The door won't open unless you give it a hard *push*. **2.** ✦ **attempt, drive, effort** ✧ **ambition, energy, enterprise** Christina is making a big push to finish her lab report.

put *verb* **1.** ✦ **place, set** ✧ **deposit, lay, position, situate** Please *put* the dishes back in the cupboard as soon as I have dried them. **2.** ✦ **assign, set** ✧ **cause, commit, make, require** I know it's really summer when Dad *puts* me to work mowing the yard. **3.** ✦ **express, formulate, phrase** ✧ **say, state, word** Sometimes I have trouble *putting* my thoughts into words.

puzzle *noun* ✦ **mystery, riddle** ✧ **problem, question** It's still a *puzzle* why the dinosaurs died out so suddenly. —*verb* ✦ **baffle, bewilder, confuse, mystify, perplex** The man's unusual symptoms *puzzled* his doctor.

Q

quaint *adjective* ✦ **old-fashioned, picturesque** ✧ **charming, cute, enchanting** The *quaint* cottage had stone walls and a slate roof.

quake *verb* ✦ **quiver, shake, shiver, shudder, tremble** ✧ **quaver, vibrate** The rabbit was so terrified that its whole body began to *quake*.

qualification *noun* 1. ✦ **condition, provision, requirement** ✧ **skill, talent** One of the main *qualifications* for this job is that applicants must have a driver's license. 2. ✦ **exception, limitation, reservation, restriction** I can say without *qualification* that Ariel is the funniest person I've ever met.

qualify *verb* 1. ✦ **authorize, entitle** ✧ **enable, fit, prepare, suit** A teaching certificate *qualifies* a person to be a teacher. 2. ✦ **limit, restrict** ✧ **change, moderate, modify** Mom *qualified* her approval by saying that I needed Dad's permission also.

quality *noun* 1. ✦ **attribute, characteristic, feature, property, trait** The candidate has many of the *qualities* necessary to make a good mayor. 2. ✦ **merit, value, worth** ✧ **excellence, status** This advertisement claims that the new discount store in our neighborhood offers goods of high *quality* for low prices.

quantity *noun* ✦ **amount, measure, volume** ✧ **mass, number, portion** My family consumes a large *quantity* of milk every week.

quarrel *noun* ✦ **argument, dispute, fight, squabble** ✧ **disagreement** My brother and I got into a *quarrel* over whose turn it was to wash the dishes. —*verb* ✦ **argue, bicker, dispute, fight, squabble** Let's not *quarrel* over who gets to sit in the easy chair.

quarter *noun* ✦ **area, district, neighborhood, zone** ✧ **part, region** New Orleans is known for its picturesque French *Quarter*. ▶

quaver *verb* ✦ **quake, quiver, shake, tremble** ✧ **shudder, vibrate** My voice *quavered* from stage fright during my audition for the school play.

queen *noun* ✦ **monarch, ruler, sovereign,** ✧ **majesty** Victoria was the *queen* of Great Britain from 1837 to 1901.

queer *adjective* ✦ **odd, peculiar, strange, weird, unusual** The clown wore a *queer* hat that looked like a flower pot.

quench *verb* ✦ **douse, extinguish, put out** ✧ **kill, suppress** The campers *quenched* their fire with a bucketful of water.

query *noun* ✦ **inquiry, question** ✧ **concern, doubt, problem** The bank manager will help all customers who have *queries* about their accounts. —*verb* ✦ **ask, question, quiz** ✧ **examine, inquire, interrogate** When I was late getting home last night, my parents *queried* me about where I had been.

question *noun* 1. ✦ **query** ✧ **inquiry** The teacher asked if anybody had *questions* about the assignment. 2. ✦ **issue, matter, subject, topic** ✧ **point, problem** The meeting dealt with the *question* of whether a new wing for the library was needed. 3. ✦ **doubt, uncertainty** ✧ **confusion, controversy, suspicion** Without any *question*, you

are my best friend. —*verb* **1. ✦ examine, interrogate, query, quiz ✧ ask, inquire** The police *questioned* two witnesses to the robbery. **2. ✦ distrust, doubt, suspect ✧ challenge, disbelieve, dispute** I never *question* my coach's judgment.

quick *adjective* **✦ fast, hasty, rapid, speedy, swift ✧ prompt** Mom said that she had to make a *quick* stop at the bakery.

quicken *verb* **✦ accelerate, speed up, step up ✧ hasten, hurry** My pulse *quickened* when our team scored the run that tied the game.

quiet *adjective* **1. ✦ noiseless, silent, soundless ✧ hushed, still** Our new air conditioner is very *quiet*. **2. ✦ calm, peaceful, restful, serene, tranquil, undisturbed** Mother said that she was looking forward to a *quiet* evening at home. —*noun* **✦ hush, quietness, silence, stillness ✧ calm, tranquility** The hikers enjoyed the *quiet* that they found in the forest. —*verb* **✦ calm, settle ✧ shut up, silence, still** If we don't *quiet* down, we might wake the baby.

quit *verb* **1. ✦ cease, discontinue, give up, stop ✧ end, halt, terminate** My uncle *quit* smoking one year ago today. **2. ✦ abandon, depart, forsake, leave ✧ resign** Our neighbors decided to *quit* the city and move to the country.

Antonyms
quit *verb*
1. begin, commence, initiate, start
2. bide, remain, stay

quite *adverb* **1. ✦ completely, entirely, fully, totally, wholly ✧ thoroughly** These two puzzle pieces don't *quite* fit together. **2. ✦ extremely, really, very ✧ rather, somewhat** It's *quite* warm in this classroom.

quiver *verb* **✦ shiver, tremble ✧ quake, quaver, shake, vibrate** My dog *quivers* with excitement whenever she hears the word "walk."

quiz *noun* **✦ exam, examination, test** We will be having a spelling *quiz* today. —*verb* **✦ check, examine, question, test ✧ ask, inquire, interrogate** Our teacher will *quiz* us tomorrow to see if we know our multiplication tables.

quota *noun* **✦ allotment, allowance, portion, ration, share ✧ part** Mom allows me two cookies a day, and I've already consumed my *quota* for today.

quotation *noun* **✦ passage, quote, selection ✧ extract, reference** Cheryl's report on Louisa May Alcott included numerous *quotations* from her novels and short stories.

quote *verb* **✦ cite ✧ extract, mention, refer to** The candidate *quoted* the Declaration of Independence when he said "all men are created equal." —*noun* **✦ passage, quotation, selection ✧ extract, reference** The newspaper article included a *quote* from the President's speech.

R

race *noun* ✦ **competition, contest** ✧ **match, meet, relay** Joe won second place in the annual bike *race*. —*verb* ✦ **bolt, dart, dash, fly, hurry, run, rush, scramble, scurry, speed, sprint** Brenda *raced* to the car to make sure that she got the front seat.

rack *noun* ✦ **frame, stand** ✧ **counter, holder, shelf** Carmen hung up her jacket on the *rack* in the hall when she came home from school.

racket *noun* ✦ **din, clamor, commotion, noise, uproar** ✧ **clatter** The *racket* from the party could be heard a block away.

radiant *adjective* **1.** ✦ **bright, brilliant, gleaming, shining, sparkling** It was a *radiant* morning without a cloud in the sky. **2.** ✦ **beaming, blissful, gay, glowing, happy, joyful, merry** My parents look *radiant* in their wedding picture.

radical *adjective* ✦ **extreme, fanatical** ✧ **revolutionary, thorough, total** The *radical* environmentalist chained himself to a tree to save it from being cut down. —*noun* ✦ **extremist, fanatic, revolutionary** ✧ **rebel** The early American patriots were considered *radicals* by those who supported the British monarchy.

rag *noun* ✦ **scrap, shred, tatter** ✧ **piece** After a few weeks on the desert island the castaway's clothes were reduced to *rags*.

rage *noun* **1.** ✦ **frenzy, fury, tantrum** ✧ **anger, wrath** My little sister flew into a *rage* when she couldn't find her favorite toy. **2.** ✦ **craze, fad, fashion, style** ✧ **passion** Hula hoops were all the *rage* in the late 1950's. —*verb* ✦ **blow up, fume, rave, seethe** ✧ **scream, yell** An angry customer *raged* at the store manager about the bad service he'd gotten.

ragged *adjective* ✦ **frayed, raggedy, tattered, worn** ✧ **ripped, torn** The old blanket was *ragged* from much use.

raid *noun* ✦ **assault, attack** ✧ **invasion, offensive, strike** The police prepared for the *raid* by putting on bulletproof vests. —*verb* ✦ **assault, attack, invade, storm** ✧ **loot, pillage, plunder** Viking warriors *raided* many European coastal towns in the Middle Ages.

rain *verb* ✦ **pour, shower, sprinkle** ✧ **heap, lavish** The guests *rained* rose petals on the bride and groom.

raise *verb* **1.** ✦ **elevate, haul up, hoist, lift, pull up** ✧ **pick up** Guards *raised* the castle's drawbridge. **2.** ✦ **boost, improve, increase** ✧ **advance, upgrade** Wendy studied hard to *raise* her test scores. **3.** ✦ **bring up, rear** ✧ **breed, cultivate, grow** When I grow up I want to *raise* a large family. **4.** ✦ **accumulate, collect, gather, get** ✧ **mass** Our Girl Scout troop *raises* money by selling cookies.

> ### Word Groups
>
> A **rake** is a tool with a long handle and teeth that is used for gardening or yardwork. ◄ **Rake** is a very specific term with no true synonyms. Here are some related words to investigate in a dictionary:
>
> cultivator, hoe, scraper, shovel, spade, trowel

✦ **best choices**
✧ **other choices**

rally *verb* **1.** ✦ **assemble, collect, gather, marshal, muster** The commander *rallied* his troops around him. **2.** ✦ **get better, improve, recover, revive** ◇ **perk up** My friend *rallied* quickly after having her tonsils removed. —*noun* ✦ **assembly, gathering, get-together, meeting** ◇ **convention** There will be a pep *rally* before the big game.

ramble *verb* **1.** ✦ **amble, roam, saunter, stroll, wander** ◇ **trek** Max and his friends like to *ramble* around the neighborhood. **2.** ✦ **babble, chatter, rattle** ◇ **speak, talk** The old man *rambled* on about his days as a gold prospector. —*noun* ✦ **saunter, stroll, walk** ◇ **hike, jaunt, trek** My dog and I went for a *ramble* in the woods.

random *adjective* ✦ **chance, haphazard, unorganized, unplanned** ◇ **accidental** The books were in *random* order on the shelf.

range *noun* **1.** ✦ **array, assortment, selection, variety** ◇ **choice, collection** I considered a wide *range* of colors before choosing the one that I wanted. **2.** ✦ **bounds, domain, limit, reach, scope, stretch** Mom feels that her new job is well within her *range* of ability. **3.** ✦ **grassland** ◇ **pasture, plains, territory** This ranch contains over 1,100 acres of open *range*. **4.** ✦ **band, chain, line, row, series** ◇ **ridge, tier** You can see many farms and a *range* of hills from my bedroom window. ◀

rank¹ *noun* ✦ **grade, level, position, status** ◇ **class, degree** George Armstrong Custer attained the *rank* of general when he was only twenty-three years old. —*verb* **1.** ✦ **count, place, rate, stand** ◇ **judge** A new camera *ranks* high on my wish list. **2.** ✦ **arrange, array, categorize, organize**

◇ **align, marshal** The teams were *ranked* according to their win-loss records.

rank² *adjective* ✦ **bad, foul, offensive, pungent, rotten** Skunks have a *rank* smell. ▶

rap *verb* ✦ **bang, hit, knock, strike, tap, thump** We were interrupted by someone *rapping* on the window.

rapid *adjective* ✦ **fast, quick, speedy, swift** ◇ **brisk, fleet, hasty** The jet made a *rapid* climb at takeoff.

rapture *noun* ✦ **bliss, delight, elation, enchantment, happiness, joy** Melissa was filled with *rapture* when she finally got to ride a pony.

rare *adjective* ✦ **scarce, uncommon, unusual** ◇ **exceptional, infrequent, unique** Dwight's hobby is collecting *rare* coins.

rarely *adverb* ✦ **infrequently, not often, seldom** ◇ **hardly, little, occasionally** It *rarely* rains in the desert.

rascal *noun* ✦ **mischief-maker, prankster, rogue** ◇ **scoundrel, villain** In Native American myth, the coyote is usually an impish *rascal*.

rash *adjective* ✦ **brash, hasty, impetuous, impulsive, reckless** ◇ **foolhardy, foolish, thoughtless** It was *rash* of me to raise my hand when I didn't know the answer.

rate *noun* **1.** ✦ **pace, speed, velocity** ◇ **tempo, time** The roller coaster was going at a breakneck *rate* when it went into the last turn. **2.** ✦ **charge, cost, price** ◇ **amount, fee** What is the *rate* for a double room at this motel? —*verb* ✦ **appraise, evaluate, grade, judge, rank** ◇ **gauge** We were asked to *rate* our favorite TV shows for a class assignment.

ratify *verb* ✦ **adopt, affirm, approve, authorize, sanction** ◇ **confirm, pass** The ambassadors met to *ratify* the trade agreement.

ratio *noun* ✦ **distribution, proportion** ✧ **percentage** The *ratio* of boys to girls on our softball team is 2 to 1.

ration *noun* ✦ **allotment, allowance, provision, quota** ✧ **portion, share** I asked Mom for a cookie, but she said that I'd had my sugar *ration* for the day. —*verb* ✦ **allot, deal out, dispense, distribute** ✧ **disperse** We *rationed* our Halloween candy so that it would last the week.

rational *adjective* ✦ **logical, prudent, reasonable, sensible, sound** ✧ **sane** When you have had a sore throat for many days, the *rational* thing to do is to see a doctor.

rattle *verb* **1.** ✦ **clink, jangle, jingle, shake** ✧ **clang, clank, clatter** I *rattled* a tambourine to amuse my baby sister. **2.** ✦ **babble, chatter, jabber, run on** Dirk apologized for *rattling* on about his new bike. **3.** ✦ **confuse, disturb, fluster, muddle, upset** It *rattled* me when I missed my cue in the school play. —*noun* ✦ **banging, clang, clanging, clank, clatter, racket** When I heard the *rattle* of pots and pans, I knew that Dad must be fixing dinner.

raw *adjective* **1.** ✦ **uncooked** ✧ **fresh** Pies can be made from either cooked or *raw* fruits. **2.** ✦ **green, inexperienced, unschooled, unskilled, untrained** The coach took the *raw* players and made them into a good team. **3.** ✦ **biting, bitter, bleak, chilly, cold, harsh, numbing, severe, wet** The cold, *raw* weather made me glad to be inside by the fire.

reach *verb* **1.** ✦ **achieve, arrive at, attain, make, realize** Barry *reached* his goal of reading ten books over the summer. **2.** ✦ **extend, go, run, span, stretch** ✧ **spread** Interstate 40 *reaches* across the entire United States. **3.** ✦ **communicate with, contact, find, get hold of** Nancy tried to *reach* you to say that she would be late. —*noun* ✦ **grasp, range** ✧ **expanse, length, span, stretch, touch** The goat poked his head through the fence and ate all the grass within *reach*.

react *verb* ✦ **respond** ✧ **act, answer, reply** Emma *reacted* with a smile when she heard the good news.

reaction *noun* ✦ **reflex, response** ✧ **answer, effect, reply** The doctor tapped my knee to check for a *reaction*.

ready *adjective* ✦ **prepared, set** ✧ **arranged, fixed, organized** It's time to get *ready* for bed. —*verb* ✦ **equip, fix, prepare** ✧ **arrange, fit, outfit** We waited while the ground crew *readied* the plane for takeoff.

real *adjective* ✦ **actual, authentic, genuine, true** ✧ **legitimate** This necklace is made of *real* gold.

reality *noun* ✦ **actuality, fact** ✧ **certainty, event, existence, truth** Our family's dream of owning a house is about to become a *reality*.

realize *verb* **1.** ✦ **comprehend, grasp, perceive, recognize, understand** I suddenly *realized* that the surprise party was for me. **2.** ✦ **accomplish, achieve, attain, complete, gain, reach** Jack *realized* his goal of learning to program his computer by taking a class.

realm *noun* ✦ **country, domain, dominion** ✧ **empire, kingdom, territory** In the past month, the ruler has traveled to all parts of her *realm*.

reap *verb* ✦ **cut, garner, harvest** ✧ **gather, glean, obtain, pick** Before the invention of modern farm machinery, scythes were used to *reap* grain.

rear¹ *noun* ✦ **back, end, tail** My cousin and I sat in the *rear* of the roller coaster car. —*adjective* ✦ **back, rearmost** ✧ **aft, hind, last** My brother and I usually sit in the *rear* seat of Mom's van.

rear² *verb* **1.** ✦ **bring up, care for, raise** ✧ **foster, develop** Grandmother *reared* three kids on her own after my grandfather died. **2.** ✦ **raise, rise** ✧ **elevate, lift, loom, soar, tower** The bear *reared* up on his hind legs when he smelled something strange.

✦   best choices
✧   other choices

reason *noun* **1.** ✦ **basis, cause, excuse, explanation, justification** I hope Gregory has a good *reason* for missing band practice. **2.** ✦ **logic, rationality, reasoning** ✧ **comprehension, sense, wisdom** Scientists are conducting experiments to see whether animals possess powers of *reason.* —*verb* **1.** ✦ **calculate, figure out, solve** ✧ **reckon, understand** Juanita *reasoned out* the math problem without assistance. **2.** ✦ **debate with, discuss with, get through to, talk to** ✧ **argue, convince, persuade** It is difficult to *reason with* someone who is angry.

reasonable *adjective* **1.** ✦ **logical, practical, rational, sensible** ✧ **intelligent, sane, wise** When I asked for a fifty-dollar allowance, Dad told me to be *reasonable*. **2.** ✦ **acceptable, fair, just, moderate** ✧ **honest** This store has good quality clothing at *reasonable* prices.

rebel *verb* ✦ **revolt, rise up, strike** ✧ **challenge, defy, mutiny, resist** The workers *rebelled* against the low pay and unsafe working conditions. —*noun* ✦ **revolutionary** ✧ **freedom fighter, mutineer, striker** Guy Fawkes was an English *rebel* who tried to blow up Parliament in 1605.

rebellion *noun* ✦ **revolt, revolution** ✧ **mutiny, uprising** The American Revolution was a *rebellion* against British control.

recall *verb* ✦ **recollect, remember, think of** ✧ **retain** I can't *recall* the name of that restaurant that I like so much. —*noun* ✦ **memory, recollection, remembrance** Amanda has such good *recall* that she can tell you the names of all her kindergarten classmates.

recede *verb* ✦ **ebb, go out, retreat, subside** ✧ **diminish, dwindle, leave** You can find lots of interesting creatures in the pools that are left when the tide *recedes*.

receive *verb* ✦ **acquire, gain, get, obtain** ✧ **accept, gather, procure** My sister *received* her high school diploma last spring. ▶

recent *adjective* ✦ **brand-new, new** ✧ **contemporary, fresh, modern** I went to the bookstore to find a *recent* book by my favorite author.

reception *noun* **1.** ✦ **greeting, welcome** ✧ **acceptance, response, treatment** We received a warm *reception* from everyone at the family reunion. **2.** ✦ **function, gathering, party** ✧ **affair, social** A *reception* for the new club members will be held next Friday night.

recess *noun* ✦ **break, intermission, rest** ✧ **halt, pause, stop** We have a fifteen-minute *recess* in the morning and another in the afternoon.

recite *verb* ✦ **quote, repeat, speak** ✧ **deliver, narrate, report, tell** Brianna can *recite* her favorite poem from memory.

reckless ✦ **careless, heedless, irresponsible, rash, thoughtless** *Reckless* driving is the cause of many accidents.

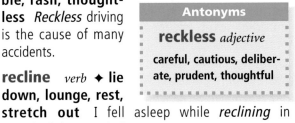

Antonyms
reckless *adjective*
careful, cautious, deliberate, prudent, thoughtful

recline *verb* ✦ **lie down, lounge, rest, stretch out** I fell asleep while *reclining* in Grandpa's lounge chair.

recognize *verb* **1.** ✦ **distinguish, identify, place, tell** ✧ **know, make out** Samantha can *recognize* many kinds of birds by their songs. **2.** ✦ **accept, acknowledge, admit** ✧ **endorse, support, sanction** I *recognize* the need to practice every day if I hope to be a good guitarist.

recollect *verb* ✦ **recall, remember, think of** ✧ **place, retain** I know Kristi told me her phone number, but I can't *recollect* it right now.

recommend *verb* ✦ **advise, advocate, counsel, endorse, promote, suggest** ✧ **back** My gym teacher *recommends* regular exercise.

recommendation *noun* ✦ **advice, counsel, endorsement, suggestion** ✧ **guidance** I am reading this book on my father's *recommendation*.

record *noun* **1.** ✦ **account, chronicle, journal, log, register** ✧ **diary, report** Liana is keeping a daily *record* of the weather as part of her science project. **2.** ✦ **mark, performance, time** ✧ **achievement** The swimmer is hoping to beat his own *record* for this event. —*verb* ✦ **chronicle, document, note, post, write down** ✧ **register** The secretary *records* everything that happens at our club meetings.

recover *verb* **1.** ✦ **get back, reclaim, regain, retrieve** ✧ **salvage** I was happy to *recover* the book that I thought was lost. **2.** ✦ **get better, improve, rally, revive** ✧ **heal, mend** You certainly *recovered* quickly from your cold.

recovery *noun* ✧ **convalescence, healing, improvement** We were pleased to hear that Mr. Bryant made a full *recovery* from his illness.

recreation *noun* ✦ **amusement, entertainment, fun, play, sport** ✧ **hobby, pastime** Mountain biking is my favorite form of *recreation*.

recruit *verb* ✦ **draft, enlist, enroll, muster** ✧ **induct, obtain** Our church is *recruiting* people to help with the craft fair.

reduce *verb* ✦ **curtail, cut, decrease, diminish, lessen** ✧ **restrict** Our team practices hard to *reduce* the number of mistakes we make.

reel *verb* ✦ **lurch, roll, spin, stagger, sway, weave, wobble** The world seemed to *reel* around me when I got off the carnival ride.

refer *verb* **1.** ✦ **direct, send, transfer, turn over** ✧ **introduce, recommend** The doctor *referred* her patient to a specialist. **2.** ✦ **consult, look at, turn to, use** ✧ **go, resort** We are not allowed to *refer to* the glossary in the back of the book while we take the test. **3.** ✦ **allude to, bring up, cite, mention, point out, touch on** My art teacher *referred to* an artist whose work is the subject of a special exhibit at the museum.

refine *verb* ✦ **process, purify** ✧ **clean, filter, strain** Sugar was first *refined* in 700 B.C.

reflect *verb* **1.** ✦ **cast back, give back, return, send back** ✧ **mirror** The windowpane *reflected* the light from my candle. **2.** ✦ **consider, contemplate, deliberate, ponder, think** My parents encourage me to stop and *reflect* before I make an important decision.

reform *verb* ✦ **alter, amend, change, correct, improve, modify, remedy, revise** Both of the candidates claim that the federal tax system needs to be *reformed*. —*noun* ✦ **change, correction, improvement, progress, revision** The 1960's were a decade of significant social *reform* in the United States.

refresh *verb* ✦ **freshen, perk (up), renew, revive** ✧ **restore, stimulate** The bicyclists took a break to *refresh* themselves.

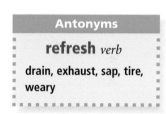

Antonyms

refresh *verb*

drain, exhaust, sap, tire, weary

refreshments *noun* ✦ **snacks** ✧ **drink, food, nourishment** We bought *refreshments* before the movie.

refrigerate *verb* ✦ **chill, cool** ✧ **ice, freeze** Mayonnaise needs to be *refrigerated* after opening to keep it from spoiling.

refuge *noun* ✦ **preserve, sanctuary** ✧ **asylum, haven, retreat, shelter** Our class took a tour of a wildlife *refuge*.

refund *verb* ✦ **give back, pay back, repay, return** ✧ **restore** The store will *refund* your money if you are not satisfied.

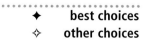

✦ **best choices**
✧ **other choices**

refuse¹ *verb* ✦ **decline, reject, spurn, turn down** ✧ **balk, resist** Rashid *refused* any help in finishing the crossword puzzle.

refuse² *noun* ✦ **garbage, rubbish, trash, waste** ✧ **litter** The *refuse* from cleaning up our yard filled several trash cans.

regard *verb* ✦ **consider, observe, scrutinize, view** ✧ **scan, watch** Morgan *regarded* the painting for several minutes before making any comments. —*noun* **1.** ✦ **admiration, appreciation, esteem, respect** ✧ **honor** We have great *regard* for the firefighters who saved our home from burning down. **2.** ✦ **attention, care, consideration, contemplation, notice** Please give more *regard* to the advice that I give you.

region *noun* ✦ **area, district, territory, tract, zone** ✧ **section** Tropical *regions* receive a lot of rainfall.

register *noun* ✦ **list, log, record, roll** The school has a *register* that contains the names and addresses of all its students. —*verb* ✦ **check in, enroll, sign up** ✧ **enlist, schedule** My brother has *registered* to take a class next fall at the community college.

regret *verb* ✦ **be sorry, feel sorry** ✧ **grieve, mourn** We *regret* that we will not be able to attend this year's New Year's Eve celebration. —*noun* ✦ **disappointment, discontent, dissatisfaction, sorrow** It was not easy at first for Gerry to switch to a different summer camp, but now he has no *regrets*.

regular *adjective* ✦ **common, customary, normal, routine, standard, usual** Bill's *regular* route to school is through the park. ▼

regulate *verb* ✦ **control, direct, govern, supervise** ✧ **adjust, modify, tune** The veterinarian told me to *regulate* my cat's diet more strictly.

rehearse *verb* ✦ **drill, practice, prepare** ✧ **review, study** The cast of the school play got together to *rehearse* their lines.

reign *noun* ✦ **dominion, regime, rule, sovereignty** ✧ **administration, monarchy** The British Empire reached its peak during the *reign* of Queen Victoria. —*verb* ✦ **govern, rule** ✧ **command, lead** Queen Victoria *reigned* from 1837 to 1901.

reinforce *verb* ✦ **bolster, brace, support, strengthen** ✧ **tighten, toughen** The beavers added twigs and branches to *reinforce* their dam. ▼

reject *verb* ✦ **deny, dismiss, refuse, spurn, turn down, veto** The city council *rejected* the proposal to build a new courthouse.

rejoice *verb* ✦ **be happy, celebrate, exult, glory** ✧ **delight** The whole family *rejoiced* when my cousin recovered from her serious illness.

relate *verb* **1.** ✦ **describe, narrate, recount, tell** ✧ **communicate, recite** The author's latest book *relates* his experiences in Africa. **2.** ✦ **apply to, bear on, concern, pertain to, refer to** Ms. Parrish showed a video that *relates* to the subject we've been studying.

relation *noun* **1.** ✦ **connection, link, relationship, similarity** ✧ **association, tie** Many movies about the Old West have almost no *relation* to the way things really were. **2. ✦ family member, relative ✧ in-law, kin, kinfolk** Mark met many distant *relations* for the first time at his grandmother's birthday party.

relax *verb* **✦ calm down, unwind ✧ ease, loosen, rest, slacken** Dad likes to *relax* after work by taking a walk in the park.

release *verb* **1. ✦ free, let go, liberate, set loose ✧ discharge** The fish hatchery will *release* the baby salmon as soon as they are big enough. **2. ✦ distribute, issue, publish, put out ✧ offer, present** The publisher plans to *release* several new books this spring.

relent *verb* **✦ give in, submit, yield ✧ soften, weaken** My parents finally *relented* and allowed me to spend the night at my friend's house.

relevant *adjective* **✦ applicable, connected, pertinent, related ✧ significant** I looked in the encyclopedia for information *relevant* to my report.

reliable *adjective* **✦ dependable, responsible, sound, trustworthy ✧ honest** I need a *reliable* person to help me organize the talent show.

relic *noun* **✦ keepsake, remembrance, souvenir ✧ heirloom** My grandfather collects medals and other *relics* from World War II.

relief *noun* **1. ✦ comfort, ease, release ✧ cure, remedy** This medicine provides immediate *relief* for an upset stomach. **2. ✦ aid, assistance, help, support ✧ rescue** The Red Cross sent *relief* to the hurricane victims.

relieve *verb* **1. ✦ aid, comfort, ease, help, lighten ✧ lessen, reduce** These lozenges should *relieve* your sore throat. **2. ✦ replace, take over for ✧ discharge, free, release** The sentry had to stay on duty until someone could *relieve* him.

religion *noun* **✦ belief, creed, faith ✧ devotion, worship** Christianity, Islam, and Judaism are three of the world's major *religions*.

religious *adjective* **✦ devout, pious, spiritual ✧ divine, holy** The *religious* woman prays several times every day.

reluctant *adjective* **✦ hesitant, resistant, unwilling ✧ averse, opposed, wary** The horse was *reluctant* to jump the wide ditch.

rely *verb* **✦ count on, depend on, trust ✧ believe, expect** I'm *relying on* you to bring the buns and potato chips to our cookout.

remain *verb* **✦ continue, last, linger, persist, stay ✧ wait** A beautiful pink glow *remained* in the sky long after sunset.

remark *noun* **✦ comment, observation, statement ✧ expression, mention** Stacey cheered me up with her *remark* about the coming weekend. —*verb* **✦ comment on, mention, note, observe ✧ express, say** Many people have *remarked on* how tall I am getting to be.

remarkable *adjective* **✦ astonishing, exceptional, extraordinary, impressive, outstanding** Modern computers can process information at *remarkable* speeds.

remedy *noun* **✦ cure, therapy, treatment ✧ antidote, medicine** The best *remedy* for a cold is to drink lots of fluids and get plenty of rest.

remember *verb* **✦ recall, recollect ✧ retain, think of** Do you *remember* who played the vampire in that movie?

remind *verb* **✦ notify, prompt ✧ admonish, caution, suggest, warn** Please *remind* me when it's time to leave for my music lesson.

remote *adjective* **1. ✦ distant, faraway, far-off, isolated, removed, secluded** The explorers were shipwrecked on a *remote* island. **2. ✦ faint, poor, slight, slim, small, unlikely** There is only a *remote* possibility that we will get another dog.

Antonyms
remote *adjective*
1. adjacent, close, nearby, neighboring

✦ **best choices**
✧ **other choices**

removal *noun* ◆ **elimination, riddance, withdrawal** ◇ **evacuation, relocation, transfer** The city made arrangements for the *removal* of debris from the empty lot.

remove *verb* **1.** ◆ **take away, withdraw** ◇ **move, shift, transfer** The landscapers *removed* the old shrubs and replaced them with rose bushes. **2.** ◆ **eliminate, extract, get rid of, take away** ◇ **clean, erase** You can *remove* some stains by soaking them with vinegar or soda water.

renew *verb* **1.** ◆ **refresh, renovate, restore** The finish on our wood floors needs to be *renewed*. **2.** ◆ **continue, extend** ◇ **begin again, restart, resume, revive** I forgot to *renew* my library card last month.

rent *noun* ◆ **payment** ◇ **cost, dues, fee, price** My parents are pleased with our new apartment because the monthly *rent* is quite reasonable. —*verb* ◆ **charter, hire** ◇ **contract, lease** My family *rented* a sailboat for the weekend.

repair *verb* ◆ **fix, mend, rebuild, restore** ◇ **overhaul, renovate, patch** I used glue to *repair* my model airplane's broken wing. —*noun* ◆ **fixing, mending, servicing** ◇ **overhaul, renovation** Our washing machine is in need of *repair*.

repeal *verb* ◆ **cancel, revoke** ◇ **abolish, reverse, withdraw** The state legislature voted to *repeal* the unpopular law.

repeat *verb* ◆ **restate, retell, say again** ◇ **recite, recount** Tonya *repeated* her instructions to make sure that everyone understood them.

repel *verb* **1.** ◆ **chase away, drive away, hold off, keep off** ◇ **resist, scatter** A porcupine's quills help it to *repel* attackers. **2.** ◆ **disgust, irritate, offend, revolt, sicken** The last scene in that movie really *repelled* me.

replace *verb* ◆ **change, substitute** ◇ **alter, restore, return** I need to *replace* the batteries in my flashlight.

reply *verb* ◆ **answer, respond to** ◇ **acknowledge, react, return** Everyone who *replies to* the survey will receive a free gift. —*noun* ◆ **answer, response** ◇ **acknowledgment, reaction** I mailed my friend a party invitation last week, and I received her *reply* today.

report *noun* ◆ **account, article, description, story** ◇ **narrative, summary** Jorge wrote a *report* for the school newspaper about visiting friends in Costa Rica. —*verb* **1.** ◆ **describe, disclose, narrate, relate, state, tell** The army scout returned to headquarters to *report* what he had seen. **2.** ◆ **check in at, go to, proceed to** ◇ **appear, arrive, reach** Please *report to* the principal's office for your classroom assignment.

represent *verb* **1.** ◆ **signify, stand for, symbolize** ◇ **characterize, illustrate, portray** The stars on the American flag *represent* the fifty states. **2.** ◆ **act for, serve, speak for** Mrs. Wong *represents* our district in the state legislature.

representative *noun* ◆ **delegate** ◇ **ambassador, deputy, emissary** In 1917, Jeannette Rankin became the first woman to be elected as a *representative* to the U.S. Congress. —*adjective* **1.** ◆ **democratic, elected, republican** The United States has a *representative* form of government. **2.** ◆ **characteristic, descriptive, illustrative, typical** This portrait is *representative* of the artist's early style. ▼

reputation *noun* ✦ **name** ◇ **position, respect, standing, stature, status** This restaurant has a good *reputation* because the food is always excellent.

request *verb* ✦ **ask for, seek** ◇ **call for, entreat, petition** I *requested* permission to leave school early because I had a doctor's appointment. —*noun* ✦ **appeal, call, plea** ◇ **demand, petition, summons** The relief agency issued an urgent *request* for food and warm clothing to give to victims of the flood.

require *verb* ✦ **command, compel, direct, oblige, order** ◇ **demand, expect** A new law *requires* bicyclists under the age of eighteen to wear a helmet.

rescue *verb* ✦ **free, help, release, save** ◇ **deliver, recover** Mom *rescued* the snake that was trapped in the garden netting. —*noun* ✦ **aid, assistance, help, relief** ◇ **recovery, salvation** My brother came to my *rescue* when I got my hand stuck in a pickle jar.

research *noun* ◇ **analysis, experimentation, inquiry, investigation, study** Kelsey went to the library to do the *research* for her history report. —*verb* ✦ **examine, explore, investigate, study** ◇ **analyze** I am *researching* the sources of air pollution for my science project.

resemblance *noun* ✦ **correspondence, likeness, similarity** ◇ **closeness, comparison, sameness** Do you see any physical *resemblance* between my cousin and me?

resentment *noun* ✦ **anger, animosity, annoyance, bitterness, indignation** I felt a lot of *resentment* when Zoe took the credit for my idea about starting a movie club.

reservation *noun* **1.** ✦ **booking, engagement** ◇ **appointment, arrangement** We have a *reservation* for two nights at the Grand Hotel. **2.** ✦ **doubt, hesitancy, misgiving, reluctance, uncertainty** My older sister is a responsible person, and my parents have no *reservations* about leaving her in charge while they're out.

reserve *verb* **1.** ✦ **conserve, hold back, keep, preserve, retain, save** The runner *reserved* some of her strength for the final lap. **2.** ✦ **book, engage** ◇ **register, retain, schedule** Dad *reserved* a train compartment for our trip. —*noun* **1.** ✦ **stock, stockpile, store, supply** ◇ **hoard, inventory** The explorers kept an emergency *reserve* of food and water at their base camp. **2.** ✦ **aloofness, coolness, restraint, self-control** The man's apparent *reserve* was really shyness.

reside *verb* ✦ **abide, dwell, live** ◇ **inhabit, stay** My uncle's family *resides* in a small town in Nebraska.

residence *noun* ✦ **abode, dwelling, habitation, home, house** ◇ **household** The President's official *residence* is the White House in Washington, D.C.

resident *noun* ✦ **citizen, dweller, householder, inhabitant, native** My grandmother is a long-time *resident* of Milwaukee.

resign *verb* ✦ **leave office, quit** ◇ **abdicate, forsake, give up** The mayor had to *resign* for reasons of health.

resist *verb* ✦ **refuse, reject, turn down** ◇ **oppose, withstand** I can't *resist* Kevin's offer of half-price tickets to the championship basketball game.

resistance *noun* ✦ **opposition, protest, struggle** ◇ **defiance, rebellion** Our dog puts up a lot of *resistance* when we try to bathe him.

resolve *verb* **1.** ✦ **decide, determine, plan** ◇ **mean, propose** Jonathan *resolved* to study harder for his next test. **2.** ✦ **clear up, fix, settle, solve** ◇ **answer** Our family holds regular meetings to *resolve* our problems.

resort *verb* ✦ **employ, refer to, turn to, use** ◇ **apply, go** I thought I knew how to load my new

✦ **best choices**
◇ **other choices**

computer game, but in the end I had to *resort to* the instruction manual. —*noun* **1.** ✦ **tourist spot, vacation place** ✧ **hideaway, retreat** Cancún, Mexico, is a popular *resort*. **2.** ✦ **alternative, choice, option, possibility** ✧ **hope, resource** If we can't get plane or train tickets, we can take the bus as a last *resort*.

resource *noun* **1.** ✦ **aid, help, source** ✧ **reserve, storehouse, support** A thesaurus is an excellent *resource* for anyone who wants to expand his or her vocabulary. **2.** ✦ **asset, capital, cash, funds, money, wealth** Dad said that we don't have the *resources* to buy a new house at this time.

respect *noun* ✦ **admiration, esteem, praise, regard** ✧ **approval, honor** I have great *respect* for people who spend their lives helping others. —*verb* ✦ **esteem, honor, regard, value** ✧ **admire, praise** My parents taught me to *respect* my elders.

respectful *adjective* ✦ **civil, considerate, courteous, mannerly, polite** ✧ **attentive, gallant, thoughtful** Our team maintained a *respectful* silence during the singing of the national anthem before the game.

respond *verb* ✦ **answer, reply** ✧ **acknowledge, act, react, return** I sent a letter to my penpal in Sweden, but she hasn't *responded* yet.

response *noun* ✦ **acknowledgment, answer, reaction** ✧ **action, reply** I knocked on the door, but got no *response*.

responsibility *noun* ✦ **charge, chore, duty, function, job, obligation, task** It is my *responsibility* to load the dishwasher this week.

responsible *adjective* ✦ **dependable, reliable, trustworthy** ✧ **accountable, capable, solid** The sixth grade needs a *responsible* person to be class treasurer.

rest¹ *noun* **1.** ✦ **break, halt, pause, time-out** ✧ **intermission, recess** Our family sat on the couch and took a *rest* from spring cleaning. **2.** ✦ **relaxation, sleep, slumber** ✧ **calm, peace, quiet** You should get plenty of *rest* before the game tomorrow. —*verb* **1.** ✦ **lie down, relax, take a break** ✧ **doze, nap, sleep** After lunch, I always *rest* for a little while before I go swimming. **2.** ✦ **lay, lean, place, position, prop, set** The worker *rested* his shovel against a tree.

rest² *noun* ✦ **balance, excess, remainder, surplus** ✧ **leftovers, remains** Take as much construction paper as you need, and put the *rest* back in the cabinet.

restless *adjective* ✦ **agitated, fidgety, jumpy, nervous, uneasy** The *restless* tiger paced back and forth in its cage.

restore *verb* ✦ **recondition, reestablish, renew, renovate, revive** ✧ **return** This wax should help to *restore* the table's original finish.

restrain *verb* ✦ **check, control, curb, hold, hold back, stop** I have to use a leash to *restrain* my dog from jumping up on people.

restrict *verb* ✦ **confine, limit** ✧ **bound, check, moderate** My parents decided to *restrict* our television time to six hours a week.

restriction *noun* ✦ **bound, check, condition, limit, limitation** ✧ **regulation** There are *restrictions* on how quickly cars can drive in the town center. ▶

result *noun* ✦ **consequence, effect, outcome, product** ✧ **end** One *result* of the election is that our city now has a new mayor. —*verb* ✦ **arise, develop, emerge, flow, follow, issue** ✧ **happen** Jerome's good grades *resulted* from his improved study habits.

resume *verb* ✦ **begin again, continue, proceed, reopen, restart** The meeting will *resume* after a one-hour lunch break.

retain *verb* ✦ **hold, keep, maintain, preserve, save** A thick layer of blubber helps whales *retain* heat even in arctic waters.

retire *verb* ✦ **depart from, give up, leave** ✧ **exit, resign, withdraw** Next month, Grandfather is going to *retire from* his job as a civil engineer.

retreat *verb* ✦ **draw back, fall back, withdraw** ✧ **depart, escape, flee** The army was forced to *retreat* when the enemy attacked. —*noun* 1. ✦ **fallback, withdrawal** ✧ **departure, escape, flight** The soldiers made an orderly *retreat*. 2. ✦ **asylum, haven, refuge, sanctuary, shelter** The doctor's private office is her *retreat* from the pressures of her job.

retrieve *verb* ✦ **fetch, get back, reclaim, recover, regain** Dad *retrieved* his hat after the wind blew it away.

return *verb* 1. ✦ **come back, go back** ✧ **reappear, revisit** The Scouts *returned* to camp after their hike. 2. ✦ **give back, hand back** ✧ **replace, restore** I will *return* your book as soon as I finish reading it. —*noun* 1. ✦ **homecoming, reappearance** ✧ **arrival** Our cat's sudden *return* delighted me because I had thought that he was lost. 2. ✦ **earnings, gain, profit, yield** ✧ **income, revenue** Mom was pleased with the *return* on her investment.

reveal *verb* ✦ **disclose, expose, give away, tell** ✧ **uncover** Please don't *reveal* how the movie ends.

reverse *adjective* ✦ **back, opposite, other** ✧ **counter, contrasting** The song that I would like to hear is on the *reverse* side of this tape. —*noun* ✦ **contrary, opposite** ✧ **contrast** I thought that you were older than I am, but it turns out that the *reverse* is true. —*verb* ✦ **counter, override,** overturn, turn around ✧ **alter, repeal** In this country, a higher court has the power to *reverse* a lower court's ruling.

review *verb* 1. ✦ **go over, reconsider, reexamine** ✧ **examine, study** We start each lesson by *reviewing* what we learned the day before. 2. ✦ **criticize, evaluate, judge** ✧ **assess, discuss** Our writing assignment is to *review* a book for the class newspaper. —*noun* 1. ✦ **drill, study** ✧ **examination, investigation** We had an oral *review* the day before we took the test. 2. ✦ **criticism, evaluation, judgment, notice** ✧ **assessment** The movie received favorable *reviews* from most of the critics I've read.

revise *verb* ✦ **alter, amend, change, modify, reconsider** The weather forced us to *revise* our vacation plans.

revive *verb* ✦ **refresh, renew, restore** ✧ **bring around** I was very tired, but a short nap *revived* me.

revoke *verb* ✦ **cancel, recall, repeal, withdraw** ✧ **abolish** If a driver has too many traffic tickets, his or her license can be *revoked*.

revolt *verb* 1. ✦ **rebel, rise up** ✧ **mutiny, protest, riot** In 1789, the people of France *revolted* against the rich noblemen who ruled the country. 2. ✦ **disgust, horrify, offend, repel, sicken** ✧ **shock** Gory movies *revolt* me. —*noun* ✦ **rebellion, revolution, uprising** ✧ **mutiny, protest, riot** Patrick Henry was one of the leaders of the American *revolt* against Great Britain.

revolution *noun* 1. ✦ **rebellion, revolt, uprising** ✧ **overthrow, upheaval** The *revolution* in Russia in 1917 created the world's first communist state. 2. ✦ **circle, cycle, rotation, turn** ✧ **spin** The second hand of my stopwatch makes one full *revolution* every thirty seconds. ▶

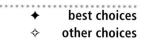

✦   **best choices**
✧   **other choices**

revolve *verb* ✦ circle, orbit ✧ reel, rotate, spin, wheel Earth *revolves around* the sun at a rate of 18.5 miles per second.

reward *noun* ✦ award, bounty, compensation, payment ✧ prize We offered a *reward* for the return of our lost cat. —*verb* ✦ compensate, pay back, repay ✧ acknowledge, award The coach *rewarded* me for my hard work by making me captain of the team.

rhythm *noun* ✦ beat, pulse, throb ✧ measure, meter, tempo The doctor listened to the *rhythm* of my heartbeat.

rich *adjective* 1. ✦ prosperous, wealthy, well-off, well-to-do Whoever owns that yacht must be very *rich*. 2. ✦ bountiful, fertile, fruitful, productive, prolific ✧ lush The Midwest region of the United States is known for its *rich* farmland. 3. ✦ creamy, fattening, heavy ✧ sweet Cheesecake is a *rich* dessert.

rid *verb* ✦ clear, free, relieve ✧ eliminate, remove Dad hired an exterminator to *rid* our house of termites.

riddle *noun* ✦ brainteaser, problem, puzzle ✧ question, mystery In many myths, the hero has to solve a *riddle* before continuing on a journey.

ride *verb* ✦ control, drive, handle ✧ take, travel in I'm learning how to *ride* a dirt bike from my friend Zack. —*noun* ✦ drive, jaunt, spin ✧ excursion, journey, trip Mom suggested that we go for a *ride* in the country.

ridicule *noun* ✦ mockery, sarcasm, scorn, sneering, teasing The inventor's idea was met with *ridicule* until he proved that it actually worked. —*verb* ✦ insult, jeer, laugh at, mock, sneer, taunt ✧ tease The politician *ridiculed* his opponent at a press conference.

ridiculous *adjective* ✦ absurd, comical, foolish, funny, laughable, silly Mick can always make me giggle with the *ridiculous* faces he makes. ▶

right *noun* 1. ✦ goodness, justice, morality, virtue ✧ honor, propriety Parents are responsible for teaching their children the difference between *right* and wrong. 2. ✦ freedom, liberty, privilege ✧ license, permission When a suspect is arrested, he or she has the *right* to remain silent. —*adjective* 1. ✦ accurate, correct ✧ exact, perfect, true, valid All of my answers on the test were *right*. 2. ✦ fair, honorable, just, noble, proper You did the *right* thing in returning the wallet.

rigid *adjective* ✦ firm, hard, immovable, inflexible, solid, stiff The frozen fish were very *rigid*.

Antonyms
rigid *adjective*
elastic, flexible, malleable, pliable, supple

rim *noun* ✦ brim, brink, edge, lip ✧ border, ledge We stood on the *rim* of Bryce Canyon and admired the magnificent view.

ring¹ *noun* ✦ circle ✧ coil, hoop, loop, wheel The Scouts sat in a *ring* around their campfire. —*verb* ✦ circle, enclose, surround ✧ encompass, hem, loop We *ringed* the fish pond with stones.

ring² *verb* ✦ sound ✧ chime, jingle, peal, toll, trill Did you hear the phone *ring*? —*noun* ✦ chime, clang, peal, ringing, sound, toll ✧ tinkle, trill Every Sunday morning I hear the *ring* of church bells.

riot *noun* ✦ disorder, disturbance, turmoil, unrest ✧ protest, uprising Many windows were broken during the *riot*.

rip *verb* ✦ slit, split, tear ✧ cut, run, shred, slash Larry *ripped* his good pants getting out of the car. —*noun* ✦ slit, split, tear ✧ cut, gash, hole, run The *rip* in my shirt is too big to mend.

ripe *adjective* ✦ **developed, full-grown, mature, ready** ✧ **plump** Pick only the *ripe* strawberries. ▼

rise *verb* **1.** ✦ **arise, ascend, climb, go up** ✧ **lift, soar** The sun *rises* in the east and sets in the west. **2.** ✦ **expand, grow, increase, swell** ✧ **strengthen, wax** It rained so heavily that the *river* rose and overflowed its banks. —*noun* ✦ **expansion, gain, increase, jump, surge** ✧ **ascent, climb** There was a *rise* in donations to the charity after their appeal on TV.

risk *noun* ✦ **chance, gamble** ✧ **danger, hazard, jeopardy, peril** The photographer took a *risk* by standing in an open field during the lightning storm. —*verb* ✦ **endanger, imperil, jeopardize** ✧ **bet, chance, gamble, hazard** The doctors *risked* their own health trying to discover the cause of the new disease.

rival *noun* ✦ **adversary, challenger, competitor, opponent** ✧ **enemy, foe** The two friends are *rivals* for the lead in the class play. —*adjective* ✦ **competing, contending, opposing** ✧ **conflicting** My cousin and I play on *rival* soccer teams. —*verb* ✦ **challenge, equal, match** ✧ **approach, compete with, meet, oppose** She *rivals* you in both scholastic and musical ability.

road *noun* ✦ **route, street** ✧ **avenue, boulevard, drive, roadway, freeway, highway, lane, thoroughfare, way** Our town is building a *road* that will lead directly from the shopping mall to the highway.

roam *verb* ✦ **drift, meander, ramble, range, stray, wander** The sheep *roamed* over a wide area of the mountainside.

roar *noun* ✧ **bawl, bay, bellow, cry, growl, howl** The gazelles stampeded when they heard the lion's *roar*. —*verb* ✦ **bawl, bellow, howl, scream, shriek** ✧ **call, cry** We *roared* with laughter during the funny play.

rob *verb* ✦ **burglarize, hold up, stick up** ✧ **pilfer, steal** The police caught the people who *robbed* a convenience store last week.

robust *adjective* ✦ **hale, healthy, hearty, lusty, strong, sturdy, vigorous** I feel much more *robust* in the summer than I do in wintertime.

rock¹ *noun* ✦ **stone** ✧ **boulder, cobblestone, pebble** The cabin's fireplace is made out of big, flat *rocks*.

rock² *verb* ✦ **heave, pitch, roll, sway, toss** ✧ **jar, shake** I almost fell in the lake when a wave *rocked* our boat.

Word Groups

A **rodent** is a mammal with large front teeth for gnawing or nibbling. **Rodent** is a very specific scientific term with no true synonyms. Here are some kinds of rodents to investigate in a dictionary:

beaver, gerbil, hamster, lemming, mouse, muskrat, porcupine, prairie dog, rat, squirrel

role *noun* ✦ **character, part** ✧ **function, place, portrayal** What *role* did you try out for in the school play?

roll *verb* **1.** ✦ **pitch, throw, toss** ✧ **revolve, rotate, tumble** Hannah *rolled* the dice and took her turn in the game. **2.** ✦ **twist, wind, wrap** ✧ **coil, curl, turn** I *rolled* the leftover wrapping paper back onto the tube. —*noun* **1.** ✦ **attendance** ✧ **lineup, list, register, schedule** The coach calls *roll* at the beginning of every practice. **2.** ✧ **biscuit, bun, croissant, pastry** We got

✦ **best choices**
✧ **other choices**

fresh *rolls* at the bakery. **3.** ◆ **boom, clap, peal, rumble** There was a drum *roll* before the announcement of the winner.

romance *noun* ◆ **adventure, excitement, mystery** ◇ **passion** Some people think that jet planes and superhighways have taken the *romance* out of travel.

room *noun* **1.** ◇ **apartment, chamber, compartment, lodging** The palace has over one hundred *rooms*. **2.** ◆ **area, space** ◇ **extent** There's no *room* to put anything more on my shelves.

root *noun* ◆ **beginning, origin, source** ◇ **base, bottom, foundation** We're trying to get to the *root* of the problem.

rot *verb* ◆ **break down, decay, decompose, go bad, spoil** The overripe bananas in the fruit basket are beginning to *rot*. —*noun* ◆ **decay, decomposition, rottenness** ◇ **blight, fungus, mildew, mold** The timbers in the old house had a lot of *rot* in them.

rotate *verb* ◆ **revolve, spin, turn, twirl, whirl** ◇ **swivel** *Rotate* this knob to focus the binoculars. ▶

rough *adjective*
1. ◆ **coarse, grainy, gritty, scratchy** ◇ **jagged, uneven** Nail files have a *rough* surface.
2. ◆ **crude, incomplete, preliminary, unfinished** ◇ **basic** The artist made a *rough* sketch before she started painting. **3.** ◆ **approximate, general, inexact, vague** ◇ **quick, hasty** We made a *rough* estimate of the amount of lumber we would need to build a fence around the entire yard. **4.** ◆ **demanding, difficult, hard, tough, unpleasant** Mom was tired because she had a *rough* day at work.

round *adjective* **1.** ◆ **circular** ◇ **elliptical, oval, spherical** The full moon looks perfectly *round* in the sky. **2.** ◆ **curved, rounded** ◇ **arched, bowed** My school desk has *round* corners. —*noun* **1.** ◆ **beat, circuit, route, tour** ◇ **watch** The museum guard makes an hourly *round* of the building. **2.** ◆ **sequence, series, string** ◇ **chain, cycle** There was a *round* of parties for the newly engaged couple. —*verb* ◆ **go around, turn** ◇ **circle** The cyclists were going at top speed when they *rounded* the bend.

rout *noun* ◆ **defeat, drubbing, thrashing** ◇ **disaster, overthrow, upset** The game ended in a complete *rout* with the home team winning by seven touchdowns. —*verb* ◆ **beat, conquer, defeat, overcome, overwhelm, triumph over** The guerrilla forces *routed* the government troops.

route *noun* ◆ **course, way** ◇ **lane, path, road, track** We planned the *route* for our trip. —*verb* ◆ **direct, dispatch, forward, send, ship** ◇ **convey** My overseas package was *routed* through San Francisco.

routine *noun* ◆ **custom, habit, pattern, procedure** ◇ **practice** Making my bed is the first step of my morning *routine*. —*adjective* ◆ **customary, familiar, normal, regular, standard, usual** We followed the *routine* procedure during the fire drill.

row *noun* ◆ **file, line, sequence, series, string** ◇ **column** When we first moved here, my parents planted a *row* of lilac bushes along the back of our property.

royal *adjective* **1.** ◇ **aristocratic, highborn, imperial, noble, regal** The *royal* family appeared on the palace balcony. **2.** ◆ **grand, magnificent, majestic, splendid, stately** The troops received a *royal* sendoff.

rub *verb* ◆ **knead, massage, stroke** ◇ **scour, scrub** *Rubbing* my temples helps me to relax. —*noun* ◆ **kneading, massage, rubdown** ◇ **scouring, scrubbing** Will you give me a back *rub*, please?

rubbish *noun* ✦ **garbage, junk, refuse, trash, waste** ✧ **litter** We threw away a lot of *rubbish* when we cleaned out the garage.

rude *adjective* **1.** ✦ **discourteous, disrespectful, impolite, inconsiderate** Please forgive me, I didn't mean to be *rude*. **2.** ✦ **coarse, crude, makeshift, primitive, rough, simple** The sheepherder built a *rude* shelter out of stones and brush.

ruffle *verb* ✦ **disorder, disturb, jumble, mess up, tangle, upset** Put on this scarf so the wind won't *ruffle* your hair.

rugged *adjective* ✦ **durable, solid, sturdy, tough** ✧ **hard, rough** I have a pair of *rugged* boots to wear when it snows. ▼

ruin *noun* **1.** ✦ **collapse, destruction, downfall** ✧ **havoc, wreck** The company is facing financial *ruin*. **2.** ✦ **debris, rubble, wreckage** ✧ **relics, remains** We explored the *ruins* of an old silver mine. —*verb* ✦ **demolish, destroy, spoil, wreck** ✧ **mangle, smash** The puppy *ruined* my leather belt by chewing on it.

rule *noun* **1.** ✦ **guideline, regulation** ✧ **law, order, principle** The lifeguard at the swimming pool enforces the safety *rules*. **2.** ✦ **dominion, reign** ✧ **administration, government** Robin Hood is said to have lived during the *rule* of King Richard the Lion-Hearted. —*verb* **1.** ✦ **govern, rein** ✧ **administer, command, control, lead** Empress Catherine the Great *ruled* Russia from 1762 until 1796. ✦ **decide, decree, determine, judge**

✧ **conclude, resolve** The referee *ruled* that the player had committed a foul.

rumble *verb* ✦ **growl** ✧ **boom, resound, roar, roll, thunder** My stomach *rumbled* because I was hungry. —*noun* ✦ **boom, roar, roll, thunder** ✧ **growl** We knew a storm was coming because we could hear the *rumble* of distant thunder.

rumor *noun* ✦ **gossip, hearsay, news, talk** ✧ **report, story** The *rumor* is that you will get the lead in the musical. —*verb* ✦ **gossip, say, suggest** ✧ **talk, tattle, whisper** It is *rumored* that there will be a field trip on Friday.

run *verb* **1.** ✦ **dash, hasten, hurry, hustle, race, rush, scurry** We must *run* to the post office before it closes. **2.** ✦ **campaign** ✧ **compete, contend, contest** The senator is going to *run* for office again. **3.** ✦ **drive, function, go, operate, perform, work** A car *runs* better after a tune-up. **4.** ✦ **direct, manage, supervise** ✧ **administer, control, maintain** My parents *run* a donut shop. —*noun* **1.** ✦ **dash, jog, race, sprint, trot** We went for a *run* around the block. **2.** ✦ **sequence, streak, stretch, string** ✧ **series** I've been having a *run* of good luck.

rupture *noun* ✦ **breach, break, crack, fracture, gap, hole, split** Our basement was flooded because of a *rupture* in our hot water tank. —*verb* ✦ **break, burst, split** ✧ **breach, crack, fracture** The water balloon *ruptured* when I filled it too full.

rural *adjective* ✦ **country** ✧ **agricultural, farm, pastoral, provincial** My family comes from a *rural* town in southern Georgia.

rush *verb* ✦ **dash, hasten, hurry, hustle, race, run** I *rushed* over to Shira's house as soon as she got home from vacation. —*noun* ✦ **haste, hurry, scramble** ✧ **dash, race, run** We were in a *rush* to finish our holiday shopping.

ruthless *adjective* ✦ **brutal, cruel, heartless, merciless** ✧ **severe** The *ruthless* queen treated her enemies harshly.

✦   **best choices**
✧   **other choices**

S

sack¹ *noun* ✦ **bag** ✧ **pack, pouch** We bought a *sack* of potatoes at the grocery store. —*verb* ✦ **bag, pack** ✧ **package** The clerk *sacked* our groceries for us.

sack² *verb* ✦ **loot, pillage, plunder** ✧ **attack, raid** The Vikings *sacked* many villages over a period of about three hundred years. —*noun* ✦ **looting, pillage, plundering** ✧ **burning, destruction, robbing** The *sack* of Rome by the Vandals occurred in 455 A.D.

sacred *adjective* ✦ **blessed, hallowed, holy, religious** ✧ **divine, saintly, spiritual** Jerusalem is a *sacred* city to Christians, Jews, and Muslims alike.

sacrifice *noun* **1.** ✦ **gift, homage, offering** ✧ **victim** The ancient Greeks made *sacrifices* to their gods by killing sheep and other animals. **2.** ✦ **concession, forfeit** ✧ **cost, loss, surrender** Our family has had to make *sacrifices* in order to put my brother through college. —*verb* ✦ **give up, let go, lose, offer up, surrender, yield** In chess, it is often necessary to *sacrifice* pieces in order to win the game.

sad *adjective* ✦ **blue, dejected, depressed, gloomy, melancholy, unhappy** ✧ **joyless** ▼ Tina

was *sad* that we had to cancel our field trip because of bad weather.

saddle *noun* ✧ **pad, perch, seat** The cowboy put a *saddle* on his horse. —*verb* ✦ **burden, load, tax, weigh down** ✧ **impose, inflict** I was *saddled* with my brother's chores when he went away to camp.

safe *adjective* ✦ **protected, secure** ✧ **defended, guarded, unhurt** The rabbit felt *safe* and comfortable in its burrow. —*noun* ✧ **chest, strongbox, vault** My parents keep their important papers in a *safe*.

sag *verb* ✦ **dip, droop, drop, sink, slump** ✧ **flop, wilt** The clothesline *sagged* when we hung up wet towels.

sail *noun* ✦ **boat trip, cruise, voyage** ✧ **excursion** We decided to go on a *sail* across the bay. —*verb* **1.** ✦ **cruise, voyage** ✧ **cross, set sail** It took us two hours to *sail* across the lake. **2.** ✦ **manage, navigate, pilot** ✧ **captain, guide, steer** My father is teaching me how to *sail* a boat. **3.** ✦ **drift, float, fly, glide, soar** ✧ **flutter, skim** A little bird *sailed* through my open window.

salary *noun* ✦ **compensation, earnings, pay, wage** ✧ **fee, income** The store owner raised her employee's *salary*.

sale *noun* **1.** ✦ **exchange, selling, transfer** ✧ **marketing, purchase** Our neighbor hopes that the *sale* of his house will go smoothly. **2.** ✦ **bargain, deal, discount, markdown** ✧ **closeout** We plan to take advantage of the big holiday *sales*.

same *adjective* ✦ **identical, matching** ✧ **duplicate, equal, exact, similar** My sister and I have eyes of the *same* color.

sample *noun* ✦ **example, specimen** ✧ **cross section, model, representative** This is just a *sample* of the kind of drawing I can make. —*verb*

taste, test, try ✧ **experience, sip** The clerk asked if we would like to *sample* the new ice cream flavor.

sanctuary *noun* ✦ **asylum, haven, protection, refuge, safety** ✧ **shelter** The refugees found *sanctuary* at the embassy.

sane *adjective* ✦ **prudent, rational, reasonable, sensible, sound, wise** I need some *sane* advice about the problems I'm having with my best friend.

sanity *noun* ✦ **common sense, judgment, mental health, reason** My grandparents questioned my *sanity* when I told them that I wanted to go bungee jumping.

sarcastic *adjective* ✦ **insulting, jeering, mocking, scornful, sneering, taunting** The politician made a *sarcastic* remark about her opponent's campaign promises.

satisfaction *noun* ✦ **contentment, fulfillment, happiness, pleasure, pride** ✧ **comfort, relief** I felt immense *satisfaction* when I completed my art project.

satisfactory *adjective* ✦ **acceptable, adequate, all right, decent, sufficient** ✧ **suitable** The teacher said that the rough draft of my report was *satisfactory*.

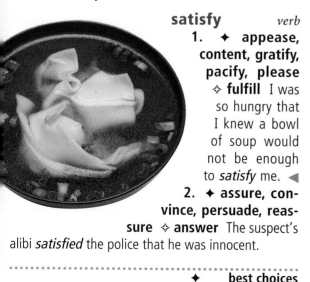

satisfy *verb*
1. ✦ **appease, content, gratify, pacify, please** ✧ **fulfill** I was so hungry that I knew a bowl of soup would not be enough to *satisfy* me. ◄
2. ✦ **assure, convince, persuade, reassure** ✧ **answer** The suspect's alibi *satisfied* the police that he was innocent.

saturate *verb* ✦ **douse, drench, soak** ✧ **fill, sop, wet** Mom *saturated* our houseplants with water before we left for the week.

savage *adjective* ✦ **brutal, cruel, ferocious, fierce, ruthless, vicious** The hungry shark made a *savage* attack on its prey.

save *verb* 1. ✦ **help, rescue** ✧ **free, protect, recover, safeguard** Many people joined in to *save* the birds that had been caught in an oil spill. 2. ✦ **keep, lay away, maintain, reserve, store** Jonah is *saving* his cereal box tops until he has enough for a free set of headphones.

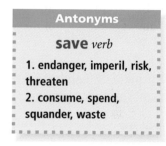

Antonyms
save *verb*
1. endanger, imperil, risk, threaten
2. consume, spend, squander, waste

say *verb* ✦ **articulate, enunciate, pronounce, recite, state, utter** Can you *say* "the frog flopped" ten times in a row? —*noun* ✦ **voice, vote** ✧ **chance, opinion, turn** All the club members had a *say* in the decision.

saying *noun* ✦ **adage, expression, motto, proverb** ✧ **statement** "There's no use crying over spilt milk" is a common *saying*.

scan *verb* ✦ **examine, inspect, search, survey** ✧ **explore, look** We *scanned* the night sky in hopes of seeing shooting stars.

scandal *noun* ✦ **disgrace, dishonor, embarrassment, outrage, shame** The mayor's dishonesty is a public *scandal*.

scant *adjective* ✦ **little, meager, poor, scanty, skimpy, sparse** ✧ **insufficient** I paid *scant* attention to the boring television show.

scar *noun* ✦ **blemish, mark** ✧ **cut, injury, wound** My mother has a *scar* from when she had her appendix removed. —*verb* ✦ **blemish, damage, deface, disfigure, injure, mark** The trees were *scarred* by the forest fire.

✦ **best choices**
✧ **other choices**

scarce *adjective* ✦ rare, uncommon, unusual ✧ infrequent, scant, scanty Water is *scarce* in the desert.

scarcely *adverb* ✦ barely, hardly, just ✧ only, slightly I had *scarcely* hung up the phone when it rang again.

scare *verb* ✦ alarm, frighten, shock, startle, terrify ✧ terrorize I had a bad dream that really *scared* me. —*noun* ✦ alarm, fright, shock, start ✧ surprise, terror You gave me quite a *scare* when you came in without knocking.

scatter *verb* ✦ disperse, distribute, spread, sprinkle ✧ separate We *scatter* rock salt on our front steps when they get icy.

scene *noun* 1. ✦ locale, location, setting, site ✧ area, place, spot The police arrived at the *scene* of the crime. 2. ✦ act, episode ✧ chapter, part, section, segment The murderer was revealed in the last *scene* of the play.

scenic *adjective* ✦ beautiful, panoramic, picturesque, pretty, spectacular Our train route through the mountains was very *scenic*. ▼

scent *noun* ✦ aroma, fragrance, odor, smell ✧ whiff I prefer soaps that don't have a *scent*. —*verb* ✦ nose out, smell, sniff ✧ detect, perceive, sense The hounds started baying when they *scented* the fox.

schedule *noun* ✦ calendar, lineup, timetable ✧ list, program, register The coach gave each player a copy of this year's game *schedule*. —*verb* ✦ arrange, book, reserve ✧ plan, prepare, program Mom *scheduled* a doctor's appointment for my annual checkup.

scheme *noun* ✦ plan, procedure, program, strategy, system ✧ plot Diet *schemes* that promise quick results usually don't work. —*verb* ✦ conspire, contrive, intrigue, plan, plot The con artist *schemed* to cheat people out of their life's savings.

scholar *noun* ✧ authority, intellectual, pupil, sage, specialist, student Many *scholars* use university libraries to do their research.

Word Groups

A **school** is a place for teaching and learning. **School** is a general term with no true synonyms. Here are some different kinds of schools to investigate in a dictionary:

academy, college, grammar school, high school, institute, kindergarten, seminary, university

scold *verb* ✦ admonish, criticize, lecture ✧ blame, denounce Mr. Cokely *scolded* us for not paying attention to the homework assignment.

scope *noun* ✦ extent, range, reach, spread ✧ realm, sphere The *scope* of my teacher's knowledge is impressive.

scorch *verb* ✦ blacken, char, singe ✧ bake, burn, roast, toast The flames *scorched* the wall but it didn't catch on fire.

score *noun* ✦ mark, grade, total ✧ count, points, record Mercedes got a *score* of 95 on her spelling quiz. —*verb* ✦ achieve, attain, earn, gain, make ◇ win The team *scored* three goals during the last quarter.

scoundrel *noun* ✦ rascal, rogue, villain ◇ crook, thief The *scoundrel* was caught and punished for his crimes.

scour *verb* ✦ buff, polish, rub, scrub ◇ cleanse, wash We *scoured* the dirty floor until it gleamed.

scout *noun* ✦ guide, lookout ◇ explorer, spy Kit Carson was a famous frontier *scout*. —*verb* ✦ examine, explore, inspect, observe, search, survey Dad sent me ahead to *scout* the next block for a place we could eat.

scramble *verb* 1. ✦ hasten, hurry, hustle, race, rush, scurry Everybody *scrambled* to put their books and papers away when the bell rang. 2. ✦ disorder, jumble, mess up, mix, shuffle I like to solve word puzzles in which all the letters are *scrambled*. —*noun* ✦ confusion, free-for-all, struggle, tumult ◇ race, rush There was a *scramble* in the end zone when one of the players dropped the ball.

scrap *noun* ✦ bit, fragment, part, piece, portion, shred Alyssa is saving *scraps* of cloth to make a quilt. ▶ —*verb* ✦ abandon, discard, dispose of, dump, junk ◇ throw away The Navy plans to *scrap* this old battleship.

scrape *verb* 1. ✦ clean off, remove, rub off ◇ peel, skin Will you help me *scrape* the ice from the windshield? 2. ✦ bruise, scratch, scuff, skin ◇ hurt, injure I wear pads when I go roller-skating so that I won't *scrape* my knees. —*noun* ✦ mark, scratch, scuff ◇ bruise, damage, injury Mom's car has a *scrape* on the right front fender.

scratch *verb* ✦ rub, scrape ◇ mar, mark, scuff Bears like to *scratch* their backs against trees. —*noun* ✦ gash, mark, scrape, scuff ◇ damage, injury This wax should cover the *scratch* on the table.

scream *verb* ✦ cry out, howl, screech, shout, shriek, yell ◇ wail Everybody *screamed* as the roller coaster looped the loop. —*noun* ✦ cry, howl, screech, shout, shriek, yell ◇ wail We heard lots of *screams* coming from the carnival's haunted house.

screech *noun* ✦ cry, scream, shriek, squawk ◇ squeal The *screech* of a blue jay woke me up. —*verb* ✦ cry out, scream, shriek ◇ squawk, squeal I *screeched* when I opened the drawer and saw the mouse.

screen *noun* 1. ✦ cover, protection, shade, shield ◇ shelter, veil This elm tree acts as a *screen* to keep the sun off our porch. 2. ✦ mesh, netting Our tent has a small *screen* that serves as a window. —*verb* ✦ cloak, conceal, hide, obscure, veil ◇ protect, shelter The dark night *screened* the attacking army.

screw *noun* ◇ bolt, fastener, pin My bookshelves are held together with metal *screws*. —*verb* ✦ turn, twirl, twist ◇ attach, fasten, tighten I had a hard time *screwing* the childproof cap off the aspirin bottle.

scribble *verb* ✦ draw, scrawl, write ◇ jot Mom says I used to *scribble* on my bedroom wall with crayons.

scrub *verb* ✦ clean, cleanse, scour, wash ◇ buff, polish, rub I *scrubbed* the kitchen counters while Marla did the dishes. —*noun* ✦ cleaning, cleansing, scouring, washing ◇ polish, rub This tub needs a good *scrub*.

✦ best choices
◇ other choices

sculpture *noun* ✦ **carving, figure, statue** ✧ **bust, figurine** My parents bought a *sculpture* of a woman's head that was made in Africa.

seal *noun* ✦ **emblem, insignia, mark, sign, stamp** ✧ **badge** Legal documents often have an official *seal* on them. —*verb* ✦ **bind, close, fasten, secure, shut** Brianna *sealed* the carton with packing tape.

search *verb* ✦ **explore, hunt, look, seek** ✧ **investigate, probe** Jeffrey likes to *search* for arrowheads. —*noun* ✦ **exploration, hunt, probe** ✧ **investigation, pursuit** The rescue team began a *search* for the missing boy.

season *noun* ✦ **period, time** ✧ **occasion, spell, term** A lot of people decorate their homes during the holiday *season*. —*verb* ✦ **flavor, spice** ✧ **enhance, salt** Mom uses curry powder to *season* her baked chicken.

secret *adjective* ✦ **confidential, private** ✧ **concealed, hidden, personal, unknown** Manuel has a *secret* password to access his E-mail account. —*noun* ✦ **confidential information** ✧ **intrigue, mystery** Don't you dare tell anyone my *secret*!

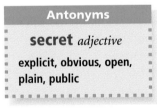

Antonyms

secret *adjective*

explicit, obvious, open, plain, public

section *noun* ✦ **part, portion, segment** ✧ **area, division, piece, slice** I like to read the sports *section* of the newspaper. —*verb* ✦ **cut, divide, separate, slice, split** Angus *sectioned* the pie into six pieces.

secure *adjective* **1.** ✦ **defended, protected, safe, sheltered** ✧ **immune** Having my dog with me when I take a walk makes me feel *secure*. **2.** ✦ **assured, certain, guaranteed, stable, steady, sure** My dad has a *secure* position with his company. —*verb* **1.** ✦ **defend, guard, protect, safeguard** ✧ **shelter, shield** The new alarm sys-

tem will help *secure* the office against burglars. **2.** ✦ **anchor, attach, bind, chain, fasten, tie** Melissa *secured* the dinghy to the dock so it would not drift away. ▼ **3.** ✦ **acquire, gain, get, obtain, procure** ✧ **win** We were able to *secure* good seats for the baseball game.

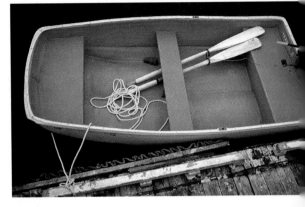

see *verb* **1.** ✦ **behold, glimpse, spot, view, watch** ✧ **notice, observe** You can *see* the ocean from here. **2.** ✦ **comprehend, grasp, perceive, understand** ✧ **detect, realize** I can *see* why you're upset. **3.** ✦ **ascertain, determine, find out** ✧ **discover, learn** Call your dad to *see* if you can spend the night.

seek *verb* ✦ **hunt for, look for, search for** ✧ **go after, pursue** Birds *seek* safe places to build their nests.

seem *verb* ✦ **appear, look** ✧ **resemble, sound, suggest** That girl over there *seems* to be waving at you.

seep *verb* ✦ **drain, dribble, drip, leak, ooze, trickle** Oil *seeped* from the car's engine onto the driveway.

segment *noun* ✦ **part, piece, portion, section, slice** ✧ **division** I gave my friend several *segments* of my orange.

seize *verb* ✦ **clutch, grab, grasp, grip, snatch** ✧ **capture, catch** I *seized* my little sister to keep her from running into the street.

seldom *adverb* ✦ **hardly ever, infrequently, not often, rarely** I *seldom* forget to brush my teeth before bed.

select *verb* ✦ **choose, decide on, elect, name, pick, settle on** Our teacher is letting us *select* our own report topics. —*adjective* ✦ **exclusive, first-class, special, superior** ◇ **choice** My friend goes to a *select* school for students who are gifted in the arts.

selection *noun* ✦ **assortment, choice, pick, range, variety** ◇ **preference** The stationery store has a large *selection* of birthday cards.

self-conscious *adjective* ✦ **bashful, modest, shy** ◇ **embarrassed, nervous** I felt a little *self-conscious* when I had to give an oral report in front of the whole class.

selfish *adjective* ✦ **greedy, self-centered, stingy, ungenerous** ◇ **inconsiderate** I was *selfish* and took the last piece of pie.

Antonyms
selfish *adjective*
bighearted, charitable, generous, giving, unselfish

sell *verb* ✦ **deal in, market, retail** ◇ **peddle, stock, trade** This bookstore *sells* both new and used books.

send *verb* ✦ **forward, mail** ◇ **dispatch, ship, transfer, transmit** I *sent* a picture of my family to my pen pal.

senior *adjective* **1.** ✦ **elder, elderly, old, older** ◇ **aged** Our neighbors are *senior* citizens. **2.** ✦ **chief, higher, leading, major, superior, top** Mom's friend is a *senior* official in the governor's office. —*noun* ✦ **elder** ◇ **better, chief, superior** I am your *senior* by four months.

sensational *adjective* ✦ **exciting, fantastic, spectacular, superb, terrific, thrilling, wonderful** The special effects in that movie were absolutely *sensational*.

sense *noun* **1.** ✦ **capability, capacity, faculty, sensation** ◇ **function** An Alsatian dog has a *sense* of smell that is about one million times stronger than a human's. **2.** ✦ **feeling, sentiment** ◇ **appreciation, understanding** I have a strong *sense* of loyalty to my school. —*verb* ✦ **detect, feel, perceive, recognize, see** ◇ **think** I *sense* that you are anxious to leave.

sensible *adjective* ✦ **intelligent, logical, prudent, rational, reasonable, wise** ◇ **thoughtful** It is *sensible* to warm up before you exercise.

sensitive *adjective* ✦ **perceptive (about), receptive, sympathetic, understanding (about)** ◇ **feeling** A teacher needs to be *sensitive* to the special needs of each student.

separate *verb* ✦ **detach, divide, part, split** ◇ **break up, detach, sever** To make vanilla pudding, you should *separate* the egg whites from the yolks. ▶ —*adjective* ✦ **different, distinct, independent, individual** ◇ **solitary** Put the light and dark laundry into *separate* piles.

sequence *noun* ✦ **arrangement, order, succession** ◇ **course, series** When I dialed the phone number out of *sequence*, I naturally got the wrong person.

serene *adjective* ✦ **calm, peaceful, placid, quiet, restful, tranquil** The lake looked *serene* in the evening twilight.

series *noun* ✦ **course, cycle, run, sequence, set, succession** ◇ **assortment, collection, group** The science channel is airing a *series* of shows on African wildlife.

✦ **best choices**
◇ **other choices**

serious *adjective* **1.** ✦ **grave, grim, sober, solemn, somber** ✧ **sad** You look very *serious* today — is there something wrong? **2.** ✦ **decided, definite, in earnest, sincere, resolved** Are you *serious* about not going to the party? **3.** ✦ **important, momentous, significant, urgent, vital** ✧ **heavy** Drug abuse is a *serious* problem. **4.** ✦ **alarming, bad, critical, dangerous, difficult, tough** The sailors were in a *serious* situation when their ship started to leak.

sermon *noun* ✦ **address, lecture, speech, talk** ✧ **lesson** The principal gave us a *sermon* on the value of a good education.

serve *verb* **1.** ✦ **act, function, labor, work** ✧ **perform** Dad *serves* as a volunteer firefighter. **2.** ✦ **aid, assist, attend, help, wait on** ✧ **support** The salesclerk was very polite when she *served* us. **3.** ✦ **give, pass** ✧ **deliver, offer, provide, supply** Please *serve* each guest a piece of your birthday cake.

service *noun* **1.** ✦ **aid, assistance, attendance, help, support** The sick man needed the *services* of a doctor. **2.** ✦ **military** ✧ **Air Force, Army, Coast Guard, Marine Corps, Navy** My uncle is home on leave from the *service*. **3.** ✦ **agency, bureau, department** ✧ **facility, utility** Many college students work for the Forest *Service* during the summer. **4.** ✦ **ceremony** ✧ **celebration, function, observance** The wedding *service* was lovely. —*verb* ✦ **fix, repair** ✧ **adjust, maintain, restore** We had our broken washing machine *serviced* by a repairman.

set[1] *verb* **1.** ✦ **lay, place, put** ✧ **install, rest, stick** Please *set* the groceries on the counter. **2.** ✦ **congeal, dry, harden, solidify, stiffen, thicken** This glue will *set* in fifteen minutes. **3.** ✦ **adjust, arrange, fix, order, prepare** Please *set* the table for dinner. **4.** ✦ **begin, commence, depart, embark, start, start out** ✧ **undertake** The cruise ship weighed anchor and *set off* on its voyage. —*adjective* ✦ **customary, definite, fixed, habitual, regular, specific** I walk a *set* route to school everyday.

set[2] *noun* ✦ **assortment, batch, collection, group** ✧ **bunch** Dad bought a *set* of metric wrenches to fix our car.

settle *verb* **1.** ✦ **agree on, arrange, choose, decide, fix, set** Let's *settle* the date for the party so I can send out invitations. **2.** ✦ **locate in, move to** ✧ **dwell, inhabit, live, reside** Many European immigrants *settled in* New York City in the 1880's. **3.** ✦ **alight, land** ✧ **descend, drop, sink** The flock of crows *settled* on the top branches of the tree. **4.** ✦ **calm, pacify, quiet, soothe** ✧ **relax** This herbal tea is guaranteed to *settle* your upset stomach.

several *adjective* ✦ **a few, some, various** ✧ **a number** That actor has been in *several* of my favorite movies.

severe *adjective* **1.** ✦ **grave, heavy, serious, stern, strict, tough** At our school there is a *severe* penalty for cheating. **2.** ✦ **bitter, brutal, difficult, hard, harsh, rough** I hope that this winter won't be as *severe* as the last one.

shack *noun* ✦ **hut, lean-to, shanty, shed** ✧ **cabin, shelter** We found an abandoned *shack* in the woods.

shade *noun* **1.** ✦ **shadow** ✧ **cover, darkness, gloom, murk** My dog likes to lie in the *shade* of our big oak tree. **2.** ✦ **color, hue, tint, tone** ✧ **tinge** The sunset turned the clouds different *shades* of pink and orange.

shadow *noun* **1.** ✧ **image, outline, reflection, silhouette, trace** Your *shadow* is always shortest at noon. **2.** ✦ **darkness, dimness, gloom, murk, shade** I can see my brother hiding in the *shadows*.

shady *adjective* ✦ **shaded, shadowy** ✧ **covered, dark, sheltered** Let's find a *shady* spot for our picnic.

shake *verb* **1.** ✦ **jiggle, rattle, vibrate** ✧ **agitate, wag** Jeremy *shook* his tambourine in time to the music. ◀ **2.** ✦ **quake, quiver, shiver, shudder, tremble** The rabbit *shook* with fear when it saw the fox. **3.** ✦ **diminish, discourage, disturb, weaken** ✧ **move, shift** No one can *shake* my determination to join the rodeo when I grow up. —*noun* ✦ **shaking** ✧ **jar, jiggle, jolt, vibration** I gave my sweater a *shake* to get the dog hair off.

shame *noun* **1.** ✦ **embarrassment, humiliation** ✧ **disgrace, regret, sorrow** The student was filled with *shame* when she was caught cheating. **2.** ✦ **disappointment, misfortune, pity** ✧ **crime, scandal** It is a *shame* that your injury kept you from playing in the last game of the season. —*verb* ✦ **disgrace, dishonor, humiliate** ✧ **discredit, embarrass** The spy *shamed* his country by selling secrets to the enemy.

shape *noun* **1.** ✦ **contour, figure, form, outline, pattern, profile** We made Christmas cookies in the *shape* of snowmen, wreaths, and candy canes. **2.** ✦ **condition, health, state, trim** ✧ **order** My cat is still in good *shape* even though he's seventeen years old. —*verb* ✦ **fashion, form, model, mold** ✧ **design, make** Mom *shaped* the bread dough into a loaf.

share *verb* ✦ **divide, split** ✧ **deal out, distribute, partition** The three friends *shared* their lunches. —*noun* ✦ **division, part, percentage, portion** ✧ **piece, segment** Each employee got a *share* of the profits.

sharp *adjective* **1.** ✦ **keen, sharp-edged** ✧ **acute, pointed, pointy** Piranhas have teeth that are as *sharp* as a razor. **2.** ✦ **abrupt, rapid, steep, sudden** ✧ **clear, distinct** The temperature took a *sharp* drop last night. **3.** ✦ **bitter, cutting, harsh, severe, stinging** ✧ **nasty** The actor was upset over the director's *sharp* criticism. **4.** ✦ **alert, bright, clever, intelligent, quick, smart** It takes a *sharp* mind to solve this riddle. —*adverb* ✦ **exactly, on time, precisely, promptly, punctually** The train will leave at 8 P.M. *sharp*.

sharpen *verb* ✦ **hone, whet** ✧ **file, grind** This carving knife needs to be *sharpened*.

shatter *verb* **1.** ✦ **break, burst, fragment, smash, splinter** ✧ **disintegrate** The jar slipped out of my hand and *shattered* on the floor. **2.** ✦ **demolish, destroy, finish, ruin, spoil, undo** Last night's loss *shattered* our dream of winning the championship.

shed *verb* **1.** ✦ **cast off, molt** ✧ **discard, drop, remove** I found a piece of skin that a snake had *shed*. **2.** ✦ **cast, emit, give, project, spread** ✧ **release, throw** The sun *sheds* little warmth on cold winter days.

sheer *adjective* **1.** ✦ **see-through, thin, translucent** ✧ **clear, transparent** The *sheer* lace curtains let a lot of sunlight into the room. **2.** ✦ **absolute, complete, pure, thorough, total, utter** My brother made up a story that was *sheer* nonsense. **3.** ✦ **abrupt, perpendicular, steep, vertical** The climbers scaled the cliff's *sheer* face.

shelter *noun* **1.** ✦ **cover, protection, refuge** ✧ **safety, security** The birds sought *shelter* when it began to rain. **2.** ✦ **asylum, haven, home, refuge, sanctuary** ✧ **hospital, retreat** Our veterinarian runs a *shelter* for homeless cats and dogs.

shield *noun* ✦ **cover, guard, protection, safeguard, screen** ✧ **defense** A power saw has a *shield* that is designed to protect the user from injury. —*verb* ✦ **cover, guard, protect, screen, shelter** ◇ **defend** I used a newspaper to *shield* my head from the hot sun.

shift *verb* **1.** ✦ **move, relocate, transfer** ◇ **carry, transport** Brad *shifted* his bookbag from one shoulder to the other. **2.** ✦ **alter, change, switch, vary** ◇ **adjust, swerve** The wind *shifted* direction. —*noun* **1.** ✦ **alteration, change, changeover, move, switch** ◇ **transfer** I haven't gotten used to the *shift* from regular to daylight savings time. **2.** ✦ **assignment, duty, tour, watch** ◇ **crew, staff** The night *shift* begins at midnight.

shimmer *verb* ✦ **flash, glimmer, glisten, glitter, sparkle, twinkle** The lights from the cruise ship *shimmered* on the dark water.

shine *verb* **1.** ✦ **beam, flash** ◇ **glare, gleam, glow, radiate** Please *shine* the flashlight over here. ◀ **2.** ✦ **buff, polish, wax** ◇ **brush, rub** I need to *shine* my shoes for the party. —*noun* ✦ **gleam, gloss, glow, luster, polish, sparkle** Dad buffed his car until it had a bright *shine*.

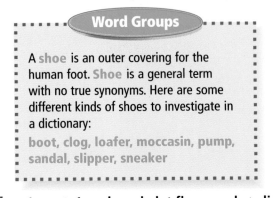

ship *noun* ✦ **boat, vessel** ◇ **freighter, ocean liner, steamer, tanker** There were more than a dozen large *ships* in the harbor. —*verb* ✦ **deliver, dispatch, forward, send, transport** ◇ **move** How much will it cost to *ship* this package to New Orleans?

shiver *verb* ✦ **shake, shudder, tremble** ◇ **quake, quiver, vibrate** The skiers *shivered* from the cold as they waited for the ski lift. —*noun* ✦ **shake, shudder, tremble, tremor** ◇ **quake, quiver** The eerie story sent a *shiver* down my spine.

shock *noun* ✦ **blow, jar, jolt** ◇ **start, surprise, upset** It was a *shock* to the family when my aunt lost her job. —*verb* ✦ **appall, dismay, stagger, startle, stun, surprise** Dad was *shocked* when he saw last month's phone bill.

Word Groups

A **shoe** is an outer covering for the human foot. **Shoe** is a general term with no true synonyms. Here are some different kinds of shoes to investigate in a dictionary:

boot, clog, loafer, moccasin, pump, sandal, slipper, sneaker

---

shoot *verb* **1.** ✦ **launch, let fly, propel** ◇ **discharge, fire, hurl** I *shot* an arrow into the air. **2.** ✦ **bolt, dart, dash, flash, rocket, run, rush** A rabbit *shot* out of the sagebrush when we rode by on our dirt bikes. —*noun* ✦ **bud, sprout** ◇ **runner, stem, sucker, tendril** The daffodils sent up new *shoots* through the spring snow.

shop *noun* ✦ **store** ◇ **boutique, department store, outlet** This mall has over a hundred different *shops*. —*verb* ✦ **browse, go shopping, look** ◇ **buy, purchase** My friend and I like to *shop* for clothes together.

shore *noun* ✦ **beach, coast, seacoast, seashore, seaside, waterside** My brothers and I built a sandcastle at the *shore*.

short *adjective* **1.** ✦ **diminutive, little, small** ◇ **low, slight, tiny, wee** My little sister is too *short* to ride this roller coaster. **2.** ✦ **brief, concise** ◇ **fast, speedy, swift** Our teacher gave us a *short* talk about the importance of being on time. —*adverb* ✦ **abruptly, instantly, quickly, suddenly, unexpectedly** The hikers stopped *short* when they came to the edge of a cliff.

shortage *noun* ✦ **deficit, lack, scarcity, shortfall** ◇ **deficiency** There are so many players on my soccer team that we have a *shortage* of game jerseys.

shortcoming *noun* ✦ drawback, fault, flaw, imperfection ✧ defect, weakness My friend's impatience is her only *shortcoming*.

shorten *verb* ✦ cut, decrease, reduce, trim ✧ abridge, condense I *shortened* the streamers on my bike so they wouldn't catch in the spokes.

shout *verb* ✦ bellow, cry out, scream, yell ✧ howl, roar I had to *shout* in order to be heard over the loud music. —*noun* ✦ cry, yell ✧ bellow, howl, roar, scream When I heard my friend's *shout*, I went outside to see what he wanted.

shove *verb* ✦ move, nudge, push ✧ press, thrust We *shoved* our desks into a circle. —*noun* ✦ nudge, push, thrust ✧ boost, prod I gave my model boat a *shove*, and it floated across the pool.

show *verb* 1. ✦ display, exhibit, present ✧ demonstrate, reveal The scientist *showed* a fossil to our group and told us how it was formed. ▼ 2. ✦ conduct, direct, escort, guide, lead, steer The usher *showed* us to our seats. —*noun* 1. ✦ display, exhibition, presentation ✧ demonstration, exhibit We entered our Border Collie in the local dog *show*. 2. ✦ performance, production, program ✧ entertainment, spectacle The school *show* was a big success.

shred *noun* ✦ bit, piece, scrap, strip, tatter ✧ fragment, particle We tore the newspapers into *shreds* for our papier-mâché project. —*verb* ✦ cut up, rip up, tear up ✧ grate, slice Dad *shredded* some lettuce for our salad.

shrewd *adjective* ✦ clever, intelligent, keen, sharp, smart, wise ✧ practical I made a *shrewd* guess and got the answer right.

shriek *noun* ✦ cry, scream, screech, shout, squeal, yell I let out a *shriek* when I saw the snake. —*verb* ✦ cry out, scream, screech, shout, squeal, yell Lots of people began *shrieking* when the rock band came onstage.

shrink *verb* 1. ✦ constrict, contract ✧ decrease, reduce, shorten, shrivel Many plastics *shrink* when they are heated. 2. ✦ back away, draw back, retreat, withdraw ✧ cower, cringe, flinch The frightened cat *shrank back* from the barking dog.

shrivel *verb* ✦ dry up, wilt, wither ✧ fade, shrink, wrinkle The rose petals *shriveled* after they fell to the ground.

shudder *verb* ✦ quake, quiver, shake, shiver, tremble ✧ convulse We all *shuddered* as we listened to the scary ghost story. —*noun* ✦ quiver, shiver, tremble, tremor ✧ convulsion, twitch I gave a *shudder* of relief when I got safely back to shore.

shuffle *verb* 1. ✦ hobble, limp, straggle ✧ drag, scuff, scuffle The injured player *shuffled* off the field. 2. ✦ jumble, mix up, rearrange, reorder, scramble ✧ shift The teacher *shuffled* the papers on her desk. —*noun* ✦ hobble, limp ✧ scuffle I walked with a *shuffle* when I sprained my ankle.

shut *verb* 1. ✦ close ✧ fasten, latch, lock, seal, secure Please *shut* the window so the rain doesn't come in. 2. ✦ cage, confine, coop up, enclose, pen ✧ imprison Tamara *shut* her budgies in their cage for the night.

✦ best choices
✧ other choices

shy *adjective* **1.** ✦ **bashful, meek, modest, reserved, timid** ◇ **coy** I felt a little *shy* on the first day at my new school. **2.** ✦ **lacking, missing, short, under** ◇ **deficient, wanting** Our volleyball team is *shy* one player. —*verb* ✦ **flinch, jerk away, recoil, shrink back** ◇ **cringe** The horse *shied away* when I reached out to pet it.

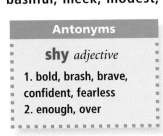

Antonyms

shy *adjective*

1. **bold, brash, brave, confident, fearless**
2. **enough, over**

sick *adjective* ✦ **ill, sickly, unwell** ◇ **ailing, unhealthy** The greasy dinner made me feel a little *sick*.

side *noun* **1.** ✦ **border, boundary, edge, end, margin** ◇ **rim** The teams lined up on opposite *sides* of the field. **2.** ✦ **face, surface** ◇ **part** I turned the letter over and read what was on the other *side*. **3.** ✦ **opinion, position, version, view, viewpoint** ◇ **aspect** The judge listened to both *sides* before she made up her mind in the case. **4.** ✦ **squad, team** ◇ **group, party, sect** Which *side* do you think will win the game?

sift *verb* ✦ **filter, screen, strain** ◇ **separate, sort** The cook *sifted* the flour into the cake batter.

sight *noun* **1.** ✦ **eye, eyesight, seeing, vision** A hawk's *sight* is very keen. **2.** ✦ **view** ◇ **appearance, glance, glimpse, look** The hot-air balloon came into *sight* over the ridge. **3.** ✦ **picture, show, spectacle** ◇ **marvel, scene, wonder** Our magnolia tree is a beautiful *sight* when it is in full bloom. —*verb* ✦ **behold, glimpse, observe, perceive, see, spot, view** The soldiers *sighted* an enemy plane approaching.

sign *noun* **1.** ✦ **gesture, mark, signal** ◇ **expression, symbol, token** The teacher raised her hand as a *sign* for the class to be quiet. **2.** ✦ **announcement, notice, poster** ◇ **billboard, bulletin** We put *signs* all around the neighborhood advertising our tag sale. **3.** ✦ **evidence,**

hint, indication, suggestion, trace The new space probe will look for *signs* of life on Mars. —*verb* ✦ **autograph, inscribe** ◇ **endorse, initial** We all *signed* our teacher's birthday card.

significance *noun* ✦ **consequence, importance, meaning** ◇ **value, weight** This test is of great *significance* to my grade.

significant *adjective* ✦ **big, consequential, historic, important, meaningful, notable** My family's move to the suburbs was a *significant* event in my life.

silence *noun* ✦ **hush, quiet, quietness, stillness** ◇ **calm, peace** A *silence* came over the room when the teacher walked in. —*verb* ✦ **calm, quiet, quieten** ◇ **muffle, shut up** The mother *silenced* her crying baby by rocking it gently.

silent *adjective* **1.** ✦ **hushed, noiseless, quiet, soundless, still** ◇ **mute** The audience was *silent* during the concert. **2.** ✦ **implied, undeclared, unexpressed, unsaid, unspoken** My brother and I have a *silent* agreement not to tell on each other.

Antonyms

silent *adjective*

1. **clamorous, loud, noisy**
2. **declared, spoken**

silly *adjective* ✦ **comical, crazy, dumb, foolish, ridiculous, stupid** Casey looked *silly* in his father's business suit. ▸

similar *adjective* ✦ **close, comparable, corresponding, equivalent, like** ◇ **identical** We have *similar* tastes when it comes to books and movies.

simple *adjective* **1.** ✦ **easy, effortless, uncomplicated** ✧ **basic, elementary** I finished the *simple* homework assignment in twenty minutes. **2.** ✦ **modest, plain** ✧ **natural, unadorned** Would you be happy with a *simple* meal of bread, fruit, and cheese?

sin *noun* ✦ **evil, misdeed, offense, trespass, violation, wrong** Many religions consider lying and stealing to be *sins*.

sincere *adjective* ✦ **earnest, genuine, heartfelt, honest, real, true** My brother's apology seemed to be *sincere*.

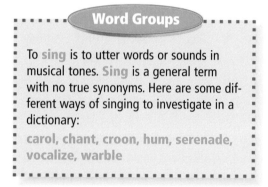

Word Groups

To **sing** is to utter words or sounds in musical tones. **Sing** is a general term with no true synonyms. Here are some different ways of singing to investigate in a dictionary:

carol, chant, croon, hum, serenade, vocalize, warble

single *adjective* ✦ **lone, one, only, sole, solitary** ✧ **individual** We were the *single* team to get its picture in the paper.

sink *verb* **1.** ✦ **go down, go under, submerge** ✧ **descend, dip, plunge** My paper boat began to *sink* after a few minutes in the water. **2.** ✦ **bore, dig, drill** ✧ **excavate** The farmer *sank* the well to a depth of two hundred feet.

sit *verb* **1.** ✦ **be seated, sit down** ✧ **rest, settle** You may *sit* wherever you like. **2.** ✦ **be located, be situated** ✧ **occupy, reside, stand** The farm *sits* on one hundred acres of rich farmland.

site *noun* ✦ **area, location, place, position, spot** We picked a level *site* on which to set up the tent.

situation *noun* ✦ **circumstance, condition, state** ✧ **place, predicament, status** The heavy rains have created a dangerous *situation* for people living near the river.

size *noun* ✦ **dimension, extent, measurement, proportion, volume** ✧ **area** A stegosaurus had a brain that was about the *size* of a walnut.

sketch *noun* ✦ **drawing, picture** ✧ **diagram, draft, portrait** Alejandra made a pencil *sketch* of the blooming cherry tree. —*verb* ✦ **depict, draw, portray** ✧ **diagram, outline** My art teacher asked us to *sketch* a horse from memory.

skill *noun* ✦ **ability, aptitude, talent, technique** ✧ **art, craft** I can skate on one foot, but I don't have the *skill* to do a jump. ▼

skillful *adjective* ✦ **adept, capable, competent, expert, good, masterful, skilled** The cellist's *skillful* performance was a pleasure to experience.

skinny *adjective* ✦ **gaunt, lean, slender, slim, spare, thin** My grandmother is always feeding me because she thinks I'm too *skinny*.

skip *verb* **1.** ✧ **bounce, bound, gambol, hop, jump, leap, spring** I was so happy that I *skipped* all the way home from school. **2.** ✦ **cut, miss, omit** ✧ **avoid, dodge, neglect** I had to *skip* Little League practice because I was away on vacation.

✦ best choices
✧ other choices

—*noun* ✦ **bounce, bound, hop, jump, leap, spring** Ava walked down the street with a *skip* in her step.

skirt *noun* ◇ **dress, frock, gown** My school uniform is a blue sweater and a plaid *skirt*. —*verb* ✦ **bypass, circle, go around** ◇ **avoid, dodge, evade** This freeway *skirts* the city to avoid the downtown traffic.

slack *adjective* **1.** ✦ **limp, loose, relaxed** ◇ **flexible, soft** My muscles felt *slack* after a few minutes in the hot tub. **2.** ✦ **down, off, slow, sluggish** ◇ **idle, weak** During the winter, business is *slack* at the beach resort.

> **Antonyms**
>
> **slack** *adjective*
>
> 1. rigid, stiff, taut, tense, tight
> 2. active, busy, employed, engaged

slam *verb* ✦ **bang, dash, smack** ◇ **hit, smash, strike** A gust of wind *slammed* the door shut. —*noun* ✦ **bang, crash, smack, smash** ◇ **blow** I dropped a book, and it hit the floor with a loud *slam*.

slant *verb* ✦ **incline, lean, pitch, slope, tilt, tip** ◇ **list** The telephone pole *slants* to one side ever since someone backed into it. —*noun* ✦ **incline, pitch, slope, tilt** ◇ **list** There is a *slant* in the ceiling of my attic bedroom.

slap *verb* ✦ **hit, smack, strike, swat, wallop** ◇ **pat, spank** My baby sister likes to *slap* the water when she takes a bath. —*noun* ✦ **blow, clap, hit, smack, swat, wallop** ◇ **pat, rap, spank** The prospector gave his mule a *slap* on the rump to get it to move.

slash *verb* **1.** ✦ **chop, cut, hack, slice** ◇ **carve, gash** The explorers *slashed* at the thick undergrowth with their machetes. **2.** ✦ **decrease, drop, lower, mark down, pare, reduce** After the holidays, stores usually *slash* prices on leftover Christmas decorations. —*noun* ✦ **cut, gash, slice,**

slit ◇ **rip, split, tear** The doctor stitched up the *slash* on my hand.

slavery *noun* ✦ **bondage, servitude** ◇ **captivity, serfdom** The 13th Amendment abolished *slavery* in the United States.

slay *verb* ✦ **exterminate, kill, slaughter** ◇ **assassinate, execute, murder** This book is about a knight who *slays* dragons.

sleek *adjective* ✦ **glistening, glossy, lustrous, shiny, silky** ◇ **polished** The seal's fur was *sleek* and smooth when it came out of the water.

sleep *noun* ✦ **slumber** ◇ **nap, rest, snooze** We spend about one-third of our lives in *sleep*. —*verb* ✦ **doze, drowse, slumber** ◇ **nap, rest, snooze** I like to *sleep* late on Saturday mornings.

slender *adjective* ✦ **lean, skinny, slim, spare, thin** ◇ **bony, gaunt, scrawny** Deer have long, *slender* legs.

slice *noun* ✦ **chunk, piece, wedge** ◇ **portion, section, segment** I had a *slice* of melon and some grapes for my snack. —*verb* ✦ **carve, cut, divide** ◇ **section, segment, separate** Renee *sliced* her birthday cake and served it to her guests.

slick *adjective* ✦ **slippery** ◇ **glossy, shiny, sleek, smooth** Be careful, the ice on the sidewalk is very *slick*.

slide *verb* ✦ **coast, glide, skid, skim, slip** ◇ **shoot** The hockey puck *slid* across the ice. —*noun* ✦ **avalanche** ◇ **landslide, mudslide, rockslide** The road was closed because it was blocked by a *slide*.

slight *adjective* **1.** ✦ **faint, insignificant, minor, small, trivial, unimportant** There is only a *slight* difference between these two colors. **2.** ✦ **skinny, slender, slim, thin** ◇ **delicate, frail** My older brother is so *slight* that he can fit into my clothes. —*verb* ✦ **affront, insult, snub, spurn** ◇ **disregard, ignore** I didn't mean to *slight* you, but I haven't had a chance to return your call. —*noun* ✦ **affront, insult, snub** ◇ **disrespect, offense** I meant my remark as a joke, not a *slight*.

slim *adjective* ✦ **lean, slender, slight, spare, thin** ◇ **gaunt, skinny** You're looking *slim* since you began exercising.

sling *verb* ✦ **cast, fling, heave, hurl, pitch, throw, toss** How far can you *sling* a rock?

slip *verb* 1. ✦ **glide, slide, steal** ◇ **move, pass, slither** The wolf *slipped* silently through the woods. 2. ✦ **skid, slide** ◇ **fall, stumble, trip, tumble** I *slipped* on the icy sidewalk. 3. ✦ **decline, decrease, drop off, fall off, lapse** ◇ **sink, vanish** My attention began to *slip* as I grew tired. —*noun* 1. ✦ **skid, slide** ◇ **fall, stumble, trip, tumble** A *slip* of the foot on this jungle gym could be dangerous. 2. ✦ **blunder, error, mistake** ◇ **lapse, oversight** I could tell Harry was distracted when he made a *slip* and called me by his sister's name.

slit *noun* ✦ **aperture, hole, opening, slot** ◇ **cut, slash** Castle walls commonly had *slits* through which archers could shoot at enemy soldiers. —*verb* ✦ **cut, slash, slice, split** ◇ **carve, rip** The clerk *slit* the cardboard box open.

slogan *noun* ✦ **motto** ◇ **expression, phrase, saying** The company printed its *slogan* on all of its packaging.

slope *verb* ✦ **angle, incline, slant** ◇ **lean, pitch, tip** The park *slopes* down to the river. —*noun* ✦ **angle, grade, incline, pitch, slant** ◇ **tilt** The *slope* of this roof is very steep.

sloppy *adjective* ✦ **disorderly, messy, slovenly, untidy** ◇ **careless** Whenever I write too fast, my handwriting looks *sloppy*.

slow *verb* ✦ **decrease, moderate, reduce, slacken** ◇ **brake, delay** The truck *slowed* its speed as it approached the icy bridge. —*adjective* ✦ **gradual, moderate, plodding, sluggish,**

unhurried The turtle made *slow* progress across the sand. ▶

sluggish *adjective* ✦ **lethargic, listless, slow** ◇ **idle, inactive, lazy** Reptiles are *sluggish* in cold weather.

slumber *verb* ✦ **doze, drowse, nap, sleep, snooze** ◇ **rest** My cat likes to *slumber* on the windowsill. —*noun* ✦ **sleep** ◇ **nap, rest, snooze** I fell into a deep *slumber* that lasted all night long.

sly *adjective* ✦ **clever, crafty, sneaky** ◇ **cunning, shrewd, tricky** Dorothy gave us a *sly* hint that today was her birthday.

smack *verb* ✦ **hit, slam, slap, strike, swat** ◇ **punch, smash, squash** I *smacked* at the mosquito that was on my arm. —*noun* ✦ **blow, hit, slam, strike, swat** ◇ **pat, slap, tap** The carpenter gave the nail a hard *smack* with his hammer.

small *adjective* 1. ✦ **little, miniature, minute, tiny, wee** ◇ **puny** Yael's laptop is *small* compared to the computers we use at school. ▼ 2. ✦ **limited, meager, scant, scanty, slight** There is only a *small* amount of seed left in the bird feeder. 3. ✦ **insignificant, minor, petty, trifling, trivial, unimportant** There's only a *small* difference between these two brands of blue jeans.

✦	**best choices**
◇	**other choices**

smart *adjective* ✦ **bright, brilliant, clever, intelligent, quick, sharp** My friend is so *smart* that she can do long division in her head. —*verb* ✦ **ache, hurt, sting, throb** ◇ **burn, itch** Does that bee sting still *smart*?

smash *verb* ✦ **break, crumble, crush, disintegrate, pound, pulverize** ◇ **demolish, splinter** We *smashed* the graham crackers to make a crust for the cheesecake.

smear *verb* 1. ✦ **apply, dab, layer, spread** ◇ **coat, cover** Chloe *smeared* sunscreen on her arms and shoulders. 2. ✦ **blur, smudge, streak** ◇ **blot, rub** Juan was careful not to *smear* the paint before it dried. —*noun* ✦ **blot, blotch, smudge, spot, stain, streak** There is a *smear* of jam on my little brother's cheek.

smell *verb* 1. ✦ **scent, sniff** ◇ **detect, nose, perceive, sense** We could *smell* bread baking in the oven. 2. ✦ **reek, stink** Rotten eggs really *smell*. —*noun* ✦ **aroma, fragrance, odor, scent** ◇ **stink, whiff** I love the *smell* of lilacs in the springtime.

smile *noun* ✦ **grin** ◇ **smirk** The photographer asked us for a big *smile*. —*verb* ✦ **beam, grin** ◇ **smirk** Jonas *smiled* at his parents when his name was called for the science award.

smooth *adjective* 1. ✦ **even, flat, level, undisturbed** ◇ **calm, tranquil** The surface of the lake turns *smooth* when the wind dies down. 2. ✦ **easy, effortless, orderly, uneventful, untroubled** The plane made a *smooth* landing. —*verb* ✦ **even, flatten, make level, straighten** ◇ **press** Please *smooth* the tablecloth before you set out the dishes.

smother *verb* ✦ **extinguish, snuff, stifle** ◇ **choke, strangle, suffocate** We threw sand on the campfire to *smother* the flames.

smudge *verb* ✦ **blur, rub, smear** ◇ **mess up, soil, spot, stain** I *smudged* the lines of my pencil drawing to give it a soft look. —*noun* ✦ **blot,** blotch, smear, spot, stain, streak Mom wiped the *smudge* of dirt off my face.

snake *verb* ✦ **meander, twist, weave, wind** ◇ **coil, spiral** A little stream *snakes* through the valley.

snap *verb* 1. ✦ **break, crack, fracture, splinter, split** ◇ **crackle, pop** The twig *snapped* when I stepped on it. 2. ✦ **bite, nip, snatch, strike** ◇ **grasp, seize** Don't put your finger in the cage or the parrot might *snap* at it. —*noun* 1. ✦ **crack, crackle, pop** ◇ **click** We could hear the *snap* of the logs as they started to burn. 2. ◇ **fastener** Dad's western shirt has mother-of-pearl *snaps*.

snare *noun* ✦ **trap** ◇ **bait, lure, net, noose** The Scouts learned how to make a *snare* in their outdoor survival class.

snatch *verb* ✦ **grab, pluck, seize, snap up, take** ◇ **catch** Joel *snatched* an apple from the bowl as he ran out the door. —*noun* ✦ **bit, fragment, part, portion, segment** ◇ **piece** The woman caught brief *snatches* of the TV news as she made dinner.

sneak *verb* 1. ✦ **creep, slink, steal** ◇ **crawl, slither** I could just see the skunk *sneaking* along the fence. 2. ✦ **slip, smuggle, spirit** ◇ **hide** Mom plans to *sneak* Dad's birthday presents into the house while I distract him.

snip *verb* ✦ **clip, cut** ◇ **nip, slice, trim** Amy *snipped* some pictures out of a magazine for her report.

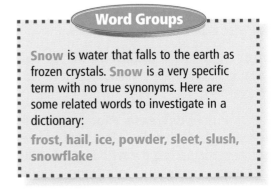

Word Groups

Snow is water that falls to the earth as frozen crystals. **Snow** is a very specific term with no true synonyms. Here are some related words to investigate in a dictionary:

frost, hail, ice, powder, sleet, slush, snowflake

snub *verb* ✦ **avoid, ignore, shun, spurn** ✧ **insult, offend, slight** My cat *snubbed* me after I left him alone for the weekend. —*noun* ✦ **discourtesy, insult, offense, slight** ✧ **oversight** It was an unintentional *snub* when I forgot to respond to my friend's invitation.

snug *adjective* **1.** ✦ **comfortable, cozy** ✧ **safe, secure, sheltered** The cabin was warm and *snug* during the storm. **2.** ✦ **confining, small, tight** ✧ **close, compact, narrow** The jacket was too *snug* in the arms so I gave it to my younger sister.

snuggle *verb* ✦ **cuddle, curl up, nestle** ✧ **embrace, hug, nuzzle** I like to *snuggle* with my kitten on the couch.

soak *verb* **1.** ✦ **drench, saturate, wet** ✧ **immerse, steep** We got *soaked* from playing with the hose. **2.** ✦ **absorb, sop up, take up** ✧ **dry, mop** I used a paper towel to *soak up* the spilled milk.

soar *verb* **1.** ✦ **float, fly, glide, hover, sail** ✧ **coast** The balloons from the parade *soared* high above us. **2.** ✦ **climb, increase, lift, mount, multiply, rise** The company's profits *soared* as their product became popular.

sob *verb* ✦ **bawl, cry, wail, weep, whimper** ✧ **yowl** The baby *sobbed* because it was tired and hungry. —*noun* ✦ **cry, wail, whimper** ✧ **yowl** There were *sobs* from the audience at the end of the sad movie.

sober *adjective* ✦ **grave, grim, sad, serious, solemn, somber** We were all in a *sober* mood after we heard the bad news.

sociable *adjective* ✦ **cordial, friendly, genial, neighborly, social** ✧ **hospitable** Our *sociable* neighbor is always coming over for a visit.

social *adjective* **1.** ✦ **civic, community, public** ✧ **common, popular** The quality of education is an important *social* issue. **2.** ✦ **amiable, cordial, friendly, outgoing, sociable** Mom says that I am a *social* person because I have lots of friends.

society *noun* **1.** ✦ **the community, the people, the public** ✧ **civilization, humanity** The criminal was sent to prison because he was a threat to *society*. **2.** ✦ **association, club, group, organization** ✧ **union** Trisha and Marianna joined a bird-watching *society*.

soft *adjective* **1.** ✦ **mushy, pulpy, spongy, squishy** ✧ **fleshy, yielding** These apples have gotten too *soft* to eat. **2.** ✦ **delicate, fine, fluffy, smooth** ✧ **satiny, silky** My pet guinea pig has *soft* fur. ▲ **3.** ✦ **hushed, low, mellow, quiet, subdued** ✧ **gentle, mild** Dad uses a *soft* voice when he's reading my little brother to sleep.

soggy *adjective* ✦ **saturated, soaked, soaking, sopping, wet** ✧ **damp** The cardboard box was *soggy* after being left outside in the rain.

soil[1] *noun* ✦ **dirt, earth, humus, loam** ✧ **ground** We mixed fertilizer with the *soil* when we planted our garden.

soil[2] *verb* ✦ **dirty, muddy, smear, smudge, stain** ✧ **foul** We *soiled* our football uniforms playing on the muddy field.

soldier *noun* ✦ **combatant, fighter** ✧ **warrior** There were hundreds of *soldiers* involved in the battle.

sole *adjective* ✦ **lone, one, only, single, solitary** ✧ **particular** My *sole* reason for going to the mall was to look for my friend Karen.

solemn *adjective* ✦ **earnest, grave, grim, serious, sober, somber** Everybody at the funeral had *solemn* expressions on their faces.

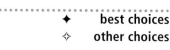

✦ **best choices**
✧ **other choices**

solid *adjective* **1.** ✦ **firm, sound, stable, sturdy, substantial** ✧ **concrete, dense, hard** The building may be old, but it has good, *solid* walls. **2.** ✦ **continual, continuous, unbroken, uninterrupted** ✧ **constant** There was a *solid* line of traffic all the way to the airport. **3.** ✦ **dependable, steady, strong** My best friend and I have a *solid* friendship.

solitary *adjective* ✦ **individual, isolated, lone, single** ✧ **alone, lonely** We passed a *solitary* runner beside the canal.

solution *noun* **1.** ✦ **blend, compound, mixture** ✧ **fluid, liquid** We cleaned the entire carpet with a special *solution* designed to remove stains. **2.** ✦ **answer, explanation, key** ✧ **interpretation, result** Lawrence guessed the *solution* to my riddle.

solve *verb* ✦ **answer, figure out, resolve, work out** ✧ **explain** It took me a long time to *solve* the tough math problem.

somber *adjective* ✦ **dismal, grim, melancholy, sad, serious, sober, solemn** We were in a *somber* mood after hearing about the accident.

sometimes *adverb* ✦ **at times, now and then, occasionally, periodically** I usually walk to school, but *sometimes* I ride my bike.

song *noun* ✦ **melody, tune** ✧ **air, anthem, ballad, carol, hymn** We sang *songs* in the car on the way to the game.

soon *adverb* ✦ **before long, promptly, quickly, rapidly, shortly** ✧ **directly** If we don't get there *soon* they might be sold out of the CD I want.

soothe *verb* ✦ **ease, relax, relieve** ✧ **calm, quiet, settle** I took a hot bath to *soothe* my stiff muscles.

Antonyms
soothe *verb*
agitate, fluster, irritate, unsettle, upset

sore *adjective* ✦ **aching, hurting, painful, sensitive, tender** My sprained wrist is still *sore*. —*noun* ✦ **hurt, injury, wound** ✧ **bruise, infection, inflammation** I need a bandage for the *sore* on my knee.

sorrow *noun* ✦ **anguish, distress, grief, heartache, sadness, unhappiness** There was *sorrow* throughout the kingdom when the young princess died.

sorry *adjective* **1.** ✦ **apologetic, contrite, regretful** ✧ **sad, sorrowful** I am *sorry* that I forgot your birthday. **2.** ✦ **inferior, miserable, pitiful, poor, ridiculous, wretched** The double chocolate cupcakes I made turned out to be a *sorry* mess.

sort *noun* ✦ **kind, manner, type, variety** ✧ **brand, category** Winona and I tried all *sorts* of different foods at the international fair. —*verb* ✦ **arrange, categorize, classify, group, organize, separate** Our class officers *sorted* the items for the school rummage sale.

sound[1] *noun* ✦ **noise** ✧ **clamor, din, racket, roar** Do you hear that strange *sound*? —*verb* **1.** ✦ **chime, peal, ring, toll** ✧ **resound** The cook *sounded* the dinner bell ten minutes before the meal was to be served. **2.** ✦ **appear, look, seem** It *sounds* as if you had a good day at school.

sound[2] *adjective* **1.** ✦ **solid, strong, sturdy, undamaged** ✧ **firm** The old barn is still *sound*. **2.** ✦ **good, logical, prudent, reasonable, sensible, wise** My older sister gave me some *sound* advice about school.

sour *adjective* **1.** ✦ **acidic, tangy, tart** ✧ **bitter, sharp** The *sour* candy made my mouth water. **2.** ✦ **bad, curdled, spoiled** ✧ **fermented** *Sour* milk has a disgusting smell. —*verb* ✦ **curdle, go bad, spoil** ✧ **ferment** Milk will *sour* if it is left unrefrigerated.

source *noun* **1.** ✦ **reference, resource** ✧ **authority, basis, fountain** An encyclopedia is a good *source* for facts. **2.** ✦ **beginning, head, origin, outset, start** The Colorado River has its *source* in the Rocky Mountains.

souvenir *noun* ✦ **keepsake** ✧ **gift, reminder, token** My friend brought me a *souvenir* from his trip to Hawaii.

sovereign *noun* ✦ **monarch, ruler** ✧ **emperor, king, queen** The United States has never had a *sovereign*. —*adjective* **1.** ✦ **regal, royal** ✧ **absolute, imperial, supreme** The queen exercised her *sovereign* power when she declared a national holiday. **2.** ✦ **free, independent, self-governing, self-ruling** Mozambique became a *sovereign* nation in 1975.

space *noun* **1.** ✦ **gap, opening, separation** ✧ **break, crack, hole** I'm wearing braces to close up the *spaces* between my teeth. **2.** ✦ **area, expanse, room** ✧ **distance, spread** Our new piano takes up a lot of *space* in the living room. —*verb* ✦ **arrange, array, place, separate** ✧ **order, organize** The trees were *spaced* far enough apart to give them room to grow.

span *noun* ✦ **duration, interval, length, period, range, term** A sequoia tree's life *span* can be several thousand years. —*verb* ✦ **bridge, cover, cross, stretch over** ✧ **reach** The fallen telephone pole *spanned* the width of the road.

spare *verb* **1.** ✦ **protect, save** ✧ **exempt, pardon, rescue** We *spared* the mouse's life by using a no-kill trap. **2.** ✦ **part with** ✧ **donate, give, lend** Can you *spare* a few sheets of paper? —*adjective* **1.** ✦ **additional, extra, reserve, substitute, unused** ✧ **surplus** We have a *spare* bedroom for overnight guests. **2.** ✦ **lean, skinny, slender, slim, thin** ✧ **gaunt** Greyhound dogs have a *spare* build.

sparkle *verb* ✦ **gleam, glimmer, glitter, shimmer, twinkle** ✧ **flash** The snow *sparkled* in the moonlight. —*noun* ✦ **flash, flicker, gleam, glimmer, glitter, twinkle** The diamond earrings gave off *sparkles* of light.

spasm *noun* ✦ **contraction, convulsion, cramp** ✧ **seizure** A muscle *spasm* can be painful.

speak *verb* **1.** ✦ **chat, converse, talk** ✧ **chatter, communicate** We were just *speaking* about you, and here you are. **2.** ✦ **declare, express, say, state, tell, utter** The witness swore that he *spoke* the truth.

spear *noun* ✧ **harpoon, javelin, lance** Roman soldiers generally carried *spears* into battle. —*verb* ✦ **jab, lance, pierce, stab, stick** ✧ **thrust** Joseph *speared* a piece of chicken with his fork.

special *adjective* ✦ **distinctive, particular, specific** ✧ **individual, unique** My grandfather is on a *special* diet to lower his cholesterol.

specialty *noun* ✦ **specialization, strong point** ✧ **accomplishment, skill, talent** As a cook, my brother's *specialties* are grilled cheese sandwiches and tuna melts.

species *noun* ✧ **category, classification, kind, sort, type, variety** There are about 750,000 known *species* of insects.

specific *adjective* ✦ **clear, definite, exact, explicit, particular, precise** The teacher gave us *specific* directions for the science project.

Antonyms

specific *adjective*

ambiguous, general, open, unclear, vague

specimen *noun* ✦ **example, sample** ✧ **item, piece, sort, type** Carl showed me some different *specimens* of quartz from his rock collection.

speck *noun* ✦ **bit, grain, particle** ✧ **drop, fleck, spot** The wind blew a *speck* of dirt into my eye.

spectacle *noun* ✦ **display, exhibition, performance, presentation, show, sight** The laser light show was a fascinating *spectacle*.

spectacular *adjective* ✦ **dramatic, impressive, magnificent, remarkable, sensational** On New Year's Eve we watched a *spectacular* display of fireworks from the roof of our building.

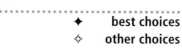

✦ **best choices**
✧ **other choices**

speculate *verb* ✦ **contemplate, deliberate about, ponder, reflect on, think about** The philosopher *speculated on* the meaning of life.

speech *noun* **1.** ✦ **speaking, talk, talking, utterance** ✧ **dialect, language** Parrots can be trained to imitate human *speech*. **2.** ✦ **address, lecture, talk** ✧ **discussion, sermon** The mayor gave a *speech* at the annual Fourth of July picnic.

speed *noun* ✦ **pace, rate, velocity** ✧ **haste, quickness, swiftness** The cheetah can run at a *speed* of about sixty miles per hour. —*verb* ✦ **bolt, dart, fly, race, rush, shoot** ✧ **whiz, zoom** The black horse *sped* past the others to win the race.

spell¹ *noun* ✦ **charm, enchantment, magic spell** ✧ **formula, incantation** We fell under the *spell* of the beautiful tropical beach. ▼

spell² *noun* ✦ **interval, period, span, stretch, time** ✧ **bout** The sunshine was very welcome after the long *spell* of rainy weather.

spend *verb* **1.** ✦ **expend, lay out, pay out** ✧ **exchange, trade** How much money did you *spend* at the book fair? **2.** ✦ **consume, fill, occupy, pass, put in, use up** Jay *spends* a lot time exploring the Internet.

sphere *noun* **1.** ✦ **ball, globe** ✧ **oval** The Earth is a *sphere* that is slightly flattened at its poles.

2. ✦ **area, domain, range, reach, realm, scope** ✧ **field** England's *sphere* of influence formerly included India and parts of Africa.

spice *noun* ✦ **flavoring, seasoning** ✧ **herb, relish, zest** Ginger is a *spice* that is commonly used in Chinese cooking. —*verb* ✦ **flavor, season** ✧ **enhance, improve** I *spiced* the hot apple cider with cinnamon, nutmeg, and cloves.

spill *verb* ✦ **flow, pour, run, slop, splash** ✧ **overflow** Root beer *spilled* all over when I dropped my glass. —*noun* ✦ **dive, fall, plunge, tumble** ✧ **accident** I took a *spill* when I went skateboarding yesterday.

spin *verb* **1.** ✦ **narrate, recount, relate, tell** ✧ **report** I like to hear Grandmother *spin* tales about her childhood. **2.** ✦ **revolve, rotate, turn, twirl, whirl** How long can you make this top *spin*? —*noun* **1.** ✦ **revolution, rotation, turn, twirl, whirl** Quinton gave the bicycle wheel a *spin* to see if it was in balance. **2.** ✦ **drive, jaunt, ride** ✧ **excursion, run** My parents took our new car for a *spin* around the neighborhood.

spirit *noun* **1.** ✦ **soul** ✧ **consciousness, essence, heart, mind** Many religions teach that the *spirit* lives on after the body dies. **2.** ✦ **ghost, phantom, specter** People say that this house is haunted by *spirits*. **3.** ✦ **energy, enthusiasm, pep, vigor** ✧ **bravery, courage, pluck** The cheerleaders shouted with lots of *spirit*. —*verb* ✦ **carry off, make off with, smuggle away, sneak away** We *spirited away* Alex's birthday gift before he could see it.

spite *noun* ✦ **animosity, ill will, malice, nastiness, resentment** He said that nasty remark out of *spite*. —*verb* ✦ **annoy, irritate, needle, nettle, provoke, upset** She withheld the information just to *spite* him.

splendid *adjective* ✦ **beautiful, glorious, impressive, magnificent, remarkable, wonderful** The peacock's tail looked *splendid* in the sun.

splendor *noun* ✦ **beauty, brilliance, glory, magnificence, majesty** We were impressed by the *splendor* of the Great Smoky Mountains.

split *verb* **1.** ✦ **carve, cut, slice** ✧ **break, burst, crack** Mom *split* the watermelon in two with a big knife. **2.** ✦ **distribute, divide, separate, share** ✧ **allot** We agreed to *split* the work so that we could get it done faster. —*noun* ✦ **rip, slash, tear** ✧ **break, crack, separation** There is a *split* in the seam of my blue jeans.

spoil *verb* **1.** ✦ **foul up, mess up, ruin, upset, wreck** ✧ **destroy** The sudden rainstorm *spoiled* our day at the beach. **2.** ✦ **decay, decompose, go bad, rot** ✧ **curdle, sour** I threw the fruit away because it had *spoiled*. **3.** ✦ **baby, cater to, coddle, indulge, pamper** The woman *spoiled* her cats by feeding them fresh fish.

sponsor *noun* ✦ **backer, contributor (to), promoter, supporter** ✧ **patron** Mom's company is one of the *sponsors* of our roller hockey team. —*verb* ✦ **back, finance, promote, support** That bakery *sponsors* an annual pie-eating contest which Toni won last year.

spontaneous *adjective* ✦ **ad-lib, improvised, impulsive, informal, unplanned** Our teacher set aside her lesson plan and gave us a *spontaneous* talk.

sport *noun* ✦ **athletics** ✧ **competition, contest, game, recreation** My dad played *sports* in high school and college.

spot *noun* **1.** ✦ **blotch, dot, fleck, mark, patch, speck** ✧ **blot, stain** Dalmatians have black *spots* on white fur. **2.** ✦ **area, location, place, point, position, site** This looks like a good *spot* to build our snow fort. —*verb* **1.** ✦ **dot, fleck, mark, spatter, sprinkle** ✧ **stain** The floor in the artist's studio was *spotted* with paint. **2.** ✦ **glimpse, observe, see, spy** ✧ **detect, find, locate** The boaters were thrilled when they *spotted* the migrating whales.

spray *noun* ✦ **mist, shower, sprinkle** ✧ **drizzle, squirt** There are birds bathing in the *spray* from the fountain. —*verb* ✦ **shoot, shower, spurt, squirt** ✧ **splash, spout, sprinkle** The firefighters *sprayed* water on the burning building.

spread *verb* **1.** ✦ **expand, extend, open up, stretch out, unfold** The pigeons *spread* their wings and flew away. **2.** ✦ **layer, put, smear, smooth** ✧ **coat, cover** Judy *spread* cream cheese on her bagel. **3.** ✦ **circulate, distribute, repeat, report** ✧ **broadcast** Mom says that it's not nice to *spread* gossip. —*noun* **1.** ✦ **advance, development, expansion, growth** ✧ **increase** This ointment can stop the *spread* of your rash. **2.** ✦ **breadth, extent, span, stretch, width** ✧ **expanse, range, size, sweep** The wandering albatross has wings with a *spread* of twelve feet. **3.** ✦ **bedspread, cover** ✧ **blanket, quilt** My aunt made me a quilted *spread* for my bed.

spring *verb* **1.** ✦ **bounce, bound, jump, leap** ✧ **hop, skip** Our dog *sprang* up and ran to the door when he heard the mail carrier. **2.** ✦ **appear, arise, emerge, grow, rise, sprout** Flowers *sprang up* in the desert after the heavy rainfall.

sprinkle *verb* **1.** ✦ **scatter, shake, spread** ✧ **dribble, dust, trickle** Nicole *sprinkled* salt on her popcorn. **2.** ✦ **drizzle, rain, shower** ✧ **mist** It *sprinkled* lightly during the first event of the track meet and then stopped. —*noun* **1.** ✦ **bit, dash, touch, trace** ✧ **dribble, trickle** Mom put a *sprinkle* of sugar on top of the cookies. **2.** ✦ **drizzle, rain, shower** ✧ **mist** This afternoon's *sprinkle* barely wet the pavement.

sprout *verb* ✦ **arise, bud, come up, germinate, grow** ✧ **bloom, flower** Everything that we planted in our garden is now beginning to *sprout*. —*noun* ✦ **seedling, shoot** ✧ **bud, runner, stem, tendril** We grew alfalfa *sprouts* in a jar.

spur *verb* ✦ **egg (on), goad, inspire, motivate, move, stimulate** ✧ **prompt, urge** The coach's pep talk *spurred* us to victory over our rivals.

✦ **best choices**
✧ **other choices**

spurt *noun* **1.** ✦ **jet, squirt, stream** ✧ **gush, spout, spray** The sprinklers in the park shoot big *spurts* of water over the grass. **2.** ✦ **burst,** ✧ **blast, gust, outbreak** Josh won the race with a final *spurt* of energy. —*verb* ✦ **gush, splash, spray, squirt** ✧ **spout** Water *spurted* all over the floor from the broken faucet.

spy *noun* ✦ **agent, secret agent, undercover agent** ✧ **informer** The *spy* stole some secret government documents. —*verb* **1.** ✦ **scout out, snoop around, watch** ✧ **eavesdrop, peep, pry** The secret agent was sent to *spy on* the enemy camp. **2.** ✦ **detect, glimpse, notice, see, spot** ✧ **observe** I *spied* Yolanda in the crowd.

squabble *verb* ✦ **argue, bicker, dispute, fight, quarrel** ✧ **feud** My sister and I *squabbled* over who would get to wear Mom's charm bracelet. —*noun* ✦ **argument, disagreement, dispute, fight, quarrel** ✧ **feud** The two friends quickly resolved their *squabble*.

squad *noun* ✦ **detail, group, unit** ✧ **company, platoon, team** A *squad* of soldiers was sent to guard the embassy.

squall *noun* ✦ **gale, storm, windstorm** ✧ **flurry, tempest** We got caught in a *squall* on our fishing trip.

square *noun* ✧ **block, box, cube, rectangle** Graph paper is marked into many small *squares*.

squash *verb* ✦ **crush, mash, smash** ✧ **compress, press, squeeze** We *squashed* the bananas to make banana bread.

squat *verb* ✦ **crouch** ✧ **bend, hunch, kneel, stoop** Dad *squatted* down to help my little brother tie his shoe.

squeal *noun* ✦ **scream, screech, shriek, yell, yowl** ✧ **wail** My little sister let out a *squeal* when she stubbed her toe. —*verb* ✦ **scream, screech, shriek, yell, yowl** ✧ **wail** We *squealed* with laughter during our pillow fight at the slumber party.

squeeze *verb* **1.** ✦ **cram, crowd, jam, pack, stuff** ✧ **compress** We were barely able to *squeeze* the Thanksgiving leftovers into the refrigerator. **2.** ✦ **force, press, twist, wring** ✧ **crush, extract** You pull this lever to *squeeze* the water from the mop. —*noun* ✦ **embrace, hug** ✧ **clasp, clutch, grasp** Dad put his arm around my shoulder and gave me a *squeeze*.

squirm *verb* ✦ **twist, wiggle, wriggle** ✧ **jerk, shift, turn** The garter snake *squirmed* out of my grasp.

squirt *verb* ✦ **discharge, eject, expel, spray, spurt** ✧ **gush, splash** An octopus *squirts* a cloud of ink when it is frightened. —*noun* ✦ **jet, spray, spurt, stream** ✧ **gush, splash** A *squirt* of water from the hose hit my face. ▶

stab *verb* ✦ **jab, plunge, prick, stick, thrust** ✧ **puncture** The zoo's veterinarian *stabbed* a big needle through the elephant's thick, wrinkled skin. —*noun* ✦ **jab, poke, thrust** ✧ **lunge, plunge** I made a *stab* at the meatball with a toothpick.

stable *adjective* ✦ **firm, fixed, immovable, secure, steady** ✧ **solid, sound** Before Mary climbed up the ladder, she made sure that it was *stable*.

Antonyms
stable *adjective*
precarious, shaky, unstable, unsteady, wobbly

stack *noun* ✦ **heap, mass, mound, pile** ✧ **batch, bundle** We have *stacks* of old magazines in the basement. —*verb* ✦ **heap, mound, pile**

◇ **assemble, group, load** I *stacked* all my tapes in one corner of my room.

staff *noun* **1.** ✦ **stave, walking stick** ◇ **cane, pole, rod, wand** The shepherd used his *staff* to herd his sheep and to lean on. **2.** ✦ **assistants, employees, help, personnel** ◇ **crew, team** The senator's *staff* did the research for her proposed bill.

stage *noun* ✦ **phase, period, step** ◇ **degree, level, point** The new housing project is in its final *stage* of development. —*verb* ✦ **act out, dramatize, perform, present, put on** ◇ **direct** My sisters and I like to *stage* plays for our friends.

stagger *verb* **1.** ✦ **lurch, reel, stumble, sway, weave, wobble** I whirled around and around until I *staggered* from dizziness. **2.** ✦ **amaze, astonish, astound, overwhelm, startle** ◇ **surprise** The man was *staggered* by the news that he had won the lottery.

stagnant *adjective* ✦ **dirty, foul, stale** ◇ **contaminated, polluted** I changed the *stagnant* water in my vase of flowers.

stain *verb* ✦ **dirty, discolor, smear, smudge, soil** ◇ **blemish, blot** The leaky ballpoint pen *stained* my fingers. —*noun* ✦ **blemish, blot, blotch, mark, smear, smudge** I hope this paint *stain* on my shirt will come out. ▼

stake *noun* ✦ **pole, post, stick** ◇ **peg, picket, pin, spike** We supported the tomato plant by tying it to a *stake*. —*verb* ✦ **mark, mark off, outline** ◇ **define, limit** We *staked out* the borders for our new flower garden.

stale *adjective* ✦ **dry, hard, old** ◇ **moldy, rotten, spoiled** Let's feed this *stale* bread to the ducks at the park.

stalk *verb* **1.** ✦ **march, stamp, stride, tramp** ◇ **swagger** The angry customer *stalked* out of the store. **2.** ✦ **follow, hunt, shadow, track, trail** ◇ **chase, pursue** The lion *stalked* its prey with great patience.

stall *noun* **1.** ✦ **enclosure, pen** ◇ **barn, corral, shed, stable** It's your turn to clean out the horse's *stall*. **2.** ✦ **booth, stand** ◇ **counter, store, table** We set up a *stall* at the swap meet to sell our comic books. —*verb* ✦ **die, halt, quit, stop** ◇ **delay, interrupt** Mom took her car to the mechanic because the engine is always *stalling*.

stammer *verb* ✦ **stutter** ◇ **falter, mumble, sputter, stumble** I *stammer* sometimes when I get excited.

stamp *verb* **1.** ✦ **step, tramp, trample, tread** ◇ **crush, mash, squash** Rashid *stamped* on the aluminum can before putting it in the recycling bin. **2.** ✦ **imprint, label, mark, print** ◇ **seal** We *stamped* the package with our return address. —*noun* ✦ **emblem, label, mark, seal** ◇ **symbol** The clerk put the bank's *stamp* on the important document.

stampede *noun* ✦ **charge, dash, flight, race, rush** ◇ **panic** There was a *stampede* to the creek when the thirsty cattle smelled the water. —*verb* ✦ **bolt, flee, scatter, take flight** ◇ **panic** The buffalo *stampeded* when they sensed danger.

stand *verb* **1.** ✦ **arise, get up, rise** We all *stood up* when the national anthem began to play. **2.** ✦ **be located, be situated** ◇ **position, rest, sit** The Eiffel Tower *stands* in Paris, France.

3. ✦ **apply, last, persist, remain, stay** ◇ **exist** I tried to change Mom's mind, but she said that her decision still *stands*. **4.** ✦ **bear, endure, take, tolerate, withstand** ◇ **deal, handle** How can you *stand* to live without a TV set? —*noun* **1.** ✦ **booth, stall** ◇ **pushcart, shop, store** We bought oranges at the fruit *stand*. **2.** ✦ **rack, support** ◇ **counter, platform, table** I need a *stand* to hold my music book while I practice. **3.** ✦ **attitude, position, viewpoint** ◇ **opinion, policy** Grandpa tends to take a conservative *stand* on political issues.

standard *noun* **1.** ✦ **guideline, ideal, principle** ◇ **example, model, pattern** Our teacher sets high *standards* for us. **2.** ✦ **banner, ensign, flag, pennant** Elizabeth carried the school *standard* in the parade. —*adjective* ✦ **customary, normal, ordinary, regular, typical, usual** ◇ **average, routine** A *standard* baseball team has nine players.

stanza *noun* ✦ **verse** ◇ **paragraph, part, section** Kimberly recited all three *stanzas* of her favorite poem.

star *noun* ✦ **lead, principal** ◇ **leading lady, leading man, hero, heroine** My best friend was the *star* of our school play. —*verb* ✦ **feature** ◇ **introduce, present, promote** This opera *stars* my favorite singer.

stare *verb* ✦ **gape, gawk, gaze, look, peer** ◇ **glare, observe, ogle, watch** My dog *stares* at me whenever I am eating something. —*noun* ✦ **glance, glare, look** ◇ **gape, gaze** The librarian gave us a disapproving *stare* when we talked too loudly.

start *verb* **1.** ✦ **depart, embark, get going, leave, set out** We'll need to *start* early if we want to get back before dark. **2.** ✦ **begin, commence, initiate, open** ◇ **activate, undertake** Adam *starts* his day by feeding the fish in his aquarium. **3.** ✦ **create, establish, found, institute, launch, pioneer** Automobiles *started* a new age of transportation. —*noun* ✦ **beginning, commence-** ment, onset, opening ◇ **initiation** I am looking forward to the *start* of the holiday season.

startle *verb* ✦ **alarm, frighten, scare, shock, surprise** You *startled* me because I hadn't heard you come home.

state *noun* **1.** ✦ **circumstance, condition, situation** ◇ **position, shape** Our house was in a *state* of confusion while we were having the kitchen remodeled. **2.** ✦ **country, nation** ◇ **dominion, land, republic** The *state* of Israel was founded in 1948. —*verb* ✦ **announce, declare, express, proclaim, say, speak** The witness *stated* her name for the record.

stately *adjective* ✦ **august, dignified, grand, solemn** ◇ **majestic, noble, regal, royal** The Presidential inauguration is a *stately* occasion.

statement *noun* ✦ **announcement, bulletin, declaration** ◇ **commentary, proclamation** The congressman's aide read a *statement* to the press.

station *noun* **1.** ✦ **position, post** ◇ **location, place, stand** The guard was instructed not to leave her *station* beside the entrance. **2.** ✦ **headquarters, office** ◇ **base, center** We went down to the police *station* to turn in the purse that we had found. **3.** ✦ **depot, terminal** ◇ **stop** The bus *station* is on Main Street. —*verb* ✦ **assign to, place at, position at, post at** ◇ **locate, situate** Carlos was *stationed at* the information booth during the school carnival.

stationary *adjective* ✦ **fixed, immobile, motionless, unmoving** ◇ **steady, still** Mom likes to read while riding her *stationary* bike.

stationery *noun* ✦ **notepaper, paper, writing paper** I wrote my grandmother a letter on a piece of my favorite *stationery*.

statue *noun* ✦ **figure, sculpture** ◇ **bust, image, likeness** The famous *statue* of Abraham Lincoln at his memorial in Washington, D.C., was sculpted by Daniel Chester French.

status *noun* ✦ **position, rank, standing** ◈ **grade, place, situation** The president of a bank holds a position of high *status*.

stay *verb* **1.** ✦ **linger, remain, wait** ◈ **loiter, pause** We *stayed* in the movie theater until everyone else had left. **2.** ✦ **abide, dwell, live, lodge, reside** ◈ **visit** I'm going to *stay* with my friend in Florida over the school holiday. —*noun* ✦ **visit** ◈ **holiday, stopover, vacation** I am looking forward to having a nice *stay* at my cousin's.

> **Antonyms**
> **stay** *verb*
> 1. depart, exit, go, leave, retire, withdraw

steady *adjective* **1.** ✦ **firm, solid, stable** ◈ **sound, strong** Is that old ladder *steady* enough to hold my weight? **2.** ✦ **constant, continuous, even, regular, uniform** The ferry made *steady* progress toward the island. —*verb* ✦ **brace, hold fast, secure, support** ◈ **balance** Please help *steady* the canoe while I get in.

steal *verb* **1.** ✦ **pilfer, snatch, thieve** ◈ **loot, plunder, rob** Magpies often *steal* shiny objects and take them back to their nests. **2.** ✦ **creep, glide, slink, slip, sneak, tiptoe** ◈ **prowl** I didn't hear my little brother *steal* into the room.

steam *noun* ✦ **condensation, mist, moisture, vapor** ◈ **fog** *Steam* from the shower fogged up the bathroom mirror. —*verb* ✦ **cruise, navigate** ◈ **run, sail, travel** During the 1800's, riverboats *steamed* up and down the Mississippi.

steep[1] *adjective* ✦ **perpendicular, sheer, upright, vertical** ◈ **high** The walls of the Grand Canyon are *steep* cliffs.

steep[2] *verb* ✦ **immerse, soak, submerge** ◈ **saturate** *Steep* the tea leaves in water that is hot but not boiling.

steer *verb* ✦ **control, direct, guide, maneuver** ◈ **navigate, pilot** I can *steer* my bicycle with no hands.

step *noun* **1.** ✦ **footstep, pace, stride** ◈ **move, tread, walk** Andrew took a *step* forward when his name was called. **2.** ✦ **act, action, measure, procedure** ◈ **level, stage** Installing a smoke alarm is an important *step* in fire safety. —*verb* ✦ **tread, walk** ◈ **pace, shuffle, stride** Laura tried not to *step* on any of the cracks in the sidewalk.

sterilize *verb* ✦ **clean, cleanse, disinfect, purify** ◈ **pasteurize** Mom *sterilized* the needle by wiping it with rubbing alcohol.

stern[1] *adjective* ✦ **hard, harsh, severe, sharp, strict** ◈ **grave, grim** I received a *stern* look when I slammed the door.

stern[2] *noun* ✦ **back, end, rear, tail** We stood at the *stern* of the boat to watch the dolphins.

stick *noun* ✦ **branch, stem, switch, twig** ◈ **limb, pole, rod, shaft** I wrote my name in the sand with a *stick*. —*verb* **1.** ✦ **jab, pierce, poke, puncture, prick, stab** Katlyn *stuck* holes in the potato so that it wouldn't explode in the microwave. **2.** ✦ **attach, fasten, put up** ◈ **glue, nail, paste, pin, tape** Kevin *stuck up* basketball posters all over his bedroom walls. **3.** ✦ **adhere, cling, hold** ◈ **bond, catch, fix, stay** Static electricity made the balloon *stick* to my hair. **4.** ✦ **extend, protrude, push, put, thrust** ◈ **place, position** My dog loves to *stick* his head out the car window when we take him for a ride.

sticky *adjective* **1.** ✦ **gluey, gummy, tacky** ◈ **adhesive, syrupy** The sap of a pine tree is very *sticky*. **2.** ✦ **clammy, humid, muggy** ◈ **damp, moist, wet** The rain was a relief after the hot and *sticky* weather.

stiff *adjective* **1.** ✦ **hard, inelastic, inflexible, rigid, unbending, unyielding** ◈ **taut** Coat hangers are made from *stiff* wire. **2.** ✦ **intense, keen, powerful, strong, tough** ◈ **forceful** Competition was not as *stiff* at the football playoffs as we had expected it to be.

✦ **best choices**
◈ **other choices**

231

stifle *verb* ✦ **control, hold back, restrain, smother, stop, suppress** I tried to *stifle* my laughter as I read the funny book in the library.

still *adjective* **1.** ✦ **hushed, noiseless, quiet, silent, soundless** The students were *still* as their teacher read them a story. **2.** ✦ **calm, motionless, placid, serene, unmoving** ◇ **stationary** The lake was perfectly *still* after the wind died down. —*noun* ✦ **hush, quiet, quietness, silence, stillness, tranquility** The *still* of the night was broken by an owl's screech. ◄ —*adverb* ✦ **nevertheless, nonetheless** ◇ **however, too, yet** Morgan's hair is getting long, but he's *still* letting it grow.

stimulate *verb* ✦ **arouse, awaken, encourage, excite, quicken, spur** Going to the air show *stimulated* my desire to become a pilot.

sting *verb* ✦ **bite, burn, chafe** ◇ **hurt, injure, smart, wound** The cold wind *stung* my cheeks.

stingy *adjective* ✦ **cheap, miserly, tight, ungenerous** ◇ **greedy** My brother is really *stingy* with his candy.

stink *verb* ✦ **reek, smell, smell bad** That rotting fish on the beach is beginning to *stink*. —*noun* ✦ **bad smell, foul odor, reek, smell** There is quite a *stink* coming from the garbage can.

stir *verb* ✦ **agitate, beat, blend, churn, mix, whip** I *stirred* the cake batter until it was smooth. —*noun* ✦ **commotion, disturbance, tumult, turmoil, uproar** Mom's long-lost brother caused quite a *stir* when he showed up at our front door.

stock *noun* **1.** ✦ **hoard, reserve, store, supply** ◇ **inventory** We keep a *stock* of canned foods for emergency use. **2.** ✦ **animals, livestock**

◇ **cattle, herd** The rancher branded her *stock* before turning them loose on the range. **3.** ✦ **ancestry, blood, line, origin, parentage** ◇ **clan, kindred, lineage** My Dad likes to say that he comes from sturdy farming *stock*. —*verb* ✦ **fill, furnish, provide, supply** ◇ **equip, store** We *stocked* our refrigerator with fresh fruits and vegetables. ▲

stocky *adjective* ✦ **heavyset, solid, stout, sturdy, thick, thickset** I'm just like my uncle—short and *stocky*.

stomach *noun* ✦ **belly, gut** ◇ **abdomen, midsection** My *stomach* is growling because I am hungry.

stone *noun* **1.** ✦ **pebble, rock** ◇ **boulder, cobble** Darryl skipped a *stone* across the pond. **2.** ✦ **gem, gemstone, jewel, precious stone** The *stone* in my ring is an opal.

stoop *verb* **1.** ✦ **bend down, lean over** ◇ **bow, crouch, duck, kneel, squat** Cynthia *stooped down* to pick up the crayons that she had dropped. **2.** ✦ **resort, sink, submit, succumb** ◇ **descend, fall** I would never *stoop* to cheating. —*noun* ✦ **slouch** ◇ **bend, bow, droop, sag** Mom always corrects my posture so that I don't develop a *stoop*.

stop *verb* **1.** ✦ **cease, discontinue, halt, quit** ◇ **pause, suspend** I had to *stop* running because I got a cramp in my leg. **2.** ✦ **bar, block, check, prevent, restrain** ◇ **intercept** The manager *stopped* us from entering the pool hall because we weren't eighteen. —*noun* ✦ **halt, standstill** ◇ **delay, end, finish, pause** At a flashing red light, drivers have to come to a full *stop*.

store *noun* **1.** ✦ **retailer, shop** ✧ **boutique, department store, market** I bought Mom's present at a stationery *store*. **2.** ✦ **accumulation, hoard, reserve, stock, supply** ✧ **inventory** We keep a *store* of candles for use when the power goes out. —*verb* ✦ **hoard, keep, put away, save, stash, stock** ✧ **collect** Squirrels *store* nuts in the fall so they'll have food in the winter.

storm *noun* **1.** ✦ **tempest** ✧ **blizzard, downpour, gale, hurricane, rainstorm, snowstorm, tornado** The *storm* was accompanied by lots of thunder and lightning. **2.** ✦ **deluge, flood, outbreak, outburst** ✧ **shower** There was a *storm* of protest against the unjust law. —*verb* **1.** ✦ **blow, bluster** ✧ **hail, pour, rain, snow** It *stormed* all night, but in the morning the sky was bright and clear. **2.** ✦ **assail, assault, attack, beset, charge, raid, rush** Enemy soldiers *stormed* the castle.

story[1] *noun* **1.** ✦ **account, anecdote, description, report** ✧ **version** My grandmother told me the *story* about how she met my grandfather. **2.** ✦ **tale, yarn** ✧ **fable, fiction, legend, narrative** Julie likes to read ghost *stories* by flashlight under the covers.

story[2] *noun* ✦ **floor, level** ✧ **layer, tier** The Empire State Building has 102 *stories*.

stout *adjective* ✦ **brawny, heavyset, husky, stocky, sturdy, thickset** Saint Bernards are big, *stout* dogs.

Antonyms

stout *adjective*

gaunt, lean, skinny, spare, thin, weedy

straggle *verb* ✦ **dawdle, lag, linger** ✧ **ramble, stray, wander** I *straggled* so far behind my parents when we went shopping that I almost lost track of them.

straight *adjective* **1.** ✦ **in line, perpendicular, upright, vertical** ✧ **even** My dance instructor often reminds me to keep my back *straight*. **2.** ✦ **direct, frank, honest, reliable, true, truthful** I gave my mom a *straight* answer when she asked where I had been. —*adverb* ✦ **at once, directly, immediately, instantly, right** When I got home from school, I went *straight* to the refrigerator for a snack.

strain *verb* **1.** ✦ **labor, strive, struggle, toil, try, work** ✧ **exert** I couldn't get the top off the jar no matter how hard I *strained*. **2.** ✦ **pull, sprain, wrench** ✧ **hurt, injure, twist** I *strained* my calf muscles by carrying such a heavy load on the hike.

strange *adjective* ✦ **bizarre, eccentric, odd, peculiar, unusual, weird** We have a *strange* cat that likes to take baths and fetch sticks.

stranger *noun* ✦ **newcomer, unknown person** ✧ **alien, foreigner, immigrant** I talked to several *strangers* at my friend's party.

strangle *verb* ✦ **choke, gag, suffocate** ✧ **smother** I loosened my tie because it was almost *strangling* me.

strap *noun* ✦ **band, strip, thong** ✧ **cord, lash, string** My sandals have two *straps* in front and one in back. —*verb* ✦ **bind, lash, tie** ✧ **attach, fasten, secure** Dad *strapped* our luggage to the roof of the car.

strategy *noun* ✦ **method, plan, procedure, scheme, system, tactic** My *strategy* for getting good grades is to pay attention at school and do my homework.

stray *verb* ✦ **drift, ramble, range, roam, wander** ✧ **digress, meander** My mind *strayed* during the boring movie. —*adjective* ✦ **abandoned, homeless, lost, wandering** We adopted the *stray* dog because it was so friendly.

streak *noun* **1.** ✦ **band, line, stripe** ✧ **bar, vein** The sparrow had *streaks* of brown on its breast. **2.** ✦ **interval, period, run, spell, stretch** ✧ **bout** I've had a *streak* of good luck lately. —*verb* **1.** ✦ **band, stripe** ✧ **mark, smear,**

✦ best choices
✧ other choices

233

smudge, stain The sky was *streaked* with red at dawn. **2.** ✦ **dash, flash, race, rush, sprint** ✧ **zoom** The runner *streaked* across the finish line.

stream *noun* **1.** ✦ **brook, creek, rill** ✧ **channel, river** This little *stream* dries up in the summer. **2.** ✦ **flow, gush, jet, spurt** ✧ **current, torrent** Dad sprayed a *stream* of water on his vegetable garden. —*verb* ✦ **course, flow, gush, pour, run, rush, spill** I was laughing so hard that tears *streamed* down my face.

street *noun* ✧ **alley, avenue, boulevard, drive, lane, road** My best friend and I live on the same *street*.

strength *noun* ✦ **brawn, might, power** ✧ **force, muscle, vigor** My brother has been working out with weights to improve his *strength*.

strengthen *verb* ✦ **brace, buttress, fortify, reinforce** ✧ **support, toughen** Workers added new beams to *strengthen* the old bridge.

strenuous *adjective* ✦ **active, brisk, dynamic, energetic, vigorous** ✧ **hard, tough** Our coach put us through a *strenuous* practice this afternoon.

stress *noun* **1.** ✦ **emphasis, importance, significance, weight** ✧ **concern** My family puts a lot of *stress* on getting a college education. **2.** ✦ **anxiety, distress, strain, tension, worry** Some people experience *stress* when they go to a dentist. —*verb* ✦ **affirm, assert, emphasize, underscore** ✧ **feature, insist** My teacher *stresses* the importance of creativity.

stretch *verb* ✦ **extend, pull** ✧ **expand, lengthen, spread, widen** It is important to *stretch* your muscles before you exercise. ◄

—*noun* ✦ **expanse, extent, length, space** ✧ **distance, reach, span** There was no one in sight on the entire *stretch* of beach.

strict *adjective* ✦ **firm, inflexible, rigid, stern, unyielding** ✧ **meticulous** My teacher is *strict* about assigned seating.

Antonyms
strict *adjective*
flexible, indulgent, lax, lenient, relaxed

strike *verb* **1.** ✦ **hit, knock, slam, smack** ✧ **pound, punch, tap** The tennis ball *struck* me on the shoulder. **2.** ✦ **impress** ✧ **affect, appear, occur, seem, touch** My cousin's joke didn't *strike* me as being very funny. **3.** ✦ **walk out** ✧ **boycott, picket, protest** The coal miners are planning to *strike* for better working conditions. —*noun* ✦ **blow, hit, stroke** ✧ **knock, punch, smack** The old oak tree was destroyed by a lightning *strike*.

strip[1] *verb* ✦ **remove, take away, take off** ✧ **peel, skin, uncover** The first step in refinishing furniture is to *strip* the old paint or varnish.

strip[2] *noun* ✦ **band, ribbon** ✧ **piece, section, segment, shred** We wove place mats out of *strips* of construction paper.

stripe *noun* ✦ **band, bar, line, streak** ✧ **strip, vein** A zebra has black and white *stripes*.

stroke *noun* **1.** ✦ **blow, hit, strike, tap** ✧ **knock, swing** I could hear the steady *strokes* of the carpenter's hammer. **2.** ✦ **act, event, feat, occurrence** ✧ **accomplishment, achievement** Getting home before the snow started was a *stroke* of good luck. —*verb* ✦ **pat, pet, rub** ✧ **brush, smooth, touch** Julia likes to *stroke* her pet rabbit's fur.

stroll *verb* ✦ **amble, hike, ramble, roam, saunter, walk, wander** I like to *stroll* through the woods behind my house. —*noun* ✦ **hike, ramble, walk** ✧ **excursion, promenade** My friend and I took a *stroll* around the neighborhood.

strong *adjective* **1. ✦ brawny, mighty, muscular, powerful ✧ forceful, hale** Elephants are *strong* enough to carry big logs with their trunks. **2. ✦ firm, secure, solid, stout, sturdy, substantial** This tree limb is *strong* enough to bear my weight.

structure *noun* **1. ✦ building ✧ construction, establishment** The ranch has a house, a barn, and several smaller *structures*. **2. ✦ arrangement, design, form, organization, pattern ✧ shape** The human brain has a complex *structure*.

struggle *verb* **✦ battle, contend with, fight, wrestle against ✧ compete, labor, toil** The tired swimmer *struggled against* the current. —*noun* **✦ effort, endeavor, strain, trouble ✧ battle, fight** It was a *struggle* to get the big chair into the small car.

stubborn *adjective* **✦ determined, headstrong, obstinate, uncooperative, unyielding** The *stubborn* camel refused to budge.

student *noun* **✦ pupil, scholar ✧ schoolboy, schoolgirl** The *students* bought a birthday present for their teacher.

study *noun* **1. ✦ analysis, examination, investigation ✧ learning, research** The *study* of bugs is called entomology. **2. ✧ den, library, office, studio, workroom** We turned the spare bedroom into a *study*. —*verb* **✦ examine, go over, learn, read over ✧ cram, meditate, research** I have to *study* my notes for tomorrow's history quiz.

stuff *noun* **✦ articles, goods, items, things ✧ belongings, possessions** Here's a list of the *stuff* that we need for the trip. —*verb* **✦ cram, crowd, fill, jam, load, pack ✧ squeeze** The piñata was *stuffed* with candy.

stuffy *adjective* **1. ✦ airless, close, stifling, suffocating ✧ muggy, sweltering** I opened the windows to air out my *stuffy* room. **2. ✦ blocked,** clogged, congested, filled My sinuses are *stuffy* because I have allergies.

stumble *verb* **✦ trip ✧ blunder, fall, slip, stagger, tumble** I *stumbled* over my brother's toy train.

stump *verb* **✦ baffle, bewilder, mystify, puzzle, thwart ✧ frustrate** The homework question *stumped* me, so I asked Mom for help.

stun *verb* **✦ amaze, astonish, overwhelm, shock, startle ✧ surprise** I was *stunned* to hear that I had won the dance contest.

stunning *adjective* **✦ astonishing, dazzling, marvelous, remarkable, sensational, spectacular** The ballerina thrilled the audience with her *stunning* performance.

stunt[1] *verb* **✦ check, curb, curtail, impede, limit, restrict ✧ retard, slow** Doctors warn that poor nutrition can *stunt* a young person's growth.

stunt[2] *noun* **✦ feat, trick ✧ act, exploit, performance** My dog's best *stunt* is to roll over and play dead.

stupid *adjective* **✦ dumb, foolish, silly, unintelligent ✧ simple-minded** I made a *stupid* mistake on the spelling quiz.

sturdy *adjective* **✦ firm, solid, stout, strong, substantial ✧ rugged, tough** I thought that the lawn chair was *sturdy* until it broke under my weight.

stutter *verb* **✦ stammer ✧ falter, mumble, sputter, stumble** My friend *stutters* when she feels shy. —*noun* **✦ speech impediment, stammer, stammering, stuttering** I'm going to a speech therapist to correct my *stutter*.

style *noun* **✦ arrangement, design, fashion ✧ mode, pattern, shape** That haircut is a great *style* for you.

subdue *verb* **✦ check, control, quiet, reduce, suppress ✧ pacify** The medicine *subdued* my coughing.

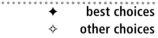

✦ **best choices**
✧ **other choices**

subject *noun* **1.** ✦ **subject matter, theme, topic** ◇ **issue, question** The teacher told us to pick a report *subject* by the end of the week. **2.** ✦ **class, course, topic** ◇ **field** My favorite *subject* is geography.

submerge *verb* **1.** ✦ **dip, douse, duck, immerse, plunge, soak** ◇ **sink** The tired hiker *submerged* her feet in the cold mountain stream. **2.** ✦ **deluge, engulf, flood, inundate, overflow, swamp** ◇ **drench, drown** It rained so heavily that the river overflowed its banks and *submerged* the downtown shopping area.

submit *verb* **1.** ✦ **defer, give in, surrender, yield** ◇ **accept, comply, obey** The duke refused to *submit* to the king's authority. **2.** ✦ **hand in, offer, present, turn in** ◇ **propose** Marissa *submitted* her test paper to her teacher at the end of class. ◀

subordinate *adjective* ✦ **junior, lower** ◇ **auxiliary, inferior, lesser, minor, secondary** The company's president accepts suggestions from *subordinate* employees. —*noun* ✦ **aide, assistant, employee, servant** ◇ **slave** It makes me angry when my older brother acts like I'm his *subordinate*.

subsequent *adjective* ✦ **following, later, succeeding, successive** ◇ **future** The misunderstanding and *subsequent* bad feelings were quickly resolved.

subside *verb* ✦ **abate, decrease, diminish, dwindle, ebb, lessen, wane** When the storm *subsided*, we went outside to play.

substance *noun* **1.** ✦ **element, ingredient, item, material** ◇ **matter, stuff** Flour is the main *substance* in cakes and breads. **2.** ✦ **essence, meaning, significance** ◇ **reality, truth** The comic book was fun to read, but it didn't have much *substance*.

substantial *adjective* ✦ **ample, considerable, generous, great, large, significant** Dad hopes to get a *substantial* raise.

substitute *noun* ✦ **alternate, alternative, equivalent, replacement, stand-in** Mom uses honey as a *substitute* for sugar when she makes some recipes. —*verb* ✦ **change, exchange, replace, swap, switch, trade** The coach *substituted* the players every ten minutes to let everyone get some experience.

subtract *verb* ✦ **deduct, remove, take off** ◇ **discount, withdraw** The clerk *subtracted* one dollar from our grocery bill because we had some coupons.

succeed *verb* ✦ **be successful, flourish, prosper, thrive** ◇ **triumph** Retail stores need a good location in order to *succeed*.

success *noun* ✦ **triumph, victory** ◇ **achievement, attainment, sensation** Our school's fund-raising drive was a big *success*.

successful *adjective* **1.** ✦ **effective, efficient, favorable, productive, winning** ◇ **perfect** My parents helped me to develop *successful* study habits. **2.** ✦ **famous, notable, popular, prominent, well-known** Susannah's dream is to be a *successful* engineer.

sudden *adjective* ✦ **abrupt, quick, rapid, unexpected, unforeseen** ◇ **instant** The driver had to make a *sudden* stop in order to avoid hitting the squirrel.

suffer *verb* ✦ **accept, bear, endure, experience, sustain, undergo** Mom said that I'll have to *suffer* the consequences if I don't study for my test.

sufficient *adjective* ✦ **adequate, enough** ✧ **abundant, satisfactory** Do we have *sufficient* time to stop at the video arcade?

suffocate *verb* ✦ **choke, smother** ✧ **gag, stifle, strangle** Dense smoke can *suffocate* a person.

suggest *verb* ✦ **offer, propose, put forward, recommend** ✧ **advise, counsel** My teacher *suggested* a report topic that she thought I might like.

suggestion *noun* ✦ **idea, proposal, proposition, recommendation** ✧ **advice, counsel** I like your *suggestion* that we go bowling after dinner.

suit *verb* ✦ **fit, please, satisfy, serve** ✧ **content, delight, gratify** My new room *suits* me better than my old one did.

suitable *adjective* ✦ **appropriate, apt, fit, good, proper, right** ✧ **acceptable** Mom bought a new dress because she didn't have anything *suitable* for her friend's wedding.

sullen *adjective* ✦ **bitter, hostile, moody, resentful, sulky** ✧ **angry, cross** Tamara gets *sullen* whenever she thinks nothing is going her way.

Antonyms
sullen *adjective*
cheerful, chipper, happy, pleasant, sunny

sum *noun* ✦ **amount, gross, sum total, total** ✧ **aggregate, entirety, number** Ticket sales for the raffle came to a larger *sum* than we had expected. —*verb* ✦ **add up, calculate, compute, figure, total** Dad *summed up* the expenses from his business trip.

summary *noun* ✦ **digest, outline, review** ✧ **abridgment, condensation** We had to read a book over the summer and turn in a *summary* of its contents in the fall.

summit *noun* ✦ **crest, peak, pinnacle, tip, top** ✧ **crown** There is snow all summer long on the mountain's *summit*.

sunrise *noun* ✦ **dawn, daybreak, sunup** ✧ **daylight, morning** Why is it that roosters always crow right around *sunrise*? ▶

sunset *noun* ✦ **dusk, nightfall, sundown, twilight** ✧ **evening** The planet Venus will be visible just after *sunset*.

superb *adjective* ✦ **excellent, fine, magnificent, splendid, superior, terrific** The actress received an award for her *superb* performance as a rookie police officer.

superior *adjective* ✦ **excellent, exceptional, first-rate, premium** ✧ **admirable, fine, high** This store carries furniture of *superior* quality.

supervise *verb* ✦ **administer, direct, manage, oversee, run** ✧ **govern, head** Ms. Spartos is going to *supervise* the after-school program.

supervisor *noun* ✦ **boss, chief, director, head, manager** ✧ **administrator** The factory has a *supervisor* in charge of each shift.

supplement *noun* ✦ **addition, complement, extra** ✧ **appendix, insert** The teacher gave us a magazine article as a *supplement* to our textbook. —*verb* ✦ **add to, augment, extend** ✧ **complete, increase** Lev *supplements* his allowance with the money that he makes recycling soda cans.

supply *verb* ✦ **equip, furnish, present, provide** ✧ **contribute, give** Our team sponsor *supplied* us with new basketball jerseys. —*noun* ✦ **quantity, stock, store** ✧ **hoard, inventory, reserve** The corner store gets a fresh *supply* of doughnuts every morning.

✦ best choices
✧ other choices

support *verb* **1.** ✦ **bear, brace, hold up, prop up** ✧ **reinforce** The cabin has a big beam that *supports* the roof. **2.** ✦ **back, encourage, foster, promote, uphold** ✧ **aid, assist, help** My parents have always *supported* my interest in music. —*noun* **1.** ✦ **backing, encouragement, help** ✧ **aid, assistance** My friends have given me lots of *support*. **2.** ✦ **brace, buttress, pillar, post, prop** ✧ **frame** We used toothpicks as *supports* for our miniature bridge.

suppose *verb* ✦ **believe, expect, guess, imagine, think** ✧ **assume** Do you *suppose* it will snow tonight?

supreme *adjective* ✦ **chief, foremost, head, highest, primary, principal, top** The U.S. President is the *supreme* commander of the nation's military forces.

sure *adjective* **1.** ✦ **certain, confident, definite, positive** I am *sure* that I can finish my chores before noon. **2.** ✦ **firm, reliable, secure, solid, steady** Mountain goats are known for their *sure* footing.

surface *noun* ✦ **exterior, outside** ✧ **cover, face, top** A pore is a tiny opening in the *surface* of the skin. —*verb* ✦ **cover, pave, top** ✧ **coat, overlay** Ancient Roman roads were *surfaced* with stone.

surpass *verb* ✦ **better, eclipse, exceed, outdo, pass, top** Robyn *surpasses* all of her classmates in speed and endurance.

surprise *verb* ✦ **amaze, astonish, astound** ✧ **shock, startle, stun** I was *surprised* by how big the redwoods really are when I saw them up close. ▶ —*noun* ✦ **amazement, astonishment, wonder** ✧ **awe, shock** Mom was filled with *surprise* when I cleaned my room without being told.

surrender *verb* ✦ **give up, submit, yield** ✧ **quit, succumb** The army *surrendered* after being surrounded by enemy troops. —*noun* ✦ **concession, submission, yielding** ✧ **resignation**

Displaying a white flag to the enemy is the traditional sign of *surrender*.

surround *verb* ✦ **circle, encircle, envelop, mob, ring** ✧ **crowd, enclose, skirt** The actor was *surrounded* by reporters after he announced his retirement.

survey *verb* ✦ **inspect, observe, regard, scan, view** ✧ **watch** The general *surveyed* the battlefield as he planned his attack.

survive *verb* ✦ **exist, live, persist, thrive** ✧ **endure, withstand** Polar bears can *survive* in extremely cold climates.

suspect *verb* ✦ **distrust, doubt, mistrust, question** ✧ **challenge** We *suspected* our neighbors' motives when they showed up for a visit right at dinnertime.

suspend *verb* **1.** ✦ **hang, sling** ✧ **attach, dangle, swing** Dad *suspended* his hammock between two trees. **2.** ✦ **break off, discontinue, interrupt, postpone** ✧ **defer, delay** The baseball game had to be *suspended* because of rain.

suspense *noun* ✦ **anticipation, apprehension, tension, uncertainty** ✧ **doubt** The mystery novel kept me in *suspense*.

suspension *noun* ✦ **halt (in), interruption, pause (in), stoppage** ◇ **break, discontinuity** The cable company announced a brief *suspension* of service while they replaced their old equipment.

suspicion *noun* **1.** ✦ **feeling, guess, hunch, idea, inkling, notion** ◇ **belief** I have a *suspicion* that my little brother is the one who left this rubber chicken in my bed. **2.** ✦ **distrust, doubt, mistrust** ◇ **question** When we discovered that the hamburger meat was missing, our *suspicions* fell on the dog.

sustain *verb* **1.** ✦ **bear, hold up, support** ◇ **brace, carry, prop** Is this branch strong enough to *sustain* a treehouse? **2.** ✦ **hold, maintain** ◇ **keep, preserve, retain** I turned off the TV program because it didn't *sustain* my interest.

swallow *verb* ◇ **bolt, consume, gulp, guzzle** Louis can *swallow* a pill without taking any water. —*noun* ✦ **drink, gulp, mouthful, sip** ◇ **bite, taste** I tried a *swallow* of coffee once, but I didn't like it very much.

swamp *noun* ✦ **bog, marsh, marshland, swampland, wetland** ◇ **mire, morass** There are alligators living in Florida's *swamps*. —*verb* ✦ **deluge, engulf, flood, overwhelm** ◇ **immerse, submerge** The post office gets *swamped* with letters during the holidays.

swarm *noun* ✦ **crowd, horde, host, mass, multitude, throng** A *swarm* of fans ran onto the field as the game ended. —*verb* ✦ **congregate, crowd, flock, mass, throng** ◇ **teem** At the school dance, most of the students *swarmed* around the refreshment table.

sway *verb* ✦ **move, ripple, wave** ◇ **beat, flap, swing** The flowers *swayed* in the evening breeze.

swear *verb* ✦ **pledge, promise, vow** ◇ **affirm, assert, state, testify** All of the witnesses *swore* to tell the whole truth and nothing but the truth.

sweep *verb* ✦ **brush, whisk** ◇ **clean, dust, tidy, wipe** I *swept* the dirt into a big pile. —*noun* ✦ **pass, stroke, swoop, thrust** ◇ **motion, movement** I cleaned off the cookie crumbs with one *sweep* of my hand.

sweet *adjective* **1.** ✦ **sugary, sweetened** ◇ **rich** Dad doesn't buy *sweet* cereals for us anymore. ▶  **2.** ✦ **considerate, courteous, friendly, gracious, kind, nice** It was *sweet* of Barry to send you a birthday card.

swell *verb* ✦ **bulge, expand, grow, puff, rise** ◇ **increase** That bee sting is really beginning to *swell*. —*noun* ✦ **wave** ◇ **breaker, comber, ripple, roller** The ocean *swells* gently rocked our boat.

swerve *verb* ✦ **dodge, turn aside, veer** ◇ **move, shift, swing, twist** The driver *swerved* in order to avoid hitting the pothole.

swift *adjective* ✦ **fast, fleet, quick, rapid, speedy** ◇ **brisk, hasty** Jamar is our *swiftest* runner.

swindle *verb* ✦ **cheat, deceive, exploit, fool, trick** ◇ **steal** The dishonest jeweler tried to *swindle* people by selling them fake diamonds. —*noun* ✦ **deception, fraud, hoax, racket, trick** After the *swindle* was discovered, the responsible people were sent to jail.

swing *verb* **1.** ✦ **dangle, hang, suspend** ◇ **move, shift, sway** I like *swinging* by my knees from the jungle gym. **2.** ✦ **circle, curve, swerve, turn** ◇ **twist** The boomerang *swung* around and came back to me. —*noun* ✦ **stroke, swat** ◇ **blow, hit, strike, thrust** The golfer took a big *swing* at the ball.

✦ **best choices**
◇ **other choices**

swirl *verb* ✦ spin, twirl, twist, whirl ✧ reel, swish The dancer's skirts *swirled* around her as she moved. ◄

switch *noun*
1. ✦ branch, rod, stick, twig ✧ cane, whip Jake improvised a fishing pole from a long *switch* and a piece of string. 2. ✦ alteration, change, shift ✧ exchange, swap, trade We had to make a last-minute *switch* in our vacation plans. —*verb* ✦ change, exchange, shift, swap, trade My sister and I sometimes *switch* rooms for the night.

symbol *noun* ✦ emblem, mark, sign, token ✧ badge The dove and the olive branch are both *symbols* of peace.

sympathize *verb* ✦ feel bad for, feel sorry for ✧ pity, relate, understand I *sympathized with* Suzanne when she told me about her Dad's accident.

sympathy *noun* ✦ comfort, compassion, support, understanding ✧ concern, pity My friends gave me lots of *sympathy* when I had my tonsils removed.

symptom *noun* ✦ indication, feature, sign, trait ✧ evidence A runny nose is often a *symptom* of a cold.

synthetic *adjective* ✦ artificial, manmade, manufactured ✧ imitation, unnatural Plastic is a *synthetic* material made from petroleum.

system *noun* 1. ✦ set, unit ✧ arrangement, combination, complex My parents just bought a new stereo *system*. 2. ✦ method, order, pattern, plan, procedure In 1876, Melvil Dewey developed a *system* for organizing library books that is still in use today.

T

table *noun* ✦ **chart, list** ✧ **appendix, graph, index, register** My encyclopedia has a *table* of facts about the planets in our solar system.

tablet *noun* ✦ **capsule, pill** ✧ **dosage, dose, medication, medicine** When I have a headache, I usually take two aspirin *tablets*.

tack *verb* ✦ **pin, stick** ✧ **attach, fasten, fix, secure** I *tacked* a poster of my favorite singer to my closet door.

tact *noun* ✦ **consideration, diplomacy, tactfulness, thoughtfulness** ✧ **courtesy, politeness** It takes *tact* to tell a person about his or her faults without offending him or her.

tag *noun* ✦ **label, sticker** ✧ **marker, slip, ticket** All items with red *tags* are on sale. —*verb* 1. ✦ **label, mark, ticket** ✧ **designate, identify** The porter *tagged* each piece of baggage to show its destination. 2. ✦ **follow, tail, trail** ✧ **accompany, attend, dog** My little brother *tags* along whenever I go outside to play with my friends.

tail *noun* ✦ **back, end, rear** ✧ **extremity, stern, tip** The airplane's identification number was painted on its *tail*. —*verb* ✦ **follow** ✧ **pursue, stalk, track, trail** A police detective *tailed* the suspect from the airport to her apartment.

take *verb* 1. ✦ **capture, gain, secure, seize** ✧ **acquire, get, obtain** The invading army was unable to *take* the enemy fort. 2. ✦ **bring, carry** ✧ **bear, convey, haul, move, transport** Kara *takes* her lunch to school every day. 3. ✦ **swallow** ✧ **chew, drink, eat** *Take* this medicine twice a day. 4. ✦ **execute, give, make, perform** ✧ **act, do** The actors each *took* a bow at the end of the play. 5. ✦ **call for, need, require** ✧ **demand, involve, want** This assignment *takes* about one hour to complete. 6. ✦ **abide, endure, suffer, tolerate, withstand** ✧ **accept** I'm not sure if I can *take* another day of this rainy weather.

7. ✦ **comprehend, interpret, understand** ✧ **assume, grasp** Did you *take* her comment the same way I did? 8. ✦ **deduct, remove, subtract, withdraw** ✧ **eliminate** If you have eighteen quarters and *take away* two, how many dollars would you have?

tale *noun* ✦ **anecdote, narration, story, yarn** ✧ **fable, tall tale** The old sailor had many *tales* to tell about his days at sea.

talent *noun* ✦ **aptitude, flair, gift, knack** ✧ **ability, capability, power, skill** Melissa has a *talent* for expressing her thoughts in an original manner.

talk *verb* ✦ **chat, converse, speak** ✧ **chatter, communicate, discuss** My friends and I can *talk* on the phone for hours. —*noun* 1. ✦ **conference, consultation, discussion** ✧ **chat, conversation** My parents had a *talk* with my teacher about my progress in school. 2. ✦ **address, presentation, speech** ✧ **commentary, lecture, sermon** A firefighter gave our social studies class a *talk* about fire safety.

tall *adjective* ✦ **high, lofty** ✧ **big, lengthy, long, towering** The *tallest* building in the world is the Sears Tower in Chicago.

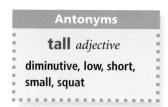

Antonyms

tall *adjective*

diminutive, low, short, small, squat

tame *adjective* ✦ **docile, gentle, mild** ✧ **broken, domesticated, meek, obedient** Our parakeet is so *tame* that he will sit on my finger. —*verb* ✦ **break, domesticate** ✧ **discipline, master, subdue, train** It's not easy to catch and *tame* a wild elephant.

tamper *verb* ✦ **fool around, meddle, mess, play, tinker** ✧ **alter, interfere** Dad told us not to *tamper* with his new fax machine.

✦ best choices
✧ other choices

tang *noun* ✦ bite, sharpness, zest ✧ flavor, relish, savor, taste Some cheeses are aged to give them a greater *tang*.

tangle *verb* ✦ kink, knot, snarl, twist ✧ disorder, scramble The wind *tangled* Rebecca's long hair. —*noun* ✦ kink, knot, snarl, twist ✧ maze, mess, muddle The kitten played with a *tangle* of ribbon. ◀

tantrum *noun* ✦ blow-up, fit, temper tantrum ✧ outburst, rage, scene When I was little I had big *tantrums* when I didn't get what I wanted.

tap¹ *verb* ✦ drum, knock, rap, thump ✧ hit, pat, slap, strike Mr. Pirelli always *taps* his pencil on his desk when he's thinking. —*noun* ✦ knock, rap, thump ✧ hit, pat, slap, strike Did you hear a *tap* on the window?

tap² *noun* ✦ faucet, spigot ✧ spout, valve We need to fix that dripping *tap*.

tape *noun* ✦ band, ribbon, strap, strip ✧ reel, roll, spool The lead runner broke the *tape* that was stretched across the finish line. —*verb* ✧ attach, clip, fasten, secure, stick Sean *taped* basketball posters all over his wall.

tardy *adjective* ✦ delayed, late ✧ belated, slow Our bus broke down this morning and we were all *tardy* getting to school.

target *noun* ✦ goal, mark, objective ✧ aim, end, object, purpose We have set a *target* of $1,000 for our fund-raising drive.

tarnish *verb* ✦ darken, dim, discolor, dull ✧ corrode, rust, stain Some metals *tarnish* after they've been exposed to air for a while. —*noun* ✦ discoloration ✧ corrosion, rust, stain The antique silver pitcher had a lot of *tarnish* on it.

tart *adjective* ✦ acid, sour ✧ bitter, dry, sharp, tangy Lemons are so *tart* that they make my mouth pucker up.

task *noun* ✦ assignment, chore, duty, job, obligation, responsibility My first *task* of the day is to make my bed.

taste *noun* 1. ✦ flavor, savor ✧ relish, tang, zest Shannon loves foods that have a sweet *taste*. 2. ✦ bit, bite, morsel, piece, sample ✧ sip, swallow May I have a little *taste* of your burrito? 3. ✦ judgment, liking, preference ✧ fashion, style You and I have the same *taste* in music. —*verb* ✦ sample, test, try ✧ eat, relish, savor Please *taste* this soup and tell me if it needs a little more salt.

tasteless *adjective* 1. ✦ bland, flat, flavorless, plain ✧ unsavory The spaghetti sauce was rather *tasteless*, so Mom added some herbs and spices. 2. ✦ crude, offensive, rude, tactless ✧ improper No one laughed at the *tasteless* joke.

taut *adjective* ✦ stretched, tight ✧ firm, rigid, stiff, tense Please hold the measuring tape *taut*.

tax *noun* ✦ assessment, levy ✧ charge, duty, tariff, toll The main way the government raises money is by *taxes*. —*verb* 1. ✦ assess ✧ charge, levy Our city government *taxes* property owners to pay for services like schools and sewers. 2. ✦ drain, exhaust, sap, weaken ✧ burden, strain Playing the whole game with no substitutes *taxed* my strength.

taxi *noun* ✦ cab, taxicab ✧ hired car, limousine Dad called a *taxi* to take us to the airport. ▼

teach *verb* ✦ **educate, inform, instruct, train** ✧ **lecture, tutor** Babies learn to crawl and walk all by themselves without having to be *taught*.

teacher *noun* ✦ **educator, instructor** ✧ **professor, trainer, tutor** It takes skill and hard work to be a really good *teacher*.

team *noun* ✦ **crew, group, squad, unit** ✧ **band, company, force** A *team* of investigators thoroughly examined the accident site. —*verb* ✦ **combine, join up, pair up, unite** ✧ **associate, connect, link** The two authors *teamed up* to write a book together.

tear¹ *verb* 1. ✦ **pull apart, rip up, shred** ✧ **cut, slice, split** My gerbils *tore up* a piece of cardboard to build a nest. 2. ✦ **charge, fly, race, rush, speed** ✧ **bolt, dash, hurry** A group of kids came *tearing* down the street on their bicycles. —*noun* ✦ **rip, split** ✧ **break, cut, gap, hole** Mom showed me how to sew up the *tear* in my jeans.

tear² *noun* ✦ **teardrop** ✧ **drop, moisture** I laughed so hard that I had *tears* running down my cheeks.

tease *verb* ✦ **annoy, bother, harass, irritate, pester, torment** The dog growled at the boys who were *teasing* him.

technique *noun* ✦ **art, craft, form, skill, style** ✧ **method, procedure, system** The guitarist practiced hard in order to improve her *technique*.

tedious *adjective* ✦ **boring, dull, tiresome, uninteresting, wearisome, weary** Pulling up weeds in the garden can be a *tedious* task.

televise *verb* ✦ **air, broadcast, show, telecast** ✧ **transmit** They're going to *televise* highlights of the Olympics tonight at eight o'clock.

tell *verb* 1. ✦ **say, speak, state, utter** ✧ **communicate, talk, voice** I always feel better when I *tell* the truth. 2. ✦ **narrate, recite, relate** ✧ **describe, report** Please *tell* the story about when the dog chewed up Grandpa's favorite shoes! 3. ✦ **disclose, expose, give away, reveal** ✧ **betray** I promised my friend that I wouldn't *tell* her secret to anyone. 4. ✦ **distinguish, know, separate** ✧ **determine, discover** Do you know how to *tell* a ripe watermelon from an unripe one? 5. ✦ **bid, command, direct, order** ✧ **demand, require** Mom *told* me to turn off the television and clean up my room.

temper *noun* 1. ✦ **disposition, mood, nature** ✧ **attitude, spirit** Our dog has a very sweet *temper*. 2. ✦ **anger, fury, rage, wrath** ✧ **irritation** When I am upset, I count to ten to control my *temper*.

temporary *adjective* ✦ **brief, short-lived, short-term** ✧ **fleeting, momentary, passing** The storm caused a *temporary* loss of power in our part of town.

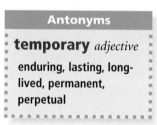

Antonyms
temporary *adjective*
enduring, lasting, long-lived, permanent, perpetual

tempt *verb* ✦ **attract, invite, lure, persuade** ✧ **coax, inspire, urge** The bakery put a gingerbread house in the window to *tempt* people on the street to come inside.

temptation *noun* ✦ **attraction, lure** ✧ **bait, draw, pull** Chocolate is a *temptation* that many people find difficult to resist.

tenant *noun* ✦ **lodger, renter** ✧ **inhabitant, occupant, resident** My parents have found a *tenant* for their rental house.

tend¹ *verb* ✦ **be apt, be inclined, be likely** ✧ **lean, slant** New Mexico's climate *tends* to be hot and dry.

tend² *verb* ✦ **attend, care for, look after, watch** ✧ **guard, protect** Our neighbor is paying me to *tend* his yard and garden while he's away on vacation.

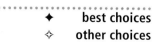

✦   **best choices**
✧   **other choices**

tendency *noun* ✦ disposition, habit, inclination ✧ bias, leaning, trend I have a *tendency* to stay up late on weekends.

tender *adjective* 1. ✦ delicate, soft ✧ fragile, frail, weak Carrots become *tender* when they are steamed. 2. ✦ painful, sensitive, sore, uncomfortable ✧ aching, throbbing I sprained my ankle last week, and it's still *tender*. 3. ✦ caring, gentle, loving ✧ compassionate, kindhearted, warm The mother cat was very *tender* with her newborn kittens.

tense *adjective* 1. ✦ rigid, stiff, strained ✧ stretched, taut When I'm frightened, my whole body gets *tense*. 2. ✦ anxious, apprehensive, nervous, restless, uneasy The actor was *tense* on the opening night of his first play.

term *noun* 1. ✦ duration, interval, period, time ✧ span, stretch Our mayor was elected for a *term* of four years. 2. ✦ expression, word ✧ designation, name, phrase This dictionary defines more than 1,500 science and computer *terms*. 3. ✦ condition, provision, qualification, requirement One of the *terms* of the loan was that it had to be paid off in two years.

terminal *noun* ✦ depot, station ✧ destination, stopping place We arrived at the *terminal* just in time to catch our bus.

terrible *adjective* 1. ✦ fierce, intense, severe, violent ✧ alarming, frightful The *terrible* storm caused damage all along the coast. ▼ 2. ✦ awful, bad, dreadful, horrible ✧ poor I'm usually pretty good at tennis, but my game was *terrible* today.

terrific *adjective* 1. ✦ fierce, intense, powerful, severe ✧ horrible, terrible The hurricane had *terrific* winds of more than 110 miles per hour. 2. ✦ great, magnificent, marvelous, splendid, superb, wonderful I had a *terrific* time at your party last night.

terrify *verb* ✦ alarm, frighten, panic, petrify, scare, terrorize Thunder and lightning *terrify* my new puppy.

territory *noun* ✦ area, domain, realm, region ✧ district, locality, terrain A grizzly bear roams over a *territory* of about one hundred square miles.

terror *noun* ✦ alarm, fear, fright ✧ dread, horror, panic The rabbit froze in *terror* when it saw a hawk circling overhead.

test *noun* ✦ exam, examination, quiz ✧ check, investigation, study We are having a *test* on Egyptian civilization tomorrow. —*verb* ✦ analyze, check, examine, investigate ✧ question, quiz Cities routinely *test* their water supplies to make sure that the water is safe to drink.

testify *verb* ✦ affirm, assert, claim, confirm, declare, swear My friends *testified* that they had seen me put my homework in my knapsack.

testimony *noun* ✦ declaration, statement ✧ evidence, proof The jury listened carefully as the witness gave her *testimony*.

text *noun* 1. ✦ contents, subject matter, words ✧ theme, topic My dictionary contains 840 pages of *text*. 2. ✦ book, schoolbook, textbook ✧ manual, primer, reader I have to read a chapter in my history *text* by tomorrow.

textile *noun* ✦ cloth, fabric, material ✧ fiber, thread, yarn Rayon was the first synthetic *textile* to be developed.

texture *noun* ✦ feel ✧ character, composition, consistency, quality Sandpaper has a rough *texture*.

thankful *adjective* ✦ **appreciative, grateful** ✧ **content, glad, pleased** We were *thankful* to be inside all warm and snug while the blizzard raged outside.

thankless *adjective* ✦ **unacknowledged, unappreciated, unrewarded** ✧ **boring, dreary, dull** Mom complains that keeping the house picked up is a *thankless* chore.

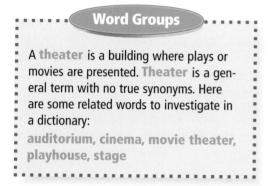

Word Groups

A **theater** is a building where plays or movies are presented. **Theater** is a general term with no true synonyms. Here are some related words to investigate in a dictionary:

auditorium, cinema, movie theater, playhouse, stage

theft *noun* ✦ **stealing** ✧ **burglary, pilfering, robbery** The man reported the *theft* of his car to the police.

theme *noun* **1.** ✦ **point, premise, subject, subject matter, topic** The *theme* of the mayor's speech was that more money is needed for law enforcement. **2.** ✦ **article, composition, essay, paper, report** ✧ **commentary, piece** We're supposed to write a *theme* about what we did during summer vacation.

theory *noun* ✦ **hypothesis, idea** ✧ **assumption, explanation, guess, speculation** I have a couple of different *theories* about how my lamp was broken.

thick *adjective* **1.** ✦ **broad, bulky, fat** ✧ **big, deep, large, thickset, wide** I picked the *thickest* carrots to cut up for the stew. **2.** ✦ **heavy, stiff** ✧ **firm, solid** We almost got stuck in the *thick* mud. **3.** ✦ **crowded, dense, packed, tight** The branches were so *thick* that we couldn't see very far into the woods.

thief *noun* ✦ **burglar, robber** ✧ **bandit, criminal, crook** The police are looking for the *thief* who broke into our neighbor's house.

thin *adjective* **1.** ✦ **lean, slender, slight, slim, spare** ✧ **gaunt, skinny** Plenty of exercise helps keep our dog *thin*. **2.** ✦ **meager, scant, scanty, scarce, sparse** ✧ **rare** Grandpa's hair is getting *thin* on top. **3.** ✦ **dilute, runny, watered-down, watery** ✧ **weak** *Thin* paint is easier to apply than thick paint. —*verb* ✦ **decrease, diminish, reduce** ✧ **dilute, water down, weaken** The crowd began to *thin* before the game was over.

thing *noun* **1.** ✦ **article, item, object** ✧ **device, gadget** I saw some really neat *things* at the museum. **2.** ✦ **act, action, deed** ✧ **accomplishment, feat** Mom said that I did the right *thing* when I returned the wallet I found. **3.** ✦ **belongings, goods, personal effects, possessions** Dad told me to pick up my *things* and take them to my room **4.** ✦ **affairs, circumstances, conditions, matters** ✧ **business** How are *things* at school?

think *verb* **1.** ✦ **consider, contemplate, deliberate, ponder, reflect** Charles had to *think* a few moments before he could solve the riddle. **2.** ✦ **assume, believe, conclude, guess, presume, suppose** People sometimes *think* that my friend and I are related because we look so much alike.

thorough *adjective* ✦ **complete, exhaustive, extensive, full, total** ✧ **careful** Tanya gave her horse a *thorough* brushing.

thought *noun* **1.** ✦ **consideration, contemplation, deliberation, reflection** I have given your suggestion a lot of *thought*. **2.** ✦ **idea, notion, opinion, view** ✧ **belief, concept** What are your *thoughts* on this subject?

thoughtful *adjective* **1.** ✦ **contemplative, meditative, reflective** ✧ **thinking** Kendra gets very quiet when she is in a *thoughtful* mood. **2.** ✦ **caring, considerate, kind, kindly**

✦ **best choices**
✧ **other choices**

◇ **courteous, polite** It was *thoughtful* of you to send me a get-well card.

thrash *verb* ✦ **beat, crush, defeat, overwhelm, trounce, whip** ◇ **conquer** Our softball team *thrashed* our opponents by a score of 7 to 0.

threat *noun* **1.** ✦ **warning** ◇ **caution, notice, notification, promise** The teacher carried out her *threat* to send the noisy students to the principal's office. **2.** ✦ **danger, hazard, menace, peril, risk** A spokesperson said that the forest fire does not pose a *threat* to any homes.

threaten *verb* **1.** ✦ **bully, intimidate, menace** ◇ **caution, warn, terrorize** The belligerent country *threatened* its neighbor by moving troops to the border. **2.** ✦ **endanger, jeopardize, put at risk, put in jeopardy** This year's harvest is being *threatened* by drought.

thrifty *adjective* ✦ **economical, frugal** ◇ **careful, prudent, saving** A *thrifty* shopper buys things on sale whenever possible.

thrill *verb* ✦ **delight, excite, please** ◇ **inspire, move, stimulate** Brooke was *thrilled* when she got a perfect score on the math test. —*noun* ✦ **excitement, fun, joy, pleasure, sensation** ◇ **adventure** I can still recall the *thrill* of my first roller coaster ride. ◀

thrive *verb* ✦ **flourish, prosper, succeed** ◇ **advance, grow, progress** Dad is pleased that his new business is *thriving*.

throb *verb* ✦ **beat, pound, thump** ◇ **flutter, tremble, vibrate** After the race, I could feel my pulse *throbbing*. —*noun* ✦ **beat,**

pulse, tremor, vibration ◇ **spasm** The crew could feel the *throb* of the engines as the tugboat began to move.

throng *noun* ✦ **crowd, flock, horde, mass, mob, multitude, swarm** A *throng* of eager visitors waited outside the gates of the amusement park. —*verb* ✦ **crowd, flock, jam, mob, press, swarm** ◇ **assemble, gather** After the game, the fans *thronged* around the players.

through *preposition* ✦ **around, in** ◇ **among, between, into, past** We took a drive *through* the countryside. —*adjective* ✦ **done, finished** ◇ **completed, ended, over** Are you *through* with your homework yet?

throw *verb* ✦ **pitch, toss** ◇ **cast, fling, heave, hurl, sling** Will you please *throw* that pillow over here? —*noun* ✦ **pitch, toss** ◇ **cast, fling, hurl** The pitcher's first *throw* was high and wide.

thrust *verb* ✦ **force, jam, push, ram, shove** ◇ **drive, plunge** The bear *thrust* its paw into the hollow tree looking for honey. —*noun* ✦ **advance, lunge** ◇ **drive, plunge, push, shove** In fencing, competitors use their swords to block their opponents' *thrusts*.

thus *adverb* ✦ **accordingly, as a result, consequently, hence, therefore** I overslept, and *thus* I was late for school.

thwart *verb* ✦ **defeat, foil, frustrate, hinder, obstruct, prevent, stop** I *thwarted* my dog's attempt to eat the cat's food.

ticket *noun* **1.** ✦ **admission, pass** ◇ **coupon, permit** Dad has two free *tickets* for tonight's concert. **2.** ✦ **marker, slip, sticker, tag** ◇ **label, tab** The price on the *ticket* says this shirt costs thirty dollars.

tickle *verb* **1.** ◇ **brush, caress, pet, scratch, stroke, touch** My little sister always squirms and giggles when I *tickle* her feet. **2.** ✦ **amuse, cheer,**

delight, entertain, gladden, please The children's performance *tickled* the entire audience.

> ## Word Groups
>
> The regular rising and falling of the surface level of oceans is the tide. Tide is a very specific term with no true synonyms. Here are some related words to investigate in a dictionary:
>
> current, drift, flow, stream, surf, undertow, wave

tidy *adjective* ✦ **neat, orderly, organized** ◇ **clean, trim** Michelle likes to keep her desk *tidy*. —*verb* ✦ **neaten, organize, straighten up** ◇ **arrange, clean** Dad asked me to help *tidy up* his tool bench when we finished rewiring the lamp.

tie *verb* **1.** ✦ **attach, bind, fasten, secure** ◇ **connect, join, knot** We used a strong cord to *tie* the mattress to the top of the car. **2.** ✦ **balance, equal, even** ◇ **draw, match, meet** That last touchdown *tied* the score. —*noun* **1.** ✦ **fastener, fastening** ◇ **cord, line, ribbon, rope, string** Do you have a *tie* for this garbage bag? **2.** ✦ **attachment, bond, connection, link, relationship** There is a strong *tie* between my brother and me. **3.** ✦ **deadlock, draw, standoff** The hockey game ended in a *tie*.

tier *noun* ✦ **layer, level** ◇ **rank, row, step, story** The wedding cake had three *tiers*.

tight *adjective* **1.** ✦ **fast, fixed, secure, set** ◇ **sealed, strong** The knot was so *tight* that I could hardly undo it. **2.** ✦ **little, small, snug** ◇ **constricted, narrow** My favorite jeans are getting too *tight* for me. **3.** ✦ **stiff, taut, tense** ◇ **firm, rigid** The lines holding up our tent weren't very *tight*, and it collapsed in the night. **4.** ✦ **close, compact, packed** ◇ **crowded, full, thick** The military jets were flying in a *tight* formation.

tighten *verb* ✦ **contract, shorten, stiffen, tense** ◇ **fortify, strengthen** Your muscles *tighten* when you pick up something heavy.

till[1] *verb* ✦ **cultivate, furrow, harrow, plow** ◇ **hoe, turn** A long time ago, farmers *tilled* their fields with horse-drawn plows.

till[2] *conjunction* ✦ **before, until** ◇ **prior to, sooner than, up to** We can't leave *till* the meeting is over.

till[3] *noun* ✦ **cash box, cash drawer, cash register** ◇ **safe, vault** The money in the *till* has to be counted every night.

tilt *verb* ✦ **incline, lean, tip** ◇ **pitch, slant, slope** I *tilted* my head toward Jenna so I could hear what she was whispering to me. —*noun* ✦ **incline, lean, slant, slope** ◇ **list, pitch** This table has a noticeable *tilt* because one of the legs is shorter than the others.

time *noun* **1.** ✦ **interval, space, span, spell, stretch, term, while** It seems like a long *time* until summer vacation. **2.** ✦ **age, day, epoch, era, period** ◇ **season** I like to read stories set in the *time* of King Arthur. **3.** ✦ **chance, moment, occasion, opening, opportunity** Now would be a good *time* to ask Dad for permission to go to a movie. —*verb* ✦ **adjust, regulate, schedule** ◇ **measure, pace, plan** Our sprinklers are *timed* to go on at regular intervals.

timid *adjective* ✦ **apprehensive, bashful, shy** ◇ **afraid, cautious, hesitant** When my little brother is feeling *timid*, he hides behind Dad's legs.

tint *noun* ✦ **hue, shade, tinge, tone** ◇ **color, dye** "Emerald" and "jade" are two different *tints* of green. —*verb* ✦ **color, dye** ◇ **shade, stain, tinge** People sometimes *tint* their hair because they want to look different.

tiny *adjective* ✦ **diminutive, little, miniature, minute, small, wee** A Chihuahua is a very *tiny* dog.

✦ best choices
◇ other choices

tip¹ *noun* ✦ **head, peak, point, top** ◇ **end, extremity** Only the *tip* of an iceberg shows above water.

tip² *verb* ✦ **knock over, overturn, upset** ◇ **overthrow, tilt, topple** I accidentally *tipped over* my glass of milk.

tip³ *noun* 1. ◇ **bonus, gift, present, reward** Dad left a generous *tip* for the waiter. 2. ✦ **pointer, suggestion** ◇ **advice, clue, hint, information** The police officer gave our class several *tips* on bicycle safety.

tire *verb* 1. ✦ **drain, exhaust, fatigue, weaken, wear out, weary** The long bike ride *tired* me. 2. ✦ **grow weary of, lose interest in** ◇ **annoy, bore, bother** Micah never seems to *tire of* playing computer games.

tired *adjective* 1. ✦ **drained, exhausted, fatigued, weary, worn-out** The *tired* wolf lay panting on the ground. 2. ✦ **bored with, exasperated by, fed up with, sick of** ◇ **impatient** I am *tired of* your constant complaining.

title *noun* 1. ✦ **name** ◇ **designation, heading** What is the *title* of that book you are reading? 2. ✦ **claim to, ownership of, possession of,** ◇ **deed, interest, right** There is some question as to who really has legal *title to* the mansion. 3. ✦ **championship, crown** ◇ **honors, laurels** The boxer that wins this bout will win the world *title*. —*verb* ✦ **call, designate, entitle, name** ◇ **label, term** The author has decided to *title* her new book *How I Survived Grade School*.

toil *verb* ✦ **labor, slave, work** ◇ **strain, strive, struggle** The farm workers *toiled* in the fields from dawn to dusk. —*noun* ✦ **drudgery, exertion, labor, work** ◇ **effort, struggle** The coal miner was finally able to retire after years of hard *toil*.

toast *verb* ✦ **heat, warm, warm up** ◇ **burn, char, roast, scorch** It felt good to *toast* our frozen feet in front of the fire.

token *noun* ✦ **expression, mark, sign, symbol** ◇ **keepsake, souvenir** The couple exchanged rings as a *token* of their love for each other.

tolerant *adjective* ✦ **open-minded (about), patient (with), understanding (toward)** ◇ **charitable, forgiving, sympathetic** I try to be *tolerant* of people who think differently from me.

tolerate *verb* 1. ✦ **allow, have, permit, stand for** ◇ **approve, authorize** Our teacher will not *tolerate* any boisterous behavior in her classroom. 2. ✦ **abide, bear, endure, suffer, take, withstand** I can *tolerate* hot weather better than cold weather.

toll¹ *noun* ✦ **charge, fee, price** ◇ **cost, expense, tariff, tax** Drivers have to pay a *toll* to use this expressway.

toll² *verb* ✦ **peal, ring, sound** ◇ **chime, strike** In Colonial days, bells were *tolled* to gather people together.

tomb *noun* ◇ **burial chamber, crypt, grave, mausoleum, sepulcher, vault** The Taj Mahal in India is a luxurious *tomb* built for an emperor's wife.

tone *noun* 1. ✦ **note, pitch, sound** ◇ **noise** This whistle has a high *tone*. 2. ✦ **hue, shade, tinge, tint** ◇ **color** Our new drapes have three *tones* of blue in them. 3. ✦ **attitude, feel, mood, spirit** ◇ **manner, mode** The brightly colored paper lanterns gave the patio a festive *tone*. 4. ✦ **firmness, fitness, strength** ◇ **health, vigor** My grandmother does yoga to maintain her muscle *tone*.

tongue *noun* ✦ **language** ◇ **dialect, speech, talk, voice** My friend Tuyen's native *tongue* is Vietnamese.

too *adverb* 1. ✦ **also, as well, likewise** ◇ **additionally, besides, furthermore** I told Mira that if she tried out for the play, I would too. 2. ✦ **excessively, overly, unduly** ◇ **extremely, greatly, very** This shirt is *too* small for me.

tool   *noun*   ✦ **implement**   ✧ **apparatus, device, instrument, machine, utensil**   A hammer is one *tool* that every carpenter is likely to have.

top   *noun*   **1.**   ✦ **crest, peak, summit, tip**   ✧ **crown, head, zenith**   The *top* of Mount Everest is 29,028 feet above sea level.   **2.**   ✦ **cap, stopper**   ✧ **cover, lid**   I can't find the *top* to my tube of toothpaste.   —*adjective*   ✦ **best, greatest, highest, topmost**   ✧ **chief, leading, main**   This car's *top* speed is one hundred miles per hour.   —*verb*   ✦ **beat, better, exceed, outdo, surpass**   ✧ **excel**   That joke *tops* the one you told yesterday.

topic   *noun*   ✦ **matter, subject, theme**   ✧ **issue, point, question**   The weather is a common *topic* of conversation.

topple   *verb*   ✦ **knock over, overturn, upset**   ✧ **drop, fall, overthrow**   The rider won the competition because she didn't *topple* any of the barrels. ▼

torch   *noun*   ✧ **fire, flame, flare, lamp, light**   At the start of the Olympic Games, a *torch* is used to light the Olympic Flame.

torment   *noun*   ✦ **agony, anguish, distress, misery, pain, suffering**   A bad toothache can be a source of great *torment*.   —*verb*   ✦ **annoy, bother, pester, plague, torture**   ✧ **distress, pain**   A thick cloud of mosquitoes *tormented* the campers all night long.

torrent   *noun*   ✦ **deluge, flood**   ✧ **downpour, flow, overflow, stream**   Heavy rain turned the gentle creek into a rushing *torrent*.

torture   *noun*   ✦ **persecution, punishment, torment**   ✧ **agony, anguish, misery, suffering**   Jumping into the icy lake felt like a form of *torture*.   —*verb*   ✦ **distress, pain, punish, torment**   ✧ **maim, mutilate**   These new boots are *torturing* my feet.

Antonyms
torture *noun*
comfort, contentment, ease, pleasure
torture *verb*
ease, relieve, soothe

toss   *verb*   **1.**   ✦ **cast, fling, sling, throw**   ✧ **heave, hurl, pitch**   Amber *tossed* her coat on the bed.   **2.**   ✦ **heave, pitch, rock, roll, thrash**   ✧ **stir, sway, writhe**   Our little rowboat *tossed* this way and that in the choppy water.   —*noun*   ✦ **cast, fling, roll, throw**   ✧ **heave, pitch**   Many games start with a *toss* of the dice.

total   *noun*   ✦ **sum, sum total**   ✧ **aggregate, amount, whole**   We collected a *total* of 241 cans during our food drive.   —*adjective*   ✦ **complete, entire, full, whole**   ✧ **absolute, thorough**   The *total* cost of the party was less than forty dollars.   —*verb*   ✦ **add, calculate, compute, figure, sum up**   When we *totaled* the score for our game, I had won by ten points.

touch   *verb*   **1.**   ✦ **feel, finger, handle**   ✧ **manipulate, stroke**   Please don't *touch* my model airplane before the paint dries.   **2.**   ✦ **come to, contact, meet, reach to**   ✧ **border, press**   Let's move the couch out so that it doesn't *touch* the wall.   **3.**   ✦ **affect, move, stir**   ✧ **impress, influence**   Your thoughtfulness *touched* me deeply.

✦   **best choices**
✧   **other choices**

—*noun* **1. ✦ contact, feel, pressure ✧ feeling, handling, touching** I looked up when I felt the *touch* of someone's hand on my shoulder. **2. ✦ bit, dash, pinch, trace ✧ crumb, dab, hint, shade, tinge** Mom added a *touch* of oregano to the spaghetti sauce.

touchy *adjective* **✦ irritable, sensitive, testy ✧ crabby, nervous, resentful** My brother is so *touchy* that he takes every remark as a criticism.

Antonyms
tough *adjective*
1. brittle, delicate, flimsy, fragile
2. easy, facile, simple

tough *adjective* **1. ✦ durable, rugged, stout, strong, sturdy ✧ hardy** Leather is a *tough* material. **2. ✦ demanding, difficult, hard ✧ rough, strenuous** Alan spent a long time trying to solve the *tough* math problem.

tour *noun* **✦ excursion, outing, trip ✧ expedition, journey, visit** If we take this *tour*, we'll be able to see the Tower of London. **—***verb* **✦ journey through, travel through, visit ✧ explore, see** My whole family *toured* Japan and Korea last summer.

tourist *noun* **✦ sightseer, traveler, visitor** *Tourists* from all over the world come to Niagara to see the magnificent falls.

tournament *noun* **✦ competition, contest, match, meet ✧ challenge, games, series** This chess *tournament* is open to players of all ages. ▼

tow *verb* **✦ draw, pull, tug ✧ drag, haul, lug** Powerful tugboats *towed* the ocean liner out of the harbor.

tower *noun* **✧ belfry, minaret, spire, steeple, turret** The clock *tower* above City Hall is the oldest building in town. **—***verb* **✦ loom, rear up, rise, soar ✧ dominate, overlook** A huge storm cloud *towered* on the horizon.

town *noun* **✦ community, municipality, settlement ✧ city, village** Dad grew up in a small *town* in the Midwest.

toxic *adjective* **✦ harmful, injurious, poisonous ✧ deadly, venomous** *Toxic* chemicals have to be handled very carefully.

toy *noun* **✦ plaything ✧ trifle, trinket** When I was younger, my favorite *toy* was a yellow dump truck. **—***verb* **✦ play, trifle ✧ putter, tease, tinker** I *toyed* with my dinner because I wasn't all that hungry.

trace *noun* **1. ✦ evidence, indications, remains, signs ✧ mark, proof** The hikers found *traces* of an old mining camp. **2. ✦ bit, dash, pinch, touch ✧ hint, inkling, suggestion, tinge** There's just a *trace* too much salt in this soup. **—***verb* **1. ✦ hunt down, track down, trail ✧ follow, pursue, search, seek** The FBI helped *trace* the missing person. **2. ✦ copy, outline, reproduce ✧ diagram, draw, portray, sketch** My little sister spends hours *tracing* pictures from her coloring book.

track *noun* **1. ✦ footprint, print ✧ mark, sign, trace, trail** Who left these dirty *tracks* all over the kitchen floor? **2. ✧ course** I like to go over to the high school and run laps around the *track*. **—***verb* **1. ✦ follow, hunt, pursue, trail ✧ search, seek, trace** The wildlife photographer *tracked* a bear and her cubs through the forest. **2. ✦ bring, carry, drag, trail ✧ bear** I took off my sandals so that I wouldn't *track* sand into the house.

tract *noun* ✦ **lot, parcel, piece, plot** ✧ **area, district, region, site** This *tract* of land is going to be used for a housing development.

trade *noun* **1.** ✦ **business, commerce** ✧ **exchange, traffic** The United States engages in *trade* with most of the countries in the world. **2.** ✦ **barter, exchange, swap, switch** ✧ **substitution** Do you think that my baseball glove would be a fair *trade* for your tennis racket? **3.** ✦ **business, craft, occupation, profession** ✧ **career, work** People in the plumbing *trade* usually have to serve an apprenticeship. —*verb* ✦ **exchange, substitute, swap, switch** ✧ **barter** My brother and I sometimes *trade* chores.

tradition *noun* ✦ **custom, habit, practice** ✧ **convention, standard** It is our family *tradition* to celebrate Passover at my grandparents' house.

traditional *adjective* ✦ **conventional, customary** ✧ **habitual, normal, routine, usual** Aunt Debbie and her fiancé decided to have a *traditional* wedding.

traffic *noun* **1.** ✦ **travel** ✧ **movement, transit, transport** *Traffic* is heavy on this freeway during rush hour. **2.** ✦ **commerce, market, trade** ✧ **business, exchange, sale** The government is trying to stop the *traffic* in illegal drugs. —*verb* ✦ **deal, trade** ✧ **barter, buy, market, sell** It is against the law to *traffic in* stolen goods.

tragedy *noun* ✦ **catastrophe, disaster, misfortune** ✧ **accident, mishap** The sinking of the *Titanic* was one of the worst maritime *tragedies* of the twentieth century.

tragic *adjective* ✦ **doomed, sad, sorrowful, unfortunate, unhappy** ✧ **dreadful, mournful** The tale of Romeo and Juliet is a *tragic* love story.

trail *verb* **1.** ✦ **drag, draw, pull, tow** ✧ **haul, lug** Danny played with his kitten by *trailing* a shoelace in front of it. **2.** ✦ **trace, track** ✧ **hunt, pursue, search, seek** The shepherd and his dog *trailed* the lost sheep. **3.** ✦ **follow, lag, straggle, tag along** ✧ **linger, tail** The lame wolf *trailed* behind the rest of the pack. —*noun* **1.** ✦ **trace, track** ✧ **mark, scent, sign** The fox followed a rabbit's *trail* through the snow. **2.** ✦ **footpath, path, route, track** ✧ **course, way** This *trail* leads to the pond.

train *noun* ✦ **caravan, procession** ✧ **column, line, string** In the Old West, mule *trains* were used to transport military supplies. —*verb* ✦ **coach, drill, instruct, teach** ✧ **educate, tutor** I'm trying to *train* my dog to roll over.

trait *noun* ✦ **attribute, characteristic, feature, quality** ✧ **property** Honesty and kindness are two of my friend Petra's best *traits*.

traitor *noun* ✦ **betrayer, double-crosser** ✧ **informer, spy** A *traitor* sold secret plans to the enemy.

tramp *verb* ✦ **hike, march, plod, stamp, trek, trudge** ✧ **trample** We got wet feet *tramping* through the snow. —*noun* ✦ **excursion, hike, march, trek** ✧ **ramble, stroll** We went for a *tramp* through the woods.

trample *verb* ✦ **crush, flatten, squash** ✧ **stamp, tramp, tread** Our dog *trampled* our newly planted petunias.

tranquil *adjective* ✦ **calm, peaceful, quiet, restful, serene, soothing** We enjoyed a *tranquil* weekend at the lake.

transfer *verb* ✦ **convey, move, shift** ✧ **carry, send, ship, transport** Jennifer used a floppy disk to *transfer* information to her computer's hard drive. —*noun* ✦ **reassignment, relocation** ✧ **change, move, shift** My uncle got a *transfer* from Pennsylvania to Oregon.

transform *verb* ✦ **alter, change, convert, modify, turn** ✧ **renew** Cinderella's fairy godmother *transformed* a pumpkin into a carriage.

transition *noun* ✦ **alteration, change, modification, shift, transformation** For my science

✦ **best choices**
✧ **other choices**

251

project, I took pictures of a caterpillar's *transition* into a butterfly.

translate *verb* ✦ **render** ✧ **alter, change, convert, modify, transform** Do you know Chinese well enough to *translate* this letter into English?

transmission *noun* **1.** ✦ **conveyance, transfer, transference** ✧ **passage, sending** Regular washing of the hands helps prevent the *transmission* of germs. **2.** ✦ **broadcast, communication, signal** ✧ **message, report** We can receive *transmissions* from radio stations that are more than 220 miles away.

transmit *verb* ✦ **convey, pass, relay, send, transfer** ✧ **deliver** Fax machines *transmit* images and written messages over telephone lines. ◄

transparent *adjective* **1.** ✦ **clear, see-through, translucent** Most jellyfish have delicate, *transparent* bodies. **2.** ✦ **apparent, evident, obvious, plain, unmistakable, visible** My sister's joke was a *transparent* attempt to change the subject.

Antonyms
transparent *adjective*
1. opaque
2. concealed, hidden, obscured

transport *verb* ✦ **carry, convey, haul, move, take, transfer** ✧ **bear, cart, ferry, shift** There is no way that we can *transport* all this luggage in our little car. —*noun* ✦ **conveyance, shipment, shipping, transfer, transportation** ✧ **delivery** Trucks, trains, and airplanes are used for the *transport* of freight.

transportation *noun* ✦ **conveyance, transit** ✧ **transport** My neighbor's favorite form of *transportation* is a motorcycle.

trap *noun* ✦ **ambush, lure, snare** ✧ **deception, hoax, trick** The police set a *trap* to catch the robbers. —*verb* ✦ **capture, catch** ✧ **net, seize, snare** Many people prefer to *trap* mice alive rather than poison them.

trash *noun* ✦ **garbage, refuse, rubbish, waste** ✧ **debris, junk** It's your turn to take out the *trash*.

travel *verb* **1.** ✦ **journey, roam, tour, trek, wander** ✧ **sightsee, visit** It would be fun to *travel* through Europe by bicycle. **2.** ✦ **go, move, pass, proceed** ✧ **advance, progress** Light *travels* at a speed of approximately 186,000 miles per second. —*noun* ✦ **excursion, journey, tour, trek, trip** ✧ **voyage** We enjoyed our *travels* through Italy and Greece.

treacherous *adjective* **1.** ✦ **deceitful, disloyal, traitorous, treasonous, unfaithful** A *treacherous* guard assassinated Indira Gandhi, Prime Minister of India, in 1984. **2.** ✦ **dangerous, hazardous, perilous, risky, unsafe** Sailing can be *treacherous* if the wind is too strong.

treason *noun* ✦ **disloyalty, treachery** ✧ **betrayal, conspiracy** Benedict Arnold committed an act of *treason* during the American Revolutionary War.

treasure *noun* ✦ **fortune, riches, wealth** ✧ **gems, gold, jewels** The divers found a sunken ship that was full of *treasure*. —*verb* ✦ **cherish, prize, value** ✧ **adore, esteem, love, revere** My mother *treasures* the rocking chair that she received from her grandmother.

treat *verb* **1.** ✦ **consider, look upon, regard** ✧ **handle, manage** My parents encourage me to *treat* everyone with respect. **2.** ✦ **care for, medicate, relieve** ✧ **cure, heal** Grandmother *treats* a sore throat with lemon juice and honey in hot water. —*noun* ✦ **delight, enjoyment, joy, pleasure** ✧ **bonus, comfort** Our Friday night *treat* is pizza and a movie.

treatment *noun* ✦ attention, care, reception ✧ approach, handling, management We appreciated the friendly *treatment* we received from the store manager.

treaty *noun* ✦ accord, agreement, compact, pact ✧ alliance, arrangement Representatives from six nations were present at the signing of the peace *treaty*.

tremble *verb* ✦ shake, shiver, shudder ✧ quake, quaver, quiver The campers *trembled* with cold until they got their fire started.

tremendous *adjective* ✦ enormous, gigantic, great, huge, immense, large ✧ intense A *tremendous* wave capsized the boat.

tremor *noun* ✦ quake, shake, shock ✧ earthquake, tremble, vibration We felt little *tremors* for several days following the earthquake.

trench *noun* ✦ ditch, furrow, trough ✧ channel, excavation, gully Workers dug a *trench* to bury the water pipe.

trend *noun* ✦ direction, inclination, movement, tendency ✧ course, fashion, style There has been an upward *trend* in the price of concert tickets recently.

trial *noun* 1. ✧ case, hearing, inquiry, lawsuit, suit The *trial* will start as soon as a jury is selected. 2. ✦ check, test, tryout ✧ analysis, examination, experiment The new plane will be put through a series of *trials* to see how it performs. 3. ✦ adversity, affliction, hardship, misfortune, ordeal, trouble For early pioneers, the westward trek was a time of both *trial* and adventure.

tribute *noun* 1. ✦ acknowledgment (of), homage, honor (of), praise (of), recognition (of) This statue was erected in *tribute* to the man who founded our town. 2. ✦ levy, money, payment, tax ✧ bribe, offering Ancient Rome received great amounts of *tribute* from the nations it conquered in battle.

trick *noun* 1. ✦ feat, stunt, technique ✧ accomplishment, skill My sister taught our cat the *trick* of rolling over to get a treat. 2. ✦ deceit, deception, device, tactic ✧ fraud, scheme An opossum will lie motionless as a *trick* to make enemies think that it is dead. 3. ✦ antic, gag, jest, joke, prank ✧ mischief My friends and I play *tricks* on each other on April Fool's Day. —*verb* ✦ deceive, fool, mislead ✧ cheat, double-cross, swindle It is against the law to *trick* a person into giving a confession.

trickle *verb* ✦ dribble, flow, ooze ✧ leak, drip, seep Sweat *trickled* down my back after playing tennis in the hot sun. —*noun* ✦ dribble ✧ crawl, creep, drip, drop This creek slows to a *trickle* during the summer.

trifle *noun* ✦ knickknack, novelty, trinket ✧ plaything, toy We bought balloons and other *trifles* to hand out as party favors. —*verb* ✦ fidget, fool, play, putter, toy Lynell *trifled* with the papers on her desk while waiting for the computer to boot up.

trim *verb* 1. ✦ clip, crop, cut, prune, snip ✧ nip, shape We *trimmed* the roses and covered them with straw for the winter. 2. ✦ adorn, decorate, edge ✧ embroider, ornament Mom and I *trimmed* my dress with lace. —*noun* 1. ✦ clip, crop, cut ✧ pruning, shortening I asked the barber to give my hair a *trim*. 3. ✦ condition, order, repair, shape, state ✧ fitness My uncle's boat is always in good *trim*. —*adjective* ✦ fit, lean, slender, slim ✧ neat, sleek, tidy Mom and Dad looked *trim* after their vacation at a health spa.

trip *noun* ✦ excursion, journey, tour ✧ jaunt, outing, voyage We went on a *trip* to Mexico to visit the Mayan ruins. —*verb* ✦ fall, stumble, tumble ✧ flounder, slip, stagger Our new puppy sometimes *trips* over its own feet.

triumph *verb* ✦ beat, defeat, prevail over, win over ✧ conquer, outdo, succeed We went wild when our team finally *triumphed over* our greatest rival. —*noun* ✦ **accomplishment, achievement, success** ✧ **conquest, victory, win** Paula had a feeling of *triumph* when she finally finished the quilt.

triumphant *adjective* ✦ **exultant, joyful, jubilant, victorious** ✧ **conquering, winning** Irena gave a *triumphant* smile as she crossed the finish line ahead of the others.

trivial *adjective* ✦ **insignificant, petty, slight, trifling, unimportant** The music students played their recital pieces with only a few *trivial* mistakes.

troop *noun* ✦ **group, unit** ✧ **band, bunch, company, corps, squad** Our Boy Scout *troop* will be going to next summer's jamboree. —*verb* ✦ **file, march, parade, step, stride** ✧ **advance, proceed** We *trooped* off the bus and headed for the science museum.

trophy *noun* ✧ **award, citation, crown, honor, laurels, prize** Our school gives *trophies* to the best students at the end of each year.

trouble *noun* **1.** ✦ **difficulty, a fix, a jam, a predicament** ✧ **problem** We'll be in *trouble* if we don't get to school on time. **2.** ✦ **annoyance, bother, inconvenience** ✧ **care, effort, work** Would it be too much *trouble* to pick up my tickets on your way home? —*verb* ✦ **annoy, bother, distress, disturb, upset, worry** Is anything *troubling* you today?

truce *noun* ✦ **armistice, cease-fire, peace** ✧ **halt, lull, stop** The fighting will end when the *truce* takes effect at midnight.

trudge *verb* ✦ **plod, toil, tramp** ✧ **hike, limp, shuffle, trek** We got our snow saucers and *trudged* back up the hill.

true *adjective* **1.** ✦ **accurate, correct, factual, right, valid** ✧ **exact** The witness swore that everything she said was *true*. **2.** ✦ **dependable, faithful, loyal, reliable, steadfast, trustworthy** My dog is a *true* companion who always wants to be

with me. **3.** ✦ **lawful, legal, legitimate, rightful** ✧ **just, official** The documents will prove who is the *true* owner of this priceless diamond necklace. **4.** ✦ **actual, authentic, genuine, real** ✧ **undoubted** This book is a *true* first edition.

truly *adverb* ✦ **definitely, genuinely, positively, really** ✧ **actually** The teacher said that my short story was *truly* original.

trust *verb* **1.** ✦ **believe in, depend on, rely on, swear by** Self-confident people *trust* their instincts. **2.** ✦ **assume, believe, presume, suppose** ✧ **anticipate, expect** I *trust* that you will keep my secret. —*noun* **1.** ✦ **confidence, conviction, faith, reliance** ✧ **belief** I value the *trust* that my friends have in me. **2.** ✦ **care, custody, guardianship, keeping, protection** Carrie left her hamster and turtle in my *trust* while she was away on vacation.

trustworthy *adjective* ✦ **dependable, reliable, responsible** ✧ **faithful, loyal** I know that Carl will pay back the money I loaned him because he is very *trustworthy*.

truth *noun* ✦ **actuality, fact, reality** ✧ **authenticity, honesty, truthfulness** The *truth* is that I did eat the last doughnut.

try *verb* **1.** ✦ **sample, taste, test** ✧ **check, examine, experience, inspect** Would you like to *try* one of the cookies I made? **2.** ✦ **consider, deliberate, hear, judge** The Supreme Court *tries* important cases that are referred to it by lower courts. **3.** ✦ **aim, attempt, endeavor, seek, strive** ✧ **struggle** Ed always *tries* to get his homework done before dinner. —*noun* ✦ **attempt, effort, endeavor, trial** ✧ **experiment, test** Our lawnmower usually doesn't start on the first *try*.

trying *adjective* ✦ **demanding, difficult, hard, rough, tough, troublesome** My parents had a *trying* time when my baby brother was sick.

tug *verb* ✦ **drag, draw, jerk, pull** ✧ **haul, heave, wrench** My dog *tugs* so hard on his leash that I can barely hold him. —*noun* ✦ **jerk, pull, yank** ✧ **heave, tow, wrench** Give this rope a *tug* to ring the bell.

tumble *verb* **1.** ✦ **roll, somersault, stumble, trip** ✧ **pitch, reel, toss** The children *tumbled* over one another to get to the candy from the piñata. ▶ **2.** ✦ **drop, fall, plunge, topple** ✧ **slip, spill** The lamp *tumbled* to the floor when I bumped the table. —*noun* ✦ **fall, spill** ✧ **dive, drop, plunge, slip** My little sister took a lot of *tumbles* while learning to walk.

tune *noun* **1.** ✦ **air, melody, refrain, song, theme** I can't think of the name of the *tune* that keeps running through my head. **2.** ✦ **harmony, pitch** ✧ **accord, agreement, conformity** I wish I could sing in *tune* like my sister. —*verb* ✦ **harmonize** ✧ **adapt, adjust, regulate, set** I haven't learned how to *tune* my new guitar yet.

tunnel *noun* ✦ **underground passage** ✧ **corridor, passageway, shaft, tube** The longest railway *tunnel* in the world is in Japan. —*verb* ✦ **burrow, dig** ✧ **excavate, mine, scoop, shovel** It looks like those gophers are *tunneling* through our back yard again.

turmoil *noun* ✦ **chaos, commotion, confusion, dither, flurry, flutter, tumult, uproar** ✧ **ferment** The ants ran around in *turmoil* when their nest was disturbed.

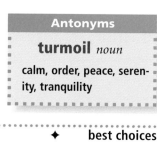

Antonyms
turmoil *noun*
calm, order, peace, serenity, tranquility

turn *verb* **1.** ✦ **pivot, revolve, rotate** ✧ **spin, twirl, whirl** *Turn* the faucet to the left to get hot water. **2.** ✧ **detour, divert, move, shift, swerve, wheel** We have to *turn* right at the corner of Almond Street to get to my aunt's house. **3.** ✦ **become, change into, transform into** ✧ **alter, convert, modify** I'm reading a story about an ugly duckling that *turns into* a beautiful swan. **4.** ✦ **sprain, twist, wrench** ✧ **hurt, strain** I *turned* my ankle playing soccer. —*noun* **1.** ✦ **angle, bend, curve** ✧ **arc, corner, rotation, twist** The path makes a *turn* to the left just before the pond. **2.** ✦ **alteration, change, shift, switch** ✧ **modification** The weather has taken a *turn* for the better. **3.** ✦ **chance, opportunity, spell, time** ✧ **attempt, go** Whose *turn* is it to bat after Janine?

tutor *noun* ✦ **educator, instructor, teacher** ✧ **coach, trainer** My school has volunteer *tutors* in every classroom. —*verb* ✦ **educate, instruct, teach** ✧ **coach, inform, train** My uncle *tutors* me in math.

twilight *noun* ✦ **dusk, nightfall, sundown, sunset** ✧ **evening** Deer come out to feed just after dawn and just before *twilight*.

twinkle *verb* ✦ **flash, flicker, gleam, glimmer, glitter, sparkle** ✧ **shine** The sequins on the singer's dress *twinkled* under the spotlight.

twirl *verb* ✦ **revolve, rotate, spin, turn, whirl** ✧ **swirl, wheel** The drum majorette *twirled* her baton and then threw it into the air.

twist *verb* **1.** ✦ **coil, roll, wind, wrap** ✧ **curl, twine, weave** The cowboy *twisted* his rope around the post. **2.** ✦ **sprain, turn, wrench** ✧ **hurt, strain** How did you *twist* your ankle? **3.** ✦ **alter, change, distort** ✧ **deform, warp** Some people *twist* the facts in order to make their story more interesting. —*noun* **1.** ✦ **angle, bend, curve, turn** ✧ **zigzag** This road is full of dangerous *twists*. **2.** ✦ **alteration, interpretation, slant, variation** ✧ **change, development,**

✦ **best choices**
✧ **other choices**

treatment A pun makes us laugh by putting an unexpected *twist* on a word's meaning.

twitch *verb* ✦ **jerk, quiver** ◇ **quaver, shake, wiggle, wriggle** The cat's whiskers *twitched* when he saw the mouse.

type *noun* **1.** ✦ **category, class, kind, sort, variety** ◇ **group** Our library has all *types* of books on its shelves. **2.** ✦ **print, printing** ◇ **character, letter, text** Grandpa likes newspapers with large *type* because they're easier to read.

typical *adjective* ✦ **average, common, normal, ordinary, standard, usual** The *typical* American household has at least one television set.

tyranny *noun* ✦ **oppression, repression, suppression** ◇ **domination** The government's *tyranny* ended when a democratic leader was finally elected.

tyrant *noun* ✦ **absolute ruler, dictator** ◇ **oppressor** The *tyrant* was overthrown by the people she had been oppressing.

U

ugly *adjective* **1.** ✦ **bad-looking, homely, unattractive, unsightly** ✧ **plain** We entered our iguana in the *ugly* pet contest. ◀ **2.** ✦ **disgusting, foul, nasty, repulsive, unpleasant, vile** ✧ **mean, rude** There was an *ugly* smell coming from the town dump.

ultimate *adjective* ✦ **highest, supreme, top** ✧ **concluding, end, final, last** The *ultimate* achievement in the Boy Scouts is to earn an Eagle badge with Silver Palm.

umpire *noun* ✧ **arbitrator, judge, ref, referee** We need an *umpire* for next week's baseball game.

unable *adjective* ✦ **incapable (of), not able** ✧ **powerless, unfit, unqualified** Baby birds are *unable* to fly until they grow feathers.

unanimous *adjective* ✦ **undivided, unified, united** ✧ **common, solid, universal** The pioneers were *unanimous* in their support of the wagon master's decision to push onward.

unaware *adjective* ✦ **ignorant, unconscious, uninformed** ✧ **blind, heedless, oblivious** I was *unaware* of how much time I was actually spending on the Internet until you pointed it out to me.

unbelievable *adjective* ✦ **absurd, dubious, flimsy, incredible, questionable, unconvincing, weak** Jasmine's story about seeing a flying monkey was a bit *unbelievable*.

uncanny *adjective* ✦ **eerie, mysterious, strange, weird** ✧ **curious, unusual** Dad says our new kitten bears an *uncanny* resemblance to the cat he had as a child.

uncertain *adjective* **1.** ✦ **unclear, undecided, unsure** ✧ **doubtful, dubious** I am *uncertain* as to whether or not I want to go to my friend's party. **2.** ✦ **erratic, unpredictable, unsettled, variable** ✧ **fickle, freakish** The *uncertain* weather forced us to cancel our fishing trip.

uncomfortable *adjective* **1.** ✦ **embarrassed, nervous, self-conscious, uneasy** ✧ **awkward, upset** I'm usually *uncomfortable* when I have to speak in front of the class. **2.** ✧ **cramped, hard, ill-fitting, painful** This old couch is lumpy and *uncomfortable*.

uncommon *adjective* ✦ **rare, unusual** ✧ **exceptional, remarkable, strange, unique** Taylor caught a beetle for her collection that is *uncommon* in this part of the country. ▶

unconcerned *adjective* ✦ **indifferent (to), uninterested (in)** ✧ **apathetic, careless, heedless** My uncle wears whatever clothes he happens to find because he is *unconcerned* about his appearance.

unconscious *adjective* **1.** ✦ **knocked out, out cold** ✧ **senseless, stunned** The man was *unconscious* for several minutes after falling and hitting his head. **2.** ✦ **ignorant, innocent, oblivious, unaware, unknowing, unmindful** The speaker was *unconscious* of the fact that her mannerisms were distracting her audience.

uncover *verb* ✦ **dig up, discover, expose, find, turn up, unearth** ✧ **disclose, reveal** Historians are always *uncovering* new facts about events of the past.

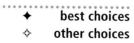

✦ **best choices**
✧ **other choices**

undecided *adjective* ✦ **indefinite, uncertain, undetermined, unresolved, unsure** My older sister is still *undecided* about which college she wants to attend.

under *preposition* **1.** ✦ **below, beneath, underneath** I finally found my calculator *under* a stack of papers on my desk. **2.** ✦ **less than, lower than, smaller than** ◇ **short, shy** Anyone *under* four feet in height may not ride this roller coaster. **3.** ✦ **according to** ◇ **controlled by, following, subject to** *Under* the rules of basketball, each team can have only five players on the court at one time.

undergo *verb* ✦ **experience, go through, have, meet with** ◇ **encounter** Babies *undergo* many significant physical changes during the first year of life.

underground *adjective* ✦ **belowground, subterranean** ◇ **buried, covered, sunken** Foxes, wolves, and coyotes typically live in *underground* dens. ▼

underneath *preposition* ✦ **beneath, under** ◇ **below** Kristen wore a heavy wool sweater *underneath* her jacket. —*adverb* ✦ **below, beneath, under** ◇ **down, lower** The leaf was green above and silver *underneath*.

understand *verb* **1.** ✦ **comprehend, follow, get, grasp, know** ◇ **realize, recognize** The teacher took great care to ensure that every student *understood* the lesson. **2.** ✦ **gather, hear** ◇ **believe, conclude, perceive, presume** I *understand* that the rehearsal might be postponed.

understanding *noun* **1.** ✦ **appreciation, comprehension, concept, grasp, idea, knowledge** My dog likes to ride in the car, but he has no *understanding* of how it moves. **2.** ✦ **agreement, arrangement** ◇ **bargain, compromise, deal, pact** I have an *understanding* with my parents that I will call home if I'm going to be late. —*adjective* ✦ **sympathetic** ◇ **compassionate, kind, tender, tolerant** Whenever I feel unhappy, I tell my troubles to an *understanding* friend.

undertake *verb* ✦ **assume, attempt, tackle, take on** ◇ **begin, start** Cleaning out the basement was a chore that no one wanted to *undertake*.

undo *verb* **1.** ✦ **cancel, erase, neutralize, reverse, wipe out** ◇ **defeat, spoil** I can't *undo* my mistakes, but at least I can apologize for them. **2.** ✦ **free, loosen, unfasten, unravel, untie** ◇ **open, unclose** Can you *undo* this knot?

uneasy *adjective* **1.** ✦ **anxious, apprehensive, nervous, worried** ◇ **tense, troubled** I felt a little *uneasy* about diving off the high board. **2.** ✦ **awkward, uncomfortable, unpleasant** ◇ **embarrassed, shy** There was an *uneasy* pause in our conversation.

unemployed *adjective* ✦ **jobless, out-of-work** ◇ **idle, inactive** The state government has a bureau that helps *unemployed* people find jobs.

unequal *adjective* **1.** ✦ **different, dissimilar, uneven** ◇ **lopsided, unbalanced** I trimmed my old jeans into a pair of shorts, but the legs are of *unequal* length. **2.** ✦ **lopsided, mismatched, unbalanced, uneven** If I raced my older brother in the fifty-yard dash, it would be an *unequal* contest.

uneven *adjective* **1.** ✦ **bumpy, irregular, rough, rugged** ◇ **coarse** We had difficulty walking across the *uneven* ground. **2.** ✦ **lopsided,**

mismatched, un-balanced, unequal ◇ **different, unlike** The basketball game was *uneven* because one team had much taller players than the other.

unexpected *adjective* ✦ **unanticipated, unforeseen** ◇ **abrupt, sudden, surprising** Lisa was delighted when she received an *unexpected* present a week after her birthday.

unfair *adjective* ✦ **one-sided, unjust, unreasonable** ◇ **biased, prejudiced** Wrestlers are matched up according to their weight so that no one has an *unfair* advantage.

unfamiliar *adjective* **1.** ✦ **strange, unknown** ◇ **different, fresh, new, novel, original, uncommon** The explorers moved cautiously through the *unfamiliar* territory. **2.** ✦ **unacquainted** ◇ **ignorant, inexperienced, unaware, uninformed** I was *unfamiliar* with many of the foods we ate on our trip to India.

unfortunate *adjective* ✦ **regrettable, unlucky** ◇ **bad, inappropriate, poor, unhappy** It was an *unfortunate* mistake to forget the map on our trip.

unfriendly *adjective* ✦ **aloof, cold, cool, distant, unsociable** ◇ **haughty, hostile** Our cat is usually *unfriendly* to strangers.

unhappy *adjective* ✦ **blue, dejected, depressed, down, downcast, gloomy, low, sad** ◇ **sorrowful** Listening to my favorite CD cheers me up when I'm feeling *unhappy*.

unhealthy *adjective* **1.** ✦ **ill, sick, sickly, unwell** ◇ **frail, weak** My plant looks *unhealthy* because it hasn't been getting enough sunlight. **2.** ✦ **dangerous, harmful, risky, unhealthful, unwholesome** People used to think that it was *unhealthy* to have fresh air in the bedroom at night.

uniform *adjective* **1.** ✦ **constant, even, regular, steady, unchanging** ◇ **same** A good refrigerator keeps everything at a *uniform* temperature. **2.** ✦ **comparable, equal, identical, like, similar, standard** ◇ **alike** Most bricks are of *uniform* size.

unify *verb* ✦ **combine, consolidate, join, merge, unite** ◇ **connect, link** In 1990, East and West Germany *unified* to form one nation.

union *noun* **1.** ✦ **combination, consolidation, joining, merger, unification** The United Arab Emirates is a country that was formed in 1971 by the *union* of seven sheikdoms. **2.** ✦ **alliance, association, federation, league, organization** ◇ **guild, society** Dad is a member of a labor *union*.

unique *adjective* ✦ **different, distinctive, individual, separate** ◇ **remarkable, sole, unusual** Every snowflake has a *unique* shape.

unit *noun* **1.** ◇ **category, classification, measure, quantity** Seconds, minutes, hours, and days are *units* used to measure time. **2.** ✦ **component, device, system** ◇ **element, item, part, piece** Our car needs a new heating *unit*.

unite *verb* ✦ **combine, consolidate, join, link, merge, unify** ◇ **connect** Chief Tecumseh's dream was to *unite* all North American tribes into one Indian nation.

universal *adjective* ✦ **all-around, broad, general, wide, widespread** ◇ **boundless, total,**

✦ **best choices**
◇ **other choices**

unlimited Some books become classics because they have *universal* appeal.

unkempt *adjective* ✦ **disheveled, messy, sloppy, slovenly, uncombed, untidy** ◇ **neglected, slipshod** The hunter had an *unkempt* appearance after spending a week in the woods.

Antonyms
unkempt *adjective*
groomed, neat, orderly, shipshape, spic-and-span, spruce, tidy, trim

unkind *adjective* ✦ **cruel, harsh, inconsiderate, mean, thoughtless** I apologize for my *unkind* remark about your new friend.

unknown *adjective* ✦ **anonymous, nameless, unidentified, unrecognized** ◇ **obscure** The mystery donation was made by a person who wished to remain *unknown*.

unlike *adjective* ✦ **different, dissimilar, distinct, diverse** ◇ **opposite, unrelated** Though a whale and a mouse are both mammals, they are quite *unlike* in appearance.

unlikely *adjective* ✦ **doubtful, improbable, unexpected** ◇ **questionable, rare, slight** When I saw the clear sky, I knew it was *unlikely* that we would have a snow day.

unlucky *adjective* ✦ **luckless, unfortunate** ◇ **cursed, doomed, unhappy** The *unlucky* gambler lost all of his money.

unnatural *adjective* ✦ **bizarre, curious, eerie, peculiar, strange, unusual, weird** We decided to investigate when we saw an *unnatural* light coming from the abandoned laboratory.

unpack *verb* ✦ **empty, unload** ◇ **clear, discharge, dump** I had to *unpack* my whole suitcase just to find my pajamas.

unpopular *adjective* ✦ **disliked, unwanted, unwelcome** ◇ **unacceptable, undesirable** The *unpopular* politician was voted out of office in the next election.

unreasonable *adjective* **1.** ✦ **absurd, foolish, illogical, irrational, senseless** It's *unreasonable* to expect to get a perfect score on every test. **2.** ✦ **excessive, extreme** ◇ **outrageous, unfair, unjust** My brother spends an *unreasonable* amount of time combing his hair.

unreliable *adjective* ✦ **questionable, uncertain, undependable, untrustworthy** The newspaper didn't print the story because the information came from an *unreliable* source.

unrest *noun* ✦ **agitation, disorder, disquiet, disturbance, trouble, turmoil** Periods of political *unrest* can occur when people are unhappy with their leaders.

unruly *adjective* ✦ **disorderly, uncontrollable, unmanageable, wild** ◇ **disobedient** More police were called in to help control the *unruly* mob.

unsatisfactory *adjective* ✦ **inadequate, insufficient, unacceptable** ◇ **bad, poor** The new employee almost lost his job because he was making *unsatisfactory* progress.

unskilled *adjective* ✦ **inexperienced, untrained** ◇ **unqualified, untalented** *Unskilled* workers usually make less money than professionals.

unsteady *adjective* ✦ **rickety, shaky, unstable, wobbly** ◇ **insecure, unsafe** The table was too *unsteady* to hold anything heavy.

untie *verb* ✦ **loosen, unbind, undo, unfasten** ◇ **detach, disconnect** Someone *untied* my shoelaces as a practical joke.

unused *adjective* **1.** ✦ **new, untouched, untried** ◇ **fresh, original** Christopher found some ice skates at a yard sale that looked like they were *unused*. ▶

2. ✦ **unaccustomed, unfamiliar (with)** ✧ **inexperienced** I am *unused* to getting up this early in the morning.

unusual *adjective* ✦ **exceptional, extraordinary, freakish, odd, peculiar, rare, strange, uncommon** ✧ **unique** An *unusual* blizzard once hit Nebraska in the middle of July.

up *adverb* ✦ **overhead, upward** ✧ **above, aloft, higher** I looked *up* just in time to see an eagle taking off from its nest.

uphold *verb* ✦ **maintain, support, sustain** ✧ **defend, preserve, protect** Police officers take an oath in which they promise to *uphold* the law.

upkeep *noun* ✦ **maintenance, repair** ✧ **preservation, operation, support** Dad has been spending a lot of money on the *upkeep* of his old car.

upper *adjective* ✦ **higher, top, uppermost** ✧ **greater, superior** There's a good view from the *upper* floors of our apartment building.

upright *adjective* **1.** ✦ **erect, raised, vertical** ✧ **perpendicular, standing** Please place your seatback in an *upright* position before takeoff. **2.** ✦ **good, honest, honorable, moral, trustworthy, virtuous** The *upright* news reporter was admired and trusted by everyone.

uproar *noun* ✦ **clamor, commotion, disturbance, noise** ✧ **tumult, turmoil** There was such an *uproar* from the audience that I almost couldn't hear the band.

upset *verb* **1.** ✦ **capsize, overturn, turn over** ✧ **knock over, topple** We all got pretty wet when Dad accidentally *upset* our canoe. **2.** ✦ **disorganize, disrupt, mess up, unsettle** ✧ **jumble, muddle** The cancellation of the flight *upset* all our travel plans. **3.** ✦ **agitate, distress, disturb, perturb, trouble** ✧ **annoy, bother** The news that our teacher was leaving *upset* everyone in the class. —*adjective* **1.** ✦ **overturned, upside-down,**

upturned ✧ **capsized, toppled** We are so late because the road was blocked by an *upset* garbage truck. **2.** ✦ **distressed, disturbed, troubled** ✧ **annoyed, bothered** Mary was very *upset* when she lost her favorite necklace.

urban *adjective* ✦ **city, metropolitan, municipal** ✧ **civic** When the Industrial Revolution began in the eighteenth century, many people moved to *urban* areas to find work.

Antonyms
urban *adjective*
agrarian, country, pastoral, rural, rustic

urge *verb* **1.** ✦ **drive, goad, press, prod** ✧ **force, push** When the cattle refused to cross the river, a cowboy *urged* them on. **2.** ✦ **advise, beg, encourage, persuade, prompt** ✧ **plead** The sick man's friends *urged* him to see a doctor. —*noun* ✦ **desire, impulse, longing, wish, yearning** ✧ **hunger, thirst** Brandon had a sudden *urge* to run outside and play in the rain.

urgent *adjective* ✦ **critical, crucial, dire, immediate, pressing** ✧ **essential, important** The charity spokesperson said that there was an *urgent* need for donations.

usage *noun* ✦ **handling, operation, treatment, use** ✧ **application** Michelle's bicycle is still in good shape despite years of hard *usage*.

use *verb* **1.** ✦ **employ, make use of, utilize** ✧ **apply, exercise, practice** My knife has a special blade to *use* for punching holes. **2.** ✦ **consume, take** ✧ **eat up, exhaust, finish, spend** Our old refrigerator *uses* too much electricity so we are getting a new one. —*noun* **1.** ✦ **operation, service** ✧ **duty, work** We will have to wait because the elevator is in *use* right now. **2.** ✦ **application, function, utilization** ✧ **advantage, purpose** A computer has many practical *uses*.

useful *adjective* ✦ **good, handy, helpful, practical, valuable** ✧ **beneficial** An electric saw is a

✦ best choices
✧ other choices

useful tool for people who do a lot of carpentry work. ◄

usher *noun* ✦ **attendant, escort, guide** ❖ **guard, leader** An *usher* showed us to our seats in the upper balcony. —*verb* ✦ **conduct, escort, guide, lead** ❖ **direct, show** The waiter *ushered* us to our table.

usual *adjective* ✦ **accustomed, customary, habitual, normal, regular, routine** I took my *usual* seat near the front of the classroom.

utensil *noun* ✦ **implement, instrument, tool** ❖ **apparatus, appliance, device, gadget** Knives, forks, and spoons are *utensils* for eating.

utter¹ *verb* ✦ **pronounce, say, speak** ❖ **articulate, talk, vocalize** The witch *uttered* a spell, and the prince was turned into a frog.

utter² *adjective* ✦ **absolute, complete, perfect, total** ❖ **entire, thorough** When the electricity went out, the house was plunged into *utter* darkness.

V

vacant *adjective* ✦ **empty, uninhabited, unoccupied** ✧ **abandoned, deserted** Someone finally moved into the apartment in our building that has been *vacant* for a year.

vacation *noun* ✦ **break, holiday, leave, recess** ✧ **furlough, rest** Shane hopes to go to camp during his summer *vacation*.

vacuum *noun* ✦ **empty space, void** ✧ **emptiness, nothingness** Sound waves cannot travel through a *vacuum*. —*verb* ✦ **clean** ✧ **brush, dust, mop, sweep** One of my weekly chores is to *vacuum* the carpet in my bedroom.

vague *adjective* ✦ **dim, faint, fuzzy, hazy, indistinct** ✧ **indefinite, uncertain** The lookout saw the *vague* outline of a ship approaching through the fog.

vain *adjective* 1. ✦ **futile, ineffective, unsuccessful, useless** ✧ **worthless** We made a *vain* attempt to get to the post office before it closed. 2. ✦ **arrogant, conceited, haughty, proud, smug** The *vain* man assumed that everyone adored him.

valiant *adjective* ✦ **brave, courageous, fearless, gallant, heroic, valorous** The good samaritan succeeded in her *valiant* effort to help a fellow passenger to safety after the train wreck.

valid *adjective* 1. ✦ **acceptable, convincing, logical, sound, suitable, true** Jeremy had a *valid* excuse for being late to school. 2. ✦ **lawful, legal, legitimate** ✧ **authentic, genuine, real** You need to have a *valid* driver's license in order to legally operate a motor vehicle.

valley *noun* ✦ **dale, dell, glen** ✧ **basin, hollow** The peaceful *valley* was nestled between two mountain ranges.

valuable *adjective* 1. ✦ **costly, expensive, high-priced** ✧ **invaluable, precious, priceless** That antique chair is very *valuable*. 2. ✦ **beneficial, helpful, important, useful, worthwhile, worthy** My brother says that his summer job gave him *valuable* experience.

value *noun* 1. ✦ **merit, use, usefulness, worth** ✧ **importance, significance** My parents' advice usually has a great deal of practical *value*. 2. ✦ **cost, price** ✧ **amount, charge, expense** The *value* of our house has gone up since we bought it. —*verb* 1. ✦ **appreciate, cherish, esteem, prize, respect, treasure** Chelsea says that she really *values* my friendship. 2. ✦ **appraise, assess, estimate, evaluate, price** A jeweler *valued* Nora's emerald ring at five hundred dollars.

vanish *verb* ✦ **disappear, go away** ✧ **dissolve, evaporate, fade** Many ships are said to have *vanished* in the Bermuda Triangle.

Antonyms
vanish *verb*
appear, arise, emerge, materialize

vanity *noun* ✦ **arrogance, conceit, pride, smugness** Harold's friends describe him as a humble person who has little or no *vanity*.

vapor *noun* ✦ **fog, mist** ✧ **haze, smog, smoke, steam** Our view of the bay was obscured by *vapor* rising from the water. ▶

variable *adjective* ✦ **changeable, erratic, unstable, unsteady** This is not a good day for sailing because the winds are so *variable*. —*noun* ✦ **circumstance, factor, unknown** ✧ **chance**

✦ best choices
✧ other choices

263

There are many *variables* that could alter the outcome of this experiment.

variety *noun* **1.** ✦ **change, diversity, variation** ◇ **difference** For the sake of *variety*, let's have something other than pepperoni on our pizza tonight. **2.** ✦ **array, assortment, collection, mixture, selection** People usually carry a *variety* of hooks and lures when they go fishing. **3.** ✦ **kind, sort, type** ◇ **brand, category, species** There are several thousand different *varieties* of apples grown around the world.

various *adjective* ✦ **assorted, different, diverse, varied** ◇ **numerous, several** This shirt is available in *various* colors.

vary *verb* ✦ **alter, change, differ, shift** ◇ **adjust, modify, switch** Fashions *vary* from season to season.

vast *adjective* ✦ **colossal, enormous, gigantic, huge, immense** ◇ **endless** When I looked at a map of North Africa, I saw that the Sahara was more *vast* than I had imagined.

vault¹ *noun* ✦ **strong room** ◇ **safe, storeroom** Bank *vaults* usually have massive steel doors.

vault² *verb* ✦ **hurdle, jump, leap, spring** ◇ **bound, hop** In a race known as a steeplechase, horses have to *vault* over fences, ditches, and other such barriers.

vegetation *noun* ✦ **flora, plant life, plants** ◇ **greenery, shrubbery** Hawaii is famous for its lush *vegetation*.

vehicle *noun* ✦ **conveyance** ◇ **transport, transportation** Cars, buses, and trucks are all motor *vehicles*.

veil *noun* ✦ **cloak, cover, curtain, mask, screen, shroud** The mountaintop was hidden behind a *veil* of clouds. —*verb* ✦ **cloak, conceal, cover, hide, mask, screen, shroud** In the spy movie I watched last night, the heroine *veiled* her face to keep her identity a secret.

vein *noun* ✦ **line, seam, streak** ◇ **layer, stripe** The prospector found a rich *vein* of gold.

velocity *noun* ✦ **pace, rate, speed** ◇ **quickness, rapidity** Sound waves travel at a *velocity* of approximately 740 miles per hour.

vendor *noun* ✦ **peddler, seller** ◇ **dealer, merchant, salesperson, supplier** We bought some fruit from a *vendor* on the corner. ▼

venom *noun* ✦ **poison, toxin** Black widow spiders produce a *venom* that is harmful to humans.

vent *noun* ✦ **opening, outlet** ◇ **aperture, hole, passage** Our clothes dryer is connected to a *vent* so that heat can be released outside the house.

venture *noun* ✦ **adventure, endeavor, enterprise, undertaking** ◇ **chance, gamble, risk** Columbus's expeditions were risky *ventures*.

verbal *adjective* ✦ **oral, spoken, unwritten** The two women had a *verbal* agreement to go into business together.

verdict *noun* ✦ **conclusion, decision, finding, judgment, ruling** The jury's *verdict* was that the defendant was not guilty.

versatile *adjective* ✦ **adaptable, all-around, flexible** ◇ **all-purpose, handy** The *versatile* hockey player was good at both defense and offense.

version *noun* ✦ **account, description, report, statement, story** Each boy gave his own *version* of how the window got broken.

vertical *adjective* ✧ **perpendicular, standing, straight up, upright** A referee's shirt has *vertical* stripes.

very *adverb* ✦ **exceedingly, exceptionally, extremely, especially, greatly, immensely** Jason was *very* angry when I lost his watch. —*adjective* ✦ **exact, precise, specific** ✧ **identical, same** The book you gave me is the *very* one that I've been wanting to read.

vessel *noun* **1.** ✦ **boat, craft, ship** ✧ **freighter, liner, tanker, yacht** Oceangoing *vessels* are usually quite large. **2.** ✦ **container, receptacle** ✧ **bottle, bowl, cup, jar, pitcher** This old earthenware *vessel* appears to have been used for storing wine.

veteran *noun* ✦ **expert, master, old hand** ✧ **professional** Our new police chief is a *veteran* with twenty years of previous experience.

veto *noun* ✦ **denial, disapproval, rejection** ✧ **ban, cancellation** The President's *veto* kept the bill from becoming law. —*verb* ✦ **disapprove, reject, turn down, void** ✧ **block, stop** State governors can *veto* bills passed by their legislatures.

vibrate *verb* ✦ **quake, quaver, quiver, shudder** ✧ **shake, tremble** When you strike a tuning fork, it *vibrates* for several moments.

vibration *noun* ✦ **quivering, shaking, throbbing, tremor** ✧ **trembling** I can feel *vibrations* inside the car whenever the engine is started.

vicinity *noun* ✦ **area, locality, neighborhood, region, surroundings** This is a good place to live in part because there are many stores and restaurants in the *vicinity*.

vicious *adjective* **1.** ✦ **cruel, hateful, hurtful, malicious, mean, spiteful** A *vicious* lie is one that is told with the intention of hurting somebody. **2.** ✦ **atrocious, bad, evil, immoral, terrible, wicked** The dictator committed many *vicious* crimes. **3.** ✦ **dangerous, ferocious, fierce,** savage, violent, wild Our neighbor's dog is not as *vicious* as he sounds.

victim *noun* ✦ **casualty** ✧ **fatality, sufferer** Paramedics rushed the *victim* of the accident to a hospital.

victorious *adjective* ✦ **successful, triumphant, winning** ✧ **champion, conquering** The *victorious* candidate thanked everyone who had helped to get him elected.

victory *noun* ✦ **success, triumph** ✧ **conquest, win** Joan of Arc was only seventeen when she led the French army to *victory* at the Battle of Orléans.

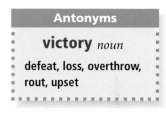

Antonyms
victory *noun*
defeat, loss, overthrow, rout, upset

view *noun* **1.** ✦ **glimpse, look (at)** ✧ **glance, peek, sight** Dad lifted my little sister up so that she could get a better *view* of the parade. **2.** ✦ **outlook, panorama, scene, scenery** ✧ **spectacle, vision** The hikers paused to admire the *view*. **3.** ✦ **belief, conviction, feeling, opinion, position, thought** What are your *views* on the television rating system? —*verb* ✦ **look at, see, watch** ✧ **behold, observe, witness** Special glasses are required to *view* 3-D movies.

vigor *noun* ✦ **energy, liveliness, power, strength, zest** ✧ **endurance** Gerald did his chores with *vigor* in order to finish them quickly.

vigorous *adjective* ✦ **active, brisk, dynamic, energetic, lively, strenuous** *Vigorous* exercise gives me an appetite!

village *noun* ✦ **hamlet, small town** ✧ **community, settlement** The *village* had just one store, two churches, and fewer than one hundred houses.

villain *noun* ✦ **bad guy, criminal, rascal, rogue, scoundrel** In old-time westerns, the good guys wore white and the *villains* wore black.

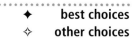

✦ **best choices**
✧ **other choices**

violate *verb* ✦ break, disobey, disregard, ignore ✧ defy, resist Police officers give tickets to drivers who *violate* traffic laws.

violence *noun* 1. ✦ brutality, savagery ✧ assault, attack Because the movie depicted fist-fights and other forms of *violence*, my parents wouldn't take me to see it. 2. ✦ ferocity, force, fury, intensity, power, severity, strength The wind blew with such *violence* that it snapped trees in two as if they were toothpicks.

violent *adjective* 1. ✦ forceful, intense, powerful, rough, strong, wild In 1988, Hurricane Gilbert's *violent* winds were clocked at 175 miles per hour. 2. ✦ fierce, fiery, furious, terrible ✧ excited, impetuous Theo was able to control his *violent* temper by counting to ten when he began to feel angry.

virgin *adjective* ✦ unspoiled, unused ✧ brand-new, fresh, new, pure Alaska has vast tracts of *virgin* wilderness that very few people have ever seen.

virtual *adjective* ✧ effective, essential, practical My mother's best friend has been a *virtual* aunt to me for many years.

virtue *noun* ✦ decency, goodness, integrity, morality ✧ honesty, honor People respect our fire chief because he is a man of great *virtue*.

visible *adjective* 1. ✦ discernible, observable, perceptible ✧ visual There are billions of stars, but fewer than six thousand are *visible* to the naked eye. 2. ✦ apparent, clear, distinct, evident, obvious, plain The doctor said that her patient was making *visible* improvement.

vision *noun* 1. ✦ eyesight, sight ✧ seeing Hawks have extremely keen *vision*. 2. ✦ imagination, perception, wisdom ✧ farsightedness, foresight Benjamin Franklin was a man of great *vision*. 3. ✦ dream, idea, notion ✧ fancy, fantasy, plan Martin Luther King, Jr. is famous for his *vision* of all races living together in harmony.

visit *verb* ✦ call on, go to, see, stay with ✧ drop by, look up Next year I will fly to Pennsylvania to *visit* my grandparents. —*noun* ✦ stay ✧ call, stopover, vacation, visitation My friend who moved away will be coming back for a *visit* sometime this summer.

visitor *noun* ✦ caller, company, guest ✧ tourist, traveler We're expecting *visitors* from out of state for the holidays.

visual *adjective* ✦ discernible, observable, perceivable, visible The footprints in the snow were *visual* proof that a fox had been checking out the chicken coop.

vital *adjective* ✦ essential, critical, crucial, important, necessary Our drama teacher reminded us that everyone's cooperation is *vital* if the play is to be a success.

Antonyms
vital *adjective*
insignificant, irrelevant, paltry, trifling, trivial

vivid *adjective* 1. ✦ bright, brilliant, colorful, rich Alicia painted her dresser a *vivid* shade of yellow. 2. ✦ acute, clear, intense, keen, sharp, strong Derek has *vivid* memories of the first time he gave a piano recital.

vocal *adjective* ✦ oral, phonetic, uttered, voiced ✧ spoken Parrots and parakeets don't really speak—they just make *vocal* imitations of sounds that they have heard.

voice *noun* 1. ✧ delivery, expression, speech, tone, utterance When I answered the telephone, I immediately recognized my best friend's *voice*. 2. ✦ part, role, say, share ✧ choice, opinion, vote In a true democracy, all citizens have a *voice* in running their government.

volume *noun* 1. ✦ book ✧ edition, publication I have read all seven *volumes* of C.S. Lewis's *Chronicles of Narnia*. 2. ✦ capacity ✧ amount, extent, measure, quantity, size This large plastic milk jug has a *volume* of one gallon. **3.** ✦ **loudness, sound** ✧ **intensity, power** Could you please turn down the *volume* on the TV?

voluntary *adjective* ✦ **free, optional, unforced, willing** ✧ **spontaneous** The *voluntary* donations that visitors make help the museum pay for new exhibits.

volunteer *noun* ✧ **unpaid person, voluntary person** The coaches for our soccer league are all *volunteers*. ▶ —*adjective* ✦ **voluntary** ✧ **nonprofessional, unpaid** Maya's father is a *volunteer* firefighter. —*verb* ✦ **contribute, donate, give, offer, provide** We *volunteered* our time to help with the community cleanup campaign.

vote *noun* ✦ **election** ✧ **choice, preference** The *vote* for class president was close this year. —*verb* ✦ **cast a ballot** ✧ **choose, elect, select** American citizens are eligible to *vote* at the age of eighteen.

vow *noun* ✦ **oath, pledge, promise** ✧ **assurance, guarantee** The knight took a *vow* of loyalty to his king. —*verb* ✦ **pledge, promise, swear** ✧ **affirm, declare** The husband and wife *vowed* to always love each other.

voyage *noun* ✦ **expedition, journey, trip** ✧ **cruise, sail** Captain James Cook discovered the Sandwich Islands on his third *voyage* to the South Pacific.

✦ **best choices**
✧ **other choices**

wad *verb* ✦ **compress, crush, press, roll, squeeze** Brian *wadded* his pajamas into a ball and stuffed them into his dresser.

wage *noun* ✦ **compensation, pay, salary** ✧ **earnings, fee, payment** My brother will receive a higher *wage* at his new job. —*verb* ✦ **carry on, carry out, conduct** ✧ **make, pursue, undertake** The senator *waged* a successful reelection campaign.

wail *verb* ✦ **bawl, cry, sob, weep** ✧ **howl, moan, whine** The movie was so sad that we were all *wailing* by the time it was over. —*noun* ✦ **cry, howl, moan** ✧ **sob, whine** The strange *wails* we heard last night were probably from a cat fight.

wait *verb* ✦ **linger, remain** ✧ **delay, stand by, stall, stay** Charlene *waited* outside the gallery for thirty minutes before her friends arrived. —*noun* ✦ **delay** ✧ **break, lull, pause, postponement, rest** There was a long *wait* before the doctor was able to see me.

wake¹ *verb* ✦ **arouse, awake, awaken, rouse, waken** ✧ **stir** My alarm clock *wakes* me at seven o'clock every morning.

wake² *noun* ✦ **path, track, trail** ✧ **aftermath, course** The tornado left many ruined buildings in its *wake*.

walk *verb* ✦ **go on foot** ✧ **amble, hike, march, stride, stroll, trek** Jessie and her friends *walk* to school every day. —*noun* **1.** ✧ **hike, jaunt, march, ramble, stroll, trek** Connor took his dog for a *walk* in the park. **2.** ✦ **footpath, path, sidewalk, walkway** ✧ **lane** There is a great view of the city from the *walk* that runs along the river. ◄

wander *verb* **1.** ✦ **amble, ramble, roam, saunter, stroll** My friends and I spent the afternoon *wandering* around the neighborhood. **2.** ✦ **drift, shift, stray, swerve** ✧ **become lost** The audience became restless when the speaker *wandered* from his subject.

want *verb* ✦ **crave, desire, long, wish, yearn** ✧ **like, need, require** Scott *wants* to get the lead part in the class play. —*noun* ✦ **desire, need, requirement** ✧ **demand, necessity** The old hermit had very few material *wants*.

war *noun* ✦ **battle, conflict, fight, struggle** ✧ **combat, warfare** The government is *waging* a war against illegal drugs.

wares *noun* ✦ **commodities, goods, merchandise, products** ✧ **stock, supplies** Peddlers used to roam the countryside to sell their *wares* at farms and villages.

warm *adjective* **1.** ✦ **lukewarm, tepid** ✧ **hot, sizzling** The recipe said to mix the ingredients with half a cup of *warm* water. **2.** ✦ **affectionate, friendly, loving, tender** ✧ **enthusiastic** Dad gave me a *warm* hug when I got home from camp. —*verb* ✦ **heat, simmer, warm up** ✧ **cook, thaw** Amy *warmed* some leftover soup on the stove.

warn *verb* ✦ **alert, caution, forewarn** ✧ **inform, make aware, notify, signal** Beavers slap their tails on the water to *warn* others when danger is present.

warning *noun* ✦ **admonition, caution, notice, notification** ✧ **alarm, precaution, signal** Hazardous products contain safety *warnings* on their labels.

warrior *noun* ✦ **brave, fighter** ✧ **combatant, soldier, trooper** Chief Sitting Bull led his *warriors* against Custer's Seventh Cavalry.

wary *adjective* ✦ **careful, cautious, suspicious** ✧ **alert, watchful** My parents taught me to be *wary* of strangers.

wash *verb* **1.** ✦ **clean, cleanse, scour, scrub** ✧ **bathe, launder** Please *wash* your hands before dinner. **2.** ✦ **carry, move, sweep** ✧ **flush, remove** The heavy rain *washed* sand and dirt over our patio. —*noun* **1.** ✦ **cleaning, cleansing, washing** ✧ **bath, shower** Dad said that his car could really use a good *wash*. **2.** ✦ **clothes washing, laundry** We do our *wash* every Tuesday at the Fluff and Fold Laundromat.

waste *verb* **1.** ✦ **lose, squander, throw away** ✧ **consume, dissipate, eat up** We *wasted* two hours trying to find a shortcut. **2.** ✧ **decline, decrease, diminish, fade, weaken, wither** Certain diseases cause the body to *waste* away. —*noun* **1.** ✦ **misuse, squandering** ✧ **abuse, extravagance, loss** Trying to fix up that outdated computer is a *waste* of both time and money. **2.** ✦ **garbage, refuse, rubbish, trash** ✧ **debris, litter** We take our household *waste* to the landfill once a week.

wasteful *adjective* ✦ **extravagant, lavish** ✧ **uneconomical** Don't be *wasteful* with the milk by taking more than you can drink.

watch *verb* **1.** ✦ **gaze at, look at, observe, see, view** ✧ **notice** Our whole class went to the air base to *watch* the space shuttle land. ▶ **2.** ✦ **attend, guard, look after, mind, tend** ✧ **care for, protect** Would you mind *watching* my jacket while I'm in the restroom? —*noun* **1.** ✦ **timepiece, wristwatch** ✧ **clock, pocket**

watch Ira needs a new band for his *watch*. **2.** ✦ **guard, lookout, vigil** ✧ **attention, observation** The mare kept a close *watch* over her newborn foal.

watchful *adjective* ✦ **alert, attentive, observant, vigilant, wary** ✧ **aware, careful** The sheepdog kept a *watchful* eye on the entire flock.

water *verb* ✦ **irrigate, saturate, soak** ✧ **dampen, moisten, spray, sprinkle, wet** In dry weather we have to *water* the vegetable garden every other day.

wave *verb* **1.** ✦ **flap, flutter, ripple** ✧ **beat, shake, sway, waver** The flags over the castle *waved* in the breeze. **2.** ✦ **gesture, motion, signal** I *waved* to Krista to get her attention. —*noun* **1.** ✦ **swell** ✧ **breaker, comber, ripple, roller** A huge *wave* almost capsized the rowboat. **2.** ✦ **gesture, motion, movement** ✧ **sign, signal, wag** The police officer gave us a *wave* of his hand when it was safe to cross the street.

way *noun* **1.** ✦ **manner, method, system, technique** ✧ **fashion, style** My friend taught me a new *way* to braid my hair. **2.** ✦ **direction, route** ✧ **course, path, road, trail** Do you know the *way* to the main library? **3.** ✦ **distance** ✧ **length, space, span, stretch** My uncle's farm is a long *way* from here. **4.** ✦ **choice, desire, preference, wish** ✧ **will** My parents usually ask my opinion, but I don't always get my *way*.

weak   *adjective* ✦ **faint, feeble** ✧ **fragile, frail, helpless, powerless** I felt *weak* because I hadn't eaten anything all day.

wealth   *noun* **1.** ✦ **assets, capital, money, riches** ✧ **fortune, treasure** The man accumulated a great deal of *wealth* by investing in the stock market. **2.** ✦ **abundance, lot, profusion, world** ✧ **much, plenty** This encyclopedia has a *wealth* of information on a large variety of subjects.

wealthy   *adjective* ✦ **affluent, prosperous, rich, well-off** The *wealthy* woman gave money to our city to build a new stadium.

wear   *verb* **1.** ✦ **don, dress in, have on, put on** ✧ **deck** Kenisha *wore* traditional African clothing for the first day of Black History Month. **2.** ✦ **rub, wear away** ✧ **abrade, erode, exhaust, fray, use up** I *wore* a hole in the elbow of my favorite sweater. —*noun* **1.** ✦ **apparel, attire, clothes, clothing, garments** This store specializes in children's *wear*. **2.** ✦ **service, use** ✧ **application, employment, utilization** You certainly have gotten a lot of *wear* out of those hiking boots.

weary   *adjective* **1.** ✦ **drained, exhausted, fatigued, tired, worn-out** My brother usually feels *weary* when he gets home from basketball practice. **2.** ✦ **dreary, tedious, tiresome, wearisome** ✧ **boring, dull** It's been a long, *weary* winter. —*verb* ✦ **drain, exhaust, fatigue, tire, wear out** The long hike *wearied* my whole family.

weather   *noun* ✦ **climate, temperature** ✧ **elements** Arizona is known for its warm *weather*. —*verb* **1.** ✦ **age, season, toughen, wrinkle** ✧ **bleach, dry** The old sailor's face has been *weathered* by long exposure to sun and wind. **2.** ✦ **come through, endure, survive, withstand** ✧ **deal with** The President thinks that his administration can *weather* the current crisis.

weave   *verb* **1.** ✧ **braid, knit, lace, plait, spin, twist** Navajo women *weave* colorful rugs and blankets from homespun wool. **2.** ✦ **wind, zigzag** ✧ **meander, twist, wander** We had to *weave* our way through the parking lot to find an exit.

web   *noun* ✦ **cobweb** ✧ **maze, net, snare, trap** Spiders spin *webs* in order to catch flies and other small insects.

wed   *verb* ✦ **marry** ✧ **combine, join, link, unite** My aunt will *wed* her fiancé next August.

weep   *verb* ✦ **cry, shed tears, sob** ✧ **bawl, blubber, wail** I began to *weep* as I read the tragic story.

weight   *noun* ✦ **heaviness** ✧ **mass, poundage, tonnage** My science book says that a person's *weight* on the moon would be only one-sixth of what it is here on Earth.

weird   *adjective* ✦ **bizarre, odd, peculiar, strange** ✧ **eerie, unnatural** Dad took his car to a mechanic because it was making *weird* noises.

welcome   *verb* ✦ **greet, meet, receive** ✧ **accept, hail** Mother went to the front door to *welcome* her guests. —*noun* ✦ **greeting, reception** ✧ **acceptance** I always receive a warm *welcome* at my best friend's house. —*adjective* ✦ **agreeable, favorable, nice, pleasant, pleasing** Sunny weather will be a *welcome* change after all of this rain.

Word Groups

A **well** is a deep hole that is dug into the ground in order to gain access to a natural deposit such as water. The noun **well** is a very specific term with no true synonyms. Here are some related words to investigate in a dictionary:

fountain, geyser, mine, pit, shaft, spring, water hole

---

well   *adverb* **1.** ✦ **agreeably, favorably, nicely, satisfactorily** ✧ **adequately, all right**

Amanda is getting along very *well* at her new school. **2.** ✦ **considerably, far, much, quite** ✧ **fully, thoroughly** I got up *well* before dawn this morning. —*adjective* ✦ **fit, hale, healthy, sound** ✧ **all right, satisfactory** I was sick last week, but I'm feeling *well* now.

wet *adjective* **1.** ✦ **drenched, soaked** ✧ **damp, moist, soggy, soppy** You might get *wet* if you don't take an umbrella. **2.** ✦ **rainy, stormy** The forecast is for another *week* of wet weather. —*verb* ✦ **dampen, moisten** ✧ **drench, saturate, soak, water** I have to *wet* my hair before I can comb it properly.

wharf *noun* ✧ **dock, jetty, pier, quay** I like to go down to the *wharf* and watch while the ships are loaded and unloaded.

whim *noun* ✦ **desire, fancy, idea, impulse, inclination, notion, wish** Dianne's dream of becoming a veterinarian is not just a passing *whim*.

whine *verb* ✦ **fuss, whimper** ✧ **complain, cry, moan, sob** Little children often *whine* when they get tired.

whip *noun* ✧ **crop, lash, strap, switch** The cowboy snapped his *whip* in the air to get the cattle moving. —*verb* **1.** ✦ **lash, thrash** ✧ **beat, strike, switch** The pirate captain threatened to *whip* anyone who disobeyed him. **2.** ✦ **crush, defeat, overcome, rout, trounce, vanquish** The Tigers *whipped* their opponents with a score of nine to nothing.

whirl *verb* ✦ **spin, turn, twirl, twist** ✧ **reel, rotate, swirl** I *whirled* around when I heard a strange noise behind me. —*noun* ✦ **spin, swirl, turn, twirl** ✧ **revolution, rotation** The ballet dancers executed a series of graceful leaps and *whirls*.

whisk *verb* **1.** ✦ **brush, flick, sweep** ✧ **wipe** Dad used a small brush to *whisk* the dirt out of his car. **2.** ✦ **bustle, hurry, hustle, rush, speed** ✧ **dash, hasten, race, scoot** When I began to feel faint, my teacher immediately *whisked* me off to the nurse's office.

whisper *verb* ✦ **speak softly** ✧ **mumble, murmur, mutter** I could hear someone *whispering* in the back of the classroom. —*noun* ✦ **undertone** ✧ **mumble, murmur, mutter** My friend lowered her voice to a *whisper* before telling me her secret.

whole *adjective* ✦ **complete, entire, full** ✧ **all, total** My brother and I ate a *whole* bag of corn chips all by ourselves. —*noun* ✦ **all, entirety** ✧ **aggregate, bulk, lot, sum, total** We spent the *whole* of our vacation at the beach.

wholesome *adjective* ✦ **healthful, healthy, nourishing, nutritious** A *wholesome* diet includes plenty of fresh fruits and vegetables.

wicked *adjective* ✦ **bad, evil, mean, nasty, vicious** ✧ **immoral, sinful** In *The Wonderful Wizard of Oz*, a *wicked* witch tries to steal Dorothy's magic slippers.

wide *adjective* ✦ **broad, extensive, large, vast** ✧ **ample, full** I tossed some confetti into the air, and the wind scattered it over a *wide* area.

width *noun* ✦ **breadth, wideness** ✧ **distance, measure, size** Standard-size typing paper has a *width* of eight and one-half inches.

wild *adjective* **1.** ✦ **native, natural, uncultivated** ✧ **undomesticated, untamed** Every summer, my family goes out to the woods to pick *wild* blueberries. **2.** ✦ **disorderly, uncontrolled, undisciplined, unruly** ✧ **crazy, frantic** The camp counselor made it clear that he would not tolerate any *wild* behavior.

will *noun* **1.** ✦ **desire, determination, drive, wish** ✧ **conviction, resolution** Robert is a good soccer player because he has a strong *will* to win. **2.** ✦ **testament** ✧ **last wishes, legacy** According to the terms of the man's *will*, his wife is to inherit all of his money. —*verb* **1.** ✧ **choose,**

✦ best choices
✧ other choices

desire, determine, resolve, want, wish The marathon runner *willed* herself to keep going even though she was very tired. **2.** ✦ **leave** ✧ **confer, endow, pass on, transfer** The wealthy man *willed* most of his money to charity.

willing *adjective* ✦ **prepared, ready** ✧ **happy, delighted** Dad said that he is *willing* to drive us to the concert.

wilt *verb* ✦ **become limp, droop, sag, wither** ✧ **die, shrivel** Plants *will* wilt if they don't get enough water.

win *verb* **1.** ✦ **prevail, triumph** ✧ **beat, conquer, defeat** My little brother usually *wins* when we play checkers. **2.** ✦ **earn, gain, get, receive** ✧ **achieve, acquire, attain, obtain** Kerri *won* a trophy for being our softball team's best player. —*noun* ✦ **triumph, victory** ✧ **conquest, success** Our football team has had five consecutive *wins* so far this season.

wind[1] *noun* **1.** ✦ **breeze** ✧ **blow, draft, gale, gust** This *wind* would be perfect for flying a kite. **2.** ✦ **breath** ✧ **air** The hard tackle knocked the *wind* out of me.

wind[2] *verb* **1.** ✦ **coil, loop, turn, wrap** ✧ **reel, roll, twist** I *wound* the rope tightly around the post to make sure that it wouldn't slip. **2.** ✦ **meander, snake, wander, weave** ✧ **bend** This road *winds* through the village and out into the country. ◄

wing *noun* ✦ **addition, annex, extension** ✧ **branch, section** The new library *wing* was built to house the children's collection.

winner *noun* ✦ **champion, victor** ✧ **conqueror, master** The *winner* in our school's spelling contest will advance to the city-wide competition.

wipe *verb* ✦ **clean, wash** ✧ **dry, dust, mop, polish, rub, scrub** I used a damp sponge to *wipe* off the kitchen table.

wire *noun* **1.** ✧ **cable, cord, filament, line, strand** The rancher had to use several coils of *wire* to repair his fences. **2.** ✦ **cable, cablegram, telegram, telegraph** The urgent message arrived by *wire*. —*verb* **1.** ✧ **bind, fasten, join, lash, secure, tie** When my kite broke, I *wired* the pieces back together. **2.** ✦ **cable, telegraph** When my brother went off to college, my parents had to *wire* him some money.

wisdom *noun* ✦ **common sense, knowledge, understanding** ✧ **intelligence, judgment** We gain *wisdom* by learning from our experiences.

wise *adjective* ✦ **intelligent, prudent, rational, sensible, smart, sound** ✧ **bright, sage** Angela made a *wise* decision not to go in swimming alone.

wish *noun* ✦ **desire, hope, longing, yearning** ✧ **need, want** Cody's fondest *wish* is to become an astronaut. —*verb* ✦ **choose, desire, like, want** ✧ **crave, long for, yearn** If you *wish*, you may go first.

wit *noun* **1.** ✦ **cleverness, comedy, humor, wittiness** ✧ **fun, joke** Kevin likes Mark Twain's books because they successfully mix *wit* and realism. **2.** ✦ **mind, senses** ✧ **intelligence, judgment, understanding** My brother scared me out of my *wits* when he crept up behind me and yelled.

witch *noun* ✦ **enchantress, sorceress** ✧ **conjurer, magician** *Witches* are said to be able to put spells on people they don't like.

withdraw *verb* **1.** ✦ **remove, take away, take back** ✧ **cancel, eliminate** We *withdrew* our suggestion when we realized that it wasn't practical. **2.** ✦ **depart, exit, go away, leave, retire**

◇ **retreat** The butler served dinner, and then he quietly *withdrew* from the room.

wither *verb* ✦ **dry up, parch, shrivel** ◇ **die, droop, fail, sag, wilt** Our grass *withered* during last summer's drought.

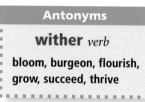

Antonyms

wither *verb*

bloom, burgeon, flourish, grow, succeed, thrive

withstand *verb* ✦ **bear, endure, stand up to, take, tolerate** ◇ **oppose, resist** Our new tent can *withstand* winds of up to ninety miles per hour.

witness *noun* ✦ **eyewitness, observer, onlooker, spectator, viewer** There have to be *witnesses* present in order for a wedding to be legal. —*verb* ✦ **observe, see, view, watch** ◇ **notice, spot** The police are hoping to find someone who *witnessed* the accident.

witty *adjective* ✦ **amusing, clever, funny, humorous** ◇ **smart** I laughed out loud when I heard the *witty* comment.

wizard *noun* 1. ✦ **magician, sorcerer** ◇ **conjurer, enchanter** The *wizard* cast a spell that made the dragon fall asleep. 2. ✦ **ace, expert, genius, prodigy, master, professional** A friend of mine at school is a computer *wizard*.

wobble *verb* ✦ **rock, shake, sway** ◇ **quake, waver** This chair *wobbles* because one of the legs is loose.

wonder *noun* 1. ✦ **marvel, sensation, spectacle** ◇ **curiosity, miracle** One of the seven *wonders* of the world was the Hanging Gardens of Babylon. 2. ✦ **awe, fascination** ◇ **amazement, astonishment, surprise** We watched in *wonder* as our cat gave birth to her kittens. —*verb* ✦ **ponder, question, reflect on, speculate about** ◇ **meditate, think** I sometimes *wonder* what my life will be like when I grow up.

wonderful *adjective* 1. ✦ **amazing, astonishing, fantastic, incredible, marvelous** The many splendors of Yosemite Valley are *wonderful* to behold. 2. ✦ **excellent, great, splendid, superb, terrific** I had a *wonderful* time at your holiday party.

wood *noun* 1. ✦ **boards, lumber, planks** ◇ **logs, timber** I need some *wood* to make more bookshelves in my room. 2. ✦ **forest, woodland** ◇ **grove, timber, timberland** My friends and I like to explore the *woods* behind my house.

word *noun* 1. ✦ **term** ◇ **designation, expression, name** "Gigantic" is a *word* that means "very large." 2. ✦ **chat, conversation, discussion, talk** The principal wants to have a *word* with us. 3. ✦ **assurance, guarantee, pledge, promise, vow, word of honor** Katie gave me her *word* that she would return the money I loaned her by the end of the week. 4. ✦ **message, news, notice** ◇ **communication, report** Our relatives sent *word* that they would be arriving a day late. —*verb* ✦ **express, phrase, put, state** ◇ **term** I *worded* my suggestion carefully so that my friend would not be offended.

work *noun* 1. ✦ **drudgery, effort, labor, toil** ◇ **exertion** Mowing a large yard by hand is a lot of *work*. 2. ✦ **employment, job, occupation, profession** ◇ **business, career, trade** Carlton's dad says that he really enjoys his *work* as a salesman. 3. ✦ **chore, task** ◇ **assignment, duty, project, responsibility** Mom said that I could go outside as soon as I finished my *work*. 4. ✦ **creation, piece, product** ◇ **accomplishment, achievement, composition** This gallery specializes in displaying the *works* of local artists. —*verb* 1. ✦ **labor, toil, strive** ◇ **endeavor, strain** Craig *worked* hard washing windows to raise money for his karate team. 2. ✦ **function, operate, perform, run** ◇ **go** Do you know how a computer *works*?

world *noun* 1. ✦ **Earth, globe** ◇ **planet** Ferdinand Magellan commanded the first expedition to sail around the *world*. 2. ✦ **humanity, humankind, the human race, mankind**

✦ **best choices**
◇ **other choices**

✧ **everyone** Conservation can help make sure that the *world* does not run out of important natural resources. **3.** ✦ **abundance, great deal, large amount, profusion, wealth** A good library contains a *world* of information on all types of subjects.

worry *verb* ✦ **concern, distress, disturb, trouble, upset** ✧ **fret** I'm *worried* that I might not pass tomorrow's math test. —*noun* ✦ **care, concern** ✧ **anxiety, apprehension, trouble** My kid brother doesn't have a *worry* in the world.

worship *noun* ✦ **adoration, glorification, reverence** ✧ **devotion, honor** A mosque is a building that Muslims use for religious *worship*. —*verb* ✦ **adore, glorify, revere** ✧ **idolize, honor** The ancient Greeks *worshiped* many different gods and goddesses.

worth *noun* ✦ **importance, merit, usefulness, value** ✧ **significance** Lauren proved her *worth* when she hit two home runs in one game.

worthless *adjective* ✦ **good-for-nothing, insignificant, unimportant, useless, valueless** This is just a *worthless* piece of junk mail.

worthwhile *adjective* ✦ **good, important, useful, valuable, worthy** ✧ **helpful** Helping to feed the homeless is a *worthwhile* cause.

worthy *adjective* ✦ **deserving** ✧ **excellent, fit, good, worthwhile** Your idea is *worthy* of further consideration.

wound *noun* ✦ **injury** ✧ **harm, hurt, sore** Our first-aid instructor showed us how to clean and bandage an open *wound*. —*verb* ✦ **injure, hurt** ✧ **harm, pain** A police officer was slightly *wounded* in the shootout.

wrap *verb* ✦ **cover, enclose, gift-wrap** ✧ **bind, bundle, package** I *wrapped* my mom's present in bright paper. ◄

wrath *noun* ✦ **anger, fury, ire, rage** ✧ **gall, indignation, rancor, resentment** The giant was filled with *wrath* when he discovered that Jack had been stealing from his castle.

wreck *verb* ✦ **damage, demolish, destroy, ruin, shatter, smash** Dad accidentally *wrecked* my bike when he backed the minivan over it. —*noun* ✦ **accident, crash, smashup** ✧ **destruction, devastation, disaster** Fortunately no one was hurt in yesterday's train *wreck*.

Antonyms
wreck *verb*
fix, mend, preserve, rebuild, renovate, repair

wrench *verb* **1.** ✦ **jerk, pull, snatch, tug, twist** ✧ **wring** My dog won our tug-of-war contest when he *wrenched* the stick out of my hand. **2.** ✦ **sprain, strain** ✧ **pull, turn** My grandfather *wrenched* his back when he tried to pick up a heavy box without help.

wrestle *verb* ✦ **grapple, scuffle, tussle** ✧ **fight, jostle, struggle** Sometimes my friends and I *wrestle* with each other in the yard just for the fun of it.

wretched *adjective* ✦ **dreadful, horrid, lousy, miserable, rotten, terrible** We've had *wretched* weather all winter long.

wring *verb* ✦ **squeeze, twist** ✧ **compress, force, wrench** I had to *wring* the water out of my socks after I fell in the wading pool.

wrinkle *noun* ✦ **crease, fold** ✧ **furrow, groove, line, pleat** Mom ironed the *wrinkles* out of her new skirt. —*verb* ✦ **crease, crinkle, furrow** ✧ **crumple, fold** My skin starts to *wrinkle* when I've been in the water a long time.

write *verb* **1.** ✦ **inscribe, jot down** ✧ **record, scrawl, scribble** Please *write* your phone number on this card. **2.** ✦ **compose, create** ✧ **author, draft, produce** I have to *write* a book report for my English class.

wrong *adjective* **1.** ✦ **inaccurate, incorrect, mistaken** ✧ **false, untrue** Marguerite had only one *wrong* answer on her final spelling test. **2.** ✦ **bad, immoral** ✧ **evil, nasty, sinful, vile, wicked** It is *wrong* to tell lies about other people and get them in trouble. **3.** ✦ **improper, inappropriate,**

unfit, unsuitable High-heeled shoes are the *wrong* thing to wear for a strenuous hike. **4.** ✦ **amiss, defective, faulty, out of order** There's something *wrong* with Dad's car. —*adverb* ✦ **badly, inaccurately, incorrectly, improperly** Most people pronounce my name *wrong*. —*noun* ✦ **misdeed, offense** ✧ **crime, evil, sin** "Two *wrongs* don't make a right" means that it isn't proper to seek revenge. —*verb* ✦ **betray, mistreat** ✧ **dishonor, harm, hurt, injure** I *wronged* my friend when I revealed the secret I had promised not to tell anyone.

Antonyms
wrong *adjective*
1. accurate, correct, right
2. decent, ethical, good, moral
3. apt, fitting, proper, respectable

XYZ

x-ray *noun* ✧ **diagnostic picture, medical photograph** When the doctor examined the *x-rays* of my injured ankle, he discovered a hairline fracture. —*verb* ✧ **film, photograph** The dentist *x-rays* my teeth once a year to make sure that I don't have any hidden cavities.

yacht *noun* ✦ **boat, ship** ✧ **cabin cruiser, sailboat, sloop** The crew of the *yacht* met to discuss the upcoming race.

yank *verb* ✦ **jerk, pull, tug, wrench** ✧ **draw, snatch** When my friend and I played tug of war, he *yanked* me off my feet. —*noun* ✦ **jerk, pull, tug, wrench** ✧ **grab** Because the door was stuck, Nicole had to give it a hard *yank* to get it to open.

yard *noun* ✦ **backyard** ✧ **courtyard, grounds, lawn, lot** Adam is out in the *yard* practicing karate.

yarn *noun* 1. ✦ **spun wool** ✧ **fiber, strand, thread** Geraldine is knitting mittens with red and blue *yarn* as a gift for her sister. ◀ 2. ✦ **anecdote, story, tale** ✧ **fable, tall tale** On career day, Gina's father told us a *yarn* about his misadventures when he first started working as a reporter.

yawn *verb* ✦ **gape** ✧ **divide, expand, extend, open, spread** The cave explorers carefully studied the deep pit that *yawned* open in front of them.

yearn *verb* ✦ **ache, desire, long, want, wish** ✧ **covet** Mrs. Takamoto *yearns* to visit her grandchildren again.

yell *verb* ✦ **bawl, bellow, call, cry, scream, shout** ✧ **roar** Terry *yelled* from his window that he would be down in a minute. —*noun* ✦ **call, cry, scream, shout** Firefighters rescued the trapped woman after they heard her *yells* for help.

yet *adverb* 1. ✦ **as yet, so far, thus far** ✧ **before, earlier** Dad hasn't gotten home *yet*. 2. ✦ **eventually, finally, someday, sometime, still** If the rain ever stops, we may *yet* go to the park. —*conjunction* ✦ **but, however, nevertheless, nonetheless** ✧ **although, though** I was pretty full, *yet* I had another slice of pizza.

yield *verb* 1. ✦ **bear, give, produce, provide** ✧ **generate** The tree in our backyard *yielded* more than one hundred oranges last year. 2. ✦ **give in, submit, succumb, surrender** ✧ **relent** Mom *yielded* to temptation and had a second piece of pie. —*noun* ✦ **crop, harvest** ✧ **output, produce, production** Tyson hopes to have a good *yield* from his garden plot this year.

yoke *verb* ✦ **harness, hitch** ✧ **attach, connect, join, link** The farmer *yoked* the oxen to his hay cart. ▼

young *adjective* ✦ **immature, juvenile, youthful** ✧ **new, undeveloped** Dad said that my little sister is still too *young* to see a scary movie with me. —*noun* ✦ **babies, offspring** ✧ **brood, family, litter** Mother bears are known for keeping a close watch over their *young*.

youngster *noun* ✦ **child, juvenile, youth** ✧ **boy, girl, lad, lass** Grandpa says that he didn't have television to watch when he was a *youngster*.

youth *noun* 1. ✦ **adolescence, childhood** ✧ **boyhood, girlhood** In his *youth*, Mr. Snyder lived in the same neighborhood as my mom. 2. ✦ **adolescent, juvenile, teen, teenager** ✧ **child** Dad started working when he was a *youth* of seventeen.

youthful *adjective* ✦ **adolescent, juvenile, young** ✧ **boyish, childish, girlish** This television series was made to appeal to a *youthful* audience.

yowl *noun* ✦ **cry, howl, moan, scream, screech, shout, wail, yell** Tobias let out a *yowl* of pain when he smashed his thumb with a hammer. —*verb* ✦ **howl, moan, screech, wail** ✧ **cry, scream, shout, yell** I was awakened by two cats *yowling* in the alley.

zenith *noun* ✦ **height, highest point, peak, pinnacle** ✧ **apex, crest, summit, top** When the actor's career was at its *zenith*, he starred in three major movies in just one year.

Antonyms
zenith *noun*
abyss, base, bottom, depths, foot

zero *noun* ✦ **naught, none, nothing, nought** Five subtracted from five equals *zero*.

zest *noun* ✦ **flavor, pungency, spice, tang, taste** Darryl puts red pepper flakes and Parmesan cheese on his pizza to give it extra *zest*.

zip *verb* ✦ **close, fasten** ✧ **button, snap** I always make sure to *zip* my backpack before I put it on. ▶

zone *noun* ✦ **area, district, neighborhood, region** ✧ **locality, territory** Our town has a business *zone* and several residential *zones*.

zoom *verb* ✦ **bolt, dart, dash, race, speed, streak** ✧ **fly, hurry, rush, sail, scoot, soar** The motorcycle *zoomed* past us so quickly that we could barely catch a glimpse of it.

✦ best choices
✧ other choices

Index to Antonyms and Word Groups

You will find Antonym and Word Group features at the following main entries:

Antonyms

abundant	happy	reckless
activity	hasten	refresh
advance	hesitant	remote
amiable	humorous	respond
apathy	immediate	rigid
assist	impair	save
barren	impulsive	secret
begin	infuriate	selfish
brittle	insult	shy
cheap	intricate	silent
combine	jumble	slack
complete	just	soothe
condemn	key	specific
conserve	leisure	stable
contrast	lock	stay
courteous	luxurious	stingy
cruel	major	stout
daring	mask	strict
defeat	merge	sullen
dense	misplace	swift
drawback	nervous	tall
dwindle	novel	temporary
easy	obvious	torture
encourage	optional	tough
eternal	outlaw	transparent
everyday	patient	turmoil
exciting	perish	uneven
expose	personal	unkempt
false	plug	urban
ferocious	portable	vanish
finish	powerful	victory
flat	principal	vital
fragile	procure	wither
fresh	prolong	wreck
fury	prosper	wrong
glee	prudent	zenith
graceful	quit	

Word Groups

alibi	kingdom
artist	knife
author	laugh
blockade	letter
borrow	mansion
button	music
castle	nail
chair	pan
citizen	pillow
council	puppet
descendant	rake
diary	rodent
diplomat	school
document	shoe
emperor	sing
envelope	snow
food	theater
guardian	tide
hotel	uniform
infect	wall
international	well
jewelry	

Picture Credits

page i Allan Landau Photography **page iii** Allan Landau Photography **page iv** Phoebe Ferguson **page v** Phoebe Ferguson **page vi** © Houghton Mifflin Studio **page vii** Tony Scarpetta Photography

ability © 1997 PhotoDisc, Inc **abundance** Picture Cube/Kathy Tarantola **adapt** © 1997 PhotoDisc, Inc. **against** Albano Ballerini **aloud** Jeroboam/Michael Mancuso **apparatus** © 1997 PhotoDisc, Inc. **arid** Zephyr Images/Cheyenne Rouse **assistance** Lightwave/John J. Stier **atmosphere** National Aeronautics and Space Administration **award** © Houghton Mifflin Studio

balance Picture Cube/Frank Siteman **bear** © Houghton Mifflin Studio **behind** Stock, Boston/Bob Daemmrich **bind** © Houghton Mifflin Studio **bit** Photo Researchers/Joseph Sohm **boost** PhotoEdit/Michael Newman **breed** © 1997 PhotoDisc, Inc. **budge** Picture Cube/E. Williamson **bundle** David Desroches Photography

cabin Picture Cube/Camerique **captain** © Houghton Mifflin Studio **caution** PhotoEdit/Richard Hutchings **chew** Photo Researchers/Alan and Sandy Carey **cliff** Zephyr Images/D. Friend **commemorate** Jeroboam/Laima Druskis **compromise** © Houghton Mifflin Studio **condition** © 1997 PhotoDisc, Inc. **control** Picture Cube/Nancy Sheehan **correct** © 1997 PhotoDisc, Inc. **costume** © Ewing Galloway, Inc. **crease** Albano Ballerini **crew** Jeroboam/Kent Reno Photo Edit/Richard Hutchings **cultivate** © Houghton Mifflin Studio **cut** Photo Edit/Richard Hutchings

dainty © 1997 PhotoDisc, Inc. **decent** PhotoEdit/David Young-Wolff **deficiency** Phoebe Ferguson **deliver** Picture Cube/Frank Siteman **demonstrate** Tony Scarpetta Photography **desire** Lightwave/Darryl Baird **dig** John Zoiner **dip** Picture Cube/Frank L. Simonetti **discussion** © Ewing Galloway, Inc. **distant** © 1997 PhotoDisc, Inc. **dive** © 1997 PhotoDisc, Inc. **domestic** © 1997 PhotoDisc, Inc. **drag** PhotoEdit/David Young-Wolff **drown** Albano Ballerini **duplicate** Picture Cube/Len Rubenstein

elder © 1997 PhotoDisc, Inc. **engage** © 1997 PhotoDisc, Inc. **equipment** PhotoEdit/Michael Newman **examination** Photo Researchers/Blair Seitz **expect** Stock, Boston/Bob Daemmrich

facility Stock, Boston/Bob Daemmrich **fast** Picture Cube/Kindra Clineff **festival** Tracey Wheeler Photography **fill** Phoebe Ferguson **flock** PhotoEdit/Alan Oddie **fortune** © Ewing Galloway, Inc. **found** © Houghton Mifflin Studio **front** Stock, Boston/Kevin Horan

gear PhotoEdit/Michael Newman **glide** Photo Researchers/Tom Leeson **globe** © Houghton Mifflin Studio **grasp** Stock, Boston/Bob Daemmrich **grip** © 1997 PhotoDisc, Inc. **growth** Stock, Boston/Kevin Horan

hand © 1997 PhotoDisc, Inc. **hazard** Stock, Boston/Stone + Neurath **heavy** Albano Ballerini **hit** Albano Ballerini **horde** Stock, Boston/Robert Fried **hurl** Zephyr Images/Michael Yada

immerse Picture Cube/Marc Alcarez **immortal** Corbis/Wolfgang Kaehler **impressive** © John Turner **incomplete** © Houghton Mifflin Studio **inflate** Phoebe Ferguson **institute** © Houghton Mifflin Studio **interrupt** © Houghton Mifflin Studio **introduce** Stock, Boston/Jeffrey Dunn **invent** © Houghton Mifflin Studio

jacket © Houghton Mifflin Studio **jewel** Gem Hut (http://www.gemhut.com) **join** Stock, Boston/Henry Horenstein **judgment** © Houghton Mifflin Studio

keg © Houghton Mifflin Studio **king** Corbis/Gianni Dagli Orti **knit** PhotoEdit/Amy C. Etra **knot** © Houghton Mifflin Studio **land** National Aeronautics and Space Administration **legible** Phoebe Ferguson **load** Stock, Boston/Jon Feingersh **logical** Tracey Wheeler Photography **luggage** Albano Ballerini **make** Zephyr Images/Melanie Carr

matter © 1997 PhotoDisc, Inc. **misfortune** PhotoEdit/Michael Newman **moor** Picture Cube/Miro Vintoniv **mount** © 1997 PhotoDisc, Inc. **mud** Stock, Boston/Stephen Swinburne

nestle Stock, Boston/Lawrence Migdale **nourishment** PhotoEdit/James Shaffer **nutritious** © Houghton Mifflin Studio

obstruct © Houghton Mifflin Studio **obstruction** Picture Cube/Steve Stone **open** Phoebe Ferguson **operation** Photo Researchers/Benelux Press **outside** Stock, Boston/Bob Daemmrich

parade Jeroboam/Billy E. Barnes **pastime** Zephyr Images/Melanie Carr **peek** © 1997 PhotoDisc, Inc. **perfect** PhotoEdit/Tony Freeman **pet** © 1997 PhotoDisc, Inc. **pick** Picture Cube/Nancy Sheehan **place** Albano Ballerini **plunge** Allan Landau Photography **power** PhotoEdit/David Young-Wolff **praise** Phoebe Ferguson **press** Stock, Boston/Martin Rogers **profession** Photo Researchers/Science Photo Library

quarter PhotoEdit/Myrleen Ferguson

rake Photo Researchers/Blair Seitz **range** © 1997 PhotoDisc, Inc. **rank²** © 1997 PhotoDisc, Inc. **receive** Stock, Boston/Bob Daemmrich **regular** John Zoiner **reinforce** © 1997 PhotoDisc, Inc./ © 1997 PhotoDisc, Inc. **representative** *Eleanor* by Frank Weston Benson, reproduced courtesy of the Museum of Fine Arts, Boston, The Hayden Collection **restriction** © 1997 PhotoDisc, Inc. **revolution** © 1997 PhotoDisc, Inc. **ridiculous** PhotoEdit/David Young-Wolff **ripe** © 1997 PhotoDisc, Inc. **rotate** © 1997 PhotoDisc, Inc. **rugged** Picture Cube/Kindra Clineff

sad Picture Cube/John Yurka **satisfy** Albano Ballerini **scenic** Photo Researchers/Renee Lynn **scrap** © Houghton Mifflin Studio **secure** Picture Cube/David Witbeck **separate** © 1997 PhotoDisc, Inc. **shake** PhotoEdit/Barbara Stitzer **shine** © Houghton Mifflin Studio **show** Stock, Boston/Bob Daemmrich **silly** Allan Landau Photography **skill** Picture Cube/Frank Siteman **slow** © 1997 PhotoDisc, Inc. **small** PhotoEdit/David Young-Wolff **soft** © 1997 PhotoDisc, Inc. **spell** Zephyr Images **squash** © 1997 PhotoDisc, Inc. **squirt** PhotoEdit/Tony Freeman **stain** © Houghton Mifflin Studio **still** © 1997 PhotoDisc, Inc. **stock** Albano Ballerini **stretch** Jeroboam/Robert Clay **submit** Photo Researchers/Richard Nowitz **sunrise** © 1997 PhotoDisc, Inc. **surprise** PhotoEdit/Jose Carrillo **sweet** Albano Ballerini **swirl** Jeroboam/Shmuel Thaler

tangle © Ewing Galloway, Inc. **taxi** © 1997 PhotoDisc, Inc. **terrible** Picture Cube/James Lemass **thrill** Photo Researchers/Bill Aron **topple** Stock, Boston/Joe Benson **tournament** © 1997 PhotoDisc, Inc. **transmit** © 1997 PhotoDisc, Inc. **tumble** © 1997 PhotoDisc, Inc. **ugly** © 1997 PhotoDisc, Inc.

uncommon © 1997 PhotoDisc, Inc. **underground** Photo Researchers/Jeffrey Lepore **unused** Albano Ballerini **useful** Jeroboam/Robert W. Ginn

vapor © 1997 PhotoDisc, Inc. **vendor** Photo Researchers/Richard Hutchings **volunteer** Zephyr Images/Melanie Carr

walk © 1997 PhotoDisc, Inc. **watch** National Aeronautics and Space Administration **wind²** Photo Researchers/Adam Jones **wrap** Phoebe Ferguson

yarn © Houghton Mifflin Studio **yoke** Stock, Boston/Daniel H. MacDonald

zip © Houghton Mifflin Studio